ISSUES IN RACE AND ETHNICITY

8th Edition

Sara Miller McCune founded SAGE Publishing in 1965 to support the dissemination of usable knowledge and educate a global community. SAGE publishes more than 1000 journals and over 800 new books each year, spanning a wide range of subject areas. Our growing selection of library products includes archives, data, case studies and video. SAGE remains majority owned by our founder and after her lifetime will become owned by a charitable trust that secures the company's continued independence.

Los Angeles | London | New Delhi | Singapore | Washington DC | Melbourne

ISSUES IN RACE AND ETHNICITY

SELECTIONS FROM *CQ RESEARCHER*

8TH EDITION

⑤SAGE | **CQPRESS**

FOR INFORMATION:

CQ Press

An Imprint of SAGE Publications, Inc.

2455 Teller Road

Thousand Oaks, California 91320

E-mail: order@sagepub.com

SAGE Publications Ltd.

1 Oliver's Yard

55 City Road

London EC1Y 1SP

United Kingdom

SAGE Publications India Pvt. Ltd.

B 1/I 1 Mohan Cooperative Industrial Area

Mathura Road, New Delhi 110 044

India

SAGE Publications Asia-Pacific Pte. Ltd.

3 Church Street

#10-04 Samsung Hub

Singapore 049483

Printed in the United States of America

ISBN (pbk): 978-1-5443-1632-1

Library of Congress Control Number: 2017955585

This book is printed on acid-free paper.

MIX
Paper from
responsible sources
FSC® C014174

Executive Publisher: Monica Eckman

Editorial Assistant: Zachary Hoskins

Production Editor: Kimaya Khashnobish

Typesetter: C&M Digitals (P) Ltd.

Cover Designer: Anupama Krishnan

Marketing Manager: Erica DeLuca

17 18 19 20 21 10 9 8 7 6 5 4 3 2 1

Contents

Annotated Contents

CHANGING DEMOGRAPHICS
"Alt-Right" Movement

The "alt-right," a loose coalition of white nationalists, white supremacists, anti-Semites and others seeking to preserve what they consider traditional Western civilization, is urging white Americans to band together and fight multiculturalism. The movement has gained more attention than any fringe group in decades because of its role in the 2016 election and its embrace of President Trump's America First agenda. Political observers say the alt-right has tapped into some whites' fears about immigration and the nation's changing demographics, where whites will soon be a minority. The alt-right remains small, but both conservatives and liberals denounce its beliefs as racist. They point with alarm to the alt-right's online use of profane language and images to attack social conventions — moves that are helping it gain followers. The movement's use of identity politics, some say, is reminiscent of how liberals used it to fight for racial and gender equality. A number of analysts note that hate crimes have been increasing since the election and urge Trump to more forcefully speak out against them.

Populism and Party Politics

Populism — the deep public mistrust of political parties and other so-called "establishment" institutions — is disrupting traditional politics in the United States as well as abroad. Analysts and academics say Donald Trump demonstrated populism's reach by winning the 2016 Republican presidential nomination, while Vermont Sen. Bernie Sanders waged what often was described as a left-wing populist challenge to Hillary Clinton for the Democratic nomination. Populist movements have spread across Europe with the rise of anti-establishment politicians in several countries, underscored by the United Kingdom's June 2016 "Brexit" vote to leave the 28-nation European Union. But the meaning of populism has become elastic, as it is applied to a wide range of politicians and movements. Today's populists are amplifying many of the movement's earlier traditions through heavy use of Twitter, Facebook and other social media to launch venomous "us-versus-them" attacks on opponents. The new-media warfare has led some experts to wonder if populism is compatible with what they think should be a sober and deliberative political process.

Diversity in Hollywood

Charges of gender and racial bias and sexual stereotyping continue to plague the film and broadcast entertainment industries despite decades of complaints from women, minorities and civil rights advocates. White males still dominate virtually all aspects of the business, from writers, directors and producers to actors starring in leading roles. But the movie industry may have reached a tipping point in 2016 following a controversy over the Academy Awards nominations for best actor and actress: For the second consecutive year, all the nominees were white. Television, meanwhile, is becoming somewhat more inclusive than movies, as are emerging internet-based shows. Still, the Equal Employment Opportunity Commission is investigating claims of bias against female directors, and many minorities remain unpersuaded by recent Hollywood diversity initiatives. Skeptics say significant industry change is unlikely, especially in the high-cost, high-risk movie business, where box-office favorites rather than untested newcomers typically determine which films receive financing.

Future of the Middle Class

The percentage of middle-income U.S. households has declined significantly in recent years, leading some economists, policy experts and politicians to argue that the American middle class is in deep trouble — or even disappearing. Globalization, automation and declining union membership have shrunk the manufacturing workforce — historically a bulwark of the middle class — and an increasing share of the nation's wealth has accrued to the richest Americans. Many experts say achieving middle-class status today is unlikely without a college education and entry into the whitecollar work world — a stark turnaround from the booming post–World War II years, when a stable blue-collar job anchored millions of families in a middle-class lifestyle. Still, some experts call fears of a middle-class decline overblown, saying poor Americans who face far tougher conditions are being overlooked. Presidential candidates in both parties responded to middle-class discontent, with Democrats promising to cut college costs and Republicans proposing changes in the tax code.

Gentrification

As rising numbers of young professionals, wealthy foreigners and baby boomers move to America's urban centers, they are bringing prosperity and new life to once-derelict neighborhoods. But the newcomers also are causing real estate values to soar, sparking concern that people with less means are being forced to move to lower-cost suburbs, where jobs and social services are scarcer and commutes longer. Some experts say fears about gentrification's negative effects are overblown. But advocates for the poor worry that gentrification is contributing to income disparity, leading several big-city mayors to seek ways to minimize the effects on low-income residents, such as expanding paid sick leave and living-wage requirements and mandating some affordable housing units in new residential developments. While many cities have embraced the prosperity that gentrification has spurred, experts question whether the changes are sustainable, especially if cities can't continue to appeal to younger residents as they begin raising families.

ETHNICITY AND IMMIGRATION
Anti-Semitism

In the run-up to the 2016 presidential election and afterward, the United States has experienced disturbing outbreaks of anti-Semitism, including a spate of incidents on more than 100 college campuses, where white supremacists have been distributing anti-Semitic fliers and openly recruiting adherents. Some human rights and Jewish activists say President Trump has emboldened right-wing hostility toward Jews, but others say such charges are unjustified. Defining anti-Semitism is controversial. Members of Congress and state legislators want to codify a definition that would include opposition to Israel's existence. But pro-Palestinian and civil liberties groups say that would violate free-speech rights. A similar debate is playing out in Europe, where some countries have seen a rise in deadly attacks on Jews in recent years, often by radicalized Muslims, such as the 2015 terrorist attack on a kosher grocery in Paris. Paradoxically, growing anti-Muslim attitudes in countries experiencing an influx of refugees have also spurred more prejudice against Jews — the target of history's longest hatred.

Native American Sovereignty

Native American lands contain $1.5 trillion in untapped coal, oil and other energy resources. The potential bounty is raising hopes among many Indians that energy development can help tribes reduce poverty on their reservations, where unemployment averages 19 percent. But development also is raising fears that it will threaten Indians' traditional way of life and harm the Earth. In addition, the dispute is raising tough questions among Indians, lawmakers and others about energy development and the limits of tribal sovereignty. The Navajo and like-minded tribes want federal regulations relaxed so Indians can develop their energy resources, providing jobs and other benefits. But other tribes argue the federal government remains obligated under treaties to protect Indian land from commercial exploitation. They are further worried about the Trump administration as it relaxes regulations on the energy industry and federal lands. Meanwhile, controversy has arisen over some tribes' disenrolling of members. Critics say the practice is a power grab by tribal leaders, but defenders say tribes have a right to decide who is a member.

Immigrants and the Economy

President Trump's vows to protect American jobs and improve national security by tightening U.S. borders are intensifying the debate over immigration's impact on the economy. Many politicians and workers argue that immigrants — legal and illegal — undercut wages and take jobs from native-born workers. They also contend undocumented immigrants burden society with welfare, medical and education costs. Immigration advocates respond that newcomers bring badly needed skills to the American economy, especially in the technology sector, where half the leaders of billion-dollar Silicon Valley companies are immigrants. Advocates also say immigrants often fill low-wage jobs short on workers, from home building to landscaping and dishwashing. Many experts fear the heated debate over immigration may cause the world's most talented young people to avoid studying at American universities or moving to the United States. Meanwhile, "Dreamers" — children brought to the United States illegally — are nervously waiting to learn whether the administration will allow them to stay in this country.

Far-Right Extremism

The massacre in June 2015 of nine African-American worshippers at the historically black Emanuel AME Church in Charleston, South Carolina, was the most lethal in a string of ideologically motivated post-9/11 attacks committed by far-right extremists. They range from white supremacists and anti-government militia members to so-called sovereign citizens, who deny the legitimacy of most U.S. laws. Dylann Roof, the 21-year-old suspect in the Charleston killings, is believed to have written an online manifesto ranting against blacks and Hispanics and explaining how a white supremacist website inspired him to commit violence. While experts say most adherents of extremist movements are not violent, a recent survey found that police agencies are more concerned about violence by anti-government extremists than by Islamic extremists. The threat of violence has spurred debate about the strength of the government's efforts to fight extremism and whether it should try to prevent far-right radicalization of young people. Meanwhile, Life After Hate, a group founded by former racist skinheads, is working to help former white supremacists find a new path in life.

RACE AND EDUCATION
Charter Schools

Charter schools — public schools with more freedom to innovate than traditional public schools — have exploded in popularity in the past 25 years. About 6,800 charters now operate in 43 states serving 5 percent of the nation's public school students. Advocates say charter schools provide a superior education, and as proof they cite studies showing that charters have been particularly successful in raising student achievement scores in troubled inner-city districts. Charters do more with less, they say, by eliminating bureaucracy and allowing teachers to try different educational approaches. Critics, however, say that while some charters excel, most do no better than traditional public schools and many do worse. They also accuse charters of cherry-picking the best students and say the charter movement is driven, at least partly, by the desire of for-profit charter operators to make money from public education. Opposition to charter expansion has grown in some states, but President Trump and his new Education secretary, Betsy DeVos, are charter supporters.

Racial Conflict

Race-centered conflicts in several U.S. cities have led to the strongest calls for policy reforms since the turbulent civil rights era of the 1960s. Propelled largely by videos of violent police confrontations with African-Americans, protesters have taken to the streets in Chicago, New York and other cities demanding changes in police tactics. Meanwhile, students — black and white — at several major universities have pressured school presidents to deal aggressively with racist incidents on campus. And activists in the emerging Black Lives Matter movement are charging that "institutional racism" persists in public institutions and laws a half century after legally sanctioned discrimination was banned. Critics of that view argue that moral failings in the black community — and not institutional racism — explain why many African-Americans lack parity with whites in such areas as wealth, employment, housing and educational attainment. But those who cite institutional racism say enormous socioeconomic gaps and entrenched housing and school segregation patterns stem from societal decisions that far outweigh individuals' life choices.

Free Speech on Campus

Several recent incidents in which college students spewed racist or misogynistic language on campus have renewed debate about how much freedom of speech the U.S. Constitution actually permits. Among the most notorious examples: the singing of a racist chant in 2015 by several University of Oklahoma fraternity members. College presidents at Oklahoma and other campuses have swiftly disciplined students for speech deemed inappropriate, but civil liberties advocates say college officials are violating students' First Amendment rights to free speech. Meanwhile, critics say a small but growing movement to give students "trigger warnings" about curriculum material that might traumatize them indicates that colleges are becoming overly protective. American universities also have come under fire for accepting money from China and other autocratic governments to create overseas branches and international institutes on their home campuses. Defenders of such programs say they are vital for global understanding, but critics say they may compromise academic freedom.

Preface

In the wake of a divisive presidential election charged with debates
around immigration and identity politics, Americans continue to
grapple with issues of race and ethnicity. These topics confound
even well-informed citizens and often lead to cultural and political
conflicts, because they raise the most formidable public policy questions: Are U.S. policies and institutions discriminatory? Should Native
Americans have more control over their land? Do the white nationalist views of far-right extremists have wide support? To promote
change and hopefully reach viable resolution, scholars, students, and
policymakers must strive to understand the context and content of
each of these issues, as well as how these debates play out in the
public sphere.

With the view that only an objective examination that synthe-
sizes all competing viewpoints can lead to sound analysis, this
eighth edition of *Issues in Race and Ethnicity* provides comprehensive and unbiased coverage of today's most pressing policy problems. It enables instructors to fairly and comprehensively uncover
opposing sides of each issue, and illustrate just how significantly
they impact citizens and the government they elect. This book is a
compilation of twelve recent reports from *CQ Researcher*, a weekly
policy backgrounder that brings into focus key issues on the public
agenda. *CQ Researcher* fully explains complex concepts in plain
English. Each article chronicles and analyzes past legislative and
judicial action as well as current and possible future maneuvering.
Each report addresses how issues affect all levels of government,
whether at the local, state, or federal level, and also the lives and
futures of all citizens. *Issues in Race and Ethnicity* is designed to
promote in-depth discussion, facilitate further research, and help

readers think critically and formulate their own positions on these crucial issues.

This collection is organized into three sections: Changing Demographics; Ethnicity and Immigration; and Race and Education. Each section spans a range of important public policy concerns. These pieces were chosen to expose students to a wide range of issues, from gentrification to illegal immigration. We are gratified to know that *Issues in Race and Ethnicity* has found a following in a wide range of departments in political science and sociology.

CQ RESEARCHER

CQ Researcher was founded in 1923 as *Editorial Research Reports* and was sold primarily to newspapers as a research tool. The magazine was renamed and redesigned in 1991 as *CQ Researcher.* Today, students are its primary audience. While still used by hundreds of journalists and newspapers, many of which reprint portions of the reports, *Researcher*'s main subscribers are now high school, college and public libraries. In 2002, *Researcher* won the American Bar Association's coveted Silver Gavel Award for magazine excellence for a series of nine reports on civil liberties and other legal issues.

Researcher writers — all highly experienced journalists — sometimes compare the experience of writing a *Researcher* report to drafting a college term paper. Indeed, there are many similarities. Each report is as long as many term papers — about 11,000 words — and is written by one person without any significant outside help. One of the key differences is that the writers interview leading experts, scholars and government officials for each issue.

Like students, the writers begin the creative process by choosing a topic. Working with *Researcher*'s editors, the writer identifies a controversial subject that has important public policy implications. After a topic is selected, the writer embarks on one to two weeks of intense research. Newspaper and magazine articles are clipped or downloaded, books are ordered and information is gathered from a wide variety of sources, including interest groups, universities and the government. Once the writers are well informed, they develop a detailed outline and begin the interview process. Each report requires a minimum of 10 to 15 interviews with academics, officials, lobbyists and people working in the field. Only after all interviews are completed does the writing begin.

CHAPTER FORMAT

Each issue of *CQ Researcher,* and therefore each selection in this book, is structured in the same way. A selection begins with an introductory overview, which is briefly explored in greater detail in the rest of the report.

The second section chronicles the most important and current debates in the field. It is structured around a number of key issues questions, such as "Has the border security buildup made the United States more secure?" and "Should employers be penalized for hiring illegal immigrants?" This section is the core of each selection. The questions raised are often highly controversial and usually the object of much argument among scholars and practitioners. Hence, the answers provided are never conclusive, but rather detail the range of opinion within the field.

Following those issue questions is the "Background" section, which provides a history of the issue being examined. This retrospective includes important legislative and executive actions and court decisions to inform readers on how current policy evolved.

Next, the "Current Situation" section examines important contemporary policy issues, legislation under consideration and action being taken. Each selection ends with an "Outlook" section that gives a sense of what new regulations, court rulings and possible policy initiatives might be put into place in the next five to ten years.

Each report contains features that augment the main text: sidebars that examine issues related to the topic, a pro/con debate by two outside experts, a chronology of key dates and events and an annotated bibliography that details the major sources used by the writer.

CUSTOM OPTIONS

Interested in building your ideal CQ Press Issues book, customized to your personal teaching needs and interests? Browse by course or date, or search for specific topics or issues from our online catalog of over 500 *CQ Researcher* issues at http://custom.cqpress.com.

ACKNOWLEDGMENTS

We wish to thank many people for helping to make this collection a reality. Thomas J. Billitteri, managing editor of *CQ Researcher,* gave us his enthusiastic support and cooperation as we developed this edition. He and his talented staff of editors have amassed a first-class collection of *Researcher* articles, and we are fortunate to have access to this rich cache. We also thankfully acknowledge the advice and feedback from current readers and are gratified by their satisfaction with the book.

Some readers may be learning about *CQ Researcher* for the first time. We expect that many readers will want regular access to this excellent weekly research tool. For subscription information or a no-obligation free trial of *Researcher,* please contact CQ Press at www.cqpress.com or toll-free at 1-866-4CQ-PRESS (1-866-427-7737).

We hope that you will be pleased by the eighth edition of *Issues in Race and Ethnicity.* We welcome your feedback and suggestions for future editions. Please direct comments to Monica Eckman, Executive Publisher, CQ Press, 2600 Virginia Avenue, NW, Suite 600, Washington, DC 20037; or send e-mail to *monica.eckman@cqpress.com.*

—The Editors of CQ Press

Contributors

Marcia Clemmitt is a veteran social-policy reporter who previously served as editor in chief of *Medicine & Health* and staff writer for *The Scientist.* She has also been a high school math and physics teacher. She holds a liberal arts and sciences degree from St. John's College, Annapolis, and a master's degree in English from Georgetown University. Her recent *CQ Researcher* reports include "The Dark Web" and "Teaching Critical Thinking."

Sarah Glazer is a London-based freelancer who contributes regularly to *CQ Researcher.* Her articles on health, education and social-policy issues also have appeared in *The New York Times* and *The Washington Post.* Her recent *CQ Researcher* reports include "Privacy and the Internet" and "Decriminalizing Prostitution." She graduated from the University of Chicago with a B.A. in American history.

Alan Greenblatt is a staff writer at *Governing* magazine. Previously he covered politics and government for NPR and *CQ Weekly*, where he won the National Press Club's Sandy Hume Award for political journalism. He graduated from San Francisco State University in 1986 and received a master's degree in English literature from the University of Virginia in 1988. His *CQ Researcher* reports include "Confronting Warming," "Future of the GOP," "Immigration Debate," "Media Bias" and "Downtown Revival."

Christina Hoag is a freelance journalist in Los Angeles. She previously worked for *The Miami Herald* and the Associated Press and was a correspondent in Latin America. She is the coauthor of *Peace in the Hood: Working with Gang Members to End the Violence.*

Reed Karaim, a freelance writer in Tucson, Ariz., has written for *The Washington Post, U.S. News & World Report, Smithsonian, American Scholar, USA Weekend* and other publications. He is the author of the novel *If Men Were Angels*, which was selected for the Barnes & Noble Discover Great New Writers series. He is also the winner of the Robin Goldstein Award for Outstanding Regional Reporting and other journalism honors. Karaim is a graduate of North Dakota State University in Fargo.

Peter Katel is a *CQ Researcher* contributing writer who previously reported on Haiti and Latin America for *Time* and *Newsweek* and covered the Southwest for newspapers in New Mexico. He has received several journalism awards, including the Bartolomé Mitre Award for coverage of drug trafficking from the Inter-American Press Association. He holds an A.B. in university studies from the University of New Mexico. His recent reports include "Police Tactics" and "Central American Gangs."

Christina L. Lyons, a freelance journalist in the Washington, D.C., area, writes primarily about U.S. government and politics. She is a contributing author for CQ Press reference books, including *CQ's Guide to Congress*, and was a contributing editor for Bloomberg BNA's *International Trade Daily*. A former editor for Congressional Quarterly, she also was coauthor of CQ's *Politics in America 2010*. Lyons began her career as a newspaper reporter in Maryland and then covered

environment and health care policy on Capitol Hill. She has a master's degree in political science from American University.

Barbara Mantel is a freelance writer in New York City. She was a 2012 Kiplinger Fellow and has won several journalism awards, including the National Press Club's Best Consumer Journalism Award and the Front Page Award from the Newswomen's Club of New York for her Nov. 1, 2009, *CQ Global Researcher* report "Terrorism and the Internet." She holds a B.A. in history and economics from the University of Virginia and an M.A. in economics from Northwestern University.

Micheline Maynard is a former senior business correspondent and Detroit bureau chief for *The New York Times* and a contributor to *Forbes*. She has reported and written extensively on global manufacturing, among other things. Her books include *Curbing Cars* (2014), *The Selling of the American Economy* (2009) and *The End of Detroit* (2003).

Chuck McCutcheon is an assistant managing editor of *CQ Researcher*. He has been a reporter and editor for *Congressional Quarterly* and Newhouse News Service and is coauthor of the 2012 and 2014 editions of *The Almanac of American Politics* and *Dog Whistles, Walk-Backs and Washington Handshakes: Decoding the Jargon, Slang and Bluster of American Political Speech*. He also has written books on climate change and nuclear waste.

1

"Alt-Right" Movement

Marcia Clemmitt

Demonstrators protest a speech at Texas A&M University on Dec. 6, 2016, by Richard Spencer, who coined the term "alt-right." Many in the movement hope white Americans eventually will live in a whites-only ethno-state that Spencer has said might be created by some means of "peaceful ethnic cleansing."

From *CQ Researcher*,
March 17, 2017

A t the Conservative Political Action Conference (CPAC) in February, where leading conservatives gather annually near Washington for four days of speeches and strategizing, organizers minced no words about one of the attendees and his beliefs.

Richard Spencer, unofficial leader of the white nationalist "alt-right" movement, had bought a ticket to the conference, but was later escorted out by security guards. "He is not welcome here," CPAC Communications Director Ian Walters said. "His views are repugnant and have absolutely nothing to do with what goes on here."[1] And in an address to the conference, organizer Dan Schneider called the alt-right a "sinister organization that is trying to worm its way into our ranks."

But some in the CPAC audience welcomed Spencer and treated him like a celebrity, posing with him for selfies. "Richard Spencer is, like, the coolest guy," said the president of a College Republicans group at a New England state university.[2]

Undaunted by the organizers' harsh words and encouraged by the audience's reception, Spencer said, "What the alt-right is doing is clearly resonating with people. You can call it names, or you can actually ask, why is it resonating? Why does a young white person feel alienated in the modern world?"[3]

White nationalists have long existed in the United States. What's surprising today, historians and political analysts say, is that over the past two years the loose assemblage of white nationalists, white supremacists and others who gather under the alt-right banner have gained more attention than any fringe group in decades because of their ties to a major-party political nominee, Donald Trump, who

1

Hate Groups Again On the Rise

The number of hate groups in the United States rose nearly 17 percent over the past three years, according to the Southern Poverty Law Center (SPLC), which monitors extremist organizations. Its count of hate group reflects only those that have a website and also undertake on-the-ground operations, such as rallies or leaflet distribution. The number of hate groups rose steadily between 1999 and 2011 before falling over the next three years. The SPLC attributed that decline to the fact that some groups moved exclusively to the Web.

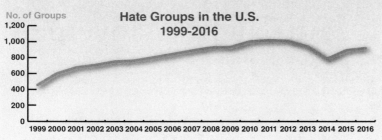

Hate Groups in the U.S.
1999-2016

Source: Mark Potok, "The Year in Hate and Extremism," Southern Poverty Law Center, Feb. 15, 2017, http://tinyurl.com/hhfvcwj.

won the presidency in November. The alt-right's use of internet attacks on Trump's behalf, and Trump's occasional retweeting during the campaign of material posted by white extremists, brought the alt-right waves of media attention and new enthusiasts, such as the Spencer fans at CPAC.

The movement also has sparked criticism and alarm at both ends of the political spectrum. Many on the Left denounce its stances and say the very term "alt-right" is a politically correct mask for its extremist views. Meanwhile, critics on the Right say the movement is racist and an affront to both conservatism and traditional Republicanism; they also note that most Trump voters reject white extremism.[4]

Political observers say several other factors are spurring interest in the movement, including its ability to tap into some whites' fears about the changing demographics of the nation, where whites will soon be a racial minority, eclipsed by Hispanics and other groups. Another factor is Trump's populist appeals to whites worried about immigration, such as his false suggestion that a high percentage of Mexican immigrants are criminals.[5]

International developments also are propelling the alt-right. In Europe, a backlash against globalization and recent surges in refugees has led to the rise of far-right political parties throughout the Continent. Moreover, some backers of the alt-right make savvy online use of profane, taboo or abusive language and images to attack political correctness and social conventions. Those tactics attract many social media users, especially young men, analysts of extremist groups say.

White nationalism's new prominence is "a reaction against the multicultural explosion in America," says Lawrence Rosenthal, chair of the Center for Right-Wing Studies at the University of California, Berkeley. "We have just had a black president. Even the South is a very different place than it was 50 years ago. California has already turned majority minority."

Whether this primarily internet-based movement can solidify and expand its influence with voters and within the Trump administration remains unclear, observers say.

"We shouldn't exaggerate the alt-right's size and influence," says George Hawley, an assistant professor of political science at the University of Alabama and the author of the 2016 book *Right-Wing Critics of American Conservatism.* In this mostly online movement, it's unknown how many people are core members — defined as those "who are really serious content creators" of, for example, original tweets or message-forum posts, he says. Hawley estimates the core group at a few thousand.

The term "alt-right" was first used in 2010, when Spencer, a writer and activist for a white nationalist think tank, the National Policy Institute (NPI), launched *Alternative Right*, an online publication featuring what were widely viewed as white racist, misogynist and anti-Semitic writings.[6] Spencer holds that alt-right thinking springs mainly from the perception that America's dominant white majority is losing ground to others.

Spencer didn't respond to *CQ Researcher*'s requests for an interview. In November he told the Center for Investigative Reporting, "Yes, white people are generally better off than many other people." But today, institutions such as government and media are acting on non-white people's behalf, he said. "And you can talk about this being fair . . . but . . . fairness has never been really a great value in my mind. I like greatness and winning and dominance and beauty."[7]

The Anti-Defamation League (ADL), a U.S.-based advocacy group that opposes anti-Semitism and other bigotry, holds that the alt-right movement is a loose network of people — mostly white males — who believe the United States is a majority white nation that should reject policies that dilute whites' influence and behave in a nationalistic fashion.

Besides fostering white identity, the alt-right also encourages "aggressive anti-feminist and misogynistic politics," says Matthew Lyons, co-author of the 2000 book *Right-Wing Populism in America*. Alt-right groups "say they have no interest in recruiting women or addressing any of women's concerns," he says.

Still, groups that accept the alt-right label aren't monolithic in their views, says Marilyn Mayo, a director of the ADL's Center on Extremism.

For example, while some are anti-Semitic neo-Nazis, others appear not to be, she says. In fact, because most alt-right activity consists of anonymous online posts, it is not even clear how many alt-right followers are racists, Mayo says. "Some certainly are attracted just because they enjoy the rejection of political correctness. But a lot are really racist," she says.

Further dooming attempts to definitively describe the alt-right are frequent squabbles and defections in the

Defining the "Alt-Right"

The alt-right movement has gained prominence since white nationalist Richard Spencer coined the term in 2008 in what some analysts call an effort to make its beliefs more acceptable to a broader audience. Believing white interests are under attack from multiculturalism, adherents are using the internet and supporting the Trump administration in an attempt to build a following.

Glossary

Alt-right: An umbrella term for various groups — white supremacists, anti-Semites and others — that espouse far-right ideologies centered on white nationalism. Spencer, its unofficial leader, wants an "ethno-state" — a territory set aside for people of European descent.

European New Right: With roots in 1930s fascism, the movement opposes multiculturalism and espouses isolationist and anti-globalization ideologies; it is a source of ideas for American white nationalists.

Paleoconservatism: An ideology founded in the 1980s that maintains the United States owes its greatness to the Founders' European heritage; it strenuously opposes immigration and other policies that might dilute that heritage.

White nationalism: A belief that the United States was founded as a white nation and whites should band together to keep it that way.

White separatism: A more extreme form of white nationalism and supremacism; its adherents advocate separation from other races in either an ethno-state or a racially segregated society.

White supremacism: The view that whites are superior to all other races and whites should dominate American society.

Sources: "Alternative Right," Southern Poverty Law Center, http://tinyurl.com/gmafta5; Dylan Matthews, "Paleoconservatism, the movement that explains Donald Trump, explained," *Vox*, May 6, 2016, http://tinyvurl.com/hdrh397.

group, for example over such questions as whether gays should be allowed to call themselves "alt-right" or whether Jews can be considered white people.[8]

Alt-right members may differ about the ideal outcome of their activism, but Spencer has made his clear, says Hawley. "He wants to see an all-white ethno-state established in North America," he says.

Spencer, however, has not clarified how the ethno-state would come about, a lack of detail that Hawley says is par for the alt-right course. The movement does not have "a lot in the way of real policy platforms," he says.

The lack of policy specifics springs from necessity, at least in part, says Brian Levin, director of the Center for the Study of Hate and Extremism at California State University, San Bernardino. "Spencer has to maintain credibility with extremists in the alt-right network, while also sending a more amorphous message that might reach mainstream voters" without frightening those voters off, says Levin.

While members of what's now called the alt-right have been active for years, they came to public attention in the last two years after various white nationalists began speaking out in favor of Trump's candidacy, and alt-right online activism caught the media's attention. Trump, who has denounced the movement, is "energizing" white nationalists in the United States, said Spencer, because of his anti-immigration, America First rhetoric.[9]

The movement's profile rose further when candidate Trump retweeted white nationalist and neo-Nazi messages, such as a fictitious crime statistic claiming that 81 percent of 2015 white murder victims were killed by blacks. (The correct figure is about 15 percent.)[10] Democratic presidential nominee Hillary Clinton accused Trump of stoking racism. The alt-right represents "a paranoid fringe in our politics," Clinton said in an August 2016 speech in Reno, Nev., and Trump had invigorated the movement by "stoking it, encouraging it and giving it a national megaphone."[11]

Over the past several years the movement also received exposure from the right-wing Breitbart News Network. Stephen Bannon, who became executive chairman after founder Andrew Breitbart died in 2012, said in August 2016 that *Breitbart News* is "the platform for the alt-right."[12] Trump named Bannon his campaign chief executive in August 2016, and then, post-election, named him chief White House strategist, moves that again raised the movement's public profile and that some observers fear could give the group a say in government policymaking.[13]

Throughout his campaign, Trump won endorsements from extremist groups, such as white supremacists and neo-Nazis, while also winning over tens of millions of mainstream voters, says Levin — something virtually unprecedented in U.S. history. "Far-right extremists have tried for decades to field candidates who could go mainstream, but they haven't ever had a charismatic leader who could do it," he says.

Still unclear, though, is the degree to which the Trump administration can or would act to turn white nationalist ideas into public policies, analysts say. In his inaugural address, Trump promised to fight for all Americans. "It is time to remember that old wisdom our soldiers will never forget: that whether we are black or brown or white, we all bleed the same red blood of patriots, we all enjoy the same glorious freedoms, and we all salute the same great American flag," he said.[14]

Advocates of race-based politics say they have only modest hopes. In his inaugural address, Trump served up "egalitarian schmaltz," self-proclaimed "race realist" Jared Taylor, founder of the alt-right American Renaissance website, said with disapproval. However, Trump does seem "to realize that at least some people don't belong [in the United States]," Taylor said, and may learn from some advisers, such as Bannon, to become more race-conscious with time.[15]

As political observers and others speculate on the alt-right's future, here are some of the questions they are asking:

Is the alt-right a white supremacist movement?

People who identify as "alt-right" view race as central to human identity and consider the mixing of races in one society as a recipe for strife. In the past, many such people professed belief in "white supremacy" — the idea that whites are by nature superior to all other races, such as blacks, and therefore deserve to dominate society.

Alt-right groups do not use the term white supremacy to describe their beliefs. Some political analysts, however, argue that many in the alt-right are traditional white supremacists who have dropped the term because it fell out of public favor.

Several terms are routinely used to describe white identity politics, says Rosenthal, of the University of California, Berkeley.

White nationalism is "the idea that this is a white country," Rosenthal says. "Then there's white separatism — the desire to have a literal place, a state, where white people can live on their own. Then there's white supremacy, which sees white people as having created all of Western civilization and asserts that they should therefore dominate in society. It's difficult to tell who holds which of these ideas, [partly because] people are very likely to say different things depending on who's there," he says.[16]

The alt-right has members with various beliefs. It "is now the main refuge of what previously was a hodge-podge of bigots, including neo-Nazis," says Levin of the Center for the Study of Hate and Extremism. Held in common "is a widespread notion that diversity and internationalism are traitorous," he says.

Many scholars of extremism, including Levin, say that the idea of white supremacy underlies the beliefs of many in the alt-right.

"Alt-right, much like white nationalism, is a rebranding of white supremacy," says Mayo of the ADL. "Some reject the term 'white supremacy,' but when you read their materials, their articles, their blogs, there's a constant focus on whites being superior," she says.

For example, the *American Renaissance* website posts a series of articles called "How I Saw the Light About Race," collating website readers' comments. One reader who grew up in an all-white area wrote, "When I did finally meet blacks, I found them to be childish, unintelligent, inarticulate, and often immoral and degenerate. That opinion has been confirmed over the decades."[17]

"Biological determinism that argues some races are objectively inferior to others isn't as easy a sell as it once was, neither politically nor scientifically," says Levin. "Most people just don't buy it any longer." As a result, arguments for white separatism or dominance based on white supremacy are seldom used today, at least publicly, he says. White nationalists still do use the biological determinism argument for some audiences, calling it "biological diversity," Levin says.

Today, the alt-right argues that "white Europeans" have singlehandedly created a superior U.S. culture that has gained nothing of value from the presence of other ethnicities, Levin says.

The shift away from the white supremacy term began as early as 1994, when some members of the Ku Klux Klan and others realized that it made many people envision "a certain kind of uncultured bigot," said Michael Waltman, an associate professor of interpersonal and organizational communication at the University of North Carolina, Chapel Hill. Many adopted "white nationalist" as a substitute. But "it is really hard to be a white nationalist and not sort of think of white people as better than other folks," Waltman said.[18]

Taylor, founder of the *American Renaissance* website, said in September that the alt-right is "in unanimity"

American white-nationalist author Jared Taylor, founder of the alt-right *American Renaissance* website, addresses the International Russian Conservative Forum in St. Petersburg, Russia, on, March 22, 2015. Taylor has said the alt-right is "in unanimity" about rejecting "the idea that the races are basically equivalent and interchangeable."

about rejecting "the idea that the races are basically equivalent and interchangeable." Genetic differences make white people more moral and more intelligent than black people, Taylor claimed.[19]

Nevertheless, Taylor added that he rejects the white supremacist term because "you could very effectively argue that East Asians are objectively superior to whites. Does that make us yellow supremacists? I don't think so."[20]

Many in the alt-right movement hope white Americans eventually will live in a whites-only ethnostate that Spencer has said might be created by some means of "peaceful ethnic cleansing."[21] The ethno-state would not be open to Jews, he said. "Jews are Jews."[22]

In a November 2016 speech to a Washington conference of the alt-right sponsored by the National Policy Institute think tank, which Spencer heads, he laid out many of his ideas.

He did not use the term white supremacy. Nevertheless, he argued that the United States was "great" through the early 1960s, citing its space program and other accomplishments, but has since lost its lead. The cause: "American society was 90 percent European" in the early 1960s, but since then ethnic diversity and racial minorities' influence in society have increased, to the country's detriment, Spencer said.[23] (The Immigration and

Nationality Act of 1965, also known as the Hart-Celler Act, abolished immigration quotas based on national origin, and the Civil Rights Act of 1964 outlawed discrimination based on race, color, religion, sex or national origin.[24])

To applause from the nearly 300 people at the conference, Spencer described white Americans as superior people continually under attack by liberals, who he said are allied with blacks and Hispanics. "The American Left is driven by anti-white hatred, full stop," he said, adding that "we have nothing in common with these people."[25]

In a multiethnic society, said Spencer, white Americans who have had their nation's greatness unfairly stripped away are ready to fight back. "We were not meant to beg for moral validation from some of the most despicable creatures to ever populate the planet," he said, referring to liberals and nonwhite Americans. "We were meant to overcome, overcome all of this, because that is natural and normal for us. Because for us, as Europeans, it is only normal again when we are great again."

Then he concluded by declaring: "Hail Trump. Hail our people. Hail victory."[26]

Does the Trump administration support alt-right ideas?

Political analysts say the alt-right owes its current prominence to the fact that, from the day he announced his presidential campaign on June 16, 2015, President Trump often asserted white nationalist-friendly ideas, such as his calls for a wall between the United States and Mexico and his broad-brush assertions to African-Americans that "you're living in poverty."[27]

White nationalists — who had not openly embraced a Democratic or Republican presidential candidate within living memory — began praising Trump's statements online. And, to some extent, at least, candidate Trump appeared to respond in kind, such as when he retweeted a depiction of his primary opponent Jeb Bush as a beggar that was originally posted by someone with the white nationalist Twitter name @WhiteGenocideTM.[28]

Taking notice of this relationship between a major-party candidate and white nationalists, the media began covering the alt-right, creating a level of public awareness of white nationalism that has not been seen for years.

Trump himself has said he rejects the alt-right, although his critics say he was slow to do so. In a Nov. 22 interview with *The New York Times* the president said of the alt-right, "I don't want to energize the group. I disavow the group."[29]

Nevertheless, two months into his presidency, signs point both for and against the Trump administration pursuing an agenda that parallels certain alt-right beliefs, experts say.

The movement's leaders are clearly supportive of many of the administration's ideas. For example, Trump's plan to aggressively deport more undocumented immigrants is nothing less than a revolution that might restore a white America, said Kevin MacDonald, editor of the online *Occidental Observer*, a leading white nationalist publication.[30]

Another sign that alt-right-friendly ideas are in play are reports that the Trump administration plans to shift a government program for monitoring violent ideologies to focus on so-called Islamic extremism, says Jasmin Mujanoviĉ, a New York City-based international relations scholar and consultant specializing in Eastern Europe.[31] In the past, the program has also monitored domestic extremists from the right, such as white nationalists, who have been responsible for many U.S. bombings and shootings, Mujanoviĉ says.

The focus on Islamic extremism is a signal the alt-right might welcome, he says.

Writers at some neo-Nazi websites associated with the alt-right have taken it just that way. "This measure would be the first step to us going fully mainstream, and beginning the process of entering the government in full-force without the fear of being attacked, financially assailed, and intimidated into silence by the nefarious Jews," wrote poster Marcus Cicero at the neo-Nazi website *Infostormer*.[32]

Trump's appointment of Bannon as White House chief strategist suggests that white nationalist ideas might get a hearing but not necessarily automatic approval, political observers say.

On the one hand, Bannon has said he has no tolerance for "some racial and anti-Semitic overtones" in alt-right thinking.[33] However, he is also an outspoken critic of immigration, free trade and international alliances and is widely reported to be the moving force behind some hardline actions that the Trump administration has taken against undocumented immigrants, refugees and travelers from several majority Muslim countries.[34]

Those moves are in tune with alt-right views, notes Hussein Ibish, a senior resident scholar and expert on hate crimes and civil liberties at the independent Arab Gulf States Institute, a Washington think tank. Trump himself, however, has taken a more pragmatic view of immigration through the years, raising questions about whether he'll fully support such hardline actions throughout his presidency or eventually move in another direction, Ibish says.

Ibish cites a *Breitbart News Daily* radio interview that Bannon conducted with Trump in 2015, in which Trump "called for using practical economic considerations" to decide which immigrants to admit, saying that "there are advantages to bringing in Indian computer scientists." "But Bannon basically said, 'Absolutely not.' If they weren't white Europeans they weren't wanted in this society," Ibish recalls.[35]

Many Trump supporters don't see his policies as racist but as pro-white, says Carol Swain, a professor of law and politics at Vanderbilt University, in Nashville, and the author of two books about contemporary white nationalism. "White people have real concerns — rising mortality rates in some places with people dying of despair, drug abuse, overdoses," she says. "Naturally when they hear about government addressing the problems of other groups they want to hear about their own problems. And Mr. Trump tapped into that."

"I don't think Donald Trump is a white nationalist," Swain says. "He was tapping into real concerns. And he was steering people toward patriotism — things that unite."

On the whole, the alt-right hopes Trump will be a transitional figure whose ideas can nudge public debate in the direction of their ideology, many analysts say.

Trump can help normalize their ideas by introducing less extreme but related concepts into the discussion as a

White Nationalists Gain on Social Media

White-nationalist movements have gained 22,000 Twitter followers since 2012, a more than sevenfold increase but still a minuscule part of social media traffic. Among Twitter accounts of white nationalists, those with pro-Nazi sympathies were more prevalent than those focusing on other alt-right ideologies.

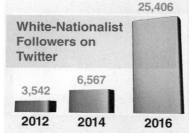

White-Nationalist Followers on Twitter

Source: J.M. Berger, "Nazis vs. ISIS on Twitter: A Comparative Study of White Nationalist and ISIS Online Social Media Networks," September 2016, pp. 3-4, http://tinyurl.com/gpc57jr.

sort of "gateway drug" to accustom people to hearing racist and isolationist views, says Mujanoviĉ. "They've been working on this for years online, and they've been looking for a carrier to bring it to a wider audience."

"They call it shifting the Overton window" — a term invented by a conservative think tank to describe a range of socially acceptable positions, says Lyons, coauthor of *Right-Wing Populism in America*.[36] "They were on the verge of saying 'This is hopeless!' Then Trump came along" and showed willingness to try widening the window. His ability to voice previously unacceptable ideas gave the movement new hope for its plan, Lyons says.

Alt-right members see some early presidential actions as less than encouraging, however. For instance, few of Trump's cabinet appointees appear to favor a U.S. exit from international alliances. "These are globalists in general. They love free trade, they love immigration — big red flags for us," said MacDonald of the *Occidental Observer*.[37]

Does the alt-right promote violence?

So far, there is no evidence the alt-right has explicitly inspired violent acts, says the University of Alabama's Hawley.

Alt-right leader Spencer said he opposes direct threats of violence but supports the free-speech rights of those who display swastikas or make racist statements. "In terms of self-expression, we're not going to condemn something like [displaying swastikas] wholesale," Spencer said.[38]

Ku Klux Klan members wearing hoods may not be the threats that some perceive them to be, Spencer told NPR. Instead, he said, such apparently provocative actions may just be people's attempt "to get in touch with their identity as a European."[39]

Guatemalan immigrants deported from the United States arrive in Guatemala City on Feb. 9, 2017. Political observers say the alt-right has tapped into some whites' fears about immigration and the nation's changing demographics, where whites will soon be a minority. President Trump's populist appeals to people worried about immigration also have resonated with alt-right supporters.

In fact, Spencer contended, the real causes of violence and hatred in society are situations in which people of different races are forced into close interaction. History demonstrates this, he argued. "When you have two really dramatically different cultures, two dramatically different races all being forced together, it's a recipe for turmoil," Spencer said. "I don't know of an historical example that contradicts that."[40]

Some psychologists, however, say that simply identifying oneself as part of a group with common interests and a shared identity — such as race or religion — makes people more likely to express and act on prejudices against non-group members, even to the point of violence.

That's because the more strongly people believe they have a rational reason to harm another person, the more likely they are to feel free to do so, wrote Daniel Effron, an assistant professor of organizational behavior at London Business School in England, and Eric Knowles, an associate professor of psychology at New York University in New York City. Moreover, people are highly likely to believe that protecting the shared interests of one's group from a suspected threat provides just such a reason, said Effron and Knowles, who conducted several studies of the matter on ordinary people, not extremist groups.[41]

"Our research therefore raises the concern that as the [the United States] continues to diversify, whites not only may develop greater hostility toward other racial groups but also may increasingly regard themselves as possessing a license to express it," Effron and Knowles wrote.[42]

History bears out that connection, says Heidi Beirich, director of the Southern Poverty Law Center's (SPLC) Intelligence Project, which monitors extremist groups. "Historically there's been violent politics when things change culturally," such as in the 1920s when the nation's white Protestant majority felt threatened by a large wave of immigration, and Ku Klux Klan violence escalated, she says.

If a recognized authority figure simply suggests that some demographic group should be feared or disliked, some people may view that statement as permission to commit violence, said Charles Taylor, professor emeritus of philosophy at McGill University in Montreal, who is an expert on xenophobia and the challenges that multicultural societies face.[43]

"Whenever political leaders propose to limit the rights of Muslims," said Taylor, "they encourage Islamophobic sentiment and disinhibit hostile acts," whether they intend to do so or not. "If highly respected leaders share that hostility, why shouldn't people who hold the same views act on them?" Trump's limitations on travel visas from Muslim-majority countries may have had that effect on Alexandre Bissonnette, who killed six Muslim men in a Quebec City, Canada, mosque, Taylor said.[44]

After Spencer spoke at a Washington conference on Nov. 19, the U.S. Holocaust Memorial Museum issued a statement arguing that the speech could incite violence. Spencer made "several direct and indirect references to Jews and other minorities, often alluding to Nazism," the statement read. "He implied that the media was protecting Jewish interests and said, 'One wonders if these people are people at all?' . . . His statement that white people face a choice of 'conquer or die' closely echoes Adolf Hitler's view of Jews and that history is a racial struggle for survival."[45]

"By the end of World War II," the museum's statement continued, "the Germans and their collaborators had murdered six million Jews and millions of other innocent citizens, many of whom were targeted for racial reasons. The Holocaust did not begin with killing; it began with words."

Words can spark violence and also help keep violence at bay, notes political consultant Mujanoviĉ, a Bosnian who in the 1990s was a young refugee from the former Yugoslavia, where ethnic and religious strife helped fuel wars and authoritarian takeover.

"I would really love it if the Republicans and Democrats could release some statement together, saying, 'There are certain things about which we'll likely always disagree, but there are some ways of talking that we all find unacceptable. Here are a handful of things that we do not support.' As a former refugee, I understand the anxiety many people say they feel in this climate. And it means so much for elder statesmen to come out and say, 'This has gone too far,' " he says.

BACKGROUND
American Racial Purity

The alt-right's beliefs are nothing new. Throughout U.S. history, many Americans have held that national greatness rested on maintaining the values of European whites. Likewise, the alt-right idea that the nation should avoid foreign alliances has had many adherents, including President George Washington.

Non-British immigration was unpopular at times during the colonial period. Benjamin Franklin, a philosopher, scientist and apostle of the Enlightenment, worried about the large number of German-speaking immigrants in Pennsylvania.

While these immigrants had "industry and frugality" that would likely be useful to the colony, Franklin wrote in a 1753 letter, it might still be advisable to cap their numbers. "Those who come hither are generally of the most ignorant Stupid Sort." Moreover, he continued, "few of their children in the Country learn English," to the point that "in a few years [interpreters] will be also necessary in the [colony's] Assembly, to tell one half of our Legislators what the other half say," he grumbled.[46]

Once the United States became an independent nation, established under a written Constitution, two competing visions emerged about what nationhood entailed, says Levin of the Center for the Study of Hate and Extremism.

"Some see the nation as having a unifying national creed that includes things such as respect for religious pluralism" and accepting as citizens all people who agree to embrace that creed, Levin says. "But for many of the electorate this is less important than another notion — seeing their nation in racial, ethnic and religious terms." The struggle between those visions persists to this day, he says.

"A foreigner can immigrate to France or Japan but never become truly French or Japanese," said Matthew Spalding, associate vice president of the Washington-based Allan P. Kirby Jr. Center for Constitutional Studies and Citizenship, a project of Michigan's Hillsdale College.[47] "But a foreigner of any ethnic heritage or racial background can immigrate to the United States and become, *in every sense of the term*, an American," he wrote.[48]

"The Founders were not afraid that immigrants, by themselves, would subvert the American republic," so long as, in the words of founder Alexander Hamilton, the new nation's first treasury secretary, they would "learn the principles and imbibe the spirit of our government," Spalding said.[49]

But many Americans also have argued strenuously against opening citizenship to all and against the idea that people of different ethnicities are equal. They needed only to look at the Constitution and its "three-fifths" compromise, which counted a slave as three-fifths of a person for the purposes of apportioning taxes and representation.

"Ours is the Government of the white man," and that is the source of its success, contended U.S. Sen. John C. Calhoun of South Carolina in 1848. Some other young countries in the Americas, colonized by Spain, were failing because they had committed the "fatal error of placing the colored race on an equality with the white," said Calhoun, arguing against a call for the United States to annex Mexico after the 1846-1848 Mexican-American War. More than half of Mexico's population were "pure Indians" and many more were of "mixed blood," and Calhoun "[protested] against the incorporation of such a people," he said.[50]

During periods when America's white Protestant majority believed its dominance was threatened, the ethnicity-based vision of nationhood strengthened and produced organizations dedicated to enforcing it, sometimes through acts of terror.

In the 1850s, the nativist party known as the Know-Nothings argued that the country was being overrun by

Irish Catholics and other immigrants, and it fought to limit immigration.

With the defeat of the South in the Civil War and the freeing of slaves, the Republican-controlled Congress embarked on a program to "reconstruct" the former Confederate states by creating biracial governments in the South and trying to integrate African-Americans into civic life. But the Ku Klux Klan, which was founded in Tennessee in 1866, fought to maintain white supremacy by using violence to terrorize newly freed slaves and their white supporters.[51]

After about a decade and a half of activity, the Klan and its sympathizers had largely achieved their goal of squelching black freedmen's attempts to exercise their voting rights or otherwise seek social equality. That success and some government action to quell the violence, led to the Klan's virtual (but temporary) disappearance by the 1880s and the rise of Jim Crow laws in the South that legalized racial segregation.[52]

The vision of a nation whose strength derived from a common creed, not a common ethnicity, remained alive for some, however, even in those times. Sen. Charles Sumner of Massachusetts, for example, argued in 1871 for a law to ensure equal civil rights for freedmen. "There is true grandeur in an example of justice, making the rights of all the same as our own, and beating down prejudice, like Satan, under our feet," Sumner said.[53]

As the 20th century began, a massive wave of immigration from across the world once again made white Protestants uneasy. Asians, Eastern Europeans, Catholics, Jews and others arrived in greater numbers. Nearly 1.3 million legal immigrants entered the country in 1907, and more than 1.2 million arrived in 1914 — annual immigration peaks that would not be matched until the 1990s.[54]

In 1915, the Ku Klux Klan announced that it would reassemble, this time establishing itself as both an anti-black and an anti-immigrant organization in the South and the Midwest.[55]

"In the 1920s, one-seventh to one-eighth of the electorate were tied to the Klan," says Levin.

In its successful outreach to middle- and upper-class Americans, the Klan published books and newspapers, ran seminars, and even tried to open its own university, said Kelly J. Baker, author of the *Gospel According to the Klan: The KKK's Appeal to Protestant America, 1915-1930*. The

Klan successfully spread the belief that biology proved white people to be the world's "leading race" and that God had ordained it so, Baker said.[56]

Some important government policies reflected those ideas.

For example, in 1924, Congress passed the Johnson-Reed Immigration Act, banning Asian immigration and capping annual immigration of other nationalities at 2 percent of the total number of people of that nationality appearing on the 1890 census. The law's "most basic purpose" was "to preserve the ideal of U.S. homogeneity," according to the U.S. State Department.[57]

During the Great Depression of the 1930s, Klan membership dropped steeply as immigration fell, the group faced some scandals and Americans focused on the economy. White supremacist groups have never regained their 1920s prominence. A resurgence of such groups began in the 1950s, however, as the civil rights movement intensified.

Far-Right Thinkers

The alt-right has roots in racist movements such as the Ku Klux Klan and similar groups that focused on intimidating people who tried to assert minority rights. But it also has roots in another area in which some advocates of white nationalism have worked — conservative political theory.

One such group, called "paleoconservatives," was the early political home of Spencer.[58]

Paleoconservatism — which is considered a far-right political movement — took shape in the 1980s as an effort to dissuade the Republican Party from following the lead of the "neoconservatives," a group of influential formerly liberal scholars and journalists who had joined the Republican ranks around 1970.

By the time President Ronald Reagan took office in 1981, neoconservatives had won significant Republican support for ideas that horrified some traditional conservatives, such as open immigration, embrace of the civil-rights movement and aggressive use of both diplomacy and military might to advance U.S. interests abroad.[59]

Although they did not burn crosses or view race as the sole unifying idea of their philosophy, paleoconservatives nevertheless embraced a white nationalist vision of America. They argued that the United States owed its greatness to the Founders' European heritage, and they

CHRONOLOGY

1990s *White supremacists use the internet to spread racist ideas.*

1995 Don Black of Florida sets up *Stormfront*, believed to be the world's first hate website, for white supremacists and neo-Nazis.

1999 Far-right parties, allies of U.S. white nationalists, win 11 percent of seats in the European Union's Parliament.

2000s *White nationalists win support by rebranding as an "identity" movement, urging whites to band together to protect common interests.*

2005 Conservative publishing-dynasty heir William Regnery II and other white nationalists open the National Policy Institute (NPI) think tank to promote white people's interests through meetings and publications.

2008 In the title of an article about "paleoconservatives" — members of a far-right group interested in preserving white dominance — *Taki's Magazine* editor Richard Spencer labels them the "alternative right."

2010s *A loose network of white-identity groups become known as the alt-right.*

2010 Leadership of NPI operations passes to Spencer. . . . He founds the online publication *Alternative Right* to publish essays on race and gender and serve as a gathering place for the alt-right.

2013 Alt-right, anti-Semitic website *Daily Stormer* is founded.

2014 Europe's far-right parties make further gains in the EU Parliament, winning just under 23 percent of the seats. . . . Russian President Vladimir Putin boosts the political fortunes of Marine Le Pen, leader of the French far-right National Front party, with a loan of 9 million euros from a Russianbacked bank.

2015 White supremacist Jared Taylor attends a March conference in Moscow on the denigration of white European traditions. . . . Republican presidential candidate Donald Trump is praised online by several alt-right members when, at his June 16 campaign launch, he labels many Mexican immigrants criminals. . . . Alt-right members

use the term #cuckservative — formed from "cuckold," a man who's been cheated on, and "conservative" — to insult conservatives they say have sold out to liberals.

2016 Stephen Bannon, executive chairman of the conservative *Breitbart News*, is appointed chief executive of the Trump presidential campaign and says *Breitbart* has been "the platform for the alt-right." . . . Alt-right members' enthusiasm for candidate Trump grows when he retweets posts from someone using the Twitter name @WhiteGenocideTM. . . . Profile of alt-right rises after Democratic nominee Hillary Clinton calls it a "paranoid fringe." . . . On Nov. 8, Trump wins the presidency. . . . Nearly 300 people attend a Nov. 20 alt-right conference in Washington, up from 172 in 2015; when conference organizer Richard Spencer closes a speech saying, "Hail Trump! Hail our people! Hail victory!" some in audience raise their arms in a Nazi salute. . . . After Spencer's speech, the U.S. Holocaust Memorial Museum said in a statement, "The Holocaust did not begin with killing. It began with words." . . . Asked on Nov. 22 about his possible alt-right connections, President-elect Trump says "I disavow the group."

2017 At the February annual meeting of the Conservative Political Action Conference (CPAC), President Trump and Bannon, now White House chief strategist, get enthusiastic welcomes from the event organizer. Self-described alt-right "fellow traveler" Milo Yiannopoulos, a former *Breitbart News* editor, whom Spencer calls an inspiration for his provocative use of hate speech as humor, is scratched from a CPAC speaking spot after a taped interview surfaced in which he appeared to sanction sex between men and underage boys. Spencer buys a ticket to sit in the CPAC audience but is escorted from the venue by hotel security because of his beliefs; some attendees enthusiastically welcome him, however. . . . Anti-Defamation League reports 63 cases of white nationalists distributing fliers on campuses in January and February, a significant increase over 2016. . . . Critics charge that some actions by President Trump tacitly encourage the alt-right; they point to travel bans for citizens of six Muslim-majority countries and a plan to publicize a list of criminal acts committed by undocumented immigrants. . . . IRS suspends the tax-exempt status of Spencer's NPI think tank because the group filed no IRS paperwork since 2013.

Researchers: Alt-Right Uses Internet to Normalize Hate

"You have all these men who see their role as internet warriors."

When David French, a writer for the conservative National Review, criticized Donald Trump during the 2016 presidential campaign and questioned his alleged ties to the "alt-right," followers of the movement began to attack him online.

One attack, French said, involved the posting of "images of my daughter's face in gas chambers, with a smiling Trump in a Nazi uniform preparing to press a button and kill her."[1]

The incident, researchers say, is one example of how the alt-right has been using its online skills over the past two years to attack opponents, raise its profile and gain members.

During the 2016 presidential campaign, people identifying themselves as alt-right followers targeted Trump's "critics, among others, with streams and streams of abuse through anonymous Twitter accounts," says Matthew Lyons, a Philadelphia-based researcher and author specializing in right-wing movements.

"It's a devastating tactic," says Lyons. "And you can't even say that anybody in particular is orchestrating it. You have all these men who see their role as internet warriors. And somebody points to a person who's perceived as an enemy, like *National Review* writer David French, who criticized Trump. And someone says, 'Let's go after his family,' " he says.

It's not surprising that the alt-right is skillfully using the Web to win followers and wield political influence, says Jessie Daniels, a sociology professor at Hunter College in New York City and the author of the 2009 book *Cyber Racism*.

Racist groups were among the earliest organizations to see the internet's potential, she says. In an early-1990s interview, for example, David Duke, founder of the Louisiana-based Knights of the Ku Klux Klan, called the internet the greatest-ever opportunity to spread racist ideologies. "I believe that the Internet will begin a chain reaction of racial enlightenment that will shake the world by the speed of its intellectual conquest," Duke wrote.[2]

Some alt-right websites, such as the anti-Semitic white nationalist site *Daily Stormer*, have been building an online following quickly, says Heidi Beirich, director of the Southern Poverty Law Center's Intelligence Project, which monitors extremist groups.

The center found that the *Daily Stormer*, which was founded in 2013, needed only three years to surpass the

strenuously opposed policies that might dilute that heritage, such as open immigration and foreign alliances.[60]

In the 1990s one prominent paleoconservative, Patrick Buchanan, a former adviser to Republican Presidents Richard Nixon, Gerald Ford and Ronald Reagan, presented the group's ideas directly to voters with some success, winning more than a fifth of the votes cast in both the 1992 and 1996 Republican presidential primaries. He especially railed against immigration. "If America is to survive as 'one nation, one people,' " Buchanan said in 1994, "we need to call a "time-out" on immigration, to assimilate the tens of millions who have lately arrived."[61]

Despite paleoconservatives' inability to get buy-in from elected officials, such ideas held some public appeal and "continued to attract young intellectuals" into the 2000s, said Lyons.[62]

In 2008, leading paleoconservative Paul Gottfried, a retired professor of humanities at Elizabethtown College in Pennsylvania, said the movement had "youth and exuberance on our side, and a membership that is largely in its twenties and thirties." The young blood might eventually overcome what he deemed a long-running media and political-establishment collaboration to block far-right challenges to mainstream Republicanism.[63]

Web traffic of the oldest hate sites online, such as *Stormfront,* which debuted in 1995, Beirich says.

Trolling — posting inflammatory messages in an attempt to provoke controversy — is one way the alt-right wins new followers, says George Hawley, an assistant professor of political science at the University of Alabama in Tuscaloosa.

"Trolling isn't done to influence the person being trolled," he says. "Other people are watching, and the trolls know they'll attract some of them if they draw the target into a fight" or simply troll in an aggressive way that seems "edgy and fun" to some people. "It sends the message that, 'Hey, if you follow us, you too can rile famous people online,'" Hawley says.

During the 2016 campaign, the alt-right also used bots — automated software — to quickly spread political memes, which are images or other material passed around online, says Daniels.

When a topic alt-rightists wanted to target came up in a Twitter feed — such as the #imwithher hashtag connected to the campaign of Democratic presidential nominee Hillary Clinton — a bot would instantly retweet the hashtagged tweet along with the cartoon Pepe the Frog meme that the alt-right adopted as a symbol, Daniels says. "Bots were able to quickly get it into the general online conversation" much faster than humans could, she says.

Extremists also have learned how to gradually shift public discourse in directions they choose, Daniels says.

For example, a website on slavery run by white supremacists can excerpt oral histories found in the public domain and twist their meaning, such as by highlighting innocent-seeming facts about slaves being allowed to grow vegetables for their own use, she says. By savvy use of linking and other methods, they can change search engine results, so that when someone types into Google "was slavery so hard?" sites that give a misleading picture turn up, Daniels says.

"So much of what we know and understand about the world happens through search engines now," and white nationalists are among the internet-savvy people who can shape the public's picture of reality without anyone being aware of the manipulation, Daniels says.

Alt-right followers use similar methods to shift public discourse toward acceptance of once forbidden racist words and images, says Lyons. Some alt-right-related websites go out of their way to use the most shocking images of bigotry possible as a way to gradually make once-shunned speech and imagery seem normal through repetition, he says.

A case in point is some posters' recent heavy use of gas-chamber jokes, Lyons says. "Thousands and thousands of tweets have gone out telling gas-chamber jokes, and even if many people are still horrified," some will begin to view the jokes as normal, which shifts the political and social climate without most people even realizing it, he says.

— *Marcia Clemmitt*

[1]David French, "The Price I've Paid for Opposing Donald Trump," National Review, Oct. 21, 2016, http://tinyurl.com/j9ddfrr.

[2]Quoted in Jessie Daniels, *Cyber Racism* (2009), p. 3; also see Mark Weitzman, "'The Internet Is Our Sword,'" *Remembering for the Future: The Holocaust in an Age of Genocide* (2001), pp. 911-925, http://tinyurl.com/jn2s4kf.

Among this younger generation was Spencer, a former graduate student at the University of Chicago and Duke University, in North Carolina, who worked as an editor at two paleoconservative publications before starting his own online publication in 2010. That website, AlternativeRight.org, which Spencer edited until 2012, gathered many far-right voices into what is now known as the alt-right.[64]

Unlike paleoconservatives, "the alt-right is about race per se," says the University of Alabama's Hawley.

Like older paleoconservatives, Spencer wrote journal essays about his political ideas. Unlike them, however, he also argued on social media and reached out to neo-Nazis and other less staid advocates of white racial politics, who used racist epithets freely and with the intention to shock.[65] The alt-right is "revolutionary," while paleoconservatives are not, Spencer said. "I think we might need a little more chaos in our politics, we might need a bit of that fascist spirit," he said.[66]

Europe's New Right

Another major source of alt-right thinking was the far-right parties that have appeared in virtually all European countries over the past few decades.[67]

Called the European New Right (ENR), the movement has roots in the highly authoritarian, nationalistic

Alt-Right Borrows a Page From the Left

The movement is using identity politics to build a bigger following.

Taking its cue from the "identity politics" of the Left — in which people rallied around campaigns for gay rights or black pride — the so-called alt-right is attempting to rally mainstream white Americans to its cause by appealing to white pride, according to researchers Carol Swain of Vanderbilt University and Russ Nieli of Princeton University.[1]

Richard Spencer, the unofficial spokesman of the alt-right — an umbrella group of people with various racist beliefs, including anti-Semites, white supremacists and white nationalists who want whites to live in a separate "ethno-state" — urged white Americans to see themselves as a unified group. Whites, he said, must band together to fight for common interests or watch "European culture" get wiped out in a multicultural United States in which whites are simply one more minority group.[2]

White identity is at the core of the alt-right's appeal to the average white person and to President Trump's supporters, Spencer claimed, even if, he said, most Trump voters "aren't willing to articulate it as such."[3] Identity language, experts say, clearly resonates with some whites.

J.P. Sheehan, president of a College Republican club, said he was an Obama voter who gradually came to believe that ethnic minorities were moving into the forefront at his expense. He said he latched onto the white-identity language Spencer uses because it gave him a sense of meaning. "People think the alt-right is just simply about being mean to other people," said Sheehan. "It's really not. The alt-right is simply identity politics for white people."[4]

The appeal of identity language for some whites isn't surprising, Swain says.

"White people have real concerns, such as rising mortality rates, with older white people in some communities dying of despair, drug overdoses," she says. "They want those concerns recognized. But in the liberal political language [of the last several decades], they were hearing about everybody else and not about themselves."

For disaffected whites — including those who argue that whites are superior to other races — the "logical next step was to copy that multiculturalist language and use it to talk about themselves," Swain says. It was clear in the early 2000s that white identity would soon become the next rallying cry for disaffected white people, both mainstream whites and white racists, she says.

Swain says she recognized then that identity politics could be an effective tool for the far right to reach mainstream whites and help build opposition to racial inclusiveness.

Walter Benn Michaels, an English professor at the University of Illinois, Chicago, made a similar argument in his 2006 book, *The Trouble With Identity: How We Learned to Love Identity and Ignore Inequality.*

In the book, Michaels argued that identity politics was a dangerous diversion that allowed politicians to ignore the country's real socioeconomic problems, which afflict people from all demographics. Michaels, like Swain, warned that identity politics could backfire by making white people see themselves as an identity group victimized by racism.

In 2006, many liberal critics rejected both those arguments. But "someone told me they'd just discovered the book last week, and now it reads like a prophecy," said Michaels last year.[5]

As identity politics and language come to dominate the public debate, "what you get is an increasing number of white people who are committed and convinced that they're

fascism that took hold in Germany and Italy in the 1930s and eventually went down to defeat in World War II, says Lyons, the coauthor of *Right-Wing Populism in America*. Beginning in the 1990s, ENR texts were translated from French to English and became a source of ideas for "Americans seeking to develop a white

nationalist movement outside of traditional neo-Nazi/Ku Klux Klan circles," he wrote.[68]

After World War II, European far-right politicians had to recast their ideas to win over a wary public, Lyons says. Classical fascism developed in an era when Europeans' imperial conquests in Africa and elsewhere

the victims of racism," something that was evident in the 2016 campaign cycle, said Michaels.

In a 2014 survey by the independent research group Public Religion Research Institute, 52 percent of white Americans, 61 percent of Republicans and 73 percent of people identifying themselves as tea party members said racial discrimination against whites was as big a problem as racial discrimination against minorities.[6] "White people are indeed victimized — they're the largest group of poor people," Michaels said. "Those people begin to think, yeah, racism is the problem. That's why what we've seen emerge during this Trump campaign is a white identity politics."[7]

To combat this view — and to prevent white nationalists from continuing to use it to build support for racism — "we have to take new approaches to problems like poverty," Swain argues. "Look at socioeconomic problems that affect whites along with other ethnic groups and address them as that — as socioeconomic problems, not as problems of this identity group or that."

Others, however, defend identity politics and warn against abandoning it. The 2016 election did not demonstrate white backlash, said Jacob T. Levy, a professor of political theory at McGill University in Montreal. Trump got a lower share of white votes than Republican nominee Mitt Romney in 2012, 58 percent versus 59 percent. Moreover, in polls white voters expressed reluctance to vote for Trump when he spoke against minorities or showed disrespect for women, Levy said.[8]

Identity politics is necessary, Levy said, because so much injustice is "targeted injustice." He pointed to laws banning gay sexual activity and to policing that leads to the disproportionate arrests of blacks. To progress as a society, "we need to be able to hear each other talking about particularized injustices, and to cheer each other on when we seek to overturn them," he said.

— *Marcia Clemmitt*

A Ku Klux Klan member in Hampton Bays, N.Y., said on Nov. 22, 2016, that his KKK branch has had some 1,000 inquiries from people interested in joining since Donald Trump's election. The alt-right has roots in racist movements such as the Klan.

[1] Carol M. Swain, *The New White Nationalism in America: Its Challenge to Integration* (2002); Carol M. Swain and Russ Nieli, eds., *Contemporary Voices of White Nationalism in America* (2003), p. 5.

[2] Maya Oppenheim, "Alt-Right Leader Richard Spencer Worries Getting Punched Will Become the 'Meme to End All Memes,' " *Independent*, January 2017, http://tinyurl.com/jzmkm5d.

[3] Joseph Goldstein, "Alt-Right Gathering Exults in Trump Election Win With Nazi-Era Salute," *The New York Times*, Nov. 20, 2016, http://tinyurl.com/jauuls5.

[4] Michelle Goldberg, "Alt-Right Facts," *Slate*, Feb. 23, 2017, http://tinyurl.com/jylf6l4.

[5] Ryan Smith, "Walter Benn Michaels on How Liberals Still Love Diversity and Ignore Equality," *Chicago Reader*, Nov. 23, 2016, http://tinyurl.com/zsesmcl.

[6] Robert P. Jones, Daniel Cox and Juhem Navarro-Rivera, "Economic Insecurity, Rising Inequality, And Doubts About The Future," Public Religion Research Institute, Sept. 23, 2014, p. 39, http://tinyurl.com/jajsus9.

[7] *Ibid.*

[8] Jacob T. Levy, "The Defense Of Liberty Can't Do Without Identity Politics," Niskanen Center, Dec. 13, 2016, http://tinyurl.com/jdrmsrv.

seemed to confirm the idea that Western Europeans were a "master race," as Germany's Nazis had declared, Lyons says.

After independence movements essentially ended colonialism in the 1960s, however, the ENR switched from the vision of a conquering European master race to a "defensive mode," says Lyons. ENR politicians, including Nigel Farage in the United Kingdom, vowed to defend European civilization and a heritage whose greatness they said was under attack, diluted by immigration and by the new mass culture that globalization of economics and media was creating, he said.[69]

The alt-right takes a similar approach, casting the United States' long-dominant white majority as a group under attack who must fight to protect their common interests, say Lyons and others.

In 2005, a small group of white nationalists launched the National Policy Institute (NPI) think tank, mostly online, to host conferences and publish writings about what they called the fast-shrinking influence of white Americans. "Within the first- or secondhand memories of people in this room, the white race may go from master of the universe to an anthropological curiosity," said chief NPI founder William Regnery II, whose father, Henry, founded the conservative publisher Regnery Publishing.

In 2010, control of NPI's operations passed to Spencer.[70] For the next several years, NPI and other white nationalist websites, online magazines and membership groups continued trying to promote their ideas but were getting little public or media attention. Members wrote blog posts, journal articles and social-media posts. Spencer, Taylor and others held small conferences for white nationalists. But it wasn't until July 2015 when white nationalists responded enthusiastically to Trump's announcement that he would be a candidate for the presidency, did the groups capture much public attention.

CURRENT SITUATION
Campus Outreach

White supremacists and other members of the alt-right are stepping up their efforts to recruit college students, according to the Anti-Defamation League.

The group said it cataloged 63 incidents of movement members distributing fliers on campuses in January and February, a significant increase from 2016. A number of activists also are giving speeches. Spencer, for example, spoke at Texas A&M in College Station in early December. The league said white supremacists are "emboldened by the 2016 elections and the current political climate."[71]

The alt-right's outreach is roiling universities. Appearances by Milo Yiannopoulos, a former *Breitbart* editor who is considered an alt-right ally, have been especially controversial. Three hours before he was scheduled to speak at the University of California, Berkeley, on Feb. 1, students gathered outside the student union to protest his speech. The protests were peaceful, according

to authorities, until several dozen protesters wearing black masks arrived and attacked police barricades, threw firecrackers and broke windows. Authorities canceled the speech. A Berkeley student told a reporter, "We won't put up with the violent rhetoric of Milo, Trump or the fascistic alt-right."[72]

On Inauguration Day, a black-clad protester punched Spencer in the face while he was being interviewed by a journalist on a Washington, D.C., street. "There was an actual anti-fascist rally going on, and I walked into it," he said.[73]

Conservative groups are increasingly speaking out against the alt-right. The Tea Party Nation — an affiliate of the tea party movement, which espouses conservative principles — calls the alt-right fake conservatism and warns that it "pits itself against 'establishment' conservatism." At CPAC in February, organizer Schneider, who is executive director of the American Conservative Union, denounced alt-right members' beliefs. "They are anti-Semitic. They are racist. They are sexist," he said. "They are not an extension of the conservative movement."[74]

On March 12, though, Rep. Steve King, R-Iowa, drew praise from former Ku Klux Klan grand wizard David Duke after tweeting support for Dutch far-right politician Geert Wilders, who has called for ending Muslim immigration, closing mosques and banning the Koran. Americans from across the political spectrum blasted as racist King's remark that "we can't build our civilization with other people's babies."[75]

Meanwhile, a number of administration critics say President Trump is tacitly encouraging the alt-right with his immigration policies, including the revised travel ban that temporarily bars new visas for citizens of six predominantly Muslim countries. They also point to Trump's issuing of an executive order on Jan. 25 for the Department of Homeland Security to make public a list of all criminal acts committed by undocumented immigrants.[76]

And they say he offered delayed responses to an attack on the Canadian mosque that killed six; to some 100 bomb threats to Jewish organizations; to vandalism at Jewish cemeteries; and to the shooting of two Indian immigrants in Kansas by a suspect who reportedly shouted, "Get out of my country!"[77]

Many mainstream Republicans defend Trump, and the White House denies the criticisms, saying the president — including in his Feb. 28 speech to Congress — has repeatedly condemned racial and religious attacks as evil. It also dismisses any links between the president's rhetoric and acts of violence. "Any loss of life is tragic," White House press secretary Sean Spicer said on Feb. 24. "To suggest that there's any correlation I think is a bit absurd."[78]

As the debate continues, experts agree that the white nationalist movement thrives on controversy and is enjoying its time in the spotlight. A search of Google's news page turns up hundres of thousands of hits for the term "alt-right."

Nevertheless, most of the public remains unfamiliar with the movement. A December poll by the Pew Research Center in Washington found that 54 percent of the public had heard "nothing at all" about the alt-right, while 28 percent had heard only "a little."[79]

Conferences held under the alt-right banner remain small but have grown recently, at the same time as the movement's press coverage has expanded. After Trump's election, nearly 300 people attended a Nov. 19, 2016, NPI-sponsored conference in Washington, according to one affiliated group, Identity Evropa (IE).[80] That was up from 172 the year before.[81]

IE is led by Nathan Damigo, a former Marine corporal who is a student at California State University, Stanislaus, and formerly headed the National Youth Front, a wing of the Neo-Nazi American Freedom Party. It's one of the few alt-right groups to try offline activism, visiting university campuses to reach out to college Republican clubs and posting signs about the importance of white European identity.[82]

For reasons not yet understood, young people's involvement in white nationalism is rising, says Hawley. At meetings of groups such as American Renaissance, he says, more people under 30 seem to turn up today than did so 10 years ago.

Among Millennials, an October poll by Ipsos Public Affairs, a market research and consulting firm in Washington, found that 34 percent had a favorable view of the alt-right and only 21 percent an unfavorable. (The rest had no opinion.)[83]

Hawley told *The Washington Post* that "the alt-right has been able to successfully brand itself as an edgy and fun and ironic movement that takes pleasure in needling both liberals and conservatives, and it's tongue-in-cheek and rebellious as opposed to just being motivated by genocidal hatred."[84]

A flare shows a damaged window at a Wells Fargo Bank in Berkeley, Calif., during protests against a scheduled speech at the University of California by former Breitbart News Network editor Milo Yiannopoulos, a political provocateur who is considered an alt-right supporter. Authorities canceled the speech after protesters broke windows and threw flares and smoke bombs.

AFP/Getty Images/Josh Edelson

Internet Savvy

Individuals and groups have long used the internet to boost their causes, and the alt-right is using it effectively on Trump's behalf, political and technology analysts say.

The alt-right "contributed in a significant way to Trump's victory by their skillful use of online activism," such as by devising internet memes, says Lyons, coauthor of *Right-Wing Populism in America*. An internet meme is a catchy phrase, video or image that encapsulates an idea and spreads quickly online, carrying the idea with it.

Two such memes were #cuckservative and #draftourdaughters.

Combining the words "cuckold" — an insulting word for a man whose wife has cheated on him — and "conservative," #cuckservative denigrates traditional Republicans, whom the alt-right sees as selling out to liberal ideas such as allowing large-scale immigration. It was used to boost the image of outsider Republican candidate Trump. For #draftourdaughters, online activists photoshopped authentic-looking fake Clinton campaign materials stating that as president Clinton would bring more women into the armed services to fight wars she planned, such as a war with Russia.[85]

The alt-right's work with memes "was effective enough that mainstream media took notice. So that's power," says Lyons. "Could Trump have won anyway?

Should online racist speech be regulated?

YES
Jessie Daniels
Professor of Sociology, Hunter College

Written for *CQ Researcher*, March 2017

The commonplace view of free speech in the United States is often attributed to this quote, supposedly from the French philosopher Voltaire: "I disapprove of what you say, but I will defend to the death your right to say it." The quote is actually from a Voltaire biographer, and it misleads us about the nature of protected speech.

In 2003, the U.S. Supreme Court ruled that a burning cross is not protected speech, because it is meant to terrorize a group of people. When we think about the hate speech that can be located online today through Google searches, the question becomes: What constitutes a burning cross in the digital era?

Before Dylann Roof decided to kill nine people in a Bible study group in Charleston, S.C., in 2015, he searched online for "black on white crime." In his manifesto, he said that what he learned left him determined "to do something."

One racist site, Stormfront, has grown from 124,000 registered users in 2008 to over 320,000 today. And, because the internet is nearly borderless, our homegrown white supremacy is available to a global audience with deadly consequences. The Southern Poverty Law Center has linked that site alone to some 100 hate-crime murders.

The misbegotten notion that white supremacist views deserve First Amendment protection is rooted in another ill-formed idea: that good ideas will rise to the top and bad ideas will sink to the bottom.

But that is not true. When white supremacist ideas have a platform, they thrive, gain legitimacy, grow in popularity and endanger lives.

The Department of Homeland Security should treat white supremacy as a terrorist threat to the government and monitor online sites that promote racial hate. Unfortunately, it gutted its monitoring program for domestic terrorism in 2010, after conservatives objected to a "politically charged" leaked report. It is time to rebuild it, and identify and outlaw the kind of online speech that can cause real harm.

Other democracies do not see free speech as an absolute right; they see it as a right that must be balanced with others, such as the human right to not be the target of violence based on race, ethnicity, religion or sexual identity.

We should refuse to allow the First Amendment to be used to protect the speech of those who wish to use that protection to harm others.

NO
Jeffrey Herbst
President and Ceo, Newseum

Written for *CQ Researcher*, March 2017

The Web and the social media revolution it spawned are in many ways the First Amendment realized. Families have been reconnected, friendships renewed across vast distances and the isolation of some relieved. At the same time, social media, perhaps inevitably, has been the vehicle for the transmission of a tremendous amount of hatred, including numerous examples of racist speech that rightfully anger many.

What to do about the racism polluting parts of the information ecosystem is an important and emotional issue. In its recent survey of high school students — the "digital natives" supposedly at the core of the social media revolution — the Knight Foundation found that only 43 percent agreed people should be allowed to say offensive things on social media.

It is still not understood that the government is not allowed to regulate many instances of racist speech. Indeed, hate speech, except under very narrow exceptions — such as direct encouragement of others to immediately commit violence — is protected speech in the United States.

As private companies, the social media platforms themselves are able to regulate what they present to the public. Although these companies, notably Facebook, initially asserted that they were merely pipes through which others posted, they have become increasingly aggressive in developing and enforcing company-specific community standards, including prohibitions on racist speech.

The challenge is that social media use is evolving quickly, and the sheer volume of posts in almost every language transmitted at great speed makes regulation exceptionally difficult. Racists also continually push to see what they can get through.

In the new information order where the gatekeepers inevitably struggle, perhaps the ultimate form of "regulation" rests with citizens themselves. Racism flourishes online in part because hateful speech is allowed to dominate conversations.

Racism should be identified and countered. However, the ultimate way to do so is for the public to speak up and make persuasive statements through posts, videos, tweets and snaps showing that the only way we will prosper as a society is to figure out how we can live together as individuals. The power of algorithms used by the social media platforms is that they figure out with great speed the sentiments that are most popular and then distribute them. By guiding searchers to anti-racist speech, algorithms can help counter an age-old evil without violating the First Amendment.

Maybe. But this certainly helped him. It made his opponents look ridiculous in the eyes of some voters. And there was no defense."

International Movement

Internet or no, the alt-right wouldn't have risen from obscurity without an international trend that's made many white voters receptive to extremist messages, political scholars say.

Support for far-right political parties has soared across Europe since 1999, according to British investigative journalist Nafeez Ahmed. The parties' voter appeal has recently risen to heights not seen since the 1930s, when Hitler came to power in Germany, he wrote. In the most recent elections, held in 2014, far-right parties won just under 23 percent of the seats in the European Union's legislative body — the European Parliament — up from just 11 percent in 1999.[86]

This spring in France, far-right nationalist anti-immigrant politician Marine Le Pen, leader of the National Front party, has a good chance of winning the presidential election.[87] Germany and the Netherlands also have far-right candidates running strongly in presidential elections this year.[88]

Many European far-right parties have relationships with Russian Federation President Vladmir Putin, who apparently hopes the rise of parties that shun international alliances can weaken the European Union, a top economic and political rival of Russia, political observers say.[89]

It can be said "with a high degree of confidence" that Putin has been building ties with Europe's far right for a decade, says Alina Polyakova, deputy director of the Dinu Patriciu Eurasia Center at the nonpartisan international affairs think tank Atlantic Council in Washington. Le Pen even received a 9 million euro campaign loan from the Moscow-based First Czech Russian Bank, which has ties to Russia's government, she says.

Putin has given European far-right politicians "a kind of ideological architecture — strongly and consistently arguing against the EU and NATO," says international-affairs consultant Mujanović. "It's a language that has proven very attractive to many people who feel as if they and their traditions have been left behind" by the newly united EU and has helped the far-right parties gain voters, Mujanović says.

In recent years, the alt-right and other American far-right groups have been building international connections, both with Europe's far-right parties and with Putin's Russia. Alt-right leaders have praised Putin for his "anti-globalist" stance and for promoting white nationalism. American Renaissance founder and alt-right ally Taylor, for example, attended a 2015 conference on nationalist and ethnic issues in Moscow. Spencer has called Russia "the sole white power in the world."[90] And Trump has repeatedly praised Putin, which critics say has further encouraged the alt-right.

Despite alt-right members' apparent outreach to Putin, the movement's situation is "profoundly different" from that of European far-right parties in ways that make it unlikely that a Putin-alt-right alliance does or even could exist, Polyakova says. For one thing, "while there is overlap in ideas, the alt-right here is very new." Moreover, because the United States has a primarily two-party political system, small interest groups such as the alt-right are in no position to work with Putin "in a strategic way" as Europe's far-right politicians can, she says.

OUTLOOK
Spreading Influence?

Whether the alt-right can expand its online influence to win more real-world support for its views is still unknown. Also unknown — and worrisome to many — is whether the alt-right's race-oriented politics will lead to social disruption or violent pushback from other groups.

"White supremacists in the alt-right are fringe still," says the ADL's Mayo. "A few different groups are trying to meet and do real-world events, but those efforts are mostly just beginning."

The alt-right may pin most hope for expanding its support base on online trolling of people they disagree with and on speeches and writings from provocateurs such as Yiannopoulos, the former *Breitbart* editor who recently resigned over tapes in which he appeared to approve of sex between men and underage boys.[91]

Yiannopoulos and some other provocateurs friendly to the movement "are not white nationalists but try to be outrageous about the same issues to get a rise out of people," Mayo says. "The thought is that if you attract people by criticizing politically correct views, you may be able to gradually nudge them" into adopting more extreme racist and misogynist political views, she says. "I think that would be a small percentage of people, but it could happen."

Unlike the alt-right, advocacy groups with true clout "have think tanks, policy papers [and] people on congressional staffs," says the University of Alabama's Hawley. The alt-right has "already put themselves on the radar in ways that the far right hasn't previously been able to do. But it's not clear how they would get additional resources [and] support. It's possible that they've already accomplished all they're ever going to."

While the alt-right's online presence has gained it some young followers, it's also not clear whether exclusionary, isolationist politics will be as attractive to younger generations as they have sometimes been to older ones, says Levin of the Center for the Study of Hate and Extremism. In general, "Millennials are far more tolerant than their grandparents."

The attempts at relationship building carried out by the alt-right and European far-right parties could be a sign of desperation, says Ibish of the Arab Gulf States Institute. "They all want a movement because they know they're a minority, so if they don't go international, really become a worldwide movement, they're likely to die."

But Ibish says that may be more easily said than done. "How do you make an international movement of nationalists?" he says. And the differences among groups are substantial, in both the European far right and in the U.S. alt-right. "Some are anti-Semitic, some accept Jews but are very anti-Islam; some accept gays and others don't. The differences seem large. And the more they try to work in unison, the more they're likely to find it harder than they imagine," Ibish says.

The threat of violence from extremists on the right and left is real, says Levin. "The progressive left is now out of power, and with the absence of leadership there we have a fringe of the hard left — the anti-fascists, the Marxists — who believe that resistance should be violent" he says. "Will there be a coalescence of the hard violent left in response" to the rise of alt-right ideas or to policies put in place by an alt-right-friendly Trump administration? "We just don't know."

NOTES

1. Alice Ollstein, "CPAC Boots White Nationalist Richard Spencer After He Crashes The Party," *Talking Points Memo*, Feb. 23, 2017, http://tinyurl.com/jrlfgb2.

2. Quoted in Michelle Goldberg, "Alt-Right Facts," *Slate*, Feb. 23, 2017, http://tinyurl.com/jylf6l4.

3. Ollstein, *op. cit.*

4. "The Alt-Right: NOT Right — NOT Conservative," Tea Party Nation, http://tinyurl.com/jo92yg8.

5. For background, see Reed Karaim, "Immigrant Detention," *CQ Researcher*, Oct. 23, 2015, pp. 889-912.

6. For background, see Matthew N. Lyons, "Calling Them 'Alt-Right' Helps Us Fight Them,'" *threewayfight*, Nov. 22, 2016, http://tinyurl.com/zh9s6wy; Christopher Caldwell, "What the Alt-Right Really Means," *The New York Times*, Dec. 2, 2016, http://tinyurl.com/jne5xtd.

7. Quoted in "A Frank Conversation With a White Nationalist," Reveal, Center for Investigative Reporting, Nov. 10, 2016, http://tinyurl.com/zbkko6c.

8. For background, see "Queer Fascism: Why White Nationalists Are Trying To Drop Homophobia," *Anti-Fascist News*, Nov. 6, 2015, http://tinyurl.com/jejle6z, and Lukas Mikelionis, "Alt-Right Meltdown After Tweets About the 'Jewish Question,'" *HeatStreet*, Dec. 27, 2016, http://tinyurl.com/grhl4j7.

9. Quoted in Garrett Haake, "White Nationalist Group to Hold Conference on Trump in DC Saturday," WUSA.com, March 2, 2016, http://tinyurl.com/zsmdl45; "Donald Trump's New York Times Interview: Full Transcript," *The New York Times*, Nov. 23, 2016, http://tinyurl.com/juymes5.

10. Nicholas Confessore, "For Whites Sensing Decline, Donald Trump Unleashes Words of Resistance," *The New York Times*, July 13, 2016, http://tinyurl.com/jh5nx69.

11. Abby Ohlheiser and Caitlin Dewey, "Hillary Clinton's alt-right speech, annotated," *The Washington Post*, Aug. 25, 2016, http://tinyurl.com/jksmlan.

12. Sarah Posner, "How Stephen Bannon Created an Online Haven for White Nationalists," The Investigative Fund, The Nation Institute, Aug. 22, 2016, http://tinyurl.com/z5wm6za.

13. Jonathan Martin, Jim Rutenberg and Maggie Haberman, "Donald Trump Appoints Media Firebrand to Run Campaign," *The New York Times*, Aug. 17, 2016, http://tinyurl.com/gmav62k; Michael D. Shear, Maggie Haberman and Alan Rappeport, "Donald Trump Picks Reince Priebus as Chief of Staff and Stephen Bannon as Strategist," *The New York Times*, Nov. 13, 2016, http://tinyurl.com/zm3fp44.

14. "Inaugural Address: Trump's Full Speech," CNN, Jan. 21, 2017, http://tinyurl.com/j6jjkkg.

15. Jared Taylor, "I Was There," *American Renaissance*, Jan. 21, 2017, http://tinyurl.com/hned8t7.

16. For background, see Josh Harkinson, "We Talked to Experts About What Terms to Use for Which Group of Racists," *Mother Jones*, Dec. 8, 2016, http://tinyurl.com/h24w9lz.

17. "How I Saw the Light About Race (Part VIII)," *American Renaissance*, Feb. 27, 2017, http://tinyurl.com/h96tlp4.

18. Quoted in Harkinson, *op. cit.*

19. Quoted in Betsy Woodruff, "Alt-Right Leaders: We Aren't Racist, We Just Hate Jews," *The Daily Beast*, Sept. 9, 2016, http://tinyurl.com/zfqh8vo.

20. Quoted in *ibid.*

21. Amanda Taub, "'White Nationalism' Explained," *The New York Times*, Nov. 21, 2016, http://tinyurl.com/zxfwxz4.

22. Woodruff, *op. cit.*

23. "Richard Spencer — NPI 2016, Full Speech," Red Ice TV, YouTube, Nov. 21, 2016, http://tinyurl.com/hgybpgh.

24. For background, see "U.S. Immigration Through 1965," History.com, http://tinyurl.com/24hemcb; "Civil Rights Act," History.com, http://tinyurl.com/pp7sa3w.

25. Spencer, *op. cit.*

26. *Ibid.*

27. Richard Fausset, Alan Blinder and John Eligon, "Donald Trump's Description of Black America Is Offending Those Living in It," *The New York Times*, Aug. 24, 2016, http://tinyurl.com/hx7fmb7.

28. Tal Kopan, "Donald Trump Retweets 'White Genocide' Twitter User," CNN.com, Jan. 22, 2016, http://tinyurl.com/gnjvh3g.

29. "Donald Trump's New York Times Interview: Full Transcript," *op. cit.*

30. Quoted in Sarah Posner and David Neiwert, "How Trump Took Hate Groups Mainstream," *Mother Jones*, Oct. 14, 2016, http://tinyurl.com/h9kfd6b.

31. For background, see Julia Edwards Ainsley, Dustin Volz and Kristina Cooke, "Exclusive: Trump to Focus Counter-Extremism Program Solely on Islam — Sources," Reuters, Feb. 2, 2017, http://tinyurl.com/zo9cmv3.

32. Marcus Cicero, "President Trump Ready to Change Definition of 'Extremis,' Will Remove White Supremacists From List," *Infostormer*, Feb. 2, 2017, http://tinyurl.com/jl3tg7g.

33. "Steve Bannon: 'Zero Tolerance' For Anti-Semitic, Racist Elements of the Alt-Right," *Breitbart*, Nov. 19, 2016, http://tinyurl.com/h4otqxb.

34. For background, see Evan Perez, Pamela Brown and Kevin Liptak, "Inside the Confusion of the Trump Executive Order and Travel Ban," CNN Politics, Jan. 30, 2017, http://tinyurl.com/zx4mfk8; John Walcott and Julia Edwards Ainsley, "Trump's Go-to Man Bannon Takes Hardline View on Immigration," Reuters, Jan. 31, 2017, http://tinyurl.com/zxx95lq.

35. For background, see David A. Fahrenthold and Frances Stead Sellers, "How Bannon Flattered and Coaxed Trump on Policies Key to the Alt-Right," *The Washington Post*, Nov. 15, 2016, http://tinyurl.com/jbsde9h.

36. For background, see Nathan J. Russell, "An Introduction to the Overton Window of Political Possibilities," Mackinac Center, Jan. 4, 2006, http://tinyurl.com/hzqlodo.

37. Frank Morris, "White Nationalists' Enthusiasm for Trump Cools," *All Things Considered*, NPR, Jan. 13, 2017, http://tinyurl.com/hgvvfna.

38. Quoted in Laurie Richards, "The Alt-Right Reveals Its Agenda to Influence Trump's Presidency," ThinkProgress, Nov. 20, 2016, http://tinyurl.com/zctstqy.

39. "'We're Not Going Away': Alt-Right Leader On Voice in Trump Administration," *All Things Considered*, NPR, Nov. 17, 2016, http://tinyurl.com/habljcy.

40. "A Frank Conversation," *op. cit.*

41. Daniel A. Effron and Eric D. Knowles, "Entitativity and Intergroup Bias: How Belonging to a Cohesive Group Allows People to Express Their Prejudices," *Journal of Personality and Social Psychology*, February 2015, pp. 234-253, http://tinyurl.com/gwfqdw9.

42. *Ibid.*

43. Nathan Gardels, "Weekly Roundup: When Leaders Disinhibit Acting Out Hate," WorldPost, *The Huffington Post*, Feb. 3, 2017, http://tinyurl.com/hrz8mc7.

44. Quoted in *ibid.* For background, see Jonathan Montpetit, "Muslim Leaders in Quebec City Find It Difficult to Ignore Tensions That Preceded Shooting," CBC News, Jan. 31, 2017, http://tinyurl.com/h6eoq9f; Les Perreaux and Eric Andrew Gee, "Quebec City mosque attack suspect known as online troll inspired by French far right," *The Globe and Mail* (Toronto), Jan. 31, 2017, http://tinyurl.com/zyslahg.

45. "Museum Condemns Hateful Rhetoric at White Nationalist Conference; Calls on the Nation to Confront Hate Speech," press release, U.S. Holocaust Memorial Museum, Nov. 21, 2016, http://tinyurl.com/zsc3fey.

46. Benjamin Franklin, "Letter to Peter Collinson," TeachingAmericanHistory.org, May 9, 1753, http://tinyurl.com/jzxxq6a.

47. Matthew Spalding, "Why Does America Welcome Immigrants?" The Heritage Foundation, June 30, 2011, http://tinyurl.com/zbxqvm3.

48. *Ibid.*

49. *Ibid.*

50. John C. Calhoun, speech on Mexico, Jan. 4, 1848, http://tinyurl.com/hvvupqf.

51. "Ku Klux Klan," *Encyclopedia Britannica*, Dec. 6, 2016, http://tinyurl.com/h4dwkfa.

52. *Ibid.*

53. Quoted in W.E.B. DuBois, *Black Reconstruction in America, 1860-1880* (1998), pp. 592-593.

54. "Legal Immigration to the United States, 1820 to Present," Migration Policy Institute, http://tinyurl.com/jd8hvym.

55. "Ku Klux Klan," *op. cit.*

56. Kelly J. Baker, "White-Collar Supremacy," *The New York Times*, Nov. 25, 2016, http://tinyurl.com/zkku59y.

57. "The Immigration Act of 1924 (The Johnson-Reed Act)," Office of the Historian, U.S. Department of State, http://tinyurl.com/qe2tnuw.

58. Jacob Siegel, "The Alt-Right's Jewish Godfather," *Tablet*, Nov. 29, 2016, http://tinyurl.com/hku86bb.

59. For background, see Matthew N. Lyons, "AlternativeRight.com: Paleoconservatism for the 21st Century," *threewayfight*, Sept. 10, 2010, http://tinyurl.com/goqww49; Euan Hague and Edward H. Sebesta, "Neo-Confederacy and Its Conservative Ancestry," in *Neo-Confederacy: A Critical Introduction*, E. Hague, Heidi Beirich, and E. H. Sebesta, eds. (2008), p. 26; and George Hawley, *Right-Wing Critics of American Conservatism* (2016).

60. Siegel, *op. cit.*

61. Patrick J. Buchanan, "Immigration Time-out," Oct. 31, 1994, http://tinyurl.com/hrut4w4; "US President-R Primaries," 1992, Our Campaigns, http://tinyurl.com/z34em5d; and "US President-R Primaries," Our Campaigns, 1996, http://tinyurl.com/hbzl9fk.

62. Lyons, "AlternativeRight.com: Paleoconservatism for the 21st Century," *op. cit.*

63. Paul Gottfried, "The Decline and Rise of the Alternative Right," *Taki's Magazine*, Dec. 1, 2008, http://tinyurl.com/j2t4mt6.

64. Lyons, "AlternativeRight.com: Paleoconservatism for the 21st Century," *op. cit.*; Richard Spencer, "Am I Not Being Outrageous Enough?" National Policy Institute, Nov. 20, 2014, http://tinyurl.com/jcmots9.

65. Siegel, *op. cit.*

66. Quoted in Siegel, *op. cit.*

67. For background, see Margaret Quigley, "Some Notes on the European 'New Right,' " Political Research Associates, Aug. 29, 2016/Jan. 1, 1991, http://tinyurl.com/h46arxf; Zack Beauchamp, "An Expert on the European Far Right Explains the Influence of Anti-Immigrant Politics," *Vox*, May 31, 2016, http://tinyurl.com/hbwapt7.

68. Matthew N. Lyons, "Crl-Alt-Delete," Political Research Associates, January 2017, p. 4, http://tinyurl.com/goay3st.

69. *Ibid.*

70. "The Groups," Southern Poverty Law Center Intelligence Report, Jan, 29, 2010, http://tinyurl.com/hwtd5pm; "About," *Radix Journal*, http://tinyurl.com/z5u42os.

71. "ADL: White Supremacists Making Unprecedented Effort on U.S. College Campuses to Spread Their Message, Recruit," Anti-Defamation League, March 6, 2017, http://tinyurl.com/jljmr5u.

72. Julia Carrie Wong, "UC Berkeley Cancels 'Alt-Right' Speaker Milo Yiannopoulos as Thousands Protest," *The Guardian*, Feb. 2, 2017, http://tinyurl.com/h2rluvn.

73. Liam Stack, "Attack on Alt-Right Leader Has Internet Asking: Is It O.K. to Punch a Nazi?" *The New York Times*, Jan. 21, 2017, http://tinyurl.com/h2avjmz.

74. Joseph Weber, "CPAC Leader Blasts 'Alt-Right,' as Conservatives Define Agenda Under Trump," Fox News, Feb. 23, 2017, http://tinyurl.com/zcehd49; Tea Party Nation, *op. cit.*

75. Brian Naylor, "Rep. Steve King Stands by Controversial Tweet About 'Somebody Else's Babies,' " NPR, March 13, 2017, http://tinyurl.com/h4frc3y; Matthew Haag, "Steve King Says Civilization Can't Be Restored With 'Somebody Else's Babies,' " *The New York Times*, March 12, 2017, http://tinyurl.com/hg8o6nh.

76. Peter Beinart, "Trump Scapegoats Unauthorized Immigrants for Crime," *The Atlantic*, March 1, 2017, http://tinyurl.com/z84kglx.

77. Jaweed Kaleem, "Trump Speaks Out Against Attacks on Jews and Shooting of Indian Immigrants," *Los Angeles Times*, Feb. 28, 2017, http://tinyurl.com/hys2cd6.

78. Ishaan Tharoor, "An Act of American Terror in Trump's Heartland," *The Washington Post*, Feb. 27, 2017, http://tinyurl.com/jb3takr.

79. John Gramlich, "Most Americans Haven't Heard of the 'Alt-Right,' " Pew Research Center, Dec. 12, 2016, http://tinyurl.com/hfaqwte.

80. Karl North, "NPI 2016," Identity Evropa, Nov. 29, 2016, http://tinyurl.com/zt8u54h.

81. Richard Spencer, "The Rainbow Coalition," America (blog), National Policy Institute, Nov. 4, 2015, http://tinyurl.com/ht6r9j4.

82. "Identity Evropa: Mapping the Alt-Right Cadre," Northern California Anti-Racist Action, ICD, Dec. 9, 2016, http://tinyurl.com/zhvpvto; Hailey Branson-Potts, "In Diverse California, a Young White Supremacist Seeks to Convert Fellow College Students," *Los Angeles Times*, Dec. 7, 2016, http://tinyurl.com/z3q9348.

83. Susan Page and Karina Shedrofsky, "Poll: How Millennials View BLM and the Alt-Right," *USA Today*, Oct. 31, 2016, http://tinyurl.com/j8szksm.

84. Max Ehrenfreund, "What the Alt-Right Really Wants, According to a Professor Writing a Book About Them," *The Washington Post*, Nov. 21, 2016, http://tinyurl.com/hjt4fqy.

85. For background, see Abby Ohlheiser, "What Was Fake on the Internet this Election: #draftourdaughters, Trump's Tax Returns," *The Washington Post*, Oct. 31, 2016, http://tinyurl.com/he4wtfx.

86. Nafeez Ahmed, "European Support for Far Right Extremism Reaches 1930s Scale," *Medium*, June 19, 2016, http://tinyurl.com/h9hu84q. Also see Brian Beary, "European Unrest," *CQ Researcher*, Jan. 9, 2015, pp. 25-48.

87. Nicole Stinson, "Marine Le Pen Defends Putin and Attacks Europe for 'Carrying Out Cold War AGAINST Russia,' " [U.K.] *Express*, March 6, 2017, http://tinyurl.com/znzlvxw.

88. Michelle Martin, "Germany's Divided Anti-Immigrant Party Faces Rocky Election Road," Reuters, March 2, 2017, http://tinyurl.com/gpjmyo4.

89. For background, see Suzanne Sataline, "U.S.-Russia Relations," *CQ Researcher*, Jan. 13, 2017, pp. 25-48.

90. Casey Michel, "Beyond Trump and Putin: The American Alt-Right's Love of the Kremlin's Policies," *The Diplomat*, Oct. 13, 2016, http://tinyurl.com/zeck4xb.

91. For background, see Shikha Dalmia, "Conservatives Made Their Bed With Milo, Now They Have to Lie In It," *Reason*, Feb. 26, 2017, http://tinyurl.com/jtmho62.

BIBLIOGRAPHY
Selected Sources
Books

Daniels, Jessie, *Cyber Racism*, Rowman & Littlefield, 2009.
A sociology professor at Hunter College in New York City recounts how white supremacists have used the internet to win followers and spread their message.

Hawley, George, *Right-Wing Critics of American Conservatism*, University Press of Kansas, 2016.
An assistant professor of political science at the University of Alabama describes how far-right thinkers — including white nationalists and "paleoconservatives" — have challenged mainstream conservatives and helped spawn the so-called alt-right.

Swain, Carol M., and Russ Nieli, *Contemporary Voices of White Nationalism in America*, Cambridge University Press, 2003.
A professor of political science and law at Vanderbilt University (Swain) and a lecturer in politics at Princeton University (Nieli) present in-depth interviews with 10 leading white nationalists in the United States, several of whom are members of the loose network that has become the "alt-right."

Articles

Beauchamp, Zack, "White Riot," *Vox*, Jan. 20, 2017, http://tinyurl.com/j57rmcf.
The rising number of minorities in the United States and Europe may have led to a white backlash against increasing ethnic diversity and multiculturalism and contributed to the election of President Trump.

Ehrenfreund, Max, "What the Alt-Right Really Wants, According to a Professor Writing a Book About Them," *The Washington Post*, Nov. 21, 2016, http://tinyurl.com/hjt4fqy.
A University of Alabama assistant professor of political science, who is interviewing alt-right members for a new book, describes what he has learned about the beliefs and demographics of the movement, saying "it is predominantly an online phenomenon, and amorphous."

Letson, Al, "A Frank Conversation With a White Nationalist," Reveal, The Center for Investigative Reporting, Nov. 10, 2016, http://tinyurl.com/hpm6n2g.
In an interview, alt-right spokesman Richard Spencer describes his hopes that the United States eventually will become a white "ethno-state" — a nation populated entirely by people of white European ancestry.

Ohlheiser, Abby, and Caitlin Dewey, "Hillary Clinton's Alt-Right Speech, Annotated," *The Washington Post*, Aug. 25, 2016, http://tinyurl.com/jksmlan.
Democratic presidential nominee Hillary Clinton brought the alt-right heightened publicity when, in a 2016 speech, she sharply criticized the movement and then-candidate Donald Trump's alleged embrace of it.

Penny, Laurie, "On the Milo Bus With the Lost Boys of America's New Right," *Pacific Standard*, Feb. 21, 2017, http://tinyurl.com/hduulp7.
A reporter describes her conversations with young men who worked for alt-right-affiliated provocateur Milo Yiannopoulos during his college lecture tour. These alt-right members were primarily involved with the movement for amusement, not because of the ideology, she says.

Roy, Avik, "Up From White Identity Politics," *National Review*, Aug. 18, 2016, http://tinyurl.com/zg334he.
A conservative columnist explains why he believes white-identity politics are bad for the country, for conservatives and for Republican priorities.

Siegel, Jacob, "The Alt-Right's Jewish Godfather," *Tablet*, Nov. 29, 2016, http://tinyurl.com/hku86bb.
Richard Spencer's alt-right network includes anti-Semites. But Spencer's philosophical mentor is Paul Gottfried, a Jewish professor and a developer of paleoconservatism, which criticizes mainstream conservatives as too friendly to social and political equality.

Tanner, Charles, Jr., "Richard Spencer: Alt-Right, White Nationalist, Anti-Semite," Institute for Research and Education on Human Rights (IREHR), Jan. 5, 2017, http://tinyurl.com/jpuqaje.
A human-rights advocate describes alt-right spokesman Richard Spencer's background in the world of far-right political theory.

Reports and Studies

Berger, J. M., "Nazis vs. ISIS on Twitter: A Comparative Study of White Nationalist and ISIS Online Social Media Networks," George Washington University Program on Extremis, September 2016, http://tinyurl .com/gpc57jr.
A university-based researcher on extremist movements describes how white nationalists and the Islamic State gather followers and communicate their views using social media.

Klapsis, Antonis, "An Unholy Alliance: The European Far Right and Putin's Russia," Wilfried Martens Center for European Studies, 2015, http://tinyurl .com/zryk9oc.
A centrist European think tank examines links between European far-right parties with similarities to the alt-right and Russian President Vladimir Putin and his government.

Lyons, Matthew N., "Ctrl-Alt-Delete: The Origins and Ideology of the Alternative Right," Political Research Associates, Jan. 20, 2017, http://tinyurl .com/zm7f7cu.
An independent researcher on right-wing extremism traces the origins of the alt-right.

For More Information

American Renaissance, www.amren.com. Alt-right-affiliated website and organization founded by white nationalist Jared Taylor that argues that race heavily determines traits such as intelligence and morality.

Anti-Defamation League, 605 Third Ave., New York, NY 10158; 212-885-7700; www.adl.org. International Jewish group that researches, monitors and opposes anti-Semitism and other forms of bigotry.

Center for Right-Wing Studies, 2420 Bowditch St., MC5670, University of California, Berkeley, CA 94720-5670; 510-643-7237; crws.berkeley.edu. Research center that studies right-wing movements around the world.

Center for the Study of Hate and Extremism, State University of California, 5500 University Parkway, San Bernardino, CA 92407-2318; 909-537-7711; http:// hatemonitor.csusb.edu. Research group that analyzes data and policy on bigotry, terrorism and extremism's effects on civil rights.

National Policy Institute, www.npiamerica.org. Alt-right think tank and publisher of material on white European identity politics.

Occidental Observer, www.theoccidentalobserver.net. Far-right Web publication on white European culture and white identity politics.

Political Research Associates, 1310 Broadway, Suite 201, Somerville, MA 02144; 617-666-5300; www.political research.org. Think tank that researches and analyzes threats to social justice from the far right.

Southern Poverty Law Center, 400 Washington Ave., Montgomery, AL 36104; 334-956-8200 www.splcenter.org. Monitors domestic hate groups and extremists and provides training and legal advocacy to oppose hate crimes.

2

Populism and Party Politics

Chuck McCutcheon

Donald Trump, campaigning in Macon, Ga., last Nov. 25, demonstrated the reach of populist disgust with traditional politicians, some analysts say, by defeating more than a dozen more experienced rivals to win the GOP presidential nomination. Populist movements also have spread across Europe with the rise of anti-establishment politicians in several countries, punctuated by the United Kingdom's "Brexit" vote in June to leave the European Union.

From *CQ Researcher*, September 9, 2016

Image credit (vertical): AP Photo/Atlanta Journal-Constitution/Curtis Compton

New Yorker Karen Bruno liked what she heard from Donald Trump. So the self-described evangelical Christian showed up at the Republican presidential candidate's Trump Plaza headquarters to volunteer for his campaign.

"The more he riles up the establishment, the better I like it," Bruno told a TV station. "I think the establishment is in cahoots to bring this country down. . . . I don't know what they're doing."[1]

Bruno's comments reflect what the media and academic researchers describe as populism, in which citizens rise up in frustration and anger against what they see as an entrenched "establishment" of "elites" in government, industry and other institutions that ignores their concerns.

John Baick, a professor of history at Western New England University in Springfield, Mass., defines populism as "a large group of people united in the suspicion that someone, some group — 'elites' is their shorthand — is controlling things to their detriment." Bart Bonikowski, a professor of sociology at Harvard University, says populists "invariably portray the people as the rightful sources of power" and often favor the use of "direct democracy," such as ballot initiatives that let voters bypass legislators to making laws.

Political analysts and academics say Trump demonstrated the reach of populism by defeating more than a dozen more experienced rivals to win the GOP nomination, revealing deep-seated voter disgust with traditional politicians. Former presidential candidate Bernie Sanders tapped into similar voter anger on the left in his unsuccessful battle with Hillary Clinton for the Democratic nomination. So-called populist movements also have spread across

Manufacturing Jobs on Steep Decline

The United States has lost more than 5 million manufacturing jobs since 2000, a decline that has helped fuel a rise in populist anger, particularly toward undocumented immigrant workers, who Republican presidential nominee Donald Trump says have taken American jobs. He also blames the loss on trade pacts such as the 1994 North American Free Trade Agreement, which lifted trade barriers among the United States, Mexico and Canada.

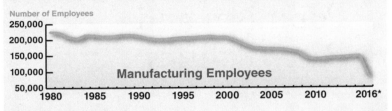

Number of Employees

* Data through July 2016

Source: "Employment, Hours, and Earnings from the Current Employment Statistics survey (National)," Bureau of Labor Statistics, July 2016, http://tinyurl.com/mgomng9.

Europe with the rise of anti-establishment politicians in several countries and the United Kingdom's "Brexit" vote in June to leave the 28-nation European Union.[2]

But the meaning of populism has become increasingly elastic. It has been invoked to describe politicians who seek to unite disparate groups as well as those who pit one group against another. And it is applied as a catchall in various contexts beyond politics, including business (the ride-hailing service Uber) and music (country artists and rock groups such as Pearl Jam that want promoters to lower ticket prices for the groups' concerts).[3]

Populism today also characterizes almost any impassioned grassroots movement, ranging from the limited-government, anti-tax tea party that rose up against President Barack Obama to the left-wing Occupy Wall Street groups challenging the financial industry to the Black Lives Matter protests of police shootings of African-Americans.[4]

"It is broadly used in scholarly, media and public affairs circles despite the fact that it has no widely accepted theoretical meaning," said Diego von Vacano, a professor of political science at Texas A&M University.[5]

In the United States, populism has existed in various forms for two centuries. Today's populism, experts say, differs from earlier versions in how politicians such as

Trump and Sanders have amplified some of its traditions — particularly appealing to a sense of "us against them" — by relying heavily on Twitter, Facebook and other forms of social media and using combative rhetoric that has drawn extensive coverage from traditional news media. As a result, they have not needed to rely on political parties or large corporate campaign contributions to pay for advertising.

"Media can no longer be treated as a side issue when it comes to understanding contemporary populism," Benjamin Moffitt, a research fellow in political science at Sweden's University of Stockholm, said in his new book, *The Global Rise of Populism.* "Media touches upon almost all aspects of modern life . . . [and] populism is particularly attuned to the contours of the contemporary mediatized landscape."[6]

The pervasiveness of social media "has changed populism as it has changed social movements in general," agrees Nancy Wadsworth, a University of Denver professor of political science. "It's provided a whole new set of resources for connectivity that are way more accessible than they used to be."

The populist-driven antagonism and hostility pervading social and news media are coarsening American culture, many experts say. Populist leaders often play on people's fear and anger by demonizing their opponents and creating and perpetuating a sense of crisis, they say.[7] Wadsworth calls this "toxic populism."

"Populism is more an emotion than it is an ideology. And that emotion is anger," said Michael Kimmel, a professor of sociology at New York's Stony Brook University and author of *Angry White Men: American Masculinity at the End of an Era.*[8]

But populism also can take a less-noxious form as a purely political style. So-called establishment politicians often make populist-sounding remarks to broaden their appeal. In 2000, Democratic Vice President Al Gore campaigned for the presidency by declaring of Republicans, "They're for the powerful; we're for the people."[9]

Similarly, Clinton, who has drawn criticism on the left for accepting large campaign donations from Wall Street and other corporations, has lambasted "special interests" that prevent citizens from making bigger financial gains. "The economy is rigged in favor of those at the top," she said.[10] The media also have applied the "populist" label to Clinton for her promises to tax multimillionaires and U.S. companies that attempt to relocate overseas.[11]

And some establishment Republicans who ran against Trump, including former Florida Gov. Jeb Bush, also castigated lobbyists and others in ways the media characterized as populist.[12]

Political scientists say populism often flourishes when wealth is concentrated at the top of society, as it is today.[13] Previous populist movements forced a realignment of political parties, with major shifts of voters from one party to the other. Some experts say that already has occurred: Most socially conservative Democrats already have switched to the Republican Party, while few socially liberal, well-off Republicans are left to move to the Democratic camp.

"The party coalitions are pretty well defined," said Michael Lind, a cofounder of New America, a center-left think tank in Washington. "The civil wars within the parties [are] about defining the party platforms more than the party coalitions."[14]

The left- and right-wing versions of American populism have different orientations. Left-leaning populists seek to check the power of banks and big business. To that end, about 800 activists representing several left-wing organizations held a "Populism 2015" conference last year in Washington to discuss how their groups can coordinate through social media and other means to blunt the influence of corporations seeking to limit the reach of government.

"As progressives reclaiming the mantle of 'populism,' our alliance is tapping a deep American tradition," said Isaiah J. Poole, one of the organizers, who is editor of OurFuture.org, a liberal website for the Campaign for America's Future. "We see the government as an instrument for the public good."[15]

Populists on the political right, meanwhile, direct their frustration at the government, arguing it favors undeserving groups over ordinary Americans — often minorities or foreigners, but also, like populists on the left, lobbyists and big business. They also blame GOP leaders for failing to stop Obama from being elected and re-elected.

Trump shares similarities with past populist presidential candidates, say experts studying populism, including Alabama Gov. George Wallace, an outspoken segregationist who ran as an independent in 1968; conservative political commentator Patrick Buchanan, who sought the GOP nomination in 1992 and 1996 (and waged a third-party candidacy in 2000) pledging to curb immigration and free trade; and business tycoon H. Ross Perot, who ran as an independent in 1992 calling for drastic cuts in Washington spending and lobbying.

Some of Trump's critics, such as Avik Roy, an aide to several former GOP presidential candidates, said Trump's success shows his supporters are driven by "white nationalism," or deep resentment of other races and cultures.[16] But Trump supporters themselves say they care more about his articulation of their anger at being left behind economically and socially than about inflammatory statements for which he has drawn criticism.

"I live in Trump's America, where working-class whites are dying from despair. . . . They're angry at Washington and Wall Street, at big corporations and big government," said Michael Cooper Jr., a lawyer in North Wilkes-boro, N.C., where manufacturing jobs have plummeted over the last two decades. "When you're earning $32,000 a year and haven't had a decent vacation in over a decade . . . you just want to win again, whoever the victim, whatever the price."[17]

Not all observers consider Trump a populist, citing his proposed breaks for upper-income Americans.[18] They also say he appears more interested in promoting himself than in representing a broad swath of voters.

"Trump is more anti-establishment than he is pro-people, as he is mainly pro-Trump," said Cas Mudde, a University of Georgia professor of international affairs.[19]

On the other hand, Sanders' campaign is widely seen as within the traditions of left-wing populism. A self-described "democratic socialist," the Vermont senator called for a political "revolution" aimed at ending what he described as both major political parties' unhealthy reliance on large campaign donors.

Sanders backer Zack Smith of New Hampshire cited Sanders' challenge to the banking industry to reduce consumer transaction fees on debit cards. "It's the average person's issues he brings up," Smith said.[20]

Americans' Confidence in Institutions Falls

Fewer than a third of Americans have strong confidence in the nation's major political, financial, religious and news media institutions. The low level is reflected in populist support for anti-establishment candidates such as Republican presidential nominee Donald Trump and Democrat Bernie Sanders, who lost his party's bid for the nomination to Hillary Clinton. Both Trump and Sanders have sharply criticized mainline institutions — the news media by Trump, and banks by Sanders.

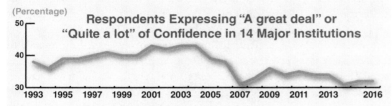

Respondents Expressing "A great deal" or "Quite a lot" of Confidence in 14 Major Institutions

Source: "Average Confidence Rating for All Institutions, 1993-2016," Gallup, June 13, 2016, http://tinyurl.com/hd3afho.

Gun rights long have been a populist issue on the right, while recent mass shootings have helped to spur left-wing grassroots efforts to address gun control. Petition drives in California, Nevada, Maine and Washington state led to the placement of gun-control measures on November ballots.[21]

As politicians, academics and commentators debate populism and its role in the presidential election, here are some questions being debated.

Does populism undermine confidence in government?

Critics of populism say its reflexive mistrust of the Democratic and Republican parties erodes confidence in government institutions and the political process. They say populists reject the necessary checks and balances of government in favor of unquestioned executive power while also rejecting their opponents' legitimacy. "Anyone with a different view speaks for 'special interests,' i.e., the elite," said the University of Georgia's Mudde.[22]

But supporters of populism counter that it has opened the political system to new people and ideas.

Americans have become less attached to the two major political parties in recent years, with the percentage of people identifying as independents rising, according to the Pew Research Center, a nonpartisan polling and

research institution in Washington.[23] Meanwhile, the parties have grown more partisan: Pew found that "Republicans and Democrats now have more negative views of the opposing party than at any point in nearly a quarter century."[24]

That situation, many political analysts say, has created an opening for widespread rejection of both parties. "Politics is polarized, and a full-throated, angry populism seems to be burning all of the oxygen in the 2016 race," wrote William Daley, a former Obama chief of staff who is now on the board at the centrist think tank Third Way.[25]

Experts describe the tea party movement, a loose confederation of conservative groups calling for strict adherence to their interpretation of the Constitution, as a form of populism directed at challenging Obama.[26]

Historian Robert Kagan, an adviser to Republican and Democratic politicians, said Obama's critics sought to persuade voters during his presidency "that government, institutions, political traditions, party leadership and even parties themselves were things to be overthrown, evaded, ignored, insulted [and] laughed at."[27]

Many observers across the political spectrum say Trump's fiery populist appeals to blue-collar whites pose risks for the Republican Party, which has been seeking to recruit more Latinos and other ethnic and minority groups as the country grows more diverse.[28]

However, some political observers say voters' disdain for the Democratic Party also has stoked populism. Arthur Brooks, president of the American Enterprise Institute, a conservative think tank in Washington, said some Democrats saw Sanders' "far-left populism" as "a pirate ship" seeking to overtake and impose its views on the rest of the party.[29]

Some populists promote conspiracy theories that critics of populism say delegitimize non-populist politicians and institutions. Before he ran for president, Trump claimed Obama was born in Kenya and implied he is a Muslim, and recently he predicted that the fall election "is going to be rigged."[30] Meanwhile, supporters of

Sanders accused Clinton's campaign of manipulating election results in several primaries.[31]

In addition, critics of populism say it oversimplifies complicated issues, such as the North American Free Trade Agreement (NAFTA), a joint agreement among the United States, Mexico and Canada that was negotiated by President George H. W. Bush and signed into law by President Bill Clinton in 1993. Trump's and Sanders' arguments that NAFTA and similar pacts caused massive losses of American manufacturing jobs are too simplistic, the critics say. And eliminating those trade deals, NAFTA supporters say, would cause long-term economic harm without restoring goodpaying blue-collar jobs. In fact, studies indicate that many of those jobs were lost due to modernization, automation and outsourcing to lower-wage countries both with and without free-trade agreements.[32]

"Populism appeals because it promises simple solutions to complex problems," said a report by two economists at the New York City-based Council on Foreign Relations, a centrist think tank studying international issues.[33]

Outside the United States, some establishment politicians say populism's impatience with the political process is at odds with how democracy works.

"Building prosperity requires caution and patience. It requires time," said Fernando Henrique Cardoso, Brazil's president from 1995 to 2003. "Populism is a shortcut that doesn't work."[34]

Cardoso is a frequent critic of the Workers' Party, a leftist populist movement whose former president, former Brazilian President Dilma Rousseff, and other leaders have become caught in widespread corruption scandals.[35] Brazil's Senate voted in August to impeach and remove Rousseff from office.[36]

But others say populism can invigorate political engagement by inviting participation from people who otherwise shun politics. "It can make politics more accessible, comprehensible and popular," the University of Stockholm's Moffitt said.[37]

Some Trump supporters say they admire his bluntness, in contrast to what they see from establishment politicians. "He talks like me," said Rozilda Greene, a 65-year-old Floridian. "If I have the truth to tell, I tell it."[38]

J. D. Vance, an investment executive in San Francisco and author of the new book *Hillbilly Elegy,* a memoir of growing up in Appalachia, said the white working-class voters who back Trump have forced better-off Americans to take their concerns more seriously. When he won Nevada's GOP primary in February, Trump cited his overwhelming popularity among those without college degrees and said, "I love the poorly educated."[39]

"The two political parties have offered essentially nothing to these people for a few decades," Vance said. "From the left, they get some smug condescension, an exasperation that the white working class votes against their economic interests because of social issues. . . . From the right, they've gotten the basic Republican policy platform of tax cuts, free trade, deregulation, and paeans to the noble businessman and economic growth."[40]

Meanwhile, Sanders' candidacy stirred interest among younger voters who applauded his attacks on the party establishment. The 75 million Americans in their teens, 20s and early 30s, known as Millennials, are the country's single biggest generation, and both Democrats and Republicans are eager to gain their long-term support.[41]

Advocates of populism say heightened participation has nudged the parties toward reflecting the broader public's wishes. They point to Sanders' influence on Hillary Clinton on trade: Clinton had said in 2012 that the TransPacific Partnership — an agreement fostering trade among the United States and 11 other countries bordering the Pacific Ocean — "sets the gold standard in trade agreements." But after Sanders criticized the pact during the Democratic primaries, she came out against it.[42]

Sanders' policy director, Warren Gunnels, also cited the inclusion of some of the senator's priorities in the Democratic platforms adopted. The platform, a nonbinding outline of a party's agenda, included Sanders' calls to reform Wall Street and raise the minimum wage to $15 an hour.[43]

Is globalization driving populism?

In seeking to explain populism's ascension, commentators have described it as a rebellion led by the economic losers of globalization — the push for free movement of goods, people and technology across international borders.

Since the end of World War II, many governments have sought to reduce or eliminate trade barriers. Globalization of trade intensified after 2001, when China joined the World Trade Organization, which sets standards for international trade.

Democratic presidential candidate Hillary Clinton greets supporters in Cleveland on Aug. 17. Clinton has sounded populist notes in her campaign, lambasting "special interests" that prevent citizens from making bigger financial gains. The media have applied the populist label to Clinton for her promises to tax multimillionaires and U.S. companies that attempt to relocate overseas.

Proponents of globalization envisioned it as a solution to deep-seated poverty and unemployment in many developing countries.[44] But the loosening of trade restrictions occurred just as revolutionary new technologies began to eliminate many jobs in developed economies, and the rise of the internet made other jobs exportable to lower-wage countries. As a result, some commentators argue, the drive to globalize free trade unintentionally delivered considerable wealth and power to a small elite while reducing the number of high-paying jobs available to lower-skilled workers.

"Most people don't understand what NAFTA did, or what the TPP is or how trade bills work," says the University of Denver's Wadsworth. "But they are getting the sense that corporate power seems to have superseded political power nationally and globally. I think Sanders tried to provide a narrative that explains and articulates that" in his criticisms of the proposed Pacific trade pact.

In 1960, about one in four Americans worked in manufacturing; less than 1 in 10 do today. Since 2000, the United States has lost 5 million jobs in that sector, many to China.[45] Trump won the GOP primaries in 89 of the 100 U.S. counties most affected by trade with China, according to *The Wall Street Journal*.[46]

But despite Sanders' anti-free trade positions, fears about globalization do not appear to motivate left-leaning populists. A June poll by the Chicago Council on Global Affairs, a think tank, found that 75 percent of Sanders' self-identified supporters agreed with the statement "Globalization is mostly good for the United States." That figure was just 1 percentage point below the share of Clinton's supporters expressing the same sentiment.[47]

Others say populism is driven less by the economic consequences of globalization than by the racial and cultural anxieties stoked by immigration. Trump has vowed to build a wall on the border with Mexico and at least temporarily bar Muslim immigrants from entering the country. After the son of Afghan immigrants killed 49 people at the Orlando, Fla., nightclub Pulse in June, Trump expanded his proposed ban to include migrants from any region with "a proven history of terrorism" against the United States or its allies.[48] Trump also has called for "extreme vetting" of would-be immigrants to determine if they reflect U.S. values.[49]

Meanwhile, some experts say the U.K. "Brexit" vote was a consequence of what many Britons see as excessive immigration. Legal annual immigration into that country is 10 times what it was in 1993, and pro-Brexit forces argued many of those immigrants have taken jobs from British natives.[50]

"Immigration is probably the number one issue driving the rise of political populism around the world, whether it's the Brexit vote . . . or the rise of Donald Trump, the Republican presidential nominee," wrote Greg Ip, *The Wall Street Journal*'s chief economics correspondent. "The backlash against immigration is less about jobs and wages — it's more about a sense of national identity and control over national borders,"[51]

Jonathan Rothwell, a researcher for the Gallup polling organization, studied the demographics of Trump's support and found cultural mistrust of other races and ethnicities to be the biggest factor, saying those viewing Trump most favorably are "disproportionately living in racially and culturally isolated ZIP codes . . . with little exposure to blacks, Asians and Hispanics."[52]

Likewise, populism's appeal in Europe appears to stem more from cultural factors than economic ones, according to a new study by Harvard and University of Michigan researchers. In addition to Brexit, they cited hostile anti-immigrant rhetoric and anxiety over recent terrorist attacks. Populism's spread in Europe, they said, "is largely due to ideological appeals to traditional values, which are concentrated among the older generation, men, the religious, ethnic majorities, and less-educated sectors of society."[53]

Daniel Gros, director of the Centre for European Policy Studies, a think tank in Brussels, Belgium, examined education and employment statistics in Europe and found that people with a college degree are more likely to get jobs and earn more than those without one. But, he said, the number of jobs requiring high levels of education has not grown in Europe in recent years, nor has the difference in unemployment rates between the highly educated and the less educated.

"But if these factors account for the rise of populism, they must have somehow intensified in the last few years, with low-skill workers' circumstances and prospects deteriorating faster vis-a-vis their high-skill counterparts," he said. "And that simply is not the case, especially in Europe."[54]

Is U.S. populism identical to Europe's?

The rise of populist movements in the United States and Europe has led many scholars, commentators and journalists to connect the two. They say populist leaders in both places have capitalized on deepening mistrust of politicians and parties.

Americans and Europeans "are more dissatisfied with mainstream politicians and parties than they have been in living memory," said Duncan McDonnell, a professor of government and international relations at Australia's Griffith University and coauthor of the 2015 book *Populists in Power.* "People go looking for other alternatives, and the one thing about populists is that they still promise people that voting can actually change something — that democracy can be saved somehow."[55]

Analysts say that attitude particularly appeals to voters on the political right, who are more skeptical of government than Democrats and who see themselves losing influence.

Constanze Stelzenmüller, a senior fellow on foreign policy at the Brookings Institution, a centrist think tank in Washington, cited several recent U.S. books and articles "about the fraying economic and social conditions which offer a potent explanation for the current dark mood of much of the American electorate. Yet 'Europe' could be substituted for 'America' in many of these studies with equal plausibility."[56]

The result, Stelzenmüller and others say, is the tendency among right-wing populists such as the Netherlands Geert Wilders, Austria's Norbert Hofer and France's Marine Le Pen to make claims similar to Trump's that increased immigration is a leading cause of their country's problems, especially crime and terrorism. Although those populists say recent terrorist attacks in Europe reinforce their concerns, critics accuse them of xenophobia, an irrational dislike or fear of foreigners.

Ongoing anti-government mistrust took hold during the global economic recession between 2007 and 2009. As the tea party movement was gaining influence in the United States, separate public pushes for secession flourished in parts of Belgium, Italy, Scotland and Spain.[57]

Some analysts described June's Brexit vote as an echo of Trump's rise. Padraig Reidy, editor of the London news and cultural magazine *Little Atoms,* wrote, "The American political establishment should take note of what has happened — what was inconceivable for Britain just a few months ago has suddenly become reality."[58]

But other experts say the U.S. and European versions of populism are more different than alike. Europe's is based more on a distrust of the EU imposing regulations on member countries than opposition to trade agreements, said Thomas Greven, a professor of political science at Germany's Free University of Berlin.[59]

Jacqueline Gehring, an assistant professor of political science at Pennsylvania's Allegheny College, said Britain "has been ambivalent about the European Union" since it was founded in the 1950s and Britain initially chose not to become a member. The Brexit vote, she added, reflected "a failure of political leadership" from then-Prime Minister David Cameron, who was criticized for failing to foresee pro-Brexit sentiment and who resigned after the referendum, which he had advocated.

"Brexit may have been pushed somewhat by recently increasing xenophobia or populism," Gehring said, "but it is not its primary motivator."[60]

The University of Georgia's Mudde also said populists in Europe and North America see immigration differently. He said Trump — unlike those on Europe's right wing — distinguishes between legal and illegal immigration, blaming the latter for what he said are the United States' problems, and "does not attack the status of the U.S. as a multicultural immigration country."[61]

Others who study populism say the different political structures of the United States and many European countries shape populism in those places. Many European nations have parliamentary systems in which a coalition of parties can form a majority, enabling populist parties to share power. Unlike the United States, where third parties still lag far behind the Republican and Democratic parties, those countries have many national parties; France, for example, has more than a dozen.[62]

"The European context looks very different" from the United States, says Joe Lowndes, a University of Oregon professor of political science. "You have actual populist parties over there and a parliamentary system."

Gros of the Centre for European Policy Studies said left-wing populism has prevailed across southern Europe as a result of the debt crisis that has afflicted Europe since 2009 and that resulted from the global recession.[63] Meanwhile, the United States' economy has rebounded in the last few years.

In the aftermath of the global recession, several EU countries — Greece, Portugal, Ireland, Spain and Cyprus — were unable to repay or refinance their government debt or to bail out overly indebted banks under their national supervision.[64]

BACKGROUND

"Passions, Not Reason"

Without using the word "populism," ancient philosophers such as Plato and Aristotle had reservations about democracy because of their concerns that angry segments of the public could rise up and undermine it.[65]

James Madison, one of the authors of the U.S. Constitution, said his biggest fear of the new United States was that "the passions . . . not the reason, of the public would sit in judgment." If that happened, the future president wrote in his famous *Federalist No. 10* essay in 1787, "the influence of factious leaders may kindle a flame."[66]

Historians say the rise of Democrat Andrew Jackson kindled the populist flame in the 1820s. The former military hero won the popular vote in 1824 but lost to John Quincy Adams. He defeated Adams four years later in what often is described as one of the nastiest campaigns in history. In 1832 Jackson said some congressional proposals, such as using federal money to support

road and canal construction, proved that "many of our rich men have not been content with equal protection and equal benefits, but have besought us to make us richer by act of Congress."[67]

The economic slump that followed the Civil War (1861-1865) and the start in the late 1800s of the so-called Gilded Age, in which the gap separating the rich and poor grew wider, also spurred populist developments. During the Greenback Movement, which began in 1868, farmers and others sought to prevent a drop in crop prices by maintaining or increasing the amount of paper money being circulated.[68] The Granger Movement of the 1870s featured a coalition of mostly Midwestern farmers fighting railroads' monopoly on transporting grain.[69]

Those alliances gave way in 1890 to the Populist (or People's) Party, a third party championing former Minnesota Rep. Ignatius Donnelly's belief that "public good is paramount to private interests."[70] Its interests overlapped with the Progressive Movement of the 1890s, which also grew out of dissatisfaction with government and the power of corporate monopolies. Progressives, however, argued for less-sweeping change; for example, they opposed the Populists' belief that government should directly control or own railroads.[71]

In 1892, the Populist Party nominated James B. Weaver of Iowa for president and demanded a graduated income tax, with the wealthy taxed at higher rates than those with lower incomes. But Weaver won in just four states, and Democrat Grover Cleveland was elected.[72]

In the next presidential election, a divided group of Populists endorsed Democrat William Jennings Bryan, one of the 19th century's most famous orators, while selecting their own vice presidential nominee.[73] Bryan staunchly opposed the gold standard, which limited the money supply but eased trade with other nations whose currency also was based on gold. He captivated voters with the famous edict, "You shall not crucify mankind on a cross of gold," but lost the election to Republican William McKinley.[74]

Another influential populist thinker of the era was Henry George, whose 1879 book *Progress and Poverty* sold 3 million copies to become the all-time best-selling book on economic theory to that point. George called for abolishing all taxes except for a single tax on land; he argued it would make land widely available to those who would use the property instead of keeping it in the hands of the wealthy. He also campaigned for the right of voters to cast secret ballots, making them less susceptible to intimidation.[75]

The Populists remained politically active until 1908, when the party combined with the Democratic Party.[76*] But its beliefs have remained influential.

"Sanders could practically have run on the Populist Party platform of 1892," said Michael Magliari, a professor of history at California State University, Chico, saying Sanders' call to let people cash checks and open savings accounts at post offices was taken directly from the earlier group's plan.[77]

Polarizing Figures

During the first half of the 20th century, outspoken populist leaders became prominent, including "the radio priest," Father Charles Coughlin. He broadcast scathing attacks alleging Jewish bankers controlled the money supply and dismissed Democratic President Franklin D. Roosevelt's New Deal — a wide-ranging series of government programs aimed at lifting the country out of the Great Depression — as a tool of banking interests.[78]

Another flamboyant populist was Huey Long, a Democratic governor and U.S. senator from Louisiana. Long denounced the wealthy and in 1934 proposed creating a "Share Our Wealth Society" whose slogan was "Every man a king." He called for the government to prevent families from owning fortunes larger than $5 million to $8 million (about $90 million to $144 million today, adjusted for inflation), with the proceeds used to provide every family in the country with an annual income.

Long drew an impassioned following, but Roosevelt and other critics dubbed him a dangerous demagogue.[79] Long was assassinated in 1935 but had an enduring influence in Louisiana, where he spearheaded an aggressive program of building and improving roads and bridges and providing free school lunches and textbooks to poor students.[80]

The 1950s saw the rise of Wisconsin Republican Sen. Joseph McCarthy, another famously polarizing figure. In seeking to expose communists and other left-wing "loyalty risks" in the U.S. government, McCarthy tried "to mobilize an anti-elite sentiment," said Daniel Bell, a Harvard professor of sociology. The Senate voted in 1954 to formally condemn McCarthy for what senators called his "inexcusable" and "vulgar" accusations. Historians say the vote greatly diminished the influence of McCarthy, who died three years later.[81]

Alabama's Wallace also used populism to divide rather than unite, historians say. He concluded his 1963 inaugural speech for governor with the infamous line, "Segregation now, segregation tomorrow, segregation forever." After surviving an assassination attempt, he issued public apologies later in his career for his earlier statements while improving health care and education for blacks as well as whites.[82]

During the 1950s and 1960s, Columbia University's Richard Hofstadter became known as one of the 20th century's most influential historians. In such books as *Anti-Intellectualism in American Life* (1963) and *The Paranoid Style in American Politics* (1965), Hofstadter argued that Jacksonian-era populist sentiments had recurred throughout U.S. history, resulting in a prejudice against intellectuals as representatives of an elite that could not be trusted.[83]

Left-wing populism gained followers in the 1970s. Oklahoma Democratic Sen. Fred Harris ran for president in 1972 with the slogan "a new populism," decrying liberal "elitism" while calling for a broader distribution of wealth. After failing to win the nomination, he mounted another failed effort four years later.[84]

Also in 1972, left-wing journalists Jack Newfield and Jeff Greenfield, in *A Populist Manifesto,* sought to mobilize workers, young people and minorities around the belief that "some institutions and people have too much money and power, most people have too little, and the first priority of politics must be to redress that imbalance."[85]

Later in the 1970s, political referendums and state ballot initiatives began attracting attention. The initiative process, which began in South Dakota in 1898, enables citizens to vote on proposed statutes or constitutional amendments at the polls. State legislatures can place initiatives on the ballot, but the initiatives often are generated by petition drives.[86]

---

*The Progressive — or Bull Moose — Party of 1912 was headed by former Republican Theodore Roosevelt who eventually rejoined the GOP. Today, the word "progressive" generally is synonymous with liberal.

CHRONOLOGY

1820s-1910s *Early populists back the interests of farmers and laborers.*

1828 Democrat Andrew Jackson, whom historians consider a leading figure in American populism, wins the presidency.

1891 The Populist (or People's) Party is founded, merging the interests of farmers and laborers. A year later, populist presidential candidate James Weaver of Iowa loses to incumbent Democratic President Grover Cleveland.

1896 Populists endorse Democrat William Jennings Bryan for president; he loses to Republican William McKinley.

1908 Populists cease to be politically active, combining with the Democratic Party.

1920s-1960s *Controversial populist politicians emerge.*

1926 Father Charles Coughlin, a Roman Catholic priest, begins anti-semitic attacks on banks and other institutions.

1928 Democrat Huey Long is elected Louisiana governor and denounces the wealthy and banks, calling for redistribution of wealth.

1962 Democrat George Wallace is elected Alabama governor on a populist, pro-segregation platform.

1965 Historian Richard Hofstadter argues that populist sentiments of Jackson's era had recurred throughout U.S. history.

1970s-1990s *Populist initiatives on taxes, immigration gain support.*

1972 Oklahoma Sen. Fred Harris unsuccessfully seeks the Democratic presidential nomination with the slogan "a new populism," denouncing liberal "elitism."

1978 California voters approve Proposition 13, which slashed property taxes.

1992 Republican Patrick Buchanan and independent H. Ross Perot wage unsuccessful populist campaigns for president.

1994 California voters approve Proposition 187, which prevents undocumented immigrants from receiving education, health care or other public services.

1996 Buchanan and Perot again run unsuccessfully for president.

2000s *Populist candidates gain national stage.*

2002 Far-right French presidential candidate Jean-Marie Le Pen defeats socialist Prime Minister Lionel Jospin in the first round of voting.

2008 Republican presidential candidate John McCain of Arizona selects as his vice presidential running mate Alaska Gov. Sarah Palin, who denounces Democratic elites.

2009 Tea party movement arises to challenge President Obama.

2011 Occupy Wall Street movement attacks the power of the financial industry.

2013 The Black Lives Matter movement forms to protest police racism and violence against African-Americans.

2014 Tea party–backed college professor Dave Brat topples House Majority Leader Eric Cantor of Virginia in GOP primary. . . . Tea party candidates help Republicans make substantial gains in November elections.

2015 Republican Donald Trump launches presidential campaign on a "Make America Great Again" populist platform. . . . Independent Sen. Bernie Sanders announces he will run for president as a Democrat.

2016 Trump wins the GOP nomination but alienates Republicans with incendiary rhetoric. . . . Sanders loses in Democratic primaries to Hillary Clinton but endorses her. . . . United Kingdom votes to withdraw from European Union. . . . North Dakota voters reject a controversial law that would have relaxed a ban on corporate farms.

California's Proposition 13 in 1978 was the era's best-known initiatives. Conservative activists proposed it in a response to rising home values that caused property taxes to skyrocket. The initiative limited annual property taxes to 1 percent of a property's assessed value and required a two-thirds majority for any state or local tax increase. Though it achieved its goal of reducing taxes, critics said it triggered drastic cuts in public spending that hurt the quality of schools and public services.[87]

California later adopted other controversial ballot initiatives. Proposition 187 in 1994 made immigrants who were in the United States illegally ineligible for public benefits (although it has never been enforced); Proposition 209 in 1996 banned affirmative action at state institutions; and Proposition 227 in 1998 restricted bilingual education in public schools. In a 2005 study, three political scientists said those measures shifted the state's politics toward the Democratic Party by alienating Latinos — who had been drifting toward the GOP — as well as many white voters.[88]

In 1984 a new Populist Party — no connection to the original — started to run far-right candidates in the presidential elections, including former Ku Klux Klan leader David Duke of Louisiana, in 1988. It failed to win any converts beyond a tiny band of extremists.[89]

Buchanan, the political commentator who first ran for president in 1992, also drew upon mistrust of elites. But he promoted an "America First" foreign policy that went against prevailing GOP sentiment by rejecting many international alliances. He also harshly criticized Wall Street and called illegal immigration "the greatest invasion [of the United States] in history."[90]

Texas entrepreneur Perot, meanwhile, reserved his harshest criticisms for lobbyists, political action committees (PACs) and the politicians allied with them. He said they had formed "a political nobility that is immune to the people's will" and called for term limits for members of Congress, a balanced budget amendment and placement of proposed laws on a national ballot for voters to decide.[91]

Neither Buchanan nor Perot attracted widespread support. Although Perot drew 19 percent of the vote, he did not win a plurality of the votes in any states and no Electoral College votes.[92] Consumer activist Ralph Nader, who built a passionate following in the 1960s with his attacks on corporations, also ran in 2000 as the Green Party's candidate. Some political experts say Nader received enough votes in Florida to cost Gore the state and hand the election to George W. Bush.[93]

Tea Party Politics

In the 2008 U.S. presidential election, GOP nominee John McCain, an Arizona senator, bypassed several experienced establishment politicians and selected first-term Alaska Gov. Sarah Palin as his running mate. Palin drew the populist tag for portraying herself as a "hockey mom" who condemned Democratic elites.[94]

The tea party movement arose shortly after McCain's loss to Obama, helping the Republican Party make substantial gains in the 2014 midterm elections. But it targeted some Republicans as well. Tea party-backed college professor Dave Brat startled the political world by toppling House Majority Leader Eric Cantor of Virginia in a June 2014 GOP primary. Brat had blasted Cantor for being too cozy with Wall Street and business leaders.[95]

The tea party was not hostile to all government programs. A Harvard study said resistance to Obama's Affordable Care Act health care overhaul "coexists with considerable acceptance, even warmth, toward long-standing federal social programs like Social Security and Medicare, to which tea partiers feel legitimately entitled. Opposition is concentrated on resentment of perceived federal government 'handouts' to 'undeserving' groups, the definition of which seems heavily influenced by racial and ethnic stereotypes."[96]

In running for president, Trump received Palin's endorsement and became "the leader the tea party never had," according to Griffith University's McDonnell.[97] However, Trump's embrace of some government programs led some tea party members to prefer Texas Sen. Ted Cruz, who in the GOP primaries campaigned as a purer example of conservative principles.[98] Cruz, however, could not beat Trump in many Eastern and Midwestern states, where blue-collar workers embraced Trump's "Make America Great Again" slogan.[99]

Trump's blaming of all politicians — not just Democrats — for what he called their inability to solve problems irked many Republicans, especially the GOP establishment, which he described as too beholden to what he said were the party's narrow interests.

During the primaries, Trump did not have to rely on the Republican Party or raise and spend significant sums

Europe a Hothouse for Populist Leaders

On the right and left, populism is sprouting across the continent.

Populism has long found the soils of Europe a fertile place to grow, thanks to a history of tensions with immigrants and a multiparty system that breeds antiestablishment views.

Experts say economic and cultural concerns have fueled populism's growth. The decline of manufacturing jobs and influx of immigrants have helped to stoke populism on the right, while suspicions about government power and institutions such as the European Union have boosted it on the left.

For populists, these developments have been translating into gains at the polls. In a new study, political scientists Ronald Inglehart of the University of Michigan and Pippa Norris of Harvard University found that the average share of the vote for populist parties in European elections has nearly tripled since the 1960s, from 5 percent to 13.2 percent.

During those five and a half decades, the share of seats in legislative bodies held by politicians considered to be populists more than tripled, from just below 4 percent to nearly 13 percent, according to Inglehart and Norris.[1]

Here are some of the most prominent right-wing and leftwing Europeans who are widely described in media and academic circles as populists:

Austria: Norbert Hofer

Hofer, 45, is the leader of Austria's Freedom Party, which Ruth Wodak, an emeritus professor of linguistics and English language at England's Lancaster University and author of a recent book on populism, described as "a far-right populist party claiming that its intention is to protect Austrian culture and national identity."[2]

Hofer lost the presidential election in April, but his party appealed the result and a court invalidated it, citing sloppiness in ballot handling. Another election is scheduled for October.[3]

The presidency is largely ceremonial, but Hofer has promised to seek to fire the coalition government in charge if it fails to control immigration more strictly. His party also has vowed speedier deportations of undocumented immigrants and increased surveillance of mosques and Muslim schools.[4]

France: Marine Le Pen

Le Pen, 48, is the daughter of Jean-Marie Le Pen, the founder of the conservative National Front party who was widely criticized for his anti-Semitism and racism. She took over as its leader in 2011.

The Washington Post described Marine Le Pen as "Europe's pioneer in attempting to cast the populist far right in a more respectable light."[5] Unlike her father, she has acknowledged and condemned the Holocaust but continued his call for drastically limiting legal immigration. She has demanded that legal immigrants who have been unemployed for six months return to their country of origin, regardless of how long they have lived in France.

Le Pen unsuccessfully ran for president in 2012 and is expected to run again in 2017. She said she would hold a referendum on her country's membership in the EU within six months.[6]

Greece: Alexis Tsipras

Tsipras, 42, is the leader of Syriza, which academics and media outlets say is a left-wing populist party. He was elected Greece's prime minister last year on a surge of public hostility to stringent austerity measures that the government had imposed after the country plunged into financial crisis.[7]

Under his leadership, Greek lawmakers in May approved some tax hikes and other, lesser austerity measures that Tsipras said were aimed at eventually making the country less reliant on aid from other European nations.[8]

Like other populist leaders, Tsipras has made frequent use of social media, putting out regular YouTube videos and frequent tweets in which he has argued that the people's will is more important than the wishes of government officials.[9]

Netherlands: Geert Wilders

Wilders, 52, is the founder and leader of the Dutch Party for Freedom, which Wodak said practices an "ethno-nationalist" populism pushing a strong national identity.[10]

Wilders is among the most controversial politicians in Europe, having said the Quran is a "fascist book" that should be banned alongside *Mein Kampf*, in which Adolf Hitler outlined his plans for Nazi Germany.[11] He has been among the loudest in condemning Muslim immigration to his country.[12]

Wilders said he would call for a referendum on Dutch membership in the EU if he is elected as prime minister in March.[13]

Spain: Pablo Iglesias

Iglesias, 37, is secretary-general of Podemos ("We Can"), which academics and media describe as a left-wing populist party. It formed in 2014 and merged in May with several minor parties to become Unidos Podemos ("United We Can"). But the party failed in June's elections to replace the center-left Socialist Party as leader of the country's political left.[14]

Iglesias is a former political science lecturer in Madrid and former member of the European Parliament. He entered politics after taking part in protests against globalization.

He said he and other protesters "understood that a big part of the important decisions weren't being taken by democratically elected governments, but rather, institutions that weren't chosen by anyone, like the International Monetary Fund (IMF) or the World Bank."[15]

United Kingdom: Nigel Farage

Farage, 52, served from 2006 to 2009 and from 2010 until July as the leader of the UK Independence Party, which many describe as a "Euroskeptic" populist party that is suspicious of alliances with other European nations.[16]

He was a prominent leader of the pro-Brexit movement along with Boris Johnson, the former mayor of London who is now the UK's secretary of state for foreign and commonwealth affairs. Farage said in August that he would consider returning to lead the party if Brexit is not implemented to his satisfaction.[17] He traveled to the United States to campaign for Donald Trump and said of Trump's supporters, "They are the same people who made Brexit happen."[18]

— *Chuck McCutcheon*

Getty Images/Matt Jelonek

Geert Wilders, founder of the ultra-nationalist Dutch Party for Freedom, is among the most controversial politicians in Europe. He has called the Quran a fascist book that should be banned.

[1]Ronald F. Inglehart and Pippa Norris, "Trump, Brexit and the Rise of Populism: Economic Have-Nots and Cultural Backlash," Kennedy School of Government, Harvard University, July 29, 2016, http://tinyurl.com/heh5aqz.

[2]Ruth Wodak, *The Politics of Fear: What Right-Wing Populist Discourses Mean* (2015), p. 191.

[3]Josh Lowe, "Far Right Takes Lead in Austria Presidential Election Re-Run," *Newsweek*, Aug. 2, 2016, http://tinyurl.com/gtjrhkb.

[4]Anthony Faiola, "Meet the Donald Trumps of Europe," *The Washington Post*, May 19, 2016, http://tinyurl.com/hv8e6z5.

[5]*Ibid.*

[6]Cecile Alduy, "The Devil's Daughter," *The Atlantic*, October 2013, http://tinyurl.com/jt6ng59; Elisabeth Zerofsky, "Marine Le Pen Prepares for a 'Frexit,' " *The New Yorker*, June 29, 2016, http://tinyurl.com/zeqmh3f.

[7]Jeff Wallenfeldt, "Alexis Tsipras," *Encyclopaedia Brittanica*, http://tinyurl.com/z8xqnlb.

[8]Niki Kitsantonis, "Greek Lawmakers Narrowly Approve Austerity Legislation," *The New York Times*, May 22, 2016, http://tinyurl.com/gksbujf.

[9]David Auerbach, "The Digital Demogogue," *Slate*, July 2, 2015, http://tinyurl. com/omqe2gp.

[10]Wodak, *op. cit.*, p. 206.

[11]Bruno Waterfield, "Ban Koran Like Mein Kampf, Says Dutch MP," *The Telegraph* (U.K.), Aug. 9, 2007, http://tinyurl.com/jsqsvbs.

[12]Faiola, *op. cit.*

[13]"Dutch anti-immigration leader Wilders calls for Dutch referendum on EU membership," Reuters, June 24, 2016, http://tinyurl.com/ht5u9m3.

[14]Jon Stone, "Spanish Leftists Podemos Boosted by New Electoral Alliance," *Newsweek*, May 16, 2015, http://tinyurl.com/j4agzjd; Tobias Buck, "Spain's Podemos Mourns Losses at 2016 Election," *Financial Times*, June 28, 2016, http://tinyurl.com/jfdzb8n.

[15]Zoe Williams, "Podemos leader Pablo Iglesias on Why He's Like Jeremy Corbyn: 'He Brings Ideas That Can Solve Problems,'" *The Guardian* (U.K.), Dec. 15, 2015, http://tinyurl.com/nk6l5k6.

[16] Wodak, *op. cit.*, p. 207.

[17]Arj Singh and Georgia Diebelius, "Nigel Farage Reveals He Would Consider Returning as Ukip Leader 'If Brexit Is Not Delivered,'" *The Mirror* (U.K.), Aug. 14, 2016, http://tinyurl.com/jqkn9ax.

[18]David Wright, "Brexit Leader Nigel Farage Calls Trump 'The New Ronald Reagan,'" CNN.com, Aug. 29, 2016, http://tinyurl.com/h62bgf8.

Are Populism and Social Media Compatible?

Some worry speed and venom can outstrip sober deliberation.

When Donald Trump tweets a populist-oriented attack, as he's done regularly throughout the presidential race, TV networks and other media often waste no time reporting on it.

"I do a tweet on something," Trump boasts, "something not even significant, and they break into their news within seconds."[1]

Trump's use of Twitter shows how it and other social media sites, such as Facebook and Instagram, thrive on the ability of politicians instantly to reach a wide audience — a perfect complement to populist rhetoric, which thrives on striking an emotional us-versus-them chord with the public.

But many experts say those features can overshadow or conflict with what they view as the sober and deliberative process of traditional politics.

Populists long have deployed the media to their advantage, going back to the People's (Populist) Party publishing its own crusading newspapers in the 1890s.[2] But Trump and unsuccessful Democratic presidential candidate Bernie Sanders have employed social media both to send messages to voters and, in newer fashion, to foster a two-way dialogue with them.

Trump and Sanders "are using social media like you or I would use social media," said Matt Lira, a Republican digital strategist. "They're using it as a platform to genuinely engage their supporters."[3]

Such populist-driven uses of social media can have positive results, such as rapidly spreading news about rallies or instantly obtaining hundreds of thousands of petition signatures, said Jill Lepore, a Harvard University professor of history and a writer for *The New Yorker*. But she cited negative consequences as well, including "the atomizing of the electorate," or making voters more individualistic and less concerned about others' well-being by encouraging them to act quickly rather than thoughtfully.

"There's a point at which political communication speeds past the last stop where democratic deliberation, the genuine consent of the governed, is possible," Lepore said. "An instant poll, of the sort that pops up on your screen while you're attempting to read debate coverage, encourages snap and solitary judgment, the very opposite of what's necessary for the exercise of good citizenship."[4]

At the same time, some in politics express concern that social media is reinforcing populist outrage at the establishment and diminishing civility among politicians, campaign workers and the public.

"I have a lot of friends working for various campaigns right now," said Republican strategist Matt Rhoades, who managed Mitt Romney's presidential campaign in 2012. "They hate each other. We have candidates running for the highest office in the United States trolling each other on social media. That's what social media also has given us."[5]

Concerns about social media's effect on political discourse are not limited to the United States. Srgjan Ivanovik, a journalist in Macedonia, said social media has increased politicians' tendency to manipulate opinion by telling the public what it wants to hear without regard for the truth.

of campaign money because of his celebrity and ability to command significant media attention. One study in March 2016 estimated that he had received the equivalent of nearly $2 billion in coverage through newspapers, television and other journalistic outlets. That was 2 1/2 times more than Clinton, and many times greater than any of his Republican rivals.[100] At the same time, Trump made frequent use of Twitter, often lashing out at opponents.

"Inside the political power structure, Trump has no power," said Nicco Mele, director of Harvard's Shorenstein Center on Media, Politics and Public Policy. "And so he is very effective at forcing himself into it through a combination of Twitter and earned media," or news articles and TV broadcasts.[101]

Sanders, as a member of Congress, was known for criticizing so-called "corporate welfare" — government

"Leaders have learned a lesson from the internet," Ivanovik said. "Our interest in their campaigns is more like [reality TV's] 'The X Factor' or 'Choose Your Idol' shows than a real political platform with adequate programs, solutions and answers. In response, our leaders simply became populist. They answer what the majority wants to hear."[6]

Ruth Wodak, an emeritus professor of linguistics and English language at England's Lancaster University, said a populist "media-democracy" in Europe and elsewhere has produced a climate "in which the individual, media-savvy performance of politics seems to become more important than the political process." Thus, she said, "politics is reduced to a few slogans thought to be comprehensible to the public at large."[7]

British multimillionaire Arron Banks, the largest financial donor to this summer's "Brexit" referendum in which the United Kingdom voted to leave the European Union, said populist strategists for the leave-the-EU effort used Facebook and other social media to make stark emotional warnings about the dangers of immigration.

By comparison, Banks said, proponents of remaining in the EU "featured fact, fact, fact, fact, fact. It just doesn't work. You have got to connect with people emotionally."[8]

Banks' comments drew a rebuke from Katharine Viner, editor-in-chief of Britain's *Guardian* and a Brexit opponent. "When 'facts don't work' and voters don't trust the media, everyone believes in their own 'truth' — and the results, as we have just seen [with Brexit], can be devastating," Viner wrote. "When the prevailing mood is anti-elite and anti-authority, trust in big institutions, including the media, begins to crumble."[9]

But Scott Adams, creator of the cartoon "Dilbert," said social media can curb some of the excesses of populism. Adams, who regularly blogs about current events, cited the fistfights and other disturbances that arose at several rallies for Trump earlier this year.

"The fear is that the small scuffles will escalate to something terrible," Adams wrote. "But social media solves that. Every person at a Trump rally knows the world is watching. And it isn't just big media that is watching. Every phone in every pocket is a direct link to the world. And Trump supporters know their candidate would be done if a big riot broke out."[10]

— ***Chuck McCutcheon***

[1] Jim Rutenberg, "The Mutual Dependence of Donald Trump and the News Media," *The New York Times,* March 20 2016, http://tinyurl.com/jg4wv9u.

[2] "Kansas populist newspapers," Kansas Historical Society, http://tinyurl.com/h8mgpsn; "People's Party," Texas State Historical Association, http://tinyurl.com/huyc8hm.

[3] Issie Lapowsky, "Trump Isn't the First Tech-Propelled Populist. But This Time It's Different," *Wired,* May 13, 2016, http://tinyurl.com/hqj372p.

[4] Jill Lepore, "The Party Crashers," *The New Yorker,* Feb. 22, 2016, http://tinyurl.com/h2onlbj.

[5] James Irwin, "America Rising Founder: Social Media Fuels Populism," *GW Today,* Feb. 19, 2016, http://tinyurl.com/z8kfgs2.

[6] Srgjan Ivanovik, "Social Media Is Making Politicians More Populist Than Ever!" The Good Men Project, Sept. 24, 2014, http://tinyurl.com/jk2gzr5.

[7] Ruth Wodak, *The Politics of Fear: What Right-Wing Populist Discourses Mean* (2015), p. 11.

[8] Robert Booth, Alan Travis and Amelia Gentleman, "Leave Donor Plans New Party to Replace Ukip — Possibly Without Farage in Charge," *The Guardian* (U.K.), June 29, 2016, http://tinyurl.com/has69a3.

[9] Katharine Viner, "How Technology Disrupted the Truth," *The Guardian* (U.K.), July 12, 2016, http://tinyurl.com/jecdlaq.

[10] Scott Adams, "Social Media Is the New Government," Scott Adams' Blog, March 21, 2016, http://tinyurl.com/hecmcam.

benefits, such as special provisions in the tax code, provided to businesses. In the wake of the housing crisis that started in 2007-2008, public resentment toward financial companies gave rise to the Occupy Wall Street movement, which Sanders endorsed.[102]

Many Democrats also supported Occupy Wall Street. Yet some, unlike Sanders, accepted campaign donations from Wall Street companies and their employees that were targets of the Occupy movement. In running against Clinton, Sanders made an issue of how much she received from the banking industry — more than $1.6 million as of August 2016, according to the nonpartisan watchdog Center for Responsive Politics.[103] Sanders refused to ally himself with "super PACs," a type of independent expenditure committee that can raise and spend unlimited amounts of money on political causes or candidates.[104]

Liberals also admired another economic populist, Elizabeth Warren, who decried Wall Street's influence. A Harvard Law School professor, she won election as a Democrat to a U.S. Senate seat in Massachusetts in 2012. She said that when she was growing up in Oklahoma, the United States was "a country of expanding opportunities. . . . Now we talk much more about protecting those who have already made it."[105]

Sanders, who became a Democrat to run for president, frequently feuded with the party's leaders and made economic issues the central focus of his campaign. That emphasis dismayed the populist Black Lives Matter movement, which urged the senator to highlight perceived abuses of African-Americans at the hands of law enforcement.

Clinton, meanwhile, met with Black Lives Matter leaders for almost a year in an attempt to win their endorsement. Although the main group did not comply, a group of mothers of Black Lives leaders did endorse her.[106]

CURRENT SITUATION
Political Races

Since winning the GOP nomination, Trump has continued to feud with establishment Republicans who say his populist appeals have damaged his chances of winning over undecided voters.

Some prominent Republicans have accused Trump of unpresidential conduct and said they will not vote for him.[107] And 50 foreign policy and national security officials who served under several Republican presidents said in an August letter that Trump would be "the most reckless president in history."[108] Also that month, Evan McMullin, a former House Republican aide and CIA officer, launched a long-shot independent bid on a stop-Trump platform.[109]

Trump said in early August that some of his supporters have urged him to lower his antagonistic tone to help him win a broader audience. But he said he is uncertain about doing so. "I am now listening to people that are telling me to be easier, nicer, be softer. And you know, that's OK, and I'm doing that," he told *Time* magazine. "Personally, I don't know if that's what the country wants."[110]

Polls taken after the July Democratic and Republican conventions showed that Trump broadened his support among blue-collar white voters, but not among other demographics. David Wasserman, an analyst for *Five ThirtyEight.com,* a website on polling and demographics, noted that the non-white share of eligible voters has risen since 2012, meaning Trump will have to gain "truly historic levels of support and turnout among working-class whites" while avoiding an erosion of support among other groups.[111]

Despite the widespread dislike for Trump among Democrats, not all of Sanders' supporters have immediately backed Clinton. Some are expected to vote for the Green Party's Jill Stein or Libertarian Party candidate Gary Johnson. But it remains unclear whether Stein or Johnson will appear on the November ballot in every state: As of early September, Johnson was not on the ballot in Rhode Island, while Stein was not on ballots in eight.[112]

Polls in early August showed that if Clinton runs against Trump without a third-party candidate on the ballot, as many as 91 percent of Sanders' backers would vote for her. But if those voters have the option of supporting a candidate other than her or Trump, that percentage drops considerably.[113]

In addition to the presidential campaign, several congressional races feature candidates who are described as populists. They include the following:

- Democrat Zephyr Teachout, who is running for a House seat in southeastern New York state to replace retiring GOP Rep. Chris Gibson. A law professor and Sanders supporter, Teachout ran unsuccessfully in the 2014 primary against Gov. Andrew Cuomo. "I like breaking up big banks, and I want to take on big cable," Teachout said, referring to large cable companies she contends are overcharging consumers.[114]
- Democrat Russ Feingold, who is running against Wisconsin Republican Sen. Ron Johnson after being unseated by Johnson in 2010. Feingold has criticized trade deals and government aid to corporations as well as the 2010 Dodd-Frank law overhauling the financial industry, saying it was too lenient.[115]
- Republican Mark Assini, who is in a rematch against veteran Democratic Rep. Louise Slaughter for a seat representing the Rochester, N.Y., area after narrowly losing to Slaughter two years ago. Assini has echoed Trump in decrying "bad trade deals" as well as calling for a crackdown on undocumented immigrants who commit crimes.[116]

Ballot Initiatives

One sign of the strength of modern populism, experts say, is the growth in the number of citizen-driven ballot initiatives appearing on state ballots across the country this fall.

As of early September, 75 petition-driven initiatives will be on the November ballot in various states — more than double the 35 in 2014 and more than in both 2010 and 2012, according to the political website Ballotpedia, which tracks such developments. That growth has come even as the total number of ballot measures — which includes state lawmakers' decisions to put issues to a public vote — has fallen in recent years.

Low turnout in recent elections that has made it easier for advocates of an issue to collect enough signatures to force an initiative vote. In all but three states — North Dakota, Idaho and Nebraska — the number of signatures required for an initiative to be included on a ballot is based on a percentage of votes cast in a previous election.[117]

This year's initiatives cover an assortment of controversial issues, including requiring background checks for all gun purchases in Nevada, closing what gun-control advocates say are legal loopholes permitting unmonitored sales at gun shows and other venues.[118] Voters in Maine and Washington state successfully petitioned for initiatives that would raise the minimum wage in those states.[119]

In North Dakota, opponents of a controversial law that relaxed a ban on corporate-owned farms gathered enough signatures to place a referendum to overturn the law on the ballot in June. The referendum passed by a 3-to-1 margin and was seen as a rebuke to large corporations that have replaced family farms in much of rural America.[120]

Such companies "could buy up all the land, and it means nothing to them," said Laurie Wagner, a Wing, N.D., farmer who sought to overturn the state law. "They could make it impossible for people like us to compete."[121]

International Populism

The U.K.'s Brexit vote has sparked debate in Europe about the broadranging implications of populism. Some

The "us-versus-them" attitude inherent in populism includes criticism of increased economic competition brought about by globalization. Donald Trump won the GOP presidential primaries in 89 of the 100 U.S. counties most affected by trade with China. Since 2000, the United States has lost 5 million manufacturing jobs, many to China. Above, women staff a textile factory in Huaibei, in eastern China.

of those who opposed the move are concerned it could have further negative impacts if the country does not address the concerns that led to its adoption.

"I have feared for many years that large-scale immigration to the U.K. would produce a harmful populist response," said Adair Turner, chairman of the Institute for New Economic Thinking, a New York City think tank. "Global elites must now learn and act upon the crucial lesson of Brexit. Contrary to glib assumptions, globalization of capital, trade, and migration flows is not good for everyone."[122]

Analysts said the vote also could inspire other European nations to hold similar votes to leave the EU. France, the Netherlands, Austria, Finland and Hungary are seen as the most likely candidates.[123] Meanwhile, anti-Brexit supporters in Scotland, which rejected seceding from the U.K. in 2014, have discussed holding another secession vote that would enable Scotland to remain in the EU.[124]

In Latin America, Brazil and other countries are dealing with the fallout from the waning popularity of leftwing populist parties. In Argentina, business-friendly centrist Mauricio Macri became president last December, succeeding Cristina Fernandez de Kirchner, whose populist rule was blamed for a sharp economic downturn.[125]

Is Donald Trump a populist?

YES

Ronald Inglehart
Political Science Professor, University of Michigan;
Pippa Norris
Political Science Professor, Harvard University

Excerpted from Paper Presented at American Political Science Association Conference, September 2016

Donald Trump's populism is rooted in claims that he is an outsider to D.C. politics, a self-made billionaire leading an insurgency movement on behalf of ordinary Americans disgusted with the corrupt establishment, incompetent politicians, dishonest Wall Street speculators, arrogant intellectuals and politically correct liberals.

The CNN exit polls across all of the 2016 GOP primaries and caucuses from Iowa onward revealed that the education gap in support for Trump was substantial; on average, only one quarter of postgraduates voted for Trump compared with almost half (45 percent) of those with high school education or less. Despite being located on opposite sides of the aisle, Trump's rhetoric taps into some of the same populist anti-elite anger articulated by Bernie Sanders when attacking big corporations, big donors and big banks.

But Trump and Sanders are far from unique. There are historical precedents in America exemplified by former Louisiana Gov. Huey Long's "Share Our Wealth" movement and former Alabama Gov. George Wallace's white backlash. And Trump's angry nativist rhetoric and nationalistic appeal fits the wave of populist leaders whose support has been swelling in many Western democracies. During the last two decades, in many countries, parties led by populist authoritarian leaders have grown in popularity, gaining legislative seats, reaching ministerial office and holding the balance of power.

Populist movements, leaders and parties provide a mechanism for channeling active resistance. Hence Trump's slogan "Make America Great Again" — and his rejection of "political correctness" — appeals nostalgically to a mythical "golden past," especially for older white men, when American society was less diverse, U.S. leadership was unrivaled among Western powers during the Cold War era, threats of terrorism pre-9/11 were in distant lands but not at home, and conventional sex roles for women and men reflected patrimonial power relationships within the family and workforce.

Similar messages can be heard echoed in the rhetoric of France's Marine Le Pen, the Netherlands' Geert Wilders and other populist leaders. This nostalgia is most likely to appeal to older citizens who have seen changes erode their cultural predominance and threaten their core social values, potentially provoking a response expressing anger, resentment and political disaffection.

NO

David Mclennan
Visiting Political Science Professor,
Meredith College

Written for *CQ Researcher*, September 2016

During his presidential campaign, Donald Trump has often been labeled a populist. Although Trump appeals to many in the country who are angry with the political establishment, a closer look shows that he is more of a demagogue than a populist.

At first glance, Trump fits the traditional definition of "populist" regarding social issues and economic policies. Stylistically, populists rail against corrupt institutions like government and business that hurt the average person. Populists often state that solutions to problems are easy to implement, once the political system is changed and the corruption removed. Sound familiar?

The classic populist in American political history was William Jennings Bryan (1860-1925), the three-time Democratic nominee for president, who was known as "The Great Commoner." He attacked the Eastern elite and their support of the gold standard and brought many populists into the Democratic Party. As an orator, Bryan spoke with empathy for the common people, but even when attacking the elites, he showed no ill will toward those who supported the gold standard or other policies.

Bryan's economic, foreign and social policy positions reflected traditional populism. His economic messages often focused on ways to improve the lives of common people, in which he supported a minimum wage, standard workweeks and inspections of food, sanitation and housing conditions.

Although Trump rails against the elites on Wall Street and in Washington and he is popular with a large segment of the working class, he fails to compare to Bryan in the talking points we've heard in his countless rallies to date.

It doesn't help that Trump's policies are constantly evolving and revolving. His positions on immigration and trade restrictions are clearly populist, but large tax cuts for the wealthy and business are not. On foreign policy, his muddled positions on military intervention in the Middle East or Europe are more idiosyncratic than philosophical. It is on social issues, however, that Trump seems more opportunistic than populist. Until his involvement in presidential politics, Trump's positions on abortion or guns were more progressive than many in his current political base.

Rhetorically, Trump sounds like a populist when he attacks the political system or political elites, but his ad hominem attacks on individuals and groups do not fit the approach taken by Bryan. Because Trump scapegoats many ethnic and religious groups, he seems more of a demagogue than a true populist.

OUTLOOK
"Here to Stay"

The dominance of social media and frustration with political parties and other institutions will continue to propel populism, according to many experts, who say Trump and Sanders have tapped an anti-establishment mood that will not disappear soon.

"Trump forces, having entered the arena, aren't likely to simply exit quietly," said Gerald Seib, the *Wall Street Journal's* Washington bureau chief. "If Mr. Trump wins, they will be empowered. If their standard-bearer fails, Republicans will have to learn to deal with an unhappy, establishment-hating army within. Eventually, Democrats may have to as well."[126]

Meanwhile, many experts say the issues that Sanders' campaign raised— such as free tuition at public colleges— will sustain left-wing populism, even if Sanders' supporters help to elect Clinton in November. "Those ideas, once they're introduced a legitimized way, are hard to tamp down," the University of Oregon's Lowndes says.

In a new book, *Populism's Power: Radical Grassroots Democracy in America,* Wellesley College professor of political science Laura Grattan said the left-wing populism of grassroots groups "can replace the traditional institutions that have failed citizens," pointing to "decimated social services, overcrowded and abandoned schools, shrinking access to higher education" and numerous other problems.

"When people in America face a heightened sense of insecurity, it is more difficult than ever to see political solutions to our problems," she said.[127]

Robert Reich, an economist and liberal activist who served as secretary of Labor under Bill Clinton, predicted that an anti-establishment "People's Party" made up of disaffected Democrats as well as some Republicans could take root as soon as 2020.[128]

But Lee Drutman, a senior fellow at the New America think tank, said the Democratic Party can incorporate populism. He predicted that over the next decade, Republicans will face a split between their populist and business-establishment wings, with the populists prevailing. Meanwhile, he said, Democrats will attract support from the business establishment while taking in the concerns of Sanders' largely city-based voters.

"Eventually, the Democrats will become the party of urban cosmopolitan business liberalism, and the Republicans will become the party of suburban and rural nationalist populism," Drutman said.[129]

Bonikowski, the Harvard sociologist, says the right-wing populism of Trump's campaign likely will encourage future candidates to run similar races playing on fears about immigration and a suspicion of other ethnic groups. "What were once private conversations around the dinner table are now okay in the public sphere — which is unusual," he says. "Even if Trump loses, the genie's out of the box."

The University of Stockholm's Moffitt predicted that in the United States and elsewhere, the lines separating populists and non-populists increasingly will diminish, as politicians of all leanings continue to seek ways to command followings through the news media and social media.

"We will see populist figures become increasingly brought into the 'mainstream' fold, while ostensibly 'mainstream' politicians will likely crib from the populist playbook," Moffitt said. "In other words, populism is here to stay."[130]

NOTES

1. "What Do Voters Think of Donald Trump?" *Manitowoc Herald Times Reporter,* Jan. 25, 2016, http://tinyurl.com/h54wyae.

2. Eduardo Porter, "In 'Brexit' and Trump, a Populist Farewell to Laissez-Faire Capitalism," *The New York Times,* June 28, 2016, http://tinyurl.com/zhahcho.

3. Scott Kirsner, "Test-Riding Uber, the Populist Car Service You Summon With a Mobile App," *Boston. com,* Oct. 18, 2011, http://tinyurl.com/zz4v8nd; Aaron A. Fox, *Real Country: Music and Language in Working-Class Culture* (2004), http://tinyurl.com/hrvh2ps; and Jay Cridlin, "Pearl Jam at 25: Back on the Road, and Bound for the Rock and Roll Hall of Fame," *Tampa Bay Times,* April 7, 2016, http://tinyurl.com/hwwvsta.

4. E. J. Dionne, "The Tea Party: Populism of the Privileged," *The Washington Post,* April 19, 2010, http://tinyurl.com/y83s9kq; Joe Lowndes and Dorian Warren, "Occupy Wall Street: A Twenty-First Century Populist Movement?" *Dissent,*

Oct. 21, 2011, http://tinyurl.com/h7ydw76; and Robert Borosage, "Embracing the New Populist Moment," Campaign for America's Future, July 19, 2016, http://tinyurl.com/hphkdup.

5. Diego von Vacano, "Hugo Chavez and the Death of Populism," Monkey Cage blog, March 6, 2013, http://tinyurl.com/j6bouk5.

6. Benjamin Moffitt, *The Global Rise of Populism* (2016), p. 160.

7. *Ibid.,* pp. 44-46. See also Tom Price, "Polarization in America," *CQ Researcher,* Feb. 24, 2014, pp. 193-216.

8. Michael Kimmel, *Angry White Men: American Masculinity at the End of an Era* (2013), http://tinyurl.com/zusrkoo.

9. David Goldstein, "Gore's Refrain: 'They're for Powerful; We're for People,' " *Deseret News,* Aug. 5, 2000, http://tinyurl.com/jfpk9bg.

10. Jennifer Epstein and Margaret Talev, "Clinton Adopts Sanders' Rhetoric of 'Rigged' Economy in Debate," Bloomberg, Feb. 11, 2016, http://tinyurl.com/hdx8paa.

11. Sheelah Kolkhatkar, "How Hillary Clinton Became a Better Economic Populist Than Donald Trump," *The New Yorker,* Aug. 12, 2016, http://tinyurl.com/hgddmga.

12. Paul Waldman, "Jeb Bush Says He's Going to Tackle Special Interests in Washington. Don't Believe Him," *The Week,* July 7, 2015, http://tinyurl.com/zez4ueh.

13. See Sarah Glazer, "Wealth and Inequality," *CQ Researcher,* April 18, 2014, pp. 337-360.

14. Mara Liasson, "How This Election's Populist Politics Are Bigger Than Trump and Sanders," NPR, April 25, 2016, http://tinyurl.com/zo5zsk2.

15. Isaiah J. Poole, "Reclaiming Populism: Progressive Movement Is Alive and Well in the 21st Century," *AlterNet,* April 29, 2015, http://tinyurl.com/m39pbzm.

16. Zack Beauchamp, "A Republican Intellectual Explains Why the Republican Party Is Going to Die," *Vox.com,* July 25, 2016, http://tinyurl.com/hkr7s79.

17. Michael Cooper Jr., "A Message From Trump's America," *U.S. News & World Report,* March 9, 2016, http://tinyurl.com/znmrjkc.

18. Patricia Cohen, "What Trump and the GOP Can Agree On: Tax Cuts for the Rich," *The New York Times,* July 10, 2016, http://tinyurl.com/zsmj8aa; Robert W. Wood, "Clinton Vows Estate Tax Hikes, While Trump Vows Repeal," *Forbes,* Aug. 9, 2016, http://tinyurl.com/gnq8k2c.

19. Farai Chideya, "What Can Europe's Far Right Tell Us About Trump's Rise?" *FiveThirtyEight.com,* May 18, 2016, http://tinyurl.com/j4p3pcb.

20. Andy Kroll, "The Bernie Revolution: What's So Appealing About a Grumpy 74-Year-Old?" Yahoo! News, Dec. 3, 2015, http://tinyurl.com/jpkad3p.

21. Kira Lerner, "Gun Control Will Be on the Ballot in 4 Big States This November," Think Progress, Aug. 16, 2016, http://tinyurl.com/j42wvf4. See also Tamara Lytle, "Gun Control," *CQ Researcher,* July 25, 2016.

22. Cas Mudde, "The Problem With Populism," *The Guardian* (U.K.), Feb. 17, 2015, http://tinyurl.com/jfjfeqv.

23. "Trends in Party Identification, 1939-2014," Pew Research Center, April 7, 2015, http://tinyurl.com/q4emnog.

24. Carroll Doherty and Jocelyn Kiley, "Key Facts About Partisanship and Political Animosity in America," Pew Research Center, June 22, 2016, http://tinyurl.com/zvmdudk.

25. William M. Daley, Jonathan Cowan and Lanae Erickson Hatalsky, "Why Bernie Sanders Can't Win," *Politico,* Dec. 8, 2015, http://tinyurl.com/hk6ssx2.

26. See Peter Katel, "Tea Party Movement," *CQ Researcher,* March 19, 2010, pp. 241-264.

27. Robert Kagan, "Trump Is the GOP's Frankenstein Monster. Now He's Strong Enough to Destroy the Party," *The Washington Post,* Feb. 25, 2016, http://tinyurl.com/h2e7gsy.

28. See Chuck McCutcheon, "Future of the GOP," *CQ Researcher,* Oct. 24, 2014, pp. 889-912.

29. Arthur C. Brooks and Gail Collins, "The Democrats Nailed It. Does It Matter?" *The New York Times,* July 29, 2016, http://tinyurl.com/zu8nsw8.

30. Reid J. Epstein, "Donald Trump: 'I'm Afraid the Election Is Going to Be Rigged,' " *The Wall Street*

Journal, Aug. 1, 2016, http://tinyurl.com/zswbbon. Chris Moody and Kristen Holmes, "Donald Trump's History of Suggesting Obama Is a Muslim," CNN, Sept. 18, 2015, http://tinyurl.com/nkdxdhj.

31. Monica Bauer, "Berning Up the Internet: Conspiracy Theories Poison the Well," *The Huffington Post,* April 21, 2016, http://tinyurl.com/ztwgcau.

32. "The Rage Against Trade," *The New York Times,* Aug. 6, 2016, http://tinyurl.com/hyc9guu. For background see Brian Beary, "U.S. Trade Policy," *CQ Researcher,* Sept. 13, 2013, pp. 765-788.

33. Robert Kahn and Steve A. Tananbaum, "Global Economics Monthly, December 2015," Council on Foreign Relations, Dec. 7, 2015, http://tinyurl.com/js25ufg.

34. "Populism and Globalization Don't Mix," *New Perspectives Quarterly*, Spring 2006, http://tinyurl.com/z793m9f.

35. Andrew Jacobs, "Brazil Workers' Party, Leaders 'Intoxicated' By Power, Falls From Grace," *The New York Times,* May 12, 2016, http://tinyurl.com/how87cf.

36. Jonathan Watts, "Brazil's Dilma Rousseff Impeached by Senate in Crushing Defeat," *The Guardian* (U.K.), Sept. 1, 2016, http://tinyurl.com/j223ejg.

37. Benjamin Moffitt, "Populism and Democracy: Friend or Foe? Rising Stars Deepen Dilemma," *The Conversation,* April 23, 2015, http://tinyurl.com/j3woayz.

38. Frank Cerabino, "From Well-Heeled to Publix Retirees, Palm Beach County Shows for Trump," *Palm Beach Post,* March 15, 2016, http://tinyurl.com/jbyc45n.

39. Rod Dreher, "Trump: Tribune of Poor White People," *The American Conservative*, July 22, 2016, http://tinyurl.com/hq6ynhp. Josh Hafner, "Donald Trump Loves the 'Poorly Educated' — and They Love Him," *USA Today,* Feb. 24, 2016, http://tinyurl.com/hqk4774.

40. *Ibid.,* Dreher.

41. See Chuck McCutcheon, "Young Voters," *CQ Researcher,* Oct. 2, 2015, pp. 817-840.

42. Timothy B. Lee, "Why Hillary Clinton's FlipFlopping on Trade May Not Matter," *Vox*, July 29, 2016, http://tinyurl.com/j7gyvqf.

43. Jamelle Bouie, "What Bernie Sanders Won," *Slate*, July 11, 2016, http://tinyurl.com/jyzrxjv.

44. Mike Collins, "The Pros and Cons of Globalization," *Forbes*, May 6, 2015, http://tinyurl.com/h7n4r9s.

45. Heather Long, "U.S. Has Lost 5 Million Manufacturing Jobs Since 2000," CNN, March 29, 2016, http://tinyurl.com/j3yfzlu.

46. Bob Davis and Jon Hilsenrath, "How the China Shock, Deep and Swift, Spurred the Rise of Trump," *The Wall Street Journal*, Aug. 11, 2016, http://tinyurl.com/j27es4y.

47. Dina Smeltz, Karl Friedhoff and Craig Kafura, "Core Sanders Supporters' Economic Pessimism Sets Them Apart From Clinton Supporters," Chicago Council on Global Affairs, July 25, 2016, http://tinyurl.com/z2yu85j.

48. For background see Christina L. Lyons, "Immigration," *CQ Researcher*, July 28, 2016.

49. Lauren Said-Moorhouse and Ryan Browne, "Donald Trump Wants 'Extreme Vetting' of Immigrants. What Is the US Doing Now?" CNN.com, Aug. 16, 2016, http://tinyurl.com/zgfo5n6.

50. Kim Hjelmgaard and Gregg Zoroya, "Exploding UK Immigration Helped Drive 'Brexit' Vote," *USA Today,* June 28, 2016, http://tinyurl.com/h8a8vpg.

51. "What Is Fueling Global Anti-Immigrant Populism?" *The Wall Street Journal* video, June 29, 2016, http://tinyurl.com/jywa2g3.

52. Jonathan T. Rothwell, "Explaining Nationalist Political Views: The Case of Donald Trump," Gallup, Aug. 11, 2016, http://tinyurl.com/z4j745z.

53. Ronald Inglehart and Pippa Norris, "Trump, Brexit, and the Rise of Populism: Economic Have-Nots and Cultural Backlash," Harvard University, Kennedy School of Government, August 2016, http://tinyurl.com/jd5u9pe.

54. Daniel Gros, "Is Globalization Really Fueling Populism?" Project Syndicate, May 6, 2016, http://tinyurl.com/hgwbe2y.

55. Orlando Crowcroft, "Generation Trump: How Donald Trump Became the Populist Leader the Tea Party Never Had," *International Business Times,* May 30, 2016, http://tinyurl.com/grcjecf.

56. Constanze Stelzenmüller, "A Donald for All of Us — How Right-Wing Populism Is Upending Politics on Both Sides of the Atlantic," Brookings Institution, March 11, 2016, http://tinyurl.com/zvyrt27.

57. Barbie Latza Nadeau, "Europe's Secession Panic," *The Daily Beast,* Sept. 18, 2014, http://tinyurl.com/my7wdmp.

58. Padraig Reidy, "Yes, It Can Happen — Populist Conservatives Led UK Out of the European Union," BillMoyers.com, June 24, 2016, http://tinyurl.com/zjrjh69.

59. Thomas Greven, "The Rise of Right-Wing Populism in Europe and the United States: A Comparative Perspective," Friedrich-Ebert Siftung (Germany), May 2016, http://tinyurl.com/zoca6qj.

60. Jacqueline S. Gehring, "Sorry Donald, Brexit Is Not About You (or the United States)," Western Political Science Association, New West blog, June 24, 2016, http://tinyurl.com/hmxwf6n.

61. Cas Mudde, "The Trump Phenomenon and the European Populist Radical Right," *The Washington Post,* Aug. 26, 2015, http://tinyurl.com/h5fwxth.

62. "France," Parties and Elections in Europe, http://tinyurl.com/q2lvzjg.

63. See Sarah Glazer, "Future of the Euro," *CQ Researcher,* May 17, 2011, pp. 237-262.

64. Gros, *op. cit.* See also Brian Beary, "European Unrest," *CQ Researcher,* Jan. 9, 2015, pp. 25-48.

65. Roger Pilon, "Populism: Good and Bad," Cato Institute, Jan. 25, 2010, http://tinyurl.com/j59el34.

66. Henry Olsen, "Populism, American Style," *National Affairs,* Summer 2010, http://tinyurl. com/zqa94vh.

67. *Ibid.*

68. "Greenback Movement," *Encyclopaedia Bri-tannica,* http://tinyurl.com/grpzo6v.

69. "Granger Movement," *Encyclopaedia Bri-tannica,* http://tinyurl.com/guestr3.

70. *Political Parties in America* (2001), p. 69.

71. Pilon, *op. cit.;* "From Populism to the Progressive Era, 1900-1912," http://tinyurl.com/z4hsdp2.

72. *Political Parties in America, op. cit.,* p. 70.

73. "The Populist Party," Vassar College 1896 history website, http://tinyurl.com/5ddyft.

74. "William Jennings Bryan," History.com, http://tinyurl.com/j7yp4de. "Bryan's 'Cross of Gold' Speech: Mesmerizing the Masses," History Matters. com, http://tinyurl.com/lxftvy.

75. M. Mason Gaffney, "Henry George 100 Years Later: The Great Reconciler," MasonGaffney.org, 1997, http://tinyurl.com/zmlsm9r; Jill Lepore, "Forget 9-9-9. Here's a Simple Plan: 1," *The New York Times,* Oct. 15, 2011, http://tinyurl.com/hkrsl3v.

76. *Political Parties in America, op. cit.,* p. 70.

77. Matthew Artz, "Trump, Sanders Following in California Populists' Footsteps," *San Jose Mercury News,* March 19, 2016, http://tinyurl.com/h3uv9oy.

78. "The Radio Priest," George Mason University Roy Rosenzweig Center for History and New Media, http://tinyurl.com/zd3zo6y. See also "New Deal Aims at the Constitution," *Editorial Research Reports (CQ Researcher),* Nov. 27, 1936.

79. "Share Our Wealth," HueyLong.com, http://tinyurl.com/ajsvsw.

80. Matt Farah, John H. Lawrence and Amanda McFillen, "From Winnfield to Washington: The Life and Career of Huey P. Long," Historic New Orleans Collection, 2015, http://tinyurl.com/zdw7kpw. Huey Long — Every Man a King," PBS. org, http://tinyurl.com/hff9hqg.

81. "Joseph R. McCarthy," History.com, http://tinyurl.com/o724hco; Daniel Bell, "McCarthy and Populism," *Commentary,* May 1, 1983, http://tinyurl.com/j47pajv.

82. "George C. Wallace," Biography.com, http://tinyurl.com/haqljf7.

83. "Richard Hofstadter," *Encylopaedia Britannica,* http://tinyurl.com/z9wzokq; David Greenberg," Richard Hofstadter's Tradition," *The Atlantic,* November 1998, http://tinyurl.com/gpy9esm.

84. Tom Hayden, "Fred Harris: A Populist With a Prayer," *Rolling Stone,* May 8, 1975, http://tinyurl.com/jnrvzys.

85. Peter Barnes, "A Populist Manifesto," *The New Republic,* April 29, 1972, http://tinyurl.com/he4tu5g.

86. "Initiative, Referendum and Recall," National Conference of State Legislatures, Sept. 20, 2012, http://tinyurl.com/ndznq67.

87. Kevin O'Leary, "How California's Fiscal Woes Began: A Crisis 30 Years in the Making," *Time,* July 1, 2009, http://tinyurl.com/zy9rbop.

88. Shaun Bowler, Stephen P. Nicholson and Gary M. Segura, "Earthquakes and Aftershocks: Race, Direct Democracy and Partisan Change," *American Journal of Political Science,* January 2006, http://tinyurl.com/hhlggl7.

89. Stephen E. Atkins, *Encyclopedia of Right Wing Extremism in Modern American History* (2011), p. 226, http://tinyurl.com/z5cfm74.

90. "Pat Buchanan on the Issues," OnTheIssues.org, http://tinyurl.com/hruuvln; Steven Stark, "Right-Wing Populist," *The Atlantic*, February 1996, http://tinyurl.com/h4udtwm.

91. Sean Wilentz, "Pox Populi," *The New Republic,* Aug. 9, 1993, http://tinyurl.com/z7yuecy; John Dickerson, "Donald Trump Isn't Another Ross Perot," *Slate,* Sept. 9, 2015, http://tinyurl.com/ pwaz84g.

92. Josh Katz, "Can Gary Johnson, the Libertarian Nominee, Swing the Election?" *The New York Times,* Aug. 4, 2016, http://tinyurl.com/hdxvx9d.

93. Bill Scher, "Nader Elected Bush: Why We Shouldn't Forget," *RealClearPolitics,* May 31, 2016, http://tinyurl.com/gpnfntw.

94. Richard E. Cohen with James A. Barnes *et al.*, *The Almanac of American Politics 2016* (2015), p. 89.

95. Geoffrey Kabaservice, "Dave Brat and the Rise of Right-Wing Populism," *Politico Magazine,* June 12, 2014, http://tinyurl.com/gqylgnc.

96. Vanessa Williamson, Theda Skocpol and John Coggin, "The Tea Party and the Remaking of American Conservatism," *American Political Science Association Perspectives on Politics 9,* March 2011, http://tinyurl.com/nl2wl36, pp. 25-43.

97. Crowcroft, *op. cit.*

98. Gerald F. Seib, "The Tea Party Eyes Donald Trump — Warily," *The Wall Street Journal,* May 16, 2016, http://tinyurl.com/jqpec38.

99. Ronald Brownstein, "Trump's Path Runs Through the Rust Belt," *The Atlantic,* March 29, 2016, http://tinyurl.com/zpcj5ws.

100. Nicholas Confessore and Karen Yourish, "$2 Billion Worth of Free Media for Trump," *The New York Times,* March 15, 2016, http://tinyurl.com/jgo7tkq.

101. Issie Lapowsky, "Trump Isn't the First Tech-Propelled Populist. But This Time's Different," *Wired,* May 13, 2016, http://tinyurl.com/hqj372p.

102. See Peter Katel, "'Occupy' Movement," *CQ Researcher,* Jan. 13, 2012, pp. 25-52.

103. "Commercial Banks," Center for Responsive Politics, http://tinyurl.com/jnw24j8.

104. Michelle Ye Hee Lee, "Sanders's Claim That He 'Does Not Have a Super PAC,' " *The Washington Post,* Feb. 11, 2016, http://tinyurl.com/z64ddba; Tom Price, "Campaign Finance," *CQ Researcher*, May 6, 2016, pp. 409-432.

105. Cohen with Barnes, *op. cit.,* p. 884.

106. Kerry Picket, "Clinton Chooses Black Lives Matter Over Law Enforcement," *Daily Caller*, Aug. 6, 2016, http://tinyurl.com/hyw7qwx.

107. Meghan Keneally, "Donald Trump Facing Increasing Resistance From Within Own Party," ABC News.com, Aug. 9, 2016, http://tinyurl.com/hgz84um.

108. Eric Bradner, Elise Labott and Dana Bash, "50 GOP National Security Experts Oppose Trump," CNN.com, Aug. 8, 2016, http://tinyurl.com/jdtr76e.

109. Andrew Prokop, "Evan McMullin: A Former GOP Staffer Is Now Running for President on an Anti-Trump Platform," *Vox.com,* Aug. 8, 2016, http://tinyurl.com/zklblss.

110. Alex Altman, Phillip Elliott and Zeke J. Miller, "Inside Donald Trump's Meltdown," *Time,* Aug. 22, 2016, http://tinyurl.com/zt8ngqj.

111. David Wasserman, " 'Missing' White Voters Might Help Trump, But Less So Where He Needs It," *FiveThirtyEight.com,* June 2, 2016, http://tinyurl.com/zc6mlf5.

112. "Help Us Put Jill Stein on the Ballot in Every State," Jill Stein for President website, http://tinyurl.com/zar8akm; "2016 Presidential Access Ballot Map," Libertarian Party, http://tinyurl.com/hbey84u.

113. Harry Enten, "About A Third Of Bernie Sanders's Supporters Still Aren't Backing Hillary Clinton," *FiveThirtyEight.com,* Aug. 8, 2016, http://tinyurl.com/ztu6f7a.

114. Mike Vilensky, "Zephyr Teachout, Who Took on Cuomo, Faces Her Own Populist Rival," *The Wall Street Journal,* June 5, 2016, http://tinyurl.com/h4fvkyr.

115. Russell Berman, "Russ Feingold Wants a Rematch," *The Atlantic,* May 15, 2015, http://tinyurl.com/zagwu27.

116. "Issues," Mark Assini for Congress, http://tinyurl.com/zgpymdk; Siobhan Hughes, "Where Donald Trump Resonates, He is Embraced Down-Ballot," *The Wall Street Journal,* April 13, 2016, http://tinyurl.com/h8cdwna.

117. "2016 Ballot Measures," Ballotpedia.org, http://tinyurl.com/jf5aj2d.

118. "Nevada Background Checks for Gun Purchases Initiative, Question 1 (2016)," Ballotpedia.org, http://tinyurl.com/j5e96jb.

119. "Maine Minimum Wage Increase Initiative, Question 4 (2016)," Ballotpedia.org, http://tinyurl.com/jknsqwv; "Washington Minimum Wage Increase, Initiative 1433 (2016)," Ballotpedia. org, http://tinyurl.com/zc9y632.

120. "North Dakota Corporate Dairy and Swine Farming Referendum, Referred Measure 1 (June 2016)," Ballotpedia.org, http://tinyurl.com/h8wvjau.

121. Julie Bosman, "North Dakotans Reconsider a Corporate Farming Ban, and Their Virtues," *The New York Times,* June 12, 2014, http://tinyurl.com/juayylh.

122. Adair Turner, "Post-Brexit Populism Will Not Be Thwarted by Ignoring Migration," *Australian Financial Review,* July 12, 2016, http://tinyurl.com/hufa2je.

123. Jonathan Owen, "End of the EU? Germany Warns FIVE More Countries Could Leave Europe After Brexit," *Express.com* (U.K.), June 26, 2016, http://tinyurl.com/zys2n92.

124. Michael Pearson, "Scotland Likely to Seek Independence After EU Vote, First minister says," CNN.com, June 26, 2016, http://tinyurl.com/zx4h5dz.

125. "The End of Populism," *The Economist,* Nov. 28, 2015, http://tinyurl.com/jntgafr.

126. Gerald F. Seib, "Separating Donald Trump from Trumpism," *The Wall Street Journal,* Aug. 8, 2016, http://tinyurl.com/zs22j24.

127. Laura Grattan, *Populism's Power: Radical Grassroots Democracy in America* (2016), pp. 4-5.

128. Robert Reich, "Robert Reich Sees the Future: Why America's Two-Party System May Collapse," Alternet.org, March 22, 2016, http://tinyurl.com/zoj3dww.

129. Lee Drutman, "Donald Trump's Candidacy Is Going to Realign the Political Parties," *Vox.com,* March 1, 2016, http://tinyurl.com/jxzk8xc.

130. Moffitt, *op. cit.,* p. 160.

BIBLIOGRAPHY
Selected Sources
Books

Albertazzi, Daniele, and Duncan McDonnell, *Populists in Power*, Taylor & Francis, 2015.
Professors of politics at England's University of Birmingham (Albertazzi) and Australia's Griffith University (McDonnell) consider whether populist parties can govern successfully by examining populism in Italy and Switzerland.

Grattan, Laura, *Populism's Power: Radical Grassroots Democracy in America*, Oxford University Press, 2016.
A Wellesley College professor of political science argues that left-wing populist movements can improve U.S. democracy.

Moffitt, Benjamin, *The Global Rise of Populism: Performance, Political Style, and Representation*, Stanford University Press, 2016.

A research fellow in political science at Sweden's University of Stockholm explores how media are influencing contemporary populism.

Wodak, Ruth, *The Politics of Fear: What Right-Wing Populist Discourses Mean*, SAGE, 2015.
A professor of discourse studies at England's Lancaster University explains how global right-wing populists are bringing what she says are extremist views into the political mainstream.

Articles

Faiola, Anthony, "Meet the Donald Trumps of Europe," *The Washington Post*, May 19, 2016, http:// tinyurl.com/hv8e6z5.
A journalist looks at right-wing populist leaders in Europe who often are compared to Donald Trump.

Ip, Greg, "Rise of Populist Right Doesn't Signal Demise of Globalization," *The Wall Street Journal*, June 8, 2016, http://tinyurl.com/gq8henb.
The newspaper's chief economics correspondent contends that immigration, rather than globalization, is fueling populism in Europe and the United States.

Jacobs, Andrew, "Brazil Workers' Party, Leaders 'Intoxicated' by Power, Falls From Grace," *The New York Times*, May 12, 2016, http://tinyurl.com/how87cf.
A reporter outlines the downfall of a left-wing populist party in Brazil whose leaders could not overcome deep economic problems and corruption.

Kolhatkar, Sheelah, "How Hillary Clinton Became a Better Economic Populist Than Donald Trump," *The New Yorker*, Aug. 12, 2016, http://tinyurl.com/hgddmga.
A journalist argues the Democratic presidential nominee is embracing economic populism.

Lapowsky, Issie, "Trump Isn't The First Tech-Propelled Populist. But This Time's Different," *Wired*, May 13, 2015, http://tinyurl.com/hqj372p.
A journalist says Donald Trump's and Bernie Sanders' use of social media differs sharply from earlier populists' use of communication tools.

Lehmann, Chris, "Donald Trump and the Long Tradition of American Populism," *Newsweek*, Aug. 22, 2015, http://tinyurl.com/ztdydmj.

A journalist compares Donald Trump to earlier populist leaders, finding similarities in their grievances against elites.

Liasson, Mara, "How This Election's Populist Politics Are Bigger Than Trump And Sanders," NPR, April 25, 2016, http://tinyurl.com/zo5zsk2.
Experts predict that Trump's and Sanders' versions of populism will extend beyond 2016.

Mudde, Cas, "The Problem With Populism," *The Guardian* (U.K.), Feb. 17, 2015, http://tinyurl.com/jfjfeqv.
A University of Georgia professor of international affairs explains the various types of populism.

Poole, Isaiah J., "Reclaiming Populism: Progressive Movement Is Alive and Well in the 21st Century," *AlterNet*, April 29, 2015, http://tinyurl.com/m39pbzm.
A left-wing activist says progressive groups are seeking to use populism to counter corporations' influence on government.

Reports and Studies

Alvares, Claudia, and Peter Dahlgren, "Populism, Extremism and Media: Mapping an Uncertain Terrain," *European Journal of Communication*, February 2016, http://tinyurl.com/zxm7rmb.
Communications researchers at Portugal's Lusófona University (Alvares) and Sweden's Lund University (Dahlgren) explore how the media are influencing populism in Europe.

Bonikowski, Bart, and Noam Gidron, "The Populist Style in American Politics: Presidential Campaign Discourse, 1952–1996," Social Forces, 2015, http:// tinyurl.com/goo4vzm.
Harvard professors of sociology (Bonikowski) and government (Gidron) find frequent use of populist themes in presidential speeches during the latter half of the 20th century.

Inglehart, Ronald, and Pippa Norris, "Trump, Brexit, and the Rise of Populism: Economic Have-Nots and Cultural Backlash," Kennedy School of Government, Harvard University, August 2016, http://tinyurl.com/jd5u9pe.
Professors of political science at the University of Michigan (Inglehart) and Harvard (Norris) examine the factors responsible for the rise of populist parties in Europe

For More Information

American Enterprise Institute, 1150 17th St., N.W., Washington, DC 20036; 202-862-5800; www.aei.org. Conservative think tank analyzing populism and other political trends.

Campaign for America's Future, 1825 K St., N.W., Washington, DC 20006; 202-955-5665; https://ourfuture .org. Liberal political advocacy organization studying left-wing populism.

Centre for European Policy Studies, 1 Place du Congres, 1000 Brussels, Belgium; +32 (0) 2 229 39 11; www.ceps .eu. Think tank studying populism and other developments in Europe.

Donald J. Trump for President, 725 Fifth Ave., New York, NY 10022; 646-736-1779; www.donaldjtrump.com. Campaign offices and website.

FiveThirtyEight.com, 147 Columbus Ave., 4th floor, New York, NY 10023; www.fivethirtyeight.com. Website founded by statistician Nate Silver that examines how populism shapes political campaigns.

Hillary for America, P.O. Box 5256, New York, NY 10185; 646-854-1432; www.hillarydinton.com. Campaign offices and website.

Our Revolution, 603 2nd St., N.E., Washington, DC 20002; https://ourrevolution.com. Political group begun by Sen. Bernie Sanders to further his populist goals.

Pew Research Center, 1615 L St., N.W., Suite 700, Washington, DC 20036; 202-419-4300; www.pew research.org. Nonpartisan think tank providing information on issues, attitudes and trends shaping the United States.

Weatherhead Center for International Affairs, Harvard University, 737 Cambridge St., Cambridge, MA 02138; 617-495-4420; http://wcfia.harvard.edu. Research center whose interests include studying international populism.

3

Diversity in Hollywood

Christina Hoag

Comedian Chris Rock, host of the 2016 Academy Awards, pointedly acknowledged the controversy over Hollywood's lack of racial and ethnic diversity in his opening bit at the ceremony: "I'm here at the Academy Awards, otherwise known as the White People's Choice Awards." For the second year in a row, only white performers were nominated for top actor and actress Oscars.

Getty Images/Kevin Winter

From *CQ Researcher,*
August 5, 2016

When African-American comic Chris Rock took the stage to host the 2016 Academy Awards, he wasted no time in confronting the issue of the day.

"I'm here at the Academy Awards, otherwise known as the White People's Choice Awards," Rock quipped. His blunt monologue reflected public outrage that the academy's 7,000-plus predominantly older, white and male members had nominated an all-white slate of actors and actresses for Hollywood's most prestigious prizes — for the second year in a row.[1]

Yet Rock himself didn't escape charges of bias and stereotyping. In a spoof that fell flat for many viewers, he introduced a group of Asian children as the accountants who tally the award votes, and Latino activists were piqued that he addressed the exclusion of blacks but not of other minorities.

"Who OK'd that script?" asks Alex Nogales, president of the National Hispanic Media Coalition. "Diversity is more than one group." Still, Rock underscored the point made by the #OscarsSoWhite hashtag that had erupted on social media in January as soon as the academy announced its 2016 nominees. "How is it possible for the second consecutive year all 20 contenders under the acting category are white?" director Spike Lee wrote on Instagram.[2]

Black Hollywood A-listers, including Lee and actor Will Smith, whose performance as a Nigerian doctor in *Concussion* had been widely considered Oscar-worthy, announced they would boycott the globally televised awards ceremony.[3] Activists holding signs saying "Shame on You" and "Hollywood Must Do Better" picketed the event.[4]

Minorities Trail Whites in Leading Roles

The percentage of minorities playing leading roles in films and broadcast shows edged up in recent years, but blacks, Hispanics and other minorities continue to fall far short of whites. Minorities filled about 13 percent of lead-actor film roles in 2014, up from 10.5 percent in 2011. In scripted broadcast programs, minorities filled about 8 percent of lead roles in the 2013-14 season, up from 5 percent in 2011-12. Minorities make up about 38 percent of the U.S. population.

Lead Actor Roles by Race in Theatrical Films, Broadcast Scripted Programming, 2011-2014

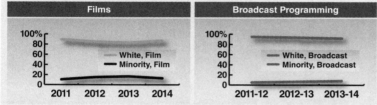

Source: "2016 Hollywood Diversity Report: Busine$$ as Usual?" Ralph J. Bunche Center for African American Studies at UCLA, Feb. 25, 2016, http://tinyurl.com/hhrdltn.

Even President Obama weighed in, saying, "As a whole, the industry should do what every other industry should do, which is to look for talent and provide opportunity to everybody."[5]

The outcry highlighted long-festering charges of bias against racial and ethnic minorities and women in the film and television industries — both in front of and behind the camera — despite decades of complaints, studies and diversity programs.

"This is a long-term problem that has proven somewhat intractable," says Darnell Hunt, professor of sociology and director of the Ralph J. Bunche Center for African American Studies at the University of California, Los Angeles (UCLA).

The issue of diversity in the film and television industries, which employ 302,000 people directly and 1.9 million indirectly, increasingly is being scrutinized as the United States becomes more heterogeneous.[6] In 2014, minorities represented 38 percent of the population; by 2060 they are projected to account for 56 percent.[7] But whites and men dominate nearly every facet of the industry, from the corporate suite to cinematography, although

studies show TV has become somewhat more diverse than movies.

A 2015 study by the Bunche Center found minorities, predominantly African-Americans, had 13 percent of lead film roles in 2014.[8] In television shows, white men filled about 70 percent of scripted roles.[9] And research by the Center for the Study of Women in Television and Film at San Diego State University said that women, who make up 51 percent of the population, occupied 19 percent of major behind-the-scenes movie jobs, such as director, writer and producer.[10] The trend is more pronounced among industry powerbrokers. The UCLA study reported that talent agents — who make the deals placing actors, writers, directors, producers and others in productions — are 91 percent white and 68 percent male.[11]

"The film industry still functions as a straight, white, boys' club," stated another study by the University of Southern California's Institute for Diversity and Empowerment at Annenberg (IDEA) that had similar findings.[12]

Studio executives admit more could be done to include women and minorities. Stacey Snider, cochair at 20th Century Fox, said she could mentor more women and "enable young female writers and directors to have access" to studios.[13] Harvey Weinstein, cochair of the Weinstein film studio, said, "The truth is that the industry needs to, and must, do better. And we will, too," he said.[14]

Activists say mass entertainment has a particular responsibility to mirror the population at-large because it wields considerable influence over popular culture and public perceptions, especially by those who may not personally know people different from themselves. Movies and TV "reflect our values but they also shape them," says Megan Townsend, entertainment media strategist for GLAAD, an LGBT rights organization known by its acronym. Adds Nogales, "The way we are perceived is the way we'll get treated."

Several factors explain why racial, ethnic and gender imbalance remains an issue in film and television, experts say. The industries' allure of glamor, wealth and fame leads to a talent supply that far outstrips demand. Thus, breaking into and advancing in the industry are highly contingent on personal relationships, which has led to the development of a clubby circle of insiders.

"It's not a merit system. Most people are disadvantaged by that," says John W. Cones, a California entertainment attorney who has written 16 books on access issues in Hollywood.

Because white males broker most deals at studios, networks and talent agencies, they tend to choose from their own circles to fill major positions, such as directors, writers and producers, Hunt and Cones say. In turn, they add, producers and directors fill production jobs with people who also tend to look like them.

"It's based on relationship and comfort zones, which is not to say that plain, old-fashioned racism isn't alive and well, too," Hunt says. "But it's very insular."

A similar dynamic appears to play out with regard to gender. In movies directed by men in 2015, women made up only 10 percent of writers, 19 percent of editors and 10 percent of cinematographers, according to the San Diego State University study. But in movies directed by women, more than half the writers were women, as were 32 percent of the editors and 12 percent of the cinematographers, the study found.[15]

Such trends are amplified in the movie business because box-office returns are unpredictable and films can cost hundreds of millions of dollars to make, researchers say. As a result, executives tend to hire people with proven success. "They go back to the same white men who have a track record," Hunt says. Because women and minorities don't get the experience they need to land the prestige studio jobs, he and others say, they end up working on smaller, independent productions.

Meanwhile, many professionals have been reluctant to complain about the system out of fear of being labeled troublemakers in a highly competitive industry, in which employment goes from project to project, researchers say.

Signs of change are afoot, however. The Oscars controversy has stirred a new push for inclusivity from Hollywood insiders. The Academy of Motion Picture Arts and Sciences, which runs the Oscars, revamped its voting rules and this year added its most diverse group of

Getty Images/Frazer Harrison

Critics blasted the selection of Hispanic actress Zoe Saldana, right, to portray beloved African-American singer Nina Simone, left, as a return to "blackface" in the movies. Saldana wore a prosthetic nose and her skin was darkened with makeup (not shown) in a trailer for the film released this year.

new members ever, with the goal of nominating more women and minorities for awards. And prominent producers J. J. Abrams and Ryan Murphy announced initiatives to hire more people from underrepresented groups as cast and crew.

Outside of Hollywood, a new generation of internet media, such as Amazon and Hulu, is providing new platforms for underrepresented groups and original story lines. They include Netflix's "Master of None," a TV comedy created by and starring an American Muslim of Indian descent, Aziz Ansari, and *Beasts of No Nation,* a searing drama about African child soldiers. Mainstream TV also is adding new shows, such as ABC's "Fresh Off the Boat," an Asian immigrant comedy, with largely ethnic casts and stories.

Actresses increasingly are speaking out against discrimination based on age, the dearth of female roles and the on-screen sexualization of women, which activists say reflect male points of view. One study shows that female characters were more likely than males to be attractive or shown nude or sexily or scantily attired.[16] Pay gender inequity also surfaced as an issue in December 2014 after hackers publicized emails from Sony Pictures that revealed Jennifer Lawrence was paid less than her male co-stars in *American Hustle* (2013).[17] Lawrence said she was shocked and angry at the disparity. And the U.S. Equal Employment Opportunity Commission is investigating

Off-Camera Jobs for Women Remain Stagnant

The share of behind-the-scenes jobs filled by women on the 250 top-grossing American films between 1998 and 2015 remained below 20 percent. In 2015, women comprised 19 percent of all directors, writers, producers, executive producers, editors and cinematographers, only 2 percentage points more than in 1998.

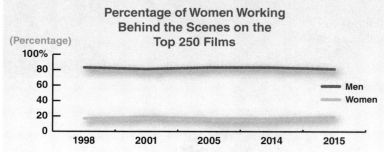

Source: "The Celluloid Ceiling: Behind-the-Scenes Employment of Women on the Top 100, 250, and 500 Films of 2015," Center for the Study of Women in Television and Film, 2016, http://tinyurl.com/h5gmn7p.

allegations of bias against female directors after the American Civil Liberties Union (ACLU) of Southern California filed a complaint against the industry.[18]

"As a result of this rapidly growing and increasingly vociferous public conversation, the explicit denial or implicit disregard of the embarrassing statistics by high-profile individuals is no longer possible," said Martha M. Lauzen, executive director of San Diego State University's Center for the Study of Women in Television and Film.[19]

As Hollywood insiders and outsiders discuss diversity in the entertainment industry, here are some of the questions being debated:

Does Hollywood discriminate against female and minority actors?

When the trailer of an upcoming movie about African-American singer Nina Simone was released this year, critics blasted it as a return to "blackface" — using makeup on white actors so they can play black characters. Hispanic actress Zoe Saldana, who had been chosen to portray Simone, was wearing a prosthetic nose and her skin had been darkened with makeup.

"There are many superb actresses of color who could more adequately represent my mother," Simone's daughter Lisa Simone Kelly said.[20]

Using white actors to portray minorities is an established practice in Hollywood. In *Exodus: Gods and Kings* (2014), English actor Christian Bale played the Middle Eastern Jewish character Moses, and white actors portrayed Egyptian characters.[21] Emma Stone portrayed a Hawaiian-Asian woman in *Aloha* (2015).[22] Joseph Fiennes plays the late pop singer Michael Jackson in *Elizabeth, Michael & Marlon* (2016).[23]

And television is not exempt. Fox's "Tyrant" stars Adam Rayner, a white actor, as the show's sympathetic Middle Eastern hero.[24]

Hollywood insiders say the problem is the bottom line: To get a movie financed, backers need a "bankable" star who can increase the film's box-office return — and most big stars are white. Director Ridley Scott responded to *Exodus* critics: "I can't mount a film of this budget, . . . and say that my lead actor is Mohammad So-and-So from such-and-such. I'm just not going to get it financed. So the question doesn't even come up."[25]

Research has shown, however, that diverse casts can boost returns. A Bunche Center study of 2014 movies found that global box-office returns for films with a 40- to 50-percent minority cast were twice that of movies with a 10 percent or less minority cast. TV shows showed similar patterns.[26]

Critics charge that it is unfair to exclude minority actors from racial and ethnic roles, especially since there are far fewer such parts and minority actors can give more nuanced performances drawn from their own experience. "How else can it be authentic?" asks Nogales of the National Hispanic Media Coalition. And playing those roles could help minority actors become bankable stars, critics say.

But Indian-American actor Ansari said in casting his Netflix series "Master of None," that it was hard to find minority actors because there are fewer of them than white actors, which leads to casting white actors in "brownface." "But I still wonder if we are trying hard enough," he said.[27]

Members of other underrepresented groups say when roles for them do arise, they often involve only limited story lines. People with disabilities, for example, are primarily played by ablebodied actors and story lines often are based on overcoming adversity or recovering from the disability, says Johnson Cheu, assistant professor at Michigan State University who studies culture, disability and media.

Rarely are people with disabilities portrayed as fully realized characters outside of their disability, Cheu says. "Disability makes for good tension and conflict, as long as [the disability] is not long-term and permanent in Hollywood. That's not progress, and it's not reality," he says.

Activists with other underrepresented groups also say their community members often are stereotyped: Transgender people are almost always women; Asian men rarely get to play romantic swashbucklers; Hispanics tend to be brown-skinned and occupy low-paying jobs. "Judges are the only role black women get to play" on television, says Rashad Robinson, executive director of ColorOfChange.org, a civil rights organization. "It makes us feel like a box was checked."

Women also face age discrimination, with fewer parts for women as they age. Maggie Gyllenhaal said that at age 37 she was deemed too old to play the love interest of a 55-year-old man.[28] The 27-year-old Stone said she's had to play opposite romantic male leads her father's age.[29]

Studies bear out their statements. Female characters in their 30s represent 28 percent of female roles, while female characters in their 40s make up only 20 percent of roles, according to research by the Center for the Study of Women in Television and Film at San Diego State University. The opposite is true for men, the study found: The percentage of older male characters increases slightly as men age: Men in their 30s represent 27 percent of male roles, while those in their 40s make up 30 percent of roles.[30]

"Portraying female characters in their 20s and 30s tends to keep the emphasis on their physical traits," said study author Lauzen.

Women actors also are speaking up about gender-based pay disparities, after WikiLeaks published the Sony emails, hacked in 2014 by the North Korean government in retaliation for the lampooning of leader Kim Jong Un in the movie *The Interview.* Lawrence learned

not only that she was paid less than her male co-stars in *American Hustle* but also that she and co-star Amy Adams received 7 percent of profits while their three male co-stars each earned 9 percent.[31]

Other actresses have spoken out as well: While Jack Nicholson received profit-sharing pay for *Something's Gotta Give* (2003), his co-star Diane Keaton did not, and triple Oscar winner Meryl Streep said she routinely is paid less than her male co-stars. Shortly after the Sony hacking revelations, Patricia Arquette underscored the issue during her acceptance speech for Best Supporting Actress at the 2015 Oscars: "It's our time to have wage equality once and for all."[32]

Lawrence, the highest-paid movie actress in 2015, earned $52 million, far less than top-paid actor, Robert Downey Jr, who made $80 million.[33]

Pay disparities also exist in television, although they are less pronounced. The two highest-paid female TV actresses — Sofia Vergara ("Modern Family") and Kaley Cuoco ("The Big Bang Theory") — each earned $28.5 million in 2015, nearly as much as the industry's highest paid actor, "Big Bang" star Jim Parsons ($29 million). But the cut-off to make *Forbes'* list of highest-paid TV actresses was $5 million — $4.5 million less than the cutoff for male actors.[34]

Is television more diverse than film?

Many experts say diversity is making visible progress in television. Fox's "Empire," a melodrama about the music industry, features a nearly all-black cast. ABC's sitcom "Fresh Off the Boat" is based on the memoir of a Taiwanese immigrant chef. The CW network has "Jane the Virgin," a comedy about a Latina who accidentally becomes pregnant.

"Television is much further along than film," says Nogales of the National Hispanic Media Coalition.

TV production companies score better on diversity overall than movie companies. Two dozen film companies were rated as not inclusive, while nine out of 10 TV companies were found to be largely or fully inclusive, according to a study by the University of Southern California's Institute for Diversity and Empowerment at Annenberg, which studies media inclusivity. The study listed the Walt Disney Co. networks (ABC, Disney, Disney Jr. and Freeform) and CW as the most diverse because they hired more women and minorities in key positions.[35]

Many experts say the nearly all-black cast of Fox's "Empire," a drama about the music industry, shows that diversity is making visible progress in television. Above, Taraji P. Henson and Terrence Howard in the show's "Et Tu, Brute?" episode.

TV always has been ahead of movies in diversity, observers say, primarily because networks, which must fill a lot of programming slots, constantly are seeking fresh stories. "There's just so much more being produced in TV than in film," says Tery Lopez, director of diversity at the Writers Guild of America West, the industry group representing screenwriters.

Television also is more nimble. Production costs tend to be lower than for movies, giving networks more latitude to try new concepts, experts say. A new show that does not attract good ratings can be yanked quickly, allowing networks to cut their losses. And television shows, which typically are produced in a matter of months as opposed to years for feature films, can incorporate fastchanging societal attitudes and current events, says GLAAD's Townsend.

Reliance on overseas sales also differs between the industries. Both studios and networks license their content abroad, but foreign sales are a vital consideration in movie financing decisions. Foreign revenue from American movies last year ($40 billion) represented 73 percent of box-office receipts — up 10 percent from 2010. By contrast, domestic movie ticket sales increased by only $4 million during the same period.[36]

As a result, studios produce more star-studded, action-driven, blockbuster movies that appeal to international audiences. Those films also appeal to the biggest U.S. movie-going demographic — 12- to 39-year-olds, who make up more than half of frequent American moviegoers.[37] Controversial themes, such as LGBT issues, thus tend to be avoided.

"There's some concern as to how films play around the world," Townsend says. "That affects the stories they are choosing to tell, or not tell."

Television, on the other hand, does not typically develop shows with foreign audiences in mind, and some U.S. ethnic shows do not translate well overseas. "Empire," for example, flopped in the United Kingdom, Germany, Australia and Canada.

"These shows are a reflection of our society, but not a reflection of all societies," said Marion Edwards, president of international TV at Fox. However, shows with mainstream themes featuring diverse casts or leads, such as ABC's "Grey's Anatomy" and "How to Get Away with Murder," have done well overseas.[38]

But ethnic content on TV could be affected as foreign sales become increasingly important to help defray rising television production costs — about $3 million for an hourlong drama in 2013.[39] "We are telling our units that they need to be aware that . . . creating too much diversity in the leads in their show means . . . problems having their shows translating to the international market," Edwards said.[40]

Behind the camera, however, television remains dominated by whites and males. During the upcoming 2016-2017 season, showrunners — those who oversee everything on a show from hiring to creative direction — at the five biggest broadcast networks are 90 percent white and 80 percent male, according to a study by the trade journal *Variety*.[41]

Industry insiders say that while most networks have programs to develop talent from diverse backgrounds, they have mostly led to tokenism rather than wide change. NBC's Diverse Staff Writing Initiative, for instance, pays a series to employ a minority staff writer, but typically only one hire is made.[42] Writer Amy Aniobi said she has seen staff lists with employees labeled "diversity writer." "Everyone knows who the diversity writer is. You're the one who's the only one," she said.[43]

That lack of minority inclusion also trickles down to production jobs. "You rarely see diversity in the crew," says Jaquita Ta'le, an African-American actress in Los Angeles.

But minorities are popular with the population at-large, says UCLA's Hunt, noting the success of African-American showrunner Shonda Rhimes, whose hit series, such as

"Scandal" and "Grey's Anatomy," use minority actors, writers and crew members.

"If more networks took that lead, they'd be more in sync with their audience," Hunt says.

Will streaming outlets lead to greater diversity?

Katie Elmore Mota was tired of seeing Latinos absent from TV so she created her own show. "East Los High," a hit soap opera depicting Hispanic teens in a fictional Los Angeles high school was recently renewed for a fourth season by the Hulu internet streaming service. Executive producer Mota says the show's 60 percent non-Latino audience underscores to the mainstream industry that TV characters don't have to all be "rich, white teenagers."[44]

To overcome barriers to hiring, women and minorities are finding internet viewing platforms — such as Amazon, Netflix, Hulu, Snapchat, Yahoo and YouTube — more welcoming than the mainstream industry. These new digital media seek different kinds of shows to lure viewers from traditional broadcast and cable channels.

In addition, many internet outlets operate under business models — such as subscriptions and limited advertising — that differ from network or cable models, so online outlets can appeal to niche audiences marginalized in the mainstream media. "Media is changing and that is . . . improving visibility for artists of color," says actress Ta'le, who has appeared in ABC's "Castle," among other shows, and voiced animated productions. "It's become the best way to get your stories told."

Some shows, such as Amazon Studios' "Transparent," created by Jill Soloway and featuring a transgender dad and his family, have turned into Emmy-winning hits. Others have helped their creators break into the mainstream industry. HBO snapped up the rights to Issa Rae's YouTube series "The Misadventures of Awkward Black Girl," which features a shy, middle-class black woman modeled on Rae, after its first webisode scored 2 million views.[45]

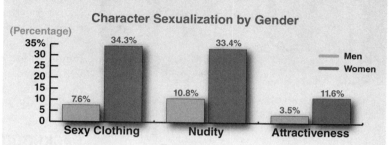

Females More Sexualized in Media Than Males

Female characters were far more likely than males to be portrayed in a sexualized manner in films, TV shows and digital series, according to a 10-year study of 10 major entertainment-media companies. The study defines sexualization as displays of sexy clothing, nudity or references to a person's physical attractiveness.

Character Sexualization by Gender

(Percentage)

	Sexy Clothing	Nudity	Attractiveness
Men	7.6%	10.8%	3.5%
Women	34.3%	33.4%	11.6%

Source: "Inclusion or Invisibility? Comprehensive Annenberg Report on Diversity in Entertainment," Media, Diversity, & Social Change Initiative, Annenberg School for Communication and Journalism, University of Southern California, Feb. 22, 2016, http://tinyurl.com/jxjyj2ps.

The internet also has evolved into a go-to place for Hollywood agents seeking fresh talent, giving exposure and critical experience to underrepresented groups, says the Writers Guild's Lopez. "The Web does give opportunities to people who put up their work," she says.

A USC study ranked Amazon and Hulu as strongly inclusive, with Amazon hiring the most female directors.[46]

Underrepresented groups also are benefiting from a boom in TV production. From 2009 to 2015, the number of scripted shows doubled — from just over 200 to 409 — leading to a shortage of experienced producers and writers and thus creating opportunities for less experienced entrants, insiders say.[47]

That's especially true in new media. Writer Gloria Calderon Kellett is making her debut as a showrunner with the Netflix remake of the 1970s sitcom "One Day at a Time," featuring a Latino family. "The fact that there is so much work is huge," she said. "People who don't normally get a chance, who are very talented, get seen."[48]

Internet companies also are producing movies. At the Cannes Film Festival in May, Amazon Studios unveiled its first slate of five feature films designed to be viewed online, including one directed by Park Chan-wook of South Korea.[49] While Netflix's first motion picture,

The hit Hulu soap opera "East Los High" depicts Hispanic teens in a fictional Los Angeles high school. Creator Katie Elmore Mota said the show's 60 percent non-Latino audience proves that TV characters don't have to all be "rich, white teenagers." Above, the cast gathers to celebrate the Season 4 premier on July 6, 2016.

Beasts of No Nation, was not a box-office hit it scored more than 3 million views via online streaming in the months after its initial release.

The internet movie trend creates "opportunities for movies to get made that audiences are going to love but are increasingly difficult to get made," said Netflix Chief Content Officer Ted Sarandos. These are "films of a certain budget, of a certain nature and certain topics."[50]

Amazon Studios' acquisition methods underscore how the internet gives underrepresented groups a chance, insiders say. While few Hollywood talent agents and producers accept unsolicited screenplays, perpetuating the insider nature of the business, Amazon Studios invites writers to submit scripts online and bases its final choices on customer feedback.[51]

Nevertheless, internet shows can be susceptible to the same tropes and criticism as traditional productions. The Netflix comedy "Unbreakable Kimmy Schmidt" has been both praised and criticized for a subplot revolving around a Lakota Indian woman disguising her heritage and then rediscovering it. Some have taken issue with a blond, white actress (Jane Krakowski) playing the role but have noted that Native Americans have been cast as her parents. Likewise, some Indians say a few of the jokes have been cringe-worthy but also reflect the truth. Others are simply glad an internet TV show features Native Americans.[52]

"There were a few moments where I cringed because it seemed like we were supposed to laugh at Native American stereotypes, which really aren't that funny," said Cutcha Risling Baldy, assistant professor of American Indian studies at San Diego State University.[53] Executive producer Robert Carlock defended the plot, saying that because some of the show's writers have Native American heritage, "we felt like we had a little room . . . to go that direction."[54]

Still, the internet is welcome news to women and minorities locked out of the traditional Hollywood system, activists say. "We have no choice but to create our own destiny," says Nogales of the National Hispanic Media Coalition.

BACKGROUND

Stereotypes and Exclusion

D. W. Griffith's *The Birth of a Nation* (1915) is famed as the first feature-length motion picture. But its use of white actors in blackface and portrayals of heroic Ku Klux Klansmen and oversexed black slaves ushered in another trend, film scholars say: Hollywood's use of racial and ethnic stereotypes.

"More than any other film, *The Birth of a Nation* gave birth to the shocking and degrading stereotypes that were to plague African-American movie images throughout the twentieth century," wrote Donald Bogle, author of *Bright Boulevards, Bold Dreams: The Story of Black Hollywood.*[55]

From Hollywood's earliest years, racial and ethnic groups — who were also battling deeply entrenched racism in society — have protested their depiction on screen and exclusion from decision-making roles. Mexican-Americans were portrayed as villains in films such as *Tony the Greaser* (1911). By 1922 the Mexican government threatened to ban Hollywood movies in Mexico, leading Hollywood producers to agree not to present Mexicans in an objectionable manner, and after that light-skinned Hispanics were cast as "Latin lovers."[56] Asian-Americans were typically laundry workers or seductresses. Fed up with Hollywood's limited roles for Asians, Anna May Wong, the biggest Asian star of the period, moved to Europe for several years in 1928.[57]

But before the studio system became entrenched — with production companies holding actors, directors, writers and others under exclusive contract and enforcing rigorous rules — the industry's initial years were years of opportunity. Women, for instance, wrote, directed, produced and edited movies and founded their own studios. "Women had a major role in the early days of the American film industry because no rigid role distinctions had yet been set. . . . Whoever could achieve a desired effect or result, male or female, got the job."[58]

Japanese actor Sessue Hayakawa, a heartthrob of silent cinema, had his own production company in 1918, writing, directing, producing and acting in 23 films.[59] African-Americans formed companies to produce "race films," with "all colored casts" in roles such as bankers and businessmen, to be shown in segregated theaters.[60] More than 30 companies produced some 500 race films by the time the genre faded around 1940.[61]

The most successful African-Americans in that era were the child actors of *Our Gang* (1922-44), which featured white and black youngsters as equals — unusual for the period.[62]

Studio Era

As silent films gave way to talkies in the 1920s and movies' popularity and profitability increased, the studio system emerged, and over the next two decades, independent filmmakers were edged out and minorities relegated to sideline roles.

Women were pushed out of behind-the-scenes jobs except writing, but then that also dropped off. In 1928, women wrote 52 of 238 screenplays. By 1940, they penned just 64 of 608 scripts.[63] Instead, women were deemed to be more suited to on-screen roles. Actresses, who fell into two main camps — sex goddesses and career women — proved to be more popular than male stars.

"The film industry during the first part of the 20th century was responsible for reinforcing patriarchal norms; with men occupying most of the positions as directors and producers, female actresses were often cast in roles and publicized in ways that led them to become the objects of the male gaze," according to a history of women in film.[64]

Faced with a backlash against "loose morals" in movies, the studios in 1930 adopted the Motion Picture Production Code, a list of 36 prohibitions designed to hold producers to high moral standards.[65] The code, which banned such things as lustful kissing, crime, nudity, suggestive dancing and interracial relationships,

In the early days of movies, white actors typically filled minority roles, including lead characters. In 1928, fed up with limited parts for Asians, Anna May Wong, perhaps the biggest Asian star of the period, moved to Europe for several years. She later was offered, and turned down in disgust, the role of a "dragon lady" in MGM's *The Good Earth*. The 1937 film notoriously cast Caucasian actors Paul Muni and Luise Rainer in "yellowface" makeup as the leads.

was voluntary and carried no penalties for violation. But theaters would not show films that did not adhere to it. The code would be abandoned in 1968 after becoming increasingly obsolete.[66]

Even when the code wasn't an issue, white actors filled minority roles, including lead characters. One of the most notorious instances was MGM's *The Good Earth* (1937). Caucasian actors Paul Muni and Luise Rainer played the married sympathetic Chinese male and female leads, in "yellowface" makeup, while Anna May Wong was offered the role as a "dragon lady," which she refused in disgust.[67]

In addition, most heroic roles went to whites, even when the heroes were minorities. Douglas Fairbanks and Tyrone Power at different times played Zorro, the Mexican masked avenger of Spanish colonial injustice.[68] Likewise, the popular Chinese-American detective Charlie Chan was played by white actors in more than 40 movies in 1930s and 1940s.[69] African-Americans were cast mostly as servants, but they won some recognition. Hattie McDaniel became the first African-American to win an Oscar, albeit for her stereotyped role as Mammy in the 1939 classic *Gone with the Wind*.

CHRONOLOGY

1910s-1930s *Stereotyped characters and "blackface" are common in films.*

1915 D. W. Griffith's *Birth of a Nation,* the first feature-length film, sparks protests over its use of white actors in blackface.

1927 The first sound film, *The Jazz Singer,* stars Al Jolson in blackface.

1939 *Gone With the Wind* actress Hattie McDaniel becomes the first African-American to win an Oscar.

1950s *Racially tinged political movies stir controversy.*

1951 Situation comedy "I Love Lucy," featuring an Anglo woman (Lucille Ball) married to a Cuban bandleader (Desi Arnaz), becomes television's most-watched show.

1952 Boxing drama *The Ring* depicts discrimination against Mexican-Americans with Latino actors in lead roles.

1954 Congress denounces *Salt of the Earth,* a film depicting striking Mexican-American mine workers, as subversive because of its creators' alleged involvement in communist politics.

1960s-1970s *Minorities and women make strides in film and TV roles.*

1961 In a widely criticized example of "yellowface," Mickey Rooney plays a stereotyped Japanese character in *Breakfast at Tiffany's.*

1962 African-Americans picket the Oscars to protest discrimination. . . . Congressional hearings are held on Hollywood bias against blacks.

1967 Sidney Poitier becomes the first black movie star with *In the Heat of the Night.*

1968 NBC's "Julia" stars Diahann Carroll, an African-American, in a non-stereotypical TV role (nurse).

1975 ABC debuts "Hot L Baltimore," featuring TV's first gay couple.

1979 Female members of the Directors Guild of America criticize the lack of opportunities for women.

1980s-1990s *Minority groups gain mainstream audiences; women enter studio executive ranks.*

1983 Directors Guild sues Warner Bros. and Columbia Pictures, alleging hiring discrimination against women and minorities.

1985 Directors Guild lawsuit is dismissed after a judge says it does not meet requirements for class-action lawsuits.

1990 Native Americans praise *Dances with Wolves* for what they call its fair depiction of tribes.

1991 Network TV's first kiss by a gay couple airs on "L.A. Law."

1994 ABC's "All-American Girl" is the first situation comedy featuring an Asian-American family.

2000-Present *Complaints rise over diversity, ageism, gender pay inequities and sexualization of women.*

2000 A group of 165 film and TV writers sue 51 studios, TV networks and talent agencies for age discrimination.

2001 Disney/ABC launches program aimed at fostering minority and female directors.

2005 *Brokeback Mountain,* one of the first movies featuring a gay love story aimed at a mainstream audience, is a critical and box office hit.

2010 Writers' age discrimination lawsuit is settled for $70 million.

2014 Networks and studios launch programs to foster careers of underrepresented directors and writers. . . . Hacked Sony Pictures emails fuel outrage over gender pay gap.

2016 Oscar nominations excluding nonwhite actors spur Academy of Motion Picture Arts and Sciences to overhaul voting rules (January) and diversify its membership (June).

Roles for African-Americans changed after 1942, when the NAACP, a civil rights organization, won pledges from studios to end stereotyped casting and hire more blacks for production jobs. The result was a raft of films featuring popular black entertainers, such as Louis Armstrong, Duke Ellington and Lena Horne, and other African-Americans who were hired as musicians and dancers.

Latin culture also boomed during this period, and depictions of Latinos changed considerably, with actors such as Cesar Romero and Ricardo Montalban portraying upper-class, educated characters in a variety of roles.

From 1947 through the 1950s, the House Un-American Activities Committee targeted political diversity in Hollywood, holding high-profile hearings aimed at rooting out communism in popular culture. Ten people, mostly writers, eventually went to prison for contempt of Congress for refusing to answer questions at the hearings, while dozens of others saw their careers ruined after being "blacklisted," or blocked from working in Hollywood.[70]

In the 1950s white filmmakers began making minority-sensitive movies. *Salt of the Earth* (1954) and *Giant* (1956) broke new ground by addressing discrimination against Hispanics, while *Viva Zapata!* (1952) depicted the life of Emiliano Zapata, with Marlon Brando playing the Mexican revolutionary. Dorothy Dandridge became the first black pinup star after her Oscar nomination for best actress for *Carmen Jones* (1954), which featured an all-black cast.[71]

By the late 1950s, the studio system had collapsed, in part due to a 1948 Supreme Court ruling in an antitrust case that forced the five major studios to sell their theater chains. The ruling allowed room for independent filmmakers and smaller studios to distribute their movies. Stars became more savvy about contracts and increasingly opted to work as free agents.

The industry also began to face significant competition from television and foreign films.

Advent of Television

Women and minorities did not fare well in early-1950s television. Women filled traditional housewife roles in shows such as "The Donna Reed Show" (1958-66), and females working off-camera were rare. Caricature-style stereotypes of blacks returned with two short-lived shows,

"The Beulah Show" (1950-53) and "The Amos 'n' Andy Show" (1951-53), which spurred NAACP protests.[72]

There were exceptions. One of the decade's biggest hits, "I Love Lucy" (1951-57) featured an ethnically mixed couple: Cuban Desi Arnaz and his zany white wife, Lucille Ball. CBS executives were initially skeptical that the mixed couple would be well received, but the show became one of television's most enduring.

"The Lone Ranger" (1949-57) TV series represented a breakthrough for Native Americans, who had largely lost major roles to white actors and had been stereotyped as whooping savages since cinema's early days. Tonto was played by Jay Silverheels, making him the first Native American star.[73]

With the civil rights movement growing powerful in the next decade, Hollywood developed more complex roles for minorities. In 1965, NBC cast Bill Cosby as a secret agent in "I Spy" (1965-68) in one of the first lead roles for an African-American. By the decade's end more than two dozen TV shows featured black actors in lead or prominent supporting roles.[74] One was "Star Trek" (1966-69), which featured a black woman (Nichelle Nichols) and an Asian man (George Takei) in what was considered revolutionary casting at the time.

Women began making inroads in other aspects of the industry, such as comedy and variety shows. After being told that women writers were not wanted on "The Smothers Brothers" comedy show (1967-70), Gail Parent was hired by another comedy program, "The Carol Burnett Show" (1967-78), the only female on CBS' staff of 100 variety show writers.[75]

The era's social tumult over civil rights and women's rights inspired moviemakers to tackle controversial themes, leading to more story lines involving minorities and women in major roles. Sidney Poitier, the first black actor to gain star status, starred in the groundbreaking 1967 interracial-relationship story *Guess Who's Coming to Dinner?* The first feature film written and directed by an African-American (Gordon Parks) was released by a major studio: *The Learning Tree* (1969).

Homosexuality, which had been featured in few films due to bans by the Motion Picture Production Code, emerged in *Inside Daisy Clover* (1965), an early-mainstream movie with a gay character who is not killed or does not commit suicide, although his sexuality is not overtly displayed.[76]

Muslims Struggle to Counter Terrorist Stereotypes

"They've been the most vilified group in the history of Hollywood."

President Obama has a message for the television and movie industry: Write more scripts depicting Muslims as regular people, not as terrorists and fanatics.

"Most Americans don't necessarily know — or at least don't know that they know — a Muslim personally," he told the Islamic Society of Baltimore in February in a speech aimed at countering negative stereotypes of Muslims and assuring them that they "fit in here" in American society.

"Many only hear about Muslims and Islam from the news after an act of terrorism, or in distorted media portrayals in TV or film, all of which gives this hugely distorted impression," Obama said. "Our television shows should have some Muslim characters that are unrelated to national security. It's not that hard to do."[1]

Muslims and Arabs have been portrayed on screen as villains and evildoers for decades. In 1,200 depictions of Arabs and Muslims in Hollywood from the early 1900s to Sept. 11, 2001, 97 percent of the portrayals were negative, said Jack Shaheen, a visiting scholar of Near East studies at New York University who has been tracking the portrayals of Arabs in popular culture since the 1970s.[2] "They've been the most vilified group in the history of Hollywood." said Shaheen.[3]

Since the 2001 terrorist attacks in New York and Washington and subsequent U.S. involvement in wars in Iraq and Afghanistan, negative stereotypes have mushroomed, particularly on hit TV shows such as Showtime's "Homeland" and Fox's "24." Such dramas have depicted both Arabs and American Muslims as terrorists threatening U.S. security.

"Hollywood and television have created an even more dangerous precedent by vilifying American Arabs and American Muslims in particular," Shaheen said. "They've blended the old stereotypes from 'over there' with new stereotypes from 'over here.'"[4]

Some say shows and movies simply reflect the current global reality of Middle East unrest and extremist bombings. "Stereotyping is common in Hollywood but tends to be factually based," wrote Melbourne University history fellow Daniel Mandel in *Middle East Quarterly.* "Because terrorism against Americans is carried out by Muslims and Arabs, there is a basic truth to the movies."[5] But others, including *Middle East Monitor* columnist Noura Mansour, say that reflection has devolved into a catch-all stereotype based on misperceptions, as well as ignorance about the Islamic religion and culture.[6] For instance, Hollywood often uses the words "Arab" and "Muslim" interchangeably, when in fact Muslims hail from 57 countries, only 22 of which are predominantly Arab.[7]

"There's a lot of misinformation about Islam and the Koran," says Suhad Obeidi, director of the Hollywood bureau of the Muslim Public Affairs Council in Los Angeles.

The Hollywood tropes help contribute to a negative view of Muslims, say Mansour, Obeidi and others. In a 2014 study by the Pew Center, Americans ranked Islam as the least favorable religion, while 58 percent associated Muslims with fanaticism and just 22 percent said they were respectful of women.[8]

The stereotypes also play into anti-Muslim sentiments expressed by some politicians, including Republican

---

The Hollywood Production Code, weakened by a 1952 Supreme Court ruling that movies were protected under the First Amendment right to free speech, became obsolete as societal attitudes liberalized and studios became reluctant to clamp down on filmmakers. When the code was officially abandoned in 1968, the Motion Picture Association of America replaced it with a ratings system that determines the age-appropriateness of movies based on the amount of sex, adult language or violence.[77]

As social attitudes became increasingly liberal in the 1970s, more opportunities opened for underrepresented groups — in both film and television.

presidential candidate Donald Trump, who has proposed registering Muslim Americans and banning foreign Muslims from entering the country.[9] Hollywood "has been presenting and reinforcing stereotypical images, which line up with belligerent and orientalist American policies towards Arabs and Muslims," wrote Mansour in the *Middle East Monitor.*[10]

Some progress has occurred, however. In ABC's "Quantico," Lebanese actress Yasmine Al Massri, who plays an FBI trainee who wears a hijab, said she took the role partly to dispel the image of a repressed, submissive Muslim woman.[11] Other shows, including Fox's "Bones," ABC's "Lost" and NBC's "Community," have featured positive Arab-American characters. And while progress in recent films has been scant, the 2009 film *Star Trek* featured a Pakistani character played by Pakistani-American Faran Tahir.[12]

Activists are working to improve Hollywood portrayals. The Muslim Public Affairs Council has been working with producers of Fox's "Tyrant," which was widely criticized for negatively stereotyped characters, to improve how it depicts Arabs. The council also has established programs to get more Muslims into the entertainment industry, which Obeidi says is the key to solving the problem.

"We want to shift it from other people telling stories about us to us telling our own stories," she says. "It's vital for us to be in the industry. TV and movies change hearts and minds."

— *Christina Hoag*

Lebanese actress Yasmine Al Massri, who plays a hijab-wearing FBI trainee in ABC's "Quantico," said she took the role partly to dispel the image of repressed, submissive Muslim women.

[1]Barack Obama, "Remarks by the President at Islamic Society of Baltimore," Office of the Press Secretary, White House, Feb. 3, 2016, http://tinyurl.com/jfocpth.

[2]Steve Rose, "Death to the Infidels! Why It's Time to Fix Hollywood's Problem with Muslims," *The Guardian,* March 8, 2016, http://tinyurl .com/j2sw86k.

[3]*Ibid.*

[4]*Ibid.*

[5]Daniel Mandel, "Muslims on the Silver Screen," *Middle East Quarterly,* Spring 2001, www.meforum.org/26/muslims-on-the-silver-screen.

[6]Noura Mansour, "Hollywood's Anti-Arab and Anti-Muslim Propaganda," *Middle East Monitor,* Jan. 29, 2015, http://tinyurl.com/ zl28xek.

[7]Helena Vanhala, *The Depiction of Arabs in Hollywood Blockbuster Films: 1980-2001* (2011), p. 119, http://tinyurl.com/zpm3cy2.

[8]Michael Lipka, "Muslims and Islam: Key findings in the U.S. and around the world," Pew Research Center, Dec. 7, 2015, http://tinyurl .com/gsmjpzj.

[9]Trip Gabriel, "Donald Trump Says He'd 'Absolutely' Require Muslims to Register," *The New York Times,* Nov. 20, 2015, http://tinyurl.com/ jglm42v.

[10]Mansour, *op. cit.*

[11]Mohamed Hassan, "Yasmine Al Massri on Fighting Arab-American Stereotypes as Twins on 'Quantico,' " NBC News, March 4, 2016, http://tinyurl.com/zrm2pun.

[12]Josie Huang, " 'Tyrant': Are There Any Positive Portrayals of Arab-Americans?" KPCC-FM, June 25, 2014, http://tinyurl.com/jha7b9a.

Chief Dan George became the first Native American to be nominated for an Oscar for his supporting role in the 1970 film *Little Big Man,* which won praise for its sensitive portrayal of American Indians.

The feminist movement also resulted in breakthrough feminist films such as *An Unmarried Woman* (1978) and *The Stepford Wives* (1975). Meanwhile, a cadre of women emerged as set and costume designers and editors, and a few as directors. Actresses such as Jane Fonda and Anne Bancroft formed their own production companies, and women attained ranking studio positions.[78] In 1976, Lina Wertmuller became the

Activists' Plea: Stop Killing Off Minorities

"Minority characters are expendable because they're not main characters."

When Lexa, a lesbian character, was killed off during a March episode of CW's hit post-apocalyptic drama "The 100," thousands of fans took to social media to protest her demise.

Tweets under the hashtags #LGBTFansDeserveBetter and #BuryTropesNotUs became trending topics nationally, with some fans writing on Twitter and Tumblr that they couldn't sleep and threatened self-harm over the loss of Lexa.[1]

A similar social media backlash occurred when Abbie Mills, an African-American female character, met an untimely death in Fox's supernatural drama "Sleepy Hollow" in April.[2] AMC's hit zombie drama "The Walking Dead" also faced criticism when three main black characters were killed in its fifth season in 2015.[3]

Along with underrepresentation of minorities on screen and a gender pay gap, treatment of minority characters is another facet of Hollywood's diversity problem, activists say. "Minority characters are expendable because they're not main characters," says Chandler Meyer, spokesperson for LGBT Fans Deserve Better, a group advocating for more protagonists from underrepresented groups. "It's part of the diversity problem behind the scenes. Most writers are straight white males."

Activists say while writers are incorporating more minority characters into story lines in an effort to be diverse, they are resorting to tropes and stereotypes when inventing plot lines for those characters, creating a more subtle pattern of discrimination.

"It's a way of being progressive without being too out there," Meyer says. "For example, bisexual women always end up with the man. Heroes are always straight and white" on television. According to LGBT group Autostraddle, 10 lesbian or bisexual characters were killed off in March alone, in shows including CW's "Jane the Virgin," AMC's "The Walking Dead" and Syfy's "The Magicians," with 20 in the first three months of 2016.[4] For LGBT people, the untimely demises hit a raw nerve, because for decades gay people have been portrayed as conflicted and rarely as happy, productive or heroic, activists say.

"When you have so few LGBT characters on TV, you're sending a message to people who identify with them that they never get a happy ending," say Megan Townsend, entertainment media strategist for GLAAD, an advocacy group that monitors how LBGT people are represented in the media.

Producers respond that plots can be a difficult balance between fans' wishes and the dramatic aims of the show.

In "The Walking Dead," two of the three black male characters who were killed — Tyreese, Bob and Noah — were white in the graphic novels on which the show is based, said producer Scott Gimple. "It's tough because I also want to be sensitive to how people feel. Two of those

first woman to be nominated for a Best Director Oscar for *Seven Beauties*.[79]

Influenced by the black power movement, African-American filmmakers, who had had little access behind the camera since the race films of the 1920s, started a genre of "blaxploitation" movies, which portrayed African-Americans as violent avengers of white injustice in movies such as *Shaft* (1971), *Super Fly* (1972) and *Foxy Brown* (1974).

In 1973, CBS appointed television's first woman executive, vice president Ethel Winant.[80] More female-centric programming came into vogue, such as the wildly popular "The Mary Tyler Moore Show" (1970-77) — the first show featuring a single career woman — and "Mary Hartman, Mary Hartman" (1976-77).

Minorities and social issues became more visible, particularly in comedies. Sitcoms depicting African-American life became a hallmark of the era, such as "The Jeffersons" (1975-85), featuring a middle-class black family, and "What's Happening!!" (1976-79), portraying life in Los Angeles housing projects. "Chico and the Man" (1974-78), with Hispanic actor Freddie Prinze in the lead role, was a Latino sitcom in a similar style and was the first show set in a Mexican-American neighborhood, East Los Angeles.

characters were destined to die, and they could've been cast in any direction, and I just cast the best people — or at least the people I just felt were best and I loved what they did with the role. It's weird to imagine not using them. But I did know those characters were dying, and I did cast those people," he said.[5]

The furor over Lexa's death has made "The 100" producers more sensitive to how characters are written, said executive producer Jason Rothenberg, noting that Lexa was killed off after she consummated her relationship with a female lover to heighten the sense of tragedy. The death was prompted because the actress who played Lexa, Alycia Debnam-Carey, was leaving the show for a role in AMC's "Fear the Walking Dead."[6]

"The end result became something else entirely — the perpetuation of the disturbing 'bury your gays' trope," Rothenberg wrote in an apology to fans. "Our aggressive promotion of the episode, and of this relationship, only fueled a feeling of betrayal. . . . I am very sorry for not recognizing this as fully as I should have. Knowing everything I know now, Lexa's death would have played out differently."[7]

While activists say they recognize that characters will die, especially in shows that pivot on violence, they hope producers can be more sensitive to the reasons for writing in deaths while also hiring more writers from underrepresented groups who can bring greater nuance to plot lines. "We're asking producers to consider the plot reasons for killing off characters, but it's also part of the larger problem of diversity," Townsend says.

— ***Christina Hoag***

The TV death of Lexa, a lesbian character played by Alycia Debnam-Carey on CW's post-apocalyptic hit drama "The 100," sparked an outcry by thousands of fans.

[1]Bethonie Butler, "TV Keeps Killing Off Lesbian Characters. The Fans of One Show Have Revolted," *The Washington Post*, April 4, 2016, http://tinyurl.com/jhq8oj2.

[2]Bethonie Butler, "After a Shocking Death on 'Sleepy Hollow,' Fans Are Questioning How the Show Treats Characters of Color," *The Washington Post*, April 12, 2016, http://tinyurl.com/z3vn9s3.

[3]Dalton Ross, "Walking Dead Showrunner on the Prominence of Black Character Deaths Last Season," *Entertainment Weekly*, Sept. 22, 2015, http://tinyurl.com/h4e9wta.

[4]Butler, "TV Keeps Killing Off Lesbian Characters," *op. cit.*

[5]Ross, *op. cit.*

[6]Maureen Ryan, " 'The 100' Showrunner Apologizes for Controversial Character Death," *Variety*, March 24, 2016, http://tinyurl.com/zgapxrj.

[7]*Ibid.*

Groundbreaking television producer Norman Lear tackled tough social issues, such as bigotry and feminism, in his hit sitcoms, "All in the Family" (1971-79) and "Maude"(1972-78).

Minority Filmmakers

In 1980, Sherry Lansing became president of 20th Century Fox, the first female to lead a major studio.[81] Her appointment heralded an age when women and minorities asserted themselves as executives, producers, directors and writers and created public awareness of hiring disparities.

Still, women were rarely found behind the camera. When Parent landed a job writing for "The Golden Girls" (1985-92), a series about a group of older women living in Miami, she was the only woman. "They allowed one of you, period," she said. "Even on shows about women."[82]

In 1983, the Directors Guild of America, the labor organization that represents film and TV directors, filed an anti-discrimination suit against Warner Bros. and Columbia Pictures on behalf of women and minority members. Although the suit was dismissed in 1985 on grounds that the guild had no a standing to sue, it drew

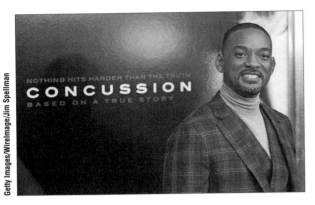

Actor Will Smith was among the Hollywood A-listers who boycotted the Academy Awards ceremony this year to protest entertainment industry diversity policies, including the nominations for best actor and actress that included no blacks for the second straight year. Smith's performance as a Nigerian doctor in *Concussion* had been widely considered Oscar-worthy.

attention to an uneven playing field and for a short time spurred the hiring of more female directors.[83]

By the late 1980s, a wave of independent black and Latino filmmakers, such as Spike Lee and Luis Valdez, emerged, winning acclaim with movies such as *She's Gotta Have It* (1986) and *La Bamba* (1987), which reflected their communities' experience but had crossover audience appeal. That coincided with a growing A-list of black actors, such as Denzel Washington and Eddie Murphy. In 1990, *Dances with Wolves* turned the tables on Native American stereotypes, depicting whites as the villains and the Lakota Indians as a benevolent people.

The television landscape changed dramatically in the 1990s, with the steady expansion of cable and satellite channels and new broadcast networks emerging. This created more programs that catered to smaller audiences.

In movies, independent filmmakers such as Quentin Tarantino became an increasingly key part of the industry.

Still, women and minorities saw only incremental progress. In 1999, the National Council of La Raza called on Hispanics to boycott TV to pressure the networks to hire more Latinos.[84] The Hispanic advocacy organization said that in two decades the percentage of Latinos playing primetime TV characters had risen only marginally — from 1 percent to 1.6 percent.[85]

In the 21st century, several barriers have been broken, but progress remains stalled, and new bias allegations

have emerged. In 2002, older writers filed a class-action suit alleging age discrimination against 51 major TV networks, studios and talent agencies. It was settled in 2010 for $70 million.[86]

Movies with gay themes received a huge boost in 2005 when *Brokeback Mountain's* male cowboy love story scored a box-office hit and three Oscars. In 2010, Kathryn Bigelow became the first woman to win a Best Director Oscar for *The Hurt Locker*.

In recent years, Mexican directors Guillermo del Toro, Alfonso Cuarón and Alejandro González Iñárritu have earned Oscar nomination and awards for mainstream movies.[87] And independently-financed African-American-themed films, including *12 Years a Slave* (2013), have been box-office hits.

In 2015, an all-white slate of acting nominees for the Academy Awards sparked a huge public outcry, and the hashtag #OscarsSoWhite lit up social media, focusing attention on Hollywood's lack of diversity. A year later, the hashtag was revived amid another wave of outrage when the nominee slate again consisted of all white actors.

CURRENT SITUATION
Gathering Momentum

Officials from the U.S. Equal Employment Opportunity Commission (EEOC) are questioning an expanded list of people in the gender discrimination investigation. The list now includes studio executives, agents, producers, actors and male directors.[88] The investigation began in 2015 after the ACLU of Southern California filed a complaint alleging that the Hollywood entertainment industry is biased against female directors.

Women accounted for 6.4 percent of motion picture directing in 2013-2014, and they tend to direct less lucrative films, according to the Directors Guild of America, the industry group representing film and TV directors.[89] In television, women directed 16 percent of episodes in 2014-2015, the guild said.[90] The EEOC investigation could spur a lawsuit against employers, mediation to increase the ranks of female directors or result in no action at all.

The inquiry is a sign that the push for more diversity in Hollywood is gathering momentum. The Academy of Motion Picture Arts and Sciences' new voting eligibility rules for Oscar nominations, announced after the

Is Hollywood taking steps to become more diverse?

YES   Rashad Robinson
Executive Director, Color of Change

Written for *CQ Researcher*, August 2016

Last year more than 51,000 Color Of Change members called for an overhaul of the Academy of Motion Picture Arts and Sciences membership process and the release of accurate diversity numbers. Since then, we have continued to work with artists and the industry to ensure that we can move toward a collective vision that promotes a standard for Hollywood that is truly representative of the diversity and intricacies of moviegoers.

We applaud the academy board for acting expediently to fix a problem that was 100-plus years in the making. But this important step cannot be the end. This isn't about "seeking validation" but about rejecting a discriminatory system that sends a message to far too many that they are unwelcome.At a time when our news media continue to make clear how little the lives of black Americans matter, and our rights continue to be rolled back on several fronts, it is especially important that we are at the center of our own narratives and that our stories receive the wide release and support they deserve.

Award recognition matters. With it comes increased financial and creative opportunities for artists and those they employ. It also provides power to confront negative depictions of our communities that shape how we're perceived.

Research continues to show that negative perceptions of black and brown men and women or the erasure of people of color from movies and television programs translate into greater chances of us being shot by the police and receiving diminished attention from doctors and less consideration when applying for jobs, loans and educational opportunities.

Let's not forget that this is about a completely flawed system — from the lack of diversity among critics who determine which movies get Oscar buzz to discrimination in casting and white-washing of historical figures to underfunding of projects helmed by people of color. Studios, guilds and agencies have a lot of work to do. The onus can't strictly be on Academy president Cheryl Boone Isaacs to create change.

Hollywood is a reflection of power structures in our country. We must take more steps to ensure real change that creates a better reality for our people both in and out of the industry.

We want actions that provide a consistent pipeline of people of color in internships, middle management and at the executive level across the industry.

NO   John W. Cones
Author, Hollywood Wars:
How Insiders Gained and Maintain Illegitimate
Control Over the Film Industry

Written for *CQ Researcher*, August 2016

Some say Hollywood is changing, but I submit the words of anthropologist Hortense Powdermaker, in her groundbreaking 1950 book, *Hollywood, the Dream Factory:* "Rarely in the history of mankind has any group with power given it up voluntarily."

Hollywood's lack-of-diversity problem finally became obvious at the two most recent Academy Awards presentations, when no African-American was nominated for an acting award. Besides some rather shallow nods toward reform, Hollywood pretty much continues to ignore the issue.

Even worse, the discrimination at the academy is just the tip of the iceberg. Hollywood's lack of diversity includes women, Latinos, Asian-Americans, Native Americans, Irish-Americans, Italian-Americans, Christians, Muslims, Mormons and many other "Hollywood outsiders." Furthermore, this massive discrimination occurs not only in the acting arena but in all professions involved in developing, producing and distributing movies.

For more than 100 years, millions of hard-working and talented people who sought employment opportunities in the film industry have been arbitrarily denied those opportunities in favor of someone else who was better connected to a narrowly defined Hollywood insider group.

And that's not all. The U.S. Supreme Court found in the 1952 *Burstyn v. Wilson* case that the motion picture is a "significant medium for the communication of ideas." That's important to a democracy that supposedly values the free marketplace of ideas. As my studies show, Hollywood movies contain patterns of bias with regard to which ideas are portrayed positively or negatively. That's because movies tend to mirror the values, interests, cultural perspectives and prejudices of their makers.

Thus, when the Supreme Court held in *Burstyn v. Wilson* that movies are protected by the First Amendment right of free speech and eliminated government censorship of movies, official censorship was simply replaced by private censorship, applied by a small group of Hollywood insiders who have used this powerful communications medium to promote their own private propaganda interests.

Many have been outraged recently by the revelation that a U.S. presidential candidate may be a racist. But it is just as outrageous for the entire government and our nation to continue to accept the massive and ongoing discrimination perpetrated by Hollywood insiders through nearly five generations.

Oscars-so-white controversy erupted in January, are aimed at enabling younger, more diverse active members to cast votes, decreasing the dominance of older, retired members who skew white.

In June, the academy unveiled a record 683 new members — 46 percent of them female and 41 percent people of color. With the new members, women now make up 27 percent of the academy's members, and people of color, 11 percent.[91]

Some said the changes were symbolic and doubted they will change nominations or hiring practices overall. "You can keep adding members — pack it like the Supreme Court — but I don't think that answers the question" of how to increase diversity, said Mike Medavoy, a producer whose movies include *The 33* (2015) and *Shutter Island* (2010).[92]

But others saw the academy's moves as important. "One good step in a long, complicated journey for people of color + women artists," tweeted Ava DuVernay, whose lack of a directing nomination for the civil rights drama *Selma* (2014) sparked an outcry in 2015. "Shame is a helluva motivator."[93]

The 2016 Oscars controversy also sparked greater awareness of Hollywood's gender and racial imbalance and spurred efforts to combat it. In February, Murphy, the producer of TV shows such as "Glee" and "American Horror Story," announced that he would fill half the directing slots on his shows with women, people of color and LGBT people, and would start a mentorship program for students. "I personally can do better," he said.[94]

Abrams, producer of the Star Wars and Star Trek movies and TV series, said his company has asked agents to include women and minorities among their candidates for acting and writing jobs. "The Oscars controversy was a wake-up call," Abrams said.[95]

The Writers Guild's Lopez said the organization has been receiving more calls from agents, managers and executives seeking minority talent. "They're asking, 'Do you have an Asian comedy writer' or 'a Latino drama writer?'" she says. "They're seeing that now is the time to really make this change and stray out of their comfort zones and open up." But others doubt the momentum will be sustained, noting that previous efforts have resulted in little more than tokenism and an eventual return to business as usual.

"The fact that the many industry programs to encourage a more diverse workforce have not achieved their desired goals speaks volumes about how deeply entrenched gender and racial bias are across an industry driven by fragmented, relationship-driven and word-of-mouth hiring practices," the directors' guild said on its website. "We continue to approach this matter from a number of angles to convince employers to take ownership of the issue. Until that happens, there may never be substantive change."[96]

Resistance to change exists. The academy's new voting rules sparked a firestorm of criticism, largely from older members. "Obviously, it's a thinly veiled ploy to kick out older, white contributors — the backbone of the industry — to make way for younger, 'politically correct' voters," said actor Tab Hunter, 84. "The academy should not cave in to media hype and change the rules without talking to or getting votes from all members first."[97]

Some members of the public also have objected to Hollywood's attempts at diversity. A 2016 remake of the 1984 hit *Ghostbusters,* with an all-female lead cast, netted a wave of criticism from fans who claimed the women would ruin the movie.

African-American actress Leslie Jones, who plays one of the ghostbusters, quit Twitter in July after being subjected to hundreds of racist and sexist tweets, saying she did not believe Twitter should be used to abusively target someone. Twitter responded by barring Milo Yiannopoulos, a prime mover of the campaign against Jones and an editor with the conservative news website Breitbart.com.[98]

Role of Government

Activists say governments can do more to encourage diversity. For instance, Illinois is the only state to give a tax credit (30 percent) to production companies that hire local minorities and women.[99] But critics say the program has a loophole that allows producers to merely show they made "a good-faith effort" to obtain a diversified workforce.

"People think you have to hire people of color. You do not. You can interview 50 minorities and you don't have to hire any of them," said Michele McGhee, a tax credit specialist with the Illinois Department of Commerce and Economic Opportunity, which runs the Illinois Film Office.[100]

Other states are considering similar programs. A pending New York bill would allot $5 million of the

$420 million Empire State Film Production Tax Credit as incentives to TV producers who hire women or minority writers or directors who are New York taxpayers, with a maximum credit of $50,000 per hire. The bill was introduced in 2013 but stalled in a Republican-controlled Senate after passing the Assembly. Backers now hope that with a Republican sponsor and the recent Oscars controversy, the measure has a better chance of passage.[101]

Robinson of ColorOfChange.org says such incentive programs would help boost minority hiring but that guilds representing Hollywood professions also must be pushed to do more. The Screen Actors Guild-American Federation of Television and Radio Artists (SAG-AFTRA), which represents the bulk of the industry's experienced actors, includes anti-discrimination provisions in the contracts producers must sign to use guild-member employees, he notes.

SAG-AFTRA also provides financial incentives for movies with budgets of up to $3.75 million that meet diversity standards. If half of the speaking roles go to actors of color, women, actors with disabilities or those who are over age 60, the union will allow concessions on how much all actors must be paid. That can include reduced overtime rates, no premiums for six-day work weeks and fewer background actors who must be paid union scale.[102] Some form of the SAG-AFTRA program and contracts could be replicated with other guilds, Robinson says.

The Motion Picture Association of America, which represents major studios, should also be pushed to take a stand, says Lauzen of San Diego State. The association could create an independent organization that aims to increase diversity on studio films, particularly in key hiring positions because they can then hire more diverse staffs, she says.

But some experts say that since the industry has not improved diversity despite years of public outcry, more forceful measures may be needed, such as lawsuits, contract provisions and more robust financial incentives.

"Because those in the industry have demonstrated little will to change, it seems likely that pressure from some external source, such as the EEOC, will be necessary to achieve significant and sustained change," says Lauzen.

OUTLOOK
Turning Point

Experts generally agree that Hollywood, particularly the movie industry, will be forced to include more women and minorities in the coming years, but they differ on what will decisively push the industry to move from tokenism to meaningful change.

If movie-going is to remain a relevant mass entertainment option, the film industry will have to echo the general trend of diversification in the U.S. population, some experts predict, especially as competition from online-viewing grows. "Diversity is a smart business decision," says Suhad Obeidi, director of the Hollywood bureau of the Muslim Public Affairs Council. "People want to see people who look like them."

The 2016 #OscarsSoWhite backlash was a watershed moment that is boosting the momentum for change, say some Hollywood observers. The Academy of Motion Picture Arts & Sciences' revised award voting rules and the admission of a new, more diversified class of members were important and symbolic first steps, they note.

"Call me a cautious optimist," says Hunt, of UCLA's Bunche Center for African American Studies. "But business as usual is really not sustainable. We've reached a turning point."

But others say it's going to take more than academy moves to prod studios out of deeply entrenched practices. Cones, the entertainment attorney, says executives are unlikely to change their business models unless compelled by government actions, such as legislation or an EEOC ruling. Over the years, he says, outcries over the lack of diversity have resulted in little progress once the initial media attention faded. "People with power do not give it up voluntarily," he says.

Jonathan Glickman, president of MGM's motion-picture group, said Hollywood is changing but slowly. "It takes time to turn the ship around to the right direction because of the amount of time it takes to produce and market a film," he said.[103]

As for television, observers are optimistic that it will continue to use more diverse characters and stories, but they say it still has a long way to go to move beyond cultural stereotypes and increase opportunities for underrepresented groups behind the camera. "We've got miles and miles to go on that frontier," Hunt says.

The push by leading producers to hire more women and minorities, plus the success of minority producers such as Rhimes, could spur other producers and networks to seek out more diverse crews, staffs and casts, experts say.

In the meantime, internet-based entertainment increasingly will become an outlet for women and minorities and make it easier for studios and networks to find diverse talent with demonstrated success. Independently produced TV shows and movies, including those made solely for online viewing, will help boost the number of diverse stories on screen, some industry observers predict, and provide needed competition for the traditional industry.

"They'll realize they're leaving a lot of money on the table," says Nogales of the Hispanic Media Coalition. "It doesn't stand to reason to not bring us in."

The programming success on newer viewing channels eventually will force the industry to open up to diverse points of view from plots to producers, says Lopez of the Writers Guild. "It'll transfer into [the mainstream business] little by little," he says. Ultimately, consumers, who can vote with their wallets and remote controls, can force progress in both the film and television industries, some experts say.

But, says actress Ta'le, "if audiences remain complicit and watch what they're given, then there's no reason to change."

NOTES

1. Michael Schulman, "Chris Rock's Oscars," *The New Yorker,* Feb. 29, 2016, http://tinyurl.com/zhruuru.

2. Brandon Griggs, "Jada Pinkett Smith, Spike Lee to Boycott Oscars Ceremony," CNN.com, Jan. 19, 2016, http://tinyurl.com/h6c65hk.

3. Cynthia Littleton, "Will Smith Won't Attend Oscars," *Variety,* Jan. 21, 2016, http://tinyurl.com/hjy64u6.

4. "Al Sharpton Leads Oscars Protest Rally in Hollywood," The Associated Press, Feb. 28, 2016, http://tinyurl.com/hg4mttu.

5. Michael Pearson, "Obama: Oscars Diversity Call Part of Broader Issue," CNN.com, Jan. 28, 2016, http://tinyurl.com/jd3hk74.

6. "Creating Jobs," Motion Picture Association of America, undated, http://tinyurl.com/heyox9z.

7. Noor Wazwaz, "It's Official: The US Is Becoming a Minority-Majority Nation," *U.S. News & World Report,* July 6, 2015, http://tinyurl.com/p4hhart.

8. Darnell Hunt, Ana-Christina Ramon and Michael Tran, "2016 Hollywood Diversity Report: Busine$$ as Usual," University of California Los Angeles, February 2016, http://tinyurl.com/hhrdltn, p. 10.

9. *Ibid.,* p. 21.

10. Martha M. Lauzen, "The Celluloid Ceiling: Behind-the-Scenes Employment of Women on the Top 100, 250, and 500 Films of 2015," Center for the Study of Women in Television and Film, San Diego State University, 2016, http://tinyurl.com/h5gmn7p.

11. *Ibid.,* p. 40.

12. Stacy L. Smith, Marc Choueiti, Katherine Piper, "Inclusion or Invisibility: Comprehensive Annenberg Report on Diversity in Entertainment," University of Southern California, http://tinyurl.com/jxjyj2p, p. 16.

13. Justin Morrow, "6 Hollywood Executives Discuss the State of the Film Industry," No Film School, Nov. 20, 2015, http://tinyurl.com/hd53hry.

14. Maria Puente and Andrea Mandell, "Hollywood Diversity Report Brings mostly Silence from Studios," *USA Today,* Feb. 23, 2016, http://tinyurl.com/jeweolp.

15. Lauzen, *op. cit.,* p. 5.

16. Smith *et al., op. cit.,* p. 3.

17. Inkoo Kang, "THR Roundtable Actresses on Ageism, the Pay Gap and Playing 'Strong Women' and Gender-Swapped Roles," *IndieWire,* Nov. 24, 2015, http://tinyurl.com/j9zcglk.

18. Martha M. Lauzen, "MPAA Must Lead — or Be Led — in Battle to Improve Diversity," *Variety,* March 17, 2016, http://tinyurl.com/hw37gpf.

19. *Ibid.*

20. Daniel Kreps, "Nina Simone's Daughter Defends Zoe Saldana, Slams Biopic," *Rolling Stone,* March 5, 2016, http://tinyurl.com/zg5zxpr.

21. Megan Gibson, "Ridley Scott Explains Why He Cast White Actors in Exodus: God and Kings," *Time.com,* Nov. 27, 2014, http://tinyurl.com/jf8577m.

22. Nigel M. Smith, "Emma Stone Says Aloha Casting Taught Her About Whitewashing in Hollywood," *The Guardian,* July 17, 2015, http://tinyurl.com/hrxzjnb.

23. Stereo Williams, "Joseph Fiennes as Michael Jackson: A Symptom of Hollywood's Deep-Seated Race Problem," *The Daily Beast,* Jan. 27, 2016, http://tinyurl.com/gqtk9qn.

24. Daniel Fienberg, "Why It Matters That FX's Tyrant Didn't Cast a Middle Eastern Actor in Its Lead Role," *HitFix,* June 24, 2014, http://tinyurl.com/zmujruy.

25. Gibson, *op. cit.*

26. Hunt *et al., op. cit.* pp. 50-53.

27. Aziz Ansari, "Aziz Anzari on Acting, Race and Hollywood," *The New York Times,* Nov. 10, 2015, http://tinyurl.com/oc6nraj.

28. Ben Childs, "Dakota Johnson Hits Out at 'Brutal' Hollywood Over Ageism," *The Guardian,* Jan. 5, 2016, http://tinyurl.com/j8pa6on.

29. Nigel Smith, *op. cit.*

30. Martha M. Lauzen, "It's a Man's (Celluloid) World: Portrayals of Female Characters in the Top 100 Films of 2015," 2016, http://tinyurl.com/zlxqvul.

31. Madeline Berg, "Everything You Need to Know About the Hollywood Pay Gap," *Forbes,* Nov. 12, 2015, http://tinyurl.com/j8r2zgp.

32. *Ibid.*

33. Peter Sciretta, "The Highest Paid Actresses and Actors of 2015," *Slash Film,* Aug. 20, 2015, http://tinyurl.com/gsdbfyv.

34. Maggie McGrath, "World's Highest Paid TV Actresses 2015," *Forbes,* Sept. 8, 2015, http://tinyurl.com/hdn84tl.

35. Stacy L. Smith *et al., op. cit.,* p. 17.

36. Ryan Faughnder, "$40 Billion in Global Box Office? Thank China and 'Star Wars,' " *Los Angeles Times,* Dec. 30, 2015, http://tinyurl.com/zpk4p9e.

37. "Theatrical Market Statistics 2014," Motion Picture Association of America, undated, http://tinyurl.com/kr3vmlq, p.12.

38. Scott Roxborough, "America's TV Exports Too Diverse for Overseas?" *The Hollywood Reporter,* March 30, 2016, http://tinyurl.com/jz3yw7d.

39. Amol Sharma, "TV Studios Court Licensing Deals in Bustling Foreign Markets," *The Wall Street Journal,* Nov. 19, 2014, http://tinyurl.com/h3kbzmo.

40. Roxborough, *op. cit.*

41. Maureen Ryan, "Showrunners for New TV Season Remain Mostly White and Male," *Variety,* June 7, 2016, http://tinyurl.com/zmjm7ah.

42. Aisha Harris, "Same Old Script," *Slate,* Oct. 18, 2015, http://tinyurl.com/om2aslu.

43. *Ibid.*

44. Maanvi Singh, " 'East Los High' Isn't Just a Soapy Teen Drama — It's Also a Science Experiment," NPR, Jan. 11, 2016, http://tinyurl.com/z6kahak.

45. Jenny Wortham, "The Misadventures of Issa Rae," *The New York Times Magazine,* Aug. 4, 2015, http://tinyurl.com/p4eq4k4.

46. "Frequently Asked Questions," Amazon Studios, undated, http://tinyurl.com/glu8mqo.

47. Josef Adalian and Maria Elena Fernandez, "The Business of Too Much TV," *Vulture,* May 2016, http://tinyurl.com/h5supdd.

48. *Ibid.*

49. Matt Donnelly, "How Amazon Studios Became the New Star of Cannes," *The Wrap,* May 10, 2016, http://tinyurl.com/zot5a5o.

50. Mike Fleming Jr., "Netflix's Ted Sarandos Says 'Beasts Of No Nation' Has Been Seen by Over 3 Million Viewers So Far: Q&A," *Deadline,* Oct. 26, 2015, http://tinyurl.com/p3jsd98.

51. "Submissions Guidelines," Amazon Studios, undated, http://tinyurl.com/j2tzho6.

52. Claire Fallon, "The Native Plot on 'Kimmy Schmidt' Makes Us Cringe, But Is It All Bad?" *The Huffington Post,* April 29, 2016, http://tinyurl.com/j86kqu6.

53. *Ibid.*

54. Alyssa Rosenberg, "Unbreakable Kimmy Schmidt's' Lakota Plot and the Fight for Diversity in TV," *The Washington Post,* March 12, 2015, http://tinyurl.com/gpqxuuk.

55. Donald Bogle, *Bright Boulevards, Bold Dreams: The Story of Black Hollywood* (2005), pp. 11-13.

56. Matthew Bernstein, *Controlling Hollywood: Censorship and Regulation in the Studio Era* (2000), p. 112, http://tinyurl.com/z9qkbn8.

57. Anne Helen Petersen, "The Forgotten Story of Classic Hollywood's First Asian American Star," *Buzzfeed,* Sept. 30, 2014, http://tinyurl.com/gm2jell.

58. Dawn B. Sova, *Women in Hollywood: From Vamp to Studio Head* (1998), p. 2.

59. "Sessue Hayakawa: The Legend," Gold Sea, undated, http://tinyurl.com/hnmvl7q.

60. Jennifer Thompson (curator), "From Blackface to Blaxploitation: Representations of African Americans in Film," Duke University Libraries, undated, http://tinyurl.com/jzszdjw.

61. Hansi Lo Wang, "Restored Race Films Find New Audiences," NPR, March 6, 2016, http://tinyurl.com/jkh749y.

62. Bogle, *op. cit.,* p. 41.

63. Sova, *op. cit.,* p. xii.

64. *Ibid.*

65. Bob Mondello, "Remembering Hollywood's Hays Code 40 Years On," NPR, Aug. 8, 2008, http://tinyurl.com/5rku7d.

66. *Ibid.*

67. Lucy Fischer and Marcia Landy, *Stars: The Film Reader* (2004), p. 189, http://tinyurl.com/ju9m9ag.

68. Markus Heide, "From Zorro to Jennifer Lopez: US-Latino History and Film for the EFL-Classroom," *American Studies Journal*, 2008, http://tinyurl.com/jpxucuv.

69. "Charlie Chan Biography," Internet Movie Database, undated, http://tinyurl.com/hjyz7ky.

70. Dan Georgakas, "The Hollywood Blacklist," *Encyclopedia of the American Left* (1992), http://tinyurl.com/pjvqara.

71. "Dorothy Dandridge," *Encyclopaedia Britannica,* undated, http://tinyurl.com/j264wwk.

72. J. Fred MacDonald, "Blacks and White TV: The Golden Age of Blacks in Television," undated, http://tinyurl.com/hsexjgl.

73. Jay Tavare, "Hollywood Indians," *The Huffington Post,* May 18, 2011, http://tinyurl.com/6y47gt7.

74. MacDonald, *op. cit.*

75. Jennifer Armstrong, "The Secret History of Women in Television," *Bust,* undated, http://tinyurl.com/zns4ksq.

76. Guy Walters, "Lesbian Gay Bisexual and Transgender Movies since 1894," *The Telegraph,* March 20, 2015, http://tinyurl.com/japw6cb.

77. Mondello, *op. cit.* For background on movie ratings system, see Brian Hansen, "Movie Ratings," *CQ Researcher*, March 28, 2003, pp. 273-296.

78. Sova, *op. cit.,* pp. 154-157.

79. "Lina Wertmüller Biography," Internet Movie Database, undated, http://tinyurl.com/zgxvjwv.

80. Pat Saperstein, "Ethel Winant," *Variety,* Dec. 3, 2003, http://tinyurl.com/zk3mkq6.

81. "Sherry Lansing Biography," Internet Movie Database, undated, http://tinyurl.com/zxnhkt8.

82. Armstrong, *op. cit.*

83. David Robb, "Feds Officially Probing Hollywood's Lack of Female Directors," *Deadline,* Oct. 6, 2015, http://tinyurl.com/j3jace6.

84. Michael A. Fletcher, "Latinos Plan Boycott of Network TV," *The Washington Post,* July 28, 1999, http://tinyurl.com/j85lm8x.

85. Dana E. Mastro and Elizabeth BehmMorawitz, "Latino Representation on Primetime Television," *Journalism and Mass Communication Quarterly,* Spring 2005, http://tinyurl.com/h9w4pfd.

86. Nikki Finke, "Huge $70M Settlement in TV Writers Age Discrimination Lawsuit," *Deadline,* Jan. 22, 2010, http://tinyurl.com/hw4c3wf.

87. Lorraine Ali, "Oscars 2015: Brutal Honesty Marks Inarritu's Bond With Cuaron, Del Toro," *Los Angeles Times,* Feb. 21, 2015, http://tinyurl.com/hrveaoo.

88. Rebecca Keegan, "Gender Bias in Hollywood? U.S. Digs Deeper to Investigate the Industry's Hiring Practices," *Los Angeles Times,* May 11, 2016, http://tinyurl.com/hznwgvq.

89. "DGA Publishes Inaugural Feature Film Diversity Report," Directors Guild of America, Dec. 9, 2015, http://tinyurl.com/qgsg438.

90. "DGA TV Diversity Report," Directors Guild of America, Aug. 25, 2015, http://tinyurl.com/ohrg2d6.

91. Alex Stedman, "Academy Invites 683 New Members in Push for More Diversity," *Variety*, June 29, 2016, http://tinyurl.com/j9vfxoh.

92. Scott Feinberg, "Academy's New Voting Rules Raise Questions, Concerns and Anger Among Members," *The Hollywood Reporter*, Jan. 23, 2016, http://tinyurl.com/j9wtbsl.

93. *Ibid.*

94. Lacey Rose, "Ryan Murphy Launches Foundation to Tackle Hollywood's Diversity Problem," *The Hollywood Reporter*, Feb. 3, 2016, http://tinyurl.com/heps8cb.

95. Rebecca Ford, "How J. J. Abrams' Bad Robot Is Bringing More Diversity to Hollywood," *The Hollywood Reporter*, March 2, 2016, http://tinyurl.com/gqm3s5f.

96. "DGA Diversity: Frequently Asked Questions," Directors Guild of America, undated, http://tinyurl.com/j56vgy5.

97. Feinberg, *op. cit.*

98. Mike Isaac, "Twitter Bars Milo Yiannopoulos in Wake of Leslie Jones' Reports of Abuse," *The New York Times*, July 20, 2016, http://tinyurl.com/jzkdpwk.

99. "Welcome to the Illinois Film Office," Illinois Department of Commerce and Economic Opportunity, http://tinyurl.com/nwpacw4.

100. La Risa Lynch, "Lights, Camera but Little Action for Blacks in Film Industry," *Austin Weekly News*, Sept. 13, 2014, http://tinyurl.com/he7275v.

101. Addie Morfoot, "New York Looks to Remedy Hollywood's Diversity Problem," *Crain's New York*, April 11, 2016, http://tinyurl.com/j3ze6z5.

102. R. B. Jefferson, "The Ultimate Guide to SAG-AFTRA Low-Budget Film Signatory Agreements for Indie Filmmakers-Part 2," *Lawyers Rock*, Oct. 20, 2014, http://tinyurl.com/jxbmv2u.

103. Puente and Mandell, *op. cit.*

BIBLIOGRAPHY
Selected Sources
Books

Cheu, Johnson, *Diversity in Disney Films: Critical Essays on Race, Ethnicity, Gender, Sexuality and Disability,* **McFarland, 2013.**
An assistant professor of American culture at Michigan State University edits an essay collection about diversity in Disney films, including race, gender, sexuality, masculinity and disability.

Cones, John W., *Patterns of Bias in Hollywood Movies,* **Algora Publishing, 2012.**
An entertainment lawyer studies why consistent complaints of bias in Hollywood have had little impact on racial and ethnic stereotyping.

Najera, Rick, *Almost White: Forced Confessions of a Latino in Hollywood,* **Smiley Books, 2013.**
A Latino writer, actor, director, comedian, playwright and producer explains how he broke into the entertainment industry and struggled against typecasting.

Scott, Ellen C., *Cinema Civil Rights: Regulation, Repression, and Race in the Classical Hollywood Era,* **Rutgers University Press, 2014.**
An expert in African-American cultural history and film explores how black audiences, activists and lobbyists influenced the representation of race in Hollywood before the 1960s.

Shaheen, Jack, *Reel Bad Arabs: How Hollywood Vilifies a People,* **Southern Illinois University, 2014.**
A Middle East scholar documents a century of offensive stereotypes about Arabs and Muslims in a review of 900 films, showing how the image of the "dirty Arab" has reemerged over the last 30 years.

Articles

Dargis, Manohla, "Lights, Camera, Taking Action," *The New York Times,* **Jan. 21, 2015, http://tinyurl.com/nandeyz.**
A film critic explores women directors' efforts to land jobs and finance their productions.

Dowd, Maureen, "Women of Hollywood Speak Out," *The New York Times Magazine*, **Nov. 20, 2015, http:// tinyurl.com/p2rtjqp.**
A columnist examines gender bias in the film industry.

Ford, Rebecca, and Borys Kit, "Hollywood's Casting Blitz: It's All About Diversity in the Wake of #OscarsSoWhite," *Hollywood Reporter,* **March 2, 2016, http://tinyurl.com/zqvag8w.**
Writers for an entertainment industry trade journal detail how colorblind casting is gaining momentum.

Kang, Cecilia, Krissah Thompson and Drew Harwell, "Hollywood's Race Problem: An Insular Industry Struggles to Change," *The Washington Post*, **Dec. 23, 2014, http://tinyurl.com/jxgwdap.**
Business reporters examine movie studios' reluctance to finance films featuring African-American stories, which has forced producers to adopt creative means to make such projects.

Scott, Ellen C., "Most Timely: Hooray for Hollywood," *Common Reader,* **Jan. 26, 2016, http:// tinyurl.com/z7runzo.**
An expert in African-American cultural history and film argues that racism in awarding the Academy Awards is not new and details the history of black actors protesting Hollywood bias in the 1960s.

Reports and Studies

Hunt, Darnell, Ana-Christina Ramon and Michael Tran, "2016 Hollywood Diversity Report: Busine$$ as Usual," UCLA Ralph J. Bunche Center for African-American Studies, February 2016, http://tinyurl .com/hhrdltn.
Researchers at an African-American academic research center analyzes films and TV shows for percentages of women and minorities in acting, writing and directing roles and looks at audience ratings and awards in the context of race and gender.

Lauzen, Martha M., "The Celluloid Ceiling: Behind-the-Scenes Employment of Women on the Top 100, 250, and 500 Films of 2015," Center for the Study of Women in Television and Film, San Diego State University, January 2016, http://tinyurl.com/h5gmn7p.
A scholar at a university academic center studying women in television and film tracks the employment of women directors, writers, producers, cinematographers and editors in the top 250 films of 2015.

Smith, Jason, "Between Colorblind and Colorconscious: Contemporary Hollywood Films and Struggles Over Racial Representation," *Journal of Black Studies,* **December 2013, http://tinyurl.com/zt4dpga.**
A George Mason University scholar in sociology examines the advances made by African-Americans in the film industry and the difference between playing colorblind and colorconscious roles.

Smith, Stacy L., Mark Choueiti and Katherine Pieper, "Inclusion or Invisibility? Comprehensive Annenberg Report on Diversity in Entertainment," Media, Diversity, & Social Change Initiative, University of Southern California, February 2016, http://tinyurl .com/jxjyj2p.
Professors at the University of Southern California's Annenberg School for Communication and Journalism look at diversity in film and television and rate entertainment companies for gender and racial balance.

For More Information

Academy of Motion Picture Arts and Sciences, 8949 Wilshire Blvd., Beverly Hills, CA 90211; 310-247-3000; www.oscars.org. Professional association whose members award the annual Oscars.

Center for the Study of Women in Television and Film, San Diego State University, 5500 Campanile Drive, San Diego, CA 92182; 619-594-6301; http://womenintvfilm .sdsu.edu. Research center that studies gender issues in the film and TV industry.

ColorOfChange.org; www.colorofchange.org. A civil rights group that works to promote racial justice and economic equality for African-Americans.

Directors Guild of America, 7920 Sunset Blvd., Los Angeles, CA 90046; 310-2892000; www.dga.org. Labor union that represents film and TV directors.

Media, Diversity, & Social Change Initiative, Annenberg School for Communication and Journalism, University of Southern California, 3502 Watt Way, Los Angeles, CA 90089; 213-740-6180; http://annenberg.usc.edu/pages/ DrStacyLSmithMDSCI. Think tank that researches gender, ethnic and racial imbalance in the entertainment industry.

Motion Picture Association of America, 1600 I St., N.W., Washington, DC 20006; 202-293-1966; www.mpaa.org. Trade association that represents major movie studios and TV networks.

Ralph J. Bunche Center for African American Studies, University of California, Los Angeles, 160 Haines Hall, Los Angeles, CA 90095; 310-825-7403; www.bunchecenter.ucla .edu. Academic research center that examines racial and ethnic bias in film and television.

Screen Actors Guild — American Federation of Television and Radio Artists, 5757 Wilshire Blvd., 7th floor, Los Angeles, CA 90036; 323-549-6644; www.sagaftra.org. Labor union that represents actors.

Writers Guild of America, 7000 W. Third St., Los Angeles, CA 90048; 323-9514000; www.wga.org. Labor union that represents television and movie writers.

4

Future of the Middle Class

Peter Katel

Jonah Devorak had been washing dishes and manning the grill at a Cleveland restaurant since he was 16. But his future brightened when he heard about a program at Cuyahoga Community College that trains students for manufacturing jobs. Now he's a full-time machine operator at Swagelok, a maker of high-pressure valves and fittings.

From *CQ Researcher,*
April 8, 2016

I n only one sentence, Sediena Barry summed up her view that the American middle-class dream has evaporated: "Young people were told, 'Get an education and work and you'll get ahead,' and none of us are."[1]

The 34-year-old office equipment installer in Reynoldsburg, Ohio, outside Columbus, spoke to *The New York Times* after voting in the most turbulent presidential primary season in decades.

Vote-seeking politicians in both parties have been pounding on the theme that the middle class is embattled. But they didn't invent the concept of declining economic mobility. A growing number of academic studies, data analyses and scholarly commentary warn that America's middle class is shrinking, its wealth far outpaced by the holdings of the rich and super-rich.

The central theme emerging from most of this work is that after decades of defining itself as an overwhelmingly middle-class country, the United States increasingly is fracturing into a nation of haves and have-nots. Many analysts fear a vision long shared by a majority of Americans is eroding: that hard work will get anyone into the middle class or from the middle class into the top reaches of society.

"The share of the American adult population that is middle income is falling, and rising shares are living in economic tiers above and below the middle," the nonpartisan Pew Research Center stated in an extensive 2015 analysis of income trends in the United States. "The hollowing of the middle has proceeded steadily for four decades, and it may have reached a tipping point."[2]

Manufacturing Jobs Vanish

The number of U.S. manufacturing jobs fell from about 19 million in 1979 to 12 million in 2015, as companies increasingly automated factories or outsourced work to countries with cheaper labor. Once a major source of middle-class income, manufacturing jobs declined most rapidly after 2000 as U.S. manufacturing productivity increased, reducing hours for factory workers, while competition from foreign countries weakened demand for U.S.-produced goods.

**U.S. Manufacturing Employment
(1970-2015 Seasonally Adjusted)**

(Millions of workers)

Source: "Manufacturing: NAICS 31-33" Workforce Statistics, U.S. Bureau of Labor Statistics, accessed March 30, 2016, http://tinyurl.com/mgomng9; "Factors Underlying the Decline in Manufacturing Employment Since 2000," Congressional Budget Office, Dec. 23, 2008, http://tinyurl.com/glhsj6z.

Many scholars — as well as numerous politicians and voters — trace the challenges facing the middle-class to the loss of good-paying manufacturing jobs that defined the post–World War II economic boom but then disappeared as U.S. companies shifted operations overseas or succumbed to foreign competition.

Stephen J. Rose, a research professor at the Center on Education and the Workforce at George Washington University in Washington, says the postwar economic boom continues to shape middle-class expectations, even though the U.S. economy — with its preeminent place in the global economic landscape — has undergone an irrevocable shift.

"We suffer from a political and emotional problem: the 30 glorious years from 1945 to 1975," Rose says. The postwar years were "a period of unbelievable growth," but one followed by the rise of major industrial competition in low-wage countries and the growth of job-killing automation.

"Europe needed us to provide a lot of capital goods to them," he continues. "Unionized and blue-collar workers with low education and fairly low skills were getting fairly good middle-class wages. That was not sustainable. No one wants to say that out loud, but that's the bottom line."

Pew's analysis highlights many of the factors that led to that stark bottom line:

- The share of adults in middle-income households fell from 61 percent of the population in 1971 to 50 percent in 2015. For the first time, they were outnumbered by those in lower- and upper-income tiers. The share of overall household income among middle-income families has declined from 62 percent in 1970 to 43 percent in 2014. On the other hand, wealthy households — representing only about one-fifth of the adult population — earned almost half the nation's household income. In 1970, they held only 29 percent of it.
- The gap between rich and poor has widened. In 2015, 20 percent of American adults were in the lowest-income tier, compared with 16 percent in 1971. On the opposite side, the share of adults in the highest income tier has more than doubled during that period, from 4 percent to 9 percent.[3]

Still, while many economic analysts agree the middle class has suffered setbacks in recent years, not all see such a grim picture.

For instance, Pew's analysis did not include ancillary forms of income, such as employee health care benefits, which other researchers routinely count in assessing middle-class conditions, notes Scott Winship, a policy analyst at the conservative Manhattan Institute for Policy

Research, a New York City think tank. When that income source is counted, the middle class is better off than it was three or four decades ago, he says.

"The middle fifth of American households is richer today than in 1979 by at least 35 percent," he says. "That translates to over $10,000 that the middle fifth has today that it didn't have in 1979."

But the wealthy have fared far better in recent decades. Incomes of the top 1 percent grew by 275 percent between 1979 and 2007, according to nonpartisan Congressional Budget Office (CBO) data, as analyzed by the liberal Center on Budget and Policy Priorities.[4]

Winship acknowledges the disparity. The growth in middle-class earnings, he says, "is much smaller than growth at the very top, and smaller than what growth was in the middle in the '50s and '60s, so it's not an unabashedly great story."

Debates about the middle class go beyond disagreements over statistical methods. They also center on the very meaning of "middle class," which can be a self-definition as much as a statistical category.[5]

A few decades ago, the notion was common that all Americans in the middle of the income distribution table shared a middle-class identity. That included blue-collar workers, who enjoyed home ownership, steady, well-paid employment and the possibility that their children would go into even better-paid white-collar work. In today's world, however, an economic — and resulting cultural and political — divide is opening between working-class Americans and those in the middle class.

Scholars say that division shows up most clearly in differences between those with and without college diplomas. "The sharpest class division is between people with four-year college degrees and everybody else," says Andrew J. Cherlin, a sociologist at Johns Hopkins University in Baltimore. "They wait to marry to have kids, their divorce rates are going down. People without degrees marry in much smaller numbers and have a much larger proportion of kids without marriage; you used to see that just among the poor."

That social distinction accompanies significant income differences. The earnings of college-educated workers consistently outpace those without bachelor's degrees. In 2013, according to the latest available statistics, median earnings for those with bachelor's degrees — $48,500 a year — amounted to $18,500 more than the earnings of high school graduates.[6]

But many ordinary Americans do not view a college diploma as a middle-class credential. An overwhelming 89 percent of respondents to a Pew survey this year said the first requirement for being considered middle class is a secure job. Only 30 percent said a college education is a necessity.[7]

Even so, Jacob Hacker, a political scientist at Yale University in New Haven, Conn., says the upper-income tiers of the college-educated middle class also are feeling uncertain about their future. "They're more likely to switch jobs and have to balance work and family, to deal with health care costs, education costs and housing in particular," he says. "Even if they feel relatively secure at the moment, they know they're going to have to put their kids through college, to save to own a home."

That uncertainty is well founded, some experts say. "Incomes are growing more slowly" in the middle class, says Lane Kenworthy, a sociologist at the University of California, San Diego.

And even though the economy is recovering from the housing crash and ensuing 2007-2009 recession, the youngest college graduates are still seeing their earnings decrease, according to data compiled by the Economic Policy Institute, a liberal think tank in Washington. Average hourly wages, inflation adjusted, for college graduates ages 21-24 have fallen from $18.41 in 2000 to $17.94 in 2015. What's more, according to a survey by Harvard University's Institute of Politics, 73 percent of current college students expect to have trouble finding a job when they graduate.[8]

As young adults continue to face struggles, they appear to be responding to political messages aimed at middle-class voters. Many young Democrats—including Barry, the office equipment installer in Ohio — have been flocking to Democratic presidential candidate Bernie Sanders, who pledges to "rebuild the American middle class." He has called for curbs on the growing concentration of wealth in the hands of the ultrarich and an end to foreign trade deals that cost American jobs. By mid-March, Sanders had won 1.5 million youth votes in the Democratic presidential primaries and caucuses — more than twice as many as his Democratic competitor, Hillary Clinton.[9]

Clinton and GOP front-runner Donald Trump, along with other Republican candidates, also are campaigning

U.S. Income Gap Widening

Median earnings of upper-income households rose to nearly $175,000 in 2014, up 47 percent since 1970 after adjusting for inflation. Earnings of middle- and lower-income households rose 34 percent and 28 percent, respectively, during the period. Incomes of all three groups fell since 2000, but middle- and lower-income households saw larger declines than wealthier ones.

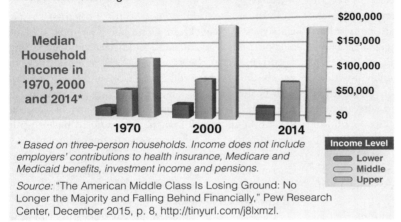

Median Household Income in 1970, 2000 and 2014*

1970   2000   2014

$200,000
$150,000
$100,000
$50,000
$0

Income Level
Lower
Middle
Upper

Based on three-person households. Income does not include employers' contributions to health insurance, Medicare and Medicaid benefits, investment income and pensions.

Source: "The American Middle Class Is Losing Ground: No Longer the Majority and Falling Behind Financially," Pew Research Center, December 2015, p. 8, http://tinyurl.com/j8lxmzl.

hard on the issue of middle-class economic prospects and income disparities. Clinton now opposes the Trans-Pacific Partnership free trade agreement, citing its potential to harm American workers.[10] And Republican Sen. Ted Cruz of Texas is pitching a 10 percent flat tax as a way to counter a situation in which "Washington pads Wall Street's pockets" through tax loopholes.[11]

Even some experts who view middle-class anxieties as well-founded argue that the political system is capable of resolving them. "The big if is [whether] we can get our political system moving," says Hacker. "Our standard of living encompasses a lot more than income, and I believe we have enormous potential in providing income security, access to high-quality health care" and other things the middle class worries about.

Analysts on the left are more pessimistic, saying growing middle-class discontent reflects a coming to terms with reality. "Your kids are not going to do better than you, and their opportunities, unless they're born into money, are very, very poor," says Alan Nasser, a professor emeritus of political economy at Evergreen State College in Olympia, Wash. "I can't imagine this wouldn't produce a significant change in consciousness."

As economists, politicians and average Americans discuss the future of the middle class, here are some of the questions being debated:

Does income stagnation mean the middle class is in decline?

In a flood tide of political rhetoric, scholarly books and journalism about the nation's changing economy and the growing disparity in America's wealth distribution, the single most explosive concept for middle-class Americans is the idea that they are an endangered species.

But experts disagree over whether the middle class is shrinking, in large part because the term "middle class" is partly an economic concept and partly a social one. In its recent report, Pew took the economic approach, defining middle-income households as those with income amounting to two-thirds to double the national median. For a three-person household, that works out to about $42,000 to $126,000 a year, in 2014 dollars.[12]

Although Pew used the terms "middle income" and "middle class" interchangeably, the report acknowledged that the terms are not necessarily synonymous. "Being middle class can connote more than income, be it a college education, white-collar work, economic security, owning a home," the report said. "Class could also be . . . a matter of self-identification."[13]

In any case, by Pew's method, the middle class is diminishing — from 61 percent of the adult population in 1971 to 50 percent last year.[14]

Some experts not affiliated with Pew agree that a variety of data support the report's conclusion. "The share of Americans with incomes in what we might call the middle has been decreasing," says Kenworthy of the University of California.

And results from a 2015 Gallup Poll were remarkably similar to Pew's: 51 percent of Americans categorized themselves as middle or upper-middle class — a sharp decline from the 61 percent, on average, who had labeled themselves as such in 2000-2008.[15]

That data may not be definitive. The respected General Social Survey, run by NORC at the University of Chicago (and which also asks respondents if they are lower class, working class or upper class), shows that the share of Americans describing themselves as middle class has been at roughly its most recently recorded level, 42 percent for 2014, since 1990.

However, Noah Smith, a finance professor at Stony Brook University in New York who analyzed the Gallup data, concluded that the Gallup results appear to show an anxiety rooted in hard financial reality. "Even if your family makes $180,000 a year, well above the national median, it might be hard to think of yourself as upper-middle class if you could be fired at any time, or one medical emergency could send you into bankruptcy."[16]

Different ways of measuring income can lead to different conclusions about the size and condition of the middle class. Using CBO's methodology of including Medicare, investment income and pensions, Winship, of the Manhattan Institute, concluded that middle-class households have grown 35 percent more prosperous since 1979.[17]

Income growth for the middle class "is much smaller than growth at the very top," Winship acknowledges, "and smaller than what growth was for the middle in the 1950s and 1960s, but we are significantly better off."

Winship argues that those in the middle class have less reason to worry about potential job and benefits losses than they seem to think. "These are real anxieties," he says, but in surveys, "about the same share of people" say they fear dying in airplane crashes or becoming victims of crime or terrorist attacks as say they worry about losing their jobs and benefits.

Kenworthy says income stagnation may be more important than the shrinking size of the middle class. Statistics from the Economic Policy Institute show a near-absence of growth in middle-income earnings between 1979 and 2013, compared with what higher-income earners made. Middle-class wages rose 6 percent during that period, while compensation for highly paid workers jumped 41 percent, the institute found.[18]

"Household income has been going up, but very slowly," Kenworthy says, and that's only because "more and more households have added a second earner."

Still, says Rose of George Washington University, earnings data not only exclude employer-paid benefits, but they also fail to account for smaller household sizes and rising living standards. "We have bigger houses, better cars; we eat out more," he says. "And we're living longer." Indeed, for the U.S. population overall, life expectancy rose from about 71 years in 1970 to 79 in 2013.[19]

Rose acknowledged that a rising mortality rate among lower-earning Americans in blue-collar jobs reflects a grimmer reality for people who may once have considered themselves, or their parents, as middle class.

"I'm not saying there's no pain and anxiety," he says. "If sons and daughters tried to follow their parents into factories, they were really in bad shape. But people who work in offices, including education and health care, do OK. And what do you see when you're in Albuquerque or Baltimore or Denver? You don't see factories. You see offices and health care and educational facilities."

Experts, such as Cherlin at Johns Hopkins University, also find that wages for those with bachelor's and advanced degrees are falling. "During the '70s, '80s and '90s, the wages of college-educated workers went up," he says, drawing a contrast with today's situation. But data from 2000 to 2014, the most recent figures available, show median annual earnings of male bachelor's degree holders fell — from $67,470 to $60,933. And those with doctorates saw a drop from almost $98,000 in 2000 to about $92,000 in 2014.[20]

Cherlin speculates that bachelor's degrees may have become an inadequate credential for middle-class status. "You have to wonder, as the economy becomes more automated and computerized, whether college graduates will have trouble achieving their economic dreams."

Since the rise of automation in workplaces of all kinds in recent decades, employment in so-called middle-skill jobs — including sales, office and administrative work — has fallen from 60 percent of the workforce in 1979 to 46 percent in 2012.[21]

But fears that highly advanced automation software may eliminate even upper-middle-class jobs that require considerable analytical capabilities — such as financial analysis — are largely unfounded, says David Autor, a Massachusetts Institute of Technology economist considered an authority on automation's effects.

"The pressure of automation on labor forces is likely to be more downward than upward," he says. "More autonomous vehicles, more dexterous robots are doing more labor-intensive tasks. Automation replaces some

J. Paul Gorman does computer coding at Bit Source, a tech startup in Pikeville, Ky., on Feb. 1, 2016. The company hired 10 coders recently but said nearly 1,000 people responded to its recent job ads. Many companies now send their coding work to firms overseas.

high-skilled workers, but often complements them as well, as with robots that doctors work with."

Would helping the poor also bolster the middle class?

Overall, the U.S. economy is recovering from the 2007-2009 recession, with unemployment falling to 5 percent this year — about half what it was in 2009 at the height of the recession. For those with bachelor's degrees or higher, unemployment was 2.5 percent by the end of 2015, a year in which nearly 2.7 million jobs were created.[22]

But the poverty rate for 2014 is 14.8 percent — representing 46.7 million people — up from 12.2 percent in 2000 and barely changed since 2010.[23]

Given those statistics, many policy experts say focusing too much on the middle class ignores the plight of the poor. "The safety net should be limited to people who are truly indigent, as opposed to being spread around in a way that metastasizes into middle-class entitlements," Arthur Brooks, president of the American Enterprise Institute, a conservative think tank, said during a panel discussion with President Obama last year.

His argument echoed a long-standing conservative view that Medicare and Social Security should be "means-tested" so rich people do not benefit. Liberals say if such programs were means-tested, they would lose their broad public support because they would be seen as anti-poverty programs.[24]

Low-wage workers have been urging local and state governments to raise the minimum wage to $15 an hour, which some say would also push up wages of higher-earning employees, thus expanding the middle class. A growing number of cities and two states — New York and California — have approved or are in the process of enacting such laws.[25]

But debates over whether to focus on helping the poor or the middle class have roiled Democrats in recent years. In late 2014, Democratic Sen. Charles Schumer of New York criticized the Obama administration and liberal Democrats for pushing the Affordable Care Act in 2010, arguing that it benefited mostly the poor because most middle-class Americans have insurance through their jobs. At that time, he said, the Democrats should have "continued to propose middle-class-oriented programs."[26]

Nevertheless, Winship of the Manhattan Institute says government initiatives focusing on the middle class would siphon resources more urgently needed by the poor.

"To focus too much on the perception that the middle class is in decline is bad for poor people," he says, citing a Department of Agriculture survey showing that 20 percent of U.S. households are worried that their food will run out before the end of the month.[27] Programs should focus instead on improving the standard of living and upward mobility of the bottom fifth of the income scale, he says.

But political will is not focused on the poor, says Anthony P. Carnevale, an economist and the director of Georgetown University's Center on Education and the Workforce. "It is morally repulsive, but the poor are not in the game," he says. "They have been disappeared in America. Strengthening the middle class is the mantra."

The most recent major government action directed at poor families, Carnevale says, was the 1996 welfare reform law, which included job training.[28] But its beneficial effects vanished when the job market tightened in the early 2000s. "When there is no surplus, the poor get nothing" because they have no political leverage, he says. "I think that, in the end, doing something for the poor will have to wait until the rest of us are taken care of."

Others, like Rose of George Washington University, say providing more for the middle class is "just too expensive," and no firm data show that the educated middle class needs rescuing. And while median household income for the highly educated may be in the $60,000 range, he says, it grows substantially with age. As of 2013, median income for those age 40 or older with an associate's or bachelor's degree was slightly less than $80,000 a year.[29]

Most members of the middle class have periods when they are doing well and times when they are doing less well. Over time, "people who play by the rules can get hurt," Rose says, "but they also can win."

Some experts, including Kenworthy of the University of California, say some programs designed to aid the middle class would also help the poor.

"For example, if we were to put in place a good-quality universal early-education system, along the lines of what Sweden and Denmark do, with some user fee or co-payment," Kenworthy says, would produce "a real increase in living standards" for both poor and for middle-class families.

Early-childhood education is a longtime liberal anti-poverty solution. Advocates cite studies showing that early education improves the earnings of adults who attended as children. Studies in Tulsa, Okla., and Boston calculate that poor children would earn about $3 more for each dollar spent on their early education.[30]

But some conservatives, most recently in Tennessee, cite studies showing that early education makes little difference in the long run.[31]

Can improved education and training protect the middle class?

Statistics show that higher education pays off. Men with bachelor's degrees earn $900,000 more in median lifetime earnings than male high-school graduates, and women $630,000 more. For those with graduate degrees, the differential amounts to $1.5 million for men and $1.1 million for women.[32] Associate's degree holders earn $798 per week — $120 more than high-school graduates.[33]

Questions remain, however, about what type of higher education — and in which fields — best prepares

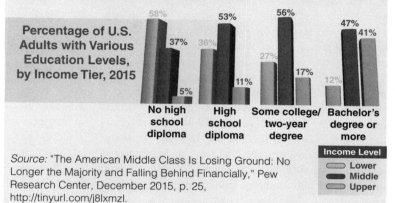

Most College Grads in Wealthier Households

Four in 10 Americans with bachelor's degrees lived in upper-income households in 2015, and nearly half lived in middle-income households. Most adults who completed high school or some college lived in middle-income households. A majority of those who did not graduate from high school lived in lower-income households.

Percentage of U.S. Adults with Various Education Levels, by Income Tier, 2015

No high school diploma: 58%, 37%, 5%
High school diploma: 37%, 36%, 11%
Some college/two-year degree: 27%, 56%, 17%
Bachelor's degree or more: 12%, 47%, 41%

Income Level: Lower, Middle, Upper

Source: "The American Middle Class Is Losing Ground: No Longer the Majority and Falling Behind Financially," Pew Research Center, December 2015, p. 25, http://tinyurl.com/j8lxmzl.

a student for the present and future economic climate. A growing number of experts say a student's training should be geared toward new technological advancements.

"Are your skills a complement to the skills of the computer?" asked Tyler Cowen, a professor of economics at George Mason University in Fairfax, Va. "If [so], your wage and labor market prospects are likely to be cheery."[34]

In his book *Average Is Over,* Cowen warns, "Lacking the right training means being shut out of opportunities like never before." The highest earners, usually those with advanced postsecondary degrees, "are earning much more," he adds. But all science and technology degrees are not automatically valuable, he writes, arguing that a trained marketer likely will do better than, say, an astronomer.[35]

Still, machines may replace a variety of careers. A 2013 study by two technology specialists at the University of Oxford in Britain estimated that 47 percent of all U.S. jobs are at high risk of being replaced by robots or other technologies in the next 20 years.[36]

But while fear of automation builds, others say demand remains high in certain jobs that do not require college or postgraduate degrees. "We might train some high-school graduates for midlevel jobs that are still around and might be growing — medical technicians, who run X-ray machines and medical devices; [and] there are factory jobs that require knowledge of computer-controlled machinery," Cherlin says.

However, the need for such vocational training, much of which can be done at community colleges, poses a policy question. "Do we give up on the dream that every young adult should have a four-year college degree, and pour resources into community colleges?" Cherlin asks. He and others favor a community college-based strategy, on the grounds that not all students will make it through a four-year college, which is also far more expensive.[37]

Winship of the Manhattan Institute rejects the argument that college is becoming unaffordable. "The cost of higher education and increases in student indebtedness have definitely led a lot of people to worry that pathways to the middle class are blocked off," he says, "but that is not reflected in rising graduation rates" at American colleges. Graduation rates at four-year colleges have increased, though modestly, from about 58 percent for those entering in 2000 to 59 percent for those students entering in 2006.[38]

And undergraduates typically accumulate far less debt than graduate students, Winship notes. In 2011-2012, the most recent years for which figures are available, 30 percent of bachelor's degree graduates owed no debt, 10 percent owed less than $10,000 and 18 percent owed less than $30,000. By contrast 54 percent of professional, doctoral-level degree graduates owed $120,000 or more.[39]

Worries over debt are "misplaced," Winship says. "People who get a degree and come out with $20,000 to $30,000 in debt — that is not nearly as big a problem as people who drop out and have $10,000 to $20,000 in debt."

But Rose of George Washington University argues that the education issue goes deeper than acquiring diplomas. The dropout rates for students seeking bachelor's degrees reflect the failure of high schools to prepare graduates for college work, he says. "What we're talking about is people who don't have skills" that enable them to succeed in college.

Consequently, he says, the most urgent task is to expand the community college system. "Otherwise we will force more people into the four-year system, in which a small number will find themselves and thrive, and another group will make it through because they're at colleges with very low standards."

And even those like Cowen, who advocate education and training geared specifically toward new technologies used in today's workplaces, say the educational infrastructure is nowhere near ready for the task.

"That takes a full generation," Cowen says. "It's a slow process. We don't even have teachers trained to do that much training. We're starting, but I wouldn't say we have started in a big way."

BACKGROUND
Early Middle Class

Even before the Civil War, long before the modern emphasis on the United States as a middle-class country, at least one writer was already celebrating the American middle class as the embodiment of national ideals.

"The most valuable class in any community is the middle class — the men of moderate means," poet and journalist Walt Whitman wrote in a Brooklyn newspaper editorial in 1858.[40]

During that era, according to sociologist C. Wright Mills, a scholar of the U.S. class system, "the middle class was so broad a stratum and of such economic weight that even by the standards of the statistician the society as a whole was a middle-class society." Mills counted professionals, self-employed manufacturers and independent farmers as members of the middle class.[41]

But Mills may have painted too romantic a picture, ignoring sharp class differences within the working population, with wage workers on one side and far-better-paid professionals and bosses on the other, according to economics professor Robert J. Gordon of Northwestern University in Evanston, Ill. If middle class in the 1870s meant a household that employed a servant — a standard definition — then the middle class accounted for only 15 percent of households and the rest were working class, writes Gordon.[42]

The period between the 1870s and America's entry into World War I in 1917 was also marked by the excesses of what is known as the Gilded Age, when industrialists such as Andrew Carnegie, John D. Rockefeller and Cornelius Vanderbilt built immense fortunes by monopolizing the steel, oil and shipping industries. Wealth was concentrated at the top of the socioeconomic ladder: By 1917 the top 1 percent of earners received more than 40 percent of the national income. Today, that percentage is even higher, leading many experts to call this America's new gilded age.[43]

Gilded Age excesses gave rise to the Progressive movement of 1900 to 1920. Led by members of the upper class and of the still relatively small professional middle class, the Progressives were outraged at big-business domination of the economy and politics. One of the movement's major champions, President Theodore Roosevelt, railed against the power of the industrial monopolies, or trusts, and used the Sherman Anti-Trust Act to break up the Northern Securities Corp., a holding company of railroads.[44]

Overall, the movement succeeded in imposing regulations on factories that improved worker safety and limited work hours of children and women. But most attempts to impose major curbs on big business failed, given the strength of the interests involved. And when the Progressive era had run its course, by 1920, it was followed by the "Roaring Twenties," when wealth was celebrated and regulation of business weakened.[45]

Government Intervention

The Great Depression, preceded by a catastrophic stock market crash in 1929, ended the hopes and dreams of vast numbers of Americans. Millions of savings accounts were wiped out when more than 10,000 banks failed.[46] By 1933, more than 25 percent of the workforce was unemployed.[47]

After taking office in 1933, President Franklin D. Roosevelt initiated a series of laws and programs known as the New Deal, designed to rescue millions of unemployed Americans devastated by the Depression. New Deal innovations included the Social Security system; legislation authorizing and regulating collective bargaining; and federal employment in public works of all kinds. The Works Progress Administration (WPA)—which sent jobless workers across the country to build and repair bridges, roads, parks and other public facilities — employed 8.5 million Americans during its eight-year existence, which ended in 1943. However, in a political compromise with segregationist Southerners in Congress, African-Americans were excluded from major New Deal programs in the South.[48]

After World War II, the Servicemen's Readjustment Act of 1944 — better known as the GI Bill of Rights — authorized federal benefits, including tuition for

A biology class meets at Massasoit Community College in Brockton, Mass. Many jobs that will be in demand in the future, such as medical technician, don't require four-year college degrees, prompting policymakers to ask whether every young adult should have a four-year degree.

college or trade school, low-cost home mortgages and business loans, to 12.4 million veterans — about 78 percent of all those who served.[49] The legislation was designed to — and did — create a bigger, more financially secure middle class.

"The increasing share of the population with high school diplomas and then college degrees helped pave the way for a transformation from a working-class society before World War II to a middle-class society afterward," Gordon writes, expressing a virtually universal view.[50]

Some 5.6 million veterans attended trade schools or took on-the-job training in fields such as auto and radio repair, accounting, construction trades, cooking, flight training and other work. As a result, the bill expanded the service sector of a diversifying economy.[51]

However, some local administrators, following racist practices common at the time and unwilling to empower African-Americans, denied GI Bill benefits to black veterans. The long-term effect was to severely limit the formation of a black middle class at a time when the white middle class was expanding.[52]

The early postwar period was also marked by an economic boom that made the United States the envy of other countries. The nation's GNP more than doubled from $200 billion in 1940 to more than $500 billion in 1960. The United States had three-quarters of the world's investment capital and two-thirds of its industrial capacity.[53]

Economic Boom

Some of America's postwar economic advantages dated back to war production in a country that, unlike war-ravaged Europe and Asia, suffered no battles on its soil (with the exception of the 1941 Japanese attack on Pearl Harbor).

For instance, thanks in part to the expanded wartime manufacture of tanks and other vehicles, American auto-makers could produce far more cars after the war. They sold 9.1 million cars and trucks in 1954, compared with only 4.7 million in 1941. The vast expansion of the national automobile fleet helped stimulate GDP and income growth. Thanks to the latter, ordinary working families could own more than one car — an advantage previously confined to the wealthy.[54]

Construction of the Interstate Highway System (begun in 1956), which allowed faster and easier shipping, accounted for a 31 percent jump in productivity during the 1950s. Northwestern's Gordon writes that 32 of 35 industries benefited from lower costs because of transportation improvements.[55]

Meanwhile, the housing market exploded, in large part because of federally backed mortgages under the GI Bill. By 1955, 57 percent of U.S. households owned a home — up from 41 percent in 1940 — strengthening the connection between homeownership and middle-class status. Middle-class Americans came to view homeownership "as an inalienable right," one scholar has written.[56]

By the mid-1950s, households in the top 1 percent of the income distribution spectrum held about 10 percent of the nation's income — down from nearly 24 percent in 1928, the year before the Great Depression. And during the period from 1947 to 1979, average overall hourly compensation rose by about 100 percent.[57]

The Reversal

As far back as 1962, sociologist Mills was warning that mostly middle-class office workers — those earning salaries rather than hourly wages — were vulnerable in ways that the early 19th-century middle class was not.[58]

By the late 1970s, Gordon and others write, the earnings of those in the middle (and bottom) of the earning scale were being held down by the growing practice of outsourcing jobs and increasing automation, which also reduced the number of jobs. These were coupled with a steep decline in labor union power.

By 1981, 26 percent of the cars, 25 percent of the steel and 60 percent of televisions and consumer electronics sold in the United States were imported.[59] The decline of American manufacturing gave rise to the term Rust Belt to describe the Midwestern region where factories were shutting and well-paying manufacturing jobs were disappearing.[60] Steel industry employment, for instance, declined from more than 1 million in 1970 to 630,000 in 1990.[61]

The 1980s and early 1990s also saw the advent of the personal computer age, which would transform office work and communications. Desktop computers came into homes and offices, and users began connecting to networks over phone lines. Email began replacing business letters. And computers put powerful search and analytical capabilities into millions of hands.

The computer revolution eliminated jobs or enabled them to be moved overseas. With the emergence of the Internet and instantaneous global connections, companies began to shift tasks such as accounting, document search and medical-image interpreting to English-speaking countries where labor was cheaper.

As the Internet rapidly expanded and the benefits of digital technology seemed limitless, a stock market frenzy took hold, with shares in virtually any Internet startup skyrocketing in value. The "dotcom bubble" burst on March 11, 2000. Within a month, the total value of all shares traded on Nasdaq, the main tech stock market, had plummeted by almost $1 trillion.[62]

A recession followed, spurred by further declines in manufacturing. Those in the middle-earnings group took the hardest hit — with 1.3 million job losses in 2001.[63] Although the recession officially ended after eight months, economist Jared Bernstein, later the chief economic adviser to Vice President Joseph Biden, warned in 2003 that the recovery was a jobless one, with 2.1 million fewer private-sector jobs than existed in 2000.[64]

Worries about labor market changes persisted as technological advances enabled employers in a growing variety of fields to "offshore" services to contractors abroad. Economist Alan S. Blinder of Princeton University, a former vice chairman of the Federal Reserve, estimated in 2006 that offshored service-sector jobs eventually could number two to three times the 14 million manufacturing jobs that existed at the time.[65]

C H R O N O L O G Y

1760-1920 *Colonial and post-independence middle class make up majority of the non-slave population.*

1760 Seventy percent of free Americans — farmers, craftspeople and professionals — are considered middle class.

1870 As the country industrializes, class distinctions sharpen, with professionals and business owners accounting for 15 percent of U.S. households.

1920 New consumer credit industry enables purchases of appliances and other consumer goods.

1929-1944 *Great Depression devastates U.S.*

1929 Stock market crash precedes a widespread financial system failure.

1933 About one-quarter of the nation's workforce — 15.5 million people — are unemployed as Great Depression reaches bottom. . . . President Franklin D. Roosevelt's New Deal authorizes labor organizing and collective bargaining and spurs massive government employment in public works.

1941 United States enters World War II, begins to expand industrial capacity for vital war materiel.

1944 GI Bill helps pay for college and vocational education and provides home mortgages and business loans for more than 12 million veterans.

1947-1981 *U.S. economy soars; home and car ownership mark middle-class status.*

1947 Average hourly compensation for workers begins steady increase.

1954 U.S. auto industry sells 9.1 million cars, nearly double the 1941 total.

1955 Fifty-seven percent of U.S. households own their homes, up from 41 percent in 1940.

1956 U.S. Interstate Highway System construction begins, leading to declines in shipping costs.

1959 At Moscow debate with Soviet Premier Nikita S. Khrushchev, Vice President Richard Nixon touts products available to U.S. steelworkers.

1962 Columbia University sociologist C. Wright Mills warns that middle-class office workers are losing economic independence that early 19th-century middle class enjoyed.

1981 As effects of globalizing world economy begin to take hold, 26 percent of cars, 25 percent of steel and 60 percent of consumer electronics are imported.

1982-Present *Continuing globalization, outsourcing and digital innovation cause disruptive economic change, sparking intense political debate.*

1982 Personal computers become commercially available.

1990 American steel industry employment falls to 630,000 from more than 1 million in 1970.

1994 Amazon, which will cause huge job losses in retail and other industries, is founded.

2006 Leading economist estimates that up to 42 million service-sector jobs face potential offshoring.

2007-2009 Major recession pushes unemployment rate to 10 percent. . . . Long-term unemployed include educated, skilled workers.

2011 "Occupy Wall Street" movement reflects growing debate over economic disparity in American society.

2013 Economist Thomas Piketty's *Capital in the Twenty-First Century* intensifies debate over fate of middle class.

2015 Pew Research Center concludes the middle-income population is shrinking. . . . Princeton University economists document death rate increase among lesser-educated whites. . . . Young college graduates' hourly pay (inflation-adjusted) is $17.94 an hour, down from $18.41 in 2000.

2016 Presidential primary candidates from both parties attack U.S. trade policy for allegedly eliminating U.S. jobs.

Recession Underscores Black-White Economic Gap

Bulk of African-American wealth tied up in homes.

The brutal recession of 2007-2009 and its aftermath spurred many Americans to talk about class distinction, but the crash and recovery also is a story about race.

Black households lost 40 percent of their wealth, on average, from 2009 to 2011, when recovery from the recession was beginning. During the same period, the median loss among white households (excluding home equity) dwindled to zero.[1]

Much of that disparity stems from the different natures of black wealth and white wealth. The Social Science Research Council, a New York-based organization of academics in sociology and related fields, examined the racial dimensions of the recession and recovery for the American Civil Liberties Union. It noted that black home-owning households depended on the values of their homes for their wealth to a greater extent than whites.

In 2007, home equity accounted for 71 percent of the total wealth of the typical black homeowner.* For white homeowners, home equity made up 51 percent of wealth.[2] That difference partly explains why median wealth — excluding home equity — was $14,200 for blacks and $92,950 for whites in 2007.[3]

Some experts conclude that this gap in resources is due, in part, to a history of housing discrimination, in which many minorities were denied mortgage loans or were required to pay higher loan rates than those charged to whites. A boom in mortgage lending that began in the 1990s eventually triggered the recession, underscoring the legacy of that discrimination, in the view of some experts.[4] A disproportionate percentage of blacks, as well as Latinos,

_____

*Home equity is a home's fair-market value minus any debt outstanding on the property.

held "subprime" mortgages, which carried higher interest rates because subprime borrowers were perceived to be at a higher risk of defaulting.[5]

"Before the subprime boom, black borrowers were more likely to be denied loans overall," wrote sociologists Jacob S. Rugh, now an assistant professor at Brigham Young University, and Douglas S. Massey, a professor at Princeton University. "During the boom, minority borrowers' underserved status made them prime targets for subprime lenders who systematically targeted their communities for aggressive marketing campaigns."[6]

Rugh and Massey said data showed that subprime mortgages went disproportionally not only to black and Latino borrowers but also to non-college-educated borrowers.[7]

Among blacks, as among whites, a college degree increasingly is seen as the dividing line between being middle class and working class. Karyn Lacy, a sociology professor at the University of Michigan in Ann Arbor, who wrote a book based on fieldwork in black communities in the Virginia and Maryland suburbs of Washington, D.C., argues that the black lower middle class is more accurately described as working class.[8] Its members earn $30,000 to $49,000 a year in jobs that don't typically require a college degree.

"Most of the rewards associated with a middle-class lifestyle, such as a safe neighborhood, quality public schools or job security are merely wishful thinking for this group," Lacy wrote in 2012.[9]

Overall, African-Americans are poorer than whites, with black median household income at $35,398 in 2014, compared to $60,256 for white non-Hispanics. But 11 percent of black Americans earn $100,000 to $200,000 a year, and 1.6 percent earn $200,000 a year or more — putting both those groups within the upper middle class.[10]

In the next few years, worries about foreign competition took a back seat to fears over possible collapse of the entire economy, as a plunge in housing prices sparked the 2007-2009 recession, in which 8.7 million jobs were lost.[66] Joblessness peaked at 10 percent in October 2009, the highest rate since the Depression.[67]

The housing crash followed a vast expansion of easy mortgage lending, financed largely by investors who

Lacy urges that the continuing plight of many black households not lead to an overly generalized conclusion that the entire black middle class has been economically devastated over the past nine years.

Now doing research in Atlanta, Lacy says, "Here you have athletes, entertainers, many not college-educated but rich, as well as very wealthy black business owners. I've interviewed some of these people, and as far as I can tell, their lifestyles have not changed. There is still a black elite middle class that have maintained their status."

Despite black communities' history with subprime mortgages, as well as other institutional barriers, Lacy finds that African-Americans who are lower down on the economic-class hierarchy are more likely to blame themselves than others for obstacles they encounter.[11]

"When lower-middle-class [black] people are not successful, they tend to think, 'I didn't make the sacrifices to go to college,'" Lacy observes. "The feeling is, 'I fell short due to some individual deficiency.'"

Blaming oneself, rather than the system, is consistent with research by other scholars, who have found young African-Americans acknowledging that the conditions they face are somewhat better than those of earlier generations. For a 2014 book, Andrew J. Cherlin, a sociologist at Johns Hopkins University, and colleague Timothy Nelson interviewed men of both races and found more optimism among African-Americans. "I think there are better opportunities now because first of all, the economy's changing," a black interviewee said. "The color barrier is not as harsh as it was back then."[12]

White men, however, were less optimistic. The gap between the races showed up in responses to survey questions about how respondents expect their children to fare. Negative responses among whites increased from 12 percent in 1994 to 15 percent in 2012. But negative responses among blacks declined during the same period, from 17 percent to 14 percent.[13]

Orlando Patterson, a Harvard University sociologist, noted last year that inner-city young blacks with little education and few possibilities tend to subscribe wholeheartedly to the classic American success doctrine. "The most hardened, disconnected youth insisted on attributing their failures to their own shortcomings and refused to blame racism," Patterson wrote.[14]

But members of the black middle and upper-middle classes, Lacy says, tend to blame institutionalized discrimination more than themselves for obstacles they encounter. "The higher you ascend on the class ladder, the more cognizant you are of barriers you have to overcome," she says.

— *Peter Katel*

---

[1] Sarah Burd-Sharps and Rebecca Rasch, "Impact of the US Housing Crisis on the Racial Wealth Gap Across Generations," Social Science Research Council, June 2015, p. 1, http://tinyurl.com/j6uoc4e.

[2] *Ibid.*, p. 12.

[3] *Ibid.*

[4] For background, see Kenneth Jost, "Housing Discrimination," *CQ Researcher*, Nov. 6, 2015, pp. 937-960.

[5] Jacob S. Rugh and Douglas S. Massey, "Racial Segregation and the American Foreclosure Crisis," *American Sociological Review*, 2010, http://tinyurl.com/jjha3jm.

[6] *Ibid.*, p. 632.

[7] *Ibid.*, p. 633.

[8] Karyn Lacy, *Blue-Chip Black* (2007).

[9] Karyn Lacy, "All's Fair? The Foreclosure Crisis and Middle-Class Black (In)Stability," *American Behavioral Scientist*, November 2012, p. 1568, http://tinyurl.com/gs592e3.

[10] Carmen DeNavas-Walt and Bernadette D. Proctor, "Income and Poverty in the United States: 2014," Current Population Reports, U.S. Census Bureau, September 2015, p. 5, http://tinyurl.com/oskydlu; "African American Income," *BlackDemographics.com*, undated, http://tinyurl.com/h8pt5px.

[11] For background, see Peter Katel, "Racial Conflict," *CQ Researcher*, Jan. 8, 2016, pp. 25-48.

[12] Andrew J. Cherlin, *Labor's Love Lost: The Rise and Fall of the Working-Class Family in America* (2014), pp. 170-171.

[13] *Ibid.*, p. 170.

[14] Orlando Patterson, "The Social and Cultural Matrix of Black Youth," p. 50, in Orlando Patterson, with Ethan Fosse, ed., *The Cultural Matrix: Understanding Black Youth* (2015).

---

bought securities based on mortgage obligations. The investments failed when homeowners couldn't make their mortgage payments. For the 30 preceding years, administrations and Congress had left financial institutions to mostly supervise themselves, relying on the self-correcting nature of the markets.

But in 1999, Congress weakened the 1933 Glass-Steagall Act, a major law governing the financial industry.

Rising Death Rates Signal Troubled Middle Class

Some despairing whites turn to alcohol, drugs.

For decades, death rates fell throughout the industrialized world as health habits and medical care improved. Lately, that trend has reversed — but only in one country, the United States, and only for middle-aged whites with a limited education.

From 1999 to 2014, the death rate for non-Latino whites with a high-school education or less shot up by 134.4 per 100,000, a jump of more than 20 percent. In the two decades before the spike, the mortality rate for all white Americans had fallen by nearly 2 percent a year, in line with the average rate of decline in other wealthy countries.[1] The findings emerged from an analysis of Centers for Disease Control and Prevention and Census Bureau data by Princeton University economists Anne Case and her husband, Angus Deaton, last year's winner of the Nobel Prize in economics.

Case and Deaton's alarming study made headlines. The immediate causes of the new trend were as troubling as the rise in death rates itself: drug overdoses, alcoholism, suicide and two illnesses associated with drug or alcohol abuse: chronic liver disease and cirrhosis. Not coincidentally, mortality rose hand in hand with a massive increase in prescriptions for opioid painkillers — chemical cousins of morphine and heroin — and an associated surge in heroin use in predominantly white regions, especially New England.[2]

Andrew Gelman, a professor of political science and statistics at Columbia University, questioned some of the Case-Deaton data analysis. He and a colleague didn't find an increase in the overall death rate for middle-aged whites — though they did find that they were doing worse in mortality than their counterparts in other countries. And those who are facing an increase are not men, Gelman said: "Actually, what we see is an increasing mortality among [white] women aged 52 and younger." That trend, he said, is geographically limited to the South and Midwest.[3] Gelman did not examine the regional discrepancy or any possible reasons for the female death-rate increase that he found in his analysis.

Deaton and Case stood by their analysis. But they acknowledged that some explanation was needed that went beyond specific causes of death. "Ties to economic insecurity are possible," Case and Deaton speculated. "Many of the baby-boom generation are the first to find, in midlife, that they will not be better off than were their parents."[4]

Deaton, who also studies global poverty, told the Council on Foreign Relations, a New York-based foreign-policy think tank, that he sees in the mortality spike the effects of a decline in manufacturing, a byproduct of globalized trade and automation. "These are the people who used to have good factory jobs with on-the-job training," he said. "These are the people who could build good lives for themselves and for their kids. And all of that has gone away."[5]

But Lane Kenworthy, a sociology professor at the University of California, San Diego, argues that the mortality data do not support that hypothesis. Notably,

---

The 1999 action allowed banks to engage in commercial activities, such as insurance and investment banking, which previously had been forbidden. Many experts say weakening Glass-Steagall contributed to the mortgage crisis by allowing banks to become "too big to fail."[68]

"The financial industry itself played a key role in weakening regulatory constraints on institutions, markets, and products," said the 2011 report of the bipartisan National Commission on the Causes of the Financial and Economic Crisis. In 1999-2008 alone, Wall Street firms spent $2.7 billion lobbying Congress and more than $1 billion on campaign contributions, the panel noted.[69]

The effects of the financial crisis were long-lasting, especially for the middle class.[70] By late 2010, nearly 6.7 million jobless Americans were considered "long-term unemployed." And many of these long-term jobless were skilled workers who had earned middle-class salaries.[71]

Anger over Wall Street firms' role in creating the mortgage crisis prompted the "Occupy Wall Street" movement, which began in New York City and spread

the death-rate increase was higher before the 2007-2009 recession — when economic conditions worsened — than after it began, he noted in a blog post.[6]

Kenworthy argues that, without a statistical analysis, the opioid boom alone could account for the death-rate increase, though he acknowledges that there could well be some connection to economic dislocation. "It is more likely that since around 1980, there has been a sizable segment of the American population who felt insecure or struggled economically but weren't addicted to pain relievers or heroin, or overdosing or killing themselves intentionally, until there was a change in the distribution of pain relievers," he says. "If all these people were happy with their lives, there might be some increase in addiction, but not enough to change the direction of the mortality rate."

Other scholars squarely defend the Case-Deaton hypothesis, arguing that changes in the class structure could well explain a sense of alienation among middle-aged white workers. The children of fathers whose working-class incomes provided a comfortable, secure existence have seen the economic environment change, says Andrew J. Cherlin, a sociology professor at Johns Hopkins University in Baltimore. And these workers, if they lacked college degrees, weren't prepared for the transformation.

"They thought they could be prosperous like their parents," he says. "College-educated people, I think they are doing just as well. It's the non-college-educated, especially whites, who feel correctly that they are not able to live up to the standards of their parents' generation."

Deaton told the Council on Foreign Relations that anguish could come not only from people's memories of their parents' generation, but also from a view of their own children's future.

"One of the things that would really make you despair in middle age is not only if you were not going to be better off than your parents," said the economist, who grew up in a coal-mining family, "but if you thought your kids were going to be even worse off than you were going to be and if the kids are turning to drugs and all of that too. I think that would make me despair."[7]

— Peter Katel

---

[1] Anne Case and Angus Deaton, "Rising Morbidity and Mortality in Midlife Among White Non-Hispanic Americans in the 21st century," *PNAS* (Proceedings of the National Academy of Sciences), Dec. 8, 2015, http://tinyurl.com/j378n6b; Gina Kolata, "Death Rates Rising for Middle-Aged White Americans, Study Finds," *The New York Times*, Nov. 2, 2015, http://tinyurl.com/nrf6d5x.

[2] Katharine Q. Seelye, "Heroin in New England, More Abundant and Deadly," *The New York Times*, July 18, 2013, http://tinyurl.com/h5tygzn; "Here and There with Dave Marash," interview, Sam Quinones, author of *Dreamland*, Feb. 25, 2016, http://tinyurl.com/j63ov6k.

[3] Andrew Gelman, "Is the Death Rate Really Increasing for Middle-Aged White Americans?," *Slate*, Nov. 11, 2015, http://tinyurl.com/h87m3y3. Andrew Gelman and Jonathan Auerbach, "Age-Aggregation Bias in Mortality Trends," undated, http://tinyurl.com/jvde4l7; "More Details on Rising Mortality Among Middle-Aged Whites," *The New York Times*, Nov. 6, 2015, http://tinyurl.com/hmautna; "Middle-Aged White Death Trends Update: It's All About Women in the South," Statistical Modeling, Causal Inference, and Social Science (blog), Jan. 19, 2016, http://tinyurl.com/jx7e5kk.

[4] Case and Deaton, *op. cit.*, p. 4.

[5] "Angus Deaton on Foreign Aid and Inequality," Council on Foreign Relations, Feb. 18, 2016, http://tinyurl.com/hysdpk5.

[6] Lane Kenworthy, "Is Economic Insecurity to Blame for the Increase in Deaths Among Middle-Aged Whites?" blog post, Nov. 5, 2015, http://tinyurl.com/h7fljux.

[7] "Angus Deaton," *op. cit.*; John Kay, "The Great Escape: Health, Wealth and the Origins of Inequality by Angus Deaton (book review)," *Prospect Magazine*, Nov. 14, 2013, http://tinyurl.com/hfrh6cf.

---

nationwide in 2011. The movement claimed to represent the "99 percent" who were losing out to those at the top of the socioeconomic ladder. In fact, the protesters were largely middle class: Eighty percent of active Occupy members in the movement's New York heart had bachelor's or graduate degrees. According to a 2012 survey, 29 percent of Occupy activists had lost their jobs in the previous five years, nearly half were professionals and 36 percent had household incomes of at least $100,000.[72]

Although the movement ebbed, it had put the growing disparity in the distribution of the nation's wealth — and the fate of the middle class — squarely on the national agenda. A 2012 Pew survey of self-described middle-class Americans found that 62 percent blamed Congress "a lot" for the mortgage crisis and 54 percent blamed financial institutions.[73]

Debate on the growing income gap — including such largely middle-class issues as student debt — took on still more urgency after the 2014 publication of French economist Thomas Piketty's bestseller *Capital in the Twenty-First Century.* He used income tax data to show that the top 1 percent of Americans had doubled their income over the past 30 years and those in the top 0.1 percent had quadrupled theirs.[74]

By late 2015, the centrist Pew center's report on the shrinking middle-income population prompted even more attention to the widening income gap and its relation to the condition of the middle class.

These conditions were accompanied by a steep drop in the power of unions, which push for higher wages and benefits for workers. By 2015, union membership had dropped from 35 percent of the workforce in the mid-1950s to 11 percent.[75]

Meanwhile, executive pay soared. Between 1997 and 2014, CEO pay increased 997 percent, according to the Economic Policy Institute. And Bloomberg, the business news service, calculated in 2015 that the difference between CEO and worker pay reached as high as 644 to 1 — $7.29 million a year for the McDonald's CEO versus $11,324 a year for the average McDonald's employee.

Reflecting growing public indignation over such disparities, the Securities and Exchange Commission voted last year to require most public companies to report on their CEO-employee pay ratio.[76]

CURRENT SITUATION
Student Debt

Experts agree that getting the best education possible is the wisest investment young people can make. But some experts say the deck is stacked against low-income students, effectively making it harder for them to earn what is becoming an essential middle-class credential.

Low-income students are held back by the high cost of four-year degree programs and fear of graduating with an untenable amount of college debt. Total outstanding student debt reached a staggering $1.3 trillion last year, about 11 percent of which was delinquent or in default for at least 90 days. Borrowers owing half of the total have sought to postpone payment.[77]

Definitive explanations for skyrocketing college debt are hard to come by. Experts at the Brookings Institution say tuition increases do not explain all of the ballooning debt: Net tuition — the amount after deducting financial aid — increased 12 percent in 2002-2012, while total student debt increased 77 percent. And enrollment increases are not large enough to explain debt growth, the think tank analysts said.[78]

Brookings researchers Michael Greenstone and Adam Looney said students seem to increasingly be relying on loans to finance higher education, possibly because of the recession's negative impact on family finances.

Recently, the growth in college debt has been slowing. And, counterintuitively, borrowers who default owe less on average than borrowers in good standing, which could reflect lower earnings in some students' post-college careers. The average debt was $22,550 in 2014, while the average debt of those in default was $14,380.[79]

Democratic presidential candidate Sanders vows to end tuition at all public colleges and universities. Clinton has a similar but somewhat more complicated plan, in which students would not pay tuition but their parents would have to pay some college costs.[80]

And President Obama is proposing a plan that would provide free community college tuition for low-income students who attend classes at least half time and maintain at least a 2.5 grade point average. The federal government would pick up 75 percent of the tab and states the remainder.[81]

Low-income students are more likely to earn certificates or associate degrees, which can be completed in fewer years, according to Sandy Baum, a senior fellow at the Urban Institute think tank who specializes in higher education finance, and Martha C. Johnson, a research associate there.[82]

The financial barriers to bachelor's and postgraduate degrees have racial and ethnic, as well as class, dimensions. According to an analysis by Demos, a liberal think tank, 81 percent of black students at public institutions — and 86 percent at private colleges — must borrow money to pay for tuition, compared with 63 percent and 72 percent, respectively, for whites. The same study concluded that middle-class black and Latino students are having the hardest time making student loan payments. For those at the bottom of the middle class, the hardship of college loan payments threatens membership in the middle class.[83]

Because of the high indebtedness rate for black and Latino students, they drop out of college owing money at a far higher rate than white students. Thirty-nine percent of black borrowers drop out, compared with 29 percent of white borrowers.

"And despite bipartisan rhetoric around closing attainment gaps among students of color and low-income students," wrote Mark Huelsman, a senior policy analyst at Demos, referring to the disproportionately low share of minority college students, "we have created a system in which more underrepresented students take on debt and drop out."[84]

Proposed Solutions

Obama's latest proposed budget contains plans designed to boost employment in high-skilled, so-called middle-class jobs.

The budget would provide $75 million for the proposed American Technical Training Fund, which would expand tuition-free job training in fields such as manufacturing, health care and information technology.[85] But it is unlikely the fund will see the light of day. Congressional Republicans, who control both the House and Senate, have announced they won't even hold hearings on Obama's proposed budget.[86]

But another Obama budget proposal — to supplement the wages of displaced manufacturing workers who take lower-paying service jobs by providing them up to $10,000 over two years — conceivably could get Republican support.

"The idea of targeting financial support to people who, especially later in their careers, are choosing between going back to a lower-wage job or potentially ending up on disability or something else — it's a win-win to have them in the workforce," said Oren Cass, a senior fellow at the Manhattan Institute and former domestic policy director for 2012 Republican presidential nominee Mitt Romney.[87]

Obama's plan to shore up the middle class and enlarge gateways to enter it takes a less ambitious approach than that of Sanders, who calls for spending $1 trillion over five years to rebuild roads, bridges, water systems and other infrastructure. "If we are truly serious about reversing the decline of the middle class, we need a major federal jobs program which puts millions of Americans back to work at decent paying jobs," Sanders said last May.[88]

Sanders is dueling Clinton on whose proposals would best help the middle class. She argues that his recommendations, which include expanding Medicare to cover all Americans, would raise middle-class taxes, which she

French economist Thomas Piketty intensified the debate on the growing income gap with his bestselling book *Capital in the Twenty-First Century*. Using income tax data, he showed that the top 1 percent of Americans had doubled their income over the past 30 years – and that those in the top 0.1 percent had quadrupled theirs.

vows not to do. She defines the middle class as individuals earning less than $200,000 a year and couples earning less than $250,000. "We need to give middle class families a break, not a tax increase," said Jake Sullivan, a senior Clinton adviser.[89]

Clinton's definition of middle class has raised considerable criticism among liberal Democrats. "But under Mrs. Clinton's pledge, some of the well off [are] lumped in for receiving a boost," Bryce Covert, economic policy editor at ThinkProgress, a left-of-center news site, wrote in *The New York Times*.[90]

The Tax Policy Center of the Urban Institute and Brookings Institution confirmed that Clinton's proposal would raise taxes on the top 1 percent of earners. Under Sanders' proposal, all income groups would pay some increases, but most would come from the highest earners, the center said.[91]

On the Republican side, Trump has proposed reducing the number of tax brackets to three and eliminating income taxes on individuals making $25,000 a year or less, or couples making $50,000 or less. He called it a "substantial reduction for the middle-income people." However, the Tax Policy Center concluded that Trump's plan would give the biggest breaks to the highest-income households. And the corporate income tax rate would be cut from 35 percent to 15 percent.[92]

Is the American middle class in permanent decline?

YES
Alan Nasser
*Professor Emeritus of Political Economy,
The Evergreen State College*

Written for *CQ Researcher*, April 2016

Capitalism does not normally produce a middle class. The middle-class myth is based on the "golden age" of 1949 to 1973. During that period, the income of one breadwinner bought many families a house, an automobile, a plethora of durable goods, higher education for the kids, health care and sufficient savings for retirement. This suggests that hard work earned a desirable standard of living as a reward — namely, the wage — for that work. But the wage of the breadwinner has never been sufficient to enable the benefits touted in the single-breadwinner story.

The "American dream" was achieved by initiating a bubble in consumption, encouraging households to augment their buying power by taking on *increasing* debt. In 1946, the ratio of household debt to disposable income stood at 24 percent, by 1950 at 38 percent, by 1955 at 53 percent, by 1960 at 62 percent, and by 1965 at 72 percent. The stagnation of real wages that began in 1974 pressured households to further increase their debt in order to maintain desirable living standards, pushing the ratio of debt to disposable income to 77 percent by 1979. Then the median wage began, in 1974, a long-term decline persisting to this day. By the mid-1980s, the ratio began a dangerous ascent, from 80 percent in 1985 to 88 percent in 1990 to 95 percent in 1995 to more than 100 percent in 2000 and 138 percent in 2007.

Rising debt was necessary not merely to purchase more consumer "toys," but to meet growing housing, health care, education and child-care costs. With soaring health care costs the leading cause of personal bankruptcy, *mounting* debt was necessary for most workers to stay out of poverty. Middle-class status was bought at the expense of *addiction* to debt.

If "middle class" connotes material security based on income from work, absent unsustainable debt addiction, there has never been an American middle class.

The debt bubble was unsustainable, and it climaxed in the debacle of September 2008, when the housing bubble finally burst. Since then, we have witnessed rising and record inequality and the further hollowing out of middle-income jobs. And automation in both manufacturing and services, more than job outsourcing, has resulted in the fastest-growing jobs being temporary, part-time and low-paying. With economists as distinguished as Paul Krugman, Lawrence Summers and Robert Gordon forecasting secular, or chronic and therefore long-term, stagnation "forever" (in Summers' words), it is unlikely that there will even *appear* to be a middle class.

NO
Scott Winship
Fellow, Manhattan Institute

Written for *CQ Researcher*, April 2016

Is the middle class in permanent decline? It's not even temporarily so. Seven years from the darkest days of the Great Recession, the American economy has almost fully rebounded to the considerable health it previously enjoyed. The unemployment rate is below 5 percent, not far from where it was before the recession started. Median hourly wages are back to their historical peak in 2007. Median annual household income also is nearly at its historic high.

Over the long run, hourly pay has risen in line with productivity growth. Median pay among male workers stagnated during the 1980s and early 1990s. But that was a historical adjustment that gradually whittled away the unfair premium that male breadwinners received in earlier decades because married women were discouraged from working. Pay among female workers increased with productivity growth, and since the boom of the 1990s, male and female pay levels both have risen with productivity gains.

Some commentators focus on relatively low labor-force participation rates to argue that the unemployment rate no longer captures the weakness of the labor market. But much of the decline in labor-force participation is due to rising school enrollment and the retirement of baby boomers. And much of the rest of it is voluntary. Fewer than 40 percent of men aged 25 to 54 who are out of the labor force tell government surveyors they want a job, and the rise between 1979 and 2006 in the number of these men who are not interested in work statistically accounts for the entire drop in labor-force participation over that period.

Claims that the middle class has shrunk use a threshold for the middle that rises as the country grows richer. They also conceal the fact that most of the "shrinking" is due to an increase in the share of Americans with enough money that they are better off than the "middle class" as it is defined in these analyses. The Congressional Budget Office, Congress' nonpartisan budget analysts, and other sources show the middle fifth of American households richer by one-third compared with 1979 — by $15,000, according to the CBO.

Finally, economic mobility rates have held steady even as inequality has risen and family disruption increased. While the income growth rates of the mid-20th century have not returned, the American middle class is far richer than its counterpart from that era, and tomorrow's will be richer than today's.

Cruz proposed a 10 percent flat tax on income, plus a consumption tax. That would give high-income taxpayers a 29.6 percent tax cut, according to the Tax Policy Center, and a 3.2 percent cut for middle-income households.[93]

For all the attention politicians are devoting to taxes, a bipartisan team of analysts from Brookings has concluded that raising taxes on the wealthy would produce "exceedingly modest" results in reducing income disparities overall.[94]

A less complicated idea is to raise the minimum wage to $15 an hour — more than double the current federal minimum of $7.25 an hour. In early June, Democratic Gov. Jerry Brown of California signed into law the first statewide $15-an-hour minimum, and Gov. Andrew Cuomo of New York, also a Democrat, enacted a $15-an-hour minimum for the New York City metropolitan area and a $12.50 minimum for the rest of the state, where the cost of living is lower.[95]

Both new minimum wages will be phased in, reaching the top level by 2022 in California, and by 2018 in New York City, with the lower wage required elsewhere in the state by 2021.[96]

Before California and New York acted, at least 14 cities and counties had already adopted the $15 minimum.[97] Many experts are unsure how the higher minimum wages will affect other wages. "It's very unclear how that's going to stack up," said Ben Zipperer, an economist at the Washington Center for Equitable Growth, a research and grantmaking organization.[98]

Some advocates argue that raising the minimum to $15 would push other wages further up, expanding the middle class. "A policy that can shore up the middle class will also reduce income inequality and serve as a foundation for job creation," wrote Oren M. Levin-Waldman, a professor of public policy at the Metropolitan College of New York.[99]

Others, like Charles Fay of Rutgers University's School of Management and Labor Relations, say employers instead will just give smaller wage increases across the board. "There's a decreasing increase so that you can maintain equity across the different wage levels," he said.[100]

OUTLOOK
Slower Growth

In a much-discussed new book, economist Gordon of Northwestern University argues that whatever the fate of the middle class, it will not be vastly expanded by a new era of massive economic growth like that triggered by life-transforming innovations in the 1870-1970 era.

Revolutionary changes, such as universal electricity, water and sewer service, paved highways and air travel, are unlikely to be equaled in the foreseeable future, he contends.[101]

"I am not predicting zero growth" in the economy, Gordon says. Citing recent advances in oil and gas drilling and other technological developments, he says, "I'm not saying we are not going to invent anything; there is plenty of room for fracking, 3-D printing, autonomous cars. But each of these innovations is evolutionary rather than revolutionary."

Nasser of Evergreen State College agrees with Gordon. "U.S. long-term growth has always been associated with things like the steam engine, railroads, electricity, automobiles, suburbanization, which transformed the country's whole way of life," says Nasser, author of the forthcoming book *United States of Emergency: American Capitalism and its Crises.* "The more you think about it, the more intuitively improbable it is that any economic system could generate large-scale transformations of that kind ad infinitum."

As for the middle class, Gordon says it will likely be smaller, barring a change in how the fruits of slow growth are distributed. "With the rise of inequality, . . . already slow growth in the income available is being siphoned off into the top 1 percent, leaving less for everyone else to share."

Hacker of Yale says political changes could lay the groundwork for greater economic growth and for ensuring that the middle class shares in whatever growth occurs. For now, "We are not making the kinds of investments we would need to make in order to have growth like we used to have. Are we putting the kind of money we need to in infrastructure, early-childhood education, research and development?" he asks rhetorically.

And as automation requires fewer workers to produce more goods and services, Nasser says, private business won't be motivated to maintain high employment. The solution, he says, is "direct government employment" in activities such as infrastructure reconstruction and repair. The alternative, he says, is "long-term imposed austerity, with an increase in social disorder, burglaries, robberies, psychological depression [and] disillusion with government."

But Winship of the Manhattan Institute argues that technological innovation promises significantly more growth than Gordon forecasts, while acknowledging that there will be less need for labor. "I see a future where things are going to get quite a bit cheaper," he says. "People won't have to work as long for the same standard of living."

However, he adds, "We do need to be concerned about people at the bottom who have few marketable skills." But that is not to say that there are no possibilities. Workers must "look ahead and think imaginatively about jobs that will be created in the future for even people with relatively few skills."

Journalist James Fallows, who spent three years visiting small cities in overlooked parts of America, writes that many small towns are undergoing "a process of revival and reinvention that has largely if understandably been overlooked in the political and media concentration on the strains of this Second Gilded Age."[102]

He found that many places considered backward and isolated are producing more innovation than the big coastal cities thought to attract talented and innovative young people.[103]

But whatever the future of fly-over country innovation, and regardless of whether Gordon is correct about a lower-growth future, says Kenworthy of the University of California, "we have had pretty decent economic growth since the late 1970s."

If that growth had been evenly distributed, "we would have good income gains for the middle class, so much so that I don't think we'd be having this conversation."

NOTES

1. Quoted in Patrick Healy and Amy Chozick, "Hillary Clinton Wins 4 Races, Rebounding From Michigan Loss," *The New York Times,* March 15, 2016, http://tinyurl.com/j3sn9te.
2. "The American Middle Class Is Losing Ground," Pew Research Center, Dec. 9, 2015, p. 13, http://tinyurl.com/j8lxmzl.
3. *Ibid.,* pp. 4-5.
4. Chad Stone *et al.,* "A Guide to Statistics on Historical Trends in Income Inequality," Center on Budget and Policy Priorities, updated Oct. 26, 2015, http://tinyurl.com/j6pqdue.
5. "The American Middle Class Is Losing Ground," *op. cit.,* p. 6.
6. "Annual Earnings of Young Adults," National Center for Education Statistics, U.S. Department of Education, updated May 2015, http://tinyurl.com/nc8vrf6.
7. Anna Brown, "What Americans Say It Takes to Be Middle Class," Pew Research Center, Feb. 4, 2016, http://tinyurl.com/hszvehw.
8. Alyssa Davis, Will Kimball and Elise Gould, "The Class of 2015: Despite an Improving Economy, Young Grads Still Face an Uphill Climb," Economic Policy Institute, May 27, 2015, pp. 21-22, http://tinyurl.com/hg9wrl3; John Wagner, "Why Millennials Love Bernie Sanders, and Why That May Not Be Enough," *The Washington Post,* Oct. 27, 2015, http://tinyurl.com/jrbu8m8.
9. Quoted in "Democratic town hall: Transcript, video," CNN, Feb. 4, 2016, http://tinyurl.com/hl6qekl; Aaron Blake, "74-year-old Bernie Sanders's Remarkable Dominance Among Young Voters, in 1 Chart," *The Washington Post,* March 17, 2016, http://tinyurl.com/hy8vt43; Wagner, *op. cit.;* John Cassidy, "What Bernie Sanders Has Achieved," *The New Yorker,* March 17, 2016, http://tinyurl.com/jygf2bd.
10. For background, see "U.S. Trade Policy," *CQ Researcher,* Sept. 13, 2013, pp. 765-788.
11. Dan Merica and Eric Bradner, "Hillary Clinton Comes Out Against TPP Trade Deal," CNN, Oct. 7, 2015, http://tinyurl.com/jpj3u5o; Joseph Lawler, "Cruz Pits Wall Street Against Middle Class in New Ad," *Washington Examiner,* March 25, 2016, http://tinyurl.com/zyfbwnp.
12. "The American Middle Class Is Losing Ground," *op. cit.*
13. *Ibid.,* p. 6.
14. *Ibid.,* p. 5.
15. Frank Newport, "Fewer Americans Identify as Middle Class in Recent Years," Gallup, April 28, 2015, http://tinyurl.com/j69rzsz.
16. Noah Smith, "Decline of the U.S. Middle Class," Bloomberg, March 28, 2016, http://tinyurl.com/

zmcxvtd. "Class (subjective class identification), General Social Survey, NORC at University of Chicago, 2014; "Class Identification," GSS Data Explorer, http://tinyurl.com/zt7on2m.

17. "The Distribution of Household Income and Federal Taxes, 2011," Congressional Budget Office, November 2014, pp. 6-7, http://tinyurl.com/zxxkc74. Scott Winship, "Sorry EPI, The Rich Did Not Steal $18,000 from the Middle-Class," The Manhattan Institute, http://tinyurl.com/h4zzfrq.

18. Lawrence Mishel, Elise Gould and Josh Bivens, "Wage Stagnation in Nine Charts," Economic Policy Institute, Jan. 6, 2015, p. 6, http://tinyurl.com/zvtrngt.

19. "Life Expectancy at Birth, at Age 65, at Age 75, by Sex, Race and Hispanic Origin: United States, Selected Years 1900-2013," U.S. Centers for Disease Control and Prevention, updated May 6, 2015, http://tinyurl.com/zlomsln.

20. "Table P-16. Educational Attainment-People 25 Years Old and Over by Median Income and Sex: 1991 to 2014," U.S. Census Bureau, http://tinyurl.com/87hwyqn.

21. David H. Autor, "Why Are There Still So Many Jobs? The History and Future of Workplace Automation," Journal of Economic Perspectives, Summer 2015, p. 14, http://tinyurl.com/zw6hboh.

22. "Unemployment rate," U.S. Bureau of Labor Statistics, March 12, 2016, http://tinyurl.com/3gss8qd; Patricia Cohen, "Robust Hiring in December Caps Solid Year for U.S. Jobs," The New York Times, Jan. 8, 2016, http://tinyurl.com/h757xna.

23. Alemayehu Bishaw, "Poverty: 2000 to 2012," U.S. Census Bureau, September 2013, p. 5, http://tinyurl.com/k9hzfer; "Income and Poverty in the United States: 2014," U.S. Census Bureau, September 2015, pp. 12, 13, http://tinyurl.com/oskydlu.

24. "Remarks by the President in Conversation on Poverty at Georgetown University," The White House, May 12, 2015, http://tinyurl.com/juhj7zf; James Pethokoukis, "Yuval Levin on Means Testing Medicare and Social Security," American Enterprise Institute, Feb. 20, 2013, http://tinyurl.com/h25fn7o; Dean Baker and Hye Jin Rho, "The Potential Savings to Social Security from Means Testing," Center for Economic and Policy Research, March 2011, pp. 1-2, 13, http://tinyurl.com/h3wjryq.

25. Jesse McKinley and Vivian Yee, "New York Budget Deal With Higher Minimum Wage Is Reached," The New York Times, March 31, 2016, http://tinyurl.com/hfs9op7.

26. Quoted in Sarah Mimms, "Chuck Schumer: Passing Obamacare in 2010 Was a Mistake," The Atlantic, Nov. 25, 2014, http://tinyurl.com/j3p97o6.

27. Alisha Coleman-Jensen et al., "Household Food Security in the United States in 2014," U.S. Department of Agriculture, September 2015, p. 8, http://tinyurl.com/o3fpopl.

28. For background, see "Welfare Reform," CQ Researcher, Aug. 3, 2001, pp. 601-632.

29. Ray Boshara, William R. Emmons and Bryan J. Noeth, "The Demographics of Wealth: How Age, Education and Race Separate Thrives from Strugglers in Today's Economy," Federal Reserve Bank of St. Louis, May 2015, p. 10, http://tinyurl.com/jx5qbs4.

30. Tim J. Bartik, "What the Available Evidence Shows About Middle-Class Benefits of Early Childhood Education," Investing in Kids (blog), Feb. 4, 2014, http://tinyurl.com/zdmphjb.

31. Kevin Huffman, "Democrats Love Universal Pre-K — and Don't Seem to Care That It May Not Work," The Washington Post, Feb. 4, 2016, http://tinyurl.com/h92ccfq; Cory Turner, "The Tennessee Pre-K Debate: Spinach Vs. Easter Grass," NPR, Sept. 29, 2015, http://tinyurl.com/ospvl7y

32. "Education and Lifetime Earnings," Office of Retirement Policy, Social Security Administration, November 2015, http://tinyurl.com/j89gymz.

33. "Earnings and Unemployment Rates by Educational Attainment," U.S. Bureau of Labor Statistics, updated March 15, 2016, http://tinyurl.com/ybn8p8p.

34. Tyler Cowen, Average Is Over: Powering America Beyond the Age of the Great Stagnation (2013), p. 4.

35. *Ibid.*, pp. 3, 21-22.

36. Carl Benedikt Frey and Michael A. Osborne, "The Future of Employment: How Susceptible Are Jobs to Computerisation?" University of Oxford, Sept. 17, 2013, http://tinyurl.com/oj67kae.

37. For background, see David Hosansky, "Community Colleges," *CQ Researcher,* May 1, 2015, pp. 385-408.

38. "Graduation Rate From First Institution Attended for First-Time, Full-Time Bachelor's Degree-Seeking Students at 4-Year Postsecondary Institutions," National Center for Education Statistics, undated, http://tinyurl.com/p58rtjk.

39. "Cumulative Debt of Bachelor's Degree Recipients by Sector Over Time," Trends in Higher Education, College Board, undated, http://tinyurl.com/h3cye3b; "Cumulative Debt for Undergraduate and Graduate Studies Over Time," Trends in Higher Education, College Board, undated, http://tinyurl.com/hujcet4.

40. Quoted in Stuart M. Blumin, *The Emergence of the Middle Class: Social Experience in the American City, 1760-1900* (1989), p. 1.

41. C. Wright Mills, *White Collar: The American Middle Classes* (1951, 2002), p. 6.

42. Robert J. Gordon, *The Rise and Fall of American Growth: The U.S Standard of Living since the Civil War* (2016), Kindle ed.

43. Emmanuel Saez, "Striking it Richer: The Evolution of Top Incomes in the United States," University of California, Berkeley, Sept. 3, 2013, figure 1, http://tinyurl.com/o3vrnwt; Paul Krugman, "Why We're in a New Gilded Age," *New York Review of Books,* May 8, 2014, http://tinyurl.com/zecxnm4.

44. "Progressive Movement," American Political History, Eagleton Institute of Politics, Rutgers University, undated, http://tinyurl.com/nuvbytj; Jacob S. Hacker and Paul Pierson, *Winner-Take-All Politics: How Washington Made the Rich Richer and Turned Its Back on the Middle Class* (2010), pp. 83-87; "Sherman Act," Theodore Roosevelt Center, Dickinson State University, undated, http://tinyurl.com/huyrkcz.

45. *Ibid.*; Gordon, *op. cit.,* Kindle edition.

46. Earl Wysong, Robert Perrucci, David Wright, *The New Class Society: Goodbye American Dream?* (2014), p. 14.

47. Irving Bernstein, "Americans in Depression and War," U.S. Department of Labor, undated, http://tinyurl.com/h2nvt2l.

48. *Ibid.*; John E. Hansan, "The Works Progress Administration," Social Welfare History Project, undated, http://tinyurl.com/zp5mf4c; for background, see Peter Katel, "Racial Conflict," *CQ Researcher,* Jan. 8, 2016, pp. 25-48.

49. Glenn C. Altschuler and Stuart M. Blumin, *The GI Bill: A New Deal for Veterans* (2009), pp. x; 132-134.

50. Gordon, *op. cit.,* Kindle edition.

51. Altschuler and Blumin, *op. cit.,* pp. 152-170.

52. Ira Katznelson, *When Affirmative Action Was White: An Untold History of Racial Inequality in Twentieth-Century America* (2005), p. 11.

53. Wysong *et al., op. cit.,* pp. 15-16; "The Postwar Economy: 1945-1960," United States History, Country Studies, Library of Congress, undated, http://tinyurl.com/h628sam.

54. *Ibid.*, Kindle edition.

55. Gordon, *op. cit.,* Kindle edition.

56. David L. Mason, *From Buildings and Loans to Bail-Outs: A History of the American Savings and Loan Industry, 1831-1995* (2004), p. 145.

57. David Weil, *The Fissured Workplace: Why Work Became So Bad for Many and What Can Be Done to Improve It* (2014), Kindle edition.

58. Mills, *op. cit.,* Kindle edition.

59. Wysong *et al.,* p. 22.

60. Lee E. Ohanian, "Competition and the Decline of the Rust Belt," Federal Reserve Bank of Minneapolis, Dec. 20, 2014, http://tinyurl.com/z85z8oc.

61. Cherlin, Love's Labor Lost, *op. cit.,* p. 122.

62. Ben Geier, "What Did We Learn From the Dotcom Bubble of 2000?" *Time Magazine,* March 12, 2015, http://tinyurl.com/grw7344.

63. David S. Langdon, Terence M. McMenamin and Thomas J. Krolik, "U.S. Labor Market in 2001: Economy Enters a Recession," U.S. Bureau of Labor

Statistics, Monthly Labor Review, February 2002, p. 19, http://tinyurl.com/jygndg5.

64. Jared Bernstein, "The Jobless Recovery," Economic Policy Institute, March 24, 2003, http://tinyurl.com/gnepwfx.

65. Alan S. Blinder, "Offshoring: The Next Industrial Revolution?" *Foreign Affairs*, March/April 2006, http://tinyurl.com/hgw4ccx.

66. For background, see Marcia Clemmitt, "Mortgage Crisis," *CQ Researcher*, Nov. 2, 2007, pp. 913-936.

67. "The Recession of 2007-2009," U.S. Bureau of Labor Statistics, February 2012, http://tinyurl.com/8tuqc8k.

68. See Jim Zarroli, "Fact Check: Did Glass-Steagall Cause the 2008 Financial Crisis?," NPR, Oct. 14, 2015, http://tinyurl.com/hssxrf2.

69. "The Financial Crisis Inquiry Report," National Commission on the Causes of the Financial and Economic Crisis in the United States, January 2011, p. xviii, http://tinyurl.com/44pkjn3.

70. For background, see Thomas J. Billitteri, "Middle-Class Squeeze," *CQ Researcher*, March 6, 2009, pp. 201-224.

71. Nancy Cook, "What the Great Recession Taught Us About Long-Term Unemployment," *The Atlantic,* March 31, 2015, http://tinyurl.com/zjcjatz.

72. Ruth Milkman, Stephanie Luce and Penny Lewis, "Changing the Subject: A Bottom-Up Account of Occupy Wall Street in New York City," Joseph S. Murphy Institute for Worker Education and Labor Studies, City University of New York, 2013, pp. 10-13, 47, http://tinyurl.com/hnjvw3x.

73. For background, see Peter Katel, " 'Occupy' Movement," *CQ Researcher,* Jan. 13, 2012, pp. 25-52; Michael Levitin, "The Triumph of Occupy Wall Street," *The Atlantic,* June 10, 2015, http://tinyurl.com/nohkdr2.

74. Paul Krugman, "Review: 'The Economics of Inequality; by Thomas Piketty," *The New York Times,* Aug. 2, 2015, http://tinyurl.com/qzlm3bc; "The Lost Decade of the Middle Class," Pew Research Center, Aug. 22, 2012, http://tinyurl.com/cqhthqa.

75. Gordon, *op. cit.,* Kindle edition; "Union Members Summary," U.S. Bureau of Labor Statistics, Jan. 28, 2016, http://tinyurl.com/27c4z5; Steven Greenhouse, "Union Membership in U.S. Fell to a 70-Year Low Last Year," *The New York Times,* Jan. 21, 2011, http://tinyurl.com/4kml6ep. For background, see Chuck McCutcheon, "Unions at a Crossroads," *CQ Researcher*, Aug. 7, 2015, pp. 673-696.

76. Peter Eavis, "S.E.C. Approves Rule on C.E.O. Pay Ratio," *The New York Times,* Aug. 5, 2015, http://tinyurl.com/nv4rep5; Dave Michaels, "These U.S. CEOs Make a Lot More Money Than Their Workers," Bloomberg, Aug. 13, 2015, http://tinyurl.com/qapde3u; Lawrence Mishel and Alyssa Davis, "CEO Pay Has Grown 90 Times Faster Than Typical Worker Pay Since 1978," Economic Policy Institute, July 1, 2015, http://tinyurl.com/zr6ura7.

77. Janet Lorin, "Borrowers Fall Further Behind on $1.3 Trillion in Student Loans," Bloomberg, Aug. 13, 2015, http://tinyurl.com/jgr66pq.

78. Michael Greenstone and Adam Looney, "Rising Student Debt Burdens: Factors Behind the Phenomenon," Brookings Institution, July 5, 2013, http://tinyurl.com/h2juov2.

79. Sandy Baum and Martha Johnson, "Student Debt: Who Borrows Most? What Lies Ahead?" Urban Institute, April 2015, pp. 1, 7, http://tinyurl.com/glzkcw6.

80. Laura Meckler and Josh Mitchell, "Hillary Clinton Proposes Debt-Free Tuition at Public Colleges," *The Wall Street Journal,* Aug. 10, 2015, http://tinyurl.com/hfr962h; Jordan Weissman, "Bernie Sanders Wants to Make College Tuition Free. Here's Why We Should Take Him Seriously," *Slate,* May 19, 2015, http://tinyurl.com/qguhtua.

81. Greg Jaffe, "Obama Announces Free Community College Plan," *The Washington Post,* Jan. 9, 2015, http://tinyurl.com/hsaa7xl.

82. *Ibid.,* p. 13.

83. Mark Huelsman, "The Debt Divide: The Racial and Class Bias Behind the 'New Normal' of Student Borrowing," *Demos,* 2015, p. 8, http://tinyurl.com/jmlgf3t.

84. *Ibid.,* p. 2.

85. "Meeting Our Great Challenges: Opportunity for All," White House, http://tinyurl.com/hc6u4ae; "Fiscal Year 2017 Budget Overview," Office of Management and Budget, undated, http://tinyurl.com/hqf9uaz.

86. Jackie Calmes, "Congressional Republicans Balk at Obama's Budget, Sight Unseen," *The New York Times,* Feb. 8, 2016, http://tinyurl.com/zxxx4cj.

87. Quoted in Noam Scheiber, "Obama Budget Seeks to Ease Economic Fears for U.S. Workers," *The New York Times,* Feb. 9, 2016, http://tinyurl.com/hf2jhql.

88. "Bernie's Announcement," Bernie 2016, May 26, 2015, http://tinyurl.com/nmh5qft.

89. Tami Luhby, "Clinton vs. Sanders: The Battle for the Middle Class," CNN, Jan. 14, 2016, http://tinyurl.com/zqegvh3.

90. Bryce Covert, "$250,000 a Year Is Not Middle Class," *The New York Times,* Dec. 28, 2015, http://tinyurl.com/jl84pdb.

91. Frank Sammartino *et al.,* "An Analysis of Senator Bernie Sanders's Tax Proposals," Tax Policy Center, March 4, 2016, http://tinyurl.com/jlrkr5m; Richard Auxier *et al.,* "An Analysis of Hillary Clinton's Tax Proposals," Tax Policy Center, March 3, 2016, http://tinyurl.com/h94yr4f.

92. Quoted in Matthew Boyle, "Donald Trump: Cut Taxes on Middle Class, End Tax Breaks for Billionaires on Wall Street," *Breitbart,* Sept. 27, 2015, http://tinyurl.com/pufqohw; James Nunns *et al.,* "An Analysis of Donald Trump's Tax Plan," Tax Policy Center, Dec. 22, 2015, http://tinyurl.com/jqbrcyl.

93. Joseph Rosenberg *et al.,* "An Analysis of Ted Cruz' Tax Plan," Tax Policy Center, Feb. 16, 2016, http://tinyurl.com/gtgze2u.

94. William G. Gale, Melissa S. Kearney, Peter R. Orszag, "Would a Significant Increase in the Top Income Tax Rate Substantially Alter Income Inequality?" Brookings Institution, September 2015, http://tinyurl.com/nmdkdlp.

95. Edward Krudy, "New York's Cuomo Signs Two-Tier Minimum Wage Law in Push for Statewide $15/ Hour," Reuters, April 4, 2016, http://preview.tinyurl.com/jzx6ug4; John Bacon, "$15 Minimum Wage Coming to New York, Calif.," *USA Today,* April 5, 2016, http://tinyurl.com/ huub28r.

96. *Ibid.*

97. "State Minimum Wages/2016 Minimum Wage by State," National Conference of State Legislatures, updated Jan. 1, 2016, http://tinyurl.com/kxlue7a; "14 Cities & States Approved $15 Minimum Wage in 2015," National Employment Law Project, Dec. 21, 2015, http://tinyurl.com/hpjbbxa.

98. Quoted in Noam Scheiber and Ian Lovett, "$15-an-Hour Minimum Wage in California? Plan Has Some Worried," *The New York Times,* March 28, 2016, http://tinyurl.com/j3z2gtm.

99. Oren M. Levin-Waldman, "How Raising the Minimum Wage Would Boost the Middle Class," *Governing,* Feb. 13, 2014, http://tinyurl.com/ jmb3k99.

100. Lydia DePillis and Jim Tankersley, "Minimum Wage Increases Haven't Grown the Middle Class. $15 might be different," *The Washington Post,* Aug. 12, 2015, http://tinyurl.com/howtdll.

101. Gordon, *The Rise and Fall of American Growth, op. cit.*

102. James Fallows, "How America Is Putting Itself Back Together," *The Atlantic,* March 2016, http:// tinyurl.com/h8gykmy.

103. *Ibid.*

BIBLIOGRAPHY
Selected Sources
Books

Cowen, Tyler, *Average Is Over: Powering America Beyond the Age of the Great Stagnation*, Dutton, 2013.
A George Mason University economist argues that because of technological changes, highly educated and imaginative individuals are becoming more valuable in the job market, but those considered ordinary are less in demand.

Gordon, Robert J., *The Rise and Fall of American Growth: The U.S. Standard of Living Since the Civil War*, Princeton University Press, 2016.
In a much-discussed study, a Northwestern University economist contends that the age of inventions that transformed daily life is over for the foreseeable future.

Hacker, Jacob, and Paul Pierson, *Winner-Take-All Politics: How Washington Made the Rich Richer — And Turned Its Back on the Middle Class*, Simon & Schuster, 2010.
Political scientists from Yale (Hacker) the University of California, Berkeley (Pierson) effectively predicted the current furor over inequality and the problems facing the middle class.

Lacy, Karyn, *Blue-Chip Black: Race, Class and Status in the New Black Middle Class*, University of California Press, 2007.
The African-American middle class — often portrayed as a single bloc — actually is divided by occupation, lifestyle and goals, much like the American middle class in general, a University of Michigan sociologist writes after conducting research in suburban Washington, D.C.

Porter, Katherine, ed., *Broke: How Debt Bankrupts the Middle Class*, Stanford University Press, 2012.
A collection of studies presents a picture of middle-class families whose finances are threatened by necessities such as higher education and medical expenses.

Articles

Balz, Dan, "Charting Donald Trump's Rise Through the Decline of the Middle Class," *The Washington Post*, Dec. 12, 2015, http://tinyurl.com/jq2km8c.
A political reporter uses a Pew Research Center report on the decline of the middle class to explain the current Republican presidential frontrunner's appeal.

Ellison, Charles D., "Are We Talking Enough About the Black Middle Class?" *Pacific Standard*, April 13, 2015, http://tinyurl.com/zu4n85l.
An African-American political analyst argues that viewing the entire black population as poor fosters biased policies that keep the black middle class from expanding.

Fletcher, Michael A., "Is the American Middle Class Doing Better Than We Think?" *The Washington Post*, Dec. 18, 2014, http://tinyurl.com/j6xc7bm.
An economics writer reports on researchers dissenting from conventional wisdom on the condition of the middle class.

Popper, Nathaniel, "The Robots Are Coming for Wall Street," *The New York Times Magazine*, Feb. 25, 2016, http://tinyurl.com/h35d429.
The success of new analytical software on Wall Street may spell the end of many high-paying jobs there, a financial journalist reports.

Scheiber, Noam, "Growth in the 'Gig Economy' Fuels Work Force Anxieties," *The New York Times*, July 12, 2015, http://tinyurl.com/nblwpuj.
A labor reporter describes the effects of companies' growing use of freelance contractors.

Searcy, Dionne, and Robert Gebeloff, "Middle Class Shrinks Further as More Fall Out Instead of Climbing Up," *The New York Times*, Jan. 25, 2016, http://tinyurl.com/mubr5at.
Journalists report that President Obama's most recent proposed budget attempts to extend a hand to middle-income households.

Reports and Studies

"The American Middle Class Is Losing Ground," Pew Research Center, Dec. 9, 2015, http://tinyurl.com/j8lxmzl.
A nonpartisan think tank finds that middle-income Americans are no longer in the majority and the middle class is losing ground financially.

Carnevale, Anthony P., Tamara Jayasundera and Artem Gulish, "Six Million Missing Jobs: The Lingering Pain of the Great Recession," Center on Education and the Workforce, Georgetown University, December 2015, http://tinyurl.com/zhvd5ts.
Researchers conclude that, despite overall economic recovery, the recession of 2007-2009 continues to affect millions of households.

Mishel, Lawrence, Elise Gould and Josh Bivens, "Wage Stagnation in Nine Charts," Economic Policy Institute, Jan. 6, 2015, http://tinyurl.com/zvtrngt.
Researchers at a liberal think tank present data showing that most Americans are not advancing under current economic conditions.

Rose, Stephen, "Beyond the Wage Stagnation Story," Urban Institute, August 2015, http://tinyurl.com/jbxg84j.
A labor economist shows that middle-income wages have increased, though at a lesser rate than for the wealthy.

For More Information

Brookings Institution, 1775 Massachusetts Ave., N.W., Washington, DC 20036; 202-797-6000; www.brookings .edu. Centrist think tank researching income disparities.

Center on Education and the Workforce, Georgetown University, 3300 Whitehaven St., N.W., Suite 3200, Washington, DC 20007; https://cew.georgetown.edu/. Conducts research on the relationship between academic training and career planning.

Manhattan Institute for Policy Research, 52 Vanderbilt Ave., New York, NY 10017; 212-599-7000; www.manhattaninstitute.org. Conservative research organization that questions whether the middle class is endangered.

Pew Research Center, 1615 L St., N.W., Washington, DC 20036, 202-419-4300; www.pewresearch.org. Nonpartisan public opinion survey and data-analysis organization studying issues involving the middle class.

Urban Institute, 2100 M St., N.W., Washington, DC 20037; 202-833-7200; www.urban.org. Nonpartisan think tank researching income disparity.

U.S. Bureau of Labor Statistics, 2 Massachusetts Ave., N.E., Washington, DC 20212; 202-691-5200; www.bls.gov. Publishes statistics on earnings.

5

Gentrification

Alan Greenblatt

Young diners reflect the changing face of Cincinnati's blossoming Over-the-Rhine neighborhood. Once crime-ridden and decaying, the historic neighborhood has undergone a resurgence in recent years, thanks in part to $500 million in public and private investment. Advocates for low-income people say gentrification contributes to income inequality, but others say it is a positive force because it occurs only after real estate has hit rock bottom.

From *CQ Researcher*, February 20, 2015

Caption credit (vertical): Getty Images/*The Washington Post*/Jahi Chikwendiu

When Ivan McCuistion began studying at the University of Cincinnati five years ago, he liked to explore the city's diverse neighborhoods in his spare time. But he never considered a foray into Over-the-Rhine, a down-at-the-heels historic neighborhood with grand 19th-century Italianate architecture. The scene of urban riots a decade earlier, it was still considered among the country's most dangerous areas.

"Different people would tell us different things, like don't even go there after dark," he says.

By the time he graduated last year, Over-the-Rhine had become one of his main hangouts. Some $500 million in public and private investment has reshaped the neighborhood, bringing in new condos and offices, craft breweries and restaurants where evening wait times can stretch to two hours.[1]

"I love the density and the close buildings and the variety of people you see here," McCuistion says on his way to meet friends for brunch.

The transformation of Over-the-Rhine is a striking but not unusual gentrification success story.* Around the country, neighborhoods once struggling or tagged as derelict have become prime real estate for young professionals and empty nesters, older couples

---

*Gentrification can mean a variety of things. Generally it refers to the population and infrastructure of a neighborhood changing character, when poorer people give way to people with greater means. The term often has racial undertones, with whites replacing people of color.

whose children are grown up and not living at home. Meanwhile, the business mix in many downtowns has gone far beyond the traditional law and financial firms, attracting a broad range of companies eager to move back in from the suburbs.

Demographics are partly driving the downtown population boom. The United States has a population bulge of young adults (18- to 35-year-olds) who may have grown up in suburbs but prefer living in denser areas. They are being joined in many cities by "empty nesters," older couples whose children are grown up and who are helping to fill condos and apartments in and around downtown areas. Those two groups have contributed to double-digit population growth in many urban cores since 2000. At the same time, people who are in their prime child-rearing years are still opting more often for suburban life.

All of this means center cities, after decades of decline and depopulation, are healthier than they've been for years. Not too long ago, urban planners worried about the "doughnut hole" left empty when prosperous suburbs surrounded a decaying city. But now, it's often the older, close-in suburbs, known as inner-ring suburbs, that are struggling.

Plenty of longstanding inner-city residents are being pushed out by rising rents and property costs, and sometimes by developers who convert apartment buildings to upscale condos. Average rents in San Francisco shot up 13.5 percent last year, and 5 percent in Boston and about 6 percent in Miami.[2] Officials are just beginning to grapple with problems of income inequality within city limits and the tensions arising between neighboring jurisdictions as populations shift.

Meanwhile, although most people and jobs remain in the suburbs, poverty has become more prevalent in suburban America even as major cities are once again thriving. In fact, cities are growing faster than their suburbs for the first time since the 1920s. "People in the suburbs escaped the city to flee the problems [of the urban core]. But that's changing," said Cincinnati Mayor John Cranley. "You're going to see cities in a better financial situation than a lot of the suburbs."[3]

Cities where industry once flourished, such as Cincinnati, Cleveland and Pittsburgh, had been losing population since the 1950s, but are now drawing tech companies and other modern businesses along with the young workers with advanced degrees they employ. Cities where the economy is thriving, such as Seattle, Los Angeles, Austin, Texas, and Denver, have become even more trendy and crowded.

Major companies are making big investments in urban cores, and workers are following them. Dan Gilman, a Pittsburgh City Council member, represents the Oakland section of town, where tech companies from Google and Apple on down have expanded operations. He says property values are climbing so fast — up 23 percent over the past year, according to the online real estate site Zillow — that he can't afford to buy a home in his own district. "I love my landlords," he said jokingly at a recent fundraiser.[4]

While professionals like Gilman may be feeling pinched, many low-income and blue-collar workers complain they are being priced out of their hometowns entirely.

And, for those who can remain, life is becoming increasingly segregated economically. "Poor people are being concentrated in places with less resources," says Jennifer Ritter, a community organizer who works on housing issues in Chicago. "It's the stratification of the city."

The idea that there are "two Chicagos" — one benefiting the rich and the other where the poor and even the middle class are struggling — has been the major complaint against Mayor Rahm Emanuel leading up to his Feb. 24 reelection bid. Similar "tale of two cities" debates are occurring in places such as Detroit New York and Philadelphia, where less-affluent residents wonder whether elected leaders can slow the growing levels of income inequality within city limits.

Some economists argue that the notion of upscale urban villages, filled with dog walkers and e-cigarette lounges, displacing low-income residents has been greatly exaggerated. For one thing, many neighborhoods described as gentrified — such as Over-the-Rhine — had been largely abandoned. Many developers are building downtown condos in vacated or underused industrial sites. Due to earlier population loss in Over-the-Rhine, the rehabbing has avoided the usual arguments about gentrification: There was almost no one to drive out. "We were able to do this because everything was boarded up, and hardly anyone was living there," says City Councilman Chris Seelbach, who lives in the neighborhood.

Maryland-based development consultant Peter Katz, founding director of the Congress for the New Urbanism, a Chicago group that promotes mixed-use development, and others say that the poor suffer less from gentrification than from lack of investment in their neighborhoods — investment such as property development or even upkeep of streets and other infrastructure. That situation had prevailed in many urban neighborhoods until recently. "I've been around long enough to remember when having the middle-class fleeing the cities was the problem," says Howard Husock, vice president for policy research at the Manhattan Institute, a conservative think tank.

Some observers believe media coverage of big cities such as New York, Los Angeles, San Francisco and Washington has created the impression that gentrification's effects are universally negative. Prices might be going up in parts of Pittsburgh and Philadelphia, but plenty of affordable housing remains available outside the trendiest neighborhoods. "If you're in Syracuse, Buffalo or even Richmond, Va., you don't really have aggressive displacement," says Ned Hill, dean of the college of urban affairs at Cleveland State University.

But even if the greatest gentrification challenges are taking place in only a handful of places, those cities account for a significant share of the U.S. economy and population. "Even if one were to say that only the greater metro areas of New York, Boston, D.C., San Francisco, Los Angeles, Portland, Chicago and Seattle are transforming, you are still talking about a combined megalopolis where around 20 percent of the [U.S.] population lives," says Suleiman Osman, an urban history scholar at George Washington University in Washington, D.C.

Rent Exceeds 40 Percent of Income in Five Cities

Renters in Los Angeles on average paid nearly half of their monthly income for housing in 2014, the highest proportion of any big city.

Cities Where Rent Consumed the Highest Percentage of Monthly Income*

Metro Area	% of Monthly Income Spent on Rent
Los Angeles, CA	47.9%
San Francisco, CA	45.9%
Miami, FL	44.5%
San Diego, CA	42.5%
New York, NY	40.5%
San Jose, CA	37.9%
Riverside, CA	36.4%
Boston, MA	34.1%
Denver, CO	32.9%
Tampa, FL	32.4%

* Based on average rents in the third quarter of 2014

Source: Press release, "New Zillow Report: Buying Twice as Affordable as Renting," Zillow/PRNewswire, Dec. 9, 2014, http://tinyurl.com/nx7f3hl.

Osman notes that gentrification and the trend toward center-city living have survived two major housing slumps, in the early 1990s and the mid-2000s, reflecting white-collar professionals' preference for downtown living. But the affluent haven't always chosen to live in the heart of cities. Some civic leaders are worried that although the combination of condos, restaurants and nightlife in dense neighborhoods has proven successful, it may not be sustainable.

Sustainability is tied to cities' need for demographic variety. That means cities need to capture more than members of the professional class at certain stages of their development. "Every mayor in America knows that to survive they need middle-class families, and if they're going to retain families they have to restore faith in the city schools," says Steven Conn, an urban historian at Ohio State University. "If they think it's impossible to send their kids to schools in the city, and they leave the city in large numbers, we may see a slump in those neighborhoods that are full of coffee shops and locally sourced foods."

As cities wrestle with ongoing demographic and population shifts, here are some of the questions people are debating:

Does gentrification displace the poor?

Vanny Arias, a lifelong resident of the Highland Park section of Los Angeles, is living in crowded quarters. After her mother was evicted from a house that was refurbished and sold, she moved into the one-bedroom apartment Arias already was sharing with her three children. Now Arias is worried that rents are rising so fast that they'll all be forced out.[5]

Portland, Ore., Is Most Gentrified City

Nearly 60 percent of low-income neighborhoods in Portland, Ore., saw home values and education levels soar between 2000 and 2013, a higher rate than in any other major U.S. city, according to *Governing* magazine. Washington D.C., Minneapolis and Seattle also experienced high gentrification rates.

Most Gentrified U.S. Cities, 2000-2013*

Metro area	Percentage of Low-Income Neighborhoods Gentrified
Portland, Ore.	58.1%
Washington, D.C.	51.9%
Minneapolis	50.6%
Seattle	50.0%
Atlanta	46.2%
Virginia Beach, Va.	46.2%
Denver	42.1%
Austin, Texas	39.7%
Sacramento, Calif.	30.0%
New York	29.8%

* Based on estimates from the U.S. Census 2009-2013 American Community Survey and 2000 and 2010 surveys

Source: Mike Maciag, "Gentrification in America Report," *Governing*, February 2015, http://tinyurl.com/pmdauf3.

Highland Park, a hilly neighborhood northeast of downtown Los Angeles, is at the center of the city's ongoing debates about gentrification. The area's traditional mix of taco stands and dive bars is making way for designer doughnut shops and fusion-burger joints. In addition to the changing commercial mix, housing prices are rising fast. According to the online real estate site Trulia, the median home price in Highland Park is $515,000 — up 60 percent just since November.

Nearly 30 apartment buildings changed hands in one Highland Park ZIP code last year. Some of the new owners plan to raise rents on existing tenants, but a bigger worry is that other owners plan to empty the buildings and redo them to draw much higher-paying tenants. "There's a handful of buyers who are doing that," Dana Coronado, a local real estate broker, told the *Los Angeles Times*. "They have tons of money, and they're willing to spend the hundreds of thousands of dollars that it takes to redo these buildings."[6]

The changes in Highland Park and other areas have sparked several protests against gentrification in recent months, with mock eviction notices pasted on some new businesses.

In Washington, a halfway house that accommodates 40 ex-offenders and has been operating for nearly 60 years is being converted into a nine-unit luxury condo building.[7] In New Orleans, a proposed condo development at the site of a bull-dozed school in the Lower Ninth Ward — badly damaged by Hurricane Katrina a decade ago — has residents worried that the once-impoverished neighborhood will, as one occupant put it, "feel like it belongs to the rich."[8]

As city centers draw more affluent residents, critics charge that they are becoming de facto city-sized gated communities, where low-income and working-class residents are no longer welcome.

In San Francisco's Tenderloin district, one of the poorest neighborhoods in the Bay Area, one-bedroom apartments are renting for $2,500 per month, says James Tracy, a housing activist and the author of *Dispatches Against Displacement,* a 2014 book about housing issues in San Francisco. "It puts up a gigantic wall so that people who are seeking housing just can't get in," he says. "It's an economic and racial wall that's going up around cities like San Francisco."

While housing prices are rising in many cities — and quickly in coastal cities such as Boston and Seattle — some economists and urban planners argue that concerns about displacement are overblown.

Journalist John Buntin wrote recently in *Slate* that there is "very little evidence" that gentrification is displacing the poor. He cited work by economists including Lance Freeman, who teaches urban planning at

Columbia University, and Jacob Vigdor, a public affairs professor at the University of Washington, that indicates residential turnover is no higher in gentrifying neighborhoods than other parts of cities.

"That gentrification displaces poor people of color by well-off white people is a claim so commonplace that most people accept it as a widespread fact of urban life. It's not," Buntin wrote. "Gentrification of this sort is actually exceedingly rare."[9]

Other research indicates that more census tracts have slipped into poverty than have been gentrified. A recent study of the nation's 51 largest metropolitan areas by the Portland, Ore.–based think tank City Observatory found that fewer than 5 percent of the neighborhoods that had high poverty rates in 1970 had climbed above the national average in income level by 2010. In other words, most poor neighborhoods remain poor over time, with very few gentrifying.[10]

Only a few metro areas — Chicago, Memphis, Tenn., New Orleans, New York, and Washington — saw a significant number of neighborhoods shift from poverty to affluence from 1970 to 2010, the study found.

Stories about displaced residents and struggling business owners in transitioning neighborhoods may be catnip to journalists, but they are "isolated vignettes" that don't represent the larger picture, says development consultant Katz.

"When people in transitioning neighborhoods are interviewed, even the poorest, most people say they like the changes in the neighborhoods," he says. "They like the fact that there's less crime and there are fresh vegetables in the store at lower cost."

Todd Swanstrom, a public policy professor at the University of Missouri, St. Louis, agrees that gentrification's effects are sometimes overblown, at least in cities with overall moderate or low home values. "An economic tipping point that pushes out low-income residents — that appears not to be happening in rebound neighborhoods of St. Louis," he says. "There's some displacement around the edges, but even then a household can move maybe eight blocks away and get an affordable apartment."

But Jennifer Ritter, executive director of ONE Northside, a social justice group that works on housing issues in Chicago, says the notion that renters and other low-income residents are not harmed when their neighborhood turns over is "infuriating."

In the neighborhoods where she works, such as Lakeview and Uptown, affordable housing has become scarce to nonexistent, with poor people turned out of their homes as apartment buildings large and small are converted into more-upscale residences.

"Most recently, a hundred-unit building that housed low-income people was emptied out, and in its place is a 60-unit, new, awesome urban dwelling for people with money," Ritter says. "The people being displaced may be going to a shelter in the neighborhood. I know one guy who moved into a storage unit."

While many neighborhoods described as gentrifying were formerly industrial areas, other urban settings once housed many more poor people of color than they do now, says Ali Modarres, director of urban studies at the University of Washington, Tacoma, and editor of *Cities: The International Journal of Urban Policy and Planning.*

"What happens is that over time there's displacement," Modarres says. "The displacement is not overnight, but it happens over time."

Can cities reduce inequality?

Bill de Blasio made income inequality a central theme of his 2013 campaign for New York City mayor and won a resounding victory. Since taking office he has sought to tackle the issue in many ways.

He expanded paid sick leave and living-wage requirements, revamped the city's workforce-development programs, imposed new hiring requirements on city contractors and is seeking to create or preserve 300,000 affordable units over the next decade. "We are confronting inequality in every way we can," he said last year.[11]

With inequality rising in much of metropolitan America, numerous big-city mayors are searching for ways to address the issue. Last year, Seattle enacted the nation's highest minimum wage, requiring that workers earn at least $15 an hour. Chicago anticipated President Obama's recent call for free community college — an idea that has yet to gain traction in Congress — by paying tuition for many of its best high school graduates. Providence, R.I., and Cambridge, Mass., have programs encouraging poor parents to expand their children's vocabularies, building on studies that found children from more affluent homes started out even in infancy with advantages because of their advanced verbal skills.

Getty Images/Kansas City Star/Jill Toyoshiba

Brooklyn's hip DUMBO (Down Under the Manhattan Bridge) neighborhood features old industrial buildings and lofts converted to high-priced residential units. Democratic Mayor Bill de Blasio has made income inequality a central focus of his agenda. In addition to seeking to create or preserve 300,000 affordable housing units over the next decade, he has expanded paid sick leave and living-wage requirements, revamped the city's workforce-development programs and imposed new hiring requirements on city contractors.

"Cities can be fantastic laboratories for social justice," says Tracy, the San Francisco housing activist. "You can raise the minimum wage and, in certain cities, you can talk about universal child care."

Indeed, when the AFL-CIO announced its policy priorities for 2015, labor officials said they would initiate efforts in seven cities to push for higher wages, paid sick leave and other measures intended to address inequality. "It's cities, not states, that have set the highest minimum-wage standards, adopted the most immigrant-friendly policies and passed the most far-reaching environmental protections," commented liberal *Washington Post* columnist Harold Meyerson.[12]

After all, the mayors of most of the largest cities are Democrats — many of them, like de Blasio, quite progressive — while more conservative Republicans hold solid majorities in state legislatures and governorships after last November's elections.

That partisan disconnect highlights some of the limits on mayors looking to address inequality. State legislators in New York approved de Blasio's effort to expand pre-kindergarten education but balked at his desire to tax the wealthy to pay for it. When San Francisco officials pressed legislators in Sacramento to

make evictions more difficult to carry out, they similarly met with defeat.

"We're strong advocates of giving cities more tools, but right now, cities largely are stuck with whatever tax system the state gives them," says Chuck Marohn, president of Strong Towns, a nonprofit group in Minnesota that studies municipal finance issues.

Cities themselves often lack the resources to do much about inequality. One of their biggest efforts — promoting affordable housing — generally relies on other actors, whether it's the federal government subsidizing rent and construction or private developers whom they call upon to set aside a certain percentage of units at below-market rates.

"That's pretty cheap for the city, because the cost is borne by developers, but the number of families helped is very small," says Vigdor of the University of Washington. "If you're going to adopt a policy that would address all the need in the area, you'd run out of money." About 20 percent of the units at some new developments are set aside at below-market rates, but competition to get into them is fierce in expensive cities such as San Francisco and New York.

Ohio State's Conn applauds cities' efforts to address inequality, but he notes that their toolbox is ultimately limited. Struggling industrial cities such as Detroit and Cleveland, he says, could do little in the face of the "tectonic shift" that drove away much of their manufacturing bases from the 1960s through the 1990s. "No individual city has control over that," Conn says. "They can't solve those problems on a large scale."[13]

The question now is whether individual cities today can do much to address the larger economic forces that are helping to make some of them successful but at the same time bastions of inequality. "It's worth noting that the cities with the biggest income inequality problems are the most prosperous in America — San Francisco, Austin, New York," says Husock, the Manhattan Institute vice president.

Several studies have found a link between cities doing well in today's knowledge economy and their rates of inequality.

"Inequality is not just an occasional bug of urban economies," according to Richard Florida, director of the Martin Prosperity Institute at the University of Toronto and a prominent chronicler of cities and the so-called knowledge economy. "It's a fundamental feature of them, an elemental byproduct of the same basic clustering force that underpins metros' rise as centers of innovation, startups and economic growth."[14]

In response to the shifting and increasingly automated economy, policymakers are working on many fronts to modernize job training and improve education. But those are long-term efforts that offer no guarantee of success for all participants. For that reason, some observers believe cities will have to make substantial efforts to redistribute wealth from those who are profiting from the growth in jobs and property values in major cities to those feeling the pinch.

Cities should "tax the benefits" property owners in global hubs are getting from population and economic growth to help pay for housing, transit, parks and other programs and services lower-income citizens rely on, says Rolf Pendall, director of the Metropolitan Housing and Communities Policy Center at the Urban Institute, a think tank in Washington.

Florida argued that cities that are prospering as they become hubs for workers with advanced degrees should adopt policies that help those less able to afford rising rents. "Certainly, the rise of urban tech creates new sources of jobs, money and municipal revenue that cities can use to address mounting inequities through initiatives that raise the minimum wage, upgrade low-wage service jobs and build more affordable housing," Florida wrote.[15]

Critics warn governments that attempts to redistribute wealth, such as by raising taxes on the wealthy, can have serious consequences. Reducing the assets of productive citizens and industries can discourage economic growth, they argue. Cities should be concerned less about inequality — an outgrowth of people being rewarded for their skills — than about creating jobs, Husock says.

Conn, the historian, is also skeptical about whether cities can create more egalitarian economies within their borders. "Cities function best when they are places for

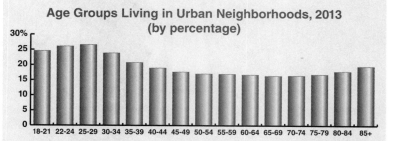

Cities Less Alluring for People Over 30

More than one-fourth of adults in their 20s live in cities, but people in their 30s are more likely to move to the suburbs, typically as they start families. The share of urban dwellers continues to fall as people age but edges up among the elderly.

Age Groups Living in Urban Neighborhoods, 2013 (by percentage)

Source: Data provided by Jed Kolko from Trulia.com; original graphic from Jed Kolko, "Urban Headwinds, Suburban Tailwinds," Trulia Trends, Jan. 22, 2015, http://tinyurl.com/o8fw93r.

economic opportunity," he says. "It's not where you get stuck but when you start going up the ladder. The question is, can cities be made to function at all levels of economic opportunity, and not just for hedge fund managers and Russian oligarchs looking to park their money in Manhattan real estate?"

Can cities retain families?

Craig Vercruysse, a hospital administrator and longtime San Francisco resident, decided to stay in the city when his son was born. Living in the city has been great for his family, he says. "The minute you go to the suburbs, you have less time for your kids because your commute is longer and you have higher transportation costs."

Many parents seem to agree. Urban neighborhoods from Philadelphia to Portland are seeing greater numbers of strollers, while associations devoted to downtown family issues have popped up in Seattle, Minneapolis and other places.

The question is whether families will stay within city limits. Vercruysse says he intends to, and he well might. But his son is only 2 — much younger than the age when many of today's urban parents are heading for the suburbs. That often happens when a child reaches school age, or after parents have a second one. "Once their children reach about 5, about half of them have left," said

Getty Images/Bloomberg/David Paul Morris (both)

Tale of Two Cities

Oakland, Calif. (top), long synonymous with crime and blight, is beginning to lure businesses and residents from San Francisco, its more famous — and pricier — neighbor. The city even has a nascent tech start-up scene. In her inaugural speech, Oakland Mayor Libby Schaaf referred to the private buses, which have become symbols of gentrification, that shuttle employees of tech companies such as Google and Apple from Silicon Valley to their homes in upscale San Francisco neighborhoods. Inviting Google to Oakland, she quipped, "You wouldn't need all those buses if you would just open an office here." Rents are notoriously high in San Francisco, even in the infamous Tenderloin (bottom), one of the city's poorest neighborhoods, where the average rent for a one-bedroom apartment is about $2,500.

Jon Scholes, president of the Downtown Seattle Association, which promotes economic development in the city's core.[16]

Public schools are perceived as offering suboptimal education in nearly every major city in the country. Some parents are optimistic about independently run charter schools, but overall such schools have not outperformed public schools.

"People in their 20s, maybe early 30s, are flooding in, but when they have families, they want a little more space and they start thinking about schools," says Sean Randolph, president of the Bay Area Council Economic Institute, a business-backed research organization in San Francisco. "Private schools are very expensive, and when you add that to the cost of housing, it's going to send a significant number of those people out of the city over time."

Some proponents of urban living are hopeful that public schools can turn around, in the same way that violent crime's big drop over the past 20 years has made cities more attractive. When enrollment grows, schools will gain resources and flexibility to solve problems, says Marohn, the Strong Towns president. Public education "becomes a lot easier to fix once you have a critical mass of people in place who want to see it fixed," Marohn says. "Parents show up, they affect change, and change starts to happen."

Reaching that critical mass, however, can be difficult. Declining enrollment has led cities such as Chicago and Kansas City, Mo., to close schools by the dozens in recent years. Meanwhile, some of the cities that are magnets for young adults in their 20s are simultaneously losing their school-age populations. San Francisco, a boom-town for young professionals, has the lowest percentage of children of any major U.S. city.[17]

In Washington, the number of residents ages 18 to 34 grew significantly between 2000 and 2010 — and perhaps even more since — but over the same period the city lost about 14,000 children under age 18.[18] A recent study found that about half of families that had a baby while living in Washington moved out of the city after five years.[19] In Atlanta, the number of children also declined, representing a loss of nearly 12.5 percent of those under 18; the loss rate was twice that in Atlanta's booming downtown and midtown.[20]

The amenities that draw young professionals and empty nesters to downtown living, such as restaurants and nightlife, aren't priorities for many young families. Singles now make up a majority of households in 46 of the nation's 51 largest metros.[21]

"We are seeing an increase in this millennial population in certain areas, but we don't know if these people will stay in the cities when and if they have families," says Lavea Brachman, executive director of the Greater Ohio Policy Center, a Columbus-based group that promotes sustainable development efforts in metropolitan areas.

The housing preferences of young adults may now be making it harder for families to raise children in the city. Denser housing — including so-called microapartments about the size of hotel rooms — may make sense for unattached young people who want to live downtown, but they won't work for families with kids. Although Seattle is experiencing a construction boom, new apartments with two or three bedrooms are like "unicorns," says Sally Clark, who chairs the City Council's housing committee.

"With the way development patterns are going right now, it's geared to the 20- to 28-year-old who's living alone, and you're not seeing any other kind of development," says Bradley Calvert, who lives in downtown Seattle and runs a website called Family Friendly Cities. Calvert notes that Vancouver and Toronto, both in Canada, require big developments to include minimum percentages of two-and three-bedroom units. Although the Vancouver example is often cited in nearby Seattle, that sort of restriction is not likely to take root in any U.S. city because of the strong value placed on private property rights.

Getty Images/Scott Olson

Redevelopment has transformed the site of Chicago's once-crime-ridden Cabrini-Green public housing complex into a mixed-use development including retail stores like Target and residential units. Affordable-housing advocates say redevelopment contributes to economic segregation in Chicago and other cities. "It's the stratification of the city," says Jennifer Ritter, a community organizer in Chicago. "Poor people are being concentrated in places with less resources." The idea that there are "two Chicagos" – one benefiting the rich and the other where the poor and even the middle class are struggling – has been a major complaint against Democratic Mayor Rahm Emanuel leading up to his Feb. 24 re-election bid.

Seattle voters in recent years have generously funded parks, libraries and schools. The city, which was planning a major waterfront park with no play area for kids, has become more proactive about consulting with parent groups.

Scholes, who notes that Seattle has long required downtown developers to help fund day care centers, says

CHRONOLOGY

1940s–1980s *Downtowns lose business, and cities lose population to the suburbs.*

1948 Downtown's share of retail trade — nearly one-third before the Great Depression — falls to 11 percent.

1949 Housing Act provides federal funds to help cities acquire and clear slum and blighted property for private redevelopment.

1956 Interstate Highway Act leads to a transportation boom that helps shift population to the suburbs.

1965 Congress creates Department of Housing and Urban Development, the first cabinet-level agency devoted to urban problems.

1970 U.S. suburban population is 74 million, double the total in 1950.

1974 Congress approves Community Development Block Grants for city infrastructure improvements.

1975 President Gerald R. Ford refuses federal aid to financially ailing New York City, prompting famous *Daily News* headline, "Ford to City: Drop Dead."

1980 Census shows that 18 of the nation's 25 largest cities in 1950 have suffered a net population loss.

1990s–2000s *Falling crime rates, rising fuel costs and changing tastes help cities begin to rebound from their postwar decline.*

1990 Congress creates the EB-5 visa program, offering green cards to foreigners who spend at least $500,000 on U.S. development projects. . . . Affordable Housing Act offers funding to revitalize public housing.

1991 Driven partly by the crack cocaine epidemic, U.S. homicide rate peaks at 9.8 per 100,000 population, largely affecting urban areas.

1995 President Bill Clinton creates urban-empowerment and enterprise zones in cities, offering federal funds and tax incentives for development and social services.

1997 New York State offers tax abatements to landlords who convert office space into apartments.

2005 An estimated 4.4 million immigrants settle in suburbs, compared with 2.8 million in cities.

2008 Share of people living in cities worldwide surpasses rural population for the first time.

2009 Following foreclosure and financial market collapses, thousands of condos sit vacant in cities. . . . President Obama creates White House Office of Urban Affairs to coordinate federal urban policies.

2010s *Center cities bounce back from the recession; corporations move back to downtowns; housing prices skyrocket in major markets.*

2011 Washington, D.C.'s black population drops below 50 percent for the first time since 1960. . . . San Francisco gives Twitter and its neighbors a payroll tax holiday, helping revitalize the mid-Market Street section of downtown.

2013 Detroit enters into the largest municipal bankruptcy in U.S. history. . . . Running on a platform of addressing income inequality, Democrat Bill De Blasio wins election as mayor of New York. Other big-city mayors are elected on similar themes.

2014 Allocation of 10,000 EB-5 visas for foreigners who invest at least $500,000 in American development projects runs out before the end of fiscal year, with Chinese nationals snapping up 85 percent. . . . National housing prices rise 4.5 percent from 2013 levels in third quarter but remain 6.2 percent below their 2007 peak. . . . First $100 million apartment is sold in New York City.

2015 Supreme Court hears arguments in a case regarding the Fair Housing Act that could determine whether legal challenges can be brought against practices that may promote segregation without proof of intentional discrimination. . . . San Francisco voters will decide whether to approve $250 million in bonds for new construction of affordable housing (Nov. 3).

the same model can be used to support elementary schools. To help meet demand from a growing school population, Seattle's school district decided recently to enter the bidding for a former Federal Reserve building downtown. Seattle has had no downtown elementary school in recent years.

Seattle Mayor Ed Murray, who has formed a high-profile housing task force, says his city must figure out how to attract not just young professionals but all manner of people at all stages of life. "We need three bedrooms — not just microhousing, but affordable housing for families," he says. "If cities like Seattle don't get this right, then what you see as great today is not sustainable."

BACKGROUND
Leaving the City

Long before the Middle Ages, affluent Europeans lived in cities. There was a strict demarcation between city and countryside, and people who lived outside the city walls sometimes had fewer rights than people who lived inside them.

Those fashions transferred across the Atlantic to colonial America. But starting in the 19th century, people began commuting daily to jobs from homes that edged out into the urban periphery. Ferries, railroads and cable cars "gave additional impetus to an exodus that would turn cities 'inside out' and inaugurate a new pattern of suburban affluence and [city] center despair," wrote historian Kenneth T. Jackson.[22]

At first, many of the new localities, such as Philadelphia's Main Line suburbs, catered to the well-to-do, who were eager to get away from the noise and grime of urban factories. With the growth of immigration around the dawn of the 20th century, cities often were crammed with poor immigrants.

Not only the wealthy but also many members of the working class aspired to move out of the center city. The advent of streetcar lines decades before World War II helped make that possible.

After the war, suburbanization exploded. The 1956 Interstate Highway Act led to massive road-building that made it easy to commute longer distances. In addition, federal housing policies, including mortgage subsidies, encouraged people to buy houses, which were cheaper in the suburbs than in cities thanks to lower land prices. By 1954, the editors of *Fortune* estimated that 9 million people had moved to the suburbs over the preceeding decade.[23]

Meanwhile, public housing for the poor became concentrated in urban centers. Federal housing agencies had built their own units in the 1930s, but court battles led to local governments having the authority to choose sites.

African-Americans flooded Northern cities during and after World War II, seeking factory work and an escape from the racially segregated South. With rapid growth — Detroit's population increased by 220,000 between 1940 and 1950 — many were shunted to dilapidated parts of town.[24]

In Chicago, the Hyde Park and Kenwood neighborhoods would not welcome African-Americans "based on behavior, not color. . . . The Negro has shown neither disposition or ability to maintain a decent American community," neighborhood association officials wrote in 1944.[25]

The 1949 Urban Renewal Act allowed local governments to create redevelopment agencies that used eminent domain to seize property in "blighted" areas.[26] Housing authorities in many cities pursued a policy of "slum clearance," displacing poor and African-American populations and concentrating them in huge housing projects located in dilapidated parts of town.

Most suburbs chose not to have any public housing programs at all, which helped to reinforce prevalent patterns of residential segregation. Suburbs such as Levittown in Long Island, New York, were completely white during the 1950s. Various suburbs had restrictive covenants that kept out members of racial and ethnic minorities, a policy of segregation that often was reinforced by lending practices.

"White flight" from cities continued during the 1960s. Laws and court decisions banning segregation led many white families to move to the suburbs — a tendency that only increased when race riots, triggered by the assassination of The Rev. Dr. Martin Luther King Jr., as well as by poverty and discrimination, plagued scores of cities during the 1960s. Between 1960 and 1970, the white population of the 20 largest Northeastern and Midwestern cities fell by 13 percent, and then declined by another 24.3 percent during the 1970s. Meanwhile, the black share of city populations shot up 725 percent from 1960 to 1968.[27]

Global Rich Buying Up U.S. Homes

Absentee owners "using our real estate market as a place to park their money."

Last year, more than 90 homes sold for prices above $2.5 million in Arcadia, a suburb of Los Angeles. Many were then torn down and replaced with far bigger properties.

For most of the buyers, such eye-popping prices were a bargain. Many were millionaires from China, happy to spend about $650 per square foot for a home in Arcadia — as opposed to nearly $2,000 per square foot in Beijing or Shanghai. "If they sell their apartment in Beijing, they can easily buy a house here," said Stone Liu, who edits *China Press,* a newspaper published in nearby Alhambra, Calif.[1]

Arcadia may be earning a reputation as the "Chinese Beverly Hills," but it's far from the only U.S. city attracting investment from Chinese and other foreign buyers. According to the National Association of Realtors, $92 billion worth of U.S. property was sold to foreign buyers in the 12 months ending in March 2014.[2]

The New York Times has found that many foreign buyers, including government officials, have set up shell companies to invest in Manhattan real estate, sometimes laundering money in the process. "About $8 billion is spent each year for New York City residences that cost more than $5 million each, more than triple the amount of a decade ago," *The Times* reported as part of a recent investigatory series. "Just over half of those sales last year were to shell companies."[3]

"We have foreign investments in our real estate markets that we've never seen before," says Tyler McKenzie, president of the Seattle-King County Association of Realtors. "We're seeing cash from China, and they're literally using our real estate market as a place to park their money."

That may be good for the real estate market, but it's making things that much more difficult for people trying to find affordable housing in many of the nation's hottest markets. Units owned by foreign buyers — and sitting empty much of the year — are helping to drive up the cost of occupied housing. "In effect, this means that absentee homeowners can price out people who are actually living in the area," wrote urban policy reporter Emily Badger. "It means that cities may be short on housing that locals can afford, even as a non-trivial share of their housing sits vacant."[4] Longtime residents are sometimes disheartened by the idea that demand for housing in their area may be driven less by regional wages than economic trends in China. "If you want a city that is diverse and a place that is something other than Disneyland for the global wealthy, no, it's not terribly healthy," says Ned Hill, dean of the College of Urban Affairs at Cleveland State University, "but in a market economy, it's hard to counter [such purchase decisions]."

About half the foreign buyers occupy their new homes, while the other half are seeking an investment. "What you're really seeing is a market expression of distrust of the Chinese government and its ability to protect wealth and pass it on to your family," says Hill. "Someone said that China is the place to make money, and the U.S. is the place you go to preserve your money."

One increasingly popular avenue is the EB-5 visa program, which offers green cards to foreign investors who spend at least $500,000 on American development projects. Last year, for the first time, Chinese nationals snapped up 85 percent of the annual allocation of 10,000 visas before the end of the fiscal year. At one development alone, about 1,200 Chinese families have put up roughly $600 million toward construction of three skyscrapers in Manhattan.[5]

Not all immigrants are wealthy, of course. Over the past two decades, immigrants have made up more than a quarter of the growth in U.S. owner-occupied households, most of the growth among households headed by those under 45, according to the Harvard Joint Center for Housing Studies.[6] "Without the foreign born, what we would've experienced would've been a much more negative impact of

In 1968, Congress passed the Fair Housing Act, which sought to deter discrimination in housing. However, federal housing policies at that time continued so-called urban renewal policies that turned out to be counterproductive at addressing urban poverty. Smaller housing units were torn down in favor of massive apartment towers in many cities, which ultimately had the effect of concentrating poverty and crime. Many such

the baby bust" — a drop in U.S. population growth due to lower fertility rates — "on the homeownership trends," said George Masnick, a senior research fellow at the center.[7]

Still, the fact that wealthy foreign nationals are buying up properties in some of the most in-demand markets bothers some public officials. Legislators in San Francisco, New York and elsewhere have proposed various "mansion" or "pied a terre" taxes aimed at raising the tax bill for foreigners and others who have bought valuable space but leave it empty most of the year. Badger suggests such taxes won't dissuade foreign buyers but can be used to subsidize affordable housing. "When places have become weekend homes for oligarchs, you'll find people in favor" of such taxes, says Jacob Vigdor, an economist at the University of Washington.

But Shirley Humphrey, director of a real estate agency in London, said, "For ultra-high-net-worth individuals who can buy anywhere in the world, it's not going to stop them."[8]

However, Vigdor and other observers doubt that the tax proposals will get very far. Americans place a strong value on private-property rights and might not warm to residency requirements.

Even if new taxes did drive some foreign buyers away, it probably would not open up enough housing to relieve demand. "[The housing] might go to slightly less rich people who actually use the units, but the 6,000-square-foot apartment on Central Park West is not going to end up housing a custodian's family," Vigdor says.

— Alan Greenblatt

At 926 feet, luxurious 30 Park Place will be the tallest residential building in downtown Manhattan.

Getty Images/Bloomberg/Victor J. Blue

[1]Christopher Hawthorne, "How Arcadia Is Remaking Itself as a Magnet for Chinese Money," *Los Angeles Times,* Dec. 3, 2014, http://tinyurl.com/kh3ognv.

[2]"Profile of International Home Buying Activity," National Association of Realtors, June 2014, http://tinyurl.com/mfdny7p.

[3]Louise Story and Stephanie Saul, "Stream of Foreign Money Flows to Elite New York Real Estate," *The New York Times,* Feb. 7, 2015, http://tinyurl.com/lqw5d8d.

[4]Emily Badger, "Foreign Investors Are Making Housing More Expensive," *The Washington Post,* May 20, 2014, http://tinyurl.com/ltv6gjs.

[5]Karen Weise, "Why Are Chinese Millionaires Buying Mansions in an L.A. Suburb?" *Bloomberg Businessweek,* Oct. 15, 2014, http://tinyurl.com/

kqfjwrf. Eliot Brown, "Hot Source of Property Financing: Visa Seekers," *The Wall Street Journal,* Dec. 9, 2014, http://www.wsj.com/articles/hot-source-of-real-estate-financing-green-card-seekers-1418146394.

[6]George Masnick, "11+ Million Undocumented Immigrants in the U.S. Could Be Important for the Housing Recovery," Harvard Joint Center for Housing Studies, Jan. 5, 2015, http://tinyurl.com/nc2gujg.

[7]Gillian B. White, "Can Immigrants Save the Housing Market?" *The Atlantic,* Jan. 8, 2015, http://tinyurl.com/kk4f6lg.

[8]Eliot Brown and Art Patnaude, "How a Mansion Tax Could Affect Wealthy Neighborhoods," *The Wall Street Journal,* Dec. 4, 2014, http://tinyurl.com/lfm7vou.

complexes were demolished over the past 20 years, but some tenants lost housing as a result because the total number of units was not always matched by new construction.

The suburbanites' sense that urban life was poor, brutal and out of control continued into the 1980s. Even through the worst of times, however, office workers still shopped downtown, because many jobs remained

Suburban Poverty on the Rise

Property values and tax bases fall steeply in "slumburbia."

For decades, poverty and inner cities often were seen as almost synonymous. But with poverty rates today growing faster in the suburbs, that's no longer the case. More poor people, in fact, now live in suburbs than center cities.

Between 2000 and 2013, the number of people living in the suburbs below the poverty line grew by 66 percent, according to the Brookings Institution, a centrist think tank in Washington — more than double the growth rate of the urban poor.[1]

For the first time, the 2010 census showed that the suburban poor outnumber their city counterparts. "This is where the poor people live now, and this is where they're going to live," said Alan Berube, deputy director of Brookings' Metropolitan Policy Program.[2]

"The old path of white flight to the suburbs is now followed by Asians, Hispanics and, to a greater degree than ever before, blacks," writes William Frey, a demographer associated with Brookings and the University of Michigan. "The black city/white suburb paradigm has almost entirely broken down."[3]

The poor have both been pushed out to the suburbs by urban gentrification and drawn there by cheaper housing, according to Berube and his colleagues. In addition, changes in federal subsidy programs have made housing vouchers more portable, allowing more of the poor to move out of the urban core.

Some suburbs that were once nearly all white have drawn minority and immigrant residents, many but not all of whom are poor. The majority of Americans live in suburbs so, of course, there are all types of suburbs. Prospering communities such as Evanston, Ill., and Bethesda, Md., feature dense housing, transit options and strong job bases. And exurbs on the outer fringe of metropolitan areas that offer big homes are continuing to grow.

But many older, inner-ring suburbs largely built after World War II are aging badly. The small tract homes are too cramped for today's tastes and, after 60 or 70 years of use, entire neighborhoods are showing signs of wear.

"The suburbs that were built after World War II have zoning that separated uses," says Todd Swanstrom, a public policy professor at the University of Missouri-St. Louis. "All the housing is in one place, and all the commerce is in another. They don't have mixed-use, which is where it's at now."

Residents of many suburbs have slipped into poverty as their communities and regions have struggled to bounce back from the recession. "People who are poor in these inner-ring suburbs may find themselves in some ways even more trapped [than the urban poor]," says Steven Conn, an urban historian at Ohio State University. That's because, among other things, suburbs typically offer fewer transit options than big cities, making it harder for people who can't afford a car to get to jobs. In addition, ever since

in the cities. But casual visitors stayed away. Parking was scarce and expensive, many retail outlets had closed and crime became a major concern, particularly after a crack epidemic in the late 1980s and early 1990s left drug addicts, homeless people and panhandlers in its wake.

Bounce-Back

During the 1980s, jobs and population continued to shift to suburban areas, but green shoots of development began to grow in many cities. It became almost a cliche that neighborhoods would change as artists, in pursuit of cheap living and working quarters, moved into lofts and warehouse spaces, soon to be followed by coffee shops and

"urban pioneers" attracted to gritty but appealing parts of the city. "Cheap rentals [began] to disappear and cheap housing [was] either torn down or adapted and. . . . packaged differently," says Modarres, the editor of *Cities: The International Journal of Urban Policy and Planning*.

Gentrification stepped up during the 1990s, as the image of the city changed from *Escape From New York* — the 1981 movie in which the island of Manhattan is depicted as a maximum security prison — to *Friends* and *Seinfeld*, the 1990s sitcoms that depicted cities as a cool place to hang with pals. Those shows reflected the reality that many young adults longed to escape the blandness of suburbia.

immigrants flooded American cities at the dawn of the 20th century, philanthropic organizations have tended to locate in downtown and center-city areas.

Although new social-service programs for the poor are cropping up in the suburbs, many areas have been unable to keep up with the rapidly growing demand for them. "They don't have the institutional framework to deal with a lot of poverty within their boundaries," says Pete Saunders, an urban planner in Peoria, Ill.

Many local officials worry about "slumburbia" — the shifting of city slums to the suburbs as poor residents move out of center cities and more-affluent whites move in. "Minority suburban poverty surrounding white city affluence will be worse than the reverse," Saunders says, "because suburbs have shorter shelf lives." As suburban housing stock ages, poor residents attracted by cheaper housing may not have the money to rehab the properties.

Moreover, there is little room for new development in inner-ring suburbs, which are generally built out.

Older homes, limited commercial activity and, in some places, lack of jobs have caused property values and tax bases to decline steeply. In Cuyahoga County (Cleveland and vicinity), total property values in several of the 1940s-1950s-era suburbs around the city have dropped by a quarter or more during the past decade.[4]

The result is a vicious cycle that could make it hard for declining suburbs or their residents to make any kind of a quick comeback.

"Once property values are down, then you're in a resource trap," and that affects the public schools, which rely heavily on property taxes, says Jacob Vigdor, a public

A foreclosed, boarded-up house is offered for sale in Harvey, Ill., a depressed suburb of Chicago.

policy professor at the University of Washington. "You let the quality of public schools decline, and it's going to make any middle-class families rethink where they're going to live."

— *Alan Greenblatt*

[1] Elizabeth Kneebone and Natalie Holmes, "New Census Data Show Few Metro Areas Made Progress Against Poverty in 2013," Brookings Institution, Sept. 19, 2014, http://tinyurl.com/n6lxpxb.

[2] Jennifer Medina, "Hardship Makes a New Home in the Suburbs," *The New York Times,* May 9, 2014, http://tinyurl.com/o37o7l4.

[3] William H. Frey, *Diversity Explosion* (2015), p. 149.

[4] Daniel J. McGraw, "The Complications of Our Deteriorating Inner Ring Suburbs," *Belt,* Jan. 5, 2015, http://tinyurl.com/pet7feu.

Federal, state and local governments all offered tax breaks to developers who worked on downtown projects. New York State, for example, amended its housing code in 1997 to offer substantial tax abatements to landlords who converted office space into apartments. A decade later, every building on the south side of Wall Street in Lower Manhattan was being used for residential purposes, save the New York Stock Exchange.[28]

Business-improvement districts (BIDs) in many cities imposed levies or helped pass tax increases that paid for new convention centers, stadiums and performing arts complexes that helped draw people downtown. BIDs invested heavily in sprucing up appearances, which

helped downtowns look cleaner and safer. The so-called FIRE industries (finance, insurance, real estate) that had remained loyal to downtowns were joined by design, advertising and software companies.

Using BIDs, downtown employers collected taxes to pay for the services they once sought from government. "They allowed people to tax themselves extra to get signage, plantings, additional police services," said Atlanta-based urban consultant Otis White. "The rise in property values more than covered whatever people have paid in taxes."[29]

Cities tried various schemes to draw people back downtown, spending billions on new sports stadiums, hotels and convention centers. Cities entered into partnerships with the private sector to construct such multimillion-dollar projects. Government used eminent domain to amass land, secured tax-exempt financing and provided fast-track approval for ambitious projects that began, in fits and starts, to attract people back downtown.

Consider the sprawling desert city of Phoenix. Having grown from 100,000 people in 1950 to more than 1.5 million today, it is a classic Sun Belt town, long better known for ranch-resort tourism than for downtown vitality. "Phoenix had sprawled out to the suburbs and pretty much abandoned the central city," City Council member Claude Mattox said in 2006. Left behind were "the homeless, vagrants and prostitutes."

In recent years, however, downtown Phoenix has used new baseball, basketball and hockey facilities, two major new museums and two concert halls, an upscale retail complex and a $600 million expansion of the convention center to draw tens of thousands of people downtown every night. Convinced that sports and tourism weren't enough to make the downtown healthy, city leaders also have promoted residential construction and a biomedical campus. Like other cities, Phoenix worked with universities to create downtown branch campuses.

With his 1997 book, *The Rise of the Creative Class,* urban studies scholar Florida persuaded many civic leaders that the path to prosperity lies not in granting tax breaks to businesses but in presenting the right blend of social and cultural amenities to attract well-educated workers. Even as ideas like Florida's became chic, broader economic forces helped push people back downtown. The decline in urban manufacturing made cities cleaner. Gas prices were rising, discouraging long commutes from the suburbs, while violent crime rates were going down, making inner cities safer.

Some major employers began moving into downtowns — NCR in Atlanta, American Eagle Outfitters in Pittsburgh, even a traditionally nonurban company like Weyerhaeuser in Seattle. Currently, the massive retailer Amazon and Vulcan, a multifaceted research company owned by Microsoft cofounder Paul Allen, between them are building 10 million square feet of office space at the northern end of downtown Seattle.

Lots of tech companies such as Twitter, Salesforce and Yelp have chosen to locate in downtown San Francisco,

rather than Silicon Valley. "Innovative companies really want to be near similar companies," says Bruce Katz, who directs the Metropolitan Policy Program at the Brookings Institution, a centrist think tank in Washington. "There's this desire — really, an imperative — for density and connectivity. Over the last decade, the story that's been told has been about millennials, but this has really kicked into high gear because of corporations."

Meanwhile, the dream of escaping city life for the suburbs became less appealing as traffic congestion got worse, given the disconnect between where people lived and where they worked. And, even as white-collar professionals became enamored of cities, low-income immigrants and other poor people became more prone to settle in suburbs, drawn by service jobs and lower housing costs. The 2010 census was the first to show that a majority of each minority group now lives in suburbs.[30]

Since the 1990s, federal housing subsidies have been more tied to individual tenants than to properties, which tended to be concentrated in cities. As many massive public housing complexes were demolished in cities such as Chicago, in hopes of addressing congestion and crime rates, some tenants were persuaded to cash out their subsidized housing assistance payments for home-ownership vouchers. This helped many first-time buyers secure loans, sometimes for homes in the suburbs. As the housing market crumbled starting in 2006, some of them defaulted on their loans.

The bursting of the housing bubble, the collapse of the financial markets in 2008 and the lingering high unemployment rates left many downtown condos in cities such as Miami and Chicago vacant for a time. But cities fared better during the recession than suburbs did, at least in terms of employment. Between December 2007 and December 2010, the number of unemployed city residents rose by 1.5 million, but the number of unemployed suburbanites increased by 3.1 million.[31]

The post-recession recovery has been uneven in metro areas. But it's clear that many center cities are seeing higher land values, population and cachet in ways that that would have been unimaginable through much of the postwar period.

"We are living at a moment in which the massive outward migration of the affluent that characterized the second half of the 20th century is coming to an end, and we need to adjust our perception of cities, suburbs and urban mobility as a result," writes longtime *Governing* editor Alan Ehrenhalt.[32]

CURRENT SITUATION

Tales of Two Cities

Perhaps no neighborhood better exemplifies the changing approaches toward urban revitalization than Pittsburgh's Hill District. When the Civic Arena was built there in 1961 and became home to the Pittsburgh Penguins, an NHL hockey team, it was part of a broad redevelopment effort that displaced an estimated 8,000 residents, demolished blocks of housing and commercial buildings and cut off the Lower Hill District from the city's downtown.[33]

The Hill District then and now is predominantly African-American, and many homeowners and tenants were not fairly compensated for their losses. "The economic heart of our neighborhood was destroyed when the Civic Arena was built," says Daniel Lavelle, who represents the Hill District on the City Council.

After the Penguins moved to a new arena a few blocks away in 2010, the team, which controlled the Civic Arena site, wanted to redevelop it. Years of negotiations ensued, resulting this past September in an agreement to build office space — including a new headquarters for U.S. Steel — and 1,100 residential units.

Not everyone was pleased with the proposal, but the discussion was far more inclusive than during the 1960s era of urban renewal. Minority developers will gain 30 percent of the construction work, with women getting 15 percent, and a special taxing district will fund at least $22 million worth of projects in other parts of the neighborhood — "extending the value of the 28 [Civic Arena] acres to the rest of the Hill District," Pittsburgh Mayor Bill Peduto said at the news conference outlining the deal.

This kind of strategy — relying on anchor developments to reshape their surroundings — has become common in American cities. Hospitals, universities and — in the case of Detroit — a billionaire (Dan Gilbert, the founder and chairman of Quicken Loans) are triggering downtown building booms.

In Salt Lake City, the Mormon church in 2012 opened the 20-acre City Creek Center, one of the largest mixed-used developments to emerge in the U.S. since

New York City's wildly popular High Line is a mile-and-a-half-long park built on an elevated section of disused New York Central Railroad tracks on the West Side. Since the first phase of the park opened in 2009, it has spurred real estate development in the neighborhoods that lie along the line - notably the popular Meatpacking District and Chelsea - and some 5 million visitors annually.

the recession. "In Salt Lake City, in everything I do, I'm working arm in arm with the private sector, both profit and nonprofit, to allow us to do the things we want to achieve for our city," said Mayor Ralph Becker. "I find it an encouraging and probably even more necessary piece of what we do going forward."[34]

However, critics of such developments often complain that the deals benefit deep-pocketed corporations and investors at the expense of residents of modest

Is gentrification good for American cities?

YES

Pete Saunders
Executive Director, Tri-County Regional Planning Commission, Peoria, Ill.

Written for *CQ Researcher*, February 2015

To paraphrase Gordon Gekko of "Wall Street" movie fame: Gentrification, for lack of a better word, is good.

There are two reasons I believe gentrification has positive benefits. I spent the first half of my planning career trying to catalyze the revitalization of impoverished communities. All too often, public-sector activity was simply not enough to stimulate such communities. The increased demand that comes from gentrification — the arrival of more affluent neighbors — can bring desired amenities to a community, amenities that it previously did not enjoy.

In addition, I've come to regard neighborhood churn as vital to neighborhood growth and sustainability. In my career, I've noted some distinctions among impoverished communities. Some poor communities are immigrant settlement points and have a transient nature. They rely on a continual influx of new residents and maintain a sense of vitality that often belies their economic status.

Then there are communities that, once the poor moved in, stagnated. Those communities collapsed. Why? Because no one came in after them. The community lost its transience and in doing so lost its vitality. I've found that revitalization cannot happen without churn.

To be sure, gentrification does present some negative side effects, but those are best addressed through communication and engagement, not by halting the process. In all, urbanists should be careful, because this is the future that we wished for.

The problem with the gentrification narrative most of us work with is that it was established in the cities that experienced the first wave of urban revitalization — such as New York, San Francisco, Boston. Too many people have adopted the mindsets that emerged as those cities went through their revitalization challenges, without considering how unique their own cities' conditions are.

Those mindsets include newcomer angst, in which those relocating into a neighborhood wonder if their decision has hurt others; activist rage, in which (usually) longtime residents vent their concerns about neighborhood change and a lack of affordable housing; and fear among low-income residents, in which those most directly impacted speak out. In each case, the underlying concern is about displacement.

But what happens if your city does not have the kind of development demand that characterizes the cities where gentrification first took hold? Perhaps they are the exception, not the rule.

NO

James Tracy
Cofounder, San Francisco Community Land Trust

Written for *CQ Researcher*, February 2015

It is easy to look at cities as a bundle of dilemmas that only the short, sharp shock of gentrification can remedy. Want to repurpose a dying waterfront? Sell it to the highest bidder. Have a struggling neighborhood in your town? Provide a tax break to businesses with little interest in uplifting the existing population.

But displacement of lower-income residents will curtail any city's efforts to achieve important goals of strong communities, thriving schools and reduced greenhouse gas emissions. Take the case of a woman I know, a medical assistant and mother of two who was evicted after living in the same San Francisco apartment for 20 years. She found rental housing in a working-class suburb about 20 miles away.

She no longer contributes to the community she'd lived in as a volunteer at a local clinic. She can't keep an eye on neighboring elders as she once did. The commute to work has made it more difficult to spend time with her kids and help them with homework. The U.S. Centers for Disease Control and Prevention stated in a 2001 study that social loss was one of the most frequent impacts of displacement. It sabotages the everyday ways that people build community. As families leave the city, public schools funded by average daily attendance ratios are also cash-starved.

Some pundits suggest that gentrification can help stop global warming. The logic goes that we should expect reduced greenhouse gas emissions as fewer people commute to the city for work. But when middle-income commuters simply trade places with low-income people, this gain is eliminated.

Some of gentrification's cheerleaders can barely conceal race and class antagonisms hidden behind coded language of neighborhood improvement. I believe that there are many who simply see no other path to improve cities and would embrace other options to develop a local economy.

Cities do have the tools to combat displacement, including zoning choices, progressive taxation to discourage quick flips of homes and creation of community land trusts. Through this long-range community-planning approach, tenants in jeopardy of displacement can convert their homes from rental units to permanently affordable cooperative arrangements. This is no pie-in-the-sky idea. There are roughly 6,000 units of community land trust housing across the United States. All that is lacking is the political will to bring this idea to scale.

means. Plenty of major deals from San Francisco to Kansas City included substantial tax breaks for developers or their tenants.

Many city officials are aware that there is a perceived conflict between investments made to promote and attract businesses and the need to fund services that average taxpayers might depend on. In Chicago, Detroit, New York and elsewhere, complaints have grown that the gap between prosperous newcomers and struggling residents is getting larger. "We do have two Pittsburghs," says Kevin Acklin, Peduto's chief of staff. "We have parts of the city that haven't seen development for generations."

Peduto himself has talked about the "bike-lash" he experienced when he installed bike lanes in some downtown streets last summer. Low-income residents typically haven't taken to commuting by bicycle or participating in bike-share programs that have become common in big cities.[35] "If you're worried about where your next meal's coming from, you're not worried about a bike lane," says Jake Wheatley, who represents the Hill District in the Pennsylvania House.

In Atlanta, some complain that planning decisions involving MARTA, the regional transit system, will be driven more by the demands of corporations than the desires of their voters. In recent months, major employers such as State Farm, Mercedes-Benz USA and NCR have all announced plans to move their headquarters or regional offices to locations accessible by mass transit.

Many city officials argue that dollars spent attracting businesses or new residents through major investments such as streetcar lines or relatively minor ones such as streetscape improvements pay dividends by enlarging the tax base. Some critics contend, however, that corporate recipients of such tax breaks aren't contributing their fair share of the cost of these urban improvements.

Cities must not lose sight of the fact that they have to offer certain levels of services to all their residents, says Husock, of the Manhattan Institute. "Cities have an absolute obligation to provide the basic public goods — schools, parks, police, clean streets," Husock says. "If cities can't do that, that's the problem, not the fact that they have some better-off newcomers. There's no reason low-income neighborhoods have to be bad neighborhoods. That's not a norm we should accept."

Regional Tensions

Cities and suburbs in the Greater Seattle and San Francisco areas are struggling to carry the affordable-housing load as rents in the urban cores have skyrocketed. "We allocate different spaces for affordable housing," says Modarres, a University of Washington urban studies professor. "We have created style destinations, places where a certain level of income can bring you certain amenities."

People who can't afford increasingly pricey city centers will have to drive. Congested suburban areas are experiencing heavy traffic because of growth and the many residents who have to commute from the suburbs, Modarres says. "Right now, the Seattle region can accommodate people working and living in different places, but we're really strained on that," says Peter Steinbrueck, a former member of the Seattle City Council.

For some neighboring communities, the idea that Seattle is outsourcing its affordable-housing problem is creating a strain. "For us, just having families live here and commute up to Seattle has its negative aspects," says Pat McCarthy, the county executive in Pierce County, which is south of the city.

It's hard to pay for transportation infrastructure and public safety without also having companies that provide jobs, she says. "On the one hand, we welcome young families, they build communities," McCarthy says. "On the other hand, we need the economic development that keeps a community thriving."

In some metropolitan areas, poverty is growing rapidly in the suburbs. In Atlanta, 88 percent of the poor now live in suburbs, with the suburban poor growing by 159 percent between 2000 and 2011, even as the number of impoverished city residents stayed flat.[36]

Similarly, in Austin — one of the fastest-growing cities in the nation — the number of poor people has decreased since 2000, while more than doubling in the suburbs. The gentrification of formerly low-cost urban neighborhoods has both city and suburban officials scrambling to address heightened traffic problems. "We tend to take the position that Austin doesn't have as much of an affordable-housing problem as it has a transportation problem," said Chris Schreck, economic development manager for the Capital Area Council of Governments. "There's lots of affordable housing not that far from downtown Austin" — but limited public transit options.[37]

Still, some suburban officials are happy to welcome the overflow of residents from their bustling urban neighbors. Oakland, Calif., has a nascent tech start-up scene, thanks to the high rents and congestion across the bay in San Francisco and Silicon Valley.

The private buses that shuttle employees of companies including Google, Yahoo, Apple and Genentech to increasingly expensive San Francisco neighborhoods have become much derided symbols of gentrification — a fact that Libby Schaaf, Oakland's new mayor, noted in her recent inaugural address. She invited Google to come set up shop in her city.

"You wouldn't need all those buses if you would just open an office here," Schaaf said.[38]

OUTLOOK
Disparate Fates?

Some observers are concerned that the economic fortunes of competing metro areas could diverge in the future.

Denser development has helped revive downtowns in recent years even in relatively small cities such as Greenville, S.C., and Dubuque, Iowa. But the formula hasn't worked everywhere.

Lots of older cities in the Midwest and Northeast are continuing to struggle, notes Brachman of the Greater Ohio Policy Center. "There are smaller cities in places like Michigan, Pennsylvania and even New Jersey that have had a couple of really big factories or industries close and are not on anyone's map," she says.

Brachman says she's "bullish" about the urban future in general but worries there may not be enough young professionals to fill all the downtown condos being built. "We can't rely on this continual funnel of new batches of 24-to 35-year-olds," she says. "After this millennial bulge, the demographics are not quite as rosy with the next generation coming up."

There's clearly a competition between cities to capture the more educated and affluent young people. "Having a success like San Francisco is a fever that everybody dreams of," says Modarres of the University of Washington. "Everybody has the condo-mixed-use development formula they think will bring in the creative class. What happens is that other cities say, we can create that for you at a cheaper price."

Although relatively inexpensive cities such as Pittsburgh and Cincinnati have attracted professionals who feel they can live better in comparatively affordable areas, larger megacities may have more "momentum" that keeps them ahead of the rest of the county, Modarres says.

Large companies, just like their young workers, seem to want to cluster in areas with nice amenities and growth industries. "It's difficult to build cities, unless you're New York and maybe Chicago, by betting on having a continual stream of middle-income young residents coming from the rest of the country," says Hill, the urban affairs dean at Cleveland State.

Cities with cheaper housing can try to market themselves as more affordable alternatives to places such as Boston and Austin, which are magnets for people with advanced degrees, says Husock of the Manhattan Institute. But, along with sprucing up their downtowns, they have to put policies in place that make it easier for entrepreneurs to do business.

"They can take steps to make themselves more attractive, and they should try to do that, but my fear would be that there's this divide [between metros] that would emerge," Husock says. "My concern is the older manufacturing cities are still not going to find a way forward."

While suburbs as a whole still have more population and jobs than the center cities — and many are building town squares and other walkable areas in ways that mirror denser downtowns — some older suburbs are falling into vicious cycles of increasing poverty, declining property values and decreasing levels of public services. Many lack the kind of job bases and commercial activity that kept people coming to urban downtowns through their lean decades.

"Those suburbs face a confluence of fiscal and job problems that are some of the toughest problems in the country," says the Brookings Institution's Bruce Katz.

With urbanization spreading worldwide, few people seem to think the trend toward people and employers locating downtown will abate anytime soon. The question is whether this phenomenon will lead to success nationwide, or be heavily concentrated in a small but significant number of places.[39]

"There are cities whose fortunes have really turned around — New York City nearly declared bankruptcy in the 1970s," says Conn, the historian from Ohio

State. "But one question for me is whether this reurbanization we've been seeing in some places extends to a wider set of somewhat smaller, less sexy but urban environments."

With affordability being such a huge issue in Seattle and other booming cities, they face questions about whether their levels of growth can be sustained. "The only long-term solution to some of the issues in these very expensive cities would be new construction on a massive scale," says Vigdor, the University of Washington economist.

He doesn't see that happening, even though many big-city mayors are talking about building tens or even hundreds of thousands of new units over the next few years. The cities that are thriving now are likely to remain prosperous — and expensive.

"Over the next 10 or 20 years, if the demand in Seattle slacks off a little bit because of these demographic shifts, with age cohorts slightly lower and maybe less immigration and lower birth rates, . . . the housing market might cool off," Vigdor says. "But I don't know that anybody around here is all that worried about that."

NOTES

1. Alan Greenblatt, "From Vacant to Vibrant: Cincinnati's Urban Transformation," *Governing,* September 2014, http://tinyurl.com/mj5j5u6.

2. "San Francisco Apartment Rents Rose by 13.5% in 2014," Zumper blog, Dec. 9, 2014, http://tinyurl.com/l7gd6bs.

3. Alan Ehrenhalt, "Are Suburbs All They're Cracked Up to Be?" *Governing,* July 2014, http://tinyurl.com/ptenyz4.

4. Alan Greenblatt, "The Progress and Promise of Pittsburgh's Turnaround," *Governing,* November 2014, http://tinyurl.com/k3huw88.

5. Tim Logan, "Highland Park Renters Feel the Squeeze of Gentrification," *Los Angeles Times,* Dec. 21, 2014, http://tinyurl.com/mqp99m5.

6. *Ibid.*

7. Shilpi Malinowski, "Halfway House in D.C.'s Shaw to Go Condo," *The Washington Post,* Feb. 17, 2015, http://tinyurl.com/q2op38u.

8. Peter Moskowitz, "New Orleans' Lower Ninth Ward Targeted for Gentrification," *The Guardian,* Jan. 23, 2015, http://tinyurl.com/pjljrkj.

9. John Buntin, "The Myth of Gentrification," *Slate,* Jan. 14, 2015, http://tinyurl.com/mwar8q9.

10. Joe Cortright, "More People in Cities Today Live in Poverty Than in 1970," *Next City,* Dec. 5, 2014, http://tinyurl.com/mr8dz3b.

11. Rachel L. Swarns, "Measuring Mayor De Blasio's First Year by a Broken Toe and a $360 Check," *The New York Times,* Dec. 21, 2014, http://tinyurl.com/l78hq25.

12. Harold Meyerson, "The AFL-CIO Is on Sound Political Ground to Push for Wage Increases," *The Washington Post,* Jan. 8, 2015, http://tinyurl.com/mw3ejnl.

13. For background, see Thomas J. Billitteri, "Blighted Cities," *CQ Researcher,* Nov. 12, 2010, pp. 941-964.

14. Richard Florida, "The Connection Between Successful Cities and Inequality," *CityLab,* Jan. 6, 2015, http://tinyurl.com/otj4xh9.

15. Richard Florida, "Tech Culture and Rising Inequality: A Complex Relationship," *CityLab,* Dec. 9, 2014, http://tinyurl.com/mb3qlxj.

16. Alan Greenblatt, "Do Cities Need Kids?" *Governing,* February 2015, http://tinyurl.com/q2nx8rw.

17. Heather Knight, "Families' Exodus Leaves S.F. Whiter, Less Diverse," *San Francisco Chronicle,* updated June 10, 2013, http://tinyurl.com/px8g7cz.

18. Peter Tatian and Serena Lei, "Washington, D.C.: Our Changing City," Urban Institute, December 2013, http://tinyurl.com/kpcatg6.

19. Ginger Moored and Lori Metcalf, "DC Parenthood: Who Stays and Who Leaves?" Office of the Chief Financial Officer, Washington, D.C., January 2015, http://tinyurl.com/ork3hrx.

20. Bradley Calvert, "Cities Need a Family Advisory Committee," *Family Friendly Cities,* Dec. 2, 2014, http://tinyurl.com/kyr497z.

21. Richard Florida, "Singles Now Make Up More Than Half the U.S. Adult Population," *CityLab,* Sept. 15, 2014, http://tinyurl.com/qb93ez9.

22. Kenneth T. Jackson, *Crabgrass Frontier* (1985), p. 20.

23. *Ibid.,* p. 233.

24. Thomas J. Sugrue, *The Origins of the Urban Crisis* (1996), p. 42.

25. Kevin M. Kruse and Thomas J. Sugrue, eds., *The New Suburban History* (2006), p. 37.

26. James Tracy, *Dispatches Against Displacement* (2014), p. 5.

27. W., Dennis Keating, *et al.,* eds, *Revitalizing Urban Neighborhoods* (1996), p. 171.

28. Alan Ehrenhalt, *The Great Inversion and the Future of the American City* (2012), p. 68.

29. Parts of this section are drawn from Alan Greenblatt, "Downtown Renaissance," *CQ Researcher,* June 23, 2006, pp. 553-576.

30. William H. Frey, *Diversity Explosion* (2015), p. 164.

31. Emily Garr, "The Landscape of Recession," Brookings Institution, March 2011, http://tinyurl.com/ mrsl839.

32. Ehrenhalt, *op. cit.,* p. 7.

33. Christine H. O'Toole, "Pittsburgh Pursues Plan to Demolish 'The Igloo,'" *The New York Times,* March 8, 2011, http://tinyurl.com/5w656yl.

34. Alan Greenblatt, "Corporate Entrepreneurs Are at the Heart of Downtown Revitalizations," *Governing,* January 2014, http://tinyurl.com/mjbhnz6.

35. Joel Rose, "Shifting Gears to Make BikeSharing More Accessible," NPR, Dec. 12, 2013, http://tinyurl.com/mwhawgj.

36. Alana Semuels, "Suburbs and the New American Poverty," *The Atlantic,* Jan. 7, 2015, http://tinyurl.com/mlkmLho8.

37. Daniel C. Vock, "Suburbs Struggle to Aid the Sprawling Poor," *Governing,* Feb. 2015, http://tinyurl.com/llndbdg.

38. Joe Garofoli, "Horrible Commute Is a Boon to East Bay Tech Firms," *San Francisco Chronicle,* Jan. 18, 2015, http://tinyurl.com/lpyyeg8.

39. For background, see Jennifer Weeks, "Rapid Urbanization," *CQ Researcher*, April 1, 2009, pp. 91-118.

BIBLIOGRAPHY
Selected Sources
Books

Ehrenhalt, Alan, *The Great Inversion and the Future of the American City,* Knopf, 2012.
The *Governing* editor examines why center cities are attracting affluent residents while some suburbs are struggling.

Freeman, Lance, *There Goes the 'Hood: Views of Gentrification From the Ground Up,* Temple University Press, 2006.
Through interviews with residents of the Clinton Hill and Harlem sections of New York, an urban planning professor finds nuanced views of gentrification.

Jackson, Kenneth T., *Crabgrass Frontier: The Suburbanization of the United States,* Oxford, 1985.
An historian traces how two centuries of change in transportation technology and federal housing policies led to explosive suburban growth.

Tracy, James, *Dispatches Against Displacement: Field Notes from San Francisco's Housing Wars,* AK Press, 2014.
A housing activist recounts how government policies have increased evictions in San Francisco.

Articles

Buntin, John, "The Myth of Gentrification," *Slate,* Jan. 14, 2015, http://tinyurl.com/mwar8q9.
A journalist contends that concerns that gentrification displaces large numbers of poor residents of color are overblown.

Florida, Richard, "The Connection Between Successful Cities and Inequality," *CityLab,* Jan. 6, 2015, http://tinyurl.com/otj4xh9.
An urban affairs expert says clustering of high-skill workers helps make some big cities successful, but also leads to income inequality.

Hengels, Adam, "Only Two Ways to Fight Gentrification," *Market Urbanism,* Jan. 28, 2015, http://tinyurl.com/l269o3l.
As residents of upscale neighborhoods fight denser development, builders are forced to do their work elsewhere,

contributing to gentrification of poor neighborhoods, says a New York real estate developer.

Logan, Tim, "Highland Park Renters Feel the Squeeze of Gentrification," *Los Angeles Times*, **Dec. 21, 2014, http://tinyurl.com/mqp99m5.**
A neighborhood northeast of downtown Los Angeles has seen protests as housing prices rise and longtime residents fear being forced to leave.

McGraw, Daniel J., "The Complications of Our Deteriorating Inner-Ring Suburbs," *Belt*, **Jan. 5, 2015, http://tinyurl.com/pet7feu.**
Close-in Cleveland neighborhoods built after World War II are declining, and prospects for redevelopment are slim.

Semuels, Alana, "Suburbs and the New American Poverty," *The Atlantic*, **Jan. 7, 2015, http://tinyurl.com/mlkmho8.**
Although the poor increasingly live in suburbs, social-service programs still tend to be concentrated in central cities.

Tang, Eric, "Recent College Graduates Are Pushing Lower-Income African Americans Out of Cities," *The Washington Post*, **Oct. 29, 2014, http://tinyurl.com/qzpzwhz.**
Cities such as Chicago, San Francisco and Washington are losing large shares of their African-American populations as college graduates comprise more of their workforces and income inequality grows.

Weise, Karen, "Why Are Chinese Millionaires Buying Mansions in an L.A. Suburb?" *Bloomberg Businessweek*, **Oct. 15, 2014, http://tinyurl.com/kqfjwrf.**
Arcadia, a Los Angeles suburb, has seen a spike in the number of properties being built by wealthy Chinese.

White, Gillian B., "Can Immigrants Save the Housing Market?" *The Atlantic*, **Jan. 8, 2015, http://tinyurl.com/kk4f6lg.**
Much of the growth of U.S. households, particularly among those under age 45, is composed of immigrants and their children buying housing.

Reports and Studies

"U.S. Metro Economies: Income and Wage Gaps Across the U.S.," U.S. Conference of Mayors, August 2014, http://tinyurl.com/mkmuquk.
Top earners are taking home larger shares of overall wealth in the recent recession's wake, and income inequality varies considerably among metropolitan regions.

"The Socioeconomic Change of Chicago's Community Areas (1970-2010)," Voorhees Center for Neighborhood and Community Improvement, October 2014, http://tinyurl.com/mgwpapk.
A University of Illinois study finds that although gentrification receives a lot of attention in Chicago, the number of neighborhoods that have experienced upgrades over the past 50 years is limited. However, many areas have slipped into poverty while far fewer neighborhoods than in the past are populated by middle-income residents.

Pffeifer, Dierdre, "Racial Equity in the Post-Civil Rights Suburbs? Evidence From U.S. Regions 2000-2012," *Urban Studies*, **Dec. 19, 2014, http://tinyurl.com/pbt5uwz.**
An Arizona State study of 88 regions finds that in most, African-American and low-income residents have fared better in the suburbs than in central cities.

For More Information

Better Cities & Towns, P.O. Box 6515, Ithaca, NY 14851; 607-275-3087; http://bettercities.net. Nonprofit group that runs an online publication providing news and analysis about mixed-used growth and development to a largely professional audience.

Harvard Joint Center for Housing Studies, 1033 Massachusetts Ave., 5th Floor, Cambridge, MA 02138; 617-495-7908; www.jchs.harvard.edu. An interdisciplinary center that produces reports and holds conferences on issues related to housing such as homeownership and rental policies, community development and housing demographics.

Lincoln Institute of Land Policy, 113 Brattle St., Cambridge, MA 02138; 617-6613016; www.lincolninst.edu. A private foundation that studies the use and regulation of land, including tax policy and urban planning.

Manhattan Institute for Policy Research, 52 Vanderbilt Ave., New York, NY 10017; 212-599-7000; http://manhattan -institute.org. A market-oriented think tank that studies public policy issues including policing, crime and education and hosts a policy center focused on urban development.

Martin Prosperity Institute, Rotman School of Management, University of Toronto, 105 St. George St., Suite 9000, Toronto, ON, Canada M5S 3E6; 416-946-7300; http://martinprosperity .org. An academic center that studies ways in which business and governments intersect in reshaping the urban landscape and crafting policies that promote growth.

Metropolitan Policy Program, Brookings Institution, 1775 Massachusetts Ave., N.W., Washington, DC 20036; 202-797-6000; www.brookings.edu/about/programs/ metro. A think-tank program that consults with cities and conducts research on issues affecting urban centers, such as transportation, immigration, economic growth and demographic change.

National Housing Law Project, 703 Market St., Suite 2000, San Francisco, CA 94103; 415-546-7000; www .nhlp.org. A nonprofit that conducts research and uses litigation and policy advocacy work to promote afford-able housing, tenants' rights and improved housing conditions.

Strong Towns, P.O. Box 8847, Minneapolis, MN 55048; 218-325-3311; www.strongtowns.org. A nonprofit member-ship organization that studies ways in which local commu-nities can shape their land use and transportation policies to improve financial sustainability.

Urban Institute, 2100 M St., N.W., Washington, DC 20037; 202-833-7200; www.urban.org. A think tank that conducts research on housing, low-income families, tax policies and many other subjects.

6

Anti-Semitism

Sarah Glazer

Michael Ron David Kadar, 18, is escorted on March 23 from a courtroom in Israel, where he was charged in connection with hundreds of bomb threats. In April, the U.S. Justice Department charged the Jewish Israeli-American teen in connection with dozens of fake bomb threats in the United States between January and March of this year, many of them targeting Jewish community centers.

From *CQ Researcher*,
May 12, 2017

"Heil Trump," said an email threatening Jews and African-Americans, received by hundreds of University of Michigan students in February from a forged, or "spoofed," faculty address. The messages, being investigated by the FBI, followed the appearance of racist fliers on campus last fall.[1]

"We've been riding this wave of Donald Trump's election — definitely," said a member of Identity Evropa, a white supremacist group that says it has distributed fliers on more than two dozen campuses. "He's the closest to us we've ever had in recent memory, although we would like to see him go a lot further."[2]

White nationalists "feel emboldened in this current political climate" and are engaged in an "unprecedented" campaign to target college campuses, said Jonathan A. Greenblatt, CEO of the Anti-Defamation League (ADL), a Jewish civil rights group. Extremist anti-Semitic and white supremacist fliers and messages have popped up on more than 100 campuses in 33 states, according to the league, in at least 145 instances since the beginning of the school year.[3] In 2016, the group counted 108 campus incidents specifically targeting Jewish students.[4]

The Southern Poverty Law Center (SPLC), a liberal hate-watch group based in Montgomery, Ala., has blamed a nationwide "wave of hate speech and harassment" against Jews and others on Trump's election.[5] SPLC senior fellow Mark Potok said such groups were "electrified" by Trump's presidential campaign.[6]

Jewish groups both here and in Europe say anti-Semitic incidents are on the rise, and not just on college campuses. Anti-Jewish incidents jumped 34 percent last year to 1,266 — up from to

U.S. Colleges Targeted by Anti-Semitism

College campuses in 24 states experienced 108 incidents of anti-Semitism last year, according to data compiled by the Anti-Defamation League. The incidents ranged from threats and slurs to distribution of hate propaganda. California and New Jersey had the highest number of incidents, 19 each.

Number of Incidents Per State, 2016

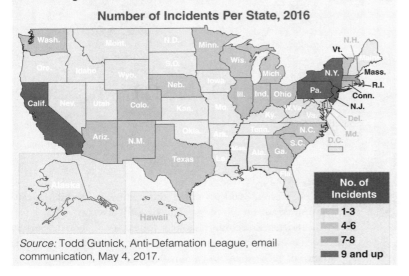

No. of Incidents
- 1-3
- 4-6
- 7-8
- 9 and up

Source: Todd Gutnick, Anti-Defamation League, email communication, May 4, 2017.

Journal, said the website fomented "a deep antagonism towards Jews," especially in its comments section.[9]

However, some Jewish observers doubt anti-Semitism is any worse under Trump; it just gets more media attention, they say. Others, such as Rep. Chris Smith, R-N.J., who has written legislation to combat anti-Semitism, strongly disagree with the accusation that Trump has inspired anti-Semitism.

"I think it's a very serious diversionary tactic by some," Smith says. "When people make those comments I think it does a disservice to the genuine and systemic causes [of anti-Semitism] we're trying to combat."

Others point out that, historically speaking, anti-Semitic incidents in both the United States and worldwide are substantially lower than they were in the mid-2000s, when Israeli-Arab conflicts were in the news, including the 2006 Israel-Lebanon war — events that experts say helped trigger waves of anti-Semitic sentiment.[10]

Criticism of Trump reached a new peak on April 11, when White House Press Secretary Sean Spicer said Nazi leader Adolf Hitler "didn't even sink to using chemical weapons" like Syrian President Bashar Assad did when he killed dozens of people with deadly sarin gas in April. Spicer seemed to have forgotten that the Nazis used poison gas to systematically kill millions of Jews.[11] Although Spicer later apologized, Jewish groups and historians said the administration was either phenomenally insensitive about Jews or verging on the anti-Semitic.

Journalists, Jewish groups and liberal bloggers cited previous occasions when the administration had "sent a clear dog-whistle of approval to anti-Semites," as a blogger from the liberal Center for American Progress in Washington described Spicer's April 11 words. For instance, the administration failed to mention Jews in its International Holocaust Remembrance Day statement and had been slow to denounce the rise in anti-Semitic incidents across the country. Earlier, Trump's campaign had tweeted a white

942 in 2015 — and continued to rise in the first quarter of this year, the ADL said. This year saw disturbing incidents of harassment or vandalism, including more than 100 bomb threats called in to Jewish schools and community centers and the desecration in February of dozens of Jewish graves at cemeteries in Philadelphia and near St. Louis, Mo.[7]

"Over the past six months we've seen a surge of bias incidents and hate crimes we haven't seen before," says Greenblatt. The Trump campaign, he says, legitimized so-called alt-right groups who "brought with them a kind of intolerance that has never before been in the center of the public debate — not just about Jews but about Mexicans, Muslims and other minorities."

The alt-right, short for "alternative right," refers to a loose amalgam of far-right groups and individuals associated with implicit or explicit racism, anti-Semitism and white supremacy.[8] President Trump's chief strategist Steve Bannon has called the *Breitbart News* website he headed before joining the Trump campaign "a platform for the alt-right." Rob Eshman, editor in chief of the *Jewish*

supremacist image showing his opponent Hillary Clinton's face atop $100 bills with a Star of David.[12]

Perhaps to deflect the criticism, Trump recently has condemned anti-Semitism and explicitly mentioned the 6 million Jews killed by Nazis during an April 25 speech at the U.S. Holocaust Memorial Museum. "We will confront anti-Semitism; we will stamp out prejudice, we will condemn hatred and we will act," he told the museum audience, which included Holocaust survivors.[13]

Meanwhile, experts have attributed a rise in anti-Semitism in some parts of Europe to increasingly popular rightwing parties as well as anti-Israel sentiment among Muslims and the political left. Anti-Jewish feeling is linked to hostility toward immigrants and any ethnic group seen as the "other," experts say, such as in the rhetoric of right-wing parties opposed to the influx of more than 2 million immigrants, mostly Muslim, from the Middle East and Africa.

"It's going to be harder and harder for visible Jews to live in France," especially those who wear religious garb such as a *kippah* (skullcap worn by Orthodox male Jews), says Bruno Chaouat, a professor of French at the University of Minnesota who studies French attitudes toward Jews. "Jews are caught in a vise between the far-right wing and anti-Semitism from Muslim youth and the left."

Hate crimes and anti-Semitic incidents spiked in Britain after the U.K. voted last June to leave the European Union (EU), according to the Community Security Trust, a London-based group that tracks anti-Semitism. Limiting immigration was a central issue in that vote.

In addition, says Mark Gardner, the trust's communications director, Jews have been "the target of jihadi terrorists" in recent years, often exacerbated by the internet. A "widespread increase" in anti-Semitism online has made the internet the main platform for "bigotry and hate," according to Tel Aviv University's Kantor Center, a watchdog group that publishes an annual report on anti-Semitic incidents globally.[14] The increase has stimulated a vigorous debate in Europe about whether to ratchet up penalties against hate speech online.

As for anti-Semitism among young Muslims, Günther Jikeli, a visiting associate professor in Jewish studies at Indiana University in Bloomington, had discovered startling sentiments among young Muslim men in London, Paris and Berlin when he interviewed them in 2007 for a book. They often said they wanted to "kill Jews before they died," Jikeli says.[15] At the time, that was not seen as a realistic possibility. "Now it is," he says, adding, "There are very explicit, detailed instructions on social media by ISIS and others calling for violence against Jews."

Jews are painfully aware of cities where deadly Islamist terrorist attacks have occurred at Jewish gathering places in recent years: a Paris kosher grocery and a Copenhagen synagogue in 2015, the Jewish Museum in Brussels in 2014 and a Jewish school in Toulouse in 2012.

The attack on the Paris grocery led to expressions of solidarity with Jews. "France without Jews is not France," said then-French Prime Minister Manuel Valls, promising to protect places of worship.[16] Officials beefed up security at Jewish institutions in Europe, and the number of violent anti-Semitic incidents worldwide fell by 12 percent — from 410 in 2015 to 361 last year.[17] But the brutality of individual events has intensified in recent years, according to the Kantor Center, such as the Paris grocery attack, which left four people dead.

Europe's refugee influx has shifted right-wing animosity more toward Muslims than Jews, according to the center. Still, many of the Muslim refugees come from Syria and Iraq, where anti-Semitic views are widespread, Jikeli points out, adding to nervousness in Europe's Jewish communities.

Some right-wing politicians in Europe have tried to capitalize on that Jewish anxiety. Marine Le Pen, who represents the anti-immigrant National Front, has tried to soften her party's historic anti-Semitism, saying French Jews have more to fear from jihadists than from organizations like hers. However, she recently declared that France was not culpable in rounding up Jews for concentration camps during World War II, which Emory University holocaust historian Deborah Lipstadt calls "soft-core Holocaust denial."[18] (Le Pen was soundly defeated by Emmanuel Macron in the May 7 election to select France's next president.)

Paradoxically, some extreme rightwing groups in Germany blame Europe's refugee influx on an international Jewish conspiracy. Once hatred turns against people seen as alien, experts say, the fallout has historically been bad news for Jews, who have been the target of what some historians call humanity's "longest hatred."[19]

As U.S. and European civil rights groups monitor anti-Semitism, here are some questions being debated in academia, national and state legislatures and the public arena:

Anti-Semitic Incidents Surged in Early 2017

The number of anti-Semitic incidents in the United States — including vandalism and harassment — jumped to 541 in the first quarter of this year — up from 291 in the same period in 2016. However, many of the 2017 incidents were fake bomb threats allegedly made by two individuals. On an annual basis, assaults declined — from 56 in 2015 to 36 in 2016 — but harassment and vandalism rose, especially in the last quarter of 2016.

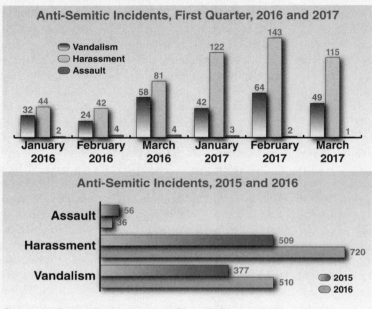

Source: "U.S. Anti-Semitic Incidents Spike 86 Percent So Far in 2017 After Surging Last Year, ADL Finds," Anti-Defamation League, April 24, 2017, http://tinyurl.com/lk2zj2d.

Is anti-Semitism on the rise?

Civil rights groups say the United States has experienced an unprecedented number of hate crimes directed at Jews since the Trump presidential campaign. According to the ADL, nearly a third of the 1,266 anti-Semitic incidents last year occurred during the last two months after Trump's election.

As an example of the role the election played, the ADL cited graffiti in Denver last year that said "Kill the Jews, Vote Trump."[20]

The surge in incidents continued into the first three months of this year, the league said, spiking 86 percent compared to last year's first quarter. By late March,

however, most of that spike was attributed to bomb hoaxes allegedly perpetrated by two disturbed individuals.[21] Israeli authorities charged an Israeli-American teenager, Michael Ron David Kadar, 18, with making hundreds of bomb threats around the world, and a man in St. Louis was charged with making a handful of them.[22]

Nevertheless, says the ADL's Greenblatt, the total number of anti-Semitic incidents spiked, even discounting the fake bomb threats, and the two individuals were not responsible for the cemetery desecrations.

Ryan Lenz, a spokesman for the SPLC, agrees with the charge that Trump's campaign contributed to the rise in anti-Semitism, citing the use of an age-old anti-Semitic stereotype in what he calls Trump's "horrifying final campaign ad, where a series of Jewish financial figures were identified by name as part of a global secret banking cabal."

Lenz adds, "While we're not saying Donald Trump caused this, he is part of a giant mix of racist expression that somehow has been legitimized."

Oren Segal, director of the ADL Center on Extremism, says such incidents "need to be seen in the context of a general resurgence of white supremacist activity in the United States."[23] In the month after the election, more than 1,000 bias crimes were reported, mostly anti-immigrant, anti-black and anti-Muslim in nature.[24]

But U.S. anti-Semitism "may have deeper roots" than Trump-inspired hate, according to Seth Frantzman, a fellow at the Jerusalem Institute for Market Studies and the op-ed editor at *The Jerusalem Post,* both based in Israel. More than 7,000 anti-Semitic incidents occurred during President Obama's eight years in office, he pointed out.[25]

"Every six days, a Jewish person in America was being attacked in 2015, and it went largely ignored," Frantzman wrote in the Jewish newspaper *The Algemeiner* in March, at the height of the bomb scares. "On average, there were threats every day against Jews and Jewish institutions over the last eight years, and most of them did not receive headlines."[26]

Mark Oppenheimer, host of *Tablet* magazine's podcast *Unorthodox*, contended that the media have focused more attention on such attacks since Trump's victory. "My best guess is that we are facing a continued march of the low-level, but ineradicable, Jew hatred that we always live with," he wrote in February.[27]

The arrest of Kadar led George Mason University law professor David Bernstein to repeat an earlier claim that the ADL "chose to hype" the numbers; he said that would worsen racism and anti-Semitism.[28]

"There's no evidence whatsoever that there's a general increase in anti-Semitic attitudes, given the Pew survey that just came out showing Jews are the most popular religious group in the United States," says Bernstein. According to the survey, half of U.S. adults expressed warm feelings toward Jews, rating them at 67 degrees on a 0-to-100 scale, ahead of Catholics and mainline Protestants.[29]

The impact of the 2016 election aside, accurately counting anti-Semitic incidents is a challenge, partly because many police departments do not report hate crimes separately. The latest FBI statistics show that Jews were the targets in more than half of religiously motivated hate crimes in 2014 and 2015.[30]

The SPLC, which monitors hate groups, has never counted hate crimes before, so it has no previous annual statistics to compare them with, according to spokesman Lenz.

Further, methods of gathering statistics on anti-Semitic hate crimes differ around the world, with some countries and organizations showing a decline while others show an uptick.

For instance, the Kantor Center in Tel Aviv, which collects data on anti-Semitism from 40 countries, found violent anti-Semitic incidents worldwide falling 12 percent in 2016 to 361, a 10-year low. And the French government reported a 61 percent plunge in all forms of anti-Semitism last year, which the center largely attributed to increased security after recent terrorist attacks.

However, contrary to claims from right-wing groups, newly arrived Muslim immigrants have not been responsible for rising anti-Semitic incidents, such as a 16 percent

uptick in Berlin, said the center. "The perpetrators continue to be the radical circles of the previous Muslim immigrants" including European-born children of Muslim immigrants, and the extreme right, the center said. New immigrants, it said, are "busy surviving," looking for work and learning a new language.[31]

Anti-Semitic hate crimes rose in some countries, including in Austria and Britain, where they reached a record last year, according to London's Community Security Trust.[32]

In addition, the Kantor Center reported "a widespread increase" in anti-Semitism on the web that "cannot be quantified."[33]

In 2016, an anti-Semitic message was posted every 83 seconds in cyberspace, mostly on Twitter, according to the World Jewish Congress.[34]

"Hate against Jews is not really dropping; it has just moved" onto the internet, where enforcement is "less well developed," said European Jewish Congress President Moshe Kantor, after whom the Kantor Center is named. As hate has migrated online, he said, the sense of security in Jewish communities "remains fragile."[35]

Is opposition to Israel a form of anti-Semitism?

Scholars and activists have debated for more than a decade whether opposition to the state of Israel is a new form of anti-Semitism. Bernard Lewis, a professor emeritus of Near Eastern Studies at Princeton University, used the term "the new antisemitism" in a 2004 paper[36]

Since then, the concept has been adopted by the State Department and some prominent scholars, but it remains highly controversial. Natan Sharansky, a Soviet dissident who became an Israeli politician, said the new anti-Semitism could be recognized by using his "three Ds" test: Demonization (comparing the Israelis to Nazis); a double standard (singling Israel out for its alleged human-rights violations when other countries are far worse); and delegitimization (denying Israel's right to exist).[37]

Since then Sharansky's three Ds have been incorporated into the State Department's "working definition" of anti-Semitism.[38] The formulation also was adopted last year as a non-legally binding definition by Britain and by the International Holocaust Remembrance Alliance — 31 nations committed to Holocaust education.[39]

The question of when criticism of Israel becomes anti-Semitism has been at the heart of two recent controversies:

Messages of sympathy, "We are all Jews," hang outside a kosher grocery store in Paris where four people were killed in a terrorist attack in 2015. Muslim extremists have been implicated in several deadly terrorist attacks in recent years on Jewish gathering places in Europe, including a Copenhagen synagogue, the Jewish Museum in Brussels and a Jewish school in Toulouse, France.

proposals to include the State Department definition in federal and state legislation and claims that the Boycott, Divestment and Sanctions (BDS) movement is anti-Semitic.

The movement is a worldwide campaign to get governments, universities and individuals to boycott Israeli products and divest themselves of investments in Israeli holdings as a way to protest Israel's 50-year occupation of the West Bank and Gaza territories. The debate over the boycott centers on whether the movement is just aimed against Israel's treatment of Palestinians living in the territories or is also a protest against Israel's existence.

Last year the Senate passed a bill to require the federal government to use the State Department definition of anti-Semitism when investigating discrimination complaints on college campuses. Known as the Anti-Semitism Awareness Act, the measure died without reaching the House floor but is expected to be reintroduced. Several prominent Jewish groups strongly support it, but the American Civil Liberties Union (ACLU) says it infringes on free speech.[40] Several state legislatures also have considered similar bills.

Kenneth Marcus, president of the Washington-based Louis D. Brandeis Center, which fights anti-Semitism, says the bill is needed because harassment of Jewish students on college campuses has been rising and is often associated with BDS demonstrations.

AMCHA, a college watchdog group named after the Hebrew word for "your people" or "grassroots," reported a 45 percent increase in anti-Semitic incidents on campuses in the first half of 2016, to 287, over the same period the previous year.[41]

But according to Mitchell Bard, executive director of the American-Israeli Cooperative Enterprise, a nonprofit that aims to strengthen relations between the two countries, more than a third of the events were lectures, "echo chambers attended by the like-minded," and some were peaceful protests against Israeli policies. "[W]hile some guerrilla theater meant to highlight Israel's alleged abuses is disturbing, it is not de facto anti-Semitic," he wrote.[42]

Marcus says the legislation is needed to deal with "campuses where there's a large amount of severe pervasive hostility to Jews, not just in protest activities but threats, vandalism and physical assaults — where the perpetrators often hide behind the notion that they're merely anti-Zionist." (Historically Zionism referred to the movement to establish a Jewish homeland in Israel; in modern times, it usually refers to support for the modern state of Israel.)

However, Kenneth S. Stern, who helped draft the original definition of anti-Semitism for a European monitoring group, strongly opposes the congressional legislation. The three Ds were intended to help countries collect data on anti-Semitic acts by using a uniform definition, says Stern, who is now executive director of the Justus and Karin Rosenberg Foundation, which combats anti-Semitism. "That's quite different from using it as a way to chill discussion on college campuses," he says.

Some Jewish groups have used the definition to try to stop protests against Israel's treatment of Palestinians, he says, such as the annual "Apartheid Week" held on many campuses or debates over the BDS movement. If the bill becomes law, university administrators would likely shut down such protests and debate to avoid losing federal funding or being sued for discrimination, he says.

Doing so would shut down a chance to develop a deeper understanding of what actually constitutes anti-Semitism, Stern says.

Yet some who are troubled by the "new anti-Semitism" say they do not oppose criticism of Israeli policies but draw a line when it evolves into opposition to Israel's existence. In a recent essay titled "Why Present-Day 'Anti-Zionism' Is Anti-Semitic," Bernard Harrison, emeritus professor of philosophy at the University of Utah, defined anti-Zionism as "political anti-Semitism," because it aims to bring about the destruction of Israel.[43]

The ADL's Greenblatt echoes that view. The BDS movement is "a global effort designed to isolate and punish Israel and end the Jewish state," he says, "denying solely to the Jewish people a universal right of self-determination."

However, Liz Jackson, a staff attorney at Palestine Legal, a group that litigates on behalf of Americans advocating for Palestinian rights, says she does not see opposition to Israel's existence as anti-Semitic. She does not believe in a separate state for Jews, she says, even though she is Jewish.

"Jews have to be safe everywhere in the world; not in just one country," she says. "You can't have a democratic society which privileges one religious group above another; anti-Jewish hatred has nothing to do with that."

In England, a similar debate is raging over the Conservative government's adoption of the State Department definition of anti-Semitism. Jewish groups supporting Palestinian rights say it could chill speech.[44]

The question of whether Israel should exist is a legitimate political argument, says Naomi Wayne, an Executive Committee member of the London-based Jews for Justice for Palestinians. "Was Israel founded in compliance with international law? People have different . . . views. What is wrong with having those debates?" she asks.

Should online anti-Semitic speech be further restricted?

In a YouTube video titled "Jews Admit Organizing White Genocide," former Ku Klux Klan Imperial Wizard David Duke says "Zionists" are "ethnically cleansing" Israel of Palestinians and planning "to do the same thing" in Europe and America by promoting the immigration of non-whites.[45]

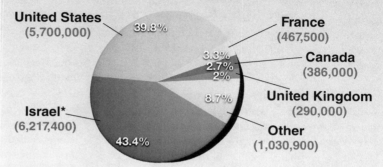

Israel, U.S. Have Biggest Jewish Populations

More than 90 percent of the global Jewish population lives in just five countries, with Israel and the United States home to the largest numbers by far.

Countries With Largest Jewish Populations and Their Percentage of World Jewish Population, 2015

United States (5,700,000) 39.8%; France (467,500) 3.3%; Canada (386,000) 2.7%; United Kingdom (290,000) 2%; Other (1,030,900) 8.7%; Israel* (6,217,400) 43.4%

* Includes Jewish residents in East Jerusalem, the West Bank and the Golan Heights.

Source: "Antisemitism Worldwide 2015," Tel Aviv University Kantor Center, p. 66, http://tinyurl.com/keubxwk.

That video triggered controversy in Britain after a Parliamentary committee investigating hate crimes recently flagged it to Google, which owns YouTube. However, Google vice president Peter Barron told the committee his company had not removed the video because it did not meet the company's standards for speech so objectionable it should be blocked.[46]

The committee's chair, Yvette Cooper, was incredulous. "You allow David Duke to upload an entire video which is all about malicious and hateful comments about Jewish people. How on Earth is that not a breach of your own guidelines?"[47]

Cooper's frustration is shared by groups fighting anti-Semitism in Europe and the United States, where online anti-Semitism is becoming increasingly hard to monitor or control. In fact, the Duke video was just one of more than 200 anti-Semitic YouTube videos discovered by a *Times of London* investigation.[48] In the United States, an ADL investigation found more than 2.6 million anti-Semitic tweets between August 2015 and July 2016, many directed at Jewish journalists.[49]

Most of the 28 EU countries ban hate speech, but debate rages over how to apply those laws to the fast-changing world of online interactions. The major hosting companies — Google, Facebook and Twitter — are based in the United States, where hate speech is constitutionally protected except when used to incite imminent violence and in other narrow circumstances.[50]

Thus, regulating the borderless internet requires negotiation between American companies and the European Union or its members.[51] Under a voluntary agreement with the EU, Google and other major media companies have agreed to review and remove illegal hate speech within 24 hours after it has been identified by an internet user.[52]

Critics say Twitter and Facebook have been even less responsive. In Germany, a recent survey by the Justice Ministry found that Twitter deletes only 1 percent of offensive content, and Facebook, about half.[53]

In response, and due to politicians' concerns that "fake news" and hate speech could sway upcoming elections, Germany became the first EU country to impose clear guidelines for penalizing online hate speech in April, when the cabinet approved controversial new fines for such speech. The law imposes fines of up to 50 million euros ($53 million) for social media companies that do not remove hate speech within 24 hours for clearly illegal content, as defined by German law, and within seven days in more ambiguous cases.[54]

The tech industry and civil liberties groups oppose the measure. Human Rights First has called it "a dangerous abridgement of free speech rights" that would embolden authoritarian governments to suppress legitimate speech. Such a broad attempt "tends to drive those sympathetic to such ideas underground, likely reinforcing their ideology," said Erika Asgeirsson, a fellow at Human Rights First. And clamping down on social media "will just change the means of dissemination."[55]

"We don't need more restrictions," says Barbora Bukovská, senior director for law and policy at Article 19, a London-based international group that advocates for free speech. Restricting speech of figures like Duke elevates them "to a pedestal as a hero and gives them exposure they don't deserve," she says.

Bitkom, an association representing digital companies, said the short deadlines and high penalties in the German law would seriously curtail free speech by forcing providers to delete doubtful content as a precaution. And the law would make "private companies rather than

the courts. . . the judges of what is illegal in Germany," said a Facebook spokesman.[56]

In Britain, it is unclear whether the government will try to penalize Google under existing law or propose legislation similar to Germany's.[57] Either step would likely raise similar objections. Stephen Pollard, the editor of the London-based *Jewish Chronicle,* has said Duke's video should remain online so his assertions can be debated. Exposure of anti-Semites' lies is what "actually defeats them," he wrote.[58]

In the United States, banning online hate speech would run afoul of the First Amendment and Section 230 of the Communications Decency Act, which immunizes internet service providers (ISPs) from prosecution for content created by others.[59]

However, Rep. Smith, a senior member of the House Foreign Relations Committee, says he wants such immunity eliminated so ISPs that host speech inciting people to violence can be penalized. "I love the First Amendment, but it is not absolute," Smith says. Some websites, he says, are getting people "ginned up to commit horrific violence."[60]

Groups such as the ADL and Human Rights First say they will continue working with Google and other media companies on a voluntary basis to help improve their ability to identify hate speech.

But the "haters have honed their skills to skirt the websites' terms of service in a skillful way," says Jonathan Vick, the ADL's associate director for investigative technology and cyber-hate response. Once a Duke video is taken down, supporters repeatedly repost it under different titles, reducing the exercise to a game of "whack-a-mole," he says.

BACKGROUND
"Blood Libel"

Anti-Semitism has endured for centuries and been almost universal — causing Jews to be repeatedly expelled from their home countries and to become the target of unparalleled levels of violence. Anti-Semitism has long been rooted in Christian teachings that Jews killed Jesus Christ, although many Christian leaders, including recent popes, have disavowed that view.[61]

One of the oldest slanders about Jews — that they killed Christian children as part of a ritual murder — originated in 12th-century Europe. The fabricated story that a young Christian boy in Norwich, England, had been killed by Jews for a religious ritual would become one of the most common incitements to anti-Jewish riots and killings during the Middle Ages.

Partly as a result of this "blood libel," Christians increasingly saw Jews as evil; in many countries Jews were forced to live apart and wear special clothing or badges to alert strangers to the dangers they supposedly posed, such as starting plagues or poisoning wells.[62]

In Europe riots against Jews erupted even as they were denied equal rights with Christians. Jews were barred from owning land and from craft guilds, forcing them to depend on moneylending or commerce, leading to the stereotype of the Jew as a greedy money-lender.

In the first large-scale deportation of Jews from a European country, King Edward expelled all Jews from England in 1290, ending their presence there for 400 years. In 1306 and 1394 Jews were expelled from France and over the next 150 years from Hungary, Austria, Lithuania and various German localities. Jews were expelled from Spain in 1492. Jews escaping Catholic persecution in Brazil in 1654 became the first Jewish settlers in North America.[63]

During the French Revolution in 1791, Jews were granted full equal rights based on the radical idea that citizenship should be granted without regard to religion or ethnicity.

"In the 19th century, France was the one country where Jews faced no legal obstacles to social and economic integration," says Maurice Samuels, director of the Yale Program for the Study of Antisemitism and author of *The Right to Difference: French Universalism and the Jews* (2016). By contrast, he notes, some American states such as New Hampshire, until 1877, still barred Jews from holding public office, even though the Constitution granted them equal rights at the federal level.

Compared to France, he says, "there was prevailing anti-Semitism in American life that lasted to the 1960s — quotas at universities, de facto exclusion from law firms and corporations, and housing covenants," which barred Jews from buying or renting in certain neighborhoods. They were also excluded from private schools and clubs and hotels.

By the late 19th century, most of continental Europe had enacted full Jewish emancipation, but that roused

Members of Jewish groups and their supporters protest in Beverly Hills, Calif., on Dec. 4, 2016, against President-elect Donald Trump for what they saw as his failure to condemn a spate of anti-Semitic incidents and his hiring of Stephen Bannon as his chief strategist. Bannon, the former head of *Breitbart News*, has called the website "a platform for the alt-right," referring to the alternative right, which includes anti-Semitic and white nationalist groups.

resentment — most famously in a German journalist and Jew-hater, Wilhelm Marr. In 1879, he coined the term "anti-Semitism" declaring himself a proud "anti-Semite." Like the Nazis later, Marr saw the Jews as a threatening race that had seized control of the German economy and society, and he argued that the only solution was their forced removal from Germany. He used the term "Semite" for Jews, according to historians, because it sounded scientifically neutral and modern.[64]

Some Jewish intellectuals began to wonder if they were welcome in Europe. Theodor Herzl, an Austro-Hungarian Jewish journalist for a Viennese newspaper, covered the notorious 1894 trial of Capt. Alfred Dreyfus, a French Jew falsely accused of spying for the Germans. During the trial Herzl witnessed anti-Jewish demonstrations in Paris, during which cries of "death to the Jews" were common; Jewish businesses, synagogues and homes were attacked and anti-Jewish riots erupted in about 70 cities. The so-called Dreyfus Affair became a watershed event for French Jews, who felt increasingly vulnerable. Dreyfus' innocence was not officially recognized until 1906.

Herzl, a secular Jew, decided that if anti-Semitism was so entrenched in the capital of the European Enlightenment, Jews could never assimilate in Europe.

In 1907 he organized the First Zionist Congress in Basel, Switzerland, which voted to establish a "publicly and legally secured home" for the Jews in the geographic region between the Mediterranean Sea and the Jordan River known as Palestine.[65]

In Herzl's utopian vision of a Jewish homeland, he imagined that Arabs in Palestine would welcome the gifts of science brought by the Jews. But Arab opposition to the influx of Jews only hardened over time, leading to the development of the Palestine national liberation movement.

Fabricated Charge

The elaborate forgery known as the "Protocols of the Learned Elders of Zion" is the most infamous document to libel the Jews. It purportedly comprised the minutes from a conference of Jewish groups plotting a takeover of the world. It first appeared in Russia between 1903 and 1905, concocted by the Russian secret police as part of a campaign against the Jews. In 1921, the *Times of London* exposed the tract as a fraud, showing how the author had copied fictional works to create it.[66]

However, "The Nazis saw its value immediately," as evidence of an alleged Jewish conspiracy theory, wrote Stephen Eric Bronner, a professor of political science at Rutgers University. "The Jew is not simply a capitalist or a communist revolutionary, but the Jew is now any enemy required by the anti-Semite," Bronner wrote.[67]

In the United States, automobile manufacturer Henry Ford was the strongest booster of the "Protocols." In 1920, he began serializing them in his newspaper, *The Dearborn Independent*. American Jews tried to persuade him it was a forgery, and in 1921 President Woodrow Wilson signed a letter denouncing *The Independent* for its anti-Semitic campaign.[68]

But the "Protocols" continued to be popular, contributing to a rise in anti-Semitism in the United States. In May 1924, President Calvin Coolidge signed the National Origins Act, effectively closing the United States to most Jewish immigrants, particularly those from eastern and southern Europe.[69]

The term Holocaust did not come into use until several years after World War II ended. In 1943, Jews were barely mentioned in Allied propaganda.[70]

Soon after the war's end, it was widely known that the Germans had killed 6 million Jews during World War II,

and 21 Nazi Party leaders were tried for war crimes in Nuremberg, Germany, in 1945 and 1946. But European Jewry's fate under the Nazis did not enter European public consciousness until the 1960s, when Israel tried Nazi official Adolf Eichmann and Germany tried former Auschwitz guards, said historian Tony Judt in his book *Postwar*.[71]

Then in 1979, the acclaimed 1978 American TV miniseries "Holocaust," starring Meryl Streep, was shown in Germany and watched by half of the German population. During discussion forums following each of the four episodes, some 10,000 phone calls poured in from viewers. For many Germans, the series was "an emotional introduction, the first encounter with the almost incomprehensible horrors of the Nazi regime," according to Jewish historian Julius H. Schoeps.[72]

Afterward, the word "Holocaust" entered common usage in Germany, and Germans became "among the best-informed Europeans on the subject of the Shoah [Hebrew for Holocaust] and at the forefront of all efforts to maintain public awareness of their country's singular crime," according to Judt.[73]

Meanwhile, the French did not acknowledge their wartime guilt in sending Jews to their death until 1995, when President Jacques Chirac admitted that the French helped to round up nearly 13,000 Jews — more than 4,000 of them children — for deportation to Auschwitz in July 1942.

Resurging Hostility

Much of the anti-Semitism that emerged in the 1990s and 2000s can be traced to the proclamation establishing the state of Israel by the Jewish community in Palestine on May 14, 1948. The U.N. General Assembly had tried to partition the territory into Jewish and Arab states in 1947, but the Arab League and Palestinian institutions rejected the plan.[74]

Israel's Arab neighbors immediately declared war, resulting in hundreds of thousands of Palestinian refugees fleeing to neighboring Jordan, Lebanon and Syria. An equal number of Jews were driven from their ancestral homes in the region.[75]

The Six-Day War in 1967 led to Israel's occupation of Gaza and the West Bank, where more than a million Palestinians still live under Israeli occupation today. In 1987 and 2000, Palestinian resentment erupted into violent

CHRONOLOGY

Middle Ages-19th Century *Ritual-murder rumors incite pogroms; Jews are persecuted during Spanish inquisition.*

1144 "Blood libel" claim that Jews murder Christian children for religious ritual emerges in England.

1290 Jews expelled from England.

1492-1498 Jews expelled from Spain, then Portugal and France.

1654 Jewish families arrive in New Amsterdam (later called New York), after fleeing Portuguese persecution in Brazil.

1791 During French Revolution France gives Jews equal rights.

1879 German journalist Wilhelm Marr coins term "anti-Semitism."

1894-1899 Capt. Alfred Dreyfus, a French Jew, is falsely accused of treason. Affair radicalizes journalist Theodor Herzl, who later leads Zionist movement.

1900s-1960s *Immigration laws aim to keep Jews out of the United States; Nazis kill 6 million Jews. Holocaust enters public consciousness.*

1903 "Protocols of the Learned Elders of Zion," a hoax claiming a Jewish plot for world domination, published in Russia.

1907 First Zionist Congress in Basel, Switzerland, votes to establish Jewish homeland in Palestine, which later becomes Israel.

1920 Industrialist Henry Ford serializes "Protocols of Zion."

1924 National Origins Law closes United States to most Jewish immigrants.

1942 Mass gassings begin at Nazis' Auschwitz-Birkenau camp. Vichy government deports 15,000 French Jews to Auschwitz.

1945 World War II ends. Allied troops liberate German concentration camps. An estimated 6 million Jews have died at Nazi hands. Nuremberg war crimes trials begin.

1948 Jewish community in Palestine proclaims state of Israel.

1962 Israelis find former Nazi official Adolf Eichmann guilty of crimes against the Jewish people; he is hanged.

2000-Present *Jews become targets of terrorist attacks in Europe and rising anti-Semitism in the United States and Britain.*

2000 Second Palestinian uprising ("intifada") spurs anti-Semitic crimes in Europe. . . . European Union begins tracking anti-Jewish incidents.

Sept. 11, 2001 Islamist terrorists fly hijacked passenger planes into the World Trade Center in New York and the Pentagon, sparking rumors that Jews knew about it in advance.

2002 Pakistani Islamist terrorists kill *Wall Street Journal* reporter Daniel Pearl.

2012 French Muslim attacks Jewish school in Toulouse, France, killing four.

2014 Four people killed at Jewish Museum of Brussels in Belgium.

2015 Islamist gunman kills four people in kosher grocery in Paris after attack on *Charlie Hebdo* magazine (Jan. 9). . . . Gunman opens fire on Copenhagen synagogue, killing one (Feb. 14).

2016 Record number of anti-Semitic attacks reported in Britain; U.S. Senate passes Anti-Semitism Awareness Act, defining anti-Semitism as including "demonization" of Israel; it dies in House.

2017 More than 100 bomb threats at U.S. Jewish institutions raise fear of growing anti-Semitism; Jewish Israeli-American man arrested, alleged to have made most of the threats. . . . Anti-Defamation League reports spikes in anti-Semitic incidents in United States in 2016 and 2017, citing increases in white supremacist activity by groups following presidential election campaign. . . . Violent attacks on Jews decline worldwide, Tel Aviv University reports, citing beefed-up security.

Anti-Semitism Persists in an Unsettled Poland

"We didn't resolve the problem of what Poles did to Jews."

The image of an ultra-orthodox Jew being burned in effigy at an anti-refugee rally in Poland in 2015 outraged many people around the world — and puzzled them as well. Why were Jews being blamed for the influx of refugees — most of them Muslims — arriving in Europe from Syria and elsewhere?

During his trial last November for inciting hatred by burning the effigy, Polish businessman Piotr Rybak, one of the rally's organizers, explained that his straw man represented billionaire Jewish-American financier George Soros.[1]

Poles with anti-Muslim views "generally blame Jews for being liberals, and there are a lot of conspiracy theories about liberals such as George Soros bringing Muslims to Europe," explains Michal Bilewicz, director of the Center for Research on Prejudice at the University of Warsaw. A survey released by the center in January, he says, showed anti-Semitism rising between 2014 and 2016 "fueled by the anti-Muslim panic that spread towards other religious and ethnic groups — for example Jewish people."

The survey also found that fewer Poles today consider anti-Semitic statements offensive. For example, a media reference to Jews as "scumbags" was offensive to only 43 percent of young people in 2016 — down from 66 percent in 2014.[2]

Bilewicz attributes the rise in anti-Semitism to an increase in anti-Semitic and right-wing rhetoric online. More than 90 percent of young people have daily contact on the internet with hate speech — against Roma (gypsies), Muslims and Jews, he says. And in a survey of 18- to 35-year-olds a week before Poland's October 2015 parliamentary elections, he found that most young voters were supporting "extremely conservative, anti-immigrant and xenophobic" political parties.

It has long been a mystery why anti-Jewish attitudes persist in a country where few Jews remained after World War II. Most of Poland's 3 million Jews were murdered in the Holocaust.[3] About 300,000 Jews survived, but the majority of them left the country after the war or never returned to their homes as word spread of Poles killing returning Jews. Most emigrated to Central Europe, the United States or Israel.[4] According to the last census, only about 10,000 Jews live in Poland, out of a population of 38 million, but there could be up to 20,000-30,000, says Bilewicz, because "it's a society where not a lot of people are open about their Jewish identity."

Poles have struggled to come to terms with the Holocaust and their role in it. A flare-up arose recently after a 2015 article by Polish-born Princeton historian Jan T. Gross, who wrote that Poles killed more Jews than Germans during the war.[5] The Polish public prosecutor has been investigating whether to charge Gross with "insulting the Polish nation," a crime punishable by up to three years in prison.[6]

In addition, a proposed law would make it a crime, also with a maximum three-year prison sentence, to say Poles were complicit in the murder of Jews during the Holocaust.[7] In his 2001 book *Neighbors,* Gross described how Polish citizens of the town Jedwabne killed their Jewish neighbors in 1941 by corralling up to 1,600 men, women and children into a barn and setting it on fire. And Gross' 2006 book *Fear* described the 1946 massacre by Poles of Jews returning to their homes in the city of Kielce after the war.[8]

Gross told the *Haaretz* newspaper that he would welcome the chance to defend his research in court, but blamed the push to prosecute him on the right-wing conservative government elected in Poland in 2015. "This strange regime works very hard on falsification of history," he said.[9]

These days, Poles are mainly interested in hearing about Polish heroes who risked their lives to save Jews, not those who killed them, says Anna Bikont, a journalist for Poland's largest paper, *Gazeta Wyborcza.* "It's all about the pride of Poland," she says. "You use Jews only to say how we [Poles] saved them . . . , how we were brave and fantastic. We have such a bad attitude towards immigrants because we didn't resolve the problem of what Poles did to Jews."

The proposed law is aimed at Gross and writers like herself, says Bikont, whose forthcoming book about Irena Sendler, a Pole who saved 2,500 Jewish children from the Warsaw Ghetto, describes those efforts as a lonely struggle amidst Poles who wanted to denounce or kill Jews.[10] "For my new book, I could theoretically be sentenced," Bikont says.

Scholars around the world protested the news that Gross was under prosecutorial investigation.[11] And the proposed legislation, widely condemned as historical censorship, is unlikely to pass, according to Maciej Kozlowski, a former Polish ambassador to Israel who teaches Holocaust history at Collegium Civitas university in Warsaw. But it could discourage writers and scholars from publishing on the controversial topic, Bikont says.

Although Bilewicz's survey has found growing anti-Semitic attitudes, Michael Schudrich, the American-born Chief Rabbi of Poland, says he hasn't sensed any recent upsurge in overt anti-Jewish behavior. Thousands of Jewish visitors come to Poland every year, he says, but "there are almost no acts of anti-Semitism."

Schudrich presides over a small but growing community of about 700 Jewish families in Warsaw, many of them converts from Catholicism. "I have people still coming to me saying, 'I discovered three months ago my grandfather is Jewish. What do I do?'"

Poland's Jewish community has a future, Schudrich maintains, "and that couldn't be said 20 years ago."

— *Sarah Glazer*

Edward Mosberg, a Holocaust survivor from New Jersey, and his granddaughter participate on April 24 in the annual March of the Living between Auschwitz and Birkenau, the sites of two former Nazi death camps in Poland. The Polish people in recent years have struggled to come to terms with their role in the Holocaust.

[2] Don Snyder, "Anti-Semitism Spikes in Poland — Stoked by Populist Surge Against Refugees," Reuters, Jan. 24, 2017, http://tinyurl.com/ml9ygtt.

[3] "Polish Victims," *Holocaust Encyclopedia,* U.S. Holocaust Memorial Museum, http://tinyurl.com/n5dycy8.

[4] Yad Vashem, "Frequently Asked Questions: In what condition were the Jews in Germany and Poland after the liberation?" http://tinyurl.com/l3xnd3x.

[5] Jan T. Gross, "Eastern Europe's Crisis of Shame," Project Syndicate, Sept. 13, 2015, http://tinyurl.com/n55ayro.

[6] Ofer Aderet, "Historian May Face Charges in Poland for Writing That Poles Killed Jews in World War II," *Haaretz,* Oct. 30, 2016, http://tinyurl.com/h7wx5s2.

[7] "Testimony of Mark Weitzman," Simon Wiesenthal Center, Subcommittee on Africa, Global Health, Global Human Rights, and International Organizations, House Committee on Foreign Affairs, March 22, 2017, p. 3, http://tinyurl.com/l4362ut.

[8] Alex Duval Smith, "Polish Move to Strip Holocaust Expert of Award Sparks Protests," *The Observer,* Feb. 14, 2016, http://tinyurl.com/lv6wd6z.

[9] "Historians May Face Charges," *op. cit.*

[10] Anna Bikont, *Sendlerowa: In Hiding* (forthcoming).

[11] "Historian May Face Charges in Poland for Writing That Poles Killed Jews in World War II," *op. cit.*

---

[1] "Polish Man Jailed for Burning Effigy of Ultra-Orthodox Jew," *The Times of Israel,* Nov. 21, 2016, http://tinyurl.com/m77zmd6. The effigy-burning occurred in Wroclaw, Poland, in November 2015. The sentence was reduced from 10 months to three months by a district court in April. See "There Is a Verdict for Burning a Jewish Puppet on a Wroclaw Market," *Newsweek,* April 13, 2017, http://tinyurl.com/kewgqf4.

Anti-Semitism Charges Roil Britain's Left

Labour Party suspends a prominent member for controversial remarks.

For the past year, Britain's opposition Labour Party, representing the country's liberal left, has been convulsed by charges of endemic anti-Semitism.

The issue came to a head in April as Labour considered whether to expel former London Mayor Ken Livingstone permanently for bringing disrepute to the party in connection with remarks he made linking Nazi leader Adolf Hitler with Zionism.

On April 4, after an 11-month inquiry, Labour's constitutional committee recommended a one-year suspension, during which Livingstone may not run for office.[1] The sanction followed a one-year suspension already imposed on him.

Livingstone's remarks came last year while defending a Labour member of Parliament, Naz Shah, against charges of anti-Semitism. In 2014 she had shared a post on Facebook proposing to "relocate" Israel to America as a "solution" to the Middle East crisis.[2]

Livingstone called the criticism against Shah "a very well-orchestrated campaign by the Israel lobby to smear anybody who criticizes Israeli policy as anti-Semitic." He told a BBC interviewer that Hitler supported Zionism "before he went mad and ended up killing 6 million Jews."[3] Zionism is the national movement to reestablish a Jewish homeland in the territory now known as Israel; since establishment of Israel in 1948, Zionism has referred to the development and protection of the Jewish nation in Israel.[4]

Livingstone apparently was referring to an agreement Hitler made in 1933 with several German Zionists to allow some Jews to emigrate to Palestine. Nazi regulations prohibited German Jews from taking their savings out of Germany. But under the agreement, the Palestinian Jewish community was allowed to buy German agricultural equipment with some of the funds blocked by the Nazis.

Jews who came to Palestine from Israel were able to "claw back a portion of their funds upon arrival," explains Emory University Holocaust historian Deborah Lipstadt.[5]

But historians dispute the idea that Hitler favored a Jewish homeland.[6] The Nazis' primary motive, it seems, was to break an economic boycott initiated by American Jews a few months' earlier.[7]

David Baddiel, a British Jewish comedian, observed that Livingstone's interpretation showed "no compassion" for this moment when the Nazis were "taking advantage of the terror and despair of fleeing refugees to get more of them to leave the country." That reflects a feeling on the left, Baddiel said, that "Jews don't quite fit into the category of The Oppressed, and so therefore don't deserve the same protections and sympathy as other minorities."[8]

"Livingstone's comments about Zionist-Nazi so-called collaboration are part of a longstanding undercurrent on the British far left of accusing Zionists of being party to the Holocaust," says Paul Bogdanor, a British writer and coeditor of the 2006 book *The Jewish Divide Over Israel.*

It's not surprising, he says, that the 2015 election of leftist Jeremy Corbyn as Labour's leader coincided with "a vast outpouring of anti-Semitism among Labour's far left forces," including thousands of anti-Semitic tweets and social-media messages received by Jewish members of Parliament. Corbyn has described Hamas and Hezbollah — labeled as terrorist groups by the United States — as "friends" and argues that Palestinian refugees who left Israel in 1948 and their descendants have the right to return to Israel and reclaim their property.[9]

Last April, Labour suspended Shah for the social-media remarks she made about Israel, for which she apologized. But the media publicity about her suspension was followed by a spike of anti-Semitic incidents in May, reaching a record high for a single month, according to the Community Security Trust (CST), a London-based group that tracks such incidents.[10]

Overall the organization counted a record 1,309 anti-Semitic incidents in 2016, up 36 percent from 2015, including a record 106 violent assaults.[11]

Anti-Semitism has been growing on the right as well. The CST attributed the increase partly to an uptick in xenophobia and racist hate crimes following Brexit — Britain's vote on June 23, 2016, to leave the European Union.

"The debate at the time turned ugly, and it was a debate about who is British and who is not and who belongs," says Mark Gardner, the group's communications director. "When you have that sort of language, Jews don't benefit."

Hate crimes rose 41 percent in the first month after the Brexit vote, but they weren't all against Jews. News reports also cited the killing of a Polish man, anti-Polish graffiti and anti-Muslim demonstrations.[12]

"The discourse is being allowed to fester in far right, far left and Islamist circles," says Gideon Falter, chairman of the Campaign Against Antisemitism, a British charity that organizes volunteers to counter anti-Semitism through education and alerting law enforcement. "If you allow this kind of hate to fester it becomes acts of hate."

Some pro-Palestinian advocates have called the recent turmoil in the Labour Party a "witch hunt" against party members for their criticism of Israel.[13]

While Livingstone's interpretation that Hitler supported Zionism was wrong, that doesn't make Livingstone anti-Semitic, said Donald Sassoon, emeritus professor of comparative history at Queen Mary University of London, one of 32 Jewish academics and Labour Party members who signed a letter condemning the disciplinary charges. "To be anti-Semitic you have to hate Jews, believe they control the world and so on," he said. "Nothing in [Livingstone's] statement suggests that."[14]

But others say the party has not gone far enough to discipline Livingstone. Nearly half of Labour's 229 members of Parliament signed an open letter protesting the decision not to expel Livingstone from the party. "[W]e will not allow our party to be a home for anti-Semitism and Holocaust revisionism," said the letter.[15]

The controversy seems unlikely to go away. Within hours of the April 4 announcement that he was being suspended, Livingstone was repeating his assertions about Nazi-Zionist collaboration in media interviews in which he appeared far from contrite.[16]

Party leader Corbyn responded by calling for Labour's ruling executive committee to consider further action based on Livingstone's new "offensive" remarks.[17]

— *Sarah Glazer*

Getty Images/Chris Ratcliffe

Former London Mayor Ken Livingstone received a one-year suspension from the Labour Party in Britain in connection with remarks – considered anti-Semitic – linking Adolf Hitler with Zionism.

[1]Rowena Mason and Jessica Elgot, "Labour Suspends Livingstone for Another Year Over Hitler Comments," *The Guardian,* April 5, 2017, http://tinyurl.com/kythu9l.

[2]Heather Stewart, "Naz Shah Suspended by Labour Party Amid Anti-Semitism Row," *The Guardian,* April 27, 2016, http://tinyurl.com/m9pxrue.

[3]"UK Rabbi: Nothing More Offensive Than Livingstone's Equation of Zionism and Nazism," *Times of Israel,* April 28, 2016, http://tinyurl.com/zy3dxtt.

[4]"Zionism," Jewish Virtual Library, http://tinyurl.com/m8d84qe.

[5]Deborah Lipstadt, "End the Misuse of Holocaust History," *The Atlantic,* April 14, 2017, http://tinyurl.com/krfzvs4.

[6]This was known as the Ha'avara ("transfer") agreement. See Edwin Black, "The Holocaust," Jewish Virtual Library, http://tinyurl.com/kfenpn7.

Also see, Paul Bogdanor, "Ken Livingstone's Claims Are an Insult to the Truth," *Jewish Chronicle,* March 31, 2017, http://tinyurl.com/lr7l34c.

[7]Black, *op. cit.*

[8]David Baddiel, "Why Ken Livingstone Has It So Wrong Over Hitler and Zionism," *The Guardian,* April 6, 2017, http://tinyurl.com/khdldo3.

[9]Paul Bogdanor, "Jeremy Corbyn Is Placing Himself at the Head of Britain's 'Palestine Solidarity' Lynch Mobs," *The Algemeiner,* Sept. 17, 2015, http://tinyurl.com/lpmbp3k.

[10]Kate McCann, "Labour Party Linked to Increase in Anti-Semitic Incidents, According to Charity Report," *The Telegraph,* Feb. 2, 2017, http://tinyurl.com/j2q6nvc.

[11]Community Security Trust, "Antisemitic Incidents Report 2016," p. 6, http://tinyurl.com/mzvoz3b.

[12]Community Security Trust, *op. cit.,* p. 13.

Also see, Katie Forster, "Hate Crimes Soared by 41 Percent After Brexit Vote," *The Independent,* Oct. 13, 2016, http://tinyurl.com/hs5wnb7.

Also see, "Brexit: Increase in Racist Attacks After EU Referendum," Aljazeera, June 28, 2016, http://tinyurl.com/gvxbvbf.

[13]Jonathan Cook, "Labour's Witch Hunt Against Ken Livingstone," Free Speech on Israel, April 2, 2017, http://tinyurl.com/mcg3c9l.

[14]Koos Couve, "Ken Livingstone's Comments Were Not Anti-Semitic, Leading Jewish Academics Say," *Islington Tribune,* April 14, 2017, http://tinyurl.com/k6zv55a.

[15]Ben Kentish, "Almost half of Labour's MPs Sign Letter Criticizing Decision to Allow Ken Livingstone to Remain in Party," *The Independent,* April 5, 2017, http://tinyurl.com/l7o9apv.

[16]See video of Ken Livingstone's remarks here: http://tinyurl.com/khdldo3.

[17]Joe Watts and Jon Stone, "Jeremy Corbyn Calls Meeting of Labour Executive to Probe Fresh Ken Livingstone Nazi-Zionist Comments," *The Independent,* April 5, 2017, http://tinyurl.com/mrkzkoc.

so-called *intifadas* ("shaking off" in Arabic).[76] Anti-Semitic incidents surged in Europe after the Second Intifada.

Muslim terrorists' hatred of Jews surfaced in a spectacular way on Sept. 11, 2001, when 19 Islamist radicals flew hijacked planes into the World Trade Center in New York City and into the Pentagon, killing approximately 3,000 people. A former member of the al-Qaeda cell that planned the attack testified that New York City was targeted because it was the "center of world Jewry." A Lebanese TV station falsely claimed the Israeli secret police knew of the impending attack and warned Jews not to go to work at the trade center that day, even though 400 Jews died there.[77]

In 2002, radical Islam's anti-Semitism resurfaced when Pakistani terrorists slit the throat of American *Wall Street Journal* reporter Daniel Pearl on camera, and later decapitated him, after forcing him to say "I am a Jew."[78]

Other deadly attacks on Jews by Muslims include the 2012 attack on a Jewish school in Toulouse, France, killing a rabbi and three children, two of them his own.[79] A French Muslim, Mehdi Nemmouche, who had reportedly returned from a stint with ISIS in Syria before killing four people at the Jewish Museum in Brussels in 2014, is awaiting trial in that case.[80]

After the 2015 attack on the Paris office of the satirical magazine *Charlie Hebdo*, a gunman who had pledged his allegiance to the Islamic State killed four people in a kosher grocery in Paris before being killed by police.[81]

A month later, a gunman killed a Jewish security guard at a Copenhagen synagogue during a bat mitzvah celebration. The suspected shooter, who grew up in Denmark and Jordan of Palestinian parentage, was killed during a shootout with police.[82]

The rise of right-wing parties in Europe has driven some of the growth of anti-Semitic crime in Europe, as politicians capitalize on xenophobic fear of new immigrants. When German hate crimes doubled in 2015, right-wing extremists were responsible for 91 percent of the anti-Jewish incidents, according to the Ministry of the Interior.[83]

In April, the U.S. Justice Department filed 36 charges against David Kadar, 18, the Israeli-American arrested in connection with the recent fake bomb threats, detailing 245 threatening calls, many targeting Jewish community centers, between January and March. Kadar appears to be linked to more than 240 hoax threats in the United States and Canada between August and December 2015.[84]

A few days later, the Israeli government indicted the teenager, whose name is under a gag order in Israel, for some 2,000 bomb threats over the past two to three years in the United States, Canada and other countries. His lawyer has said he has a brain tumor and suffers from autism.[85]

CURRENT SITUATION
Criticizing Trump

President Trump has been criticized by Jewish groups for being slow to condemn the rise in anti-Semitic incidents, but he recently made two statements sharply denouncing anti-Jewish hatred.

In a video address on April 21, Israel's Holocaust Remembrance Day, Trump called the murder of 6 million Jews by the Nazis the "darkest chapter in human history," adding, "The mind cannot fathom the pain, the horror and the loss" of the Holocaust.[86] Four days later he made his comments during the U.S. Holocaust Memorial Museum's annual days of remembrance.

But those comments followed at least two missteps by his administration — the failure to mention Jews in the International Holocaust Remembrance Day statement and his press secretary Sean Spicer's inaccurate claim that Hitler had never used poison gas on his own people.[87]

More worrying, however, says Susan Corke, director of countering anti-Semitism at Human Rights First, an international human-rights organization based in New York and Washington, are reports that Trump's counterterrorism adviser, Sebastian Gorka, was a sworn member of the anti-Semitic, quasi-Nazi Hungarian nationalist group, Vitezi Rend. Gorka has denied the charge.[88]

Human Rights First has asked Trump to fire him.[89] His status remained unclear at press time.[90]

In April, the State Department announced that it would appoint a special envoy to monitor and counter anti-Semitism, a position created by Congress in 2004 but that has been vacant since January. Several watchdog groups have expressed concern that Trump's proposed budget cuts and a hiring freeze could cripple the office.[91] GOP Rep. Smith, who wrote the 2004 legislation, has introduced a bill to elevate the position to that of ambassador, saying the office must be "adequately staffed and resourced."[92]

In other legislation, opposing sides are gearing up to debate the Anti-Semitism Awareness Act, expected to be reintroduced. It would require the Education Department's Office of Civil Rights (OCR) to use the State Department's definition of anti-Semitism when investigating claims of discrimination and harassment on college campuses. The controversy centers on the State Department explanation of when anti-Israel criticism crosses the line into anti-Semitism—such as "demonizing" Israel by comparing it to Nazi Germany.

Under Title VI of the Civil Rights Act of 1964, the Education Department can withhold federal funding from a university found to have discriminated on the basis of race, color, or national origin. In 2004, the office said Jewish, Sikh and Muslim students also were protected from discrimination under Title VI.[93]

Yet the Brandeis Center's Marcus, who drafted the policy while serving as an official at the OCR, says the department has not found any civil rights violation in any anti-Semitism case it has investigated. "That system just isn't working. And Congress really needs to take action," he says. The proposed law "is the best solution because it gets to the root of OCR's and the universities' problems [about how to define anti-Semitism], while fully protecting freedom of speech and academic freedom."

Opponents of the measure say the department never found discrimination in any of these cases because there wasn't any. "Exposure to such discordant and robust expressions, even when offensive and hurtful, is a circumstance that a reasonable student in higher education may experience," the OCR said in dismissing a 2012 harassment complaint at the University of California about two anti-Israel speakers.[94]

The ACLU likely will oppose the bill, as it did last year, saying it could infringe on freedom of expression. "You don't want government making decisions about whether people have access to federal programs simply based upon their expression of political beliefs," says Michael W. Macleod-Ball, chief of staff and First Amendment counsel at the ACLU's Washington office. The organization and other opponents have complained the bill was passed without hearings or floor debate under the Senate's expedited unanimous consent procedure.

However, several prominent Jewish groups, including the ADL, strongly support the measure. Jewish students frequently say they feel uncomfortable or ostracized by demonstrations favoring boycotts of Israel or during Apartheid Week, especially if demonstrators use Nazi images or call Israelis "baby-killers" — reminiscent of the historic blood libel against Jews. "The effect is to isolate and to alienate Jews," says the ADL's Greenblatt.

Jackson of Palestine Legal, which opposes the bill, agrees that "criticism of Israeli policy often is vigorous, emotional, passionate, upsetting and uncomfortable for Jewish students; I experienced it as a Jewish student myself." But the goal of a university is "to have your ideas and world views challenged; that discomfort is not something universities should protect students from." Legislatures in Tennessee, South Carolina and Virginia have been considering bills to require public universities or state agencies to use the State Department definition of anti-Semitism when investigating allegations of discrimination, but states do not have the power to threaten the ultimate penalty — to withdraw federal funding. The South Carolina bill passed the House.[95] A similar measure died in Virginia's short legislative session this spring.[96] Another is pending in Tennessee.[97]

International Action

Britain is one of the first countries to declare sweeping condemnation of Israel a form of anti-Semitism. The Conservative government announced the decision last December after it was agreed upon by the International Holocaust Remembrance Alliance in May 2016.

While the U.S. State Department has a similar definition, it is employed only in diplomatic efforts. The British government has said the new definition should apply to anti-Israel activities at home and was needed to "ensure that culprits will not be able to get away with being anti-Semitic because the term is ill-defined or because different organizations or bodies have different interpretations of it."[98]

Jewish groups in Britain who advocate for Palestinian rights oppose widespread adoption of the definition, citing two universities' decision to cancel their Israel Apartheid Week events in February 2017 as examples of the potential "chilling" effect of the measure.[99] The cancellations followed a letter to universities from government minister Jo Johnson just ahead of Apartheid Week saying they should have "zero tolerance" for anti-Semitism following recent anti-Semitic incidents on British campuses.[100]

Has President Trump spurred anti-Semitism in the United States?

YES
Rob Eshman
Publisher and Editor-in-Chief, Jewish Journal.com and Tribe Media Corp.

Written for *CQ Researcher*, May 2017

There has been an increase in anti-Semitic acts since Donald Trump's presidential campaign got underway. Nonprofit groups have documented an increase, as have government agencies such as the Los Angeles and New York City police departments. The only institution yet to weigh in is the FBI, which won't release its 2016 hate-crime statistics until year-end. Maybe the FBI will give a different picture, but as of now, anti-Semitism is worse.

To argue that Trump bears some responsibility for this is not to accuse him of being anti-Semitic. In fact, the Trump White House may be the most "Jewish" in American history. His two top advisers, daughter Ivanka and son-in-law Jared Kushner, are Jewish, as are senior officials such as Treasury Secretary Steven Mnuchin, National Economic Council Director Gary Cohn, senior adviser Steven Miller and Jason Greenblatt, special representative for international negotiations. If Trump is an anti-Semite, he's really bad at it.

But one doesn't have to be anti-Semitic to give cover to anti-Semites, and here is where Trump's campaign and administration are guilty.

During the campaign Trump refused to reject an endorsement from white supremacist David Duke. He retweeted an image of Hillary Clinton under the influence of stacks of $100 bills and a Star of David. By retweeting several posts from white supremacists, he garnered what the Southern Poverty Law Center called "unprecedented support" from this radical fringe. That support grew when Trump brought on Steve Bannon as a senior adviser. Bannon took over the website Breitbart.com and — in his words — recreated it as a "platform for the alt-right."

And these alt-right trolls unleashed their bile on Trump's Jewish critics. There has been truly unprecedented online harassment of Jewish journalists who dare criticize Trump.

"I've experienced more pure, unadulterated anti-Semitism since coming out against Trump's candidacy than at any other time in my political career," the conservative columnist Ben Shapiro wrote in the *National Review*.

Long after the campaign was over, Trump finally took a stand against this hate in his address to Congress. But he never explained why his administration left the mention of Jews out of its Holocaust Memorial Day announcement. De-Judaizing the Holocaust is a long-term goal of the radical right.

Trump an anti-Semite? No. Trump as someone who out of ignorance, instinct or connivance has used and given cover to anti-Semites? The evidence for that is strong, and unforgiveable.

NO
David E. Bernstein
Professor, George Mason University School of Law

Written for *CQ Researcher*, May 2017

Donald Trump has not inspired a new wave of American anti-Semitism. A Pew survey early in 2017 showed that Jews are the most admired religious group in the United States. A March Anti-Defamation League (ADL) survey shows a slight uptick in the percentage of Americans deemed anti-Semitic, but it was still near a historic low at 14 percent.

Nevertheless, some American Jews, especially among those who lean liberal politically, have been in something of an unwarranted panic over a purported surge in American anti-Semitism they attribute to Trump.

Part of this is Trump's fault. Trump has a Jewish daughter and grandchildren and a record of friendship with the Jewish community and has been an outspoken supporter of Israel, but his behavior during the campaign raised concerns that he is at best indifferent to anti-Semitism and at worst was purposely stoking it for political gain. Trump seemed to hesitate to renounce David Duke's support, failed to condemn anti-Semitic Twitter attacks on Jewish reporters and opponents, and retweeted memes with anti-Semitic origins. More generally, Trump's Euro-right style of nationalistic populism and insulting remarks about Muslims and Mexicans have raised concerns about rising intolerance against minorities, from which Jews are unlikely to be immune.

Much of the panic over anti-Semitism, however, ranged from overreaction to outright fantasy. Trump adviser Steve Bannon, for example, was widely but unfairly depicted as an anti-Semitic white nationalist. A few acts of vandalism at Jewish cemeteries, common during the Obama administration, were treated as an unprecedented outgrowth of Trumpism. A handful of alt-right provocateurs meeting in a hotel ballroom near Washington received wildly outsized media attention.

The hysteria reached a fever pitch in early 2017 when a wave of bomb threats against Jewish institutions was widely but prematurely attributed to white supremacists emboldened by the anti-Semitic environment purportedly created by Trump. In fact, the threats were the product of a psychologically disturbed Jewish Israeli and a copycat left-wing journalist angry at his girlfriend.

Unfortunately, the ADL, America's leading anti-Semitism watchdog, has fanned the flames. Leader Jonathan Greenblatt made the absurd claim that anti-Semitic discourse in the United States was at its worst level since the 1930s. Such overheated rhetoric may be good for fundraising, but it stoked unwarranted panic.

Americans, and especially American Jews, should always be vigilant about anti-Semitism. But anti-Semitism didn't disappear during the Obama years, and it hasn't suddenly become a crisis under Trump.

While pro-Palestinian groups and some professors condemned the cancellations as suppression of free speech, the British watchdog group Campaign Against Anti-Semitism hailed them as successfully preventing expressions of anti-Jewish hatred.[101]

In April, the Austrian government joined Britain and Israel in defining anti-Semitism as including assaults on Israel's legitimacy, following reports that anti-Jewish incidents had reached a record high last year.[102]

BDS Movement

Local and national governments worldwide are writing legislation and Jewish groups are filing lawsuits aimed at blocking the Boycott, Divestment and Sanctions (BDS) movement to boycott Israeli products and academic institutions. Proponents describe the movement, launched by pro-Palestinian groups in 2005, as a protest against Israel's occupation of Palestinian territories. Opponents call it an effort to bring about the end of Israel as a Jewish state.

In the United States, 17 states have passed laws either barring government contracts with groups that support the boycott or requiring state pension funds to divest themselves of companies that support it. Several states — including Texas, Washington, Nevada and New York — are considering anti-BDS legislation, as are some local governments.[103]

The Palestine Legal group says such laws are unconstitutional, citing legal opinions that boycotts are a form of protected speech.[104] In any case, says Palestine Legal attorney Jackson, the movement is growing in popularity. "People's interest in BDS is growing," especially as the peace process between Israel and Palestine seems perpetually stalled, she says. "There is no alternative to a peaceful solution; this is the only thing out there," Jackson says.

Numerous efforts are underway on campuses to persuade universities to join the boycott, but so far no American university has agreed to divest of its Israeli investments. Since 2012, however, 51 campuses have voted on resolutions urging divestment, mostly by student governments. Slightly fewer than half have passed.[105]

Last December Fordham University in New York City denied a student group's application to form a chapter of Students for Justice in Palestine, which supports the BDS movement. Dean of Students Keith Eldredge said in rejecting the application that the movement "presents a barrier to open dialogue and mutual learning and understanding" and creates the potential for campus "polarization."[106]

Four students, represented by Palestine Legal and the Center for Constitutional Rights, sued Fordham on April 26, saying the rejection represents discrimination based on students' political viewpoint and violates the university's free-speech policies.[107]

In Britain, the government has prohibited local governments from boycotting Israeli products.[108] The Palestine Solidarity Campaign, a British organization that supports Palestinian human rights, is taking the government to court over the prohibition, calling it a threat to freedom of expression.

Campaign director Ben Jamal says boycotts are "used across the world to oppose human rights violations and in situations where diplomatic routes have failed." He adds, "The line that it's anti-Semitic doesn't hold and is a very dangerous line, because it conflates criticism of Israel with hatred of the Jewish people and by doing so undermines the fight against racism."

U.S. associations representing professors in academic specialties, such as the American Anthropological Association, have been bitterly divided over BDS resolutions, which some critics have said would prevent Israeli scholars from participating in conferences in the United States or other two-country exchanges. Both sides have raised concerns about academic freedom.[109]

After the American Studies Association voted for an academic boycott in 2013, eight academic organizations followed suit, according to Jackson. Four professors have sued the association, saying the boycott violated the association's own rules on how votes should be conducted.[110]

However, several larger academic organizations, including the American Anthropological Association and the Modern Language Association, have rejected the boycott, and numerous university presidents have condemned it.

OUTLOOK
"New Era"

The recent wave of bomb threats and cemetery desecrations created an unusual sense of uncertainty among American Jews, who until now have felt mostly comfortable in their home country compared to Jews in Europe. American Jews have rarely had to ask — as

French Jews did after the 2012 attack on a Jewish school in Toulouse — whether they have a future in their own country. Nearly 7,000 Jews left France and immigrated to Israel in 2014.[111]

Perhaps the greatest fear in Europe remains the threat of another terrorist attack by radical Islamists animated by anti-Jewish hatred.

In Germany, young Muslim male refugees often hold "conspiratorial notions of Jewish power," according to Alvin H. Rosenfeld, director of the Institute for the Study of Contemporary Antisemitism at Indiana University in Bloomington, who is interviewing the refugees for a book.

Those underlying views, combined with a conservative religious upbringing, "don't mesh with liberal societies in the democratic West. It will take a generation or two to resolve," Rosenfeld says. "The last thing Germany wants, given its history, is a return of anti-Semitism. But whether Germany is successful remains to be seen."

With anti-Jewish screeds migrating to the internet, some experts fear the impact of thousands of widely shared toxic messages could be enormous. "One person who was sitting in a basement 10 years ago using a printer to print Nazi leaflets can now reach tens of thousands with a single click," says Paul Goldenberg, national director of the Secure Community Network in New York, which works with law enforcement officials and Jewish communities to provide security against attacks.

Yet French anti-Semitism expert Chaouat predicts that a government clampdown on anti-Semitic expression, online or off, could be "counterproductive." When the French government has banned the shows of anti-Semitic comedian Dieudonné M'Bala M'Bala, it only boosts his popularity, he says.[112] "The more Dieudonné is sued, the more people go to his shows," he says.

Today's anti-Semitism is fundamentally different from that of centuries past, when it was driven by Christian teachings that Jews killed Christ, says Rosenfeld. Instead, he says, Jews now must be aware of threats from all directions — rising populist nationalist movements hostile to minorities, radicalized Muslims, far-left politicians and hate-filled cyberspace.

That increased uncertainty can give Jews an ominous feeling about the future, even in America. Rosenfeld says he was taken aback upon seeing armed security guards inside and outside of a synagogue in Boca Raton, Fla., where he recently attended services. Another worshiper told him it was now normal.

"I wasn't used to that in America," Rosenfeld says. "It told me we've entered a new era."

NOTES

1. Amy Crawford, "White Nationalists Are Targeting College Campuses," Southern Poverty Law Center, May 2, 2017, http://tinyurl.com/lu4cc4c.

2. "Reports of Hate Crimes on the Rise at American Universities," CBS News, May 3, 2017, http://tinyurl.com/m7o2bys.

3. "ADL: White Supremacists Making Unprecedented Effort on U.S. College Campuses to Spread Their Message, Recruit," Anti-Defamation League, April 24, 2017, http://tinyurl.com/jljmr5u.

4. Todd Gutnick, email communication, Anti-Defamation League, May 4, 2017.

5. Crawford, op. cit.

6. Mark Potok, "The Year in Hate and Extremism," Intelligence Report, Spring 2015, Southern Poverty Law Center, http://tinyurl.com/hhfvcwj.

7. Daniel Victor, "Muslims Give Money to Jewish Institutions That Are Attacked," The New York Times, Feb. 27, 2017, http://tinyurl.com/zr5vzrp.

8. Marcia Clemmitt, "'Alt-Right' Movement," CQ Researcher, March 17, 2017, pp. 241-264.

9. Rachael Revesz, "Steve Bannon Connects Network of White Nationalists at the White House," The Independent, Feb. 7, 2017, http://tinyurl.com/zwof6m2.

10. "Study: Anti-Semitic Incidents Worldwide Doubled in 2006," Haaretz, April 15, 2007, http://tinyurl.com/n4ydxca.

11. "Gassing Operations," Holocaust Encyclopedia, U.S. Holocaust Memorial Museum, http://tinyurl.com/n32az25.

12. Laurel Raymond, "The Trump Team's History of Flirting With Holocaust Deniers," Think Progress, April 11, 2017, http://tinyurl.com/ll5cw4w.

13. "Watch: Trump Remarks at the U.S. Holocaust Memorial Museum's National Days of Remembrance," USA Today, April 25, 2017, http://tinyurl.com/lyobqcx.

14. "Antisemitism Worldwide 2016," Tel Aviv University Kantor Center for the Study of Contemporary

Antisemitism and Racism, April 23, 2017, p. 5, http://tinyurl.com/mhwg98n.

15. The book was: *European Muslim Anti-semitism: Why Young Urban Males Say They Don't Like Jews* (2015).

16. "'France Without Jews Is Not France,'" *The New York Times,* Jan. 13, 2015, http://tinyurl.com/l78yu4o.

17. "Antisemitism Worldwide 2016," *op. cit.* Also see "Antisemitism Worldwide 2015," Kantor Center, May 4, 2016, http://tinyurl.com/keubxwk.

18. Deborah Lipstadt, "End the Misuse of Holocaust History," *The Atlantic,* April 14, 2017, http://tinyurl.com/krfzvs4.

19. Robert S. Wistrich, *Antisemitism: The Longest Hatred* (1991).

20. "U.S. Anti-Semitic Incidents Spike 86 Percent So Far in 2017 After Surging Last Year, ADL Finds," Anti-Defamation League, April 24, 2017, http://tinyurl.com/lk2zj2d.

21. *Ibid.*

22. In early March, Juan Thompson, a former reporter was arrested and charged with fewer than a dozen of the bomb threats. See Benjamin Weiser, "Ex-Reporter Charged With Making Bomb Threats Against Jewish Sites," *The New York Times,* March 3, 2017, http://tinyurl.com/hcvz7ao.

23. "U.S. Anti-Semitic Incidents Spike 86 Percent So Far in 2017 After Surging Last Year, ADL Finds," *op. cit.*

24. "Hatewatch, Update," Southern Poverty Law Center, Dec. 16, 2016, http://tinyurl.com/j8asg8e.

25. Seth Frantzman, "Why Were the 7,000 Incidents Under Obama Largely Ignored?" *The Algemeiner,* March 1, 2017, http://tinyurl.com/k69uexw.

26. *Ibid.*

27. Mark Oppenheimer, "Is Anti-Semitism Truly on the Rise in the U.S.? It's Not So Clear," *The Washington Post,* Feb. 17, 2017, http://tinyurl.com/kvs4jmj.

28. David Bernstein, "19-Year-Old American-Israeli Jew Arrested in JCC Bomb Threats," *The Washington Post,* March 23, 2017, http://tinyurl.com/mgh6dvm.

29. "Americans Express Increasingly Warm Feelings Toward Religious Groups," Pew Research Center, Feb. 15, 2017, http://tinyurl.com/grkmch5.

30. "2015 Hate Crime Statistics," FBI, http://tinyurl.com/kl854ot.

31. "Antisemitism Worldwide 2016," *op. cit.,* pp. 5-8.

32. Community Security Trust, "Antisemitic Incidents Report 2016," p. 6, http://tinyurl.com/mzvoz3b.

33. "Antisemitism Worldwide 2016," *op. cit.,* p. 5.

34. *Ibid.,* p. 8.

35. See video at "Antisemitism Worldwide 2016," *op. cit.*

36. Bernard Lewis, "The New Anti-Semitism," *The American Scholar,* Dec. 1, 2005, http://tinyurl.com/mgbx5qf.

37. Natan Sharansky, "3D Test of Anti-Semitism: Demonization, Double Standards, Delegitimization," *Jewish Political Studies Review,* Fall 2004, http://tinyurl.com/lbep7tk.

38. "What Is Anti-Semitism Relative to Israel?" U.S. Department of State, http://tinyurl.com/ljysro7.

39. "Working Definition of Anti-Semitism," International Holocaust Remembrance Alliance, Dec. 12, 2016, http://tinyurl.com/lhjxokq.

40. Tana Ganeva, "How Legitimate Fear Over Bias-Motivated Crimes Is Generating Potentially Unconstitutional Policies," *The Washington Post,* Dec. 7, 2016, http://tinyurl.com/ltmm98g. 41 "Study: 45 Percent Spike in Anti-Semitic Campus Incidents," *The Jewish News of Northern California,* June 29, 2016, http://tinyurl.com/lapeg63.

42. Mitchell Bard, "Facts vs. Hysteria," *The Times of Israel,* Dec. 1, 2016, http://tinyurl.com/ny7dtnv.

43. Bernard Harrison, "Why Present-Day 'Anti-Zionism' Is Anti-Semitic," paper presented at University of Bristol-Sheffield Hallam Colloquium on Contemporary Anti-semitism, Sept. 13-15, 2016.

44. "QC's Opinion: Major Faults With Government IHRA Anti-Semitism Definition," Jews for Justice for Palestinians, March 27, 2017, http://tinyurl.com/kn3fxyy.

45. "Jews Admit Organizing White Genocide," YouTube, http://tinyurl.com/n5jndln.

46. "Oral Evidence: Hate Crime and Its Violent Consequences," House of Commons Home Affairs Committee, March 21, 2017, http://tinyurl.com/gnflr5w.

47. Rob Merrick, "Google Condemned by MPs After Refusing to Ban Anti-Semitic YouTube Video by Ex KKK Leader," *The Independent,* March 14, 2017, http://tinyurl.com/mhalv5l.

48. Mark Bridge, "Google Lets Anti-Semitic Videos Stay on YouTube," *The Times* (London), March 18, 2017, http://tinyurl.com/luyb27n.

49. "ADL Task Force Issues Report Detailing Widespread Anti-Semitic Harassment of Journalists on Twitter During 2016 Campaign," Anti-Defamation League, Oct. 19, 2016, http://tinyurl.com/mssooan.

50. Eugene Volokh, "No, There's No 'Hate Speech' Exception to the First Amendment," *The Washington Post,* May 7, 2015, http://tinyurl.com/mxoblkt.

51. "Antisemitism Worldwide 2016," *op. cit.*

52. "European Commission and IT companies Announce Code of Conduct on Illegal Online Hate Speech," press release, European Commission, May 31, 2016, http://tinyurl.com/jlhbcqp.

53. "Antisemitism Worldwide 2016," *op. cit.*

54. "German Justice Minister Calls for Hefty Fines to Combat Online Hate Speech," *DW,* April 6, 2017, http://tinyurl.com/lxe2tef.

55. Erika Asgeirsson, "German Social Media Law Threatens Free Speech," Human Rights First, April 10, 2017, http://tinyurl.com/ljr7tbd.

56. Emma Thomasson, "German Cabinet Agrees to Fine Social Media Over Hate Speech," Reuters, April 5, 2017, http://tinyurl.com/mevkwy7.

57. "Seedier Media," *The Times* (London), March 16, 2017, http://tinyurl.com/kv35ctr. Also see, "Clean Up YouTube or Face Fines, Bosses Told," *The Times,* March 18, 2017, http://tiny url.com/l3bfaap.

58. Stephen Pollard, "Why I, Editor of the Jewish Chronicle, Think Anti-Semites Should Be Allowed on YouTube," *The Telegraph,* March 15, 2017, http://tinyurl.com/homrwyk.

59. "CDA 230," Electronic Frontier Foundation, http://tinyurl.com/klr7ohb.

60. Rep. Chris Smith is chairman of the House Foreign Affairs Committee Subcommittee on Africa, Global Health, Global Human Rights, and International Organizations. His subcommittee held a hearing,

"Anti-Semitism Across Borders," on March 22, 2017, http://tinyurl.com/n7vocq4.

61. Dennis Prager and Joseph Telushkin, *Why the Jews?* (2016), p. 3. Also see "Declaration on the Relation of the Church to Non-Christian Religions, Nostra Aetate, Proclaimed by His Holiness Pope Paul VI, on October 28, 1965," Vatican, http://tinyurl.com/k4dj.

62. Phyllis Goldstein, *A Convenient Hatred* (2012), pp. 75-91.

63. Prager and Telushkin, *op. cit.,* p. 4. Also see, Nathan Glazer, *American Judaism* (1957), p. 45.

64. Robert Fine and Philip Spencer, *Antisemitism and the Left* (2017), pp. 3-4. Also see Sarah Glazer, "Anti-Semitism in Europe," *CQ Researcher,* June 1, 2008, pp. 149-181.

65. *Ibid.,* Glazer, p. 169.

66. Goldstein, *op cit.,* p. 250.

67. Sarah Glazer, *op. cit.,* p. 168.

68. Goldstein, *op. cit.,* p. 252.

69. *Ibid.,* p. 256.

70. See Sarah Glazer, *op. cit.,* p. 170.

71. Tony Judt, *Postwar* (2007), p. 811.

72. "The Emotional Impact of the Airing of 'Holocaust,' an American TV Miniseries, in the Federal Republic," Two Germanies, 1961-1989 (1979), http://tinyurl.com/kl3qh7y.

73. Judt, *op. cit,* p. 811.

74. "UN Partition Plan," BBC News, http://tinyurl.com/2igr.

75. Goldstein, *op cit.,* p. 311. Also see "The Six-Day War," Jewish Virtual Library, http://tinyurl.com/m8aqca7. Also see "Six-Day War," *Encyclopedia Britannica,* http://tinyurl.com/lt68lqg.

76. For background, see David Masci, "Middle East Conflict," *CQ Researcher,* April 6, 2001, pp. 273-296.

77. Goldstein, *op cit.,* p. 343, and p. 3 of foreword.

78. "Philosopher on the Trail of Daniel Pearl's Killer," *The New York Times,* Aug. 30, 2003, http://tinyurl.com/l5gl54n.

79. Joseph Strich, "On Two-Year Anniversary of Toulouse Shooting, Europe's Jews Still Wary of

Terrorism," *The Jerusalem Post,* March 19, 2014, http://tinyurl.com/l57qcbd. Also see Jeffrey Goldberg, "Is It Time for the Jews to Leave Europe?" *The Atlantic,* April 2015, http://tinyurl.com/ksu3c6s.

80. Alan Hope, "Jewish Museum Shooting Investigation Complete," *Flanders Today,* April 17, 2017, http://tinyurl.com/kcrudfa.

81. Julian Borger, "Paris Gunman Amedy Coulibaly Declared Allegiance to Isis," *The Guardian,* Jan. 12, 2015, http://tinyurl.com/kbd5pvm.

82. "Four Charged With Helping Gunman Attack Copenhagen Synagogue," The Associated Press, *Times of Israel,* Feb. 3, 2016, http://tinyurl.com/jt3o2og.

83. "Germany Conflicted," Human Rights First, Feb. 6, 2017, http://tinyurl.com/l8jljcr.

84. Joseph Ax, "U.S. Identifies, Charges Israeli Teen Accused of Jewish Threats," Reuters, April 21, 2017, http://tinyurl.com/kq8tm6g.

85. "Teen Accused of JCC Bomb Threats," *Times of Israel,* April 24, 2017, http://tinyurl.com/ka4kdk8.

86. "Trump Condemns Anti-Semitism on Israel's Holocaust Remembrance Day," Reuters, April 23, 2017, http://tinyurl.com/mquacfc.

87. *Ibid.*

88. David A. Graham, "Sebastian Gorka and the White House's Questionable Vetting," *The Atlantic,* March 16, 2017, http://tinyurl.com/k8lsxfj.

89. Dora Illei, "Sebastian Gorka's Shady Ties to Racist Groups," Human Rights First, April 11, 2017, http://tinyurl.com/kp7saar.

90. Vivian Salama, "Trump Advisor to Leave White House," The Associated Press, *The Washington Post,* April 30, 2017, http://tinyurl.com/kshk7hz.

91. "Anti-Semitism Envoy Post to Be Filled, State Dept. Says," *New York Jewish Week,* April 16, 2017, http://tinyurl.com/m52n5gm.

92. Rep. Chris Smith, press release: "Smith Introduces Legislation to Help Combat Anti-Semitism," U.S. House of Representatives, April 5, 2017, http://tinyurl.com/myjpx4o.

93. Kenneth Marcus, "How the Government Can Crack Down on anti-Semitism on College campuses," *Politico,* Jan. 11, 2017, http://tinyurl.com/j3co77f.

94. "Anti-Semitism Complaints Against Two California Universities Are Dismissed," Jewish Telegraphic Agency, Aug. 28, 2013, http://tinyurl.com/ma2r69j.

95. Avery G. Wilks, "Anti-Semitism Bill Passes SC House," *The State,* March 9, 2017, http://tinyurl.com/mnype28.

96. "Update: Victory!" *Palestine Legal,* Feb. 8, 2017, http://tinyurl.com/kaw87jv. Also see, "Controversial Anti-Semitism Bill Dies in House," Jewish Telegraphic Agency, Dec. 10, 2016, http://tinyurl.com/m8hhs8r.

97. See "Brandeis Center Calls on Tennessee Lawmakers to Combat Rising Anti-Semitism," press release, Louis B. Brandeis Center for Human Rights Under Law, March 29, 2017, http://tinyurl.com/k7vb36h.

98. Peter Walker, "UK Adopts Antisemitism Definition to Combat Hate Crime Against Jews," *The Guardian,* Dec. 12, 2016, http://tinyurl.com/jpdocvb.

99. "QC's Opinion," Free Speech on Israel, March 27, 2017, http://tinyurl.com/kn3fxyy.

100. Jasmin Gray, "Universities Urged to Adopt 'Zero Tolerance' Policy to Anti-Semitism Ahead of Israel Apartheid Week," *The Huffington Post,* Feb. 27, 2017, http://tinyurl.com/mrhe5wa.

101. "Universities Spark Free-Speech Row After Halting Pro-Palestinian Events," *The Guardian,* Feb. 27, 2017, http://tinyurl.com/ztdmn3b.

102. Tamara Zieve, "Jewish Officials Hail Austria's Decision to Adopt Anti-Semitism Definition," *The Jerusalem Post,* April 28, 2017, http://tinyurl.com/l6xz675.

103. "What to Know About Anti-BDS Legislation," Palestine Legal, April 4, 2017, http://tinyurl.com/krgqnfg.

104. *Ibid.*

105. "Antisemitic Divestment from Israel Initiatives Scorecard on U.S. Campuses 2012-2016,"

AMCHA, April 4, 2017, http://tinyurl.com/
k8uk3a4.

106. Elizabeth Redden, "Pro-Palestinian Group Banned
on Political Grounds," *Inside Higher Ed*, Jan. 18,
2017, http://tinyurl.com/kdjf3cd.

107. *Ahmad Awad v. Fordham University*, http://tinyurl
.com/mhqxu6q.

108. "Javid to Place Israeli Boycott Restrictions on
Legal Footing," *Public Finance*, Feb. 15, 2017,
http://tinyurl.com/k8uk3a4.

109. See Sarah Glazer, "Free Speech on Campus," *CQ
Researcher*, May 8, 2015, pp. 409-432.

110. "Federal Judge Advances Lawsuit Challenging
Academia Boycotting Israel," Brandeis Center,
April 4, 2017, http://tinyurl.com/kedsvun.

111. "France Without Jews Is Not France," *op. cit.*

112. See Laurence Dodds, "Who Is Dieudonne," *The
Telegraph*, Nov. 25, 2015, http://tinyurl.com/
lsmj8o5.

BIBLIOGRAPHY
Selected Sources
Books

Beller, Steven, *Antisemitism: A Very Short
Introduction,* **Oxford University Press, 2015.**
An independent scholar in Washington, D.C., discusses
the history of anti-Semitism from antiquity to today,
focusing on schools of philosophical thought, including
nationalism and romanticism, that have been marshaled
to support it.

Fine, Robert, and Philip Spencer, *Antisemitism and
the Left,* **Manchester University Press, 2017.**
An emeritus professor of sociology at the University of
Warwick, England, (Fine) and an emeritus professor in
holocaust studies at the University of London (Spencer)
analyze anti-Semitism on the left historically from
Marxism to today's anti-Zionism.

Goldstein, Phyllis, *A Convenient Hatred: The History
of Antisemitism,* **Facing History and Ourselves, 2012.**
Facing History and Ourselves, an educational organization in Brookline, Mass., that helps students study the
Holocaust in order to put today's moral choices in

perspective, produced this history from ancient times to
the post-Cold War era in Europe, the Middle East and
the United States.

Jewish Voice for Peace, ed., *On Anti-Semitism:
Solidarity and the Struggle for Justice,* **Haymarket
Books, 2017.**
In a collection of essays edited by a national advocacy
group for Palestinian rights, academics and activists
argue that criticism of Israel, including the boycott
movement, does not constitute anti-Semitism.

Julius, Anthony, *Trials of the Diaspora: A History of
Anti-Semitism in England,* **Oxford University Press,
2010.**
A British lawyer who famously headed the legal team
defending historian Deborah Lipstadt against a libel suit
brought by Holocaust-denier David Irving provides a
comprehensive history of anti-Semitism in England.

Articles

Bikont, Anna, "Jan Gross' Order of Merit," *Tablet,*
March 15, 2016, http://tinyurl.com/mnz2ajh.
A Polish journalist describes the controversy over histo-
rian Jan Gross' accounts of Poles who killed Jews during
World War II.

Hankes, Keegan, "Eye of the Stormer," *Intelligence
Report,* **Feb. 9, 2017, http://tinyurl.com/mdnzuod.**
The magazine of the Southern Poverty Law Center
describes how "The Daily Stormer" became the top hate
site in America.

Lipstadt, Deborah, "End the Misuse of Holocaust
History," *The Atlantic,* **April 14, 2017, http://tinyurl
.com/krfzvs4.**
A professor of modern Jewish history and Holocaust
studies at Emory University and author of *Denying the
Holocaust* says politicians who manipulate Nazi history
for their own ends are guilty of "soft-core" Holocaust
denial — a form of anti-Semitism.

Oppenheimer, Mark, "Is Anti-Semitism Truly on the
Rise in the U.S.? It's Not So Clear," *The Washington
Post,* **Feb. 17, 2017, http://tinyurl.com/kvs4jmj.**
The host of *Tablet Magazine's* podcast "Unorthodox"
raises questions about whether hate crimes and anti-
Semitic incidents in the United States have been rising,
noting the data are often faulty.

Raymond, Laurel, "The Trump Team's History of Flirting With Holocaust Deniers," Think Progress, April 11, 2017, http://tinyurl.com/mbkwqck.
A blogger for Think Progress, part of the liberal Center for American Progress think tank in Washington, asserts that President Trump and his White House team have a long history of thinly veiled anti-Semitism.

Reports and Studies

"ADL Audit: U.S. Anti-Semitic Incidents Surged in 2016-2017," Anti-Defamation League, April 24, 2017, http://tinyurl.com/mro6ds7.
In its annual report, the Jewish civil rights group finds that anti-Semitic incidents in the United States surged by one-third in 2016 compared to 2015. The report also says anti-Semitic incidents spiked 86 percent in the first three months of 2017, compared to the same period last year, but about two-thirds of that was due to bomb threats attributed to two individuals. "The 2016 presidential election and the heightened political atmosphere played a role in the increase," the report says.

"Antisemitism: Overview of Data Available in the European Union, 2005-2015," European Union Agency for Fundamental Rights, November 2016, http://tinyurl.com/lsl46m9.
The European Union agency that tracks anti-Semitic incidents in each of its 28 member countries reported increased security measures and closed schools in Jewish communities in the wake of terrorist attacks in Europe in 2012, 2014 and 2015.

"Antisemitism Worldwide 2016," Kantor Center for the Study of Contemporary European Jewry, 2017, http://tinyurl.com/mv6x947.
A Tel Aviv University center issues an annual report on the level of anti-Semitism worldwide.

"Special Status Report," Center for the Study of Hate and Extremism, 2017, http://tinyurl.com/lb6dq4u.
A research center at California State University San Bernardino found that hate crimes in New York City doubled in the first four months of this year compared to the same period in 2016, led by a surge in anti-Semitic incidents.

For More Information

AMCHA (Hebrew for "Your People" or "grassroots") Initiative, PO. Box 408, Santa Cruz, CA 95061; www .amchainitiative.org. Investigates, documents and combats anti-Semitism on college campuses.

American Jewish Committee, 212-751-4000; www.ajc.org. Global Jewish advocacy organization.

Anti-Defamation League, www.adl.org. International organization fighting anti-Semitism, headquartered in New York City.

Community Security Trust, https://cst.org.uk/about-cst. British charity that seeks to protect British Jews from anti-Semitism; issues annual report on anti-Semitism in Britain.

Human Rights First, 75 Broad St., 31st Floor, New York, NY 10004; 202-370-3323; www.humanrightsfirst.org. International advocacy organization that monitors hate crimes in Germany and France and government policies affecting anti-Semitism.

Jewish Voice for Peace, 1611 Telegraph Ave., Suite 1020, Oakland, CA 94612; 510-465-1777; https://jewishvoice forpeace.org. Supports Palestinian rights and the boycott against Israel.

Kantor Center for the Study of Contemporary European Jewry, Gilman Building, Room 454 C [454 Gimmel] Tel Aviv University, P.O.B. 39040, Ramat Aviv, Tel Aviv, 6139001, Israel; 972-3-6406073; http://kantorcenter.tau.ac.il. Research center that issues annual report on anti-Semitism worldwide.

Palestine Legal, 637 S. Dearborn St., 3rd Floor, Chicago, IL 60605; 312-212-0448; http://palestinelegal.org. Provides legal advice, advocacy and litigation support to those advocating justice in Palestine.

Southern Poverty Law Center, 400 Washington Ave., Montgomery, AL 36104; 888-414-7752; www.splcenter.org. Litigation and education group aimed at fighting bigotry; tracks hate crimes; has filed landmark suits against racism, anti-Semitism.

7

Native American Sovereignty

Christina L. Lyons

Former Crow Nation Chairman Darrin Old Coyote says the tribe has the right to develop coal reserves on its vast Montana reservation. Other tribes nearby, however, oppose fossil fuel development as a threat to Native Americans' distinct way of life and want the federal government to protect the land.

From *CQ Researcher,*
May 5, 2017

O n rolling hills in south-central Montana, near where Lt.Col. George Armstrong Custer and his 7th Cavalry made their Last Stand in 1876, the Crow Nation sees the future.

The tribe's 2.2-million-acre reservation is rich in coal, and unlocking its potential is critical to the tribe's economy, tribal leaders say. The Crow's main source of income is the 43-year-old Absaloka Mine in Hardin. The tribe for the past several years has pushed to open a second mine that could produce 1.4 billion tons of coal and generate $10 million for the tribe in five years.

But the tribe's attempts to open the new mine have been stymied in part by federal land-use and environmental rules that the tribal government says tread on its sovereignty.[1]

"I don't want to be dependent on the U.S. government," former Crow tribal Chairman Darrin Old Coyote said. "We have the resources, we have the manpower, we have the capability of being self-sufficient." Noting that the tribe's unemployment rate ranges between 25 percent and 50 percent, he added, "There's no reason why we should be this poor."[2]

But nearby tribes say fossil fuel development threatens the environment and Native Americans' distinct way of life, which they believe the federal government is obligated to protect under centuries-old treaties. Energy development "threatens the cultural heritage of what it means to be Northern Cheyenne," tribal council member Conrad Fisher said. "It has to do with being environmental stewards of the land and appreciating this beautiful country we call home."[3]

The tribes' contrasting views highlight a spirited debate among Native Americans, economists, environmentalists, scholars and

Navajo Nation Is Biggest U.S. Tribe by Far

The five largest Indian reservations in the continental United States are in the West. The Navajo Nation — spanning Arizona, New Mexico and Utah and covering nearly 27,100 square miles — is nearly eight times bigger than the second-largest reservation.
It also has the largest population.

Five Largest Native American Reservations

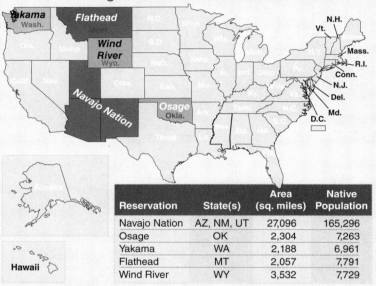

Reservation	State(s)	Area (sq. miles)	Native Population
Navajo Nation	AZ, NM, UT	27,096	165,296
Osage	OK	2,304	7,263
Yakama	WA	2,188	6,961
Flathead	MT	2,057	7,791
Wind River	WY	3,532	7,729

Sources: Amber Pariona, "Biggest Indian Reservations in the United States," *World Atlas*, July 20, 2016, http://tinyurl.com/lzve6ne; Tina Norris, Paula L. Vines and Elizabeth M. Hoeffel, "My Tribal Area," U.S. Census Bureau, 2011-2015 American Community Survey 5-Year Estimates, http://tinyurl.com/lwavjnn; "Indian Lands of Federally Recognized Tribes of the United States," Bureau of Indian Affairs, http://tinyurl.com/lm2vekh.

remains obligated to protect Indian land and natural resources from outside commercial exploitation or corrupt tribal governments.

"It's not about business anymore," David Kenny, a member of the Seneca Nation, said as he marched past the White House on March 17 protesting the completion of the Dakota Access Pipeline. The controversial oil pipeline runs under land sacred to Native Americans just outside the Standing Rock Sioux's reservation in North Dakota. "Everybody is going to die if this continues. The Earth is dying."[5]

The debate over energy development has taken on added urgency in recent years because of entrenched poverty on reservations and the growing lure of energy and mineral riches, driven in part by the Trump administration's plans to revitalize the domestic energy industry.

In 2010, 5.2 million people identified as members of one of the nation's 567 American Indian or Alaska Native tribes. About 22 percent of the Native Americans live on one of 334 reservations, which cover 100 million acres scattered across 35 states.

Those reservations contain almost 30 percent of the nation's coal reserves west of the Mississippi River, half of its potential uranium reserves and one-fifth of the known oil and natural gas reserves. Yet the Interior Department in 2008 estimated that 15 million acres of reservations' energy rich lands were undeveloped.[6]

Some tribes reside on lands with abundant natural resources for timbering, agriculture or fishing — such as in the Pacific Northwest or Great Lakes areas. Other tribes have rich fossil fuel or mineral reserves, but not all want to harvest them.

The issue of whether to exploit fossil fuel or mineral resources can put tribes at odds with each other or cause divisions within tribes.

lawmakers about energy development and tribal sovereignty. Some tribal governments — including the Navajo in the Southwest and the Southern Ute in Colorado — favor authorizing tribes to develop their energy resources or implement their own environmental safeguards without restrictions from the federal government and outsiders.

"It's about sovereignty," said Mark Fox, chairman of the Three Affiliated Tribes of the Mandan, Hidatsa and Arikara Nation, known as MHA Nation, which has profited from an oil and gas boom on its Fort Berthold reservation in North Dakota.[4]

But other tribal governments, numerous individual natives and environmentalists say the federal government

"The Navajo Nation has some members who are pro-economic development and want to provide jobs [in areas] where there is significant unemployment," says Walter Stern, a lawyer in New Mexico who represents energy companies. "And there are members who are opposed to any kind of disturbance of Mother Earth, so they don't want to see any coal development or anything."

Federal regulations can limit resource development on tribal lands, legal experts say. The regulations are based on the "trustee doctrine," which stems from an 1831 Supreme Court ruling describing tribes as "domestic dependent nations" with a relationship to the U.S. government similar to that of wards to guardians.[7]

Much of the energy development that has occurred on reservations was initiated decades ago, when changing federal policies left reservations with checkerboard land ownership patterns. The Dawes Act of 1887 divvied up native territories and allotted plots to individual Indians, to be held in trust for 25 years or until the United States deemed the individuals competent to be granted ownership. Surplus lands were sold to non-Indians.

When the allotment process ended in 1934, lands remaining in trust were frozen in the trust, while any individuals who had been granted deeds to their lots were free to lease or sell them. According to a 2011 study, about 75 percent of tribal land remains in trust protection for the tribe, 20 percent entail individual lots held in trust (primarily for heirs of the Indians originally granted the lots) and 5 percent is privately owned by Indians or non-Indians.[8]

Before Congress ended the allotment process, it allowed the U.S. government to approve any energy development contracts on tribal trust lands. Many contracts provided only limited royalties to tribes. Tribes regained some authority over development projects on their lands in the 1980s, but the Bureau of Indian Affairs (BIA) retained final approval.

Today, a "complex" regulatory framework governs BIA management of energy development on trust lands, according to the Government Accountability Office (GAO).

"Trusteeship wraps these reservations in red tape," says Terry Anderson, a senior fellow at the Property and Environmental Research Center in Bozeman, Mont., noting that energy development proposals require approval from four federal agencies and compliance with 49 regulations.

He says tribes should have "authority over the land within reservation boundaries. I think from there, tribes can decide what they want to do."

But Jacqueline Pata, executive director of the National Congress of American Indians, a lobbying organization for tribal interests based in Washington, D.C., says the trust status is necessary to prevent exploitation. "The protection of our land is so important to tribes," she says.

At the same time, Pata says, the government must recognize tribes' sovereignty. Various laws, court rulings and treaties pledged the U.S. government to honor tribal self-governance while also providing support for health care, education, housing and economic development.[9]

Yet in 2011 an estimated 40 percent of the American Indians and Alaska Natives on reservations were living in poverty. The unemployment rate averages about 19 percent, nearly a quarter of reservation homes lack plumbing, and health, education and income statistics rank near the bottom of all minority groups nationwide. Employment options are few. According to the National Congress of American Indians, 4 percent of Indians work in agriculture, forestry, fishing/hunting or mining. About one-third work in education, health care or social services; the rest are in public administration, hold odd jobs or are unemployed.[10]

Because tribes cannot tax property, they must get innovative to generate more revenue, experts say.*

Since the 1970s, many tribes have opened casinos or run bingo games. In 2015, 474 tribal gambling operations generated nearly $30 billion in revenue nationwide.[11] The most successful operations, experts note, are those located near major metropolitan areas.

The Southern Ute tribe now generates about 30 percent of its income from oil and natural gas production. But navigating the regulatory process took eight years, during which the tribe lost more than $95 million in potential revenue from permitting fees, oil and gas severance taxes and royalties, according to the GAO.[12]

Matthew Fletcher, a University of Michigan law professor and member of the Grand Traverse Band in Michigan, says the Southern Ute's success is unusual. Energy development often devastates Native American

---

*Tribes cannot levy property taxes because of the trust status of their land. They can impose sales and excise taxes.

Many Native Homes Lack Phones, Plumbing

Homes on Indian reservations and in Alaska Native villages are in poorer condition than in the general U.S. population, according to the latest census data. Nearly one-fifth of reservation households had no telephone in 2006-2010, and a quarter of the homes in Alaska Native villages lacked complete plumbing.

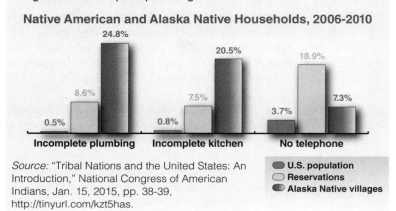

Native American and Alaska Native Households, 2006-2010

Source: "Tribal Nations and the United States: An Introduction," National Congress of American Indians, Jan. 15, 2015, pp. 38-39, http://tinyurl.com/kzt5has.

- U.S. population
- Reservations
- Alaska Native villages

lands. Radioactive material from fracking — the process of injecting high-pressure liquid into underground rock to reach oil or gas — has been dumped on reservation lands, and heavy trucks have damaged roads. In addition, with non-natives entering the reservation to work, crime has risen.[13]

Kevin Washburn, former BIA director for the Obama administration, says Congress needs to alter some outdated, "paternalistic" regulations on Indian lands, but he is wary of too much deregulation.

"All over Indian country are abandoned mines where someone made a lot of money and then left," he says. "We can't just say we trust the oil and gas companies to do the right thing."

As debate continues, these are some of the questions being considered:

Should tribes have full control over their reservations?

MHA Nation council member Fred Fox said the United States should treat tribes on reservations as sovereign nations. "We have ancestors that owned these lands. . . . Let us collect our own taxes. Let us create economic viability for our people. Let us create the regulatory system."[14]

Former *Wall Street Journal* reporter Naomi Schaefer Riley in her 2016 book, *The New Trail of Tears,* suggests tribes could become more economically self-sufficient if the federal government granted natives private-property rights over the trust lands so they can use it as collateral to start businesses.[15]

Chris Edwards, director of tax policy studies at the Cato Institute, a libertarian think tank in Washington, D.C., agrees. He suggests if the government ended the trustee relationship and created private property, reservations could reach their economic potential.

Most tribal leaders reject any proposals that would move the land out of trust protection and into private ownership. Indeed, many tribes were fearful when they read news accounts in late 2016 indicating that Donald Trump intended to privatize Indian lands after becoming president, accounts the new administration has denied.

Many experts say the current system holds several advantages for tribes, particularly financial. Federal subsidies to Native American tribes total about $20 billion a year, although the level of support varies widely by tribe.[16]

"There are tribes that are worried that if you end the trust responsibility, you will simultaneously end funding" from the federal government, says Joseph Kalt, codirector of the Harvard Project on American Indian Economic Development in Cambridge, Mass.

Furthermore, the trust system gives tribes some political voice, Kalt says. The Indian population is tiny — about 1.5 percent of the U.S. population — "so, a city like Tucson with a million people might be [able to adequately represent itself on a bigger stage, but not] a Potawatomi tribe with just a couple thousand people," he says.

Other experts question tribes' ability to manage their affairs, citing poorly run councils as well as political and regulatory instability that makes companies reluctant to invest in Native American projects. At Fort Berthold, for example, former chairman Tex Hall lost reelection in 2014 after many tribal members accused him of improperly benefiting from oil business contracts.[17]

Many tribes, however, have successfully exercised their sovereignty and built solid regulatory and economic systems and could thrive outside the trust system, Kalt says. The Confederated Salish and Kootenai Tribes on the Flathead Reservation in Montana oversees everything from road construction and maintenance to schools and natural resources. The tribal nation formed a professional services company, S&K Technologies, in 1999. Since 2002, S&K has obtained federal and commercial contracts, generating more than $25 million — paid in yearly dividends — to run the tribal government and employs about 400 tribal members.[18]

"Tribes are not perfect institutions, nor is the federal government," says Brian Gunn, an attorney in Washington, D.C, who represents tribal groups. "They go through election cycles. Sometimes a tribe will have good leadership, other times not so good."

But the U.S. government should be willing to allow tribes to try and even to fail, suggests Gunn, a member of the Confederated Tribes of the Colville reservation in Washington state.

He says lawmakers are moving in that direction. The Indian Trust Asset Reform Act, passed by Congress last year, allows tribes to manage their assets at a lesser standard than the BIA's standard, but waives the U.S. government's liability if something goes wrong, Gunn says. "So basically it puts the choice in the tribe's hands."[19]

A 2005 law similarly allowed tribes to enter agreements with the BIA to pursue land agreements for energy development on their own. But the law left in place a maze of regulations, which dissuade tribes from pursuing lease agreements, the GAO reported in 2015.[20]

Elizabeth Kronk Warner, director of the Tribal Law and Government Center at the University of Kansas and a member of the Sault Ste. Marie Tribe of Chippewa Indians, criticizes the law because it waives the government's liability if anything goes wrong with the project, even though the government retains supervisory authority. "I think tribes should be . . . fully sovereign and liable, or the federal government [should] maintain its management responsibility" and liability, she says.

Most Native Americans like the idea of federal protection entailed in the government's trust responsibility,

"but they don't want the . . . government making decisions," Kalt says.

Kevin Gover, former assistant secretary for Indian affairs under President Bill Clinton and a member of the Pawnee Nation of Oklahoma, has suggested Congress change the trust system by making tribal governments "permanent components of the American federalist system."[21] In other words, tribal reservations would be treated as jurisdictions much like counties or states, he says.

Gover, who now is director of the Smithsonian's National Museum of the American Indian in Washington, says the government could grant tribes the option of managing their own lands — including leveraging them as a capital asset — without federal oversight. If their economic enterprises fail, the land could be foreclosed upon but remain within the tribal jurisdiction.

Fletcher says he can't see how a system outside the trust could work. "The over-arching theory of federal Indian affairs is that the United States has a trust obligation to Indian tribes — that goes back to the original treaties that say the U.S. has a duty of protection to Indian tribes. . . . I do believe that duty of protection is something that can't and should never be given up."

Would energy development improve tribes' economies?

Some economists and legal experts say energy development could help tribes, especially in places like Oklahoma or Wyoming, where large oil reserves are located, or Montana and North Dakota, with their rich coal deposits. "Some reservations have energy resources worth developing, and others [are] less fortunate," attorney Stern says.

In February, Tyson Thompson, a Southern Ute tribal council member, urged Congress to ease federal regulations to encourage more energy development on Indian lands. "Our energy-related economic successes have resulted in a higher standard of living for our [approximately 1,400] tribal members," Thompson told the House Oversight and Government Reform Committee.[22]

In October, Bloomberg News had reported that the tribe "has a higher long-term credit rating than Wells Fargo and Co. and more oil and natural gas wells than it has members." The Ute now control 1,600 wells across four states and are one of the richest tribes in the nation.[23]

An oil and natural gas boom on the MHA Nation's Fort Berthold reservation in North Dakota has been at the center of the ongoing debate over Indian sovereignty versus what some see as the federal government's obligation to protect Indian land and natural resources. Entrenched poverty on reservations and the growing lure of energy and mineral riches have intensified the debate in recent years.

Anderson of the Property and Environment Research Center says if federal lawmakers streamline regulations to make it easier for tribes to tap into the energy reserves on their lands, badly needed jobs and royalties would be generated for tribal members.

The Navajo Nation formed the Navajo Transitional Energy Co. in 2013. It purchased a coal mine from BHP Billiton and has signed coal agreements with North American Coal subsidiary Bisti Fuels Co. and the Four Corners Power Plant. It has about 800 employees and announced a year ago it had returned $35 million in royalties to the tribe in 2015.[24]

The Crow government generates 70 percent of its revenue from a coal mining operation on the edge of its reservation, says James Allison, an assistant professor of history at Christopher Newport University in Newport News, Va. The revenue enables it to provide housing, police, water services and more. At the same time, he says, "you wouldn't go onto the Crow reservation and say, look at the prosperity it has produced."

History has proven that energy development is no panacea, he says; successful energy development also depends on timing, Allison warns.

A downturn in oil prices from $100 per barrel in 2013 to $30 per barrel in 2016 particularly hurt the Northern Arapaho and Eastern Shoshone on the Wind River Reservation in central-western Wyoming. Both tribes have long been dependent on oil revenues. Now the Northern Arapaho are investigating solar and wind projects, Allison says.[25]

Many tribes worry a hunger for profit will destroy their culture and ultimately erode their communities.

The Turtle Mountain Band of Chippewa Indians in north-central North Dakota, located about 190 miles from the Fort Berthold reservation, banned fracking because of concerns about its potential to contaminate drinking water and lakes and produce large volumes of waste.[26] Many other tribes also oppose fracking.[27]

In Minnesota, the Fond du Lac Band of the Lake Superior Chippewa Indians sees mining as a threat to its culture. For years the tribe has tried to halt or reverse environmental damage from a century-old iron mine. And it is fighting plans for a copper mine on land the tribe ceded to the U.S. government in 1854 in exchange for continued rights to its hunting, fishing and gathering resources.

"A hundred years of mining has already left a pretty rugged footprint on the landscape, and it has destroyed wild rice waters," says Nancy Schuldt, water projects coordinator for the Fond du Lac Environmental Program in Cloquet, Minn. "It has exacerbated a problem with mercury in fish, it has destroyed wetlands, it has destroyed headwater streams, destroyed habitat for important species, destroyed cultural resources, sacred sites, all of that."

In the Pacific Northwest, the Lummi Nation, along with other area tribes, has battled the proposed Gateway Pacific Terminal near Bellingham, Wash., that would export coal and other commodities to Asia. The Lummi said spills or maritime accidents could destroy fishing beds and threaten its treaty-protected fishing rights. The Army Corps of Engineers agreed and denied a permit for the project last May. The Crow Nation, however, continues to push for the terminal so it can sell to coal markets in Southeast Asia.[28]

Conservationists at Fort Berthold for years have denounced the tribal council's oversight of energy development, accusing it of choosing monetary profit over the well-being of the land and the people.[29]

At a February hearing in New Mexico before a United Nations representative, Navajo tribal member Leoyla Cowboy said she wanted help for her people to restore sacred lands and build infrastructure for renewable energy. Between 1944 and 1986, uranium extraction on Indian land created hazardous waste sites and contaminated drinking water. "Coal, oil and gas, as well as uranium, have had a huge negative impact on our lands, and have taken us away from our lands," she said.[30]

Fletcher says energy is not the answer for struggling reservations. "It gives a windfall to political and economic elites in Indian country, just as it does elsewhere in the country. There'll be an influx of cash, and then you'll have a series of tribal governments who fight over that cash, just as the MHA Nation does at Fort Berthold," he says. "That is just going to repeat over and over again if there's a so-called successful influx of cash resources into a tribal community where a tribe is just not used to that sort of thing."

He adds, "What I do see is massive amounts of environmental devastation and cultural devastation too."

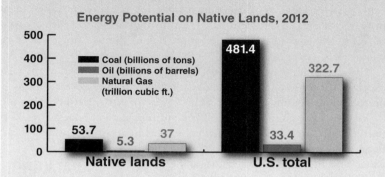

Native Lands Hold Vast Resources

Untapped energy resources on Indian lands were valued at $1.5 trillion in 2012, the most recent data available. The largest reserves are in coal and natural gas; the Crow reservation alone has 17 billion tons of coal, according to the Department of the Interior.

Energy Potential on Native Lands, 2012

Legend:
- Coal (billions of tons)
- Oil (billions of barrels)
- Natural Gas (trillion cubic ft.)

Native lands: Coal 53.7, Oil 5.3, Natural Gas 37
U.S. total: Coal 481.4, Oil 33.4, Natural Gas 322.7

Sources: Shawn Regan and Terry L. Anderson, "The Energy Wealth of Indian Nations," George W. Bush Institute, Property and Environment Research Center, pp. 17, 19, http://tinyurl.com/jwoxgfl; "Annual Coal Report 2012," U.S. Energy Information Administration, December 2013, p. 23, http://tinyurl.com/n5j6gh9; "U.S. Crude Oil and Natural Gas Proved Reserves, Year-end 2015," U.S. Energy Information Administration, December 2016, p. 2, http://tinyurl.com/lzw3579.

Must tribes be consulted on projects outside their borders?

The Standing Rock Sioux tribe and its supporters protesting the completion of the Dakota Access Pipeline said they were demanding their right to "sovereignty" — in this case, their right to protect sacred land and block potential threats to their groundwater from a project that snaked near the reservation boundary.

"It's not that they are against development," says Pata of the National Congress of American Indians, "but they want to make sure the tribe's considerations and concerns are part of the discussion."

In the 18th and 19th centuries, hundreds of tribes signed treaties with the U.S. government where they agreed to smaller territories in return for continued rights to the ceded land for spiritual, cultural or economic purposes. In the case of the Sioux, supporters say the tribe did not legally cede rights to the Missouri River or its shoreline when the government constructed five major dams between the 1930s and 1950s. They say the

construction also contravened a 1908 Supreme Court decision, known as the Winters Doctrine, which guaranteed tribes water rights on their reservations.[31]

But disagreements remain about how much say tribes actually have on projects outside their borders, even if the tribes believe the project could affect treaty land or ultimately impede life on their reservations.

In recent years, tribal lawyers have successfully convinced courts of tribes' treaty rights, according to Jan Hasselman, a staff attorney for the nonprofit environmental law firm EarthJustice, based in San Francisco. "Federal court precedent says that where a tribe opposes a project based on its impacts on treaty-reserved fishing, a federal agency cannot authorize anything more than a 'de minis' [minimal] impact," he said.[32]

Kandi Mossett, organizer of the Native Energy and Climate Campaign for the Indigenous Environmental Network, a grassroots organization in Bemidji, Minn., joined thousands of Dakota Access Pipeline protesters who ultimately were removed from their campsites outside the Sioux reservation. "We were forced off of our treaty land again. In 2017," she said. "Because that is what this country was founded upon: the taking, raping and pillaging of Native American land."[33]

Schuldt warns that tribes don't have veto power over land ceded to the government now outside their reservations. "If you go back before 1492, everything was tribal land." She adds that some tribes are looking for a "free prior informed consent right or . . . a veto right as it relates to things even off the reservation. I don't think that, frankly, is workable."

However, many tribes — but not all — do have clearly outlined treaty rights to hunt, fish, collect plants on and off reservation land, she says.

Victoria Tauli-Corpuz, a United Nations special rapporteur, in March faulted the federal government for frequently failing to consult with Native Americans on issues "affecting their land, territory and resources." In a draft report, she said, the Army Corps of Engineers approved an environmental assessment regarding the Dakota Access Pipeline that ignored tribal interests.[34]

Native Americans say the federal government thus violated the 2007 U.N. Declaration on the Rights of Indigenous Peoples, which President Barack Obama in 2010 said the United States would support. The declaration, in part, requires governments to obtain tribes' "free and informed consent" prior to the approval of any project affecting their lands or territories and other resources, particularly in connection with the development, utilization or exploitation of mineral, water or other resources.[35]

Even before adopting that declaration, however, previous administrations had mandated such consultation. Museum Director Gover says that, during the Clinton administration, "our big mantra was consultation." The Bush and Obama administrations adopted the same policy by executive memoranda, although the Trump administration has not reissued the same policy or clearly withdrawn it.

Nevertheless, Gover says the requirement that tribes be consulted is scattered through some federal statutes. "But it's not thorough going," he says.

Former BIA Director Washburn says the National Historic Preservation Act, a 1966 law that seeks to protect the nation's historical and archaeological sites, clearly states that tribes must be consulted. However, "consultation [is a] word that gets thrown around a lot of different ways," he says. It's unclear how much weight a tribal vote

has on a project outside its boundaries. "That's the issue. If it's outside tribal lands, they just don't really have sovereignty," Washburn says. "But it's not a matter of sovereignty; it's a matter of . . . good government relations."

Attorney Stern says various statutes, regulations, executive orders and other policy statements describe the federal government's obligations to consult with tribes.

"It's my view, however, that the consultation obligation that is required under the National Historic Preservation Act is not clear," he says. "For example, that statute and its regulations require that federal agencies exercise 'reasonable good faith' in consulting with the tribes. That term 'reasonable good faith,' to my mind, doesn't really provide clear guidance on the extent of consultation that must be required along the way."

BACKGROUND
Allies and Enemies

The treatment of indigenous people in North America by white settlers and later the U.S. government has fluctuated since 1492, when Italian explorer Christopher Columbus stepped foot on what is now the Bahamas.

Many of the earliest Europeans settlers were eager to trade with Native Americans and saw them as allies in their efforts to survive in the New World. However, the European powers also wanted to exploit North America's minerals, furs and fish, while colonists desired land to farm and to establish settlements.[36]

Over time, increasingly violent battles ensued between the settlers and tribes. On March 22, 1622, the Powhatan Confederacy, angry over English expansion in Virginia, launched surprise attacks on settlements along the James River, nearly wiping out the fledgling colony. A few years later, the director of the New Netherland colony, Willem Kieft, tried to tax natives on behalf of the Dutch West India Company. When the Indians refused to pay, Kieft ordered attacks on their villages, prompting the tribes to counterattack.[37]

During the French and Indian War (1754-63), the European combatants wanted the tribes as allies, as did the Americans and British during the American Revolution. Each side attacked tribes that sided with their enemies. After the Revolution, European immigration resumed and settlers pushed farther west, forcing tribes off their lands and leading to more friction.[38]

The Second Continental Congress adopted the Northwest Ordinance in 1787, which allowed new states to be added to the Union but said, "The utmost good faith shall always be observed towards the Indians; their land and property shall never be taken from them without their consent."[39]

Two years later, the U.S. Constitution empowered Congress to "regulate Commerce with . . . the Indian Tribes" and declared treaties to be the "supreme law of the land." And in 1790, Congress barred the purchase of Indian land without federal approval.[40]

But "a relentlessly expansionist white population [drove] the Indians westward without regard to treaty obligations, or . . . even simply humanity," historian Peter Cozzens said.[41]

President James Monroe told Gen. Andrew Jackson in 1817 that "the savage requires a greater extent of territory to sustain it than is compatible with the progress and just claims of civilized life, and must yield to it."[42]

Whites believed they possessed "discoverer rights" to the land — a position upheld by the Supreme Court in 1823, which stated that only the federal government, and not the tribes, could sell land to private interests.[43]

Congress in May 1830 passed the Indian Removal Act, allowing Jackson, who by then was president, to grant Indians lands west of the Mississippi in exchange for their lands within existing state borders.[44] The Cherokee Nation tried to stop the state of Georgia from clearing its members from the land, but in 1831 the Supreme Court refused to hear the case, declaring the tribe a dependent nation under the care of the federal government.[45]

A year later, the court ruled that the federal government, and not states, could regulate Indian affairs and said the Cherokees had rights acknowledged by the U.S. government. Jackson refused to enforce the ruling, however, and Georgia seized the tribe's lands for whites eager to mine newly discovered gold.[46]

About 4,000 out of 15,000 Cherokees died in the 1838-1839 march, known as the Trail of Tears, to lands west of the Mississippi River.[47]

More Indians found themselves in the whites' path after the 1848 Treaty of Guadalupe Hidalgo ended the Mexican-American War, paving the way for U.S. expansion to the Pacific Ocean.

As whites occupied more and more territory, Native Americans lost their traditional hunting grounds and much of their land and way of life. White hunters wiped out the buffalo on the Great Plains, and deadly European diseases for which Native Americans had no immunity decimated many tribes. In 1849 alone, cholera killed half of the native population in the southern plains.[48]

By 1871, when Congress limited the president's power to enter into treaties, the federal government had signed more than 400 treaties, many of which were broken by subsequent waves of settlers, or challenged by tribes throughout the "Indian wars" (about 1860 to 1880).[49]

Forced Assimilation

On July 18, 1885, Republican Sen. Henry Laurens Dawes of Massachusetts wrote to a white-run advocacy group called the Indian Rights Association, lamenting the continued fighting between whites and Indians. He urged work be done with "haste to teach [the Native American] habits of industry, self-reliance, knowledge of property, and a desire for its acquisition."[50]

Two years later, Congress passed the General Allotment Act, or Dawes Act, subdivided reservations into plots and aimed to assimilate Indians into white society by making them landowners and farmers in the European tradition. Non-native settlers rushed to claim surplus lands not given to Indians. In one day in April 1889, 50,000 prospective settlers raced across Oklahoma and claimed nearl 2 million acres by the end of the day.[51] The allotment process ultimately resulted in more than half of those living on reservations to be non-Indians.[52]

A number of whites cheated Indians out of their land. "Indians were easy marks, especially in a place like Oklahoma, where there was very valuable land, mostly because of oil and gas," Gover of the National Museum of American Indians says.

By the late 1920s, "Indians were poorer than ever," Gover says. "They were still uneducated, and under the thumb of a very oppressive bureaucracy that had told them you may not practice your religion, you may not practice your traditional means of governance, you may not speak your language. Your children will be taken and sent away for education."

The policies "were, in fact, meant to exterminate not the individual Indians but certainly the Indian nations as effective polities and social and cultural institutions," he says.

CHRONOLOGY

1700s-1850s *Federal government forces tribes from their lands.*

1789 Constitution empowers federal government to negotiate with tribes.

1790 Congress enacts the first of six Non-Intercourse Acts, requiring federal approval for any private purchase of Indian land.

1824 Secretary of War John C. Calhoun creates Office of Indian Affairs, which later becomes Bureau of Indian Affairs (BIA).

1838-1839 After gold is discovered on Cherokee lands in Georgia, tribe is forced to move west; thousands perish during infamous "Trail of Tears" march.

1831 Supreme Court rules tribes are dependent nations under U.S. guardianship.

1851 Indian Appropriations Act allocates funds to move Western tribes onto reservations.

1880s-1930s *Federal government seeks to force Native Americans to assimilate.*

1887 Dawes Act divides Indian lands into parcels to be allotted to Native and non-Native Americans.

1903 Supreme Court says treaties can be modified or terminated without tribes' consent.

1924 Indian Citizenship Act grants constitutional rights to Native Americans.

1934 Indian Reorganization Act ends land allotment process.

1938 Indian Mineral Leasing Act restores tribal control over energy development on reservations.

1970s-1980s *U.S. limits tribes' sovereignty, then promotes self-determination.*

1975 Indian Self-Determination and Education Assistance Act funnels federal grants directly to tribes.

1982 Indian Mineral Development Act enables tribes to negotiate energy extraction agreements.

1984 A Reagan administration report assails BIA, says it "thrives on the failure of Indian tribes."

1987 In *California vs. Cabazon Band of Mission Indians,* Supreme Court says tribes can open casinos.

1990s-Present *Federal government increasingly recognizes tribal self-government.*

1996 Blackfeet activist Elouise Cobell files class-action suit against federal government for mismanaging trust lands.

2002 U.S. government settles Indian claims over Missouri River dams.

2005 Indian Tribal Energy Development and Self-Determination Act gives tribes greater control over energy development on their lands.

2009 Settlement of Cobell lawsuit awards plaintiffs $3.4 billion.

2010 President Barack Obama signs Tribal Law and Order Act giving tribal courts more authority.

2011 National Wildlife Federation study finds reservations disproportionately suffer more from climate change.

2015 Government Accountability Office concludes BIA mismanagement hinders energy development on Indian lands.

2016 Indian Trust Asset Management Reform Act gives tribes more control over trust lands.

2017 A federal judge refuses request by the Standing Rock Sioux to block Dakota Access Pipeline; Indians march in Washington, D.C., to protest its completion. . . . Trump administration ends moratorium on new coal leasing on federal, including some Indian, lands. Over the objections of Native Americans, the administration also approves completing the 1,179-mile Keystone XL oil pipeline that would cross the land of numerous tribes.

Many U.S. lawmakers did raise concerns about the natives' plight. In 1921, Congress passed the Snyder Act requiring the federal government to direct money "from time to time" for health care, education, economic development, governing and policing. A 1924 law awarded citizenship to many American Indians and Alaska Natives.[53]

The measures, however, did not reverse the effects of forced assimilation. In 1928, the Institute for Government Research (later renamed the Brookings Institution) reported to the Department of the Interior: "An overwhelming majority of the Indians are poor, even extremely poor, and they are not adjusted to the economic and social system of the dominant white civilization." Among other deficiencies, the report cited the exclusion of Indians from management of their own affairs and the poor quality of public services.[54]

In the 1930s, Commissioner of Indian Affairs John Collier decried the plight of the estimated 350,000 Native Americans. He created the Emergency Conservation Work program for Indians, focused on training natives to use their own lands and resources. Before its demise in 1943, the program employed 85,349 natives from 71 reservations.[55]

In 1934, the Indian Reorganization Act ended the allotment process and began returning Indian land to the federal trust.

The Supreme Court in 1938 recognized the Native Americans' ownership of minerals and timber on their land, and Congress authorized them to lease their minerals through the Indian Mineral Leasing Act of 1938 with approval from the federal government. And Congress in 1942 passed the Indian Claims Commission Act to allow Native Americans to sue the government for compensation for lands taken from them.[56]

But tribes faced renewed threats as federal policy shifted again.

Termination Period

In 1944, Congress' Pick-Sloan Plan aimed to provide irrigation, generate hydropower and employ World War II veterans by constructing five dams on the Missouri River (including a dam already built at Fort Peck, Mont., in 1937). The Army Corps of Engineers saw condemnation as the best way to acquire Native American lands needed for the project.[57]

The plan reduced the land base of the five Missouri River Sioux reservations by 6 percent and forced the relocation of one-third of the population. The tribes' best land was flooded, and residents were forced to move to land barren of natural resources.[58]

Then, with the BIA under attack and the belief growing that Indians were ready to assimilate, Congress in 1953 adopted a resolution that Native Americans should no longer be treated as wards of the United States. Between 1953 and 1964, approximately 2.5 million acres of tribal lands were removed from protection under the trust. The losses affected over 100 tribes occupying valuable lands, including the Klamath in Oregon's timber forests.[59]

Gover says federal leaders believed the so-called termination policy was in the best interest of Native Americans, 10 percent of whom served in the armed forces during World War II. "It occurred to everybody they don't need protection, they're perfectly capable," he says.

But federal lawmakers gradually came to realize the policy wasn't helping Indians and renewed support for tribes.

Presidents John F. Kennedy (1961-63) and Lyndon B. Johnson (1963-68) called for investments in economic development on reservations. The 1968 Indian Civil Rights Act prevented states from assuming jurisdiction over Indian lands without tribal consent and barred Indian tribes from impeding on the constitutional rights of their people.[60]

President Richard M. Nixon (1969-74) formally denounced termination, mandated BIA reform and recognized the rights of tribal governments. On July 8, 1970, he told Congress, "Self-determination among the Indian people can and must be encouraged. . . . This, then, must be the goal of any new national policy toward the Indian people."[61]

Initially, however, internal conflict impeded BIA reform efforts aimed at improving relations with the tribes and led to a series of Native Americans protests. In spring 1973, 200 followers of the militant American Indian Movement occupied the village of Wounded Knee on the Pine Ridge Reservation in South Dakota, demanding that the federal government fulfill its treaty obligations. Two Indians died and an FBI agent was critically wounded in a shootout, violence that cost the movement critical support.[62]

Climate Change Threatens Tribal Lands

"It is the federal government's responsibility to protect our fishing rights."

Ancestors of the Fond du Lac Band of Lake Superior Chippewa settled centuries ago near the headwaters of the St. Louis River in Minnesota, where lush wild rice grasses swayed above wetlands, sustaining the tribe with nutrients and an abundance of wildlife.

White settlers later moved the band to a 100,000-acre reservation off the lake in northeastern Minnesota. Treaties signed in 1837 and 1854 guaranteed tribal members harvesting rights on their original lands crossing into Wisconsin. But years of pollution and climate change-related shifts in weather patterns have diminished the grasses.

"We are doing all we can to restore our wild rice resources," says Nancy Schuldt, water projects coordinator for the tribe. "We're already seeing impacts from climate change. . . . We've had whole years [of harvests] wiped out from big storms." The Fond du Lac Band and hundreds of other Native American groups say they didn't contribute to the greenhouse gases linked to global warming, and they insist the federal government is duty-bound to protect them.

"Tribes are really contributing very little, if anything, to the [carbon] footprint and are really the ones who are getting" hurt by climate change, says Elizabeth Kronk Warner, director of the Tribal Law and Government Center at the University of Kansas. She says the U.S. government is legally and morally obligated to protect tribes that it forced onto lands now among the most vulnerable to environmental change.

In 2011, the National Wildlife Federation, with several other environmental groups, detailed how climate change disproportionately affects tribal communities because they are more heavily dependent on natural resources for economic, cultural and spiritual purposes.[1]

Many indigenous communities in the United States "are literally on the forefront of losing their land . . . because of climate change," Warner says. Coastal tribal villages in Alaska, Louisiana and South Carolina lose land every year due to rising seas and severe storms, she says.

Fawn Sharp, president of the Quinault Indian Nation in Taholah, Wash., is working with specialists to relocate her tribe's village to higher ground. Rising seas caused by melting glaciers have breached barriers, and storms frequently flood the village.[2]

The Trump administration's stance on climate change has further alarmed Native Americans.

President Trump's fiscal 2018 budget blueprint, submitted to Congress on March 16, would cut $2.6 billion from the Environmental Protection Agency (EPA). Climate change programs would be hit particularly hard.[3]

"We're not spending money on that anymore," Mick Mulvaney, director of the Office of Management and Budget, told reporters. "We consider that to be a waste of your money to go out and do that."[4]

Trump also has ordered the rollback of regulations, including the landmark Clean Power Plan, designed to reduce carbon emissions.

Many tribes fear these actions will hamper their efforts to adjust to climate change.

"The utter disdain for science demonstrated by this administration is insufferable," Sharp wrote in a blog shortly after Trump revealed his budget.

She called the administration's plans unconstitutional and a violation of treaty rights. She said "it is the federal government's responsibility to protect our fishing, hunting and gathering rights, on our ceded areas and in the ocean."[5]

Meanwhile, multinational companies began encroaching on tribal lands seeking subbituminous coal found under the Northern Cheyenne and Crow reservations in Montana. "To access this coal, . . . multinational companies exploited a broken and outdated legal regime that sought to promote the development of western resources at the expense of tribal sovereignty, ecological health, and simple equity," Allison of Christopher Newport University said in his 2015 book, *Sovereignty for Survival: American Energy Development and Indian Self-Determination.*[63]

By 1973, energy companies controlled hundreds of thousands of acres on Indian lands. On Northern Cheyenne and Crow reservations, more than 600,000 acres were opened for mining, causing John Woodenlegs

Warner agrees that multiple treaties obligate the government to protect tribes and their critical natural resources. The federal government has recognized such obligations in recent years. Since 1980, the EPA has funded 6,179 grants, totaling $1.7 billion, for tribal projects, many of which have supported innovative ways to protect natural resources and respond to climate change.[6]

Trump's budget plan also would cut $6 billion from the U.S. Department of Housing and Urban Development, which awarded the Biloxi-Chitimacha-Choctaw tribe a $48 million natural disaster grant last year to move from its flooding land.[7]

Not all tribes can easily relocate, says Warner, a member of the Sault Ste. Marie Tribe of Chippewa Indians. "While they could theoretically leave, they would lose all their legal protection and legal status," she says. Many tribes also have cultural and spiritual connections to the land. "For a lot of us, our religious practices are land-based, so we're connected to a particular area," Warner says.

The Fond du Lac Band developed air and water quality monitoring programs and pursued alternative and renewable energy sources. In 2007, it adopted the international Kyoto Protocol on climate change and committed to reducing its fossil fuel use by 20 percent by 2020 — a target it hit last year. But the band can't completely avoid the greenhouse gases around it.

The Bureau of Indian Affairs under the Obama administration oversaw a Tribal Climate Resilience Program to provide resources to tribes to help them adapt to changes. But it is unclear how funding for the program will be affected under Trump.

The tribe, however, is bracing for broad federal budget cuts that could affect their local efforts. "We have tried to prepare our tribal leadership to anticipate if all our tribal grants were zeroed out," Schuldt says. "I honestly don't know what is going to happen."

— *Christina L. Lyons*

A Yupik child crosses a boardwalk in Newtok, Alaska. Rising temperatures from global climate change are threatening this and other indigenous villages with flooding.

Getty Images/Andrew Burton

[1] "Facing the Storm: Indian Tribes, Climate-Induced Weather Extremes, and the Future for Indian Country," National Wildlife Federation, 2011, http://tinyurl.com/mcjmprg.

[2] "Climate Stressors on the Olympic Peninsula," U.S. Climate Resilience Toolkit, National Oceanic and Atmospheric Administration, accessed April 6, 2017, http://tinyurl.com/ltk3hvm.

[3] Ben Wolfgang, "Trump's EPA Budget Proposes Harshest Funding, Staffing Cuts in Agency's History," *The Washington Times,* March 21, 2017, http://tinyurl.com/jvt28j3.

[4] Dan Merica and Rene Marsh, "Trump Budget Chief on Climate Change: 'We Consider That to Be a Waste of Money,'" CNN, March 16, 2017, http://tinyurl.com/n4jbu3l.

[5] Fawn Sharp, " 'Trump's Utter Disdain for Science is 'Insufferable,' " *The Daily World,* March 31, 2017, http://tinyurl.com/lzhypp4.

[6] Grant Awards Database, Environmental Protection Agency, updated March 17, 2017, http://tinyurl.com/m7oygy8.

[7] Autumn Spanne, "The lucky Ones: Native American Tribe Receives $48m to Flee Climate Change," *The Guardian,* March 23, 2016, http://tinyurl.com/kgn9yax; Jose A. DelReal, "Trump Budget Asks for $6 Billion in HUD Cuts, Drops Development Grants," *The Washington Post,* March 16, 2017, http://tinyurl.com/mu9a7yx.

of the Northern Cheyenne to lament, "The impact of uncontrolled coal development could finish us off."[64] He and other natives feared multinationals would destroy their land and way of life.

Other tribes complained the federal bureaucracy barred them from seeking economic self-sufficiency. In October 1973, Navajo Chairman Peter MacDonald told

the U.S. Commission on Civil Rights that federal bureaucrats had sabotaged or ignored the council's development programs for its 14-million-acre reservation.

"Most Indian tribes know what they want, where they want programs and in what time frame they want to accomplish these things, but the problem comes at the top," he said.[65]

Tribal Councils Increasingly Expel Members

"Disenrollment is never about who belongs in the tribe."

The U.S. government's growing recognition of tribal sovereignty has correlated with a trend that worries many Indian law experts: tribal councils disenrolling members. From 2009-2016, up to 79 tribes in 20 states disenrolled 9,000 tribal members, costing those individuals their cultural identity, civil rights, federal subsidies and — in many cases — royalties from tribal enterprises, says David Wilkins, a professor of American Indian studies at the University of Minnesota Law School.

Gabriel S. Galanda, a Native American attorney who is fighting the disenrollment of more than 300 members of the Nooksack Indian Tribe in northwest Washington state, attributes the trend to "power and greed" sparked by increasing economic capitalism on native lands.

But the Nooksack government said the members it disenrolled lacked proof of ancestry. Most had enrolled in the 1980s, basing their eligibility on an ancestor named Annie George. But George was not in the 1942 census, the tribal government said, and lineage could not be verified.[1]

Other tribal councils said they disenroll members because the individuals did not have sufficient "blood quantum" — the percentage of their tribal blood is too low due to generations of intermarriage with outsiders. Each of the 567 federally recognized tribes sets its own criteria for membership, usually based on a blood quantum or lineal descent from a tribal member.[2]

Wilkins' studies suggest that tribal leaders sometimes seek to disenroll members because of family feuds or to secure political power or limit distribution of royalties.

The first documented case of a tribe disenrolling members involved the Northern Ute in Utah. The disenrollments began in 1951 after the tribe received a $17.5 million federal payout, under the Indian Claims Commission Act, for its claim that the government improperly took its land.[3]

The payout — most of which was to be used for tribal projects, with some of the money distributed as per capita payments to tribal members — widened an existing rift between full-blood Utes and "mixed-blood" Utes, Wilkins says. Full-blood Utes wanted to maintain a relationship with the government and disenrolled the mixed-blood Utes who disagreed, he says.

The government has stayed out of such battles, particularly after the Supreme Court in 1978 affirmed a tribe's right to establish its own membership requirements.[4]

In 2009, the Bureau of Indian Affairs announced it would adhere to a "policy of Indian self-determination and self-government," Galanda says. Based on that decision, the U.S. District Court in *Timbisha Shoshone Tribe v. Kennedy* said in 2009 it would not interfere in disenrollment.[5]

More recently, some groups have pushed for a new policy. In June 2015, the National Native American Bar Association said stripping tribal citizenship without due process was a human rights issue.[6] Later that year, the Association of American Indian Physicians passed a resolution asking tribes to reconsider the disenrollment of members on health grounds, saying the process caused grief and depression for those cast aside.[7]

Galanda says disenrollment is a non-native concept that stems from federal policies that required tribes to determine who belonged.

Wilkins says when tribes began banishing members charged with committing crimes in the 1980s, tribal leaders said it was a tradition to expel members who violated social norms. But he notes that the disenrollments also coincided with increased casino gambling on tribal lands. In California, among 30 tribes that are now disenrolling members, about 23 distribute gambling royalties on a per-capita basis, Wilkins has found. "In some cases, tribes appear to be making rational, economic-based calculations," he says.

A series of court rulings and laws gave tribes slightly more control over their affairs. In 1974, the *Boldt* decision, drafted by George Boldt, the U.S. District judge for the Western District of Washington, granted fishing rights to Indians in the Pacific Northwest. And the Indian Self-Determination and Education Assistance Act of 1975 funneled federal money to tribes through contracts and grants to enable tribal councils — rather than the federal government — to control school, health, housing, law enforcement and other programs.[66]

NATIVE AMERICAN SOVEREIGNTY

In Washington state, meanwhile, the battle over the Nooksack disenrollments continues. Tribal Chairman Bob Kelly said a Nov. 4 referendum — in which those facing disenrollment were barred from voting — showed overwhelming support for disenrollment.[8]

But the Interior Department said the election was illegitimate because the members under a disenrollment cloud were not allowed to vote, and it threatened to withhold federal funds from the Nooksack Tribe until a legitimate vote took place. The department and other agencies did cut off tribal funding earlier this year.[9]

The tribe, in turn, sued the U.S. government, saying it wrongfully denied the Nooksack $13.7 million in federal and state funds. The Nooksack government argued it has the power to disenroll members who had "failed to demonstrate legally sufficient blood connections to the tribe," and it has authority to interpret tribal law and determine the legitimacy of the governing body.[10]

For four years, Galanda has represented Nooksack members facing disenrollment. He says finding proof, such as a birth or death certificate, to confirm proper enrollment of an ancestor — and thereby establish a member's direct lineage to the tribe — can be nearly impossible. "Indians were not [U.S.] citizens until 1924," Galanda says.

But he says he remains hopeful about a possible reversal of the disenrollment trend. The Grand Ronde Tribal Appeals Court in Oregon last year reversed the disenrollment of 66 members who were descended directly from Tumulth, the chief who signed the Willamette Valley Treaty of 1855.[11]

Others, like the Graton Rancheria Tribe in California and the Spokane Tribe in Washington state, have in recent years modified their constitutions to bar disenrollment of tribal members, according to Galanda.

— *Christina L. Lyons*

Native American attorney Gabriel S. Galanda says "power and greed" are behind efforts to disenroll more than 300 members of the Nooksack Indian Tribe in northwest Washington state.

Courtesy of Gabriel S. Galanda

[2] For more on disenrollment, see David E. Wilkins and Shelly Hulse Wilkins, *Dismembered: Native Disenrollment and the Battle for Human Rights* (2017).

[3] *Ibid.,* pp. 60-62. Also see Public Law 671, Chapter 1009, 68 Stat. 868.

[4] The case is *Santa Clara Pueblo v. Martinez*, 436 U.S. 49 (1978), http://tinyurl.com/madukjt.

[5] Gabriel S. Galanda, "Obama's Disenrollment Legacy," Indian Country Media Network, Jan. 25, 2017, http://tinyurl.com/m6b2vep.

[6] "Duties of Tribal Court Advocates to Ensure Due Process Afforded to All Individuals Targeted for Disenrollment," National Native American Bar Association, June 26, 2015, http://tinyurl.com/l5jjccn.

[7] "AAIP Resolution on Disenrollment," Association of American Indian Physicians, Oct 22, 2105, http://tinyurl.com/mnsjf22.

[8] Gene Johnson, "Nooksack Tribe Says It Has Booted 289 people off Rolls," *The Bellingham Herald,* Nov. 23, 2016, http://tinyurl.com/kb6nqru.

[9] Nina Shapiro, "Feds Call Nooksack Tribal Council 'Illegitimate' and 'Abusive,'" *The Seattle Times,* April 6, 2017, http://tinyurl.com/m6pje5k.

[10] *Ibid.*

[1] Liz Jones, "Nooksack Tribe Cites 'Missing Ancestor' as Reason to Disenroll 306 Members," KUOW, Dec. 17, 2013, http://tinyurl.com/kcnar8m.

[11] Dean Rhodes, "Tribal Appeals Court Reverses Disenrollments," The Confederated Tribes of Grand Ronde, Aug. 9, 2016, http://tinyurl.com/l3q6869.

Rise of Casinos

In the 1980s, President Ronald Reagan (1981-89) reaffirmed support for Indian self-determination, but his federal budget cuts sharply reduced funding for tribes, which were struggling with poverty and high unemployment.

Congress, meanwhile, passed the Indian Mineral Development Act of 1982 to allow tribes to enter into energy extraction agreements and set lease terms and royalty amounts. Allison said this gave tribes more control over reservation development.[67]

Getty Images/Chip Somodevilla

Many tribal leaders view Interior Secretary Ryan Zinke, here testifying before the Senate Indian Affairs Committee on March 8, 2017, as a supporter of Native American interests. "Our sovereign Indian nations and territories must have the respect and freedom they deserve," Zinke said when his nomination was announced.

In 1984, the President's Commission on Indian Reservation Economies assailed the BIA system, saying it "is designed for paternalistic control, and it thrives on the failure of Indian tribes."[68]

Tribal leaders, however, balked at the commission's calls to develop reservations through private ownership and profit models. They rejected recommendations to abolish the bureau and waive the tribes' immunity from lawsuits on some issues, and to subordinate tribal courts to the federal judiciary on certain questions. The commission also proposed forming an Indian Trust Services Administration aimed at protecting oil, gas, minerals, timber, water and agricultural land.[69]

In 1987, the Supreme Court opened the door for a new economic enterprise on reservations: gambling. The court, in *California vs. Cabazon Band of Mission Indians,* said tribes could legally engage in gambling not expressly prohibited by the state, and it barred states from regulating tribal gaming.[70] Complaints about a "wasteful and patriarchal" Bureau of Indian Affairs persisted into the 1990s. Rep. Bill Richardson, D-N.M., chairman of the Subcommittee on Native American Affairs, in 1993 said the bureau "has held back tribes from helping themselves."[71]

Then in 1996, Blackfeet activist Elouise Cobell launched the largest class-action lawsuit ever filed against the federal government. She accused the BIA of mismanaging payments for allotted property and said many allotment landowners lived in poverty despite the drilling of oil and gas on their property under lease arrangements. The lawsuit was settled in 2009 for about $3.4 billion; $1.9 billion went to a Trust Land Consolidation Fund set aside to buy back tribal trust lands, and $1.5 billion was to be disbursed to individual plaintiffs.[72]

President Clinton vowed to change federal attitudes toward tribes. After listening to more than 300 tribal leaders, he issued an executive memorandum mandating federal consultation with tribes "in order to ensure that the rights of the sovereign tribal governments are fully respected."[73]

President George W. Bush continued Clinton's efforts to make amends to tribes and to recognize their sovereignty. He signed a law providing $28 million to the Yankton Sioux of South Dakota and the Santee Sioux of Nebraska for damage caused by the government when the Missouri River, as a result of dams built in the 1950s and 1960s, submerged about 4,000 acres of their land.[74]

Nevertheless, tribes remained poor. The U.S. Commission on Civil Rights in 2003 reported that federal funding "has not been sufficient to address the basic and very urgent needs of indigenous" people in health care, education, public safety, housing and rural development."[75]

Many tribes also fared poorly when outside companies made deals directly with the government — deals that the Supreme Court upheld in 2003. In *United States v. Navajo Nation,* the court ruled against the tribe, which had sought to negotiate royalties for coal from a mining company. The court said only federal officials could approve the final rate and determine what was in the tribe's best interest. The Navajo Nation later sued the government when it learned the coal company had lobbied the Interior secretary to reject the tribe's higher price and forced it to accept a minimum royalty rate. The Supreme Court, however, ultimately denied the tribe's claim.[76]

In 2005, Congress sought to give tribes more autonomy by passing the Indian Tribal Energy Development and Self-Determination Act. It allowed tribes to enter agreements with the BIA to pursue lease agreements with energy companies on their own, but the law left in place the thicket of rules and regulations that have discouraged tribes from pursuing such agreements.[77]

During the Obama administration, lawmakers made some progress for self-determination. In 2012, Obama signed the HEARTH Act — Helping Expedite and Advance Responsible Tribal Home Ownership — which aimed to create an alternative process for tribes to lease trust land without further approval of the government. He also signed the Trust Asset Management Reform Act, and during his tenure returned about 542,000 acres to federal trust protection for Native Americans.[78]

Tribes frequently embraced Obama as a strong supporter of sovereignty, although some became disenchanted when his administration waited until December 2016 to halt completion of the Dakota Access Pipeline.

CURRENT SITUATION
Questions About Trump

Native Americans are uncertain about plans of the Trump administration and the Republican-controlled Congress, but they hope to have a voice in discussions on energy regulation, tax reform and other issues vital to Indians.

When Trump took office, many tribes recalled his 1993 testimony before a House Natural Resources Committee on gambling when he said he thought the Indian Gaming Regulatory Act gave tribes an unfair advantage over his own casinos. "Go up to Connecticut," he said, referring to the Mashantucket Pequot tribe, which owned Foxwoods Resort Casino. "They [the Pequot] don't look like Indians to me."[79] And during the 2016 presidential campaign, he repeatedly called Democratic Sen. Elizabeth Warren of Massachusetts "Pocahontas" after she said she was part Native American.

Trump's decision to create a Native American Coalition during the presidential transition and to appoint Rep. Markwayne Mullin, R-Okla., a Cherokee tribal member, as its chairman, reassured some tribes.[80]

Some Indians believe Trump's attitude toward tribal sovereignty was reflected in his decision to ignore the wishes of the Standing Rock Sioux and allow completion of the Dakota Access Pipeline under Lake Oahe, just north of the tribe's reservation. Over the objections of Native Americans, he also approved Keystone XL, the 1,179-mile oil pipeline that would cross the land of numerous tribes.

But others are not sure where the president stands on Indian sovereignty.

Many tribal leaders see Interior Secretary Ryan Zinke, a former one-term Republican congressman from Montana, as a supporter of Native American interests. When his nomination was announced, Zinke said, "Our sovereign Indian nations and territories must have the respect and freedom they deserve." And during his Senate confirmation hearing, he said he had no intention of selling federal lands.[81] The National Congress of American Indians supported his nomination.

Sen. Maria Cantwell, D-Wash., ranking member of the Senate Energy and Natural Resources Committee, opposed Zinke's confirmation, in part because of his support for the Dakota Access Pipeline and his opposition to Obama's coal-leasing moratorium. And Cantwell worried about Zinke's support for energy development on federal lands, noting it clashes with the government's obligation to protect tribal trust lands.[82]

Zinke also expressed support for the proposed Gateway Pacific Terminal, calling it "literally the gateway to economic prosperity" for the Crow tribe and for blue-collar workers in Washington state.[83]

Meanwhile, Trump's budget blueprint would slash funding for the Environmental Protection Agency by one-third while increasing spending for energy development on federal lands. Under the executive order he issued in March, the president plans to dismantle the Clean Power Plan that would have led to the closure of many coal-fired power plants, halted construction on new plants and replaced them with wind and solar farms. Tribes are split on the power plan.[84]

In Congress

Many tribes are closely watching as Congress considers legislation to ease energy regulations on tribal lands — legislation that failed to move during previous sessions of Congress despite bipartisan support. The Senate Indian Affairs Committee in February approved a bill by its chairman, John Hoeven, R-N.D., that aims to simplify the regulatory process for energy projects on reservations by establishing a pilot program.[85]

Hoeven told the National Congress of American Indians in February that the bill is "a big step toward tribal self-determination in developing its tribal resources."

Other committees are exploring the issue as well. In February, Frank Rusco, the GAO's director of natural resources and environment issues, told a House oversight panel that regulatory uncertainty continues to impede tribal energy projects.[86]

AT ISSUE

Could energy development lift tribes out of poverty?

YES

Terry L. Anderson
Senior Fellow, Hoover Institution;
Senior Fellow, Property and Environment
Research Center

Written for *CQ Researcher*, May 2017

Indian country contains almost 30 percent of the nation's coal reserves west of the Mississippi, as well as significant deposits of oil, natural gas and uranium.

The Council of Energy Resource Tribes, a tribal energy consortium, estimates the value of these resources at nearly $1.5 trillion. Yet these resources remain largely untapped. Developing them could help lift Native Americans out of poverty.

The negative effects of federal regulations can be seen in former President Barack Obama's "war on coal." The Crow tribe has 9 billion tons of coal that could easily be shipped to generating plants anywhere in the United States or exported to Asia. But many cities and towns along rail routes, citing concerns about train safety and the health effects of coal dust, are trying to limit coal-train traffic. And port cities such as Seattle and Portland, Ore., are holding up construction of export terminals on the ground that coal, including that from the Crow reservation, would exacerbate global warming.

Making matters worse, the Bureau of Indian Affairs (BIA) limits energy development on reservations. On the Fort Peck reservation in northeastern Montana, the BIA required an archaeological assessment before a company could begin oil and gas exploration. Fort Peck tribal councilman Stoney Anketell noted the absurdity of this requirement: "We're not shortchanging the need for archaeological reviews, but on land that has been farmed for 70 years? It's been tilled, plowed, planted, harvested. There's no teepee rings."

Legislation passed in 1999 for the Fort Berthold reservation in North Dakota reduced from 49 to four the number of regulations from four different federal agencies that must be met before oil and gas can be leased on the reservation. As a result, since the Bakken shale-oil boom started in 2000, hundreds of reservation wells have earned the tribal nation more than $500 million. Still, roughly twice as many oil and gas wells are drilled per acre outside the reservation as inside.

Some bright spots regarding potential development on reservations have come from the Trump administration. For example, the president's executive order "Promoting Energy Independence and Economic Growth" will make it more likely that Indian coal reserves can be developed. In addition, Interior Secretary Ryan Zinke issued a secretarial order to end the coal-leasing moratorium and reinstate the department's royalty advisory committee.

NO

James R. Allison III
Assistant Professor of History, Christopher
Newport University

Written for *CQ Researcher*, May 2017

No population needs economic development more than the first Americans. The poverty rate among Native Americans runs north of 25 percent and unemployment remains mired in double-digits. As recently as November, the U.S. Census Bureau declared American Indians the country's most impoverished racial group. Sadly, this is an annual tradition.

Yet since the 1930s, when federal Indian policy shifted to halt previous attempts at cultural genocide, tribal and federal officials alike have pointed to Native Americans' abundant energy resources as the panacea for Indian poverty. In oft-cited statistics, we are told that reservations contain almost 30 percent of all coal west of the Mississippi, as much as 50 percent of the nation's uranium deposits and upwards of 20 percent of known oil and gas reserves. As LaDonna Harris, a Comanche who founded Americans for Indian Opportunity, once said, "Collectively, [we] are the biggest private owners of energy in the country."

During the 1970s energy crises, Harris and others orchestrated a pan-tribal movement to throw off decades of paternalistic mismanagement by federal officials, who had transferred control over Indian energy to multinational firms for minuscule royalties. By 1982, efforts to undue this injustice had equipped Indians with expertise in managing minerals and produced legal changes that recognized Native American control over tribal resources. It was a remarkable victory.

But then little changed, and herein lies the hard lesson for any group dependent upon a single commodity, such as a fossil fuel, for economic prosperity. After securing the right to manage their own minerals, tribes watched as global events transformed the energy scarcity of the 1970s into the "oil glut" of the 1980s. A world flooded with cheap oil left little room for rural reservation development, and projects were scrapped by the dozens. Meanwhile, intense internal debates raged over the social and environmental costs of reservation mining. All the while poverty deepened.

The lesson here is not that fossil fuel development cannot help tribal communities. It can. But rarely do nations build sustainable prosperity on fossil fuel foundations alone. Those that have — such as in the Middle East — possessed full sovereignty and popular support for such development. They also happened to be on the right side of market trends. Tribal nations do not enjoy such benefits, and so should focus on projects that align better with long-term economic forecasts; federal Indian, environmental and energy policies; and a broader range of communal values. On many reservations, alternative energy presents one such option.

House Natural Resources Committee ranking member Raúl Grijalva, D-Ariz., has long opposed easing regulations for energy development for tribal and other federal lands.

"There's a fundamental lust on the part of industry for the extraction that they want out of the public lands, and there is a fundamental lust by industry for what they see in Indian country on reservations as possibilities as well," Grijalva said. He said he is particularly concerned about a controversial copper mine being reviewed for federal permits, because Congress authorized a land swap allowing the Rio Tinto Group to open the mine on former federal land sacred to Native Americans.

"If the Trump administration and [the Interior Department] go through this whole deregulation agenda that they're on — expediting, streamlining, whatever euphemism they want to use — on the public lands for extraction purposes, then what's happening with Resolution Copper and Oak Flat and those areas is the harbinger of what can happen, across the West," he said.[87]

Grijalva also wants Zinke to testify on Trump's proposed $1.5 billion budget cuts to the Interior Department. He asked how the department would "honor the federal government's trust responsibilities to Native American tribes using $1.5 billion less in funding."[88]

Meanwhile, tribes, including the MHA Nation at Fort Berthold, intend to push Congress and the administration to bar states from taxing non–Native American energy companies that extract resources on tribal lands. They say only tribal governments should be able to levy taxes on those projects.[89]

The GAO in 2015 listed dual taxation of energy projects (by states and tribes) as impediments to Indian energy development, along with tribes' limited access to capital and federal tax credits.[90]

In the Courts

The National Congress of American Indians supported the Supreme Court nomination of U.S. Appeals Judge Neil M. Gorsuch, who was confirmed on April 7.

Gorsuch's "opinions recognize tribes as sovereign governments and address issues of significance to tribes," the group's president, Brian Cladoosby, and Native American Rights Fund Executive Director John Echohawk wrote in a letter. "Judge Gorsuch appears to be both attentive to the details and respectful to the fundamental principles of tribal sovereignty and the federal trust responsibility."[91]

A series of cases regarding tribal sovereignty and land rights is making its way through the courts and could end up before the Supreme Court.

In what some consider a potentially landmark decision, a federal appeals court in Palm Springs, Calif., in March upheld a ruling that the Agua Caliente Band of Cahuilla Indians has federally established rights to groundwater beneath its reservation in Palm Springs and surrounding areas. The appeals court said the creation of the Agua Caliente reservation in the 1870s "carried with it an implied right to use water from the Coachella Valley aquifer." The local water districts could appeal to the U.S. Supreme Court.

Meanwhile, a lawsuit filed by the Standing Rock Sioux and Cheyenne River Sioux tribes accuses the Army Corps of Engineers and the company building the Dakota Access Pipeline of ignoring the risk of oil spills and their potential effects on the tribe. The project, the suit said, violates the 1970 National Environmental Policy Act requiring federal agencies to conduct environmental assessments on projects submitted for federal approval or funding.[92]

The Northern Cheyenne Tribe is suing the Interior Department over the Trump administration's decision to lift the moratorium on coal leasing on federal lands. The tribe said it should have been consulted. Tribe President L. Jace Killsback said he is worried about mining's effect on "our pristine air and water quality . . . [and] sacred cultural properties and traditional spiritual practices."[93]

OUTLOOK
"Backsliding" Feared

Christopher Newport University's Allison says he expects to see tribes gaining more control over their land.

Former Bureau of Indian Affairs Director Washburn, however, warns that federal regulations could tip the other way, as evidenced by Trump's push to complete the Dakota pipeline over tribes' objections. "I hope we don't get backsliding to a federal-control model where tribes are shut out of their own decisions on their land," he says, but adds that "tribes have a lot more clout now. . . . We may see a rolling back of baseline protections of tribal lands, but we may also see tribes creating their own regimes."

Another possibility, Washburn says, is that under the Trump administration's crusade to roll back federal regulations, the president may grant more control to tribes, "so we might see more tribal self-determination and self-governance."

Many legal experts, economists and scholars say the federal government still needs to find a way to resolve the checkerboard pattern of property ownership that remains from the allotment era and complicates tribal governing on reservations.

A "fractionalized" ownership of lots remains an issue that vexes economists and developers, and which the GAO has noted continues to impede energy development on many reservations.

Fractionalized interests refers to lots held in trust by hundreds of individuals. When owners of allotted land died without wills, heirs inherited the property under U.S. law, a process that has continued through the generations with the property divided further among subsequent heirs. Anderson at the Property and Environment Research Center says many of those lots remain undeveloped because of the difficulty in obtaining consensus from all the property owners.

"Every administration since Kennedy has looked at those reservations and said, 'We've got to do something,' including the Obama administration," Gover of the National Museum of American Indians says.

"And everyone walks away saying, 'I don't know what the hell to do.' It's not an absence of caring. It's not an absence of good will," Gover says. "To really turn those reservations around would require an enormous influx of money. Just good-old Yankee dollars that would allow an economy to begin to grow."

NOTES

1. T. J. Raphael, "A Native American Tribe in Montana Hopes Its Coal Reserves Will Provide Economic Opportunity," Public Radio International, Oct. 29, 2015, http://tinyurl.com/lah2eye.

2. Amy Martin, "Why Montana's Crow Tribe Turns to Coal as Others Turn Away," *Inside Energy,* Oct. 23, 2015, http://tinyurl.com/k5uzequ.

3. Brittany Patterson, "Tribes Divided Over Unlocking Energy Wealth," *Climatewire,* Nov. 16, 2016, http://tinyurl.com/m9jh66w.

4. Julie Turkewitz, "Tribes That Live Off Coal Hold Tight to Trump's Promises," *The New York Times,* April 1, 2017, http://tinyurl.com/kqebzf7.

5. Baynard Woods, "Out of the Standing Rock, the Birth of a New Environmental Movement," *Nashville Scene,* March 18, 2017, http://tinyurl.com/n8l3ath.

6. Shawn E. Regan and Terry L. Anderson, "The Energy Wealth of Indian Nations," *Journal of Energy Law and Resources,* Fall 2014, p. 196, http://tinyurl.com/mdo7bpp.

7. *Cherokee Nation v. Georgia,* 30 U.S. 1 (1831), http://tinyurl.com/kk628sr.

8. Regan and Anderson, *op. cit.,* pp. 110-111; Terry Anderson and Dominic Parker, "UnAmerican Reservations," Hoover Institution, Feb. 24, 2011, http://tinyurl.com/l9j6j7u.

9. "Tribal Nations and the United States: An Introduction," National Congress of American Indians, p. 16, http://tinyurl.com/kdnqsan.

10. *Ibid.,* pp. 38-41.

11. "Gaming Revenues by Region," National Indian Gaming Commission, July 2016, http://tinyurl.com/kh7865w.

12. "Poor Management by BIA Has Hindered Energy Development on Indian Lands," Government Accountability Office, June 2015, p. 22, http://tinyurl.com/mddw2ja.

13. Sarah van Gelder, "In North Dakota's Booming Oil Patch, One Tribe Beat Back Fracking," *Yes Magazine,* Jan. 21, 2016, http://tinyurl.com/jsc2f8y; "National Drug Control Strategy," Executive Office of the President, 2014, p. 47, http://tinyurl.com/m7zp4kf.

14. Valerie Volcovici, "Red Tape Chokes Off Drilling on Native American Reservations," Reuters, Jan. 27, 2017, http://tinyurl.com/mdoywlu.

15. Naomi Schaefer Riley, *The New Trail of Tears: How Washington Is Destroying American Indians* (2016).

16. "FY 2017 Federal Funding for Programs Serving Tribes and Native American Communities," Department of the Interior, http://tinyurl.com/lfxg2lk.

17. Deborah Sontag and Brent McDonald, "In North Dakota, a Tale of Oil, Corruption and Death," *The New York Times,* Dec. 28, 2014, http://tinyurl.com/mvgyhtr; Jodi Rave Spotted Bear, "Tex Hall Takes Witness Stand in Murder-for-Hire Trial," *Native Sun News Today,* March 9, 2016, http://tinyurl.com/m2s9luv; and Josh Wood, "Oil-Rich ND Reservation to Get New Leader," *The Washington Times,* Sept. 17, 2014, http://tinyurl.com/n5lbj88.

18. Jack McNeel, "S&K Technologies: A Major World Class Enterprise," Indian Country Media Network, March 26, 2017, http://tinyurl.com/kgq8geb.

19. Indian Trust Asset Reform Act, Public Law 114-178, June 22, 2016, http://tinyurl.com/kmdwtde.

20. "Poor Management by BIA Has Hindered Energy Development on Indian Lands," *op. cit.,* p. 22.

21. Kevin Gover, "An Indian Trust for the Twenty-First Century," *Natural Resources Journal,* Spring 2006, http://tinyurl.com/mclxnyx.

22. "Prepared Statement of Honorable Tyson Thompson, Councilman, Southern Ute Indian Tribal Council, at Hearing: Examining Federal Programs That Service Tribes and Their Members," Subcommittee on the Interior, Energy, and Environment, U.S. House Committee on Oversight and Government Reform, Feb. 15, 2017, http://tinyurl.com/mb77p52.

23. Catherine Traywick, "A Tale of Two Tribes: Colorado's Southern Utes Want to Drill While Sioux Battle Pipeline," Bloomberg News, *The Denver Post,* Oct. 14, 2016, http://tinyurl.com/m2ktd3m.

24. Joe Cardillo, "New Energy Player in New Mexico Already Scoring Big Firsts," *Albuquerque Business First,* May 4, 2016, http://tinyurl.com/mt24wyl.

25. Brittany Patterson, "Tribes Divided Over Unlocking Energy Wealth," *E&E News,* Nov. 16, 2016, http://tinyurl.com/m9jh66w.

26. Van Gelder, *op. cit.*

27. Dan Bacher, "Hundreds of Tribal Representatives Join Huge Rally to Oppose Fracking," *Tulalip News,* March 18, 2014, http://tinyurl.com/kg9aexq.

28. Kirk Johnson, "U.S. Denies Permit for Coal Terminal in Washington State," *The New York Times,* May 9, 2016, http://tinyurl.com/lc9pgws.

29. Deborah Sontag and Brent McDonald, "In North Dakota, a Tale of Oil, Corruption and Death," *The New York Times*, Dec. 28, 2014, http://tinyurl.com/mvgyhtr.

30. Celia Raney, "Indigenous People Speak Out Against Pollution of Tribal Lands," *DailyLobo.com,* March 5, 2017, http://tinyurl.com/knwg9kn.

31. *Winters v. United States,* 207 U.S. 564 (1908), http://tinyurl.com/kovz9tc; Jeffrey Ostler and Nick Estes, "'The Supreme Law of the Land': Standing Rock and the Dakota Access Pipeline," *Indian Country Today,* Jan. 16, 2017, http://tinyurl.com/k8cukxl.

32. Jan Hasselman, "A New Front in the Battle Against Coal Exports: Treaties," EarthJustice, July 14, 2015, http://tinyurl.com/ks7x59a.

33. Kandi Mossett, keynote at Local Environmental Action Conference 2017, http://tinyurl.com/mly8ehs.

34. Joe Helm, "U.N. Human Rights Official Criticizes Federal Relationship With Indian tribes," *The Washington Post,* March 3, 2017, http://tinyurl.com/lfcbo8k.

35. Valerie Richardson, "Obama Adopts U.N. Manifesto on Rights of Indigenous Peoples," *The Washington Times,* Dec. 16, 2010, http://tinyurl.com/365ag4f; "United Nations Declaration on the Rights of Indigenous Peoples," United Nations, March 2008, p. 12, http://tinyurl.com/7ans84.

36. Wilcomb E. Washburn, ed., *Handbook of North American Indians: History of Indian-White Relations* (1988), p. 3.

37. Tyler Anbinder, *City of Dreams: The 400-Year Epic History of Immigrant New York* (2016), pp. 19-22.

38. Washburn, *op. cit.,* pp. 3-5.

39. "History of BIA," Bureau of Indian Affairs, http://tinyurl.com/k4kh6cx.

40. Peter Cozzens, *The Earth Is Weeping: The Epic Story of the Indian Wars for the American West* (2016), p. 11.

41. *Ibid.*

42. *Ibid.,* pp. 11, 14.

43. *Johnson v. McIntosh,* 21 U.S. 543 (1823), http://tinyurl.com/h8ocs4a.

44. "Indian Removal Act," Library of Congress, http://tinyurl.com/pgcudn7.

45. *Cherokee Nation v. Georgia,* 30 U.S. 1 (1831).

46. *Worcester v. Georgia,* 31 U.S. 515 (1832).

47. "Primary Documents in American History: Indian Removal Act," Library of Congress, http://tinyurl.com/pgcudn7.

48. Cozzens, *op. cit.,* pp. 16, 17.

49. 25 U.S. Code Sec. 71, http://tinyurl.com/nxnrfh6.

50. "The Indian Problem: Senator Dawes and Gen. Armstrong Give Their Views Regarding It," *The New York Times,* July 22, 1885, http://tinyurl.com/mqz3xfr.

51. Trevor Hammond, "First Oklahoma Land Rush: April 22, 1889," Newspapers.com, http://tinyurl.com/lrotjf8.

52. Mary H. Cooper, "Native Americans' Future," *CQ Researcher,* July 12, 1996, pp. 601-624.

53. "The Indian Citizenship Act," History.com, 2010, http://tinyurl.com/3oprgrk.

54. "The Problem of Indian Administration," Institute for Government Research, Feb. 21, 1928, p. 3, http://tinyurl.com/m24e7hd; Felix S. Cohen, "The Erosion of Indian Rights," Yale Law School Legal Scholarship Repository, Jan. 1, 1953, http://tinyurl.com/k8gxaj6.

55. John Collier, "A Life for the Forgotten Red Man Too," May 6, 1934, http://tinyurl.com/lhwatq8; *Encyclopedia of American Indian History,* edited by Bruce E. Johansen and Barry M. Pritzker, pp. 554-555, http://tinyurl.com/mrv43db.

56. Cohen, *op. cit.* Also see Nancy Oestreich Lurie, "The Indian Claims Commission Act," *The ANNALS of the American Academy of Political Science,* May 1, 1957, http://tinyurl.com/k99axq5.

57. Judith Graham, "Compensation at Last for Tribes That Lost Lands to Dams," *Chicago Tribune,* http://tinyurl.com/m92c34r.

58. Janet McDonnell, "Review of Dammed Indians: The Pick-Sloan Plan and the Missouri River Sioux, 1944-1980," *Great Plains Quarterly,* Spring 1984, pp. 137-38, http://tinyurl.com/mtqt939.

59. Washburn, *op. cit.,* p. 314; "History and Culture: Termination Policy — 1953-1968," Northern Plains Reservation Aid, http://tinyurl.com/k9m7ers.

60. Indian Civil Rights Act of 1968, 25 U.S.C. §§ 1301-1304, http://tinyurl.com/ltmlgx2.

61. Homer Bigart, "American Indian Activists Winning Bureau Reform," *The New York Times,* Jan. 8, 1972, http://tinyurl.com/ld2tkxq; Richard Nixon, "213-Special Message to the Congress on Indian Affairs, July 8, 1970," American Presidency Project, http://tinyurl.com/olxfhhg.

62. Roger L. Nichols, *The American Indian: Past and Present* (2014), pp. 303-305, http://tinyurl.com/m2wllev.

63. Allison, *op. cit.,* p. 1.

64. *Ibid.*

65. James P Sterba, "Navajo Leader Assails Federal Unit," *The New York Times,* Oct. 23, 1973, http://tinyurl.com/k3dxjz6.

66. Alex Tizon, "The Boldt Decision / 25 Years — The Fish Tale That Changed History," *The Seattle Times,* Feb. 7, 1999, http://tinyurl.com/kpgrn6d.

67. Indian Mineral Development Act of 1982, Public Law 97-382, Dec. 22, 1982, http://tinyurl.com/mfyk7lp; Allison, *op. cit.,* p. 6.

68. "U.S. Indian Bureau Assailed in Report," *The New York Times,* Dec. 1, 1984, http://tinyurl.com/m9twu4h.

69. Iver Peterson, "Indians Resist Shift in Economic Goals Urged by U.S. Panel," *The New York Times,* Jan. 13, 1985, http://tinyurl.com/k3zmrun.

70. Cooper, *op. cit.* For more on Indians and casinos, see Peter Katel, "American Indians," *CQ Researcher,* April 28, 2006, pp. 361-384.

71. Bill Richardson, "More Power to the Tribes," *The New York Times,* July 7, 1993, http://tinyurl.com/lplm8gu.

72. Shanna Lewis, "American Indian Activist Led a Landmark Suit Against the Federal Government," Colorado Public Radio, Feb. 9, 2017, http://tinyurl.com/kxq8wpw.

73. "Memorandum for the Heads of Executive Departments and Agencies," The White House, April 29, 1994, available at http://tinyurl.com/l4owjpz.

74. Graham, *op. cit.*

75. "A Quiet Crisis: Federal Funding and Unmet Needs in Indian Country," U.S. Commission on Civil Rights, July 2003, p. iii, http://tinyurl.com/lnahf8h.

76. Kevin K. Washburn, "What the Future Holds: The Changing Landscape of Federal Indian Policy," University of New Mexico Law, forthcoming, p. 18, http://tinyurl.com/kwkbekq.

77. Regan and Anderson, *op. cit.,* p. 206.

78. HEARTH ACT of 2012, U.S. Department of the Interior, Indian Affairs, http://tinyurl.com/nyxbrd4; "Obama Administration Exceeds Ambitious Goal to Restore 500,000 Acres of Tribal Homelands," press release, U.S. Department of the Interior, Oct. 12, 2016, http:// tinyurl.com/kx466rg.

79. Bryan Newland, "Donald Trump and Federal Indian Policy: 'They Don't Look Like Indians to Me,'" *Indian Country Today,* July 28, 2016, http://tinyurl.com/lnox8pa.

80. "Oklahoma Representative to Chair Donald Trump's Native American Coalition," KOCO News 5, Jan. 4, 2017, http://tinyurl.com/kwth98s; Valerie Volcovici, "Trump Advisors Aim to Privatize Oil-Rich Indian Reservations," Reuters, Dec. 5, 2016, http://tinyurl.com/z9eqace.

81. Andrew Restuccia and Anna Palmer, "Trump Team Reaches Out to Native Americans," *Politico,* Dec. 16, 2016, http://politi.co/2gPor4o; Darryl Fears, "Ryan Zinke Is One Step Closer to Becoming Interior Secretary," *The Washington Post,* Jan. 31, 2017, http://tinyurl.com/malkhz3.

82. "Cantwell Details Her Opposition to Zinke's Nomination to be Secretary of the Interior," press release, U.S. Senate Committee on Energy and Natural Resources, Feb. 28, 2017, http://tinyurl .com/mfockuk.

83. "Staunch Supporter of Cherry Point Coal Project Is Trump's Interior Secretary," The Associated Press, *The Bellingham Herald,* March 1, 2017, http:// tinyurl.com/lbt2dhz.

84. "White House Budget Increases Funding for Energy Development on Public Lands and Offshore, Continues to Streamline Permitting," *Oil & Gas 360,* March 16, 2017, http://tinyurl.com/mh67tq4; Coral Davenport, "Trump Signs Executive Order Unwinding Obama Climate Policies," *The New York Times,* March 28, 2017, http://tinyurl.com/k5hzovs.

85. "Committee Passes Nine Bills During Business Meeting," press release, U.S. Senate Committee on Indian Affairs, Feb. 8, 2017, http://tinyurl.com/lhga7rd.

86. Frank Rusco, "Federal Management Challenges Related to Indian Energy Resources: Testimony Before the Subcommittee on the Interior, Energy, and Environment, Committee on Oversight and Government Reform, House of Representatives," Feb. 15, 2017, http://tinyurl.com/k84xs3x.

87. Andrew Westney, "House Dem Laments Energy Cos.' 'Lust' For Tribal Lands," *Law360,* March 31, 2017, http://tinyurl.com/maqfzb9.

88. Charlie Passut, "House Democrat Wants Zinke to Testify on Interior's Budget," *Natural Gas Intelligence,* March 23, 2017, http://tinyurl.com/jvohgpb.

89. Valeri Volcovici, "Native American Tribes Decry State Taxation of Reservation Energy Projects," Reuters, Jan. 17, 2017, http://tinyurl.com/kv2j3y3.

90. "Poor Management by BIA Has Hindered Energy Development on Indian Lands," *op. cit.*

91. Ryan Lovelace, "Support for Gorsuch From Native American Groups Could Put Pressure on Western Democrats," *Washington Examiner,* March 27, 2017, http://tinyurl.com/l7bhlgz.

92. "The Dakota Access Pipeline: Case Overview," EarthJustice, http://tinyurl.com/kkky576.

93. *Northern Cheyenne Tribe v. Department of the Interior,* March 29, 2017, http://tinyurl.com/ks4vjav; "The Northern Cheyenne Tribe Challenges Trump Administration's Decision to Lift Moratorium on Federal Coal Leases," press release, Northern Cheyenne Tribe Administration, March 29, 2017, http://tinyurl.com/ylog6vm.

BIBLIOGRAPHY
Selected Sources
Books

Allison, James R., *Sovereignty for Survival: American Energy Development and Indian Self-Determination,* Yale University Press, 2015.
An assistant professor of history at Christopher Newport University in Newport News, Va., explores how tribal

resistance to energy development on Indian lands led to increased Native American sovereignty and sparked debate about land management.

Grann, David, *Killers of the Flower Moon: The Osage Murders and the Birth of the FBI,* **Doubleday, 2017.**
A staff writer for *The New Yorker* examines the 1920s killings of members of Oklahoma's Osage Nation who had become wealthy from oil discovered under their land.

Riley, Naomi Schaefer, *The New Trail of Tears: How Washington Is Destroying American Indians,* **Encounter Books, 2016.**
A former *Wall Street Journal* reporter concludes that Native Americans' lack of property rights, access to the free market and proper education — combined with continued dependency on federal subsidies — have limited economic growth on reservations.

Wilkins, David E., and Shelly Hulse Wilkins, *Dismembered: Native Disenrollment and the Battle for Human Rights,* **University of Washington Press, 2017.**
An American Indian studies professor at the University of Minnesota Law School (Wilkins) and a specialist in tribal governmental relations (Hulse Wilkins) analyze an epidemic of disenrollment of members by tribal leaders.

Articles

Mosteller, Kelli, "For Native Americans, Land Is More Than Just the Ground Beneath Their Feet," *The Atlantic,* **Sept. 17, 2016, https://tinyurl.com/mfttnl4.**
The director of the Citizen Potawatomi Nation Cultural Heritage Center in Oklahoma says proponents of privatization of tribal lands disregard Indian culture and values.

Volcovici, Valerie, "Red Tape Chokes Off Drilling on Native American Reservations," Reuters, Jan. 27, 2017, https://tinyurl.com/mdoywlu.
Tribes complain that federal energy regulations delay projects on reservations, reduce revenue and undermine tribal sovereignty.

Warner, Elizabeth Ann Kronk, "Everything Old Is New Again: Enforcing Treaty Provisions to Protect Climate Change-Threatened Resources," *Nebraska Law Review,* **2016, http://tinyurl.com/kmglybk.**
The director of the Tribal Law and Government Center at the University of Kansas argues that existing treaties could provide useful tools for tribes seeking environmental

justice for damage to their land, natural resources and health caused by climate change.

Woodard, Stephanie, "How the U.S. Government Is Helping Corporations Plunder Native Lands," *In These Times,* **Sept. 6, 2016, https://tinyurl.com/zmemulc.**
The Bureau of Indian Affairs enables outside corporations to profit from energy development and other economic projects on Indian lands, according to a journalist's investigative report.

Reports and Studies

"Improving Tribal Consultation and Tribal Involvement in Federal Infrastructure Decisions," Departments of the Interior, Army and Justice, January 2017, https://tinyurl.com/j5huwe2.
The Obama administration recommended ways that federal decision-making on infrastructure and other projects can include input from Native American tribes.

"Poor Management by BIA Has Hindered Energy Development on Indian Lands," Government Accountability Office, June 15, 2015, p. 22, http://tinyurl.com/mddw2ja.
The Government Accountability Office, the investigative arm of Congress, recommends ways the Bureau of Indian Affairs can enable more energy development on Indians lands and encourage tribes to pursue energy resource agreements with the bureau.

Audio/Video

"How Federal Policy Affects Native Americans: Naomi Schaefer Riley on Her Book, 'The New Trail of Tears: How Washington Is Destroying American Indians,'" American Enterprise Institute, Jan. 30, 2017, http://tinyurl.com/lknzbjv.
A free-market think tank hosts a forum featuring a former Bureau of Indian Education director, a representative of the libertarian Cato Institute and author Riley discussing impediments to economic improvement on Native American reservations.

"Keynote: Kandi Mossett," Local Environmental Action 2017, March 5, 2017, http://tinyurl.com/mly8ehs.
A member of the Mandan, Hidatsa and Arikara Nation in North Dakota and the lead organizer of the Extreme Energy and Just Transition Campaign for the Indigenous Environmental Network, a Native American grassroots environmental group, discusses the environmental and cultural effects of oil drilling at Fort Berthold, N.D.

For More Information

Bureau of Indian Affairs, MS-3658-MIB, 1849 C St., N.W., Washington, DC 20240; 202-208-3710; www.bia .gov. Department of the Interior agency that provides services to Native Americans.

Earth Justice, 50 California St., Suite 500, San Francisco, CA 94111; 800-584-6460; http://earthjustice.org. Nonprofit environmental law firm that represents several tribes suing the federal government over treaty rights and environmental justice.

Indigenous Environmental Network, PO Box 485, Bemidji, MN 56619; 218-751-4967; www.ienearth.org. Grassroots organization that helps tribes protect natural resources, sacred lands and health.

National Congress of American Indians, 1516 P St., N.W., Washington, DC 20005; 202-466-7767; www.ncai .org. Advocacy group representing tribal governments and communities.

Native American Rights Fund, 1506 Broadway, Boulder, CO 80302-6269; 303-447-8769; www.narf .org. Provides legal assistance to Indian tribes, organizations and individuals.

Property and Environment Research Center, 2048 Analysis Drive, Suite A, Bozeman, MT 59718; 406-587-9591; www.perc.org. Free-market research institute that advocates for property rights to encourage resolution to environmental conflicts.

8

Immigrants and the Economy

Micheline Maynard

Syrian-Americans Ed Hyder and his son Gregory operate a popular Mediterranean grocery in Worcester, Mass. Friendly immigration policies enabled Ed's grandfather to immigrate to the United States in 1906, where he got his start peddling dry goods. Americans worried about homeland security and jobs praised President Trump's immigration actions, while potential immigrants and businesses that rely on foreign workers called them harmful to the economy.

From *CQ Researcher*, February 24, 2017

After emigrating from Syria to the United States in 1906, Ed Hyder's grandfather got his start peddling shirt collars and dry goods to men maintaining the Erie Canal and railroads in New York state. Hyder's father and uncles eventually took over the business, opening shops that sold meat and groceries.

The first two generations of Hyders would have been dazzled to see what the third and fourth generations of the family have done with the business. In a converted firehouse in Worcester, Mass., Hyder and his son Gregory run a popular Mediterranean market with a staff of 15 workers, drawing an avid foodie audience with far more upscale tastes than the working-class customers who gave the early Hyders their start. The shelves are filled with big containers of flour and racks of exotic spices, and refrigerator cases contain home-made Middle Eastern specialties and soups.

For Hyder, the heated debate over the Trump administration's hard-nosed immigration plans hits home. Friendly immigration policies allowed his ancestors to immigrate to the United States, he says; restrictive ones would have kept them out. "Limiting immigration limits the possibilities of what we can achieve as Americans," Hyder says. "I don't want to indiscriminately let in people who hate America. But it's a hard call, who's good and who's bad."

Since taking office, President Trump has moved on several fronts to tighten immigration policy. On Jan. 25, he signed an executive order to build a wall on the U.S.-Mexico border to keep migrants from Mexico and Central America from crossing into the United States. He then signed a second order on Jan. 27 temporarily blocking immigration from seven predominantly Muslim Middle East

181

Asians Are Wealthiest U.S. Immigrants

Almost 1.5 million Asian-American households in the United States had annual incomes of $100,000 or more in 2012, the most of any immigrant group.

Household Incomes by Place of Birth, 2012

* Data cover both legal and undocumented immigrants.

** Includes the Caribbean and Central and South America.

Source: "Total Money Income of Foreign-Born Households by Household Type and World Region of Birth of the Householder: 2012," U.S. Census Bureau, 2012, http://tinyurl.com/j3ha2s8.

countries. And on Feb. 21, the Department of Homeland Security detailed a more aggressive approach to arresting and deporting undocumented immigrants — even those who have committed minor offenses — including enlisting local police as enforcers, building new detention facilities and speeding up deportations.[1]

Reaction was swift on all sides. Supporters of the tough new policies believe they will protect the country's security and provide more jobs to American citizens. But other Americans and businesses that rely on immigrants to spur innovation and keep operations flowing voiced deep reservations.

The furor underscored how deeply conflicted Americans are over the impact of immigration on jobs and the overall U.S. economy. Opponents focus mainly on illegal immigration and say it takes jobs from Americans and costs the treasury billions of dollars. Supporters discount these concerns and say immigration — especially legal immigration of highly educated foreigners — is a boon to the economy.

After a federal judge issued a stay on implementing parts of Trump's executive order on refugees and travel — which the Trump administration appealed — more than 100 chief executives from technology and other

companies filed a brief with the Ninth U.S. Circuit Court of Appeals, arguing the President's so-called "Muslim ban" violated the U.S. Constitution and would badly hurt their businesses.

"The backbone of our engineering team is from overseas," said Randy Wootton, CEO of the advertising-technology firm Rocket Fuel, which signed the brief. "Imagine not having access to that talent — it's a real disservice to American business."[2]

In addition, a coalition of nearly 600 colleges and universities sent a letter to Homeland Security Secretary John Kelly saying the country could maintain its "global scientific and economic leadership position" only if it encouraged talented people to come to the United States.[3]

A number of experts and others dispute these arguments, saying undocumented workers take jobs from Americans and cost state, local and federal governments billions of dollars in educational, health and welfare benefits. Some also oppose legal immigration. Trump's chief strategist, Stephen Bannon, who is pushing an "America First" agenda, said last March that Asian immigrants have been filling American graduate schools and keeping American students from finding work in Silicon Valley and elsewhere. "Twenty percent of this country is immigrants. Is that not the beating heart of this [unemployment] problem?" he asked.[4]

Boston College political science professor Peter Skerry, who has written extensively on immigration issues, says anti-immigration arguments resonate with Americans who believe globalization and the free movement of workers across borders have hurt them. "If you're some white American in a disadvantaged situation, you wouldn't have to be a mean-spirited bigot to say, 'Gee, do we really want more of these guys?'" he says.

The stakes in the debate over the impact of immigration on the U.S. economy are high. The 35 million people who identify as Hispanic are a significant economic force in the United States, representing a consumer market of $1.3 trillion.[5]

Close behind in economic importance are the nation's 12.7 million people who identify as being of Asian descent.[6] If current population trends continue, Asian immigrants will outnumber Hispanic immigrants by 2055, according to the Pew Research Center, relying on census data.[7]

The nation's 42 million immigrants are more likely to start businesses than native-born Americans.[8] As a result, immigrants represent 18 percent of all small-business owners but only about 13 percent of the population.[9]

Regarding the impact of legal immigrants on the U.S. economy, experts mostly debate how many additional skilled foreign workers should be encouraged to come to the United States through visas and other means. Richard Florida, a University of Toronto professor of management who coined the phrase "the creative class," warned that Trump's effort to restrict immigration threatens "the very core of America's innovative edge — the ability to attract global talent."[10]

But at the other end of the economic scale, says Skerry, "if you haven't got a high school diploma, you're bound to be competing with immigrants."

Much of the president's focus has been on the nation's 11 million undocumented immigrants, who critics say are more of a drain than a boon to the economy.

The 8 million undocumented immigrants who are working pay about $13 billion a year in state, local and federal taxes, says the Federation for American Immigration Reform (FAIR), a conservative group that wants to restrict immigration. But in a widely quoted 2013 study, the group contended that undocumented immigrants cost the economy $113 billion a year, largely in state and local services — a figure that immigrant advocates dispute.[11]

"Right or wrong, opponents are concerned about the risks of market competition" from immigrant workers who often are willing to work for less, said Cass R. Sunstein, who directs the Program on Behavioral

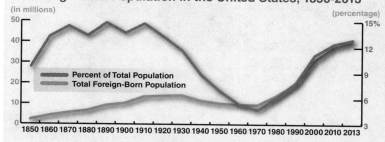

U.S. Immigrant Count on the Rise

The nation's foreign-born population has doubled in the past quarter-century, with more than 40 million legal and undocumented immigrants making up almost 13 percent of the total U.S. population in 2013, the latest tally. The immigrant count dipped in the 1960s and 1970s, hitting a low of 4.7 percent of the total, before beginning a sharp increase.

Foreign-Born Population in the United States, 1850-2013

Sources: "Nativity of the Population and Place of Birth of the Native Population: 1850 to 2000," U.S. Census Bureau, http://tinyurl.com/h27pl2d; "Population by Sex, Age, Nativity, and U.S. Citizenship Status: 2010," U.S. Census Bureau, http://tinyurl.com/gmjsent; and "Population by Sex, Age, Nativity, and U.S. Citizenship Status: 2013," U.S. Census Bureau, http://tinyurl.com/h6q28yr.

Economics and Public Policy at Harvard Law School. Among the factors he thinks are driving immigrant opponents, he says, "they want native-born Americans to keep their jobs, and they don't want them to face wage cuts."[12]

Because the number of undocumented immigrants equals about 5 percent of the working population, some critics say the nation's unemployment rate could be reduced to zero if authorities expelled as many as 3 million of these people. Others argue they should be allowed to stay legally, which would enable them to earn higher incomes and pay more in taxes.

AnnaLee Saxenian, dean of the University of California, Berkeley School of Information and an expert on Silicon Valley and technology, says much of this discussion misses the point. "The debate over immigration is deteriorating into a conversation over, 'Are they stealing jobs?'" she says.

Undocumented immigrants hold large numbers of jobs in construction, health care and restaurants, especially in Texas, which has the second-largest number of undocumented immigrants behind California. Evicting them, Saxenian says, might mean immediate hardships

Mexican farmworkers harvest lettuce in California's Imperial Valley. Immigration supporters say many industries would suffer without undocumented workers. For example, migrants - most of whom are from Mexico and Puerto Rico -constitute about 50 percent of U.S. farmworkers. A study of undocumented workers in Texas acknowledges they "lubricate" the economy, but on the negative side, the researchers note, many migrant farmworkers live in or near poverty and draw heavily on state social programs.

for the companies that employ them, because of a worker shortage in a tight job market.

Such concerns did not stop Arizona from enacting a series of tough laws between 2000 and 2010 aimed at stemming the flow of illegal immigration.

The state's undocumented immigrant population peaked at about 500,000 in 2007 and has dropped 40 percent since then, in part because the 2008 recession caused construction jobs to dry up. Nationwide, the number of undocumented immigrants has been basically unchanged since 2008, partly because economic opportunities have increased in Mexico due to new investments there, according to the Pew Research Center, a Washington, D.C., polling and research organization.[13]

Saxenian says that although technology and other business sectors highly value immigrants, foreign-born workers look at the controversies over immigration as evidence of an unwelcome American climate. This, she says, could lead some foreign entrepreneurs to establish their companies elsewhere.

"In the 1970s and '80s, everybody felt they were welcome in the U.S.," she says. "And since 9/11, they've encountered a pretty hostile immigration system. Making them feel welcome is important. These are people who would like to stay."

As the immigration debate continues among economists, politicians and the public, here are some of the questions they are asking:

Are undocumented immigrants good for the U.S. economy?

As a candidate and now as president, Trump has cited a widely quoted figure from the Federation for American Immigration Reform: Illegal immigration costs U.S. taxpayers about $113 billion a year at the federal, state and local level.[14]

Other conservative think tanks and countless opinion pieces also cite the $113 billion figure as they seek to ban undocumented immigrants or expel them from the country. "Illegal immigration increases income inequality and corrupts our democracy," wrote University of Maryland economics professor Peter Morici in *The Washington Times*.[15]

He added, "When the nation is flooded with immigrants in skill categories without genuine shortages," such as jobs in which employers would have to pay higher wages in order to find qualified applicants, "illegal immigration drives down wages and increases unemployment, especially for America's lowest-paid workers."

That $113 billion figure, according to FAIR, includes federal expenses for education, medical treatment and law enforcement, as well as other expenditures covering undocumented immigrants, who have been blocked from receiving federal welfare since passage of the 1996 welfare reform law.[16] The bulk of the expense, however, is paid by state and local governments, estimated by FAIR at $84 billion.

The American Immigration Council, a pro-immigrant think tank in Washington, said FAIR's report relied "upon flawed and empirically baseless assumptions to inflate its estimate of the costs." It added, "Much of what FAIR counts as the cost of unauthorized immigration is actually the cost of education and health care for U.S. citizen children." PolitiFact, a Pulitzer Prize-winning fact-checking website, said the cost of undocumented immigrants to the country was as low as $1.9 billion, but noted that the estimates vary widely.

"It's uncertain how much immigrants in the United States illegally cost taxpayers," said PolitiFact.[17]

The Center for American Progress, a liberal think tank, argues that undocumented immigrants contribute significantly to the U.S. economy — and that the country is missing an economic opportunity by creating an atmosphere hostile to newcomers. "Immigrants in fact are makers, not takers," wrote three experts on immigration and the economy.[18]

They cited research by Raúl Hinojosa-Ojeda, an immigration expert at the University of California, Los Angeles, concluding that undocumented residents could contribute $1.5 trillion to the U.S. gross domestic product (GDP) over a decade if all 11 million were granted legal resident status. His reasoning: Legal workers earn higher wages than undocumented workers, and they use those higher wages to buy homes, cars, appliances and electronics. As this money flows into the economy, businesses expand to meet demand, and jobs are added.

James H. Johnson Jr., a professor of strategy and entrepreneurship at the University of North Carolina's Kenan-Flagler Business School, says immigrants have an economic ripple effect that is not widely recognized. "People are not fully accounting for the way that immigrants add value to the economy," Johnson says. "They create additional jobs that would not be there." For instance, undocumented immigrants need attorneys to help them navigate U.S. laws. Or they may need translators or help filing their tax returns.

In addition, some industries might have trouble functioning without undocumented workers. For instance, undocumented immigrants constitute about 50 percent of hired farmworkers, down about 5 percentage points from the peak in 1999-2001, according to a 2016 report by the U.S. Department of Agriculture. About 69 percent of agricultural employees are from Mexico. The same is true in the construction industry; experts say immigrants are helping to fill labor shortages, and they constitute more than 25 percent of the housing construction workforce.[19]

Even as the number of undocumented workers has fallen in recent years in many places, Texas has continued to see its immigrant population rise. In construction, for example, about 25 percent of jobs go to undocumented workers, according to an in-depth series in *The Texas Tribune*. "There are almost always jobs waiting for them," it said, because of a building boom in the state's biggest cities.[20]

But using undocumented workers carries both benefits and costs, according to a study on immigrants'

impact on the Texas economy by two researchers for the Texas Public Policy Foundation, a conservative think tank in Austin. "The peripatetic ways of immigrants, both legal and illegal, serve as an economic lubricant," they said. But on the negative side, the authors continued, 65 percent of the state's illegal immigrants are in or near poverty, and a majority are forced to use a "major [Texas] welfare program."[21]

Restaurant owners are among those concerned about a crackdown on undocumented workers. "If every one of [the undocumented immigrants] working in a restaurant was gone tomorrow, you'd have to close down the entire industry," says Mike Monahan, owner of Monahan's Seafood in Ann Arbor, Mich.

The true cost of undocumented workers to American society may be debatable, but Maria Minniti, a professor of entrepreneurship at the Whitman School of Management at Syracuse University, sees advantages, both to the country and the workers themselves.

Many would not be employable in parts of the job market that require higher skill levels, she says. But working in restaurants or in similar jobs lets the newcomers get their bearings while they learn English and the ways of American society, Minniti says. "It's one of the great diversifying features of the country, the importance of freedom, the stress on the market, the commitment to work that gets you where you are," she says.

Do local economies benefit from the arrival of legal immigrants?

In Durham, N.C., City Council member Steve Schewel says his community's economy needs immigrants to prosper.

"Durham is [experiencing] a construction boom and a cultural renaissance," Schewel says. "None of that would be possible without our immigrant population, both documented and undocumented."

Durham is best known as the home of Duke University and Research Triangle Park, one of the nation's leading centers of biotechnology and life sciences research, with more than 200 companies. The city's restaurant scene is flourishing, and Durham has attracted new residents from around the world.[22]

Durham's population has grown from 149,000 in 1990, when only 4 percent were foreign born, to more than 295,000 in 2016, with 14 percent foreign born,

H-1B Applications Hit New High

Applications for the H-1B visa program, which allows employers to hire foreign workers in specialty occupations, hit a record 348,699 in 2015, with 257,317 approved.

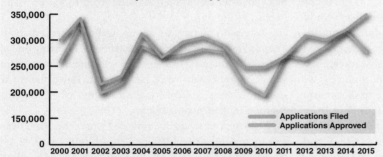

H-1B Visa Requests and Approvals, 2000-2015

Source: "Reports and Studies," U.S. Citizenship and Immigration Services, Jan. 10, 2017, http://tinyurl.com/gqrb9hd.

primarily from Latin America and Asia, according to the Census Bureau.[23]

The newcomers help fill both lower-paying jobs and positions at startups, Schewel says. "There is almost nothing that we're doing that doesn't depend on immigrant brain power," he says. "We're very much a foodie town, and immigrants are vital to that. We have a massive cluster of startup companies, and immigrants are vital to that."

Immigration opponents see things differently. Trump adviser Bannon has argued that legal immigration hurts American communities and the fabric of American life. "A country's more than an economy. We're a civic society," Bannon said in 2015. Bannon advocates an economic nationalism that puts native-born Americans first.[24]

Ohio real estate agent Mary Theis backs Trump's proposals to limit immigration and renegotiate trade deals that she said favored other countries. Citing the president's business skills as a deal maker, Theis said that "with Donald Trump negotiating on trade, maybe we'll get some of these [lost] jobs back."[25]

Schewel says he can understand such frustrations, especially among older, white Americans who have been displaced by economic change. "I think that's real. I acknowledge and affirm that experience," he says. "But keeping immigrants out won't help them. It will hurt

them [because limiting immigration will limit economic growth]. We need the kind of economy that can grow and be prosperous."

A number of economists argue that legal immigrants boost local economies in several ways. One is their impact on small businesses — the lifeblood of small towns. According to a 2012 report, 18 percent of small-business owners in the United States are immigrants, employing an estimated 4.7 million people and generating revenue of more than $776 billion annually. They are especially well represented in retail, including restaurants, groceries and dry cleaning.[26]

California and New Jersey benefit the most from immigrant-owned businesses in terms of jobs created, said a 2017 study by the personal finance website WalletHub.[27]

Another benefit of immigration is its ability to help revive struggling rural communities, according to the American Immigration Council.[28]

One example the council cited is Ottumwa, a town of 25,000 in southeastern Iowa. Its Hispanic population rose from 1 percent in 2000 to 11.3 percent in the latest U.S. census, with mostly legal Hispanic workers being drawn by the lure of jobs at a Cargill pork processing plant. As the Hispanic population rose, Latino-owned groceries and restaurants followed. The influx helped spark a downtown revival, city officials said, with new businesses opening, including a home-improvement store and a Kohl's department store. "Hispanics," said loan officer Nicole Banner of U.S Bank, "are pulling this town out of a long recession."[29]

Ottumwa was not alone. The Hispanic population in the Midwest jumped 49 percent between 2000 and 2010, according to the census.[30]

In Michigan, Republican Gov. Rick Snyder said he supports legal immigration because of its potential to boost the state economy. The state's population fell seven years in a row, from 2005 to 2011, reflecting an economy battered by the 2008 recession and job cuts resulting from the auto industry's struggles.

In 2014, Snyder created the Michigan Office for New Americans in an effort to attract foreign entrepreneurs and encourage foreign students to stay in Michigan to get advanced degrees. "We want the world to know Michigan is a welcoming state," Snyder said.[31]

Michigan's efforts to attract more immigrants are paying off in small ways so far. Between 2000 and 2014, Detroit lost 36,000 native-born residents but gained 4,400 immigrants, hardly enough to offset the loss, but at least a sign the city was appealing to newcomers. Statewide, Michigan has gained 50,000 immigrants in the past six years, Snyder said in his most recent state-of-the-state address.[32]

Citing the impact of foreigners in Silicon Valley, the University of California's Saxenian says immigrants bring energy to communities, creating a flow of ideas between their new and old homes — what she calls "brain circulation."

She says she discovered this phenomenon in the 1990s, when she began studying Silicon Valley's venture capitalists.

These company founders set up satellite offices in their home countries, such as India and Taiwan. The practice has encouraged companies in those countries to invest in the United States, too, Saxenian says. More than 600 Taiwanese companies have operations in the United States, while 100 Indian firms have collectively invested more than $15 billion in American operations.[33]

Says Saxenian, "This circulation has been mutually beneficial. It's clear there's so much opportunity elsewhere in the world. People can move quickly, and communication is much cheaper."

Should more H-1B visa holders be allowed to remain in the United States?

Every April, foreigners from around the world take part in the H-1B lottery to get one of the coveted, special visas that allow a limited number of highly skilled foreigners into the country each year. The winning applicants are allowed to work in the United States for three years, with the possibility of applying for additional time when their visas expire. Competition is stiff: In 2015, a record 348,699 people applied and 257,317 slots were approved.[34]

Each applicant must have a corporate sponsor, who must show that the applicant is earning as much as native-born employees, that the company has unsuccessfully tried to recruit Americans with similar skills and that the applicant's work is essential to the company's operations.

Applicants generally are scientists, engineers or computer programmers working in highly skilled "specialty occupations." A 2014 estimate said 65 percent of H-1B visas went to tech workers, mostly from India. H-1B visas also are available for those with other graduate degrees, such as MBAs.[35]

Critics say companies use the visas to import cheaper labor to suppress wages across the country. They say universities and hospitals also use the visas to hire low-wage teaching assistants and nurses.

Then-Sen. Jeff Sessions, R-Ala., now the U.S. attorney general, said in 2016 Congress should consider eliminating the program.

"We shouldn't be bringing in people where we've got workers," Sessions said in Indianola, Iowa. "There are a number of ways to fix it. I don't think the republic would collapse if it was totally eliminated."[36]

Trump senior policy adviser Stephen Miller has proposed scrapping the lottery system used to award the visas and potentially replacing it with a program that would seek to prevent foreign workers from undercutting domestic salaries.[37]

Yet, Labor Department records showed that Trump's golf club and model management companies had received two dozen H-1B visas for employees in the past five years, and he later said the United States needed to ensure that companies could retain employees brought to the U.S. under the H-1B program.[38]

The month before Trump took office, he convened a group of tech company CEOs, whose top priorities include expanding the H-1B program in order, they say, to recruit the most talented workers.[39] For years, many executives have been urging the White House and Congress to allow more immigration. In 2013, Facebook CEO Mark Zuckerberg co-founded FWD.us, an effort backed by Silicon Valley companies that is pushing for "commonsense" reform solutions that will satisfy both sides in the debate.

However, some startups and other small firms see the H-1B visa program as favoring bigger tech companies. If employees cannot obtain H-1B visas, they must apply for legal residence, which can take years. "Small companies can't afford to put them through the green-card process," says Syracuse University's Minniti, referring to a permit that allows a foreigner to live and work permanently in the United States.

Infosys, an Indian company whose U.S. operations are based in Plano, Texas, is the country's top applicant for H-1B visas, according to MyVisaJobs.com, a website that tracks companies' applications. Between 2014 and 2016, Infosys filed 82,506 applications for H-1B visas on behalf of its employees. Of that figure, just 57 were denied or withdrawn, said MyVisaJobs.com. Infosys was sued for visa fraud to circumvent the H-1B system.[40]

In addition to Infosys, Tata Consultancy Services and Wipro, a global technology and consulting firm, both based in India, have made heavy use of H-1B visas to staff their U.S. operations.[41]

The government can bar companies from receiving H-1B visas if they're found to be "willful violators" by displacing U.S. workers with foreign-born ones by failing to recruit Americans for the jobs. Sixteen companies are on the Labor Department's banned list, including technology and fashion firms and even a dairy.[42]

Jiangtao Liu, the business development manager for autonomous driving at Intel, who went to the University of Michigan, is among those working in the United States on an H-1B visa, which he obtained in 2015. Says Liu, "The whole U.S. immigration system is a mess."

But Liu says the H-1B lottery is a crapshoot. "There is no guarantee you will win," says Liu, who was sponsored by Intel. At least 10 of his foreign-born Michigan classmates failed to get H-1B visas and had to leave the country — some to the United Kingdom, others to Australia. In a few cases, their companies reassigned them to subsidiaries abroad.

Liu says he received a three-year H-1B visa that will expire in 2019 and is eligible to apply for a three-year extension. But he also is thinking about applying for permanent residency. "It's a painful process," says Liu.

BACKGROUND

Immigrants Spur Economy

In the 13 colonies that became the United States, immigration and economic growth went hand in hand.

At Jamestown, Va., the first permanent English colony in North America, the settlers struggled to survive in the early years until they developed a marketable crop — tobacco. But planters needed a labor force, and they first tried indentured servants, an arrangement in which they paid for an English worker's passage to the colonies in return for several years of servitude — usually seven. When the system did not meet the needs of a growing economy, planters increasingly turned to using slaves, who were first brought to Jamestown from Africa in 1619.[43]

Outside of Virginia, immigration surged, with the Scotch-Irish and Germans making up the two largest groups. Between 1683 and 1775, more than 200,000 Scotch-Irish arrived, followed by some 111,000 Germans. By 1750, the colonial population had reached 1.1 million — a sixfold increase from 1700. The polyglot colonies were peopled by immigrants from across Europe; Pennsylvania alone was believed to be one-third German. The new arrivals built an agriculture-based economy, since most colonists were farmers or planters. The rest were artisans, shopkeepers, merchants or lawyers.[44]

Upon the outbreak of the Revolutionary War in 1775, immigration for the most part ceased and did not resume until after the fighting ended in 1781. In 1789 the U.S. Constitution took effect, and Article 1, Section 8, Clause 4 gave Congress the authority "to establish a uniform Rule of Naturalization." Congress then undertook a long line of legislative efforts to define and regulate immigration in the United States.

The Naturalization Act of 1790 declared that any alien who was a "free white person" was eligible to become a citizen after living in the United States for two years. At the time, about 4,000 white people a year were immigrating to the United States.[45] But that figure was about to swell.

In the 19th century the Irish and Germans were the dominant immigrant groups, along with many Chinese. Then Italian immigration surged with more than 4 million coming between 1880 and 1914, while Caribbean natives and more Chinese arrived later in the 20th century.[46]

One of the most notable British immigrants was William Colgate, who left Kent, England, with his family as a boy in 1795. Colgate settled in New York City in 1803 and soon decided that what New Yorkers needed was soap.

In those days, wrote historian Tyler Anbinder, "manufactured soap was considered a luxury item only the wealthy could afford." Most people either used no soap at all, leading to the term "the unwashed masses," or made a crude version by boiling fat drippings from their food with potash. This homemade soap, according to Anbinder, was "greasy, foul smelling and extremely abrasive."[47]

Colgate discovered that if he could significantly cut the price of soap, New Yorkers would be willing to buy it. By 1817, after much experimentation, Colgate was the leading soap in the New York market. By the 1840s, after he had added scent to his soap, Colgate's Manhattan factory was producing 20 tons of soap a day to keep up with demand.

Colgate later expanded well beyond soap to toothpaste, toothbrushes and mouthwash. Today, Colgate is one of the nation's best-known brands.

Great Famine

Ireland's Great Famine, a period of mass starvation and disease caused by catastrophic failures of the potato crop, killed 1 million people and led to the emigration of possibly 2 million more between 1845 and 1849. Most went to the United States, especially Boston and New York.[48]

Some of the earliest Irish arrivals joined New York City's ranks of prosperous businessmen, becoming known as "lace curtain Irish" because they took on an air of respectability. Other, less-educated Irish immigrants, known as "shanty Irish," worked on ships and raised pigs in the city's teeming neighborhoods.

Irish immigrants who settled near City Hall in lower Manhattan received an especially hostile reception. A nativist political party that opposed both immigrants and Catholics — the Native American Democratic Association — condemned the appointment of Irish-Americans to political office. In 1836, the party ran Samuel F. B. Morse, inventor of the single-wire telegraph system, as its candidate for mayor. However, Morse received only 6 percent of the vote, and the party soon faded.[49]

By 1860, the Irish had become New York's largest ethnic group — and they achieved a milestone of sorts in gender history that year: 35 percent of Irish-born women worked at jobs outside their homes, compared with 18 percent of other immigrant women.[50]

The leading jobs were in garment factories, domestic service and needle trades such as sewing; 4 percent of

Mexican visitors enter the United States at a border crossing in Nogales, Ariz. Homeland Security Secretary John Kelly has signed sweeping guidelines that empower federal authorities to more aggressively detain and deport undocumented immigrants. The department also plans to hire thousands of additional enforcement agents and enlist local law enforcement to help make arrests - plans that alarm immigration advocates.

Getty Images/John Moore

Irish women were listed as business owners, twice as many as other immigrant women.[51]

German immigrants were outnumbered by their Irish counterparts in New York, but they were numerous enough that a swath of the city was called Kleindeutschland — Little Germany. "What multitudes from Germany are in our midst," *The New York Times* wrote in 1855.[52] German influence spread far beyond New York to Chicago, Milwaukee, Cincinnati and smaller cities such as Ann Arbor, Mich.

Many German immigrants prospered, including artisans such as cabinetmakers and gilders, shoemakers, bakers, locksmiths, brewers and cigar makers. Germans owned half the grocery stores in New York, even in Irish neighborhoods.

German Levi Strauss arrived in New York just as men and women from all over the country were streaming to California and points west for the 1849 Gold Rush. He followed them to San Francisco in 1853 and by 1860 was selling tents, clothing and other dry goods to stores from Nevada to Hawaii.

After the Civil War, a tailor came to him with an idea for a more rugged pair of overalls with pockets reinforced with metal rivets. Blue jeans were born in 1873.[53]

But by far, German influence was felt most significantly in big business. John Jacob Astor, the country's first multimillionaire, was of German descent. So was Harvey Firestone, the founder of Firestone Tire and Rubber Co. Others included Henry Heinz, the ketchup company founder; Otto Kahn, the investment banker; Conrad Hilton, founder of the hotel chain; and Isaac Singer of the sewing machine company.

Nevertheless, German immigrants endured two waves of anti-German sentiment, one before and during World War I, the other during World War II.

"World War I had a devastating effect on German-Americans and their cultural heritage," wrote Katja Wüstenbecker, a historian of migration at the University of Jena, Germany.[54]

Until the war's outbreak in 1914, she said, German-Americans were viewed mostly as well-integrated and esteemed. "All this changed with the outbreak of the war. At once, German ancestry was a liability." In 1910, German-Americans made up about 10 percent of the U.S. population, and their presence in virtually every major U.S. city made them instant targets.

"The battle against all things German" ran from business to entertainment, Wüstenbecker said. Music halls closed. Teachers had to sign loyalty oaths. By March 1918, the teaching of German in schools had been restricted or ended in 38 of the 48 states, Wüstenbecker wrote.

In 1918, President Woodrow Wilson declared German-Americans to be "alien enemies." About 2,000 people were confined to internment camps in Utah, Georgia and North Carolina. To protect themselves, some German-Americans anglicized their family and business names. (In Britain, the royal family did so as well, changing its name from the House of Saxe-Coburg and Gotha to the House of Windsor.)

German-Americans were barred from living near military facilities and airports, and business owners had to turn over their books to an "alien property custodian."

After the war ended, Congress passed the Quota Act of 1921, which restricted immigration, and the Johnson-Reed Act of 1924, which banned immigration by anyone from Asian countries. The latter act also set quotas on immigrants from other places.

For instance, 34,000 visas were allotted to Great Britain, but just 6,000 to Poland and 100 to Greece. In all, quotas cut immigration to 164,000 annually in the late 1920s. The figures were not revised until after World War II.[55]

German immigrants faced a new round of trouble when the world went to war in 1939 and the United States entered it in December 1941. Some 11,000 German-Americans were interned during World War II. Ten times that many Japanese-Americans were sent to camps in the United States.[56]

Chinese Contributions

In the nation's early years prejudice stalked another important immigrant group: the Chinese. Migration from China to the United States came in two waves: the 1850s to the 1880s, when Congress halted Chinese migration, and from the 1970s to the present, after U.S.-China relations were normalized in 1972. As a result, Chinese immigrants are now the third-largest ethnic group in the United States, behind natives of Mexico and India.[57]

In the early years, Chinese immigrants took mostly low-skilled and temporary jobs, working in mining, construction (especially helping build the nation's expanding railroads), manufacturing and service industries such as laundries and restaurants. Immigration records show that as many as 300,000 Chinese entered the United States in the first wave, although many returned to China, especially after Congress passed the Chinese Exclusion Act in 1882. That law barred Chinese immigrants from becoming U.S. citizens, a restriction that was not lifted until 1943.

In the 1950s, Chinese immigrants began to return to the United States. Some were escaping the oppressive policies of Communist leader Mao Zedong, while many came from the then British colony of Hong Kong, some arriving illegally.

However, Chinese immigration did not truly accelerate until President Richard M. Nixon and Mao normalized relations between the two countries in 1972. In 1980, Chinese immigrants in the United States numbered 385,000; by 2013, the figure topped 2 million, according to the U.S. Census Bureau.[58]

Unlike the first wave of Chinese migration, the second, still underway, tends to include immigrants who are well-educated and highly skilled. Most Chinese settle in California and New York; Chicago and Boston also are popular.

Nearly half of Chinese immigrants ages 25 or over hold a bachelor's degree or higher, compared with

C H R O N O L O G Y

1600s-1800s *Immigration fuels economy.*

1607 Virginia Company founds the first permanent English settlement in North America at Jamestown.

1619 First slaves arrive in Virginia.

1775 Revolutionary War causes a near halt to immigration.

1790 Naturalization Act declares that "any alien, being a free white person, may be admitted to become a citizen."

1820 German immigration expands, peaking with about 1.4 million arriving between 1880 and 1890.

1845 Ireland's Great Famine prompts migration to the U.S. As many as 4.5 million Irish arrive between 1820 and 1930.

1849 Chinese immigration accelerates.

1882 After riots, Congress passes the Chinese Exclusion Act, virtually halting Chinese immigration.

1900s-1950s *Immigration backlash grows.*

1907 Peak year for immigration as 1.3 million enter U.S.

1917 Anti-German sentiment builds with U.S. entry into World War I.

1924 Johnson-Reed Act curtails immigration; Asian immigrants are barred entry.

1930s During the Depression, hundreds of thousands of Mexican immigrants are deported.

1941 U.S. enters World War II. Tens of thousands of Americans, most of Japanese descent, are declared "enemy aliens."

1942 Bracero Program allows Mexican workers to enter the U.S., easing a wartime labor shortage.

1952 McCarren-Walter Act ends Asian exclusion.

1960s-1990s *Illegal immigrations grows.*

1965 Hart-Celler Act removes immigration quotas based on nationality.

1972 President Richard Nixon visits China and begins normalization of relations. The move opens the door to increased Chinese immigration.

1975 Vietnam War ends with fall of Saigon to communist forces; emigration from Vietnam, Thailand and Cambodia picks up.

1986 Immigration Reform and Control Act sets fines for employers who knowingly hire undocumented immigrants and amnesty for some 3.2 million undocumented immigrants.

1990 Congress creates the H-1B visa program for skilled foreign workers, allowing them to work in the U.S. for three years.

1996 Undocumented immigrant population reaches 5 million.

2000s-Present *Presidents Bush, Obama and Trump seek to change immigration policy.*

2000 H-1B cap is raised to 195,000; in 2004, Congress lowers it to 65,000.

2006 Number of undocumented immigrants reaches 11.6 million.

2007 Congress rejects George W. Bush administration's attempt to create pathway to citizenship for longtime undocumented immigrants.

2012 President Barack Obama signs an executive order protecting undocumented children, known as "Dreamers." An appeals court blocks his actions; the Supreme Court upheld the ruling in 2016.

2014 Immigration reform efforts fail in Congress.

2017 President Trump tightens immigration policy, signing an executive order blocking refugee immigration and temporarily banning entry by nationals from seven Muslim-majority countries. An appeals court upholds a lower court's stay of the order.

A "Dreamer" Fears for Her Family

Children who were undocumented when they arrived could face deportation.

Surf through the videos Maria Garcia posts on YouTube and you'll get a joyous picture of a young woman who loves the camera. She posts videos about eye makeup, nail polish, the Halloween costumes she makes and last-minute Christmas shopping.[1]

But one of her videos tells a far less upbeat story. Garcia, 20, of Los Angeles is a "Dreamer" — the child of parents who brought her to the United States as an undocumented immigrant. The name comes from a 2012 executive order, signed by then-President Barack Obama, called the Deferred Action for Childhood Arrivals program (DACA).

Under it, more than 725,000 young people provided personal information such as their passport numbers, school records and travel histories in order to obtain work permits, access to driver's licenses and the ability to get college educations. They received a renewable two-year moratorium on deportation.[2]

But DACA has been hotly debated, with opponents saying it encourages illegal immigration. Throughout his campaign for the White House, Republican candidate Donald Trump vowed to quickly repeal the act as part of his broader plan to expel undocumented immigrants. He has not moved to repeal DACA during his first weeks as president, during which he issued a temporary ban on entry to the United States of all refugees as well as immigrants from seven predominantly Muslim countries. (The ban has been stayed by a federal court.) Asked at a Feb. 16 news conference whether he will repeal DACA, Trump did not indicate what he will do, saying this "is a very, very difficult subject for me, I will tell you, . . . because you know, I love these kids."[3]

Garcia says she is watching the immigration debate with dread. "I'm scared for everyone in this undocumented situation," she says. "I can already see the number of families who are going to be affected by Trump's actions. I'm put in a situation where I would be very concerned over my family's safety and unity."

In 2014, House Republicans voted to defund DACA, saying it amounted to a temporary legalization program that ran counter to U.S. immigration law. (The vote had no impact on the program, because defunding failed in the Senate.)[4]

Mark Krikorian, executive director of the conservative Center for Immigration Studies, which wants to reduce immigration, derided the Dreamers act as "green-card lite" — a way for children of undocumented immigrants to permanently stay in the United States.[5]

Garcia, a junior at California State University who is majoring in communications, defends DACA. Her goal, she says, is to become an American citizen. She says her

28 percent of the total immigrant population and 30 percent of the native-born population. Their professions include management, business, science and the arts.[59]

Mexico's Ups, Downs

Today, Mexican immigrants are greeted warily in some parts of the country. The story was different during World War II.

In 1942, the United States and Mexico agreed on what became known as the Bracero Program, which allowed Mexican "guest workers" to fill agricultural jobs left vacant when American servicemen went to war. The Mexicans signed contracts allowing them to work in the United States, with some people coming back multiple times. In all, 4.6 million contracts were signed under the Mexican Farm Labor Program.[60]

Employers were supposed to hire *braceros* (manual laborers) only for jobs certified to have a domestic labor shortage. They also were barred from using the workers as strike breakers. In practice, employers took full advantage of this cheap labor, paying workers 30 cents an hour, according to government statistics. That was slightly higher than the rate for Texas agricultural workers in 1940 but well below the 81 cents an hour that agricultural workers were earning by the end of the war in 1945.[61]

parents emigrated from Jalisco, Mexico, when she was a child and that her younger brother and sister — both born after her parents moved to California — are citizens. But she and her parents are undocumented. She says her father is working, but she declines to be more specific. Her mother is a homemaker.

Garcia says her parents "didn't see much of a bright future in our native country due to the lack of resources and poverty. This caused them to take the risk and migrate to the U.S. That decision has turned into a greater opportunity in education and well-being for myself and my siblings."

Garcia says she faces obstacles that American-born students do not. Obtaining financial aid in the form of student loans is one difficulty. Undocumented students are not eligible for federal assistance and must turn to private aid.[6]

Although she's been able to get small grants, "it is not enough," she says. "I've paid my taxes since I started working when I was 17. I have had to work a bit harder" than native-born students "for the chance to continue to pursue higher education," Garcia says.

It is also difficult for Garcia to travel outside the United States. Many of her fellow students have spent semesters abroad or have vacationed in other countries. For Dreamers, however, "the opportunity is very rare. You have to go through a lot of paperwork and investigation just to be allowed to go."

Says Garcia, "I yearn to learn and experience other cultures. I've heard from my professors that it is an experience that can open your mind and help you grow."

Garcia says her video about her Dreamer status generated personal stories and messages of support from her YouTube followers, but a number of people posted negative comments expressing opposition to the Dreamers act. "You are an illegal student, draining our resources," wrote one, who called himself Julio Iglesias, the same name as the Spanish singer.

"Dreamer = illegal immigrant. I think it's better you cut the bull and get to the point. You want something. For nothing," wrote another, called Onaturalia.[7]

Garcia calls the comments "very upsetting." But she says she will continue posting YouTube videos and, after graduation, will try to become an entrepreneur and create a scholarship fund for undocumented and low-income students.

Beyond that, she wants to create financial security for her family. That would be "part of achieving the American dream," she says.

— *Micheline Maynard*

[1]Maria Garcia's YouTube videos can be found at http://tinyurl.com/h9uvshj.

[2]Griselda Nevarez, "4 Years Later, Lives Built by DACA at Risk in 2016 Election," NBC News, June 15, 2016, http://tinyurl.com/hxzggkw.

[3]"Full Transcript: President Donald Trump's News Conference," CNN, Feb. 17, 2017, http://tinyuil.com/h2ceucw.

[4]Miriam Jordan, "Immigrants Benefit From White House Initiative," *The Wall Street Journal*, Sept. 5, 2014, http://tinyurl.com/hqa6oy3.

[5]*Ibid.*

[6]Federal Student Aid, U.S. Department of Education, http://tinyurl.com/ho9b48e.

[7]The comments were posted on YouTube at http://tinyurl.com/h73zucx.

Despite the low wages, workers routinely overstayed their contracts, prompting the Immigration and Naturalization Service in 1954 to undertake Operation Wetback, a pejoratively named policy in which more than 1 million Mexicans and their children were deported. But some major farmers protested and persuaded Congress to extend the Bracero Program.[62]

In 1980, 2.1 million Mexican immigrants were in the United States, according to the Census Bureau. By 2010, the total number of Mexican immigrants had mushroomed to 11.7 million.

Historians say a search for economic opportunity, political instability in Mexico and fears about crime spurred Mexican immigration to the United States.[63] Also, says Boston College's Skerry, many older Mexican immigrants did not intend to stay; their plan was to earn money and then return home.

Once in the United States, Mexican immigrants tend to achieve less than other immigrants and native-born Americans, according to the Migration Policy Institute, a Washington think tank that researches immigration. Only 6 percent have college degrees, compared with 28 percent of all immigrants.[64]

Mexican immigrants, both legal and undocumented, are more likely to be employed in service occupations, construction and maintenance jobs than other immigrants

Immigrants Help Tech Engine Run

"I don't know if we can close our borders and be self-sustaining."

Lesli Ann Mie Agcaoili, an engineer at Tesla Motors in Fremont, Calif., has a front-row seat to the role that immigrants play in the technology sector — and to their fears of the Trump administration's restrictive plans on immigration.

Throughout the day, she says, she interacts with co-workers from Mexico, Canada, Germany and Australia. She socializes with people from India, who shop in their own section of Fremont called Little India.

Agcaoili says it's normal to hear conversations in different languages. Lately, much of the talk has been about President Trump's executive order — which several federal courts have blocked — temporarily barring entry to nationals from seven Muslim-majority countries.

"It has crossed peoples' minds: 'What if I have to go back?'" Agcaoili says. "People who are here legally ought to be fine, but I think there is some fear and apprehension about the [Trump] administration."

Founded by Elon Musk, who was born in South Africa, Tesla sits among a sea of companies started by people from outside the United States. More than half of 87 technology companies individually worth $1 billion or more have at least one foreign-born founder, according to the National Foundation for American Policy, an immigration research group in Arlington, Va.[1]

About two-thirds of people working in computing and mathematics jobs in San Mateo and Santa Clara counties, which comprise Silicon Valley, were born outside the United States, said the Silicon Valley Institute for Regional Studies, the research arm of Joint Venture Silicon Valley, an organization studying the region's economy. Immigrants make up 60 percent of those working in engineering and architectural jobs.

Critics say Silicon Valley recruits cheap labor from overseas. The tech industry, they say, is especially misusing the H-1B program — special visas that allow a limited number of highly skilled foreigners into the country each year. Sixty-five percent of H-1B petitions approved in the 2014 fiscal year went to tech workers, most of whom were from India, according to the U.S. Citizenship and Immigration Services.[2]

Trump senior adviser Stephen Bannon has denounced "progressive plutocrats in Silicon Valley" who want the freedom to bring overseas workers into the United States. American graduates, as a result, can't find work in the tech field, Bannon complained in March 2016.[3]

However, Trump told technology executives in a recent meeting that his immigration order was intended to stop "bad people" from entering the United States, but said he

or the native-born population, the institute said. Their wages are significantly lower than other immigrants', with their average household income in 2014 at $37,390, compared with $49,487 for all immigrants and $54,565 for native-born residents.[65]

But Mexican immigrants' income in the United States is three times the average household income in Mexico, according to the Organisation for Economic Co-operation and Development (OECD), a Paris-based economic research organization, made up of 34 developed nations, that promotes market-based economic policies. About 28 percent of workers in Mexico work more than 10 hours a day, compared with 13 percent of workers in other OECD member countries.[66]

The higher income helps explain why so many Mexicans risk crossing the border illegally, experts say.

The federal government in recent years has attempted to reform immigration policy, with much of the debate focusing on the economic implications of legal and illegal immigration.

In 1986 the Republican-controlled Senate and Democratic-controlled House passed, and Republican President Ronald Reagan signed, the Immigration Reform and Control Act, which among other things required employers to verify that their workers were in the country legally and created fines for businesses that knowingly hired undocumented immigrants. It also awarded "amnesty" to undocumented immigrants who had entered

was open to amending the H-1B program so talented workers can come.[4]

To Agcaoili, the thought of a technology sector minus immigrants makes no sense. "Just in terms of labor, they're vital to the companies and helping make them run," she says. "I just don't think it's going to be good for the economy" if the administration imposes immigration limits. "I don't know if we can close our borders and be self-sustaining."

For Agcaoili, a 45-year-old Asian-American, the issue is personal. Her father is Filipino and her mother's roots are in Japan. Born in Los Angeles, Agcaoili spent her childhood traveling between there and Hawaii, where her ancestors emigrated to work on plantations. Some of her mother's relatives were placed in internment camps during World War II.

Agcaoili, who has also worked for Ford Motor Co. in Dearborn, Mich., and the parent company of BlackBerry in Waterloo, Ontario, says immigration scares have happened before. In the early 2000s, when jobs were scarce, she says foreign-born classmates in business school were worried about whether they would be able to stay in the United States after they earned their degrees.

"It was a huge, huge deal," she says. "'Will you sponsor a visa?' That was the first thing anyone would talk about before figuring out if a job was a good fit."

Agcaoili says the multiculturalism of Silicon Valley is key to its companies' success. Tech CEOs argue much the same. The problem, they say, is not just a shortage of workers but the need to find the best talent possible. Restricting immigration "will make it far more difficult and expensive for U.S. companies to hire some of the world's best talent — and impede them from competing in the global marketplace," the CEOs of 100 tech companies said in a legal filing opposing Trump's executive order.[5]

Executives say this need extends far beyond Silicon Valley. Manufacturers in Columbus, Ind. — the hometown of Vice President Mike Pence — are heavily dependent on skilled immigrants. Dave Glass, CEO of LHP Engineering Solutions, said his company makes hiring American engineers a priority, but he can't find enough of them to fill openings. "In the last few years, we've had, like, three [Americans] apply," he said. So relying solely on domestic labor is "not an option" for his company, he said.[6]

— *Micheline Maynard*

[1]Shira Ovide, "Trump Win Is Silicon Valley's Loss on Immigration," Bloomberg News, Nov. 9, 2016, http://tinyurl.com/hx33jzr.

[2]Mica Rosenberg, Stephen Nellis and Emily Stephenson, "Trump, Tech Tycoons Talk Overhaul of H1B Visas," Reuters, Jan. 12, 2017, http://tinyurl.com/grtljcr.

[3]Frances Stead Sellers and David A. Fahrenthold, " 'Why Even Let 'Em In?' Understanding Bannon's Worldview and the Policies That Follow," *The Washington Post*, Jan. 31, 2017, http://tinyurl.com/htcvuhf.

[4]Rosenberg, Nellis and Stephenson, *op. cit.*

[5]Elizabeth Dwoskin and Craig Timberg, "How Canada Is Trying to Capitalize on Trump's Executive Order," *The Washington Post*, Feb. 10, 2017, http://tinyurl.com/hw2cogg.

[6]Annie Ropeik, "Immigration Executive Order Causes Anxiety In VP Mike Pence's Hometown," NPR, Feb. 16, 2017, http://tinyurl.com/hxsa5l6.

the United States before Jan. 1, 1982. But experts say the act did little to reduce illegal immigration.[67]

Since then, immigration-reform measures have repeatedly failed to pass, regardless of which party controlled the White House or the chambers of Congress. In 2007, Republican President George W. Bush pushed a comprehensive reform that sought to satisfy supporters and foes of immigration by providing legal status to undocumented migrants and giving them a pathway to citizenship while tightening border security.

He also proposed a controversial temporary worker program that he said would help meet the demands of a growing economy. "This program would create a legal way to match willing foreign workers with willing American employers to fill jobs that Americans will not do," Bush said. "Workers would be able to register for legal status for a fixed period of time, and then be required to go home." But critics opposed the temporary worker program, saying it would harm American workers, and they denounced the granting of citizenship to undocumented immigrants as "amnesty" for lawbreakers. The bill passed the House but died in the Senate. (Democrats controlled both chambers.)[68]

Democratic President Obama's administration tried again in 2013, proposing a reform package that went beyond Bush's. Besides giving undocumented workers a chance at citizenship and tightening border security, it included a new visa program for lesser-skilled workers and

Gkrishnan Ganapathy, a Hindu priest from Fremont, Calif., takes part in a ceremony during the grand opening of the Hindu Temple and Cultural Center in Centennial, Colo., on June 7, 2015. Supporters of immigration celebrate the diversity that people from different cultures bring to the American "melting pot." Critics complain that some newcomers take American jobs and are slow to learn English.

provisions designed to attract immigrants with needed work skills, such as in technology. Despite having bipartisan support and being passed by the Democratic-controlled Senate, the measure died after House Republicans opposed the citizenship provision as amnesty.[69]

The Obama administration, meanwhile, was aggressively expelling undocumented immigrants. In all, it deported about 3 million people during Obama's eight years in office, earning him the title of "Deporter-in-Chief" from some immigration groups critical of his policies.[70]

CURRENT SITUATION

Immigration in Crosshairs

President Trump is moving aggressively against illegal immigration by cracking down on "sanctuary cities" (places that provide haven to undocumented immigrants) and loosening the rules on who can be deported. Businesses and immigrant advocates are warning in response that limiting immigration will hurt the U.S. economy.

To dramatize the importance of immigrants to the economy, advocates staged a "Day Without Immigrants" on Feb. 16 in which shops and restaurants nationwide closed for the day. Their goal was to show what would

happen if the United States were to lose large numbers of foreign-born residents in a crackdown on illegal immigration.

"From doctors to dishwashers, immigrants are integral to daily life in the U.S.," said Janet Murguía, president and CEO of the National Council of La Raza, a Latino advocacy group.[71]

The protest was spurred by Trump's executive order on immigration, his proposal to build a wall on the Mexican border and his crackdown on sanctuary cities, as well as recent federal raids on workplaces.

Homeland Security Secretary John Kelly has signed sweeping guidelines that empower federal authorities to more aggressively detain and deport undocumented immigrants. The department also plans to hire thousands of additional enforcement agents and enlist local law enforcement to help make arrests.[72]

During the week of Feb. 5, U.S. Immigration and Customs Enforcement (ICE) agents arrested hundreds of undocumented immigrants in raids in Atlanta, Chicago, Los Angeles, New York and other cities. The raids and roundups created great fear among undocumented immigrants and their defenders. ICE, however, said the raids were not unusual and the alarms raised are greatly exaggerated. "We do not have the personnel, time or resources to go into communities and round up people and do all kinds of mass throwing folks on buses. That's entirely a figment of folks' imagination," a Department of Homeland Security official told reporters on a conference call. "This is not intended to produce mass roundups, mass deportations."[73]

In Durham, N.C., City Council member Schewel says he hopes authorities do not deport undocumented immigrants or restrict legal immigration. "I think this is one world, and to shut off the immigration spigot is to shut off the way this country was built and made great."

Immigration Restrictions

Tech companies, meanwhile, are campaigning against Trump's plans to tighten immigration controls. Immigration is the lifeblood of the technology sector, they say, with immigrants bringing much innovation to the economy. Half of the technology companies in the United States worth $1 billion or more are headed by chief executives with roots elsewhere, according to a letter signed by more than 200 industry leaders and investors.

Will limiting illegal immigration protect U.S. economic interests?

YES
Steven Camarota
Research Director,
Center for Immigration Studies

Written for *CQ Researcher*, February 2017

The notion that enforcing our immigration laws will harm the economy is not supported by the facts. First, illegal immigration is a trivial share of the United States' $18 trillion economy, accounting for 2 or 3 percent of gross domestic product (GDP), according to Harvard's George Borjas, the nation's top immigration economist. This tiny addition to GDP almost entirely goes to the illegal immigrants themselves as wages and benefits.

Yes, the aggregate size of the U.S. economy would fall a little if these immigrants went home — fewer people means a slightly smaller economy. But what matters is the per capita GDP — the nation's total output, divided by the number of people in the United States — and not aggregate GDP. And there is no indication that reducing illegal immigration would reduce the per capita GDP of natives or legal immigrants.

The best way to think about enforcement is that it creates winners and losers. If more immigrants here illegally went home, low-skilled Americans who compete with them would benefit. Borjas has estimated that by increasing the supply of workers, illegal immigrants may reduce wages by $99 billion to $118 billion a year. Their departure would mean higher wages at the bottom of the labor market. It also would mean that some of the 23 million working-age Americans with no education beyond high school who are not employed might find work.

The other winners from enforcement would be taxpayers. On average, adult illegal immigrants have only about a 10th-grade education. As a result, they tend to earn low wages, and this allows them — or more often their U.S.-born children — to qualify for welfare programs.

My own research indicates that 62 percent of such households use one or more major welfare programs. Consistent with all prior research, a 2016 report by the National Academies of Sciences, Engineering and Medicine found that immigrants with no education beyond high school create significantly more costs for government than they pay in taxes. As a result, the departure of those immigrants in the United States illegally would save taxpayers billions.

It is true that some low-wage employers and the illegal immigrants themselves would lose if we enforced our immigration laws. But the poorest and least-educated Americans would benefit, as would taxpayers. Furthermore, enforcing immigration laws could help reduce crime, enhance national security and restore the rule of law.

NO
Ediberto Román
Law Professor; Director of Citizenship
and Nationatity Initiatives,
Florida International University

Written for *CQ Researcher*, February 2017

Limiting immigration and undertaking mass deportations are not the solutions to the purported immigration crisis. In fact, the leading studies on the subject conclude mass deportation will harm the economy and is an irresponsible policy that will fail, especially if businesses' demands for undocumented labor continue.

The Immigration Policy Center, for instance, said mass deportation would reduce U.S. GDP by 1.46 percent a year. Over 10 years, the cumulative GDP loss would be $2.6 trillion, not including the actual cost of deportation. This approach would lower wages for higher-skilled natives and lead to widespread job loss.

Similarly, the Center for American Progress concluded the "costs of a massive deportation policy would not only be substantial, but in many ways, financially reckless."

A number of prominent Republicans agree. Tom Ridge, former secretary of Homeland Security, for instance, stated, "Attempting to deport everybody is neither feasible nor wise." Sen. John McCain, R-Ariz., said, "I have listened to and understand the concerns of those who simply advocate . . . rounding up and deporting undocumented workers. . . . But that's easier said than done. . . . I have yet to hear a single proponent of this point of view offer one realistic proposal for locating, apprehending and returning to their countries of origin over 11 million people."

Besides the economic costs, mass deportation is simply inhumane. The advocacy group Families for Freedom observed, "Every year, nearly 200,000 non-citizens — many with kids who are U.S. citizens — are deported and torn away from their families . . . resulting in more single-parent households and psychological and financial hardship, or forcing their U.S. citizen children into deportation with them."

It continued: "These American children may have to start over in a country with a new language, fewer resources and an uncertain future. America's immigration laws force American children to lose their parent or their country. Mandatory deportation is a life sentence of exile. Such a severe 'one size fits all' punishment cannot be the basis of our immigration system."

It is thus time to end to baseless assertions that immigration restrictions are a viable option to the immigration debate. We must turn to data, not demagoguery; we must demand facts and not merely accept economically baseless as well as inhumane rhetoric.

The roster includes Microsoft and Google, while firms such as Apple have sizable numbers of non-U.S. natives in their management and staff ranks.[74]

"In my conversations with officials here in Washington this week, I've made it clear that Apple believes deeply in the importance of immigration — both to our company and to our nation's future," Apple CEO Tim Cook said in a memo to staff in late January after Trump's immigration order was announced. "Apple would not exist without immigration, let alone thrive and innovate the way we do."[75]

"The reality is that high-skilled immigrants can choose where to go," said the University of Toronto's Florida. "Countries like Canada and Australia have come to understand the economic advantages of attracting immigrants, and have upped their efforts to attract the top talent from around the globe."[76]

On Feb. 9, Trump suffered another legal setback in his effort to temporarily ban immigrants from seven Middle East countries and halt the flow of refugees for 120 days. The San Francisco-based Ninth U.S. Circuit Court of Appeals refused to lift a lower-court suspension of his executive order, the result of a lawsuit filed by the state of Washington. Trump reacted harshly, saying the judges' motivations were political, the decision was "disgraceful" and the country's security was in peril.[77]

Trump's executive order had caught airports, airlines and immigration officials off guard. *The Washington Post* reported that administration officials were divided over the breadth of the order, especially when it came to holders of green cards, who also were temporarily barred entry back into the United States.[78]

In challenging the order, Washington state's attorney general argued that Trump's actions represented executive overreach and would hurt those who "have, overnight, lost the right to travel, lost the right to visit their families, lost the right to go perform research, lost the right to go speak at conferences around the world."[79]

Throughout the legal wrangling, Trump insisted that the Constitution gives the president wide latitude to set immigration policy, and government lawyers told the appeals court that the president has "unreviewable authority to suspend the admission of any class of aliens" — an assertion the three-judge panel rejected. The Justice Department told the appeals court on Feb. 16 that the administration will rescind the executive order and replace it with a new one.[80]

Sanctuary Cities

Businesses also are worried about the economic impact of Trump's crackdown on sanctuary cities, in which he is threatening to cut off federal funding to any municipality that offers safe haven to undocumented immigrants.

Currently, five states and at least 633 counties have adopted practices meant to shield undocumented residents and refugees from deportation, according to the Immigrant Legal Resource Center in San Francisco. Methods range from declining federal requests to hold arrestees in jail because of their immigration status to limiting police cooperation with federal agents.[81]

Twenty-eight universities also have declared themselves sanctuaries, including Columbia, Wesleyan and all 23 campuses of the California State University system.[82]

University of Michigan President Mark Schlissel said his school would continue to welcome applications from undocumented students and would not disclose information about the immigration status of its international students beyond what was required by law.[83]

But foes of illegal immigration, and some who want legal immigration reduced, say the United States needs to regain control of its borders so it can both keep potential terrorists out and protect American jobs. "Decades of record immigration have produced lower wages and higher unemployment for our citizens, especially for African-American and Latino workers," Trump said in his July acceptance speech at the Republican National Convention.[84]

No matter the outcome of the immigration debate and the court battle over Trump's executive order, Boston College's Skerry says the country is likely to remain divided.

Many Americans, he says, passionately believe immigrants should be allowed to enter the country and undocumented workers should be able to stay, because their own family members had made similar journeys in search of prosperity.

Several advertisements broadcast during this year's Super Bowl made pleas for inclusion and tolerance. An ad by Airbnb, for example, showed a series of people from different races, including a man with a turban. The subtitles read, "We believe no matter who you are, where you're from, who you love, or who you worship, we all belong. The world is more beautiful the more you accept." And in the most-talked about ad, Anheuser-Busch depicted

German-born founder Adolphus Busch arriving in America, where he's greeted by people shouting, "Go back home!"[85]

Others, however, feel just as passionately that both legal and illegal immigration harms the economy because foreigners create more competition for jobs that Americans need and are often willing to work for less so they suppress wages.

When the supply of workers goes up, the price that firms have to pay to hire workers goes down" said George J. Borjas, an economics professor at Harvard University. "Wage trends over the past half-century suggest that a 10 percent increase in the number of workers with a particular set of skills probably lowers the wage of that group by at least 3 percent."[86]

Skerry thinks attitudes on both sides of the debate "are pretty dug in right now. The people who are going to feel sympathetic will feel sympathetic, and those who are angry will be angry, and they're going to feed off each other."

OUTLOOK

Searching for Solutions

President Trump remains determined to suspend immigration from seven Muslim-majority countries, and legal experts believe the Supreme Court ultimately may tackle the issue.[87]

In the meantime, Saxenian at Berkeley says immigrant executives and venture capitalists in Silicon Valley are watching closely to gauge whether to invest in the United States or in their overseas operations. She hopes the debate does not scare them — or their potential employees — away.

"To the extent that these ecosystems develop outside the United States, we want to make sure the U.S. remains attractive," Saxenian says. "We're in a space where anxieties over globalization are so strong that we could see a slowing down" of investment.

Minniti at Syracuse University says attracting younger immigrants is critical to keeping the U.S. economy competitive. "There is a strong correlation between age and starting a business," Minniti says, noting many businesses are started by people between the ages of 24 and 35 years old.

"You don't immigrate when you're 70," she says. "You immigrate when you're young." That's equally true for lesser-skilled immigrants, who continue to come to the United States in search of advancement.

"When you come, you want to work," Minniti says. "That is something that's innately entrepreneurial. They don't have the skills that others do in the workforce. But they are able and willing to do a lot of work, usually work that is physically demanding. These are usually the people who are accused of stealing American labor, but it is not true."

Boston College's Skerry says a compromise on immigration is possible. One solution conservatives could embrace, he says, is to establish a nationwide, government-sponsored effort to teach immigrants to become fluent in English. "It needs the oomph of a national campaign to encourage immigrants to learn English," he says, similar to the way Scottish-American industrialist Andrew Carnegie jump-started the library system by building libraries across the United States.

Such a campaign could "placate people who supported Trump who understandably have been concerned about the cultural changes that have been taking place," he says. "You tell all those people, 'English is really important. It's our language, and we want people to learn it.' I've never met many immigrants who don't want to learn English."

In the end, Minniti says immigrants everywhere are an easy target for changes caused by technology and changing consumer tastes. "It's not immigrants' fault. It's not the Chinese's fault. Unfortunately, the marketplace changes and requires readjustment. Who pays the price? People with lower skills."

Trump adviser Bannon would agree that Americans with fewer skills are the ones paying the price for globalization. But more immigration is not the answer, he said. The solution, he argued, is to gain control of national borders and construct an economic nationalism that focuses on the needs of the American economy over internationalism.

"Strong countries and strong nationalist movements in countries make strong neighbors," he said. "And that is really the building blocks that built Western Europe and the United States, and I think it's what can see us forward."[88]

NOTES

1. "Full Executive Order Text: Trump's Action Limiting Refugees Into the U.S.," *The New York Times,* Jan. 27, 2017, http://tinyurl.com/huz723.;

Michael D. Shear and Ron Nixon, "New Trump Deportation Rules Allow Far More Deportations," *The New York Times,* Feb. 21, 2017, http://tinyurl.com/jtr2qmq.

2. Greg Bensinger and Rachael King, "Tech CEOs Take a Stand Against Donald Trump's Immigration Order," *The Wall Street Journal,* Feb. 6, 2017, http://tinyurl.com/hh893na.

3. Letter from the American Council on Education to Homeland Security Secretary John Kelly, Feb. 3, 2017, http://tinyurl.com/zptvsum.

4. Frances Stead Sellers and David A. Fahrenthold, "'Why Even Let 'em in?' Understanding Bannon's worldview and the policies that follow," *The Washington Post,* Jan. 31, 2017, http://tinyurl.com/htcvuhf.

5. Renee Stepler and Anna Brown, "Statistical Portrait of Hispanics in the United States," Pew Research Center, April 19, 2016, http://tinyurl.com/z7axefn. The definition of "Hispanic" varies by study, and the U.S. census permits people to self-identify as Hispanic or "Latino." See "Hispanic Origin Main," U.S. Census Bureau, http://tinyurl.com/hqbmd2s.

6. Jie Zong and Jeanne Batalova, "Asian Immigrants in the United States," Migration Policy Institute, Jan. 6, 2016, http://tinyurl.com/gqtyet4; "Asian-Americans Are Expanding Their Footprint in the U.S. and Making an Impact," Nielsen Company, May 19, 2016, http://tinyurl.com/hrq882b.

7. "Modern Immigration Wave Brings 59 Million to U.S., Driving Population Growth and Change Through 2065," Pew Research Center, Sept. 28, 2015, http://tinyurl.com/qhfo8js.

8. Jason Furman and Danielle Gray, "10 Ways Immigrants Help Build and Strengthen Our Economy," Obama White House Archives, July 12, 2012, http://tinyurl.com/hto2rum.

9. "Foreign Born Population," U.S. Census Bureau, 2017, http://tinyurl.com/jsbzqc5.

10. Richard Florida, "How Trump Threatens America's Talent Edge," *CityLab,* Jan. 31, 2017, http://tinyurl.com/jros2wj.

11. Alexia Fernández Campbell, "The Truth About Undocumented Immigrants and Taxes," *The Atlantic,* Sept. 12, 2016, http://tinyurl.com/zs9ud27; "The Fiscal Burden of Illegal Immigration

on the United States Taxpayer," Federation for American Immigration Reform, 2013, http://tinyurl.com/od66dx3.

12. Cass R. Sunstein, "The Real Reason So Many Americans Oppose Immigration," *Real Clear Politics,* Sept. 28, 2016, http://tinyurl.com/gs9fa27.

13. Jeffrey S. Passel and D'Vera Cohn, "Size of U.S. Unauthorized Immigrant Workforce Stable After the Great Recession," Pew Research Center, Nov. 3, 2016, http://tinyurl.com/hvyqz7j; Anthony Cave, "Has Arizona's Economy Improved Because of Its Immigration Laws?" Politifact Arizona, March 3, 2016, http://tinyurl.com/z99ar2c.

14. "The Fiscal Burden of Illegal Immigration on United States Taxpayers," *op. cit.*

15. Peter Morici, "The Real Cost of Illegal Immigration," *The Washington Times,* Sept. 6, 2016, http://tinyurl.com/hd59gwf

16. For background, see Sarah Glazer, "Welfare Reform," *CQ Researcher,* Aug. 3, 2001, pp. 601–632.

17. "Statistical Hot Air: FAIR's USA Report Lacks Credibility," American Immigration Council, March 29, 2011, http://tinyurl.com/hkdu5gz; Miriam Valverde, "Donald Trump Says Illegal Immigration Costs $113 Billion," PolitiFact, Sept. 1, 2016, http://tinyurl.com/hnuzdsa.

18. Marshall Fitz, Philip E. Wolgin and Patrick Oakford, "Immigrants Are Makers, Not Takers," Center for American Progress, Feb. 8, 2013, http://tinyurl.com/zlzc585.

19. Farm Labor Background Report, Economic Research Service, U.S. Department of Agriculture, 2017, pp. 3, 7, http://tinyurl.com/glrf3ar; Kenneth Megan, "Labor Shortages Make the Case for Immigration," Bipartisan Policy Center, Oct. 23, 2015, http://tinyurl.com/zht7oox.

20. Travis Putnam Hill, "In Texas, Undocumented Immigrants Have No Shortage of Work," *The Texas Tribune,* Dec. 16, 2016, http://tinyurl.com/hhdxy34.

21. Ike Brannon and Logan Albright, "Immigrations' Impact on the Texas Economy," Texas Public Policy Foundation, March 2016, http://tinyurl.com/jzcffbt.

22. Economic Profile, Greater Durham Chamber of Commerce, 2017, http://tinyurl.com/gu5t3bp.

23. Demographics, City of Durham, N.C., 2017, http://tinyurl.com/hdjx4oa; "Durham's Immigrant Communities: Looking to the Future," Latino Migrant Project, 2016, http://tinyurl.com/ztcwpzh.

24. Benjamin Wallace-Wells, "The Trump Administration's Dark View Of Immigrants," *The New Yorker,* Feb. 2, 2017, http://tinyurl.com/hpuk999.

25. Farei Chideya, "Trump's Blue Collar Base Wants More Jobs and an America Like the Past," *Five Thirty Eight,* Sept. 13, 2016, http://tinyurl.com/jrsvsas.

26. "Immigrant Small Business Owners: A Significant and Growing Part of the Economy," Immigration Research Initiative, Fiscal Policy Institute, June 2012, http://tinyurl.com/6vt5fae.

27. "Economic Impact of Immigration by State," WalletHub, Feb. 14, 2017, http://tinyurl.com/hvpc4yt.

28. "How States and Local Economies Benefit From Immigrants," American Immigration Council, http://tinyurl.com/goj2sge.

29. Miriam Jordan, "Heartland Draws Hispanics to Help Revive Small Towns," *The Wall Street Journal,* Nov, 8, 2012, http://tinyurl.com/z2vvqet.

30. *Ibid.*

31. Michigan Population Trends, Michigan Department of Health And Human Services, 2017, http://tinyurl.com/jdjdsk7; "Snyder Creates Office for New Americans," press release, Office of Governor Rick Snyder, Jan. 31, 2014, http://tinyurl.com/gu7e5d2.

32. "How Immigrants Are Helping Detroit's Recovery," *The Economist,* Feb. 16, 2017, http://tinyurl.com/zqjqvbk.

33. "Taiwanese Companies in the U.S.," U.S.-Taiwan Connect, 2017, http://tinyurl.com/z3l28el; "Indian Companies Invest Billions in the U.S.," *The Wall Street Journal,* July 15, 2015, http://tinyurl.com/z5wsusa.

34. Sara Ashley O'Brien, "High-Skilled Visa Applications Hit Record High — Again," CNN Money, April 12, 2016, http://tinyurl.com/zs473gb.

35. Mica Rosenberg, Stephen Nellis and Emily Stephenson, "Trump, Tech Tycoons Talk Overhaul of H1B Visas," Reuters, Jan. 12, 2017, http://tinyurl.com/grtljcr.

36. Paige Godden, "Jeff Sessions Considers Eliminating H-1B Program," *Des Moines Register,* Oct. 25, 2016, http://tinyurl.com/zrksa79.

37. Rosenberg, Nellis and Stephenson, *op. cit.*

38. *Ibid.*

39. *Ibid.*

40. Profile of Infosys, My Visa Jobs, 2017, http://tinyurl.com/jdqut2w, http://tinyurl.com/z7tdykv.

41. "Fearing Tighter U.S. Visa Regime, Indian IT Firms like Infosys, TCS Rush To Hire, Acquire," Reuters, Nov. 29, 2016, http://tinyurl.com/hoyw9h3.

42. "H-1B Debarred/Disqualified List of Employers," U.S. Labor Department, 2017, http://tinyurl.com/zhgkvmr,

43. Edmund S. Morgan, *American Slavery, American Freedom* (reprinted 2003).

44. Richard Hofstadter, *America at 1750: A Social Portrait* (1971), p. 19; Marianne S. Wokeck, *Trade in Strangers: The Beginnings of Mass Migration to North America* (1999), p. 46.

45. Naturalization Acts of 1790 And 1795, George Washington's Mount Vernon, http://tinyurl.com/zhc729m.

46. Tyler Anbinder, *City Of Dreams, The 400-Year Epic History of Immigrant New York* (2016), p. xxv.

47. *Ibid.,* p. 110.

48. "Great Famine," *Encyclopedia Britannica,* Jan. 28, 2016, http://tinyurl.com/z7ntujp.

49. *Ibid.,* p. 124.

50. *Ibid.*

51. *Ibid.,* p. 188.

52. "New-York City: Germans in America," *The New York Times,* June 27, 1855. (URL not available.)

53. Our History, Levi Strauss & Company, http://tinyurl.com/zujk3n4.

54. Katja Wüstenbecker, "German-Americans in World War I," *Immigrant Entreprenuership,* Sept. 19, 2014, http://tinyurl.com/jpcxm8y.

55. "Who Was Shut Out?" *History Matters,* George Mason University, http://tinyurl.com/hzjoutz.

56. Tetsuden Kashima, *Judgment Without Trial: Japanese American Imprisonment During World War II* (2003), p. 124.

57. Kate Hooper and Jeanne Batalova, "Chinese Immigrants in the United States," Migration Policy Institute, Jan. 28, 2015, http://tinyurl.com/jqovnxs.

58. *Ibid.*

59. *Ibid.*

60. Bracero History Archive, 2017, http://tinyurl.com/82huf75.

61. Marilyn Sworzin, "Wartime Wages, Income and Wage Regulation in Agriculture," *Bulletin of the U.S. Bureau of Labor Statistics,* 1946, Federal Reserve, http://tinyurl.com/gvutub4.

62. *Ibid.*

63. "Most Mexicans See a Better Life in the U.S.; One-In-Three Would Migrate," Pew Research Center, Sept. 23, 2009, http://tinyurl.com/nos7k7c.

64. Jie Zong and Jeanne Batalova, "Mexican Immigrants in the United States," Migration Policy Institute, March 17, 2016, http://tinyurl.com/ln449qb.

65. *Ibid.*

66. Mexico, OECD Better Life Index, Organisation for Economic Co-operation and Development, 2017, http://tinyurl.com/3h6oasu.

67. Caroline Mimbs Nyce and Chris Bodenner, "Looking Back at Amnesty Under Reagan," *The Atlantic,* May 23, 2016, http://tinyurl.com/jn6o627.

68. Mark Knoller, "The Last President Who Couldn't Get Congress to Act on Immigration," CBS News, Nov. 21, 2014, http://tinyurl.com/hc4qpy2.

69. Seung Min Kim, "Senate Passes Immigration Bill," *Politico,* June 28, 2013, http://tinyurl.com/hth3g3m.

70. Serena Marshall, "Obama Has Deported More People Than Any Other President," ABC News, Aug. 29, 2016, http://tinyurl.com/j7y6wy9. For more see, Reed Karaim, "Immigration Detention," *CQ Researcher,* Oct. 23, 2015, pp. 889-912.

71. Doug Stanglin, "Businesses Across U.S. Close, Students Skip School on 'Day Without Immigrants,'" *USA Today,* Feb. 16, 2017, http://tinyurl.com/jptxfhe.

72. David Nakamura, "Memos Signed by DHS Secretary Describe Sweeping New Guidelines for Deporting Illegal Immigrants," *The Washington Post,* Feb. 18, 2017, http://tinyurl.com/zdg6mln.

73. Nicholas Kulish, Caitlin Dickerson and Liz Robbins, "Reports of Raids Have Immigrants Bracing for Enforcement Surge," *The New York Times,* Feb. 10, 2017, http://tinyurl.com/hwgbj5j; and Lisa Rein, Abigail Hauslohner and Sandhya Somashekhar, "Federal Agents Conduct Immigration Enforcement Raids in at least Six States," *The Washington Post,* Feb. 11, 2017, http://tinyurl.com/jg2wcgm; David Nakamura, "Trump Administration Issues New Immigration Enforcement Policies, Says Goal Is Not 'Mass Deportations,'" *The Washington Post,* Feb. 21, 2017, http://tinyurl.com/jh7xlk3.

74. April Glaser, "What Silicon Valley Can Expect Under Trump," *Recode,* Jan. 23, 2017, http://tinyurl.com/j5jchlq.

75. Jonathan Shieber, "Apple CEO Tim Cook Sent a Memo to Employees About the Immigration Ban," *Tech Crunch,* Jan. 28, 2017, http://tinyurl.com/jdrndk4.

76. Florida, *op. cit.*

77. Matt Zapotosky, "Federal Appeals Court Rules 3 to 0 Against Trump on Travel Ban," *The Washington Post,* Feb. 9, 2017, http://tinyurl.com/hxc6vd8.

78. Josh Rogin, "Inside the White House-Cabinet battle over Trump's immigration order," *The Washington Post,* Feb. 4, 2017, http://tinyurl.com/gpyx832.

79. Adam Liptak, "The President Has Much Power Over Immigration, but How Much?" *The New York Times,* Feb. 5, 2017, http://tinyurl.com/zu6rm79.

80. "The Ninth Circuit Makes the Right Call on Trump's Travel Ban," *The Washington Post,* Feb. 10, 2017, http://tinyurl.com/j92wj6x; Julie Hirschfeld Davis, "Supreme Court Nominee Calls Trump's Attacks on Judiciary 'Demoralizing,'" *The New York Times,* Feb. 8, 2017, http://tinyurl.com/gs6b8tl; and Brent Kendall and Laura Meckler, "Trump Administration Plans New Executive Order Next Week, Ends Legal Push in Appeals Court," *The Wall Street Journal,* Feb. 16, 2017, http://tinyurl.com/z4g fjvg.

81. Jasmine C. Lee, Rudy Omri and Julia Preston, "What Are Sanctuary Cities?" *The New York Times,* Feb. 6, 2017, http://tinyurl.com/hyrw4qc.

82. Yara Simon, "28 Universities That Vow to Offer Sanctuary to their Undocumented Students," *Remezcla,* November 2017, http://tinyurl.com/gqx4mor.

83. Mark Schlissel, "Protecting the Interests of Our International Community of Scholars," University of Michigan, Jan. 28, 2017, http://tinyurl.com/z8pgh8r.

84. "Full Text: Donald Trump 2016 RNC draft speech transcript," *Politico*, July 21, 2016, http://tinyurl.com/gt4clje.

85. Michelle Castillo, "AirBnb cofounders personally edited the company's controversial Super Bowl Ad," CNBC, Feb. 6, 2017, http://tinyurl.com/hxkethm; Claire Atkinson, "Anheuser-Busch's Super Bowl ad tackles immigration," *New York Post*, Jan. 31, 2017, http://tinyurl.com/z3y6asl.

86. George J. Borjas, "Yes, Immigration Hurts American Workers," *Politico Magazine*, September/October 2016, http://tinyurl.com/hol5pmp.

87. Jeff John Roberts, "Trump's Travel Ban: The Supreme Court and What Happens Next," *Fortune*, Feb. 6, 2017, http://tinyurl.com/z9rgmah.

88. Sellers and Fahrenthold, *op. cit.*

BIBLIOGRAPHY
Selected Sources
Books

Anbinder, Tyler, *City of Dreams: The 400-Year Epic History of Immigrant New York*, Houghton Mifflin Harcourt, 2016.
A George Washington University history professor tells the stories of immigrants and the role they played in defining a polyglot New York City.

Hsu, Madeline T., *The Good Immigrants: How the Yellow Peril Became the Model Minority*, Princeton University Press, 2015.
An associate professor of history at the University of Texas, Austin tells the history of Chinese immigrants and their path from a loathed ethnic group to an educated and admired migrant group.

Peralta, Dan-el Padilla, *Undocumented: A Dominican Boy's Odyssey From a Homeless Shelter to the Ivy League*, Penguin Press, 2015.
The author, whose family migrated from the Dominican Republic and became homeless, describes his impoverished childhood — and his rise to salutatorian at Princeton University.

Urrea, Luis Alberto, *The Devil's Highway: A True Story*, Back Bay Books, 2005.
A writer tells the story of a group of 26 Mexican immigrants who got lost in the Arizona desert, of whom just 12 survived.

Articles

Borjas, George J., "Yes, Immigration Hurts American Workers," *Politico Magazine*, September/October 2016, http://tinyurl.com/hol5pmp.
An economics professor at Harvard's Kennedy School of Government argues that during the 2016 presidential campaign, neither Republican Donald Trump nor Democrat Hillary Clinton gave a complete picture of immigration's impact on the United States.

Campbell, Alexia Fernández, "The Truth About Undocumented Immigrants and Taxes," *The Atlantic*, Sept. 12, 2016, http://tinyurl.com/zs9ud27.
A journalist explains how many undocumented immigrants collectively pay millions of dollars annually in Social Security taxes, even though they are ineligible to collect retirement benefits.

Davis, Bob, "The Thorny Economics of Illegal Immigration," *The Wall Street Journal*, Feb. 9, 2016, http://tinyurl.com/jo3pfbm.
A journalist explores the steps Arizona took to limit undocumented immigration and how it affected the state's economy, in both negative and positive ways.

Fitz, Marshall, Philip E. Wolgin and Patrick Oakford, "Immigrants Are Makers, Not Takers," Center for American Progress, Feb. 8, 2013, http://tinyurl.com/zlzc585.
Analysts at a liberal public policy think tank look at ways undocumented immigrants contribute to the American economy and their potential for providing more value.

Glaser, April, "What Silicon Valley Can Expect Under Trump," *Recode*, Jan. 23, 2017, http://tinyurl.com/j5jchlq.
Technology industry CEOs discuss their priorities, including immigration reform, during the Trump presidency.

Goodman, H.A., "Illegal Immigrants Benefit the U.S. Economy," *The Hill*, April 23, 2014, http://tinyurl.com/kefo83e.
The author looks at various data about undocumented immigrants, arguing that they make a positive contribution to the U.S. economy.

Koch, Edward, "Why Americans Oppose Amnesty for Illegal Immigrants," *Real Clear Politics*, June 2, 2010, http://tinyurl.com/255ulm3.
The late New York City mayor argued the United States should expand quotas for legal immigrants rather than allow those here illegally to stay.

Reports and Studies

Brannon, Ike, and Logan Albright, "Immigration's Impact on the Texas Economy," Texas Public Policy Foundation, March 2016, http://tinyurl.com/jzcffbt.
Researchers from a conservative think tank look at the impact of legal and undocumented immigration on the economy of Texas, which has the nation's second-largest number of undocumented immigrants.

Cadman, Dan, "President Trump's Immigration-Related Executive Orders," Center for Immigration Studies, February 2017, http://tinyurl.com/z442bxg.
A fellow at the Center for Immigration Studies, which favors limiting legal immigration, analyzes President Trump's actions on immigration.

Dimock, Michael, "How America Changed During Barack Obama's Presidency," Pew Research Center, Jan. 10, 2017, http://tinyurl.com/hwb8kbk.
A political scientist discusses the changes that took place during the Obama years, including the administration's policy moves on immigration.

Krogstad, Jens Manuel, Jeffrey S. Passel and D'Vera Cohn, "Five Facts About Illegal Immigration in the U.S.," Pew Research Center, Nov. 3, 2016, http://tinyurl.com/gtmhrft.
The authors look at the demographics of the undocumented immigrant population and the immigrants' impact on the broader U.S. population.

For More Information

American Civil Liberties Union, 125 Broad St., 18th Floor, New York, NY 10004; 212-549-2500; www.aclu.org. Civil rights group that defends immigrants' legal rights.

American Immigrants Lawyers Association, 331 G St., N.W. Suite 300, Washington, DC 20005; 202-507-7600; www.aila.org. Association for immigration lawyers.

Arab-American Institute, 1600 K St., N.W., Suite 601, Washington, DC 20006; 202-429-9210; www.aaiusa.org. Represents Arab-American causes, including discrimination matters and immigration.

Center for Immigration Studies, 1629 K St., N.W., Suite 600, Washington, DC 20006; 202-466-8185; http://cis.org/. Conservative research group whose goal is to restrict illegal and legal immigration.

Federation for American Immigration Reform, 25 Massachusetts Ave., N.W. Suite 330, Washington, DC 20001; 202-328-7004; www.fairus.org. Advocacy group seeking limits on immigration that produced a widely quoted study on undocumented immigration.

Hispanic Federation, 555 Exchange Place, New York, NY 10005; 212-233-8955; http://hispanicfederation.org/. Network of 100 grassroots Hispanic organizations that provides education and job training resources to immigrants and their families.

National Council of Agricultural Employers, 525 9th St., N.W., Suite 800, Washington, DC 20004; 202-629-9320; www.ncaeonline.org. Lobbies on immigration issues and provides guidance to its members on immigration matters.

NumbersUSA, 400 Crystal Drive, Suite 240, Arlington, VA 22202; 703-816-8820; www.numbersusa.com. Advocacy group that wants to reduce legal immigration.

U.S. Border Control, PO Box 97115, Washington, DC 20090; 703-740-8668; www.usbc.org. Federal agency responsible for securing U.S. borders.

9

Far-Right Extremism

Barbara Mantel

Twenty-one-year-old Dylann Roof has been charged with hate crimes, murder and other offenses in connection with the shooting deaths of nine parishioners at the historically black Emanuel AME Church in Charleston, S.C., in June. The massacre is the most lethal of several recent ideologically motivated fatal attacks by far-right extremists.

From *CQ Researcher,*
September 18, 2015

After the June slaying of nine parishioners at the historically black Emanuel AME Church in Charleston, S.C., the motives of 21-year-old suspect Dylann Roof came under intense scrutiny. A blogger tipped investigators to a website, initially registered in Roof's name, containing a 2,500-word manifesto ranting against Hispanics and "Negroes" that Roof's friends said they believe he wrote.[1]

"I chose Charleston because it is [the] most historic city in my state, and at one time had the highest ratio of blacks to Whites in the country," the manifesto reads. "We have no skinheads, no real KKK, no one doing anything but talking on the internet. Well someone has to have the bravery to take it to the real world, and I guess that has to be me."[2]

Roof has been charged with hate crimes and other offenses by federal prosecutors, who have yet to say whether they will seek the death penalty. Until then, Roof's lawyer said he cannot advise his client how to plead, so a judge entered a not guilty plea on the federal charges on his behalf. Roof also faces state murder charges, for which state prosecutors are seeking the death penalty. Roof also has yet to enter a plea on those charges.[3]

The Charleston shooting is the most lethal in a string of ideologically motivated fatal attacks committed since 9/11 by people aligned with far-right extremism, including white supremacy, antigovernment militias and the sovereign citizens movement, which denies the legitimacy of most local, state and federal laws. In the 14 years since al Qaeda killed nearly 3,000 people in strikes against the World Trade Center and the Pentagon, far-right extremists have

205

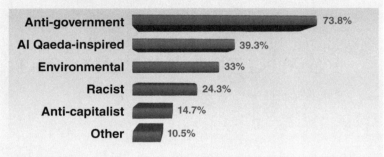

Police: Anti-Government Extremists a Top Threat

Nearly three-fourths of 382 local law enforcement agencies surveyed rated anti-government extremism among the top three terrorist threats in their jurisdictions in 2014, far more than those that listed al Qaeda-inspired threats.

Percentage of Law Enforcement Agencies Rating Types of Extremism Among the Top Three Terrorist Threats, 2014

Anti-government	73.8%
Al Qaeda-inspired	39.3%
Environmental	33%
Racist	24.3%
Anti-capitalist	14.7%
Other	10.5%

Source: Charles Kurzman and David Schanzer, "Law Enforcement Assessment of the Violent Extremism Threat," Triangle Center on Terrorism and Homeland Security, p. 4, http://tinyurl.com/pa6333f.

killed 48 people in 19 attacks in the United States, nearly twice the 26 people killed in seven Islamist extremist attacks, according to a study by the New America Foundation, a Washington-based centrist research organization.[4] Far-left animal rights and environmental extremists have caused millions of dollars in property damage but no deaths, according to researchers.

Some terrorism experts say the American public and the federal government should be paying more attention to far-right extremism and its potential for mass-casualty violence. They point to the 1995 truck bombing of the Oklahoma City federal building by two antigovernment conspirators, in which 168 people died and hundreds were wounded, and to more recent, disrupted plots.

But federal law enforcement officials say they can nimbly move resources as needed, and are doing everything necessary against the threat.

Meanwhile, there is debate about whether the federal government should broaden its controversial community outreach programs, designed to prevent Islamist extremist groups from radicalizing American Muslim youths, to include prevention of the radicalization of American youth by far-right extremists.

"These programs should be expanded beyond the Muslim community. A lot of the risk factors towards radicalization are common across ideological groups," says Susan Szmania, a senior researcher at the National Consortium for the Study of Terrorism and Responses to Terrorism (START), based at the University of Maryland.

But Michael German, a former FBI agent and a fellow at the New York-based Brennan Center for Justice, a law and policy institute, said anti-radicalization programs are based on the false notion that individuals follow a discernible path to violent extremism. "Instead of wasting resources chasing false leads, police should focus their resources where they have evidence of criminal activity," he said.[5]

Far-right, right-wing or radical-right extremism — all such terms are used — is primarily composed of two spheres, says Mark Pitcavage, investigative research director at the Anti-Defamation League (ADL), a New York-based civil rights organization. One sphere is white supremacy, consisting of neo-Nazis; racist skinheads; Ku Klux Klan groups; a religious sect called Christian Identity; and white supremacist prison gangs. The other sphere is anti-government — the so-called Patriot movement — which includes militias and sovereign citizens. Many, but not all, of its adherents hold conspiracy theories.

According to a prominent conspiracy theory, "the United Nations, which is usually seen as spearheading the 'New World Order,' is imposing a global plan, called Agenda 21, to take away citizens' property rights," according to the Southern Poverty Law Center (SPLC), an advocacy group in Montgomery, Ala., that tracks hate and anti-government groups. Another theory holds that the government has a secret plan to place citizens in concentration camps.[6] This summer, an eight-week, military training exercise across six Southern and Southwestern states prompted some residents' concern about a military takeover of Texas, causing at least some

Texans to stock up on ammunition and bury their guns. The exercise passed without incident.[7]

"We're very careful in saying that our listing of hate and anti-government groups has nothing to do with criminality, violence or any kind of estimate we're making for the potential for those things," says Mark Potok, a senior fellow at the center. "It's all about ideology."

In fact, most U.S.-based extremist ideologies do not explicitly call for violence, says Pitcavage. "They tend to present a view in which there is some sort of danger, and only imminent action can solve the problem," he says. "That's OK if you can do the action through legal means or civil disobedience, but some people will say, 'We have to go beyond that.'" He says the majority of extremist movement adherents typically are not violent.

Events of the past seven years have galvanized far-right extremists, say analysts. The 2008 election of Barack Obama, the United States' first African-American president, "greatly upset white supremacists," said an Anti-Defamation League report. "At the same time, anti-government extremists quickly linked Obama to their 'New World Order' conspiracy theories."

Sovereign citizens, in particular, tapped into the desperation that the 2007-2009 recession and mortgage crisis created.

But while "white supremacists became angrier, more agitated and also more violent, they did not appreciably increase in numbers," said the ADL report, largely because of leader deaths and group fragmentation in the previous decade. On the other hand, the number of active militia groups more than quintupled between 2008 and 2010, and the growth of the sovereign-citizen movement, which consists mostly of unaffiliated individuals, "was even more spectacular," according to the report.[8]

While the Southern Poverty Law Center estimates the number of hate and anti-government groups, the Anti-Defamation League tracks individual white supremacists. But, their numbers are best estimates and subject to outside scrutiny and critique.[9]

Increasingly, far-right extremists are finding each other online, making joining an organized group, such as a Ku Klux Klan group, far less relevant. Unaffiliated white supremacists far outnumber those belonging to specific organizations, which these days are often quite small, according to the ADL.[10]

"If people want to meet or have a demonstration, they can do it through us or through social media," says Don Black, a former Alabama Klan leader and the founder of Stormfront, a white nationalist online discussion forum. The number of registered Stormfront users has grown from 5,000 in 2002 to nearly 300,000 today, although many are inactive.[11] The site attracts about 31,000 unique visitors a day, roughly 60 percent from the United States, and takes in from $3,000 to $7,000 a month in dues and donations.[12]

Black, who advocates for a whites-only homeland, says Stormfront does not encourage violence: "People either get banned if they express their intent to conduct illegal violence or they recognize that it is counterproductive."

But Tony McAleer, a former organizer for the neo-Nazi group White Aryan Resistance and now director of Chicago-based Life After Hate, which helps white supremacists leave the movement, says it's necessary to look carefully at hate sites' language. "It's often really the implied threat of violence. By openly advocating violence, you expose yourself to all kinds of legal hot water," he says.

A few Stormfront users have gone on to commit mass murder. They include anti-immigrant extremist Anders Behring Breivik, who killed 77 adults and children in Norway in 2011, and racist skinhead Wade Michael Page, who fatally shot six people at a Sikh temple in Oak Creek, Wis., in 2012. Breivik had visited Stormfront only briefly, says Black. Page "posted 15 times on Stormfront, and he posted other places, too. We're not responsible for him," he says.

As researchers, law enforcement officials and others study the future of extremist groups in the United States, here are some of the issues being debated:

Should the public be worried about violent far-right extremists?

While the FBI maintains a database of hate crimes, which include crimes committed by individuals who aren't followers of any particular movement, it does not maintain a database of ideologically motivated far-right extremist violence. That task is up to researchers, and their estimates vary.

For example, START-funded researchers' estimates in their Extremist Crime Database are higher than the

Extremism's Deadly Legacy

Far-right extremists killed 245 people in the U.S. in ideologically motivated attacks between 1990 and 2014, compared with 62 killed by extremists associated with al Qaeda and affiliated movements.*

Number of Homicide Victims of Extremist Groups, 1990-2014*

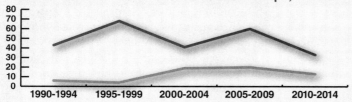

* The data exclude the nearly 3,000 who died in the Sept. 11 terrorist attacks and the 168 killed in the 1995 bombing of the Alfred P. Murrah Federal Building in Oklahoma City.

Far-Right Extremists

Inspired by al Qaeda and associated movements

Source: William S. Parkin *et al.*, "Twenty-five Years of Ideological Homicide Victimization in the United States of America," National Consortium for the Study of Terrorism & Responses to Terrorism, August 2015

New America Foundation's numbers. START researchers calculate that 134 people were killed in ideologically motivated far-right extremist attacks in the United States between 2000 and 2014, compared to 52 people killed by Islamic extremists, excluding the 9/11 victims.[13]

Yet both sets of data tell a comparable story. Far-right extremists are responsible for more deaths in the United States than Islamic extremists in recent years. Law enforcement concerns reflect those statistics.

"Three quarters of the 382 local law enforcement agencies that we surveyed [in 2014] expressed concern about antigovernment violent extremism, nearly double the number who expressed concern about al Qaeda-inspired and other Islamist extremists," says Charles Kurz-man, a sociology professor at the University of North Carolina-Chapel Hill and coauthor of a working paper about the survey results.

Law enforcement officers' concern makes sense, considering that they often are the target of violent antigovernment extremists. A July 2014 Department of Homeland Security (DHS) intelligence assessment noted a spike in militia-linked violence against law enforcement, while a February 2015 assessment predicted a continuation of sporadic, unplanned violence by sovereign citizens against law enforcement officers during routine traffic stops and home visits.[14]

One of the more notorious recent examples of such violence occurred in June 2014, when Jerad Miller and his wife, Amanda, ambushed and fatally shot two police officers eating lunch at a Las Vegas pizza restaurant. A note they left on one officer's body said the murders were "the start of the revolution." And their social media profiles talked about their willingness to "die fighting" to stop government oppression. From the restaurant, the two entered a nearby Walmart, where they killed a civilian and wounded another officer before Jerad Miller died in a shootout with police and Amanda Miller died by suicide.[15]

Such crimes may be shocking, but the number of all kinds of extremist violence, including al Qaeda-inspired, pales in comparison to the number of overall murders. "With more than 14,000 murders in the U.S. annually, violent extremism counts for less than 1 percent of fatalities in recent years," says Kurz-man. "Many Americans have greater fear of extremist attacks than other forms of violence, but the statistics suggest that we should be concerned about mundane violence that doesn't make the national news."

While surveyed law enforcement agencies ranked anti-government extremism a top concern in their jurisdictions, 66 percent gauged that threat to be moderate or low. And 83 percent rated the threat from al Qaeda-inspired violent extremism as moderate or low.[16]

"Of the list of things I lose sleep over at night, terrorism and violent extremism are not at the top of my list, and it's my profession," says William Braniff, START's executive director. "I worry much more about traffic accidents, gangs and other kinds of violence and criminality in the United States. I think something like gang violence is horrifically damaging to communities."

But Potok of the Southern Poverty Law Center (SPLC) says the public "absolutely should be worried about violence from the radical right. All you need is one or two to get through." Some of the plots the FBI has disrupted over the years have been quite scary, Potok says, including one in which a self-professed member of the Ku Klux Klan was convicted in August of conspiring to use a weapon of mass destruction to kill American Muslims.

Glendon Scott Crawford, a General Electric industrial mechanic in Schenectady, N.Y., took steps to purchase and then weaponize a commercially available industrial X-ray machine that he planned to install in a van or truck, park near the entrance to mosques and an Islamic community center and school and remotely activate, exposing people entering and exiting the facilities to lethal doses of radiation, according to the Department of Justice.[17]

"In terms of lethal violence, there's no doubt. White supremacists rule the roost," says Pitcavage of the Anti-Defamation League. He calculates that in the past 10 years, ideologically motivated killings by white supremacists greatly outnumbered those by all other far-right extremist movements. That conforms with data from the Extremist Crime Database.[18]

Steven Chermak and Joshua Freilich, criminologists at Michigan State University and the John Jay College of Criminal Justice in New York City, respectively, helped to create that database. Two years ago, they published a study exploring the characteristics that distinguish violent far-right hate groups from nonviolent hate organizations. They examined groups from the SPLC's database that had been in existence for at least three years. In a sample of 275 organizations, 21 percent had members who had committed at least one ideologically motivated violent act.[19]

The researchers found that as groups get older or increase in size, "they're more likely to be involved in violence," says Chermak.

But perhaps the most robust variable linked to violence were groups that advocated leaderless resistance, in which everyone serves in an equal position and contacts between individuals and other groups are minimized, says Chermak. Leaderless resistance reduces the chance that an informant or an arrested member would have valuable information to share with law enforcement.

"Interestingly, groups that distributed ideological literature were less likely to be involved in violence," says Chermak. Violence and the resulting attention from law

President Obama addresses the White House Summit on Countering Violent Extremism on Feb. 19, 2015. The White House favors a strategy - known as countering violent extremism, or CVE - to prevent violent extremists from recruiting and radicalizing U.S. residents.

Getty Images/Winn McNamee

enforcement "might not only harm their propaganda efforts, but it could also hurt their bottom line, because many try to profit by selling literature," he says.

But this study compared only groups. It did not compare nonviolent far-right extremists unaffiliated with any groups to violent lone wolves, such as accused Charleston shooter Dylann Roof. Freilich says lone wolves account for about 35 percent of ideologically motivated far-right extremists' homicides in the Extremist Crime Database.

In a way, they are more worrisome than attacks planned by a group, Freilich says. "The general consensus among law enforcement and scholars has been that loner attacks are harder to prevent," says Freilich. "An individual acting alone is flying beneath the radar, not emailing anyone, not calling anyone, planning in secret."

But there is a flip side, says Freilich: "When you act alone, you have less of an infrastructure and may do less damage than a group."

Is the federal government doing enough to fight far-right extremist violence?

A chorus of voices, from members of Congress to advocacy groups, is demanding that the federal government pay greater attention to violent far-right extremists.

"The United States allocates significant resources towards combating Islamic violent extremism while

Ex-skinheads Help Former Racists Rejoin Society

Life After Hate offers counseling and support.

As a young man, Tony McAleer of Toronto managed a racist skinhead rock band, recruited others for a neo-Nazi organization called White Aryan Resistance and became notorious for running a phone service that provided recorded hate messages. After a legal battle, the Canadian government shut the service down in the early 1990s.

McAleer says he was bullied both at school and by his father as a child, and that joining the racist skinhead movement gave him a sense of acceptance and power that he was lacking.

But at age 24, single-parenthood and financial hardship led McAleer to question his choices.

"I was virtually unemployable," says McAleer, who is now 48 and runs his own wealth-management company. "The birth of my daughter was the moment that began my transformation. It was the first time that I thought of somebody other than myself." Having spent years stockpiling weapons and preparing for a coming "race war," McAleer says he fully expected to be dead by age 30 and faced the prospect of leaving his baby daughter an orphan.

But it took six years before he actually started distancing himself from the activities of the white power movement and another eight years before he began to truly shed his commitment to its ideology by entering therapy with a psychologist. In addition, he says, doing business in China as a software developer opened his eyes to other cultures.

Extricating oneself from the extremist far right can be a long and difficult process, McAleer says. In 2011 he joined Life After Hate, a Chicago-based nonprofit founded in 2009 by former racist skinheads as a place for ex-members of the movement, known as "formers," to share their stories and come together. But people still in the white supremacist movement also began to contact the group for help in getting out.

This spring, McAleer, Life After Hate's volunteer president and executive director, started a formal deradicalization program called Exit USA, modeled after Exit Sweden, which helps neo-Nazis leave the movement. McAleer estimates that Life After Hate, both informally and through Exit USA, has helped 100 individuals so far.

"We know what they are feeling, what their fears are, and we can help them through that," says McAleer. "Most of the time, there are deep emotional wounds. We're not therapists, so we encourage people to get therapy because it's critical to the healing process."

The most challenging part is the initial isolation, he says. "When people leave any extreme group, they get

failing to devote adequate resources to rightwing extremism," wrote 20 House Democrats in July to President Obama and Secretary of Homeland Security Jeh Johnson. "When efforts are made to address right-wing extremism, they are often met with significant political backlash."[20]

The reference was to a 2009 Department of Homeland Security (DHS) intelligence assessment, which warned of growing recruitment by "domestic right-wing terrorists" and said that a small percentage of military personnel were joining far-right extremist groups.[21]

The document, meant for state and local law enforcement, was leaked and prompted a swift backlash from conservatives, who called the assessment a slur against veterans. "That was simply not true," says Potok of the Southern Poverty Law Center, adding that the intelligence assessment was accurate. Then-Homeland Security Secretary Janet Napolitano withdrew it and publicly criticized its authors, some of whom quit.

Some conservatives are on guard once again after then-U.S. Attorney General Eric Holder announced in June 2014 that he was reviving the Domestic Terrorism Executive Committee (DTEC), originally established after the 1995 bombing of the Alfred P. Murrah Federal Building in Oklahoma City but abruptly discontinued after 9/11. It's composed of leaders within the Department of Justice who coordinate with federal U.S.

excommunicated from their entire social circle. And if you've been a neo-Nazi or a racist skinhead for a number of years, I'll bet my bottom dollar that the rest of society has excommunicated you as well," McAleer says. "So you get stuck in this void, and there is intense loneliness."

The "formers" of Life After Hate will travel if necessary to meet with someone, and they rely on a board member with a master's degree in social work to provide guidance. The group also has a private Facebook page, called Formers Anonymous, to provide support.

"Everyone is vetted," McAleer says. "The last thing we want is a 'current' getting in there and finding out who are the 'formers.'"

Life After Hate is working with academic researchers to better understand why and how people join and leave extremist groups. Pete Simi, a criminologist at the University of Nebraska, Omaha, and colleagues have received funding from the U.S. Department of Justice to conduct interviews with former members of primarily white supremacist groups with the help of Life After Hate.

"We will use those interviews as a baseline to try and help inform the development of Life After Hate's intervention efforts," Simi says.

Life After Hate doesn't seek out individual white supremacists and try to persuade them to change.

"We can only help people who want to be helped," says McAleer. "We can make our presence known in those communities, but we can't go beyond that. I think, ethically, we have to wait for people to contact us."

To get its message out through social media, Life After Hate is producing two 30-second public service video announcements as well as banner ads, which will go live

Tony McAleer abandoned the white power movement and has started Exit USA, a deradicalization program that helps white supremacists leave the movement.

sometime this month. McAleer won't discuss their content but did describe how they will work. "For example, someone who did a search for 'white power music videos' on YouTube might see our public service announcement," he says.

Simi says the federal government may want to consider supporting such ground-level efforts. And Life After Hate, which relies on donations to finance its work, would consider accepting government funding, says McAleer, even though it could taint the message.

"The government is the enemy to people in the far right," he says. "But what is the alternative? It needs to be a partnership."

— Barbara Mantel

attorneys in districts across the country on non-jihadist domestic terrorism cases.[22]

Holder said that while law enforcement must remain vigilant against threats from al Qaeda affiliates and individuals they inspire, "we also must concern ourselves with the continued danger we face from individuals within our own borders who may be motivated by a variety of other causes, from anti-government animus to racial prejudice."[23]

At a hearing days later, Rep. Bob Goodlatte, R-Va., chairman of the House Judiciary Committee, expressed reservations. "What and whom does the attorney general really intend to target via the DTEC?" asked Goodlatte.

"Would a group advocating strenuously for smaller government and lower taxes be included in the attorney general's definition of a group with 'anti-government animus'?"[24]

But several analysts who track domestic extremism welcomed the task force's resurrection and said that even more should be done. The restoration of the Homeland Security unit that issued the 2009 report should be first on the agenda, says Potok.

"DHS has allowed its non-Islamic domestic terrorism unit, essentially, to go fallow," he says.

Daryl Johnson, a former senior domestic terrorism analyst at DHS who was the primary author of the

Ex-Supremacists Cite History of Drugs, Abuse

Former members of violent white-supremacist groups said they had dealt with substance abuse, attempted and/or considered suicide or experienced mental health problems, according to interviews with 44 ex-members. Common childhood trauma included neglect, physical abuse and sexual abuse.

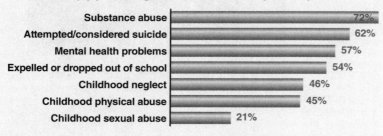

Backgrounds of Former Violent White Supremacists
(by percentage of those with each problem)

Substance abuse	72%
Attempted/considered suicide	62%
Mental health problems	57%
Expelled or dropped out of school	54%
Childhood neglect	46%
Childhood physical abuse	45%
Childhood sexual abuse	21%

Source: Pete Simi *et al.*, "Trauma as a Precursor to Violent Extremism," National Consortium for the Study of Terrorism and Responses to Terrorism, April 2015, http://tinyurl.com/opz2wcw.

controversial report, agrees with Potok. "Over the past year or so, they've had a modest effort to publish a few finished intelligence reports related to this topic," says Johnson, now a private consultant on domestic terrorism. "Nevertheless, the number of analysts at DHS's Office of Intelligence and Assessment monitoring this subject is three, compared to nearly 100 looking at Islamic terrorism. There's a clear imbalance of resources." A DHS spokesman would not confirm the figures.

Johnson says the FBI also could be doing more analysis. "The FBI has a very small domestic terrorism analysis unit — 10 analysts — but they don't put out a lot of reports," he says.

The Anti-Defamation League's Pitcavage says, "Some of the complaints about the federal government not doing enough are not quite fair to the many people in law enforcement who deal with right-wing extremism on a regular basis." He praises the work of the FBI's Joint Terrorism Task Forces, which are small teams of investigators, analysts, linguists and other specialists drawn from the FBI and federal, state and local agencies.[25]

The teams are located in each of the FBI's 56 field offices and are divided into domestic and international terrorism squads. The domestic terrorism squads "routinely make cases, and they routinely make arrests of right-wing extremists," says Pitcavage. Still, he would like to see more FBI agents assigned to them, without diminishing the focus on international terrorism.

"It's a zero-sum game. We only have so many agents," says David Gomez, a retired FBI executive, who estimates that about one-quarter to one-third of task force FBI agents are working on domestic terrorism. In any case, he says, "The FBI is pretty good at allocating resources to where they are needed."

A senior U.S. law enforcement official who spoke on condition of anonymity concurred with Gomez. "I can't give you specific numbers," the official says, but "on a regular basis, the FBI looks at the threats and its resources and adjusts accordingly. And we feel comfortable that we are properly resourced."

The FBI cannot surf the Internet looking for troubling posts or begin investigations of individuals based solely on their Internet postings, which are constitutionally protected. Evidence or probable cause must exist to believe that someone is "moving towards criminal activity," says Gomez. That can come from public tips or a confidential source, he says.

For Pitcavage, the biggest concern is that the government is not training enough state and local law enforcement personnel to deal with domestic extremism. He says law enforcement officers need to understand domestic extremists' ideologies and recognize potentially violent far-right extremists through tattoos and other indicators in order to avoid being shot during routine encounters.

The Department of Justice funds the State and Local Anti-Terrorism Training Program (SLATT), which focuses on both domestic and international terrorism. SLATT has trained more than 142,600 state, local and tribal law enforcement officers since its founding in 1996, says a Justice spokeswoman. The Anti-Defamation League is the largest nongovernment provider of such training, reaching 10,000 to 12,000 law enforcement officers a year, says Pitcavage.

"But we're both just a drop in the bucket," he says. "There are nearly a million law enforcement personnel in this country, and there's a lot of turnover."

However, the funding for SLATT may be in jeopardy, say Johnson and others. The congressional ban on earmarks, or items that lawmakers can add to spending bills independently of the executive branch, has limited Congress' ability to appropriate funding directly to SLATT. The Department of Justice was able to find money for SLATT this fiscal year, but next year's funding level is in question.

Should the federal government try to prevent young people from becoming extremists?

The Obama administration has recognized that just disrupting extremist plots and making arrests is not a sustainable strategy, says START's Braniff. "You're constantly reacting and not getting ahead of the issue," he says.

The White House announced an approach in 2011 — known as countering violent extremism, or CVE — to prevent violent extremists from recruiting and radicalizing U.S. residents.[26] The plan called for the Department of Justice, the FBI, Department of Homeland Security (DHS), the National Counterterrorism Center and U.S. attorneys in key regions to partner with communities to develop anti-radicalization programs. Although the plan said that CVE should focus primarily on Islamist extremism, it said it should not ignore "other forms of violent extremism."[27]

But that is what happened, said a June report from George Washington University: "Between 2000 and 2013, the vast majority of attacks in the homeland were carried out by non-Islamist extremists. Yet 100 percent of federal CVE efforts are aimed at Muslim communities."[28]

A three-day summit at the White House in February on countering violent extremism is a prime example of misplaced priorities, says Potok of the Southern Poverty Law Center.

"Much fine lip service was given by the president and others to the idea that this summit would cover all kinds of terrorism," he says. "But virtually all of the discussion was about Islamist terrorism."

Asked for examples of how CVE applies to non-Islamist extremism, Justice Department spokesman

Getty Images/Alex Wong

Anti-immigrant extremist Anders Behring Breivik, who killed 77 adults and children in Norway in 2011, was known to have visited Stormfront, a white nationalist online discussion forum. The number of registered Stormfront users has grown from 5,000 in 2002 to nearly 300,000 today, although many are inactive.

Mark Raimondi would only say, "CVE programs are designed to counter all violent extremists. They are not limited to any single group or demographic."

The CVE approach is not new; anti-extremism programs have existed sporadically for nearly a decade. They include everything from raising awareness through DHS-led community meetings about radicalization, to building trust through an FBI agent's sharing a meal at a mosque to break the daily Ramadan fast, to improving community resilience through leadership training for American Muslim youths.

The summit highlighted three new pilot programs led by U.S. attorneys in Boston, Minneapolis and Los Angeles that, the George Washington University researchers said, are aimed chiefly at ISIS radicalization.* The Los Angeles program seems to build on existing outreach to the Muslim community. Boston's program would send resources to organizations providing "vulnerable individuals" with mental-health services, educational assistance and transitional job opportunities.[29]

---

*ISIS is a terrorist organization that aims to create an Islamic state across Sunni areas of Iraq and in Syria and tries to radicalize European and North American youths through the Internet and social media.

CHRONOLOGY

1950s-1960s *Ku Klux Klan reemerges amid civil rights movement; neo-Nazi groups form.*

1954 Supreme Court landmark ruling in *Brown v. Board of Education* declaring segregated public schools unconstitutional spurs Klan growth.

1959 Navy veteran George Lincoln Rockwell founds American Nazi Party.

1961 Klan leaders form United Klans of America, by mid-decade the nation's largest Klan group, with an estimated 26,000 members.

1963 Bombing of 16th Street Baptist Church in Birmingham, Ala., kills four black girls; four Klan members are suspects, but no arrests are made.

1964 Congress passes Civil Rights Act, spurred in part by outrage over the 1963 church bombing. . . . White Knights of the Ku Klux Klan of Mississippi founded; members murder three civil rights workers.

1967 Seven Klan members are convicted of federal conspiracy charges in the 1964 murders of the three civil rights workers. . . . American Nazi Party founder Rockwell is assassinated; the party fractures.

1970s-1980s *Ku Klux Klan declines; neo-Nazis organize.*

1970 Rockwell disciple William Pierce founds the National Alliance, the most dangerous and best organized neo-Nazi group to emerge in the next several decades.

1977 One Klan member is convicted of murder in the 16th Street Baptist Church bombing; two others are not convicted for decades; the fourth dies before prosecution.

1979 FBI infiltrates Klan groups, and civil rights movement's victories lead to steep decline in Klan membership.

1980 A Klan grand wizard, David Duke, leaves Klan to form National Association for the Advancement of White People and in 1989 wins a seat in the Louisiana legislature as a Republican; he later loses races for the U.S. Senate and Louisiana governorship.

1989 Hammerskin Nation unifies dispersed, racist skinheads, who hold neo-Nazi ideas and have shaved heads and unique tattoos.

1992-Present *Anti-government extremists bomb federal building in Oklahoma City; al Qaeda kills nearly 3,000.*

1992 Federal agents conduct a much-criticized siege of a white supremacist compound in Ruby Ridge, Idaho. Several people are killed, including a teenage boy.

1993 Federal agents lay siege to Branch Davidian compound in Waco, Texas, resulting in the deaths of more than 80; the raids fuel anti-government militia movements.

1994 Jeff Schoep, a neo-Nazi from Minnesota, founds the National Socialist Movement.

1995 Anti-government militants detonate a truck bomb at Oklahoma City's federal building, killing 168; government cracks down on far-right violent extremists, whose numbers plummet by decade's end.

2001 Al Qaeda operatives kill nearly 3,000 people in attacks on the World Trade Center in New York and the Pentagon and the crash of a hijacked plane.

2002 National Alliance loses most members following Pierce's death; many neo-Nazis remain unaffiliated over the next decades.

2008 Election of Barak Obama, nation's first black president, the 2007-2009 recession and the mortgage crisis anger white supremacists and fuel revival of anti-government extremism.

2012 Racist skinhead Wade Michael Page attacks an Oak Creek, Wis., Sikh temple, killing six and wounding four before killing himself.

2015 Dylann Roof is charged with killing nine black parishioners in a church in Charleston, S.C.

But there are myriad problems with CVE, including no evidence that it works, say critics. It also stigmatizes American Muslims as inherently suspect, says Hina Shamsi, director of the National Security Project at the New York-based American Civil Liberties Union (ACLU), by setting "them apart from their neighbors based on their faith, their race, their ethnicity." In some cases, the FBI has secretly used "community outreach to actually gather intelligence," alienating communities, she says.[30] Several Muslim organizations in pilot cities have refused to participate.[31]

Critics have difficulty imagining the government using the same model to combat far-right radicalization. "You'd have to go to churches in places where there has been white supremacist violence and say, 'Hi, I'm DHS and I want to tell you the 12 signs of racism in your child that lead him or her to violence.' Do you think anybody would stand for that?" says Faiza Patel, co-director of the Liberty & National Security Program at the Brennan Center for Justice.

Szmania of START says the United States could take a page from Europe and emulate Exit Sweden, a non-profit run by former neo-Nazis that helps people leave the movement. Its members also talk to schools "about the negative experience of being part of a violent extremist group," says Szmania. Life After Hate began its own Exit program this past spring.

Braniff says the government could focus on prisons. "We have more white supremacists in the U.S. prison system than we'll ever have jihadists," he says. "Yet there is no formal reintegration and rehabilitation for them."

And, he says, the federal government could help communities concerned about racial violence raise awareness, provide prevention programming and create intervention teams. That way, "if the next Dylann Roof mentions to friends or acquaintances that he's going to shoot black people, there is an intervention team that can talk to him."

People must understand laws that protect behavior and speech and the privacy of students, says Braniff, "but there are also exceptions to those laws, such as when a student talks about shooting other students."

These efforts would depend on continued government funding of organizations like START that conduct violent-extremism research, says Braniff. The research results could be made accessible in one- or two-page summaries "for nongovernmental organizations to hand

out to teachers, administrators and counselors," he says. In fact, START produces such bite-size digests.

Pete Simi, a criminologist at the University of Nebraska-Omaha, is the author of a two-page research brief. He and colleagues examined the life histories of 44 violent white supremacists and found that nearly half reported being physically abused as children. Almost two-thirds said they had attempted and/or seriously considered suicide, and nearly three-quarters reported having problems with alcohol and/or illegal drugs. Slightly more than half had either been expelled from school or dropped out. These rates are higher than in the general population.[32]

Simi cautions that there is no way to predict whether someone with these experiences will become a violent extremist. "It is never a simple cause and effect," he says. But there is heightened risk, and he says a young person with such a background is vulnerable to chance encounters. The person may attend a white-power concert, for example, and meet a neoNazi skinhead who can "become a mentor of sorts in a very unfortunate way."

Simi's research did not look at nonviolent white supremacists for comparison, which makes the findings of limited utility. But Simi says the research indicates that the nation needs to better provide at-risk youths with mental health services and other supports.

"Some of these youth join street gangs, some become runaways, drugs addicts or lead otherwise dysfunctional lives, and some become violent extremists," he says. "I'm not suggesting that CVE is a bad idea, but I am suggesting that we need to think bigger than a CVE-only approach."

Providing needed mental health services, after-school programs and other outreach is a good idea, says the ACLU's Shamsi, but it "shouldn't be done in an effort led by law enforcement agencies, and it shouldn't be done in ways that say to the world at large that these communities are being targeted because we think they are a threat."

BACKGROUND
Extreme Dissatisfaction

The United States has seen multiple extremist movements throughout its history, especially during times of crisis.

Militias Score Successes in Standoffs With Feds

Some criticize government's inaction, but officials cite safety concerns.

In April 2014, Eric Parker stood on an overpass in the Nevada desert, holding a semi-automatic rifle and watching as the crowd below faced off against agents of the federal Bureau of Land Management (BLM).

Parker had traveled from central Idaho, one of hundreds of armed militia members, states' rights advocates, gun rights activists and other protesters who had gathered to support renegade rancher Cliven Bundy. The week before, BLM agents had begun rounding up hundreds of Bundy's cattle that were grazing illegally on federal land. Bundy denies federal authority over the land and refuses to pay federal grazing fees and penalties, which amount to more than $1 million.[1]

Five days after the armed contingent arrived, the BLM halted the roundup and released the cattle. BLM director Neil Kornze cited "serious concern about the safety of employees and members of the public."[2]

Militia experts, however, say it was an unprecedented retreat by the government. "It's not the groups, it's not their concerns, it's not their anger, all of that is old, but the federal government backing down? I was like, 'Wow! Seriously?'" said Catherine Stock, a history professor at Connecticut College in New London who studies rural militias.[3]

The federal agency's stance led Robert Crooks to assert, "BLM no longer exists in this section of Nevada," at a Bundy ranch celebration marking the one-year anniversary of the standoff. Crooks, founder of the Tecate, Calif.-based Mountain Minutemen group opposed to illegal immigration, had spent much of the past year living in his RV on the Bundy ranch.[4]

The FBI is reportedly investigating Bundy's armed supporters, but a year and a half later, authorities have not charged anyone with pointing weapons at federal agents or tried to collect the money Bundy owes, and his cattle continue to roam federal land.[5]

"Our primary goal remains, as it was a year ago, to resolve this matter safely and according to the rule of the law," agency spokeswoman Celia Boddington said in April.[6]

Bundy has become a hero to anti-government activists and met privately in June with Sen. Rand Paul, R-Ky., who is running for president.[7]

"It's clear that the 'victory' of Bundy and his sympathizers has already encouraged a number of similar defiant stands against government authority," said Ryan Lenz, a senior writer with the Southern Poverty Law Center (SPLC), an advocacy group in Montgomery, Ala., that researches antigovernment groups.[8]

In July, inspired by Bundy's resistance, the Filippini ranching family defied the BLM and released hundreds of cattle onto drought-stressed federal land in Nevada that the agency had placed off limits to grazing in 2013. The

"Extremists seek either a radical change in the status quo . . . or the defense of privileges they perceive to be threatened," said Martha Crenshaw, a senior fellow at Stanford University's Freeman Spogli Institute for International Studies. "Their dissatisfaction with the policies of the government is extreme, and their demands usually involve the displacement of existing political elites."[33]

Movements considered extreme in one age can, over time, occasionally become part of the mainstream.

"Sometimes, those who take an inflexible, radical position hasten a purpose that years later is widely hailed as legitimate and just," said Michael Kazin, a professor of history at Georgetown University. For instance, "moderate authorities in politics and the media" once lambasted extreme abolitionists, pioneering woman suffragists and militant opponents of Jim Crow.[34]

And sometimes, mainstream movements come to be considered extreme. In the 1920s, the Ku Klux Klan had widespread support. The post–World War I waves of

family had sued and protested, but nothing had changed the government's mind.

Nevada ranchers are "pretty close to being extinct," said matriarch Eddyann Filippini, "and they're using the drought as the ax to cut our heads off." A few days later, the government and the family reached an agreement allowing the cattle to graze for three more years in exchange for a $106 fine.[9]

"The BLM really needs to take care of the public's land, needs to regulate the ranchers' exploitation of this privilege to graze on public lands," said Kirsten Stade, advocacy director for the Washington-based Public Employees for Environmental Responsibility. But "they're scared."[10]

In August, more than 20 armed members of Patriot groups that describe themselves as defenders of the Constitution arrived in Lincoln, Mont. Two local miners embroiled in a dispute with the U.S. Forest Service over the legality of their mining operations sought the groups' help. Federal prosecutors have asked a federal judge in Montana to prevent the miners and their supporters from blocking access to public lands and threatening government officials.[11]

The government's caution in the field traces to two seminal events of the early 1990s. In 1992, federal agents laid siege to a compound of white separatists in Ruby Ridge, Idaho, which ended with several people killed, including a teenage boy. The next year, agents raided the Branch Davidian compound in Waco, Texas. The apocalyptic religious sect was believed to be amassing a weapons arsenal. A gun battle between federal agents and the Davidians, in which four agents and six Davidians died, led to a 51-day siege, broken when the FBI fired tear gas and the Davidians then set fire to the compound. When the siege was over, 75 Davidians, a third of them children, had died.[12]

"What they learned from Waco was that a heavy-handed approach risks a major loss of life," said the SPLC in a 2014 report. "Yet allowing the anti-government movement to flout the law at gunpoint is surely not the answer."[13]

— *Barbara Mantel*

[1]Jonathan Allen, "After Nevada Ranch Stand-Off, Emboldened Militias Ask: Where Next?" Reuters, April 17, 2014, http://tinyurl.com/kwwt9zm.

[2]"Nevada Cattle Issue Stalled," *The Richfield Reaper* (Utah), April 16, 2014, http://tinyurl.com/pj4kkur.

[3]Allen, *op. cit.*

[4]Kirk Siegler, "Year After Denying Federal Control, Bundy Still Runs His Bit of Nevada," NPR, April 14, 2015, http://tinyurl.com/owafag3.

[5]*Ibid.*

[6]Caroline Connolly, "'Liberty Celebration' at Bundy Ranch Marks One-Year Since Armed Confrontation With BLM," Fox 13-Salt Lake City, April 10, 2015, http://tinyurl.com/nj5ow37.

[7]Adam B. Lerner, "Rand Paul Meets With Rogue Rancher Cliven Bundy," *Politico,* June 30, 2015, http://tinyurl.com/pdxjdud.

[8]Ryan Lenz, "Free Radicals," Intelligence Report, Southern Poverty Law Center, June 10, 2015, http://tinyurl.com/ojuct2t.

[9]Julie Turkewitz, "Drought Pushes Nevada Ranchers to Take On Washington," *The New York Times,* July 2, 2015, http://tinyurl.com/p7ksk3a.

[10]*Ibid.*

[11]Matt Volz, "US Government Seeks Ruling Against Miners, Armed Protesters," The Associated Press, Aug. 11, 2015, http://tinyurl.com/pe5vxrb.

[12]Clyde Haberman, "Memories of Waco Siege Continue to Fuel Far-Right Groups," *The New York Times,* July 12, 2015, http://tinyurl.com/ns3qeq9.

[13]Haberman, *op. cit.*

Catholic and Jewish immigration and Prohibition-related crime "brought the Klan millions of recruits," wrote University of Florida historian David Chalmers in *Hooded Americanism: The History of the Ku Klux Klan.*[35]

Here are brief histories of the some of today's far-right extremist movements.

Ku Klux Klan

The Klan was born in 1865 in the wake of the Civil War, quickly becoming a vigilante group intent on intimidating Southern blacks and their white supporters and preventing blacks from exercising basic civil rights. It became especially infamous for lynchings and burning crosses.[36]

"Outlandish titles (like imperial wizard and exalted cyclops), hooded costumes, violent 'night rides,' and the notion that the group comprised an 'invisible empire' conferred a mystique that only added to the Klan's popularity," according to the Southern Poverty Law Center (SPLC). "Lynchings, tar-and-featherings, rapes and

Getty Images/Richard Ellis

David Duke, a Ku Klux Klan grand wizard, left the Klan in 1980 to form the National Association for the Advancement of White People. He won a seat in the Louisiana legislature in 1989 before running unsuccessfully for multiple offices, including Louisiana governor and U.S. president.

other violent attacks on those challenging white supremacy became a hallmark of the Klan."[37]

After Jim Crow laws enforced racial segregation in the South, Imperial Wizard Nathan Bedford Forrest — a former Confederate general — formally disbanded the Klan in 1869. But during its resurgence 50 years later the Klan "picked up its first genuine Klan senator in Texas," "helped capture the governorship" in Oregon, and "with business support, elected two U.S. Senators and swept the state" in Colorado, wrote Chalmers. From Indiana to Wisconsin to New Jersey and New York, the Klan organized in thousands of localities and influenced local and state elections.[38]

But internal power struggles, sex scandals, newspaper exposes and a growing public revulsion with its terror and violence eventually reduced the Klan's influence. By the beginning of the 1930s, the group that had numbered in the millions in the 1920s had no more than 100,000 members.[39]

The Klan experienced its third surge in the 1960s in response to the civil rights movement. In efforts to preserve segregation, the Klan conducted nocturnal cross burnings and mass meetings that began to draw growing turnouts in Alabama and Georgia. The group returned to its violent ways, according to the SPLC, and its bombings, murders and other attacks "took a great many lives."[40] Bombing targets included the 16th Street Baptist Church in Birmingham, Ala., in September 1963, in which four young girls died and 22 others were injured.[41] The resulting public outrage helped to spur passage of the Civil Rights Act of 1964 and the Voting Rights Act of 1965.

Within a decade, the Klan had waned in the wake of the civil rights movement's achievements. "The black marchers were gone from the city streets but were taking their places in the schools and factories, legislatures, city commissions, and even Southern police forces. Klansmen seemed even more likely to end up in jail," wrote Chalmers.

Since the 1970s, "the Klan has been greatly weakened by internal conflicts, court cases, a seemingly endless series of splits and government infiltration," said the SPLC, which estimates its current membership, divided among competing factions, at no more than 8,000 individuals.[42] One prominent former grand wizard, David Duke, won a seat in the Louisiana state legislature in 1989, before running unsuccessfully for multiple offices, including Louisiana governor and U.S. president.

Neo-Nazis and Skinheads

The modern American neo-Nazi movement is rooted in the late 1930s, when Adolf Hitler's Germany and Benito Mussolini's Italy inspired the proliferation of more than 100 Nazi and fascist groups in the United States. Four had a national impact, wrote Stephen Atkins, a former Texas A&M University librarian, in *The Encyclopedia of Right-Wing Extremism in Modern American History*:[43]

- The Khaki Shirts of America — whose goal was to seize the federal government, abolish Congress, build the world's largest military and kill Jews — had fewer than 200 active members.
- The Silver Shirts, modeled after Hitler's Brown Shirts and Mussolini's Black Shirts, had up to 50,000 members at its peak in 1934.
- The German American Bund, with close ties to Nazi Germany, spread pro-Nazi and anti-Semitic propaganda in public meetings and at youth camps.

- The America First Committee, an alliance of conservatives, fascists and politicians who wanted to keep the United States out of World War II, became increasingly extremist as Fascist and Nazi supporters flocked to it.

Leadership problems, as well as the United States' entry into World War II, ended some groups and significantly reduced the influence of others, wrote Atkins.[44]

The American Nazi Party of the 1950s and 1960s was the first significant neo-Nazi group to emerge in the post-war years. Its founder, World War II and Korean War Navy veteran George Lincoln Rockwell, blamed Jews for fomenting the civil rights movement and called for the execution of Jews and blacks. After an expelled member assassinated Rockwell in 1967, the party "fractured into a variety of squabbling small neo-Nazi groups," according to the Anti-Defamation League (ADL).[45]

In 1970, West Virginia physicist and Rockwell disciple William Pierce founded the National Alliance, which the SPLC said was "for decades the most dangerous and best organized neo-Nazi formation in America." The group called for the eradication of the Jews and non-white races as well as creation of an all-white homeland. Pierce's novel, *The Turner Diaries*, described a race war in which Jews and others are slaughtered. It inspired the 1995 bombing of the federal building in Oklahoma City, whose perpetrators had ties to both white supremacy and anti-government extremism, and many other acts of terror.[46]

The National Alliance reached its peak in the 1990s. "At its height, it had chapters in several European countries, and *The Turner Diaries* was translated and made available free in half a dozen languages," said the SPLC, which estimates that by 2002, the Alliance had 1,400 "carefully vetted, dues-paying members." However, after Pierce's death in 2002, the group lost most of its members.[47]

The resulting power vacuum was filled by the National Socialist Movement, currently the nation's largest neo-Nazi organization, with an estimated 350 members.[48] Led by Jeff Schoep, a neo-Nazi since his teen years in Minnesota, the group has been known for its theatrical protests — in full Nazi uniforms until 2007 and in black uniforms since then.

The movement has set up a youth corps for recruiting teens and women and skinhead divisions. It owns a

Timothy McVeigh, a supporter of the militia movement, detonated the truck bomb in Oklahoma City that killed 168 people in 1995. He said he was seeking revenge for the government sieges at a white separatist camp in Ruby Ridge, Idaho, in 1992 and an apocalyptic religious sect in Waco, Texas, the next year. McVeigh was executed by lethal injection in June 2001.

AFP/Getty Images/Bob Daemmerich

so-called hate-rock music (also known as white power music) label and a popular white supremacist social networking site. The group idolizes Hitler and believes that only "pure-blood whites" should be U.S. citizens, while everyone else should be deported. Its recent protests have focused on illegal immigrants.[49]

Overall, "the organized portion of the neo-Nazi movement has for some years been in relatively poor health," according to the ADL. "However, there still remains a large number of unaffiliated neo-Nazis in the United States, many of whom could come back 'into the fold' if a group began to experience significant success."[50]

The racist skinhead movement, which first emerged among British youth in the 1970s, also has been stagnant in recent years, according to the ADL. (The two other branches of the skinhead movement are traditional skinheads and anti-racist skinheads.) By the 1980s the racist skinhead subculture had spread across Western Europe and North America, its members sporting shaved heads and unique tattoos and holding essentially the same beliefs as neo-Nazis. They are largely unaffiliated with any organized groups, although there are two prominent racist skinhead gangs, the Hammerskin Nation, a national league of regional crews, and the Midwest-based Vinlanders Social Club.

Page, the racist skinhead who attacked the Sikh temple in Oak Creek, Wis., in 2012, played in several hate-music bands.[51]

Militia Movement and Sovereign Citizens

In 1994 and 1995, hundreds of militias with a total of as many as 100,000 members had formed across the United States, wrote University of Hartford historian Robert Churchill in *To Shake Their Guns in the Tyrant's Face,* a chronicle of the militia movement.[52]

Churchill said the movement grew out of its members' perception "that their government had turned increasingly violent." The government sieges at a white separatist compound in Ruby Ridge, Idaho, in 1992 and of an apocalyptic religious sect in Waco, Texas, the next year — both ending in multiple deaths and later criticized in official reports — "were the most important events driving this perception," said Churchill. "Finally, militia men and women feared that recently passed gun-control legislation would be enforced with the same violence exhibited at Waco and Ruby Ridge."

The militia members argued that popular violence was a legitimate response to a government's denial of fundamental rights or to state-sponsored violence against citizens.[53] Timothy McVeigh, who detonated the truck bomb in Oklahoma City that killed 168 people in 1995, said he was seeking revenge for Ruby Ridge and Waco. McVeigh was executed by lethal injection in June 2001.

The militia movement included some African-Americans, such as J. J. Johnson, the leader of the largest militia group in Ohio in the 1990s. Johnson denounced "the militarization of our law enforcement, those 'peace officers' who can be found clad in their black ninja suits while they storm inner-city neighborhoods indiscriminately shooting and beating residents while fighting their 'war on drugs.'"[54]

Many of these militias were led by constitutional fundamentalists, who argued that the federal government had exceeded its powers. Other militia leaders were more conspiracy-minded, arguing that Waco and Ruby Ridge were "dress rehearsals for an impending invasion by the forces of the New World Order," and that the federal government was stripping citizens of their guns through legislation in advance of the plot, wrote Churchill.[55]

After the Oklahoma City bombing, state and federal law enforcement agencies made "major arrests of militia group members who were engaged in a variety of plots and conspiracies in West Virginia, Georgia, Arizona, Washington, Michigan, Florida and many other states," according to the ADL. By the end of the 1990s, "many anti-government extremists had lost their energy, while a number of them were in prison," and the movement went into a steep decline.[56]

The 2008 election of Democrat Barack Obama, the nation's first African-American president, along with the recession, mortgage crisis and renewed discussion of gun-control legislation, helped to spur a second surge in the militia movement. The number of militia groups tracked by the ADL and the SPLC grew sharply between 2009 and 2010, although the numbers have declined since 2012.

The sovereign citizen movement, in particular, was galvanized by the mortgage crisis. The movement had begun in the 1970s and grew in numbers during the deep recession and farm crisis of the 1980s. Its core belief is that "many years ago an insidious conspiracy infiltrated and subverted the U.S. government, slowly replacing parts of the original, legitimate government (often referred to by sovereigns as the 'de jure' government) with an illegitimate, tyrannical government (the 'de facto' government)," according to a 2012 ADL report.[57]

Sovereign citizens believe they can tear up what they see as the illegitimate government's contracts, such as driver's licenses and Social Security cards, and thus regain their sovereignty and freedom from the illegitimate government's laws. Sovereign citizens typically eschew organized groups but rather are a loosely formed mass of individuals who follow sovereign citizen "gurus."[58]

To try to avoid paying taxes and fines, sovereign citizens resort to what is commonly called paper terrorism. "Paper terrorism involves the use of bogus legal documents and filings, or the misuse of legitimate ones, to intimidate, harass, threaten, or retaliate against public officials, law enforcement officers, or private citizens," said the ADL.

Perhaps the oldest tactic is the filing of false or nuisance liens against the personal properties of law enforcement officials and public officials, who then have to hire lawyers to clear the title at considerable expense.[59]

CURRENT SITUATION

Countering Extremists

Congress is considering legislation aimed at coordinating and funding the federal government's efforts to prevent violent extremism in the United States.

In mid-July, the House Committee on Homeland Security approved the Countering Violent Extremism Act of 2015, which defines violent extremism as "ideologically motivated terrorist activities."

The measure would establish an Office for Countering Violent Extremism within the Department of Homeland Security (DHS), to be run by a new assistant secretary, with a budget of $10 million a year.[60]

"In the face of mounting threats, our government is doing far too little to counter violent extremism here in the United States," said Rep. Michael McCaul, R-Texas, the committee chair and the bill's sponsor. "Whether it is the long reach of international terrorists into our communities or the homegrown hate spread by domestic extremist groups, we are ill-equipped to prevent Americans from being recruited by dangerous fanatics."[61]

The new office would coordinate with other federal agencies and manage DHS' activities to counter violent extremism, which the legislation says should include

- identifying risk factors that contribute to violent extremism and potential remedies;
- identifying populations targeted by violent extremist recruitment;
- managing outreach and engagement programs in communities at risk;
- assessing the methods used by violent extremists to disseminate propaganda, and
- establishing a counter-messaging program via the Internet and social media.[62]

All activities would be supported by empirical research and "respect the privacy, civil rights and civil liberties of all Americans," according to the proposed bill.[63]

Conservative opinion on beefing up DHS prevention and deradicalization efforts is mixed. For example, the Heritage Foundation, a Washington think tank, supports such change, but several grassroots conservative and libertarian bloggers oppose it for what they consider its excessively broad definition of violent extremism.[64]

A Ku Klux Klan member shouts racial slurs during a Klan demonstration protesting the removal of the Confederate flag at the statehouse in Columbia, S.C., on July 18, 2015. Controversy over displays of the Confederate flag erupted after the fatal shooting in June of nine black parishioners at a church in Charleston, when images of alleged shooter Dylann Roof holding a Confederate flag showed up on a website.

"We certainly don't need to give the government carte blanche to declare 'ideological' enemies in such a nebulous manner," said the Bastrop County Tea Party in Texas in a blog post. The group is calling for the bill to be killed.[65]

Forty-eight human rights, civil liberties and community-based organizations, including the ACLU, the Council on American-Islamic Relations and the National Association for the Advancement of Colored People (NAACP), also have strong objections to the legislation. In a letter to the House committee before the vote, the organizations outlined their many long-standing objections to CVE programs, including the lack of evidence that such programs help to reduce terrorism, the threats they pose to freedoms of speech, association and religion and their almost exclusive focus on Muslim communities.

"Our organizations believe that this effort is misguided and likely to be harmful," they wrote.[66]

Rep. Bennie Thompson of Mississippi, the Homeland Security Committee's ranking Democrat, said that he could not support the bill as currently written.[67] He introduced an amendment that tried to address some of the concerns. It would have required DHS to analyze the risk posed by extremist violence based on documented threats and empirical data; to explain its efforts to identify programs whose effectiveness has been validated by independent researchers; to provide safeguards against

Should hate speech be regulated in the United States?

YES

Michel Rosenfeld
Professor of Law and Comparative Democracy and Human Rights, Yeshiva University; Author of Law, Justice, Democracy, and the Clashes of Cultures: A Pluralist Account

Written for *CQ Researcher*, September 2015

The United States protects hate speech unless it amounts to incitement to violence, whereas Canada and European democracies prohibit hate speech if it incites racial hatred. American exceptionalism regarding hate speech mirrors the country's extraordinary devotion to free speech and has several palpable advantages. The American approach carves out clear boundaries between permissible and impermissible speech while encouraging discussion over suppression of hateful ideas, convinced that reason can best hate. One notorious example was the proposed 1978 neo-Nazi march in Skokie, Ill., a Chicago suburb where many Holocaust survivors live. The courts cleared the way for the march, and the thrust of the marchers' message fell on overwhelmingly deaf ears.

The Skokie case underscores a sharp contrast between the United States and Germany, where hate speech and Holocaust denial are criminalized in vigilance against any resurgence of Nazism. Any comparison centering on the swastika is, however, misleading, as the closest analogy in this country to what the swastika symbolizes in Germany is cross burning. The latter embodies racial hatred, intimidation and a history of extreme violence against the country's African-American minority. Yet in 1992, a unanimous U.S. Supreme Court held in *R.A.V. v. City of St. Paul* that a city's effort to punish the perpetrators of a cross burning on the lawn of an African-American family was unconstitutional. The perpetrators were not intent on violence, but on scaring and intimidating their victims so they would move out of a white neighborhood.

For the German courts, punishing Holocaust denial was imperative to uphold the dignity and cement the communal bonds of postwar German Jewish citizens. Analogously, banning cross burning in the United States would somewhat heal the dignitary wounds stemming from the legacy of U.S. racism — which is far from eradicated, as sadly attested by the recent Charleston church massacre.

Besides demeaning those it targets, hate speech often circumvents reason and fuels prejudice. Most whites living in the neighborhood of the victims in R.A.V. undoubtedly found the cross burning despicable, but several of them nonetheless preferred that their neighborhood not become truly racially mixed.

In the case of African-Americans, just as with German Jews, it is important that the state weigh in against hatred and officially sanction unmistakable hate speech. Such sanction is not likely to eradicate hate, but it will enhance dignity for all.

NO

James Weinstein
Professor of Constitutional Law, Sandra Day O'Connor College of Law, Arizona State University; Author of Hate Speech, Pornography and the Radical Attack on Free Speech Doctrine

Written for *CQ Researcher*, September 2015

Free and open discussion of matters of public concern is the lifeblood of democracy. The Supreme Court has accordingly interpreted the First Amendment — properly, in my view — to guarantee each individual the right to participate in this discussion by expressing any viewpoint, even those that the vast majority of Americans finds offensive, disturbing or even morally repugnant.

A "hate speech" exception allowing government to ban speech that demeans people on the basis of race, ethnicity, sexual orientation or similar characteristics would likely undermine this vigorous protection of public discourse. It would be most difficult for the Supreme Court to articulate a principle excluding hate speech from First Amendment protection that would not also apply to other types of expression. A long-standing justification for banning hate speech is that it might persuade others to discriminate against minorities. But by that reasoning, anti-war speech could be punished because it might persuade conscripts to resist the draft, just as radical environmentalist literature could be suppressed lest it lead to acts of eco-terrorism.

More recently, it has been argued that hate speech alienates minorities from society. It can seriously be questioned, however, whether public expression of bigoted ideas significantly contributes to such alienation in America. Indeed, in recent years, hate speech incidents often elicit massive condemnation from all segments of society in ways likely to reassure those vilified by the bigoted expression.

But even if it were possible to identify a rationale for suppressing hate speech that would not lead to a proliferation of other viewpoint-based First Amendment exceptions, banning hate speech would nevertheless likely impede public discussion of important issues. Though hate-speech laws may be intended to suppress only the most virulent forms of bigoted expression, experience in other democracies has shown that their actual reach is not so limited. For instance, under such laws, the leader of a far-right Dutch political party was imprisoned for advocating that guest-workers be removed from the Netherlands; a Catholic bishop in Belgium was arrested for saying that homosexuality was a "blockage in their normal psychological development, rendering them abnormal"; and French actress Brigitte Bardot was fined for protesting on her website the slaughter of sheep during a Muslim festival and complaining that Muslims were destroying France by "imposing their ways."

In a free and democratic society, bigoted ideas should be refuted, not censored.

religious, ethnic and racial discrimination; and to assess the compatibility of all materials and training with constitutionally protected speech, belief and activities. It would have required the DHS secretary to submit this "comprehensive strategy" to Congress within 90 days of the legislation's enactment.[68]

However, the committee voted down Thompson's amendment.

McCaul said at the time that neither the White House nor DHS had expressed any opposition to the bill.[69] It's now up to the full House to consider the legislation.

Convicting Extremists

Three important criminal cases involving far-right extremists involved in violence or conspiracies have been resolved this summer.

A Kansas jury in September sentenced long-time white supremacist and self-described anti-Semite Frazier Glenn Miller Jr. to death for the murder of three people outside two Jewish facilities in the Kansas City suburb of Overland Park, Kan., on April 13, 2014. Miller, 74, the founder and former grand dragon of the Carolina Knights of the Ku Klux Klan, a paramilitary group, shot William Corporon, 69, and Corporon's 14-year-old grandson, Reat Underwood, outside the town's Jewish Community Center. A few minutes later, he killed Terri LaManno, 53, outside the Village Shalom care center, where her mother lived. None of the victims was Jewish.

Representing himself, Miller dared jurors, whom he called "whores of the Jews," to sentence him to death, ending with a Nazi salute and "Heil Hitler."[70]

In late August, a federal judge in Sacramento, Calif., sentenced sovereign citizen Brent Douglas Cole to nearly 30 years in prison for shooting and wounding two law enforcement officers at a campsite on public land. According to their trial testimony, the officers were attempting to impound a stolen motorcycle at the campsite when Cole, 61, admitted to being armed. One of the officers withdrew a pair of handcuffs, prompting Cole to draw his revolver and begin shooting.

"Take the right to bear arms away, and this country will fall like a ripe tomato," Cole said in an interview at the county jail. "You will see genocide."[71]

That same month, a federal judge in Atlanta sentenced three members of a Georgia militia to 12-year prison terms for conspiring to use weapons of mass destruction to attack federal government agencies.

A concerned participant in a chat room frequented by militia members notified the FBI in early 2014 after Brian Cannon, 37, Terry Peace, 47, and Cory Williamson, 29, discussed online their plans for attacking federal government facilities in Georgia. The FBI then mounted a sting operation, in which a cooperating witness supplied the three men with inert pipe bombs that they planned to use against a local police department.[72]

Flag Controversy

Controversy over displays of the Confederate flag erupted after the racially motivated massacre in Charleston in June, when images of alleged shooter Roof holding a Confederate flag showed up on a website he is believed to have created. He was wearing a jacket emblazoned with the flags of two former African apartheid nations and displaying his .45 caliber Glock pistol, according to the federal indictment.[73]

Defenders of the flag say it is a symbol of Confederate heritage and honor, while opponents say it represents racism, oppression, and slavery. Less than a week after the murders, South Carolina's Republican Gov. Nikki Haley urged state lawmakers to pass legislation to remove the flag from state property.

"This flag, while an integral part of our past, does not represent the future of our great state," she said.[74] A few days later, Alabama Gov. Robert Bentley ordered Confederate flags removed from the grounds of his state capital. "This had the potential to become a major distraction as we go forward," said Bentley, a Republican.[75]

In early July, after several days of emotional debate, South Carolina lawmakers passed, and Haley signed, a bill ordering the flag's removal. On July 10, in the state where the Civil War began in 1861, the flag was permanently lowered from its perch on the grounds of the statehouse in Columbia.[76]

The state's action prompted rallies in support of the flag across the nation. Meanwhile, local governments also are removing Confederate symbols. For example, in early August Albuquerque, N.M., took down the four "Stars and Bars" flags, an earlier version of the Confederate flag, hanging over the city's historic district. And Danville, Va., passed an ordinance to remove the Confederate flag from city-owned flagpoles.[77]

Major retailers were some of the earliest to act. Walmart, Sears, Amazon and eBay removed Confederate flag merchandise from their online marketplaces within a week of the Charleston murders. "We have decided to prohibit Confederate flags, and many items containing this image, because we believe it has become a contemporary symbol of divisiveness and racism," said eBay spokesperson Johnna Hoff.[78]

OUTLOOK

Ebbs and Flows

Far-right extremist activities, including violence, have tended to move in cycles over the past 50 years, and several analysts expect the same ebb and flow over the next decade.

"Since the mid-1980s, right-wing extremism has consistently been the most lethal type of extremism in the United States, and nothing is going to change that in the near future," the ADL's Pit-cavage says.

Former white supremacist McAleer, of Life After Hate, says much depends on the economy. "If there is a serious economic downturn, all bets are off, and radical solutions become more palatable," he says. "Then all it takes is for a charismatic leader to show up and harness that."

Former DHS analyst Johnson predicts that 2016 "will be another active year for right-wing extremist violence." How the country handles polarizing issues, such as immigration and gun control, will help determine what happens during the next administration, he says.

The SPLC's Potok also is pessimistic about the future. "It's very possible that the number of extremist groups will remain very high, as the country continues its transition from a white-majority nation to a truly multicultural one," he says. "I also think that it is entirely possible that we will see attacks on the scale of the Oklahoma City bombing in the years ahead."

Pitcavage doesn't expect much change in the government's response to far-right extremist violence, such as an increase in funding for training law enforcement. "The recent Charleston shooting — the third most-lethal domestic terrorist event in the past five decades — seems to have done nothing at all to motivate the government to increase its resources in combating right-wing violence, so perhaps it would take an even worse tragedy . . . to focus attention on the problem," he says. "That's not a happy prospect."

START's Szmania is optimistic that countering violent extremism programming in the United States will increase across ideologies, including far-right extremism, in the next five to 10 years. "Mostly likely, far-right programs will build on successful examples like Life After Hate and Exit," she says.

The ACLU's Shamsi expects CVE programs to be a thing of the past in a decade. "Key aspects raise significant federal constitutional concerns and are possibly also open to challenge under state constitutions as well as privacy statutes or regulations," she says.

Researchers predict that violent-extremism studies will become more grounded in scientific methods. "In the next 10 years, we will see an increase in studies that compare violent terrorists to nonviolent extremists who share the terrorists' ideologies but don't commit violent acts," says criminologist Freilich.

Szmania says that "research will probably never be able to predict who will become a violent extremist." But, she says, it could lead to "a better understanding of the effectiveness of interventions aimed at supporting youth to stay in school, addressing mental health needs, limiting the availability of weapons, and addressing gateway criminal behavior, such as petty crime leading to involvement in more serious infractions."

NOTES

1. Frances Robles, "Dylann Roof Photos and a Manifesto Are Posted on Website," *The New York Times,* June 20, 2015, http://tinyurl.com/od5che9.

2. *Ibid.*

3. "Not Guilty Plea in Federal Court for Accused Charleston Shooter," CBSNews, July 31, 2015, http://tinyurl.com/pmwfdoe; "S.C. To Seek Death Penalty For Dylann Roof In Charleston Shooting," NPR, Sept. 3, 2015, http://tinyurl.com/ppfapol.

4. "Homegrown Extremists," New America Foundation, http://tinyurl.com/nhsrzxx.

5. Michael German, "Stigmatizing Boston's Muslim Community Is No Way to Build Trust," Brennan Center for Justice, Oct. 9, 2014, http://tinyurl.com/o79xgeb.

6. "Antigovernment Movement," Southern Poverty Law Center, http://tinyurl.com/oazpdl2.

7. Manny Fernandez, "As Jade Helm 15 Military Exercise Begins, Texans Keep Watch 'Just in Case,'"

The New York Times, July 15, 2015, http://tinyurl
.com/pjpztol.

8. "Then and Now: Right-Wing Extremism in 1995
and 2015," Anti-Defamation League, March 25,
2015, pp. 3, 5, 7, http://tinyurl.com/o6cs5sa.

9. See J. M. Berger, "The Hate List: Is America Really
Being Overrun by Right-Wing Militants?" *Foreign
Policy,* March 12, 2013, http://tinyurl.com/
ogkjmeu.

10. "With Hate in Their Hearts: The State of White
Supremacy in the United States," Anti-Defamation
League, July 2015, p. 5, http://tinyurl.com/o7ryzzz.

11. "Don Black," Southern Poverty Law Center, http://
tinyurl.com/obc9pxw.

12. Stormfront statistics, Aug. 24, 2015, http://tinyurl
.com/pg7398d; "Contributions in August 2015,"
http://tinyurl.com/or825tz.

13. William S. Parkin *et al.,* "Twenty-five Years of
Ideological Homicide Victimization in the United
States of America," August 2015, unpublished, p. 5.

14. "Domestic Violent Extremists Pose Increased Threat
to Government Officials and Law Enforcement,"
Homeland Security Office of Intelligence and
Analysis, July 22, 2014, p. 1, http://tinyurl.com/
qy9fvkb; "Sovereign Citizen Extremist Ideology
Will Drive Violence at Home, During Travel, and at
Government Facilities," Homeland Security Office
of Intelligence and Analysis, Feb. 5, 2015, p. 1,
http://tinyurl.com/pkx6wo6.

15. "Domestic Violent Extremists Pose Increased Threat
to Government Officials and Law Enforcement,"
ibid.; "Terror From the Right: Plots, Conspiracies
and Racist Rampages Since Oklahoma City,"
Southern Poverty Law Center, 2015, http://tinyurl
.com/qhp8hkw.

16. Charles Kurzman and David Schanzer, "Law
Enforcement Assessment of the Violent Extremism
Threat," Triangle Center on Terrorism and
Homeland Security, June 25, 2015, p. 3, http://
tinyurl.com/pa6333f.

17. "Upstate New York Man Convicted for His Role in
Attempting to Develop Lethal Radiation Device,"
Department of Justice News, U.S. Department of
Justice, Aug. 21, 2015, http://tinyurl.com/osj879z.

18. Parkin *et al., op. cit.,* p. 7.

19. Steven Chermak *et al.,* "The Organizational Dynamics
of Far-Right Hate Groups in the United States:
Comparing Violent to Nonviolent Organizations,"
Studies in Conflict & Terrorism, Feb. 14, 2013, p. 203,
http://tinyurl.com/pae4bmr.

20. "Letter to Barack H. Obama and The Honorable
Jeh Johnson," U.S. Congress, July 15, 2015, http://
tinyurl.com/oobq7ky.

21. "Rightwing Extremism: Current Economic and
Political Climate Fueling Resurgence in
Radicalization and Recruitment," U.S. Department
of Homeland Security, April 7, 2009, http://tinyurl
.com/k3ghvbo.

22. "Reestablishment of Committee on Domestic
Terrorism: Statement of Atty. Gen. Eric Holder,"
Department of Justice, June 3, 2014, http://tinyurl
.com/otwflbd.

23. *Ibid.*

24. Bob Goodlatte, "Hearing: Oversight of the Federal
Bureau of Investigation," House Judiciary
Committee, June 11, 2014, http://tinyurl.com/
ow3xder.

25. "Protecting America from Terrorist Attack: Our
Joint Terrorism Task Forces," FBI, http://tinyurl
.com/6f6sddq.

26. "Strategic Implementation Plan for Empowering
Local Partners to Prevent Violent Extremism in the
United States," Executive Office of the President of
the United States, December 2011, p. 1, http://
tinyurl.com/d2kavs8.

27. *Ibid.,* p. 2.

28. Lorenzo Vidino and Seamus Hughes, "Countering
Violent Extremism in America," Center for Cyber
& Homeland Security, The George Washington
University, June 2015, p. 11, http://tinyurl.com/
ozbw5nw.

29. *Ibid.,* pp. 7-8.

30. Cora Currier, "Spies Among Us," *The Intercept,* Jan.
21, 2015, http://tinyurl.com/p2rq9cc.

31. Bryan Bender, "Islamic Leader Says US Officials
Unfairly Target Muslims," *The Boston Globe,* Feb. 18,
2015, http://tinyurl.com/ouc9o3b.

32. Pete Simi, "Trauma as a Precursor to Violent Extremism," START Research Brief, April, 2015, http://tinyurl.com/q8qgwra.

33. Stephen E. Atkins, *Encyclopedia of Right-Wing Extremism in Modern American History* (2011), p. xii.

34. Michael Kazin, "A Kind Word for Ted Cruz: America Was Built on Extremism," *The New Republic,* Oct. 29, 2013, http://tinyurl.com/ngwpaat.

35. David M. Chalmers, *Hooded Americanism: The History of the Ku Klux Klan* (1987), pp. 2-3.

36. Brendan Koerner, "Why Does the Ku Klux Klan Burn Crosses?" *Slate,* Dec. 2, 2002, http://tinyurl.com/mle8o3a.

37. "Ku Klux Klan," Extremist Files, Southern Poverty Law Center, http://tinyurl.com/p3tagdh.

38. Chalmers, *op. cit.,* p. 3.

39. *Ibid.,* p. 5.

40. "Ku Klux Klan," *op. cit.*

41. *Ibid.*

42. *Ibid.*

43. Atkins, *op. cit.,* pp. 65-66.

44. *Ibid,* pp. 66-68, 72, 74-75.

45. "With Hate in Their Hearts: The State of White Supremacy in the United States," *op. cit,* p. 8; Chalmers, *op. cit.,* p. 91.

46. "National Alliance," Extremist Files, Southern Poverty Law Center, http://tinyuri.com/nnkaq56; "Then and Now: Right-Wing Extremism in 1995 and 2015," *op. cit.,* p. 6.

47. *Ibid.*

48. "With Hate in Their Hearts," *op. cit.,* p. 8.

49. "National Socialist Movement," Extremist Files, Southern Poverty Law Center, http://tinyurl.com/nax598q.

50. "With Hate in Their Hearts," *op. cit.,* p. 9.

51. *Ibid.,* pp. 9-10.

52. Robert H. Churchill, *To Shake Their Guns in the Tyrant's Face: Libertarian Political Violence and the Origins of the Militia Movement* (2012), p. 2.

53. *Ibid.,* p. 5.

54. *Ibid.,* p. 238.

55. *Ibid.,* pp. 241-242.

56. "Then and Now," *op. cit,* pp. 6-7.

57. "The Lawless Ones: The Resurgence of the Sovereign Citizen Movement," Anti-Defamation League, 2012, p. 3, http://tinyurl.com/pyd2ujn.

58. *Ibid.,* p. 6.

59. *Ibid.,* p. 16.

60. "Amendment in the Nature of a Substitute to H.R. 2899," U.S. House of Representatives, July 15, 2015, pp. 1, 8, http://tinyurl.com/nc4ev6n.

61. "Bipartisan Support in Congress to Counter Violent Extremism: McCaul's CVE Bill Unanimously Passes Committee," House Committee on Homeland Security, July 15, 2015, http://tinyurl.com/p9syl4p.

62. "Amendment in the Nature of a Substitute to H.R. 2899," *op. cit.,* pp. 3-5.

63. *Ibid.*

64. David Inserra, "Revisiting Efforts to Counter Violent Extremism: Leadership Needed," The Heritage Foundation, April 20, 2015, http://tinyurl.com/nn6khh7.

65. Allen West, "H.R.2899 Countering Violent Extremism Act — Should Not See the Light of Day," Bastrop County Tea Party, July 28, 2015, http://tinyurl.com/p5cct7n.

66. "Re: H.R. 2899, Countering Violent Extremism Act of 2015," July 10, 2015, http://tinyurl.com/nfzdf2r.

67. Rep. Bennie G. Thompson, "No Case for Countering Violent Extremism Office," U.S. House of Representatives, July 13, 2015, http://tinyurl.com/qxdj6gy.

68. "Substitute to the Amendment in the Nature of a Substitute to H.R. 2899 Offered by Mr. Thompson of Mississippi," House Committee on Homeland Security, July 15, 2015, pp. 1-4, http://tinyurl.com/nrjvmsr.

69. Dibya Sarkar, "House Panel Unanimously OKs Bill Creating Countering Violent Extremism Office Within DHS," FierceHomelandSecurity.com, July 16, 2015, http://tinyurl.com/ojkq3h4.

70. Tony Rizzo, "F. Glenn Miller Deserves Death for Killings Outside Jewish Facilities, Jury Says," *The*

Kansas City Star, Sept. 8, 2015, http://tinyurl.com/ogh7efk; "Frazier Glenn Miller," Extremist Files, Southern Poverty Law Center, http://tinyurl.com/npv4qw4.

71. Liz Kellar, "'Sovereign Citizen' Brent Cole Sentenced in Shootout," *The Union,* Aug. 31, 2015, http://tinyurl.com/no4xn52.

72. "Men Sentenced for Conspiracy to Use Weapons of Mass Destruction," U.S. Attorney's Office, Northern District of Georgia, Aug. 28, 2015, http://tinyurl.com/nszq963.

73. Bill Chappell, "Charleston Shooting Suspect Roof Could Face Death Penalty Over Federal Charges," NPR, July 22, 2015, http://tinyurl.com/nk44xsz.

74. Jeremy Diamond and Dana Bash, "Nikki Haley Calls for Removal of Confederate Flag From Capital Grounds," CNN, June 24, 2015, http://tinyurl.com/nludak9.

75. Amanda Terkel, "Alabama Governor Removes Confederate Flags From State Capital," *The Huffington Post,* June 24, 2015, http://tinyurl.com/pdeshbz.

76. Richard Fausset and Alan Blinder, "Era Ends as South Carolina Lowers Confederate Flag," *The New York Times,* July 10, 2015, http://tinyurl.com/nl3qsp3.

77. Dan McKay, "Mayor Strikes Confederate Flag in Old Town," *Albuquerque Journal,* Aug. 3, 2015, http://tinyurl.com/p7nlgg5; Shayne Dwyer, "New Danville Flag Ordinance Brings Down Other Flags in City as Well," WDBJ7 WDBJ (Roanoke-Lynchburg, Virginia), Aug. 7, 2015, http://tinyurl.com/q4gskns.

78. MJ Lee, "eBay to Ban Sale of Confederate Flag Merchandise," CNN, June 24, 2015, http://tinyurl.com/oksu227.

BIBLIOGRAPHY
Selected Sources
Books

Atkins, Stephen E., *Encyclopedia of Right-Wing Extremism in Modern American History,* **ABC-CLIO, 2011.**
A former Texas A&M University librarian examines the history of right-wing extremism in the U.S.

Churchill, Robert H., *To Shake Their Guns in the Tyrant's Face: Libertarian Political Violence and the Origins of the Militia Movement,* **University of Michigan Press, 2012.**
A University of Hartford history professor traces the origins of the modern American militia movement.

Articles

"S.C. to Seek Death Penalty for Dylann Roof in Charleston Shooting," NPR, Sept. 3, 2015, http://tinyurl.com/ppfapol.
Prosecutors have not yet decided whether to seek the death penalty for the suspect in the Charleston, S.C., church shooting.

Bender, Bryan, "Islamic Leader Says US Officials Unfairly Target Muslims," *The Boston Globe,* **Feb. 18, 2015, http://tinyurl.com/omg5ssm.**
A Boston Islamic leader criticizes the federal government's deradicalization program, saying it stigmatizes Muslims and assumes they are predisposed to violence.

Currier, Cora, "Spies Among Us," *The Intercept,* **Jan. 21, 2015, http://tinyurl.com/p2rq9cc.**
The government's outreach to Muslim communities blurs the line between outreach and intelligence gathering.

Fausset, Richard, and Alan Blinder, "Era Ends as South Carolina Lowers Confederate Flag," *The New York Times,* **July 10, 2015, http://tinyurl.com/nl3qsp3.**
The Confederate battle flag is removed from the grounds of the South Carolina State House.

Robles, Frances, "Dylann Roof Photos and a Manifesto Are Posted on Website," *The New York Times,* **June 20, 2015, http://tinyurl.com/od5che9.**
An online racist manifesto is discovered and is presumed written by the accused Charleston church shooter.

Shapiro, Emily, "Charleston Shooting: A Closer Look at Alleged Gunman Dylann Roof," ABC News, June 18, 2015, http://tinyurl.com/nklm2eo.
Accused Charleston shooter Dylann Roof planned his attack for six months, according to Roof's roommate.

Siegler, Kirk, "Year After Denying Federal Control, Bundy Still Runs His Bit of Nevada," NPR, April 14, 2015, http://tinyurl.com/owafag3.

A renegade rancher continues to refuse to pay federal grazing fees and penalties after armed supporters confronted federal agents a year earlier.

Reports and Studies

"The Strategic Implementation Plan for Empowering Local Partners to Prevent Violent Extremism in the United States," Executive Office of the President of the United States, December 2011, http://tinyurl.com/d2kavs8.
The Obama administration explains how it plans to work with local communities to prevent the recruitment and radicalization of individuals in the United States by violent extremists.

"Then and Now: Right-Wing Extremism in 1995 and 2015," Anti-Defamation League, March 25, 2015, http://tinyurl.com/o6cs5sa.
A civil rights organization takes stock of right-wing extremism on the 20th anniversary of the bombing of the Oklahoma City federal building and says a recent surge has gone largely unnoticed.

Chermak, Steven, *et al.*, "The Organizational Dynamics of Far-Right Hate Groups in the United States: Comparing Violent to Nonviolent Organizations," Studies in Conflict Terrorism, Feb. 14, 2013, http://tinyurl.com/pae4bmr.
Three university criminologists compare the characteristics of nonviolent and violent far right hate groups.

Kurzman, Charles, and David Schanzer, "Law Enforcement Assessment of the Violent Extremism Threat," June 25, 2015, http://tinyurl.com/pa6333f.
Two university terrorism experts ask law enforcement agencies to rank their concerns about violent extremist movements.

Pitcavage, Mark, "With Hate in Their Hearts: The State of White Supremacy in the United States,"Anti-Defamation League, July 13, 2015, http://tinyurl.com/o7ryzzz.
A researcher at a civil rights organization explains white supremacy movements.

Simi, Pete, "Trauma as a Precursor to Violent Extremism," START Research Brief, April 2015, http://tinyurl.com/q8qgwra.
A criminologist at the University of Nebraska, Omaha, and colleagues examine the life histories of 44 violent white supremacists and conclude that many suffered childhood trauma.

Vidino, Lorenzo, and Seamus Hughes, "Countering Violent Extremism in America," Center for Cyber and Homeland Security, The George Washington University, June 2015, http://tinyurl.com/ozbw5nw.
Two George Washington University experts on extremism assess the U.S. program to prevent violent extremists from recruiting adherents.

For More Information

American Civil Liberties Union (ACLU), 125 Broad St., 18th Floor, New York, NY 10004; 212-549-2500; www.aclu.org. Advocacy group working to preserve legal and constitutional individual rights.

Anti-Defamation League (ADL), 605 Third Ave., New York, NY 10158; 212-885-7700; www.adl.org. National civil rights organization combating bigotry.

Brennan Center for Justice, 161 Avenue of the Americas, 12th Floor, New York, NY 10013; 646-292-8310; www.brennancenter.org. Law and policy institute at New York University School of Law.

Federal Bureau of Investigation, 935 Pennsylvania Ave., N.W., Washington, DC 20535; 202-324-3000; www.fbi.gov. National security and law enforcement agency.

Life After Hate, 917 W. Washington Blvd., Suite 212, Chicago, IL 60607; http://lifeafterhate.org. Nonprofit helping individuals wishing to leave far-right extremist movements.

National Consortium for the Study of Terrorism and Responses to Terrorism (START), 8400 Baltimore Ave., Suite 250, College Park, MD 20740; 301-405-6600; www.start.umd.edu. Research group that is part of the University of Maryland and that maintains terrorism databases.

Southern Poverty Law Center (SPLC), 400 Washington Ave., Montgomery, AL 36104; 334-956-8200; www.splc.org. Advocacy group fighting hate and bigotry.

U.S. Department of Homeland Security, Washington, DC 20528; 202-282-8000; www.dhs.gov. Government agency charged with keeping America safe.

10

Charter Schools

Reed Karaim

Anti-charter school activists in Massachusetts celebrate the overwhelming defeat of Question 2, a referendum last Nov. 8 that would have allowed up to 12 new or expanded charter schools a year in the state. About 6,800 charter schools in 43 states serve 5 percent of the nation's public school students.

Getty Images/*The Boston Globe*/Barry Chin

From *CQ Researcher*,
March 10, 2017

The average ninth-grader enters Thurgood Marshall Academy in Washington, D.C.'s impoverished Anacostia neighborhood lagging behind in basic skills by three or more grade levels.[1] Then the public charter high school's challenging college-prep curriculum kicks in. In addition to an academic summer program, freshmen and sophomores take double-blocks of English and math. Later come AP courses in calculus, literature and other subjects. And every year, a self-assessment program encourages students to examine their academic struggles and achievements and present their plans for the future to a panel of teachers, staff and parents.[2]

Since Thurgood Marshall opened in 2001, every one of its graduates, virtually all of whom are African-American, have been accepted to college, and about two-thirds have graduated — eight times the college-graduation rate for the city's public schools overall. The D.C. board that authorizes and reviews city charter schools called the academy's record of college acceptances "outstanding."[3]

While Thurgood Marshall exemplifies the innovative educational approaches that help some charters succeed, the for-profit Celerity Educational Group, which operates seven charter schools in Southern California, demonstrates the perils. In January, FBI and Homeland Security agents raided Celerity's Los Angeles headquarters, seizing computers and records. The federal government has not disclosed the reason for the raid, but the Los Angeles Unified School District's inspector general has been investigating allegations of fraud and mismanagement by the company.[4]

A former Celerity teacher described the disconnect she felt between conditions at her school — which she said lacked a library,

229

Charters Show Mixed Results

More than half the nation's charter schools showed the same level of improvement in reading as traditional public institutions, and nearly half had the same improvement in math. Students at about a quarter of charter schools showed greater improvement than students at traditional public schools in reading and math in 2013, the latest year for which data are available.

Percentage of Charter Schools Showing Improvement in Reading and Math Versus Traditional Schools, 2013

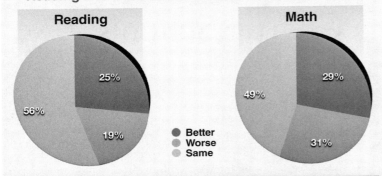

Types of Schools
Traditional public: Taxpayer-supported school governed by school district as part of a free public education system for primary and secondary students.
Charter: Tuition-free, taxpayer-supported independently run public school that operates under a charter and can be run by school districts, nonprofit groups, for-profit companies or others.
Magnet: Public school that specializes in a particular field, such as math, science or the arts.
Private: Nonpublic school run by a private organization or individuals and paid for through tuition and fees. Some students use publicly funded vouchers to pay tuition.
Religious: Private school run by religious organization. Some students use publicly funded vouchers to pay tuition.

Source: "National Charter School Study 2013," Center for Research on Education Outcomes, Stanford University, 2013, p. 57, http://tinyurl.com/npr5wq6.

this expensive party? . . . For a public school it was not normal."[5]

As these sharply differing portraits illustrate, the education community is divided on whether charter schools, which today serve 2.9 million children, or 5 percent of public school students, improve K-12 education.[6]

Charters are tuition-free, taxpayer-supported, independently run public schools that operate under a charter, a kind of contract, often with a particular mission, such as fostering college preparation or educating low-income students. They can be run by nonprofit groups, school districts, for-profit companies or others. Charter students must take all required standardized tests, but teachers can use innovative educational approaches, a fundamental goal of charter schools. Charters are part of the "school choice" movement, which advocates giving parents of K-12 students the option to select from a wide array of alternatives to traditional public schools, plus taxpayer funded vouchers for students to attend private and religious schools.

Charter school critics question their overall academic performance, their accountability and the motives of supporters, such as newly appointed Education Secretary Betsy DeVos, who strongly support for-profit companies running charter schools. The overarching question is whether the dramatic growth of charter schools — from a single school in Minnesota in 1992 to more than 6,800 schools today — has helped or hurt public education.[7]

cafeteria, gym or basic supplies — and the spending behavior of administrators, who threw a lavish party for themselves and staff. "I remember being really confused that night," Tien Le said. "When I asked for basic supplies, I couldn't get those things, yet you have money for

Because states regulate charters and each state has its own standards and requirements for charter schools, it is difficult to assess their overall performance. States differ on what kind of groups can create a charter school, and the authorizing charters also vary by state.[8]

"When you look at the preambles of all the state charter school laws, every state approached the reason they created a charter school law differently," says Nina Rees, president and CEO of the Washington-based National Alliance for Public Charter Schools.

Much media attention has focused on success stories, particularly in low-income, inner-city neighborhoods where traditional schools have struggled. Some charter schools, including those run by the for-profit BASIS and KIPP charter school chains, which operate in several states, have established a record of academic achievement based on test scores and college acceptance rates.

"Have they done better? Unequivocally, yes," says Jeanne Allen, founder and CEO of the Center for Education Reform, a charter advocacy organization in Washington. "They were intended to create a new path, new opportunities and new patterns of accountability. They have done better in all these areas."

A 2015 study of charter schools in 41 urban school districts by the Center for Research on Education Outcomes (CREDO) at Stanford University supports claims that many urban charters outperform their public school counterparts.[9] Charter supporters also cite studies indicating that traditional schools that convert to charters often improve academic performance while receiving less money per student.[10]

But critics cite an earlier CREDO study that found a large majority of charter schools in 2013 did no better or worse than traditional schools. Even among schools that did better, the authors said other factors, such as the composition of the student body, can explain the differences.[11] They also reject straight spending comparisons, saying most charters do not provide the level of services for physically disabled and special-needs children that traditional public schools are required to provide.

Moreover, the authors said, charters, which are governed by appointed boards in many states, lack the accountability and transparency of traditional schools governed by elected school boards, making it difficult or impossible for taxpayers to determine whether charter schools are using their money wisely.

A study by the Center for Popular Democracy, a liberal advocacy group in Washington, found that at least $216 million has been lost in waste, fraud or abuse in charter schools since 1994, which it said was "just the tip of the iceberg."[12]

"There's definitely a disconnect between what the well-oiled charter PR machine is championing and what is actually happening in the charter sector," says Bob Tate, a senior policy analyst with the National Education Association (NEA), a teachers union based in Washington. "Questions over accountability only scratch the surface." The NEA does not oppose charter schools but is highly skeptical and critical of how they have evolved. The union opposes private, for-profit charters and online charter schools for home schooling, which it believes neglect the socialization aspect of education.

Many critics say some for-profit charter chains appear more interested in making money than in educating students. For-profit companies manage more than 900 charter schools around the United States, according to one study.[13] The charter industry has attracted support among hedge funds and real estate companies, which have sought to take advantage of tax credits tied to locating charter schools in underserved areas. The charter movement also has been promoted by several wealthy private foundations, including the Walton Family Foundation and the Bill & Melinda Gates Foundation.[14]

Other critics question the disciplinary practices and high rates of student suspensions in some charter school chains, such as the Success Academy in New York City and the KIPP network of schools, which have zero-tolerance policies for misbehavior. Last June, then-Secretary of Education John King suggested some charters should rethink their approaches to discipline to make sure students are not being unnecessarily pushed out of school.[15]

Concerns about how charters operate led the National Association for the Advancement of Colored People (NAACP), the nation's oldest civil rights organization, based in Baltimore, to call last fall for a moratorium on charter expansion until questions about accountability and performance could be answered.[16]

Charter school advocates don't claim charters are superior in every case, or that some charters don't have problems. But they say the ability to try alternative approaches to discipline and other facets of schooling are necessary to better serve students with different interests or capabilities. "As a movement, a lot of us came to the charter camp because we didn't want to have a one-size-fits-all solution," says Rees.

Most Students Attend Traditional Public Schools

Although school-choice options have increased in the past two decades, 71 percent of school-age children still attend traditional neighborhood public schools. Another 16 percent attend alternative public schools, such as charter (4 percent), magnet (4 percent) or non-neighborhood (8 percent) schools.

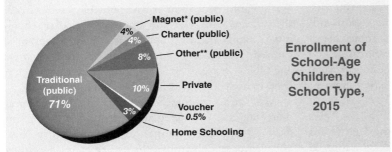

Enrollment of School-Age Children by School Type, 2015

Note: Percentages do not add to 100 because of rounding.

* Magnet public schools specialize in a particular field, such as math, science or the arts.

** Covers students who may attend a non-neighborhood public school within or outside their districts if space is available.

Source: "School Choice: What the Research Says," Center for Public Education, October 2015, Updated January 2017, http://tinyurl.com/gl4spl4.

The debate over charters is likely to intensify as the Trump administration institutes its education policy. President Trump has vowed to spend up to $20 billion to promote school choice, which includes charters as well as vouchers and tax credits for parents to use to send their children to private schools.

As educators, parents and administrators debate the value of charter schools, here are some of the questions central to the debate:

Do charter schools provide a better education than traditional public schools?

The fundamental question for many education analysts and parents is how charter schools stack up academically compared to traditional public schools. The charter movement was born in the 1990s out of concern that the nation's public school system was failing to provide children with a high-quality education.

Many defenders of traditional schools, which still educate 95 percent of public school students, say the spread of charter schools is built on a false belief that traditional schools are failing.[17]

"It's discouraging to be constantly told that American schools are failing, when by many indicators they're actually improving quite a bit," says Patte Barth, director of the Center for Public Education, a research initiative of the National School Boards Association in Alexandria, Va.

Traditional schools have made significant gains in student performance over the last 20 years, she says. In 1995, for example, U.S. eighth-graders scored below the international average in math, but in 2015 they were well above average, outscored by only six of 33 countries.[18] High-school graduation rates also are at historic highs, with 82 percent of seniors graduating on time in 2014, the most recent data available.[19]

"We know we have to continue to do better, but by some measures we're performing better than ever," Barth says.

Priscilla Wohlstetter, an education professor at Columbia University in New York City, says that, overall, charter school performance parallels public school performance. "There are some high performers, many in the middle and some in the lower rank," she says. "It kind of mirrors a bell curve."

The 2013 CREDO study backs those conclusions. It found that while one in four charter schools outperformed a comparable traditional public school in reading, more than half of charters and traditional schools performed about the same. About one in five charters did worse. For mathematics, 29 percent of charters did better, 31 percent did worse and about 40 percent did the same as traditional public schools.[20]

Some states' charter schools performed better than others, Wohlstetter says. Ohio's charter schools performed at a subpar level, for instance, with their students lagging behind those in traditional public schools in math and reading. Analysts blame the state's relatively lax charter standards.[21]

But charter supporters cite other studies to bolster the claim that, in many places, charters provide a superior education. In particular, they cite CREDO's 2015 analysis showing that more than half of the charter schools in 41 urban districts outperformed their traditional public school counterparts in math and reading. The gains were larger for black, Hispanic, low-income and special-education students.[22]

"These are communities where students have significant education challenges and are in great need of effective approaches to achieve academic success," CREDO Director Margaret Raymond said. "This research shows that many urban charter schools are providing superior academic learning for their students, in many cases quite dramatically better."[23]

However, charter critics question the fairness of such comparisons because charters' populations are, by definition, mostly self-selected. Although charters are open to all applicants, skeptics note they often require families to make a substantial commitment in travel or homework time, so only the most motivated families end up in charters.

In addition, critics say, many charter schools focus on high-performing students, who are the least expensive to educate. For instance, because many charter schools lack support programs for children with learning or physical disabilities, fewer of those students apply to charter schools, critics say.

They add that some charters are quick to push out students who can't keep up academically — an option not available to traditional public schools — resulting in distorted test-score results. One school in the Success Academy chain in New York City reportedly kept a "Got to Go" list of students that administrators wished to see forced out of the school.[24]

"Give me the story of a miracle charter, and I'm almost guaranteed there's going to be some sort of

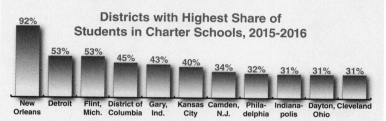

New Orleans Leads Charter Enrollment

More than half of the public school students in three cities attended charter schools during the 2015-2016 academic year, with New Orleans topping the list at 92 percent. After Hurricane Katrina destroyed many of New Orleans' public schools in 2005, the city rebuilt and reopened them as charter schools. Two Michigan school districts each had charter enrollment of 53 percent.

Districts with Highest Share of Students in Charter Schools, 2015-2016

New Orleans 92%; Detroit 53%; Flint, Mich. 53%; District of Columbia 45%; Gary, Ind. 43%; Kansas City 40%; Camden, N.J. 34%; Philadelphia 32%; Indianapolis 31%; Dayton, Ohio 31%; Cleveland 31%

Source: "A Growing Movement: America's Largest Charter Public School Communities and Their Impact on Student Outcomes," National Alliance for Public Charter Schools, Nov. 3, 2016, http://tinyurl.com/zdusry2.

shenanigans about student population — who's let in, who's kicked out, that sort of thing," says Wayne Au, a professor of education at the University of Washington in Seattle.

Susan Aud Pendergrass, vice president of research and evaluation for the National Alliance for Public Charter Schools, acknowledges that research shows charters have a slightly smaller percentage of students with disabilities, differences that increase for students with more severe disabilities. While charters are open to these students, she says, their families may be drawn to traditional schools with programs that can better serve their needs.

But Pendergrass says studies contradict the idea that self-selection of motivated students is responsible for charter performance. "The couple of studies that have been done on that have looked at public schools that were converted to charters. Basically, what they have found is that when the school converted to a charter school, there was a positive academic effect at that school," says Pendergrass "These were kids who are already there, so these aren't cases where students were self-selecting."

Rees, of the National Alliance for Public Charter Schools, notes that many charters have taken steps to ensure students spend more time learning, providing a simple explanation for some of the gains.

New Education Secretary Favors Charters

"We must revolutionize our education delivery system."

President Trump's cabinet nominees have included several controversial choices, but none has aroused more passionate debate than Secretary of Education Betsy DeVos, who was confirmed by the Senate only after Vice President Mike Pence cast a tie-breaking vote.[1]

DeVos and her husband, Dick, Michigan billionaires and longtime Republican political activists, are fierce advocates for education options outside of traditional public schools, particularly charter schools run by for-profit companies and vouchers that allow children to use public funds to attend private schools. The couple has spent millions of dollars lobbying officials, setting up advocacy groups, backing political candidates and supporting ballot measures to boost charters and "school choice."[2]

Dick DeVos' family fortune comes from the Amway marketing company, which his father co-founded. Betsy also comes from a wealthy, politically conservative family: Her father founded a successful auto parts company and was one of the early financial supporters of the Family Research Council, a conservative Christian organization.[3]

The charter school movement considers Betsy one of its own. "She has been a great supporter of parental choice," says Nina Rees, president and CEO of the National Alliance for Public Charter Schools, in Washington. "She has invested money in elected officials who have supported choice. You have someone [as Education secretary] who truly believes that parents will make better choices than bureaucrats. I know that alarms some people, but I think that's very refreshing."

Indeed, to many supporters of traditional public schools, the DeVoses have placed free-market ideology ahead of concern for children. "The whole DeVos family has used their wealth to drive an agenda that says profits are more important than kids," says Doug Pratt, director of public affairs for the Michigan Education Association, a teachers union. "Michigan has the highest concentration of for-profit charters in the country, and that's a direct result of policies the DeVoses have pushed over the years. This isn't about kids. It's about companies being able to make a profit off of public education."

About 80 percent of Michigan's charter schools are for-profit, the highest ratio in the United States.[4] Michigan schools overall rank near the bottom in national assessments of reading and math skills, and the state's charter schools rank below the state average.[5]

An investigation by the *Detroit Free Press* also found the state's charter schools almost completely lacking in transparency and accountability. Among the abuses the paper found, "[w]asteful spending and double-dipping. Board members, school founders and employees steering lucrative deals to themselves or insiders. Schools allowed to operate for years despite poor academic records. No state standards for who operates charter schools or how to oversee them."[6] The investigation also found that a lack of transparency in the state system makes it almost impossible to determine how for-profit charters are spending their money.

Yet the DeVoses have fought state legislative efforts to impose greater oversight of Detroit charter schools, contributing heavily last summer to lawmakers who helped to defeat a bipartisan effort to increase accountability.[7] Betsy DeVos personally holds a range of investments in for-profit enterprises connected to education, according to an analysis of her financial disclosure forms by the Center for American Progress, a liberal think tank and advocacy group in Washington.[8]

DeVos also has been a strong supporter of online charter schools, which even charter advocacy groups say have largely had dismal results. In 2006, *Politico*, the political news website, reported that Dick DeVos had invested in K12 Inc., one of the nation's largest for-profit chains of online schools and one that has been accused of suspect practices in several states, including requiring students to log in for as little as a minute a day to be counted present.[9]

DeVos' supporters say she has worked to bring market forces to bear in education and strip away unnecessary regulation, and they hope she takes the same approach as Education secretary. "What she should be doing is working to explore every single rule and regulation and piece of guidance and looking into ways to loosen up those restrictions for all educators and schools," says Jeanne Allen, founder and CEO of the Center for Education Reform, a pro-charter advocacy organization in Washington.

Speaking to an educator's conference in Texas in 2015, DeVos described the American system of education as "antiquated" and "embarrassing" because of what she described as poor performance stretching back half a century — a view that education analysts say ignores recent gains. "We must revolutionize our education delivery system," DeVos said. "That's it — that's all I'm asking for. Open education up; allow for choice, innovation, and freedom."[10]

But to her critics, DeVos's track record in Michigan promoting charters while opposing stronger oversight is the final argument against her approach to public education. Diane Ravitch, a research professor and historian of education at New York University, says, "Detroit, which has one of the highest concentrations of charter schools, is the lowest performing district in the country. Is this supposed to be the model under Betsy DeVos?"

Ravitch, a former Assistant Secretary of Education and school choice advocate, now takes a negative view of charters, outlined in her 2013 book, *Reign of Error: The Hoax of the Privatization Movement and the Danger to America's Public Schools.*

— *Reed Karaim*

Betsy DeVos, the new secretary of Education, is a strong advocate of charter schools and vouchers, which allow parents to use public funds to send their children to private schools.

[1] Emma Brown, "With Historic Tiebreaker From Pence, DeVos Confirmed as Education Secretary," *The Washington Post*, Feb. 7, 2017, http://tinyurl.com/jpwtmh7.

[2] Stephen Henderson, "Betsy DeVos and the Twilight of Public Education," *The Detroit Free Press*, Dec. 3, 2016, http://tinyurl.com/gtm242s.

[3] Noam Scheiber, "Betsy DeVos, Trump's Education Pick, Plays Hardball With Her Wealth," *The New York Times*, Jan. 9, 2017, http://tinyurl.com/gr4e9hw.

[4] Zack Stanton, "How Betsy DeVos Used God and Amway to Take Over Michigan Politics," *Politico Magazine*, Jan. 15, 2017, http://tinyurl.com/zltoblr.

[5] Caitlin Emma, Benjamin Wermund and Kimberly Hefling, "DeVos' Michigan Schools Experiment Gets Poor Grades," *Politico*, Dec. 9, 2016, http://tinyurl.com/hqrw8w9.

[6] Jennifer Dixon, "Michigan Spends $1B on Charter Schools but Fails to Hold Them Accountable," *Detroit Free Press*, June 22, 2014, http://tinyurl.com/jpkmp9f.

[7] Henderson, *op. cit.*

[8] Ben Miller and Laura Jimenez, "Inside the Financial Holdings of Billionaire Betsy DeVos," Center for American Progress, Jan. 27, 2017, http://tinyurl.com/jarteyj.

[9] Matt Barnum, "Betsy DeVos, Trump's EdSec Pick, Promoted Virtual Schools Despite Dismal Results," *The 74*, Dec. 1, 2016, http://tinyurl.com/j9urc4z.

[10] Valerie Strauss, "The Telling Speech Betsy DeVos Gave About Education — Full Text," *The Washington Post*, Dec. 21, 2016, http://tinyurl.com/h38ysl9.

"By and large, they do expand the school day, they do expand the school year, they do bring some kids in on Saturday," she says, "so there's more focus on content and an effort to make sure the child is achieving to the best of their potential."

Are charter schools publicly accountable?

One of the sharpest differences between charter proponents and skeptics involves accountability and transparency. Elected school boards govern traditional public schools, and they are generally subject to open-meeting and public-records laws, which means the public can scrutinize spending and budgets.

That is not the case for charters in many states. "Some states have more oversight than others, but, generally, I would say they don't have enough accountability," says the University of Washington's Au. "Basically, charter schools are using public money without actual public oversight. [Individual] charter school boards are appointed, and usually the charter school state authorizing boards are appointed."

Allen, of the Center for Education Reform, sees the charter structure as making them more accountable than public schools.

"What's wonderful about the nongovernmental boards that manage charter schools is that they're not elected. Charter schools take the politics out of schools," she says. "It's the board that files for a charter; it's the board that's accountable for everything. A [traditional public] school board isn't directly responsible for performance. Nobody is going to hold them accountable."

Allen also says charter schools face an ultimate standard: The charters under which they operate can run 100 pages or more. Those charters are in effect only for a certain number of years, often 5 or 10, and schools that fail to live up to their charter requirements can be closed. An average of about 500 charter schools have closed per year over the last 10 years, although all those closures are not necessarily tied to performance, says Pendergrass of the National Alliance for Public Charter Schools.

Supporters of traditional schools say school board members are accountable to the voters, who can throw them out of office, and school board meetings are open to the public. Indeed, Julian Vasquez Heilig, a professor of educational leadership and policy studies at California State University Sacramento, says too many

underperforming charter schools remain open. Without direct accountability to voters, he says, charter schools should really be considered private schools that receive public money.

"They're not public schools because they're run by private boards," Vasquez Heilig says. "They do get public money, but so do defense contractors. Is anybody going to argue that Grumman or Boeing are public entities? They can say they're public schools until they're blue in the face, but they're privately run."

Rees, of the National Alliance for Public Charter Schools, responds that charters are public schools because they are open to everyone, and they're free. But requiring full transparency of private charter boards could hurt their effectiveness, she says. "I fear that sometimes our opponents use transparency to discourage certain people from joining our boards and turn us into the same inefficient system that existed before," she says.

But Columbia University's Wohlstetter notes that charters vary widely from state to state, although she says there has been a movement toward holding charter schools to more thorough requirements.

In addition, charter critics say, states allow charters to escape public scrutiny in other ways as well. Of the 43 states with charter school laws, "a third do not require that the charters comply with the same open-meeting laws that govern traditional school boards," says the NEA's Tate.[25]

In 35 states, charter school finances are kept from the public through a structure in which a school contracts out control of its operations to a private for-profit company — called an education charter management organization (EMO), which does not have to disclose how the money is spent. EMOs manage between 35 to 40 percent of U.S. charter schools, according to a study by Bruce Baker, an education professor at Rutgers University in New Brunswick, N.J., and Gary Miron, a professor of evaluation, measurement and research at Western Michigan University in Kalamazoo.[26]

"The charter school is a public entity, but what happens is the charter school is run by a private management entity, so all the charter school says is, 'We got a million dollars to educate these kids and we handed this money over to this private company to run his school,' and that's what the public knows," says Doug Pratt, director of public affairs for the Michigan Education Association, the state NEA chapter. So it's "impossible to determine" how much of the money is being used to educate the students, he adds.

The private-management structure also raises potential conflicts-of-interest questions. In 2012, an investigation by *The Arizona Republic* found that 40 nonprofit charter schools paid $70 million to companies run by the schools' board members, executives or their relatives. Through EMOs, the salaries of top executives in charter chains also can be kept secret.[27]

Baker and Miron said the combination of weak oversight and the financial management structures used by some charter schools makes it likely that improper behavior or wasteful procedures are going undetected. As a result, it is possible that "a substantial share of public expenditure intended for the delivery of direct educational services to children is being extracted inadvertently or intentionally for personal or business financial gain," they wrote.[28]

Should charter schools be required to follow the same rules as other public schools?

Charter school students must take the same state and federal standardized performance tests as children in traditional public schools. Charters also must abide by federal laws that prohibit discrimination based on race, sex, national origin or disability.[29]

But U.S. public education is largely governed by the states, and state laws and regulations governing charter schools vary widely. For instance, some states, such as Arizona and Wisconsin, exempt charter schools from most state regulations and laws governing public schools. Others, such as Massachusetts and Maryland, require charters to comply with state laws and regulations that apply to traditional public schools, but charters can seek waivers in certain cases.[30]

Even teacher-training requirements differ by state. Some states require charter school teachers to be fully certified in line with teachers at traditional schools, while others require only that a certain percentage of a charter school's teachers be certified. Still other states have no certification requirements for charter teachers.[31]

A number of education experts believe states should require charters to meet the same standards as other public schools in a district, such as those concerning teacher qualifications or student suspensions. Sometimes, critics

Getty Images/Michael Buckner

Diane Ravitch, a former Assistant Secretary of Education, says charter schools should not be able to cherry-pick the best students but should be required to have student bodies that reflect the district's overall public school population, with the same proportion of students with disabilities and immigrants with weak English skills. "Absolutely, they should have to follow the same rules," says Ravitch, now a historian of education at New York University.

say, some backers have supported charters — the vast majority of which are not unionized — as a way to undermine teachers unions.

Diane Ravitch, an historian of education at New York University's Steinhardt School of Culture, Education and Human Development, says charter schools should be required to have student bodies that reflect the district's overall public school population, including those who cost the most to educate: students with disabilities and immigrants with weak English skills.

"Absolutely, they should have to follow the same rules. They should also have the same proportion of students with disabilities and the same proportion of kids who don't speak English," says Ravitch, who supported charter schools before becoming one of their foremost critics. She is author of *Reign of Error: The Hoax of the Privatization Movement and the Danger to America's Public Schools.*

Other analysts believe charters should be given more latitude in certain areas. Columbia's Wohlstetter says charters should follow the same health and safety rules as other public schools and continue to give their students "the same tests as other district kids take" so they're being measured by the same achievement standards. But when it comes to regulating classroom work, such as length of the school day or the hours teachers spend in the classroom, she says, "I'm a big proponent of deregulation in terms of the education program. Without the freedom to try new approaches, charters will be failing their essential mission to find innovative ways to improve school performance."

Charters also should be allowed more latitude with curriculum, she says, noting that charters have embraced a wide variety of teaching approaches beyond the traditional public school template. "Some use project-based learning; some are dual immersion, in which students learn two languages; some are focused on a particular area, such as the arts; some have a team-teaching approach."

Allen, of the Center for Education Reform, says many of the rules and regulations imposed on traditional schools do not correlate with the quality of education. "A charter school [in many states] doesn't have to report how often its teachers show up and their sick days and that sort of thing. Those are inputs. Charter schools are output-driven," or measured by results, she says. "All of the bureaucracy that surrounded public education before charters showed up is the kind of stuff that critics are used to, and they think that if you're not sending those keystrokes into the state [you're not doing your job]."

Rees, of the National Alliance for Public Charter Schools, says "over-regulation" is a danger as states react to the growth of the charter movement. The urge can be toward standardization, she notes, and even though 25 years of charter experience has provided models of what's successful, "we need to be careful because if we want to stay vibrant, we do need to stay open to new ideas and new people."

But charter critics note that some of the concerns about charter schools involve discipline and suspension policies, particularly in regard to minority students and children with disabilities. A 2016 study by the Center for Civil Rights Remedies at the University of California, Los Angeles, found that charter schools suspend black children and children with disabilities at higher rates than other schools do, particularly in high school.[32]

The disciplinary policies at some successful charters, such as the Success Academy chain in New York, have been the subject of public criticism. Teachers from the chain told *The New York Times* that a culture existed of belittling and embarrassing children, including tearing up incorrect homework in front of the class. "It's this culture of, 'If you've made them cry, you've succeeded in getting your point across,' " Jessica Reid Sliwerski, a former Success Academy teacher, said.[33]

Eva Moskowitz, founder and CEO of the chain, said its training materials say teachers should never shame or embarrass students and that the incidents reported were isolated cases of teachers behaving improperly.[34]

Many of the rules and regulations that govern traditional schools are there to protect both teachers and students, says the University of Washington's Au. "The education bureaucracy can be burdensome," he says. "But that same bureaucracy means there is also regulatory oversight to make sure all kids can be served, and we're just not seeing that in charter schools."

BACKGROUND
Budding Movement

The beginnings of the charter school movement can be traced to Ray Budde, a former junior high school administrator who became a professor of education at the University of Massachusetts, Amherst. Budde, who had an interest in organizational theory, presented a paper to a research society in 1974 titled "Education by Charter."[35]

His idea was different from how today's charter schools work, however. He envisioned charters as a way to cut down on educational bureaucracy within existing school systems. Essentially, teachers would have a contractual relationship through a "charter" agreement with the school board that would give them direct responsibility for effective teaching.[36]

Budde's paper received almost no attention at the time. But in 1983, the National Commission on Excellence in Education created by President Ronald Reagan issued a report, "A Nation at Risk," warning that American schools were declining academically and falling behind internationally.

"If an unfriendly foreign power had attempted to impose on America the mediocre educational performance that exists today, we might well have viewed it as

CHRONOLOGY

1970s-1991 *Charter school concept introduced after concern grows about U.S. public education.*

1974 Ray Budde, a former junior high school principal, proposes that school districts sign contracts (charters) with teachers to improve educational outcomes; his idea attracts little attention.

1983 National Commission on Excellence in Education's report, "A Nation at Risk," says U.S schools are not adequately educating students and calls for raising educational standards, spurring reform movement.

1988 American Federation of Teachers union president Albert Shanker suggests teachers set up innovative, independent schools within existing schools, which he calls "charter schools." . . . The Citizen's League, a Minnesota think tank, modifies the charter school idea to include entire schools established outside traditional ones, chartered by groups such as universities or the state.

1991 Minnesota is first state to allow school districts to create charters.

1992-2000 *Charter movement expands.*

1992 City Academy in St. Paul, Minn., opens with 53 students, becoming nation's first charter school.

1994 Improving America's Schools Act, which includes grants to states for establishing charter schools, gets bipartisan support. . . . Two young teachers start Knowledge Is Power Program (KIPP) charter school, which expands into a network of 200 schools serving nearly 80,000 students.

1996 Congress passes D.C. School Reform Act, leading to first charter school in the nation's capital.

2000 U.S. has nearly 2,000 charter schools.

2001-2011 *Charter schools proliferate and movement's political power grows, but questions arise about their performance and approaches.*

2005 National Alliance for Public Charter Schools, is founded. . . . After Hurricane Katrina devastates New Orleans' public schools, city converts to a largely charter system, which improves performance.

2006 Former New York City Council member Eva Moskowitz opens Success Academy, the first of what will become a controversial 41-school for-profit charter network in the city known for rigorous academics and strict discipline.

2009 Stanford University-based Center for Research on Educational Outcomes (CREDO) finds that 17 percent of charter schools are outperforming comparable public schools, but 37 percent are doing worse.

2011 On the 20th anniversary of the passage of the first state law authorizing charter schools, the nation has more than 5,000 charters, but they enroll only 5 percent of all public school students.

2012-Present *Charter school performance improves, but concern grows about the schools' racial composition, accountability and standards.*

2012 Education Department inspector general says the department has not effectively overseen and monitored disbursement of federal charter school grants to states and state oversight has been lax.

2013 CREDO finds charter school performance improving, but unevenly.

2015 Washington's Supreme Court rules the state's charter schools are unconstitutional because they are governed by appointed, rather than elected, boards. Legislature moves to keep charters open.

2016 NAACP calls for moratorium on new charter schools amid concerns they are increasing racial segregation. . . . Massachusetts voters defeat a referendum to allow more charter schools. . . . Number of charter schools nationally tops 6,800.

2017 Longtime charter advocate Betsy DeVos becomes Education secretary after Vice President Mike Pence casts a tie-breaking vote in the Senate.

New Orleans Becomes Movement's Poster Child

City's experiment illustrates potential and pitfalls of charter schools.

Hurricane Katrina, which devastated New Orleans in 2005, led to an unparalleled educational experiment: When the city rebuilt its schools, they reopened as a nearly all-charter school system.

By 2015, 92 percent of New Orleans' 47,880 public school students were attending charter schools, by far the highest percentage in the United States. Detroit and Flint, Mich., tied for having the second-highest charter school attendance rates, at 53 percent.[1]

Under the new system, New Orleans students have shown some significant educational gains, making it a poster child for many in the charter movement. By 2014, 63 percent of elementary and middle schools were proficient on state achievement tests, up from 37 percent the year Katrina struck.[2] High school graduation rates also improved dramatically, with 73 percent of students graduating on time in 2015, compared to 54 percent in 2004.[3]

The gains appeared so impressive that in 2010 U.S. Education Secretary Arne Duncan said, "I think the best thing that happened to the education system in New Orleans was Hurricane Katrina."[4]

But many of those involved in the New Orleans makeover say the truth is far more complicated, and the New Orleans experiment illustrates both the potential and the pitfalls of such an approach.

The academic gains have been real, they say, but at a cost. "We don't want to replicate a lot of the things that took place to get here," said Andre Perry, who was one of the city's few black charter-school CEOs. "There were some pretty nefarious things done in the pursuit of academic gain."[5]

For instance, Perry and others say, in their drive to improve performance, schools sought to skim the best students, counseled out those who were not keeping up and did not provide enough support for special-needs children.[6] A former state school official said expulsions were "out of control" and that charters used the few remaining traditional public schools as "dumping grounds" for difficult or academically struggling students.[7]

A chaotic admissions system also made it hard for many parents to get their children into the charter schools they wanted. As a result, the average distance children had to travel to attend school rose significantly.[8]

During the reorganization, nearly all 7,000 New Orleans public school system employees were fired, including all 4,600 teachers.[9] Even before the hurricane, state officials had set up a special authority to take control of the district's low-performing schools, and as the system was rebuilt, officials felt they needed a clean slate.

The Louisiana Federation of Teachers, the local educators' union, brought a class-action lawsuit on behalf of the fired teachers, but in 2015 the state Supreme Court declined to hear a final appeal on behalf of the teachers.[10]

The firings were devastating for many of the city's longtime teachers. As they were replaced by a younger group of teachers, the racial composition of the city's teaching staff also changed. Before Katrina, 71 percent of the city's 1,300 public school teachers were black; in 2015, 49 percent were black, with 45 percent white. The student population, however, remains 90 percent African-American.[11]

an act of war," the report said. "As it stands, we have allowed this to happen to ourselves."[37]

The report received national attention and ignited interest in educational reform. When Budde republished his original paper in 1988, it attracted a new audience. Albert Shanker, then head of the American Federation of Teachers, an educators union, expanded on Budde's idea. Speaking at the National Press Club in Washington, Shanker proposed creating separate schools within existing schools to serve as laboratories of innovation. Teachers would have greater autonomy to try different education approaches, such as team teaching or tailoring educational programs to the different ways children learn.[38]

School leaders have taken several steps to mitigate some of the problems. For instance, the city introduced a centralized application system that makes it easier for parents to enroll their students and harder for charters to manipulate the composition of their student bodies. The district also has increased funding for educating special-needs students.[12]

In addition, a citywide code of conduct now bans expulsions for minor offenses and has established a review process for students who are expelled.[13] Some city charter schools that formerly took a zero-tolerance approach to discipline also have shifted to an approach that works individually with students to help resolve behavior that has been getting them into trouble.[14]

New Orleans' educators say efforts to improve the system continue, defying those who want to see the transition to charters as either a simple success or a failure.

"Yes, we've come a long way, and we have a long way left to go," Rahel Wondwossen, the principal of Cohen College Prep charter school, told *Education Week*. "And that's not as clean of an answer as sometimes folks want."[15]

— *Reed Karaim*

Students have shown educational gains since New Orleans converted most of its traditional public schools — many of them rebuilt after being destroyed in 2005 by Hurricane Katrina — to charters. Above, kindergartners line up for class at the Dr. Martin Luther King Jr. Charter School for Science and Technology.

[1] "A Growing Movement: America's Largest Charter Public School Communities and Their Impact on Student Outcomes," 11th Annual Edition, National Alliance for Public Charter Schools, November 2016, http://tinyurl.com/hv7pt28.

[2] Andrea Gabor, "The Myth of the New Orleans School Makeover," *The New York Times*, Aug. 22, 2015, http://tinyurl.com/jpyveo5.

[3] Emma Brown, "Katrina Swept Away New Orleans' School System, Ushering in New Era," *The Washington Post*, Sept. 3, 2015, http://tinyurl.com/zp55lev.

[4] Nick Anderson, "Education Secretary Duncan Calls Hurricane Katrina Good for New Orleans Schools," *The Washington Post*, Jan. 30, 2010, http://tinyurl.com/ycnbomk.

[5] Gabor, *op. cit.*

[6] *Ibid.*

[7] Thomas Toch, "The Big Easy's Grand Experiment," *U.S. News & World Report*, Aug. 18, 2015, http://tinyurl.com/hfls27t.

[8] Brown, *op. cit.*

[9] Corey Mitchell, " 'Death of My Career' — What Happened to New Orleans' Veteran black Teachers?" *Education Week*, Aug. 19, 2015, http://tinyurl.com/hgkmftw.

[10] *Ibid.*

[11] *Ibid.*

[12] Toch, *op. cit.*

[13] *Ibid.*

[14] Mallory Falk and Eve Troeh, "A 'No Excuses' New Orleans Charter School Has a Change of Heart," WWNO, New Orleans Public Radio, Jan, 23, 3017, http://tinyurl.com/zmmvrbk.

[15] Rahel Wondwossen, "The last Word: Can New Orleans Deliver a High Quality Education for All Its Children?" video, *Education Week*, Aug. 19, 2015, http://tinyurl.com/hp5oahl.

Such schools-within-schools would operate with a charter outlining their approach and guaranteeing their operation for a certain number of years — Shanker suggested 5 to 10 years — to give their ideas a fair tryout. The schools would be exempt from many of the rules imposed on traditional schools, which he felt restricted teachers' ability to meet the needs of their students. But

Shanker envisioned these schools as unionized parts of the overall school system.[39]

"The school district and the teacher union would develop a procedure that would encourage any group of six or more teachers to submit a proposal to create a new school," Shanker told the press club. In Shanker's vision, these charter schools would have to be approved by a

Students plant a "teaching garden" at the KIPP Infinity Charter School in New York City's Harlem neighborhood. Some charters boast high academic achievement, particularly in low-income, inner-city neighborhoods. But even when charters outperform traditional public schools, critics say other factors, such as cherry-picking applicants, could explain some of the differences.

special board and accept a student population that reflected the overall district composition — so they could not cherry-pick their students.[40]

He also imagined a central database where the best ideas could be shared, spurring improvement in public schools nationwide. "Other teachers could then dig into that and find the eight or 12 or 15 ways that have been found by other teachers to work, and add their own comments," he said.[41] Shanker would later call the schools-within-schools he envisioned "charter schools."[42]

His ideas were taken up most enthusiastically by the Citizens League, an advocacy and policy group in Minneapolis. The league published a report advocating the establishment of charter schools and worked with Minnesota legislators to pass the first state law enabling charter schools in 1991.[43]

In a key change from Shanker's vision, however, the Minnesota law allowed charter schools to be established outside and independent of traditional public schools. In 1992, a year after the law passed, a small group of teachers set up City Academy in St. Paul, the nation's first

publicly funded, privately run charter school. It opened with only 53 students but would become the first of a wave of charters that would spread across the nation.[44]

Charters Catch Fire

That same year, California became the second state with a charter school law. In 1993 five other states passed charter laws, and by 1996, 25 states and the District of Columbia had embraced charters as a way to spur competition and improvement in public education.[45]

The charter movement received a federal boost in 1994 when President Bill Clinton supported including creation of the Charter School Program in a larger education bill signed into law. Under the program, the U.S. Department of Education provided grants to state and local education agencies to support the planning, development and start-up of new charter schools.[46]

Speaking in 1998, Clinton said, "Across our nation, public school choice, and in particular charter schools are renewing public education with their energy and new ideas." He stressed, however, that charter schools should remain open only so long as they met rigorous standards of accountability.[47]

During Clinton's eight years as president the number of charter schools in the country grew from one to more than 2,000. Federal grants for charters totaled $4.5 million in 1995; in 2016, they were $245 million.[48] Since the beginning of the program, the federal government has invested more than $3 billion in charter school development through an expanded set of grants. The U.S. Education Department says that in the past decade, those investments have enabled the launch of more than 2,500 charter schools serving approximately 1 million students.[49]

As the movement caught fire in the 1990s, many states wrote laws that made it relatively easy to open charter schools. The goal was to spur growth and allow charters to experiment. But support and training programs for operating schools were often lacking, according to some people involved in the early expansion.

"With the schools that opened in the first two years [of the state charter program], it was basically, 'Here's your charter, and good luck,'"said Cassandra A. Larsen, executive director of the Arizona State Board for Charter Schools in a 2001 interview with *Education Week*.[50]

The combination of minimal state oversight and rapid expansion led to problems in some states. In Arizona, the state auditor in 2002 found that 21 of 43 schools were in financial trouble. Embarrassing cases also surfaced in the press, including one in the Phoenix area, in which the state briefly could not locate a school to which it was sending money. It turned out the school had lost its lease and was meeting under a tree in a city park.[51]

But many new charter schools showed the kind of innovation and results that advocates had hoped to see flower. The Minnesota New Country School, a rural charter created in Henderson in 1994, works with families to devise individualized learning programs for every student. The school has no grades, bells or formal classes and is organized as a cooperative without a principal. The teachers share administrative responsibilities. The school's academic achievements were significant enough that the Bill & Melinda Gates Foundation provided $4 million to help the school replicate its model in other charters.[52]

In Boston, the Academy for the Pacific Rim, founded in 1995, combines Asian and American approaches to learning and cultural practices. Classes begin with students and teachers standing, bowing and thanking one another for their efforts. Each school day starts with an assembly, in which the school regularly hands out its "gambette award." *Gambette* is Japanese for "to persist." The school's academic track record places it among the best in the Boston area.[53]

But as the charter movement expanded, some analysts say its size and scope began to exceed the concept envisioned by its original supporters.

"It was never intended to create a parallel, market-based alternative to the public school system," says Stan Karp, a longtime high school educator who serves on the board of Rethinking Schools, a nonprofit education publisher and advocacy group in Milwaukee. "It was about creating model programs that might have some innovation, which could then generate useful reforms [in] the public school system."

A key part of the original charter idea had been individual schools operating locally. Karp says a fundamental shift came about in the late 1990s or 2000s, with the development of charter chains and for-profit schools. "These charter networks began to develop nationally and began to attract a lot of funding from people whose interests were not education reform," he says. Instead, people began to see charters as a "source of revenue, a way to promote a free-market ideology or undermine teachers unions."

Only about 11 percent of charter teachers belong to unions, according to Pendergrass, from the National Alliance for Public Charter Schools, compared to the 68 percent of public school teachers who were union members as of 2014, according to the National Bureau of Labor Statistics.[54]

A U.S. Department of Education survey for the 2011-2012 school year found that charter school teachers' salaries averaged 17 percent less than those of teachers at traditional schools. However, that could be because charter teachers were also younger on average, with fewer years of teaching experience. Teacher turnover at charter schools was higher, the survey found, than at traditional schools, although it had declined significantly since the 2004-2005 school year, while turnover rates at traditional schools crept slightly higher.[55]

Charter school growth continued to be strong through the first decade of the 21st century, topping 5,000 in the 2010-2011 school year.[56] Charter schools also continued to draw bipartisan political support. In the 2008 presidential campaign, both Republican John McCain and Democrat Barack Obama backed more assistance to charters.[57]

But as charter schools took an expanding share of public education spending, a backlash began to develop in parts of the United States.

Backlash

California, the nation's most populous state, has the largest number of charter schools — 1,234 as of the 2015-2016 school year, according to the National Alliance for Public Charter Schools.[58] But in recent years, the state has been the center of a bitter battle over further charter expansion.

In Los Angeles, the teachers union gathered a coalition of other unions and public supporters to oppose a plan led by the Eli and Edythe Broad Foundation to enroll half of the city's public school students in charter schools over the next eight years.[59] The Los Angeles–based foundation, created by billionaire homebuilder Eli Broad and his wife, says it works to promote "entrepreneurship for the public good in education, the science and arts." The plan also has attracted support from the Walton Family Foundation, the founders of the Walmart chain and one of several philanthropic groups that have invested heavily in promoting charters.[60]

Union leaders said the large-scale transfer of the city's education funds to the charter schools created under the plan would devastate the city's traditional public schools.

Resistance to further charter growth has emerged elsewhere in California as well. The City Council of Huntington Park in suburban Los Angeles voted last October to extend a moratorium on charter expansion until September 2017. The city already has 10 charters among its 24 schools, and unionized local teachers and others have opposed further expansion on the grounds that the city has plenty of education options.[61] A citizens group also attempted to get a measure on the state ballot last November that would have repealed the 1992 California law allowing charters, but the organization failed to secure the nearly 400,000 signatures required to get an initiative on the ballot.[62]

Charters did not fare as well in two other states last November. In Massachusetts, voters decisively defeated a measure that would have allowed up to 12 new or expanded charter schools annually beyond a current cap, which limits charter expansion in school districts according to a complex formula based on school enrollment and funding.

Charter opponents prevailed in Massachusetts despite being outspent — $26 million to $15 million — by charter supporters.[63] Opponents argued the measure would undermine traditional public schools. Massachusetts, which regulates its charter schools more tightly than most states, has the nation's best public school system, according to at least one study.[64]

Voters in Georgia also defeated an amendment that would have allowed the state to seize control of the worst-performing public schools and turn them over to charter operators. Polls before the election showed that voters did not like the idea of turning over local control of schools.[65]

"As more communities start to experience the hidden downfalls of charters, that's where we're seeing more pushback," the NEA's Tate says, calling the referendums in Massachusetts and Georgia "examples of growing public concern."

But despite resistance in some states, Pendergrass, of the National Alliance for Public Charter Schools, says charters remain popular with the general public. An alliance survey of 1,000 parents with school-age children, she says, found that "60 percent-plus have a positive opinion of charter schools."

Independent polling also has found majority support for charter schools over the years, although a 2005 Gallup Poll found that only 28 percent of respondents would support a charter school in their community if it meant taking money from traditional public schools.[66]

CURRENT SITUATION
Administration Action

After more than six weeks in office, the Trump administration has yet to formally present its education policy.

However, in an address to Congress on Feb. 28, President Trump labeled education "the civil rights issue of our time," and called on Congress to pass an education bill "that funds school choice for disadvantaged youth, including millions of African-American and Latino children. These families should be free to choose the public, private, charter, magnet, religious or home school that is right for them."[67]

Three days later he visited a Catholic school in Orlando, Fla., to tout the use of vouchers, or public subsidies for children to attend private or religious schools. Teachers unions say Trump's preference for vouchers shows he is hostile toward public schools and that he intends to turn education into a profit-making industry.[68]

During his campaign, Trump promised to spend up to $20 billion to promote school choice, which includes not only charters but also vouchers.[69] If combined with $110 billion in state funding, that money "could provide $12,000 in school choice funds to every single K-12 student who today is living in poverty," Trump said at a campaign event in Cleveland in September.[70]

Analysts point out that such a plan would require each state to dedicate more than $2 billion, which they are not likely to do. More significantly, charter critics ask, if Trump and the Republican-controlled Congress plan to hold the line on federal spending, how would Congress fund the program?

"We think it's a terrible idea," says the NEA's Tate. "Where is the money going to come from?"

Because of the size of Trump's campaign proposal, several education experts say they fear the money would likely come from the budgets for two education programs: the Every Student Succeeds Act and Title I education funding.

The Every Student Succeeds Act, signed into law by President Obama in 2015, replaces the No Child Left Behind Act as the principal federal tool to ensure equal access to education for all students and establishment of achievement standards and annual statewide tests to measure educational progress.[71] Title I of the Elementary and Secondary Education Act provides financial assistance to public schools with large numbers or percentages of low-income children to help all children meet challenging academic content and achievement standards.[72]

"Traditional school districts all across the country benefit from and rely on these [Title I] funds," says Tate. "If they're going to be diverted to pay for this voucher-charter scheme, that's really going to raise a lot of concern."

Charter school supporters, however, say they hope for greater federal attention and financial support. "We are cautiously optimistic," says Rees of the National Alliance for Public Charter Schools. "A lot remains to be seen in what they produce in terms of a budget, and how they use the regulatory and guidance [capabilities] of the Education Department, but we are optimistic."

Part of that optimism, charter supporters say, stems from the fact that Education Secretary DeVos, a long-time advocate of school choice and charter schools, would be charged with implementing Trump's plan. DeVos, whose Senate confirmation was highly contentious and required Vice President Mike Pence to cast a tie-breaking vote, continues to raise the ire of supporters of traditional schools.[73] After visiting a public school in Washington in February, she made what many called disparaging remarks about the teachers at the school.[74]

DeVos also said she has taken the helm of a federal cabinet agency that she wouldn't mind eliminating. "It would be fine with me if I worked myself out of a job," she said. She added that while the federal government needed to get involved in important educational issues in the past — such as ending school segregation — she said she can't think of any current issues requiring federal intervention.[75]

State Action

Although opponents of charter expansion won victories in Georgia and Massachusetts last fall, proponents of charter schools continue to press their cases in the seven states without charter school laws.

In Kentucky, several bills authorizing charters are pending in the legislature. One, introduced by Rep. John "Bam" Carney, the Republican chair of the Kentucky House Education Committee, has received the most attention. It would allow only local school districts to review and approve charter schools. Other proposed measures would allow a wider variety of organizations to authorize charters.[76]

In Montana, state Rep. Jonathan Windy Boy, a Democrat, has introduced a bill that would allow the state to authorize charter schools. He said charters would provide additional options for students in school districts with poorer schools. However, opposition to charters remains strong in Montana, with Democratic Gov. Steve Bullock and the executive director of the Board of Public Education both expressing skepticism about the legislation.[77]

In North Dakota, legislation is pending in the Senate that calls for a legislative study of charters and other school choice options, to be conducted during the period between legislative sessions. Initially, the measure — which has passed the House — would have allowed the creation of charter schools and educational savings accounts that could be used for private school tuition and home schooling, but that provision was deleted.[78]

Charter school supporters are holding rallies and lobbying public officials in other non-charter states. In Nebraska and Vermont, pro-charter crowds rallied on the state Capitol steps in January as part of School Choice Week, an annual event started in 2011 by supporters of choice. In Nebraska, a group supporting traditional public schools, Nebraska Loves Public Schools, scheduled a counter-campaign the same week that included house parties to view a film supporting traditional schools, a sign of the growing division between those supporting and opposing school choice.[79]

In Washington state, a battle over charter schools is being fought in the courts and the Legislature. In 2015, the state Supreme Court ruled that the funding mechanism for charter schools was unconstitutional because it did not provide for elected oversight. The legislature then passed a new law in 2016 funding the state's eight charter schools through the state lottery. But a coalition of charter opponents, including parents, civic and education groups, sued again, saying the new bill still did not meet constitutional muster.

AT ISSUE

Do charter schools hurt traditional public schools?

YES Lily Eskelsen García
President, National Education Association and Utah Teacher of the Year 1989

Written for *CQ Researcher*, March 2017

NO Nina Rees
President and Ceo, National Alliance for Public Charter Schools

Written for *CQ Researcher*, March 2017

Charter schools have delayed and distracted us from achieving equal access for all students to the same opportunities available to students in our best public schools. Charters dismantle our system of neighborhood public schools and diminish the community's responsibility to fight for all students, turning education into an individual commodity instead of a public good and a civil right. For a century, our system has allowed gross inequities among public schools. What we do for some students, we do not do for all. Charters have only made that problem worse.

Look at the disaster in Michigan — home of unlimited, unregulated and overwhelmingly for-profit charters — and you will see the reality of "school choice" as a magic cure-all. Parents from Detroit came to Washington to speak against the confirmation of Betsy DeVos as Education secretary because they believe charters have devastated their public schools and surrounded them with an illusion of "choice" where none of the options are good.

The fact is, America has the best public schools in the world — but those schools are most often located in affluent communities. Any good reformer would begin with an analysis of what's happening in our best public schools to see if there's something different from what's happening in our struggling schools.

The answer is not a mystery: Resources. Programs. Student supports and services. A good school might have arts programs, a girls' volleyball team, AP courses, a library and a librarian. Wouldn't it be interesting to take an inventory of the programs and services in our best schools and compare that list with what struggling schools have?

I once asked an advocate for charters why we shouldn't give students in poor communities the opportunities that affluent public schools offer. She smiled and said, "Well, that would be nice. But do you know what that would cost to provide?"

Of course we know. Because we provide it for some children. The moral question before us is whether we will provide the same for all children.

This is about more than spending equal dollars; the issue is equity in programs and services to support students. Our most affluent and well-connected parents are able to choose a great, fully resourced neighborhood public school. Why is that the rare choice for parents in poorer communities?

Charter public schools do not hurt traditional public schools. In fact, when school districts and charter schools work together, the presence of charter schools enhances the quality of district schools and the overall public school system.

Nowhere is this clearer than in Washington, D.C., where charter schools have been on the public education landscape for about 20 years. Over that time, D.C. public schools have experienced a renaissance, with rising scores on the National Assessment of Educational Progress at both district and charter schools. Perhaps even more encouraging: Washington has seen enrollment in its public schools increase over the past decade. Parents of all backgrounds no longer feel the need to flee to suburban Maryland or Virginia to give their children access to better schools.

The improvement in D.C.'s schools isn't only because of the presence of charter schools. The city has benefited from a procession of big-thinking mayors and education chancellors who took bold steps to make schools safer and more qualityfocused. But the presence of charter schools also has helped to drive this improvement. As the percentage of D.C. students attending charter schools climbed to nearly half, the district system has found ways to deossify itself and make its own schools better and more appealing to parents.

D.C.'s success is partly due to the almost unparalleled level of cooperation between the city's Public Charter School Board and the district school system. Through combined efforts like annual school quality reports and a common enrollment system, charter and district leaders have improved the quality of education, enhanced equity and reduced discipline rates.

Other cities are working hard to foster cooperation between the public school system and charter schools, with positive results. The Center on Reinventing Public Education found that sustained collaboration between charters and district schools benefits students in both types of school. This may seem obvious. Yet, too many school district leaders and mayors still chafe at the very existence of charter schools. Exhibit A: New York City has some of the nation's best charter schools, but the mayor is intent on preventing more students from gaining access to them.

After 25 years of charter schooling, the evidence shows that charter schools give students and families better options. Nowhere is this greater than in school districts that are willing to see charters as partners rather than adversaries.

On Feb. 17, King County Superior Court Judge John H. Chun ruled against the coalition, saying they had failed to prove their claim that charters were improperly diverting public funds to charter schools. Coalition members say they haven't decided whether to appeal but plan to press the Legislature to fully fund traditional public schools.[80]

NAACP Acts

Charter schools have recorded some of their strongest academic achievements in inner-city neighborhoods with high minority populations, but the NAACP's board of directors has called for a moratorium on charter school expansion until schools strengthen governance and performance.[81]

"This came from the bottom up," Cornell William Brooks, NAACP president, says about the moratorium resolution. "It was generated by the consequences and concerns about charter schools our rank-and-file members had."

Those concerns, Brooks says, include "charter schools that open and close in the twinkling of the eye and in a fraction of the school year," leaving families stranded. The NAACP's concerns also include what Brooks says is a lack of accountability and a focus on high-performing students who are the least expensive to educate.

NAACP members also are worried about the overly punitive disciplinary practices of some charters, Brooks says, and the impact that increased state spending on charter schools will have on traditional public schools.

To solicit input about these concerns, the civil rights group is holding a series of public hearings around the country.[82] Brooks says the association is not calling for a permanent ban on charter expansion but a "reasoned pause" to examine the challenges and consequences of charter expansion.

The NAACP president says it's too early to know what the hearings will find, but, "we absolutely know that something must be done to ensure that charter schools operate as public schools, really responsible for educating all the public and that means not manipulating the system so you get a select few, as opposed to the many."

Virtual Charters

Both sides of the charter school debate share concerns about the performance of online or "virtual" charter schools. About 200 such schools are serving 200,000 elementary, middle and high school students across the country, according to the most recent information available.[83] But various studies have shown that students in online charters are not learning at a rate equal to their peers in either traditional schools or other charters.

"Across all grades and subjects, students in online charter schools perform worse on standardized assessments and are significantly less likely to pass Ohio's test for high school graduation than their peers in traditional charter and traditional public schools," said Andrew McEachin, a policy researcher at the RAND Corp. think tank and one of the authors of a New York University study released in February.[84]

A 2015 CREDO study found even bleaker results: Students attending an online charter school fell behind by 72 days' worth of learning in reading and 180 days in math in a single 180-day school year.[85] In other words, said CREDO director Macke Raymond, when it came to math it was "literally as though the student did not go to school for the entire year."[86]

Charter school advocates acknowledge the problems. Last year the National Alliance for Public Charter Schools and the National Association for Charter School Authorizers issued a joint report on online charters, calling for the closure of poorly performing online charter schools and the establishment of stronger accountability procedures.[87]

"Basically, we challenge [the online charter companies] to create better models because the current ones don't seem to be very effective," says Pendergrass, of the National Alliance for Public Charter Schools.

OUTLOOK
Privatization Push

Some education experts believe the Trump administration, supported by Education Secretary DeVos, could bring the most profound shift in U.S. education policy since compulsory public education began to take hold in the 1850s.

"I expect to see a concerted effort to destroy public education," says New York University's Ravitch. "It will be a push for privatization, and whether it's charters or vouchers, it will be the same thing. . . . We're heading back toward the 19th century before there was public education. People went to church schools; they went to private schools; they were home schooled, and some kids got no education at all. We've had a 200-year battle to try to create a universal public school system, and now that's under assault."

Other charter school critics don't see the future as quite so bleak, but they still expect a dramatic shift of resources away from traditional schools. "I suspect that we're going to see a double-down on private control of schools and finding ways to make schools profit mechanisms for corporations and individuals — so voucher programs and perhaps more for-profit charter schools," says California State University's Vasquez Heilig.

The University of Washington's Au believes the administration's expected retreat from support for traditional public education "means everything will get kicked down to the states. You will have some states with some strong educational systems and some with terrible ones, but no federal watchdog saying you need to take care of stuff like equal treatment for LGBT [lesbian, gay, bisexual and transgender] students or minority students."

In fact, on Feb. 22, the Trump administration announced it was rescinding Obama administration guidelines requiring that transgender students be allowed to use public school bathrooms matching the gender with which they identify, rather than their birth gender. Trump administration officials said the issue is best dealt with at the state and local levels.[88]

Charter advocates see the administration's deemphasis of the federal role as empowering for communities and individual schools. "The school should be the focal point of all efforts. Money should flow to schools. Decision-making should be at schools. Choices of whether or not that's the school for you, parents should make those decisions," says Allen, of the Center for Education Reform.

Rees, of the National Alliance for Public Charter Schools, hopes charter school officials will be "brought to the table" to play a larger role in state education policy. She also wants to see the charter movement, which has been strongest in urban areas, expand to less populated parts of the country. "I think that's been neglected for a long time," she says.

Barth, of the Center for Public Education, believes the number of charters will continue to grow, but increased attention to charter performance by authorizers could slow the movement. That would improve the quality of charters, she says, "but if you're turning down charters at a higher rate, you're not likely to be growing as fast."

Pratt, of the Michigan Education Association, says the wave of public opposition that greeted DeVos' nomination as education secretary "speaks to the fact that people have wised up and are going to push back" on further expansion of charters and school choice.

But charter school supporters believe their movement has plenty of room for growth, despite opposition in some quarters. "When we asked parents what would be their No. 1 choice for a school, one in 10 said a charter school," says Pendergrass, of the National Alliance for Public Charter Schools. "That's nearly twice the percentage [of public school students] currently in a charter school. . . . I definitely don't feel like we're anywhere near saturation."

Looking further ahead, Pendergrass believes the nation has made a long-term shift toward school choice. "We're not going to turn back the clock and start assigning more kids to school," she says. "Support for charters and school choice actually increases as you get younger. It's highest among Millennials. They fully expect that as they go forward they will get to pick a school for their children. We, as a people, always want more choices, rather than less."

NOTES

1. Debra Bruno, "D.C.'s Education in School Reform," *Politico*, July 16, 2015, http://tinyurl.com/pq98dxk.

2. "College Preparatory Curriculum," Thurgood Marshall Academy, 2017, http://tinyurl.com/z9o6hxd.

3. "2015-2016 Renewal Report, Thurgood Marshall Academy Public Charter School," District of Columbia Public Charter School Board, Jan. 27, 2016, p. 3, http://tinyurl.com/zx6e2rk.

4. Anna M. Phillips, Howard Blume and Matt Hamilton, "Federal Agents Raid Los Angeles Charter School Network," *Los Angeles Times*, Jan. 25, 2017, http://tinyurl.com/juoe23r.

5. Anna M. Phillips, "Few School Supplies but a Lavish Party: At Charter School, Teachers Saw a Clash Between Scarcity and Extravagance," *Los Angeles Times*, Jan. 31, 2017, http://tinyurl.com/zd67wte.

6. "A Closer Look at the Charter School Movement: Charter Schools, Students, and Management Organizations 2015-2016," National Alliance for Public Charter Schools, 2016, http://tinyurl.com/j85ztlh.

7. *Ibid.*

8. "Charter School Enrollment," National Center for Education Statistics, April 2016, http://tinyurl.com/hv4bc39. Also see Arianna Prothero, "More States Create Independent Charter-Approval Boards," *Education Week*, Aug. 19, 2014, http://tinyurl.com/z236o9p.

9. "Urban Charter School Study Report on 41 Regions, 2015," Center for Research on Education Outcomes, Stanford University, 2015, p. v, http://tinyurl.com/q5wmh4v.

10. Meagan Batdorff *et al.*, "Buckets of Water Into the Ocean: Non-Public Revenue in Public Charter and Traditional Public Schools," School Choice Demonstration Project, Department of Education Reform, University of Arkansas, June 2015, http://tinyurl.com/gn33bfg. Also see Atila Abdulkadiroglu *et al.*, "Charters Without Lotteries: Testing Takeovers in New Orleans and Boston," National Bureau of Economic Research, December 2014, http://tinyurl.com/zpcxavn.

11. "National Charter School Study 2013," Center for Research on Education Outcomes, Stanford University, 2013, p. 57, http://tinyurl.com/npr5wq6.

12. "Charter School Vulnerabilities to Waste, Fraud, and Abuse," Center for Popular Democracy, May 2016, http://tinyurl.com/zkfk9mf.

13. Bruce Baker and Gary Miron, "The Business of Charter Schooling: Understanding the Policies that Charter Operators Use for Financial Benefit," National Education Policy Center, Colorado University, December 2015, http://tinyurl.com/jnludyq.

14. Abby Jackson, "The Walmart Family Is Teaching Hedge Funds How to Profit From Publicly Funded Schools," *Business Insider*, May 17, 2015, http://tinyurl.com/zh8wdwr.

15. Lauren Camera, "Education Secretary to Charter Schools: Rethink School Discipline," *U.S. News &*

World Report, June 28, 2016, http://tinyurl.com/grg4pvs.

16. Valerie Strauss, "NAACP Ratifies Controversial Resolution for a Moratorium on Charter Schools," *The Washington Post*, Oct. 15, 2016, http://tinyurl.com/grrr5tk.

17. "Charter School Enrollment," National Center for Education Statistics, April 2016, http://tinyurl.com/hv4bc39.

18. "School Choice: What the Research Says," Center for Public Education, National School Boards Association, January 2017, p. 5, http://tinyurl.com/gl4spl4.

19. "Public High School Graduation Rates," National Center for Education Statistics, May 2016, http://tinyurl.com/j6ubcbu.

20. "National Charter School Study 2013," *op. cit.*

21. Patrick O'Donnell, "Ohio's Charter School Performance Is 'Grim' and Needs State Attention, Stanford Researcher Tells the City Club," *The Cleveland Plain Dealer*, Dec. 10, 2014, http://tinyurl.com/hujasey.

22. "Urban Charter School Study 2015," *op. cit.*

23. "CREDO Study Finds Urban Charter Schools Outperform Traditional School Peers," Center for Research on Education Outcomes, Stanford University, March 18, 2015, http://tinyurl.com/zgjlpjy.

24. Kate Taylor, "At a Success Academy Charter School, Singling Out Pupils Who Have 'Got to Go,' " *The New York Times*, Oct. 29, 2015, http://tinyurl.com/z9h7oby.

25. For a list of the seven states without charter school laws, see "Charter Schools — Does the State Have a Charter School Law?" Education Commission of the States, January 2016, http://tinyurl.com/hzldwhy.

26. Baker and Miron, *op. cit.*

27. "Charters, be Transparent," *The Arizona Republic*, Nov. 21, 2012, http://tinyurl.com/gue4sqy.

28. Baker and Miron, *op. cit.*

29. Evie Blad, "Federal Civil Rights Laws Apply Equally to Charter Schools, Guidance Says," *Education Week*, May 14, 2014, http://tinyurl.com/jv6scqt.

30. "Charter Schools — What Rules Are Waived for Charter Schools?" Education Commission of the States, January 2016, http://tinyurl.com/zqxxabm.

31. "Charter Schools: Do Teachers in a Charter School Have to Be Certified?" Education Commission of the States, January 2016, http://tinyurl.com/h9u5to5.

32. Daniel J. Losen *et al.*, "Charter Schools, Civil Rights and School Discipline: A Comprehensive Review," The Civil Rights Project, University of California, Los Angeles, March 31, 2016, http://tinyurl.com/j6k5r82.

33. Kate Taylor, "At Success Academy School, a Stumble in Math and a Teacher's Anger on Video," *The New York Times*, Feb. 12, 2016, http://tinyurl.com/hpm84hq.

34. *Ibid.*

35. Ted Kolderie, "Ray Budde and the Origins of the 'Charter Concept,' " education/evolving, the Center for Policy Studies and Hamline University, June 2005, http://tinyurl.com/h3g4k4n.

36. *Ibid.*

37. Edward Graham, "'A Nation at Risk' Turns 30: Where Did It Take Us?" *NEA Today*, April 25, 2013, http://tinyurl.com/j67vqff.

38. Albert Shanker, "National Press Club Speech," National Press Club, March 31, 1988, http://tinyurl.com/hp9sl7c.

39. *Ibid.*

40. *Ibid.*

41. *Ibid.*

42. Richard D. Kahlenberg and Halley Potter, "Restoring Shanker's Vision for Charter Schools," American Federation of Teachers, 2014, http://tinyurl.com/zvdppjk.

43. Ted Kolderie, "How the Idea of 'Chartering' Schools Came About, What Role Did the Citizen's League Play?" *Minnesota Journal*, 2008, http://tinyurl.com/hxkhzxf.

44. Claudio Sanchez, "From a Single Charter School, a Movement Grows," WSIU National Public Broadcasting, Sept. 2, 2012, http://tinyurl.com/z8m3gnt.

45. "Charter School Law Rankings and Scorecard 2015," Center For Education Reform, 2015, http://tinyurl.com/lerk86m.

46. "President Bill Clinton Honored With Lifetime Achievement Award at National Charter Schools Conference," National Alliance for Public Charter Schools, June 13, 2011, http://tinyurl.com/hutlt2n.

47. William J. Clinton, "Remarks to the American Legion Boys Nation," The American Presidency Project, July 24, 1998, http://tinyurl.com/zbuw8yj.

48. "Charter School Law Rankings and Scorecard 2015," *op. cit.*

49. "U.S. Department of Education Awards $245 Million to Support High-Quality Public Charter Schools," U.S. Department of Education, Sept. 28, 2016, http://tinyurl.com/h4fdk8a. Also see "Charter Schools Program State Educational Agencies (SEA) Grant — Funding Status," U.S. Department of Education, Sept. 26, 2016, http://tinyurl.com/glngrwg.

50. "The Charter School Movement: 25 Years in the Making," *Education Week*, 2016, http://tinyurl.com/gsbqy5x.

51. Reed Karaim, "The New School Beat," *The Children's Beat*, Winter 2004, http://tinyurl.com/gr7lz6o.

52. "The Charter School Movement, 25 Years in the Making," *op. cit.*

53. *Ibid.*, p. 27.

54. Rachel M. Cohen, "When Charters Go Union," *The American Prospect*, June 18, 2015, http://tinyurl.com/hgngy95.

55. "Who Teaches at Charter Schools, and How Do They Differ From Teachers at traditional Public Schools?" *Charter Schools in Perspective*, 2013, http://tinyurl.com/zqfld9h.

56. The Hechinger Report, "Number of U.S. Charter Schools Up 7 Percent, Report Shows," *U.S. News & World Report*, Nov. 3, 2014, http://tinyurl.com/nh8hmcn.

57. Shan Carter *et al.*, "On the Issues: Education, Election Guide 2008," *The New York Times*, May 23, 2012, http://tinyurl.com/zeh9uvx.

58. "A Closer Look at the Charter School Movement," *op. cit.*

59. Howard Blume, "Unions Forge Alliance to Fight Growth of Charter Schools in L.A.," *Los Angeles Times*, Oct. 13, 2015, http://tinyurl.com/j2b32oq.

60. The Eli and Edythe Broad Foundation, 2017, http://tinyurl.com/jnr6w93.

61. Sonali Kohli, "Huntington Park Leaders Vote to Ban New Charter Schools for a Year," *Los Angeles Times*, Oct. 18, 2016, http://tinyurl.com/hpkn2gg.

62. Maureen Magee, "Inside the Fight Against California's Charter Schools," *Los Angeles Times*, Feb. 18, 2016, http://tinyurl.com/z4gdx6u.

63. Shira Schoenburg, "Massachusetts Votes Against Expanding Charter Schools, Saying No to Question 2," *Masslive*, Nov. 8, 2016, http://tinyurl.com/jop5725.

64. "2016 Report Ranks States with the Best and Worst School Systems," *Education World*, Aug. 1, 2016, http://tinyurl.com/zab4rwh.

65. Ty Tagami, "Voters Say 'No' to Opportunity School District," *Atlanta Journal-Constitution*, Nov. 9, 2016, http://tinyurl.com/jam2gb7.

66. "Public Opinion," *Charter Schools in Perspective,* http://tinyurl.com/j3kw7dp.

67. Jake Miller, "Trump to Pitch School Vouchers at Orlando Catholic School," CBS News, March 2, 2017, http://tinyurl.com/jrjmy3s.

68. "Trump to Visit Orlando Private School Today to Promote School Choice," WESH News, March 3, 2017, http://tinyurl.com/hz6cukg.

69. Ben Kasimar, "Trump Pledges to Earmark $20B for School Choice," *The Hill*, Sept. 8, 2016, http://tinyurl.com/j8f49p7.

70. *Ibid.*

71. "Every Student Succeeds Act (ESSA)," U.S. Department of Education, http://tinyurl.com/hdc62y4.

72. "Improving Basic Programs Operated by Local Educational Agencies (Title I, Part A)," U.S. Department of Education, http://tinyurl.com/zgt4ysn.

73. Emma Brown, "With Historic Tiebreaker From Pence, DeVos Confirmed as Education Secretary," *The Washington Post*, Feb. 7, 2017, http://tinyurl.com/gsuj2bd.

74. Yamiche Alcindor, "Rough First Week Gives Betsy DeVos a Glimpse of the Fight Ahead," *The New York Times*, Feb. 19, 2017, http://tinyurl.com/h3vrh8g.

75. *Ibid.*

76. Ryland Barton, "House Education Chair Files New Charter School Bill," WFPL Kentucky Public Radio, Feb. 20, 2017, http://tinyurl.com/gn2r7zq.

77. Michael Siebert and Freddy Monares, "Charter Schools, Non-Discrimination Laws, Wine Define Legislature's Seventh Week," *Bozeman Daily Chronicle*, Feb. 20, 2017, http://tinyurl.com/zrkb4y6.

78. "Bill Actions for HB1382," North Dakota Legislative Branch, 2017, http://tinyurl.com/hhs5pxr.

79. "Parents, Students, and Teachers Across the State Will Be Joined by Governor Scott and Kevin Chavou," *Business Wire*, Jan. 20, 2017, http://tinyurl.com/hbqbg6w. Also see Joe Dejka, "Charter School Debate: Hundreds Rally in Lincoln in Support School Choice," *Omaha World-Herald*, Jan. 28, 2016, http://tinyurl.com/h49pjtg.

80. Paige Cornwell, "King County Judge Rules State's Charter-School Law Is Constitutional," *The Seattle Times*, Feb. 17, 2017, http://tinyurl.com/h9p4vbm.

81. "Statement Regarding the NAACP's Resolution on a Moratorium on Charter Schools," NAACP, Oct. 15, 2016, http://tinyurl.com/ho86knp.

82. "NAACP Task Force to Hold Hearing on Education Quality," NAACP, Dec. 2, 2016, http://tinyurl.com/jdk7eom.

83. Brian Gill *et al.*, "Inside Online Charter Schools," *Mathematica*, Oct. 27, 2015, http://tinyurl.com/hpckr7b.

84. "Students in Ohio's Online Charter Schools Perform Worse Than Peers in Traditional Schools," New York University, Feb. 16, 2017, http://tinyurl.com/j9u6sbg.

85. "Online Charter School Students Falling Behind Their Peers," Center for Research on Education

Outcomes (CREDO), Stanford University, Oct. 27, 2015, http://tinyurl.com/zr5a32m.

86. Benjamin Herold, "Cyber Charters Have 'Overwhelming Negative Impact,' CREDO Study Finds," *Education Week*, Oct. 27, 2017, http://tinyurl.com/zaftmfa.

87. "A Call to Action to Improve the Quality of Fulltime Virtual Charter Schools," National Alliance for Public Charter Schools, June 16, 2016, http://tinyurl.com/jbzjaes.

88. Sandhya Somashekhar, Emma Brown and Moriah Balingit, "Trump Administration Rolls Back Protections for Transgender Students," *The Washington Post*, Feb. 22, 2017, http://tinyurl.com/hh5knjz.

BIBLIOGRAPHY
Selected Sources
Books

Moskowitz, Eva, and Arin Lavinia, *Mission Possible: How the Secrets of the Success Academies Can Work in Any School*, Jossey-Bass, 2012.
The founder and CEO (Moskowitz) of the Success Charter Network in Harlem, N.Y., and her coauthor offer lessons learned at their charter schools that they believe can improve teaching and learning for all students.

Ravitch, Diane, *Reign of Error: The Hoax of the Privatization Movement and the Danger to America's Public Schools*, Knopf, 2013.
A New York University professor and former U.S. assistant secretary of Education says the school charter and privatization movement is an effort to destroy public education, led in part by investors driven by the profit motive.

Russakoff, Dale, *The Prize: Who's in Charge of America's Schools?* Houghton Mifflin Harcourt, 2016.
A veteran journalist examines the challenges that ensued in Newark, N.J., after Republican Gov. Chris Christie and Democratic Mayor Cory Booker — backed by $100 million from Facebook founder Mark Zuckerberg — introduced charter schools and more choice into the Newark school system in 2010.

Wohlstetter, Priscilla, Joanna Smith and Caitlin Farrell, *Choices and Challenges: Charter School Performance in Perspective*, Harvard Education Press, 2013.
Three academic experts on choice in education sift through the main studies on charter school performance to determine how well they are meeting the wide range of goals established for charters across the country.

Articles

Calefati, Jessica, "California Virtual Academies: Is Online Charter School Network Cashing in on Failure?" *The* [San Jose] *Mercury News*, April 16, 2016, http://tinyurl.com/j49237b.
An investigation of a California online charter school operated by K12, one of the nation's largest online charter companies, finds questionable practices required of teachers and a failure of students to learn.

Mead, Sara, "Charters Score in Cities," *U.S. News & World Report*, March 19, 2015, http://tinyurl.com/nmdne9y.
A study by a Stanford University research center shows charter schools are making a difference in urban areas, with students learning significantly more than their peers in the 41 school districts studied.

Smith, Morgan, "When Private Firms Run Schools, Financial Secrecy Is Allowed," *The New York Times*, Dec. 14, 2013, http://tinyurl.com/zghhfx4.
An examination of charter school applications in Texas finds that charter schools are using private management firms to keep much of their financial records private, allowing them to sidestep public records and transparency laws.

Strauss, Valerie, "Separating Fact From Fiction in 21 Claims About Charter Schools," *The Washington Post*, Feb. 28, 2015, http://tinyurl.com/hz6mstv.
Academic experts examine some of the key claims and counterclaims made in the debate over charter schools, including whether they receive more or less money than traditional public schools and whether they are sufficiently accountable and transparent.

Zernike, Kate, "Condemnation of Charter Schools Exposes a Rift Over Black Students," *The New York Times*, Aug. 20, 2016, http://tinyurl.com/j5qrorn.
The National Association for the Advancement of Colored People (NAACP), the civil rights organization, and the Movement for Black Lives, an association of civil rights groups organized by Black Lives Matter, have both

called for a moratorium on charter schools, citing various concerns.

Reports and Studies

"Charter School Vulnerabilities to Waste, Fraud, And Abuse," Center for Popular Democracy, May 2016, http://tinyurl.com/zkfk9mf.
A study by a nonprofit group that promotes equity, opportunity and democracy, finds $203 million in financial fraud, waste, abuse and mismanagement in charter schools in 15 states.

"A Growing Movement: America's Largest Charter School Communities and Their Impact on Student Outcomes," National Alliance for Public Charter Schools, November 2016, http://tinyurl.com/zdusry2.
A report by a national charter school group finds that as enrollment continues to grow, school districts with the most charter schools are producing a disproportionate share of students who test as proficient or above in assessment tests.

"School Choice: What the Research Says, Center for Public Education," National School Boards Association, October 2015, http://tinyurl.com/hlmvwbh.
An examination of independent research on charter schools finds that school choice, including charter schools, works for some students, is worse than traditional public schools for some and often is no better or worse.

Candal, Cara, *Just the Facts: Success, Innovation and Opportunity in Charter Schools*, The Center for Education Reform, 2017, http://tinyurl.com/zffnzka.
A pro-charter school group analyzes negative charges about charters and concludes they are more accountable, more efficient and provide better outcomes than traditional public schools.

For More Information

Center for Education Reform, 1901 L St., N.W., Suite 705, Washington, DC 20036; 202-750-0016; www.edreform.com/home-page/. A charter school advocacy and research group that promotes school choice and innovation.

Center for Public Education, 1680 Duke St., Alexandria, VA 22314; 703-838-6722; www.centerforpubliceducation.org. An initiative of the National School Boards Association that provides research, data and analysis on education issues and engages public support for public schools.

Center for Research on Education Outcomes (CREDO), 434 Galvez Mall, Stanford University, Stanford, CA 94305; 650-725-3431; https://credo.stanford.edu. Regularly assesses charter school performance and compares student achievement at charter schools with that of students in traditional public schools.

National Alliance of Public Charter Schools, 1101 15th St., N.W., Suite 1010, Washington, DC 20005; 202-289-2700; www.publiccharters.org. The leading national nonprofit committed to advancing the public charter school movement.

National Association for the Advancement of Colored People (NAACP), 4805 Mt. Hope Dr., Baltimore, MD 21215; 877-NAACP-98; www.naacp.org. The nation's oldest and largest grassroots civil rights organization; works to ensure equal rights for all, including in education.

National Education Association (NEA), 1201 16th St., N.W., Washington, DC 20036; 202-833-4000; www.nea.org. The nation's largest labor union, with 3 million members working at every level of education, from preschool to university graduate programs.

U.S. Department of Education, Lyndon Baines Johnson Department of Education Building, 400 Maryland Ave., S.W., Washington, DC 20202; 800-872-5327; www.ed.gov. Cabinet-level department responsible for administering and coordinating federal aid to education, collecting data on schools and enforcing federal education laws.

11

Racial Conflict

Peter Katel

Following a hung jury in December, Baltimore police officer William G. Porter, right, here with his lawyer, will be retried on charges stemming from the death of Freddie Gray, 25, last April. Gray died from spinal cord injuries allegedly sustained while he was being transported in a police van after his arrest for carrying a pocket knife. Porter is one of six officers charged in Gray's death.

From *CQ Researcher,*
January 8, 2016

Chicago's Magnificent Mile, a 13-block stretch of upscale shops, sleek office towers and tony hotels, usually buzzes with post-Thanksgiving holiday shopping. But late last year it became a focal point of perhaps the most urgent social issue wracking the nation: relations between whites and minorities, particularly African-Americans.

"Sixteen shots! Thirteen months!" demonstrators shouted as they virtually shut down "Black Friday" commerce in Chicago's main shopping zone. The catalyst was a just-released video showing a Chicago police officer shooting 17-year-old Laquan McDonald 16 times on a city street, killing him. City officials had kept the video under wraps for 13 months until a reporter forced its release through a freedom-of-information request. [1]

Then, one day after Christmas, Chicago police accidentally shot and killed an unarmed grandmother while also fatally shooting an allegedly mentally troubled 19-year-old college student who was reportedly threatening family members with a baseball bat. The Chicago events followed other deadly incidents — in Ferguson, Mo., New York City, North Charleston, S.C., and elsewhere — in which white police officers used deadly force against black suspects, many of them unarmed. Tensions over these deaths ratcheted up again at year's end when a Cleveland grand jury declined to indict a policeman who shot to death 12-year-old Tamir Rice, who had been holding a toy replica of a pistol. What's more, those incidents have followed decades of frustration over large gaps between African-Americans and whites in household wealth, housing, education and employment. [2]

More than 50 years after the official end of segregation and efforts by the Rev. Martin Luther King Jr. and other leaders to protect minorities' civil rights, many activists and some scholars charge that nothing less than institutional racism still grip the nation.

"We still have segregation across America geospatially, with housing practices and banking practices that actually retarded if not prevented integration opportunities," says Maya Rockeymoore, president and CEO of Global Policy Solutions, an advocacy think tank on racial and economic inequality. "And students who have been systematically impoverished are attending impoverished schools in inner-city neighborhoods [and] are never prepared to even qualify to get into higher education. They are victims of structural barriers to opportunity."

Others deny that racism is institutionalized, saying such characterizations are designed to mask the black community's failure to meet the challenges that came after legal discrimination ended in the 1960s. They note that as the nation's first African-American president winds up his second term, a record 48 black lawmakers are serving in Congress and countless more African-Americans preside as big-city mayors, police chiefs and even the U.S. attorney general.[3]

"There is no de jure [legal] segregation in the United States anymore," says Walter E. Williams, an African-American economics professor at George Mason University in Fairfax, Va. "At one time, black Americans did not have the guarantees that everyone else did, but the civil rights struggle is over and won. That does not mean there are not major problems in the black community. When blacks were no more than a generation or more out of slavery, there was greater family stability and there weren't all these problems we see among black folks today."

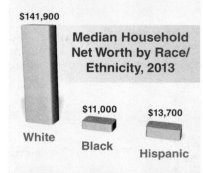

Wealth Gap Divides Whites, Minorities

The median net worth of white households in 2013 was more than 10 times that of Hispanics and nearly 13 times that of blacks, according to the latest federal data.

Median Household Net Worth by Race/ Ethnicity, 2013

$141,900 — White
$11,000 — Black
$13,700 — Hispanic

Source: Rakesh Kochhar and Richard Fry, "Wealth Inequality Has Widened Along Racial, Ethnic Lines Since End of Great Recession," Pew Research Center, Dec. 12, 2014, http://tinyurl.com/kww2vpo.

As the debate continues, a new generation of activists is challenging racial inequities that have lingered long after pundits declared a "post-racial America" following Barack Obama's 2008 election. Police encounters with black citizen are only one impetus for renewed activism. Also key, advocates say, are the socioeconomic differences between black and white Americans:

- The $11,000 median net worth of black households is about 13 times less than the median white household net worth of $141,900.
- African-Americans die 3.6 years earlier, on average, than whites.
- Only 22 percent of African-Americans earn college degrees, compared with 34 percent of whites.
- About one in 12 black men ages 25-54 are in jail or prison, versus one in 60 white men; and
- Black Americans are almost eight times more likely than white Americans to die by homicide.[4]

For the activists, these outcomes show that America has not shaken off a legacy of race-based oppression. "The [1965] Voting Rights Act and desegregation gave [blacks] more access to a still-racist system," says DeRay Mckesson, a Baltimore-based organizer with the Black Lives Matter movement, which emerged in response to widely publicized cellphone videos of police shootings or violent arrests of African-Americans in the past year.

In a year-long investigation of nearly 1,000 fatal shootings by police in the United States in 2015 (as of late December) *The Washington Post* showed stark racial disproportion in the use of deadly force. Although African-American males account for only 6 percent of the U.S. population, they represent 40 percent — or 37 — of the 90 unarmed men shot to death by police, *The*

Post reported. Overall, however, fatal shootings of unarmed black men by white officers accounted for less than 4 percent of such events. *(The Guardian,* a London newspaper, reported its own figure of 1,134 deaths at police hands — including deaths from Taser stun guns and deaths in custody — with African-American 15-to-34-year-old males accounting for 15 percent of the deaths.)[5]

Cellphone, dashboard and other videos, however, do not convey the complexities of America's racial history, many scholars say. They point to what they see as a systematic preference for whites encoded in America's institutional DNA.

Joe R. Feagin, a sociology professor at Texas A&M University, traces the socioeconomic racial divide to centuries of government policies that implicitly or explicitly provided preferential treatment for whites, especially when it came to land grants, government-guaranteed mortgages and college tuition aid — government largesse that has been the foundation of upward mobility for millions of families.

"We white families have had 20 generations to unjustly enrich ourselves," Feagin says. "Even whites who came from working-class backgrounds like mine had access to the marvelous aspects of this country — programs and services."[6]

Many black conservatives, however, reject the notion of present-day institutional racism. "Many times, people use the term when they can't find a racist," Williams says. "A lot of times they can't show you a live, breathing individual or company, so now they call it institutionalized racism." Williams continues, "Next year, I'll be 80 years old. I saw racial discrimination."

Williams blames "the welfare state" for many problems in the black community, saying that government assistance to single mothers "has done what slavery and Jim Crow could not have done: destroy the black family and create a high rate of illegitimacy and family breakdown."

He and other African-American conservatives say that with racial discrimination outlawed for a half-century, ongoing law enforcement issues and poverty in black communities stem from a breakdown of values. "One of the reasons that relations between police and poor blacks are so bad," says Derryck Green, a doctoral candidate at Azusa Pacific University, near Los Angeles, and a member of the

National Leadership Network of Black Conservatives, an online think tank for the African-American political right, "is the number of children who grow up in families without a male authority figure."

Jack Hunter, a white libertarian conservative and the political editor of the online news site *Rare,* says many conservatives "cannot wrap their heads around" discriminatory police practices. "Part of that is a lack of recognition that black Americans do have it worse — something that many conservative Republicans are not willing to accept."

For example, "young white men and black men use marijuana at the same rate," he says. "But young black men are jailed at four times the rate for whites" for marijuana violations.[7]

Some scholars cite historical and economic forces for concentrated black poverty, including deficient schools and a loss of manufacturing jobs that once provided a decent living to people with limited education — leaving criminal activities as a major alternative. "Youth unemployment is not some magical problem that dropped from the sky," Feagin says. "When you suffer discrimination on a large scale, where do you go for a job? The crime economy."

In the view of some liberal academics, think tanks and Democratic presidential candidates, government programs to boost employment, educational opportunities and homeownership for all low-income Americans are among the antidotes to racial inequality. And generations of activists and writers — most recently bestselling African-American author Ta-Nehisi Coates — have proposed preferential programs (or reparations) for victims of past institutional discrimination in the distribution of land, home mortgage guarantees and college tuition grants.[8]

But providing racial preferences in anti-poverty programs is widely seen as politically impossible — and unfair, given that many poor people are white. The standard white American's response to racially based criteria would be, "'My tax dollars shouldn't be used to fix something I'm not responsible for,'" says Leslie Hinkson, a sociology professor at Georgetown University in Washington. Hinkson says most people do not know that "structural racism . . . limits the life chances of people because of their race."

That idea had wide acceptance in the mid-1960s. The landmark civil rights laws enacted then "helped a lot of

Blacks Highest in Police Stops

African-Americans make up less than a third of Chicago's population but represented nearly three-fourths of the people stopped and frisked by Chicago police over a four-month period in 2014. In New York City, where blacks make up less than a fourth of the population, they accounted for more than half of police stops.

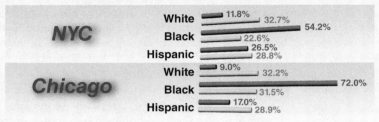

Percentage of Whites, Blacks and Hispanics Stopped and Frisked in Chicago and New York City (from May-August 2014)

NYC
- White: 11.8% / 32.7%
- Black: 54.2% / 22.6%
- Hispanic: 26.5% / 28.8%

Chicago
- White: 9.0% / 32.2%
- Black: 72.0% / 31.5%
- Hispanic: 17.0% / 28.9%

■ Percentage of People Stopped
□ Percentage of Population

Sources: Chicago stop-and-frisk data from ACLU Chicago affiliate, http://tinyurl.com/zpepgmd; New York City stop-and-frisk data from ACLU New York City affiliate, http://tinyurl.com/8vuhkp2; population data from 2014 American Community Survey, U.S. Census Bureau, http://tinyurl.com/o8op597.

black middle-class folks, but didn't do much for the urban black poor," says Michael Javen Fortner, urban studies director at the City University of New York's School of Professional Studies. "Middle-class people could use . . . laws and policies to leave neighborhoods, to get into schools that in the past they couldn't get into."

Paradoxically, the renewed attention to black-white racial tensions comes as the non-Hispanic white majority is becoming a minority.[9] Hispanics have long endured discrimination (reflected in a history of 547 documented lynchings of Mexicans and Mexican-Americans between 1848-1928 in the West and Mid-west), and American Indians have been the targets of military campaigns, mass removals and massacres that modern tribal leaders call genocide.[10]

But the African-American experience occupies a unique place in U.S. life because of slavery's legacy and the fact that the nation's culture is partly a black creation. The Smithsonian National Museum of African American History and Culture, due to open this fall on the National Mall in Washington, is designed to introduce a mass audience to that often-hidden side of the American story.[11]

As activists, scholars and others debate race relations, here are some of the questions being asked:

Would improving police interactions with African-Americans significantly advance race relations in America?

Today's conflicts between police and African-Americans have stirred debate about the larger issue of race in America, just as urban riots in the 1960s — often triggered by confrontations between police and black citizens — led to similar soul-searching.[12]

With cellphone video now ubiquitous, the public is seeing what happens in police-citizen interactions that turn ugly. In the past year alone, videos have shown these, among other incidents:

- a white police officer at a Columbia, S.C., school overturning an allegedly disobedient black student's chair with her in it before handcuffing her;
- a white officer in McKinney, Texas, slamming a black, bikini-clad girl to the ground at a pool party, then drawing his gun on her companions; and
- a white, Charlotte, N.C., officer shooting and killing an unarmed black man after a one-car accident.[13]

Videos, or "the C-Span of the streets," according to Paul Butler, a professor at Georgetown University Law School and a former prosecutor, corroborate "what African-Americans have been saying for years."[14]

Some police chiefs have accepted video as evidence of misconduct. In South Carolina, the North Charleston chief — saying he was "sickened" by the video of a cop shooting an unarmed black to death — fired the officer, who was later charged with murder.[15]

But videos also can be used unfairly against officers, said Bill Johnson, executive director of the National Association of Police Organizations. "Even if we do everything right, if we do it by the law and the investigation shows that we did, we can still just be so dragged through the mud unfairly and inaccurately by community activists, by the media," he said.[16]

Johnson said the omnipresence of videos today makes police reluctant to be "as aggressive as we used to be," something FBI Director James Comey has said might be causing an uptick in crime. But Comey conceded that police can fall into a habit of linking criminal behavior to race. "The two young black men on one side of the street look like so many others the officer has locked up," Comey said in a speech last February. "Two white men on the other side of the street — even in the same clothes — do not."[17]

Despite the outrage generated by videos, some in the Black Lives Matter movement — which emerged after the 2014 police shooting of Michael Brown, 18, in Ferguson, Mo. — say discriminatory law enforcement is not the worst problem facing African-Americans.[18] Schools, health care and other structures and institutions affect people "along the lines of race and class," says Black Lives activist Mckesson, who has coauthored a plan to limit police use of deadly force.[19]

Nevertheless, Mckesson says, the potentially deadly consequences of confrontations with police make changing relations with cops a priority. "The impact of the criminal justice system, because it means jail for people, means the police are violently interacting with your body. That is a loss of freedom and safety right now."

Some black conservatives argue that confrontations between police and African-Americans typically reflect high crime rates and moral decay in black communities. Williams of George Mason cites statistics showing that most homicide victims are black people killed by other African-Americans.[20] From 1980 to 2008, according to FBI data, 93 percent of black homicide victims were killed by other African-Americans. Overall, 28 percent of the FBI's "known offenders" are black, significantly above the black population share, the data show.[21]

"This is not a civil rights problem," Williams says. "It's not the Klan murdering blacks."

But for others, the high crime rates in poor black neighborhoods do not justify discriminatory police action. Rockeymoore of Global Policy Solutions says

Brandon Risher is comforted at the casket of his grandmother, Ethel Lance, 70, who was one of nine victims killed in a mass shooting at historic Emanuel African Methodist Episcopal Church in Charleston, S.C., on June 17, 2015. Dylann Roof, 21, a white supremacist, is accused in the shootings, which occurred during a prayer meeting.

police and others in the criminal justice system often automatically link race with criminality. "You have situations where innocents are being slaughtered or wrongly arrested," she says.

Last October, *The New York Times* — using data from police traffic stops and arrests in Greensboro, N.C. — concluded that African-Americans accounted for 54 percent of drivers pulled over even though they made up only 39 percent of the city's driving-age population. Cars driven by blacks were searched more than twice as often as cars driven by whites, and force was used more frequently with blacks than with whites. Statistics from six other states showed similar results.[22]

Nevertheless, Rockeymoore, who lives in Baltimore — a black-majority city plagued by violence — acknowledges that the high crime rates in poor, African-American neighborhoods mean those neighborhoods need more police. "It's not a function of race, but of class," she says. "When you combine poor people with primary needs and no way to meet those immediate needs outside of what they perceive as criminality, . . . that increases the rate of people wanting and needing police officers."

Lisa L. Miller, a political scientist at Rutgers University in New Brunswick, N.J., who specializes in crime and race, goes further, arguing that the Black

Lives Matter movement's intense focus on policing reinforces fundamental distrust of government, a vision that doesn't match the concerns of people in impoverished minority communities. "My worry about the fixation on state violence is that it reinforces the anti-statist narrative," Miller says. "But we don't need the state to do less; we need it to do more."

Would new laws and government programs reduce institutional racism?

Experts representing all political persuasions agree that the landmark 1954 Supreme Court decision *Brown v. Board of Education* outlawing school segregation, along with three major civil rights laws of the 1960s, were essential to correcting injustices that persisted 100 years after slavery ended.*

But experts are divided over how the government can narrow today's racial gaps in education and employment.

Hillary Clinton, the leading candidate for the Democratic presidential nomination, debated the issue in New Hampshire last summer during a meeting with Black Lives Matter activists.

Clinton acknowledged that a 1994 crime law — endorsed by her husband, President Bill Clinton — brought unintended negative consequences, including a vast increase in imprisonment, especially for African-Americans convicted of drug use.

After candidate Clinton's comments, activist Julius Jones of Worcester, Mass., referring to racism's historical roots, said, "America's first drug [was] free black labor. . . . Until someone . . . speaks that truth to white people in this country so that we can finally take on anti-blackness as a founding problem in this country, I don't believe there's going to be a solution."[23]

Clinton said that approach would accomplish little because too many whites would say, "We get it, we get it, we're going to be nicer." But she added, "That's not enough in my book, that's not how I see politics."

To address racial inequality, Clinton has called for measures intended to fight poverty and reduce income inequality — measures, she says, that would begin to curb disparities in the criminal justice system. Mass

incarceration condemns ex-prisoners and their families to poverty, Clinton said.[24]

But citing persistent housing segregation despite the 1968 Fair Housing Act, which banned racial discrimination in housing, Hinkson of Georgetown says, "Hillary Clinton believes too much in the power of the law to effect substantial change. With laws, you have a possibility of change, but you can't have actual change without having mechanisms in place to ensure that the law is upheld."

Furthermore, she continued, "you also need to effect cultural shifts so that people don't feel, 'You're forcing me to do something. I'm going to find ways around it.'"[25]

Without white acknowledgment of racism, Hinkson argues, the majority white view will continue to be "Sure we understand that racism exists, but we're not willing to have our government do anything to alleviate it because we have this understanding that if I do not overtly discriminate against someone because of their race, then I do not contribute to racism."

Even during slavery times, official, systematic discrimination has led some to argue that the government owes compensation to black victims of government policies. In more recent decades, some activists and politicians have called for "reparations." But even author Coates, among the latest to take up the cause, acknowledges that getting today's lawmakers to agree on a compensation system might be impossible — though, he writes, the debate would be worth it.[26]

Global Policy Solutions, Rockeymoore's organization, proposes a series of government programs aimed at closing the racial wealth gap, including financing infrastructure projects that would provide jobs and subcontracts in the African-American community. But the programs, despite their racial-justice impulse, would be open to all, regardless of color. "I don't think that there has been much political will or public will for racially specific solutions," Rockeymoore says.

Nevertheless, another of the center's proposals calls for reviving the "10-20-30 plan" — a provision of the American Recovery and Reinvestment Act of 2009.[27] The so-called "economic stimulus" poured federal money into food stamps and other aid, as well as infrastructure projects that designated 10 percent of stimulus money toward communities with at least 20 percent of the population living below the poverty line for at least 30 years.

---

*The three laws were the Civil Rights Act of 1964, the Voting Rights act of 1965 and the Fair Housing Act of 1968.

But Green of the National Leadership Network of Black Conservatives, organized by the conservative advocacy group the National Center for Public Policy Research, which supports environmental deregulation, opposes expanding government-funded health care and works to get black conservatives elected, doubts that programs and laws will do much good. "Racism and racial discrimination are a manifestation of sin," he says. "We have to deal with it from a moral perspective."

Green dismisses a major liberal policy proposal — raising the minimum wage nationally to $15 an hour — because, he says, doing so would kill jobs. "Increasing the minimum wage increases the unemployment of black people, whether teens or adults," he says. "If you increased to $15 for entry-level workers, business owners are not going to hire those who need employment the most. . . . [So] how are they going to develop work skills and overcome the socioeconomic differences between black and white?"

Those who favor government activism acknowledge that government programs can hurt some intended beneficiaries. "The ghetto has become a slum," says William Sampson, chair of the public policy studies department at DePaul University in Chicago. "When it was a ghetto, everybody black lived in it; it didn't matter if you were a lawyer or a dentist or on welfare, the folkways and mores were determined by the middle-income folks. Integration allowed them to leave, and they did, which took away the role models and compass of those communities."

Sampson stresses that he doesn't mean ending legal segregation was bad. "But there was a downside," he says. Some of that negative effect could be counteracted by a massive government program to train families in effective child-rearing techniques, he says.

"Kids who do well in school have quiet, orderly, structured home environments," Sampson says, "and are disciplined, with high self-esteem, internally controlled and responsible."

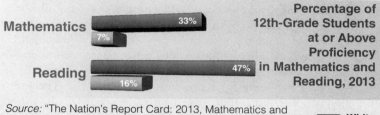

Black Students Lag in Math, Reading

Only 7 percent of black 12th-graders performed at or above proficiency in mathematics in 2013, compared to a third of white students, the latest federal data show. A wider gap existed in reading, with nearly half of white students proficient, compared with only about one-sixth of black students.

Mathematics — 33% / 7%

Reading — 47% / 16%

Percentage of 12th-Grade Students at or Above Proficiency in Mathematics and Reading, 2013

White
Black

Source: "The Nation's Report Card: 2013, Mathematics and Reading: Grade 12," National Assessment of Educational Progress, undated, http://tinyurl.com/mn6snpf.

Does government need to recommit to school desegregation?

Desegregation of public schools, a major victory of the 20th-century civil rights movement, essentially ended after 1991, when the Supreme Court allowed the termination of plans based on busing students to schools outside their neighborhoods to achieve racial balance.[28]

School integration levels began dropping after the decision, in part because blacks and whites remained residentially segregated. But by 1997, even black families who moved to suburbs found public schools there increasingly divided by race.[29]

As a result, according to the Civil Rights Project, a research organization at the University of California, Los Angeles, a statistically typical white student's class of 30 in 2011-2012 had 22 whites, two blacks and four Latinos, while the class of a typical black or Latino student had at least 20 blacks or Latinos and eight whites.[30]

"Black and Latino students tend to be in schools with a substantial majority of poor children," a research report concluded, "but white and Asian students are typically in middle-class schools."[31]

Standardized test results also reflect sharp racial divisions. The most recent report of the National Assessment of Educational Progress shows that in 2013, only 7 percent of black 12th-graders — compared with 33 percent of their white counterparts — were at or above proficiency in math. In reading, 16 percent of black students were proficient, compared with 47 percent of whites.[32]

Some education experts link blacks' poor academic performance to the resegregation of public schools. Sampson of DePaul says schools serving black and Latino students don't get the same level of resources that go to predominantly white schools. "White parents can move" if they are dissatisfied with their children's schools, he says. "Black and Latino parents can't."

George Theoharis, chair of the teaching department at Syracuse University's School of Education and a former Wisconsin school principal, advocates integration. "Certainly, there are other things that matter," he says. "Teaching matters, curriculum matters, leadership matters. But we have disregarded the fact that desegregation really matters. We have enough history in this country of being unable to achieve separate but equal schools."

But rather than pushing for reintegrating public schools, some education experts call for more publicly financed charter schools or more school vouchers, which currently provide subsidies for private-school tuition for low-income and special-needs students in 13 states and Washington, D.C.

Charter schools typically focus on trying to raise academic performance rather than on integration. "Charter schools make no bones" about their focus on academics over race, says Theoharis, who sees charter schools as "part of the whole reform agenda of the past 30 years that has really moved away from desegregation."

Proponents of charter schools, in fact, call those institutions the best way to eliminate academic-performance gaps. Charter schools provide "exciting and viable education in an inclusive, individual manner," said the Center for Education Reform, a leading charter-advocacy organization, citing statistics that show charter students in New York City outperform their public school counterparts.[33]

"In theory, charter schools make some sense," Sampson says. "In practice, they're horrible. They take only the best students. But charter schools on the whole don't outperform public schools." Lotteries that some school districts hold for charter school admissions don't avoid that selection bias, he says, because parents who enter lotteries are by definition more involved in looking for the best schools for their children.

Sampson says having black and white students mix is socially positive for all the students. Georgetown's Hinkson also supports reintegration, pointing out that in her doctoral research at Princeton she found that in the armed forces — often called the most integrated part of America — racial test score gaps at schools for children of military personnel "were smaller there than in any other state in this country."[34]

But Williams of George Mason says, "There is no evidence that in order for black kids to get a high-quality education, we have to capture white kids to sit beside them."

Theoharis says resuming desegregation would be difficult, although "magnet" schools — public schools devoted to one field — could help accomplish more integration, he says, if they were available to all students.

Williams says the need for alternatives is far more urgent than changing schools' racial makeup. He favors school vouchers or tuition tax credits so black parents could have "some kind of alternative to these rotten public schools in many of these neighborhoods."

Green of the National Leadership Network of Black Conservatives argues that public schools should get the kind of scrutiny that Sampson applied to charters. "Some charter schools are going to be terrible and should fail," he says, "and [bad] public schools should fail, too."

BACKGROUND
Slavery and Jim Crow

Today's racial tensions were born in the trans-Atlantic slave trade, which forcibly brought as many as 388,000 Africans to colonial America and the United States between 1619 and 1865, when Congress abolished slavery nationwide by passing the 13th Amendment to the Constitution.[35]

Seventy-eight years earlier, when delegates gathered in Philadelphia in 1787 to write the Constitution, they compromised on slavery in order to keep the South in the Union. Delegates from the North, where several states had banned slavery within their borders years before the constitutional convention convened, wanted to end the trans-Atlantic slave trade. But Southerners refused to accept an immediate ban. The compromise allowed the trade to continue until 1808 and slavery to survive in states where it already existed.[36]

Historians still debate whether the United States was founded as a "slave" nation. Sean Wilentz of Princeton University argued that toleration of regional slavery "did not sanction slavery in national law, as a national institution."[37] But Patrick Rael, of Bowdoin College in Brunswick, Maine, wrote, "If slavery was not legal in every state, it was nonetheless 'national law,' protected and upheld by the Constitution."[38]

The Constitution did contain sections favorable to slave owners, particularly Article 4, Section 2, which held that slaves who escaped to states that had abolished slavery remained slaves and had to be returned to their owners.[39] In 1850 Congress passed a law strengthening slave owners' rights to seize their fugitive "property."[40] Then, in 1857, the Supreme Court ruled in the *Dred Scott* decision that Scott, a slave born in Virginia, did not become free when his master took him temporarily to the free states of Illinois and Wisconsin because he was not a U.S. citizen — nor was any other person of African ancestry.[41]

During the Civil War, President Abraham Lincoln issued the Emancipation Proclamation of 1863, freeing the slaves in Confederate states. In 1865 the 13th Amendment abolishing slavery was ratified, followed three years later by the 14th Amendment, defining anyone born in the United States as a citizen entitled to "equal protection of the laws."[42]

Lincoln's successor, President Andrew Johnson, embarked on Reconstruction, the attempt to establish social and political racial equality in the South. But white resistance won out, with the acquiescence or support of some Northern politicians and judges. The post–Civil War system of white domination became known in the 1890s as Jim Crow. Southern state governments also adopted laws that decreed the arrest of all jobless black people. The penalty was forced labor — essentially, slavery.[43]

In response to white resistance, President Ulysses S. Grant stationed federal troops in nine South Carolina counties.[44] And in 1870 Congress adopted the 15th Amendment, prohibiting states from denying or limiting the right to vote because of "race, color, or previous condition of servitude." Congress followed up with the Enforcement Act, which defined racist violence as a federal crime.[45]

But anti-black violence continued, and in the 1870s, the national political tide shifted against Reconstruction, as Southern white resistance solidified and many Northern politicians proved unwilling to crush the opposition.[46] In 1877, disputed presidential election results led to a Democratic-Republican deal: The Democrats would recognize Republican Rutherford B. Hayes as the winner, and Hayes would pull federal troops out of Louisiana and South Carolina. As a result, white-supremacist politicians' power was cemented throughout the South.[47]

The end of Reconstruction took a deadly toll: Nearly 4,000 blacks were lynched in 12 Southern states between 1887 and 1950, according to the Equal Justice Initiative in Montgomery, Ala.[48]

In several Deep South states — notably Alabama, Florida and Georgia — a forced-labor system was developed in which thousands of black men were worked, often to death, in mines, steel mills and lumber camps. *Slavery by Another Name,* a Pulitzer Prize-winning 2008 book by reporter Douglas A. Blackmon, chronicled how black men were trapped in the labor system by arrests for crimes such as "vagrancy," then "leased" to companies by county sheriffs.[49]

"White Affirmative Action"

After Democrat Franklin D. Roosevelt became president in 1933, his administration's "New Deal" sought to revive the Depression-crippled economy and protect workers' rights through such laws and regulations as the Social Security Act, the Fair Labor Standards Act, the Civilian Conservation Corps, the Works Project Administration and dozens of other efforts.[50]

But whites were the primary beneficiaries, according to historians such as Ira Katznelson of Columbia University, author of the 2005 book *When Affirmative Action Was White.* Maids and farmworkers — the two kinds of jobs disproportionately held by black people — were excluded from laws protecting unionization and establishing minimum wages and work hours as well as coverage under the new Social Security system. Social Security did not cover those two job categories until the 1950s.[51]

Although Roosevelt and many Northern Democrats didn't share Southerners' racial prejudices, the administration accommodated their racial attitudes because FDR needed support from Southern Democrats to pass New Deal measures.[52] The black press argued that African-Americans were paying the price for the New

Deal. Nonetheless, some black commentators did credit FDR and his allies — particularly his wife, Eleanor — with trying to advance racial equality.[53]

After World War II, the GI Bill of Rights — which financed college educations, home mortgages and business ventures — vastly expanded the American middle class.[54] But the bill ensured that Southern black veterans received only minimal benefits — if any. Moreover, blacks were significantly underrepresented in the armed forces during World War II, with only half of military-age African-Americans serving. The military, which remained segregated until 1948, cited poor performance on health, literacy and aptitude tests for many of the rejections, although the all-black 477th Bombardment Group of airmen performed with distinction.[55]

Three years after the GI Bill was enacted, a report on how black vets were faring said it was "as though the GI Bill had been earmarked 'For White Veterans Only.'"[56]

While the South remained the African-American heartland, about 6 million blacks fled Jim Crow to cities in other regions during the "Great Migration" of 1915 to 1970. The politics and culture of Chicago, New York, Detroit, Los Angeles and many other cities soon reflected the effects of this massive population shift.[57]

In some places, the GI Bill was more equitably administered than in the South. But well into the 1960s, federal housing policy effectively blocked black home-ownership — even outside the South — by preventing homes in those areas from qualifying for government-backed mortgages.

"Neighborhoods where black people lived . . . were usually considered ineligible for FHA [Federal Housing Administration] backing," journalist Coates wrote last year, centering his reporting on Chicago. In effect, black people were denied access to mortgages or sometimes forced to rely on extortionate "contract" home purchases, which allowed the sellers to evict families for missing a single payment, leaving the buyers with no equity in the property, Coates reported.[58]

Civil Rights

In the 1950s, the civil rights movement gained fresh momentum, spurred in part by the Supreme Court's 1954 *Brown v. Board of Education* ruling, which called segregated schools inherently unequal.[59]

Then African-Americans and their white allies began a campaign of nonviolent disobedience against state segregation laws, with marches, boycotts and sit-ins that sought to register black voters and end discriminatory practices that, among other things, forced blacks to sit in backs of buses and prevented them from getting served at lunch counters.[60] By the mid-1960s, the movement was challenging racist housing, school and job policies and laws throughout the country.

Within five years of the epic 1963 March on Washington, when 250,000 white and black Americans gathered on the National Mall to demand an end to segregation and job discrimination, Congress had passed the three landmark civil rights laws. They prohibited discrimination in employment, housing, schools and all other public facilities, and mandated that states provide equal access to the polls, with Justice Department prior review — or preclearance — required of any laws that might impede voting in four Deep South states.[*][61]

School desegregation efforts begun after the *Brown v. Board of Education* ruling prompted major resistance, including in the North. In Boston, years of sometimes violent protests followed a federal court order in 1974 that both white and black students be bused to schools outside their neighborhoods in order to achieve racial integration.[62]

The busing order was based on a 1970 Supreme Court decision. But four years after the 1974 court order, the high court blocked lower courts from combining city and suburban school districts as part of desegregation plans.[63] Because housing patterns were often racially defined, neighborhood schools remained largely segregated by race.[64]

While residential patterns changed little, national politics were transformed because of the civil rights movement. Democratic President Lyndon B. Johnson, a Texan proud of his Southern roots, championed civil rights and pushed the landmark legislation through a Democratic-controlled Congress; as a result, his party became identified with the movement, and Republicans successfully appealed to Southern white Democrats to switch political allegiances.[65]

---

*This "preclearance" requirement was later extended to Alaska and Arizona and selected counties and townships in California, New York and Michigan.

C H R O N O L O G Y

1789-1863 *Founders compromise on slavery; issue eventually tears country apart.*

1789 Constitution allows slavery and return of fugitive slaves as "property."

1857 Supreme Court rules in *Dred Scott* case that slaves are not citizens.

1863 In midst of Civil War, President Abraham Lincoln issues Emancipation Proclamation, freeing slaves in 10 Confederate states.

1865-1940 *Civil War ends; racist Jim Crow regime in South survives New Deal labor and welfare laws.*

1865 13th Amendment frees all slaves. As Reconstruction attempts to establish racial equality in the South, ex-Confederate Gen. Nathan Bedford Forrest founds Ku Klux Klan to terrorize black population.

1877 Rutherford B. Hayes is recognized as the winner of presidential election in return for pulling federal troops from the South; Jim Crow system follows.

1915 African-Americans begin their "Great Migration" out of the South; the number eventually reaches 6 million.

1933 Compromises with segregationist Southern Democrats restrict black access to New Deal labor benefits.

1940 The number of African-Americans lynched in the South since 1887 approaches 4,000.

1944-1980 *Anger over obstacles to black access to veterans' benefits helps fuel civil rights movement, which wins landmark legislation.*

1944 Local administrators restrict black access to veterans' education grants and business and mortgage loans.

1954 Supreme Court unanimously rules school segregation unconstitutional in *Brown v. Board of Education.*

1964 Civil Rights Act outlaws job, school and public facilities discrimination.

1965 Voting Rights Act prohibits discriminatory obstructions to voting.

1967 Civil disorders erupt in 160 cities.

1968 National commission studying causes of urban riots concludes the nation is moving toward two "separate and unequal" societies. . . . Civil rights leader Rev. Martin Luther King Jr. is assassinated, sparking urban riots. . . . Congress passes Fair Housing Act, banning racial discrimination in housing. . . . Richard M. Nixon is elected president on promise to restore law and order to cities.

1974 Supreme Court rules against combining urban and suburban school districts to desegregate, dealing a blow to desegregation plans.

1994-Present *Crack epidemic prompts harsher sentencing laws for drug-related crimes, later viewed as impetus to mass incarceration of African-Americans.*

1994 Congress and states pass tough anti-crime bills.

2000 Incarcerated population reaches nearly 2 million, up from 474,000 in 1980, with disproportionally high black imprisonment rate.

2008 Democratic Sen. Barack Obama of Illinois is elected president, leading to hopes that America had overcome its racist past.

2012 A neighborhood watch volunteer kills black teenager Trayvon Martin in Florida, focusing new attention on dangers to black males.

2014 Death of Michael Brown at the hands of police in Missouri sparks Black Lives Matter protests and "All Lives Matter" backlash.

2015 President Obama defends Black Lives Matter slogan and movement. . . . Black Lives activists disrupt Democratic candidates' primary speeches, force changes in their campaigns. . . . Demonstrations at the University of Missouri, Yale and elsewhere raise issues of racial discrimination on campus. . . . Chicago police officer is charged with murder in shooting death of 17-year-old Laquan McDonald. . . . Justice Department opens investigation of Chicago police. . . . Chicago Mayor Rahm Emanuel fires police chief; protesters call for Emanuel's resignation.

"Black Lives Matter" Slogan Praised and Condemned

Backers point to police brutality, but critics say the slogan is anti-cop.

Three words — Black Lives Matter — have sparked a new argument over race in America. Demonstrators chanting and tweeting that slogan have protested the deaths of African-Americans, many of them unarmed, at the hands of police officers — most of them white — in cities across the country in the past two years. As Black Lives Matter activist Melina Abdullah, Pan-African studies chair at California State University in Los Angeles, said on CNN, the slogan first showed up in media reports of demonstrations after the Aug. 9, 2014, shooting death of black teenager Michael Brown by then-Ferguson, Mo., police officer Darren Wilson.[1]

A series of ensuing demonstrations evolved into the Black Lives Matter movement after unarmed black men or boys were killed by police in New York City; Beavercreek, Ohio; North Charleston, S.C.; and Baltimore. Then, a young white supremacist was charged in the shooting deaths of nine parishioners at a historic African-American church in Charleston, S.C., last July.[2]

The slogan reflects reality, says Leslie L. Hinkson, a sociology professor at Georgetown University in Washington. "We're told in so many ways that 'no, your lives don't matter,'" she says, "You don't have good services, your schools are horrible. There are constant reminders."

Some police officials and political conservatives argue, however, that the slogan and movement behind it are anti-cop. Even some sympathizers say the movement is ignoring the fact that most black homicides are perpetrated by African-Americans (as most homicides of whites are white-on-white).[3]

President Obama has defended the slogan, saying the organizers used the phrase "not because . . . they were suggesting nobody else's lives matter. Rather, what they were suggesting was there is a specific problem that is happening in the African-American community that's not happening in other communities. And that is a legitimate issue that we've got to address."[4]

Criticism of the movement, however, grew more heated after a handful of African-Americans were accused of attacking police. Those incidents included the December 2014 killing of two New York City officers and the September 2015 shooting death of Houston Deputy Sheriff Darren Goforth. "Police Lives Matter" was the rallying cry for a memorial march in his honor.[5]

"Black Lives Matter has blood on their hands . . . blue blood on their hands," Fox News host Eric Bolling said in November, accusing the movement of stoking violence against police.[6]

On the political front, the slogan has given Democratic presidential primary candidates some trouble. In June, at a speech to a black church audience in Missouri, Hillary Clinton said, paraphrasing her mother, "All lives matter." After push-back from activists, she was embracing the slogan by July. "This is not just a slogan, this should be a guiding principle," Clinton said in South Carolina. "We have some serious problems with race and justice and systemic racism."[7]

Among Republican primary candidates, the strongest reaction to Black Lives Matter has come from New Jersey Gov. Chris Christie, who accused members of calling for the killing of police officers, apparently a reference to a chant during a Minneapolis demonstration that one activist said was a joke.[8]

But some conservatives back the slogan. Jack Hunter, a libertarian former aide to Republican presidential primary candidate Rand Paul, says Obama had it right. "It's not that all lives don't matter," Hunter says. "Black Lives Matter is saying that there is something specifically wrong with our society, our criminal justice system, and that is a fact. That is what that phrase means."

Still, the movement could trigger a backlash if critics persuade enough non-African-Americans that the slogan means that only black lives matter, and only when black people are killed or injured by police.

Citing the high death-by-homicide rate for African-Americans at the hands of African-Americans, Hinkson of Georgetown asks, "Don't people within the [black] community also need to be reminded that black lives matter?"

John McWhorter, a linguistics professor at Columbia University in New York, agreed. Calling himself sympathetic to the movement, he said the movement should also direct its "fierceness" at preventing the "minority of black men from killing one another all the time."[9]

Filmmaker Spike Lee spoke in even tougher terms. "We as a people can't talk only about Black Lives Matter," he told *Chicago* magazine, "and then not talk about this self-inflicted genocide. . . . Only by talking about both and addressing both can we bring change."[10]

About two weeks after Lee's interview, a 9-year-old Chicago boy, TyShawn Lee, was shot to death in an alley in the city's largely black South Side. Police said the boy was executed because of his father's alleged gang ties; they later charged 27-year-old African-American gang member Corey Morgan with first-degree murder.[11]

Then attention shifted back to police killings after the release of a video showing a Chicago police officer fatally shooting a black 17-year-old, Laquan McDonald, 16 times; protests led to the early December firing of the police chief.[12]

Black Lives activist DeRay Mckesson, organizer of "Campaign Zero," which advocates new restrictions on police use of force and related measures, says Lee and McWhorter are missing the point. "To see people with such exposure and intellect not be able to grasp the fundamental difference between community violence and police violence is nothing short of stunning," he says. "Police are powerful not only because they have guns but because they are allowed to use guns and have protection when they use them. That makes them different from anyone else."[13]

— *Peter Katel*

A demonstrator on the National Mall on Oct.10, 2015, holds a sign that answers critics who see racism in the Black Lives Matter slogan. The Justice or Else! rally was held to commemorate the 20th anniversary of the Million Man March.

[1] "CNN Newsroom," Oct. 2, 2015, Nexis.

[2] Matt Apuzzo, "Dylann Roof, Charleston Shooting Suspect, Is Indicted on Federal Hate Crime Charges," *The New York Times,* July 22, 2015, http://tinyurl.com/qcwlj8b; Sheryl Gay Stolberg, "Trial Set for First of 6 Baltimore Officers Charged in Freddie Gray Case," *The New York Times,* Sept. 29, 2015, http://tinyurl.com/pnfc22m; Al Baker, J. David Goodman and Benjamin Mueller, "Beyond the Chokehold: The Path to Eric Garner's Death," *The New York Times,* June 13, 2015, http://tinyurl.com/nflggzh. For background, see Barbara Mantel, "Far-right Extremism," *CQ Researcher,* Sept. 18, 2015, pp. 769-792.

[3] Amy Sherman, "An Updated Look at Statistics on Black-on-Black Murders," *Politifact Florida,* May 21, 2015, http://tinyurl.com/nmvpj4l.

[4] "Remarks by the President in Arm Chair Discussion on Criminal Justice with Law Enforcement Leaders," the White House, Oct. 22, 2015, http://tinyurl.com/qguv37k.

[5] Radley Balko, "Once again: There Is No 'War on Cops,'" *The Washington Post,* Sept. 10, 2015, http://tinyurl.com/ohbeune; "Community holds

'Police Lives Matter' March in Memory of Slain Deputy," KHOU-TV, *USA Today,* Sept. 12, 2015, http://tinyurl.com/q5lz2ho; Larry Celona *et al.,* "Gunman Executes 2 NYPD Cops in Garner 'Revenge,'" *New York Post,* Dec. 20, 2014, http://tinyurl.com/lgubufb.

[6] "Quentin Tarantino Defends Anti-Cop Comments," Fox News, Nov. 5, 2015, http://tinyurl.com/pzrd7te.

[7] Cameron Joseph, "'Black Lives Matter': Hillary Clinton Addresses Nation's Racial Inequality in Meeting With South Carolina Democrats," *New York Daily News,* July 23, 2015, http://tinyurl.com/otyrq4m; Tamara Keith, "Hillary Clinton's 3-Word Misstep: 'All Lives Matter,'" NPR, June 24, 2015, http://tinyurl.com/nc4ndro.

[8] Quoted in Caitlin Dickson, "Chris Christie Doubles Down on Black Lives Matter Claims," Yahoo News, Oct. 31, 2015, http://tinyurl.com/h4pa59v; "Black Lives Matter Activist: 'Pigs in a Blanket' Chant Was 'More Playful Than Anything,'" *Breitbart,* Sept. 1, 2015, http://tinyurl.com/phsasgl; Rich Zeoli, "Executive Director of the FOP: Comey Wrong About Ferguson Effect," CBS News, Oct. 28, 2015, http://tinyurl.com/hp7r9d3.

[9] "CNN Tonight," CNN, Sept. 29, 2015; John McWhorter, "Black Lives Matter Should Also Take on 'Black-on-Black Crime,'" *The Washington Post,* Oct. 22, 2015, http://tinyurl.com/jjfqpys.

[10] Bryan Smith, "Spike Lee Sounds Off on Chi-Raq, Gun Violence, and Rahm," *Chicago* magazine, Oct. 22, 2015, http://tinyurl.com/zsmlhsv.

[11] Sarah Kaplan, "Chicago Police: Slain 9-Year-Old Was Targeted, Lured Into Alley," *The Washington Post,* Nov. 6, 2015, http://tinyurl.com/hts7spv. See also Jason Keyser, "Charges Filed in Murder of 9-Year-Old Chicago Boy Tyshawn Lee," The Associated Press, *The Huffington Post,* Nov. 29, 2015, http://tinyurl.com/qfm62o6.

[12] "Chicago Mayor Fires Police Chief in Wake of Video Release," The Associated Press, Yahoo! News, Dec. 1, 2015, http://tinyurl.com/j7z7zxx.

[13] "Campaign Zero," undated, http://tinyurl.com/p6vknog.

Race Becomes Big Issue in Upcoming Primaries

Activists demand more action from Democrats.

Race is becoming — again — a headline issue in U.S. life just as the two main political parties are preparing to nominate presidential candidates.

Democratic candidates' speeches have been interrupted by demonstrators demanding more responsiveness on race questions, prompting some changes in how the Hillary Clinton and Bernie Sanders campaigns deal with the issue.

Most members of the larger Republican field have devoted little time to the causes associated with Black Lives Matter — above all, the issue of law enforcement in minority communities.

Nevertheless, the only black candidate from either party is Republican Ben Carson, a retired pediatric neurosurgeon. He had written earlier in his career that blacks and whites received different treatment from the law enforcement system. Now, he is calling the focus on criminal justice a mistake. "I just don't agree that that's where the emphasis needs to be," he said.[1]

The Democratic Party's relations with the black community, forged in the civil rights battles of a half century ago, have not guaranteed an easy ride with the new generation of activists.

Since Democratic front-runner Clinton argued politely with Black Lives Matter activists last summer, she has stepped up her attacks on racial inequities. "Race still plays a significant role in determining who gets ahead in America and who gets left behind," Clinton said in a speech in Atlanta in October. "Racial profiling is wrong." Her campaign website does not single out racial inequality as an issue. But, in her criminal justice proposals she calls for legislation to end racial profiling by federal, state and local law enforcement officials.[2]

Clinton's leading primary opponent, Sen. Sanders of Vermont, a "democratic socialist," had his own tussles with Black Lives Matter activists. He started his campaign by stating that more jobs are the answer to racial injustice. But after activists disrupted some of his speeches, Sanders unveiled a criminal justice policy to address "violence waged against black and brown Americans: physical, political, legal and economic." He advocates "community policing," which promotes closer ties between officers and neighborhood residents; more racial and ethnic diversity on police forces; and aggressive prosecution of lawbreaking police.[3]

Clinton and Sanders' decisions to embrace the activists' cause was good politics, some analysts say. "For Democrats to win the White House in 2016, African-Americans must give 90 to 95 percent of our votes to that party's nominee," wrote Van Jones, the president of two social justice advocacy groups, Dream Corps and Rebuild the Dream, which promote innovative solutions for America's economy. "Given that fact, younger African-Americans rightfully expect each and every Democratic candidate to explicitly, loudly and enthusiastically address the pain and needs of black lives — to their satisfaction."[4]

Donald Trump, the New York real estate developer who has polled highest among the GOP candidates, has a troubled history on racial matters. In July, he reprised his past support of the conspiracy theory — embraced by white supremacists — that President Obama was not U.S.-born.[5]

When Trump opened his presidential campaign in June, he said of Mexican immigrants, "They're bringing drugs, they're bringing crime, they're rapists."[6]

Then in November, Trump defended the punching of a Black Lives Matter protester who disrupted a speech by the candidate in Birmingham, Ala. "Maybe he should have been roughed up because it was absolutely disgusting what he was doing," Trump said after the incident.[7]

Soon after, Trump announced that 100 black ministers and religious leaders would endorse him at a public event. But the event instead became a private meeting with a smaller group, where the beating of the protester was discussed. After the session, Trump got one endorsement, from the Rev. Darrell Scott, a Cleveland-area pastor who had helped organize the event.[8]

Before the meeting, the Rev. Al Sharpton, a prominent black civil rights activist, cited the candidate's recent comments about undocumented Mexican immigrants as a reason not to attend. "I don't know how you preach Jesus, a refugee, on Sunday and then deal with a refugee-basher on Monday," Sharpton said.[9]

Two Republican candidates stand apart from their competitors on racial issues. Sen. Marco Rubio of Florida spoke sympathetically of protests against discriminatory policing. "This is a legitimate issue," he said on Fox News in August. "It is a fact that in the African-American community around this country there has been, for a number of years now, a growing resentment toward the way law enforcement and the criminal justice system interacts with the community."[10]

Sen. Rand Paul of Kentucky, spoke along similar lines. "There's no justification for violence, but there is anger," he said, also on Fox. "I am starting to understand where the anger comes from, and that we need to fix things . . . in our system, because [justice] isn't being meted out fairly."[11]

But one other Republican candidate's statements on racial matters have been characterized by some as insulting or hostile. Former Florida Gov. Jeb Bush, asked during a South Carolina appearance how he would attract black voters, said, "Our message is one of hope and aspiration. It isn't one of division and 'get in line and we'll take care of you with free stuff.'"[12] Bush immediately came under fire for seemingly echoing a conservative view that government aid has sapped African-Americans' initiative.

Statistics on race and party affiliation give Republicans little political incentive to reach out to black voters in primary races. Only 11 percent of the black population "lean" Republican, according to a 2015 study by the Pew Research Center. By contrast, 80 percent of African-Americans lean Democratic.[13]

Nevertheless, candidates from both parties have been invited to two February town hall meetings on race-related issues. DeRay Mckesson, an African-American activist who is helping to organize the sessions, says, "Whoever the next president is will need to engage on a range of issues, including those that don't necessarily align with their viewpoint."

— *Peter Katel*

[1] Quoted in Kelefa Sanneh, "A Wing and a Prayer," *The New Yorker,* Nov. 30, 2015, http://tinyurl.com/pu9vdsh.

[2] Sabrina Siddiqui, "Black Lives Matter Protest Interrupts Clinton Speech on Criminal Justice," *The Guardian,* Oct. 30, 2015, http://tinyurl.com/p8dvba3; "Our Criminal Justice System Is Out of Balance," hillaryclinton.com, undated, http://tinyurl.com/pfneqjb.

[3] "Racial Justice," Bernie 2016, http://tinyurl.com/pp8bfja; Brandon Ellington Patterson, "Black Lives Matter Just Officially Became Part of the Democratic Primary," *Mother Jones,* Oct. 21, 2015, http://tinyurl.com/onc9sjm.

[4] Van Jones, "Disrupting Bernie Sanders and the Democrats: 5 lessons," CNN, Aug. 13, 2015, http://tinyurl.com/ouubgf7.

[5] Meghan Keneally, "Donald Trump's History of Raising Birther Questions About President Obama," ABC News, Sept. 18, 2015, http://tinyurl.com/qdtdlu5; Evan Osnos, "The Fearful and the Frustrated," *The New Yorker,* Aug. 31, 2015, http://tinyurl.com/q4dhgs9.

[6] Adam B. Lerner, "The 10 Best Lines from Donald Trump's Announcement Speech," *Politico,* June 16, 2015, http://tinyurl.com/or9bsht.

[7] Jeremy Diamond, "Trump on Protester: 'Maybe He Should Have Been Roughed Up,'" CNN Politics, Nov. 23, 2015.

[8] Michael Barbaro and John Corrales, "'Love' and Disbelief Follow Donald Trump Meeting With Black Leaders," *The New York Times,* Nov. 30, 2015, http://tinyurl.com/osd7opc.

[9] *Ibid.*

[10] German Lopez, "Marco Rubio Shows Other Republicans How to Respond to Black Lives Matter," *Vox,* Sept. 30, 2015, http://tinyurl.com/otdbvzb.

[11] Katherine Krueger, "Rand Paul: 'Not a Big Fan' of Black Lives Matter, But I Get 'the Anger,'" TPM Livewire, Oct. 23, 2015, http://tinyurl.com/og9j74m.

[12] Sean Sullivan, "Jeb Bush: Win Black Voters With Aspiration, Not 'Free Stuff,'" *The Washington Post,* Sept. 24, 2015, http://tinyurl.com/nbpnpz8.

[13] "A Deep Dive Into Party Affiliation," Pew Research Center, April 7, 2015, http://tinyurl.com/lbed829.

"The more Negroes who register as Democrats in the South, the sooner the Negrophobe whites will quit the Democrats and become Republicans," a strategist for Republican President Richard M. Nixon, elected in 1968, later told *The New York Times*. "That's where the votes are."[66] By the 1980s, Republican presidential candidates were winning an average of 67 percent of the white Southern vote.[67]

A major factor in the anti-civil rights backlash was riots in largely black and poor inner-city districts that erupted in Los Angeles, Newark, Detroit and about 160 other cities in 1967. A report by a commission appointed to investigate the cause of the riots concluded, "Our nation is moving toward two societies, one black, one white — separate and unequal."[68]

Just after the report was issued, more riots broke out, following the April assassination of the Rev. King, the unquestioned leader of the civil rights movement. Within a week, at Johnson's urging, Congress had passed the Fair Housing Act, outlawing housing discrimination based on race, religion, sex or national origin.

But Nixon — elected months later on a "law and order" platform — blocked efforts by Housing and Urban Development Secretary George Romney to use the new law to "affirmatively further" housing integration. Romney considered the nation's segregated housing patterns a "high-income white noose" around black inner cities and saw poverty in black ghettos as a major cause of the 1967 urban riots.[69]

"Equal opportunity for all Americans in education and housing is essential if we are going to keep our nation from being torn apart," Romney wrote at the time, according to a 2014 investigation by the public interest journalism organization Pro Publica. Romney ordered HUD to reject applications for federal water, sewer and highway projects in places that fostered segregated housing.[70] Nixon promptly shut down Romney's program, explaining in a memo, "I am convinced that while legal segregation is totally wrong, . . . forced integration of housing or education is just as wrong." He acknowledged that his decision would leave blacks and whites living apart and attending separate schools.[71]

Economic Shifts

Major economic shifts followed the civil rights victories of the 1960s. Labor-intensive manufacturing, including textile mills in the South, began moving to Asia and Mexico, putting many unskilled blacks out of work. Many well-paying, blue-collar jobs migrated to predominantly white suburbs.[72]

Drugs, already a presence in some black urban areas, provided steady — albeit illegal — work for some individuals in urban neighborhoods. As addiction spread, so did robberies and burglaries committed by addicts, prompting demands for tougher penalties for users and dealers. In 1973, with strong support from some in the black community, New York Gov. Nelson Rockefeller, a Republican, pushed through tough, new anti-drug laws, the first major attempt to deal with the drug scourge by ratcheting up prison sentences.[73]

Urban crime skyrocketed during a crack cocaine boom in the late 1980s: In Washington, D.C., alone, the rate of homicide deaths of black men jumped eightfold between 1985 and 1991.[74] Congress reacted in 1994 by passing the largest anti-crime bill in U.S. history, mandating life imprisonment without parole after three violent or drug-trafficking convictions and providing nearly $10 billion for prisons.[75]

States adopted similar measures, spurring a major increase in the prison population. From 1990 to 2000, the number of inmates in prisons and jails more than quadrupled, from 474,000 to nearly 2 million. As the prison population rose, so did racial disparity. In 1993, the imprisonment rate among blacks was seven times that of whites. By 2000, nearly 10 percent of all black males ages 25-29 were in prison, compared with 1.1 percent of whites in the same age range.[76]

The skyrocketing prison population led Michelle Alexander, an Ohio State University law professor, to dub the U.S. criminal justice system "the new Jim Crow."[77] She was referring to, among other things, police racial profiling and over-focusing on drug enforcement in African-American communities.[78]

In a forerunner of today's police-violence cellphone videos, a civilian in 1991 recorded four Los Angeles police officers repeatedly kicking and striking an unarmed black motorist, Rodney King, after a high-speed car chase. The video, showing King being struck 56 times with metal batons, aroused nationwide outrage, and the officers were charged with assault and use of excessive force. In 1992, however, an all-white jury acquitted three of them and deadlocked on the fourth, setting off five days of riots in predominantly black South Los Angeles. More than 60 people died in the mayhem. A federal grand jury later indicted the officers on charges of violating King's civil rights; two were convicted and went to prison, and two were acquitted.[79]

Fifteen years later, Obama's election aroused hopes the country had moved into a post-racial era, but reality proved otherwise. A long-running effort on the right to challenge Obama's U.S. citizenship — joined by current Republican presidential candidate Donald Trump — was seen by commentator Fareed Zakaria as "shame[ful] coded racism," a view shared by many others.[80]

Then a series of deaths of black people, mostly at police hands (and one, Trayvon Martin, 17, killed by a neighborhood watch volunteer in Sanford, Fla.), propelled racial issues back to the top of the national agenda.

CURRENT SITUATION

Police on Trial

Police officers face criminal charges in the deaths of two young black men in separate incidents in Baltimore and Chicago. The deaths sparked shock across the nation, riots in Baltimore, dismissal of the Chicago police chief and demands that Chicago's mayor resign.

In Baltimore, six police officers face charges in connection with the death of Freddie Gray, 25, arrested for carrying a knife after running from patrol officers on April 12, 2015. A video showed Gray being dragged, groaning, to a police van, where his hands and legs were shackled but he was not secured with a seatbelt. Hospitalized after losing consciousness, he died from spinal cord injuries allegedly sustained in the van.[81]

In December, William G. Porter was the first officer to go on trial on charges of manslaughter, assault and reckless endangerment — all stemming from his failure to secure Gray with a seatbelt. In mid-December, a mistrial was declared after a jury of seven blacks and five whites deadlocked. Prosecutors said they will retry the officer. The van's driver faces second-degree murder charges, while two other officers are accused of manslaughter and two others with second-degree assault.[82]

Porter's defense focused on his testimony that he had asked Gray if he needed a medic and helped him onto a van bench.[83]

Acclaimed author Ta-Nehisi Coates, right, discusses racial issues with sociology professor Bruce Western at Harvard University's John F. Kennedy School of Government on Nov. 11, 2015. A MacArthur fellow and national correspondent for *The Atlantic*, Coates won the 2015 National Book Award for *Between the World and Me*, about the centuries-old legacy of violence inflicted upon African-Americans.

Getty Images/Paul Marotta

The McDonald shooting in Chicago presents an even starker picture of what can happen in interactions between police and residents of poor, tough neighborhoods. The 17-year-old was shot in Chicago's predominantly black South Side on Oct. 20, 2014, by police responding to a call that a man had punctured a car tire with a knife. Police reports at the time depicted McDonald advancing on officer Jason Van Dyke and threatening violence by attempting to get up from the ground after being shot.[84]

But a police car dashcam video, released more than a year later, showed McDonald walking away from police and then spinning around and collapsing as he is hit by the first of Van Dyke's 16 bullets.[85] The video became public after a journalist sued to get it released and only hours after Van Dyke was charged with first-degree murder in the death. He was freed on bail, and in late December pleaded not guilty.[86]

A week later, as protests of police practices grew, Mayor Rahm Emanuel fired police superintendent Garry F. McCarthy, saying he "had become an issue rather than dealing with the issue." Emanuel later apologized for the killing and took responsibility for it. But protesters demanded that he resign.[87]

Pressure on Emanuel increased again after the post-Christmas police killings of a grandmother and college student. The mayor announced "a major overhaul" of use-of-force policies. Every officer assigned to respond to incidents will be required, by June 1, to carry a non-lethal electric stun gun (Taser).

Meanwhile, new revelations have emerged about the department's treatment of African-Americans. The Cook County prosecutor released another long-held video, of a police shooting of Ronald Johnson III, 25, fatally shot in the back a week before the McDonald incident. Another video, from 2012, showed officers using a stun gun against a jail inmate, then dragging him down a hallway by his handcuffed wrists. The prisoner, Philip Coleman, a University of Chicago graduate with a master's degree from the University of Illinois, was suffering from a mental health crisis when he died in custody, according to his family.[88]

Chicago police shot and killed 70 people, most of them black, in a five-year period ending in 2014 — more than any other of the nation's 10 largest cities, *The New York Times* reported. The city's police oversight panel upheld misconduct claims in only two cases out of more than 400 police shootings since 2007. But the city has paid out more than $500 million since 2004 to settle lawsuits or complaints involving police.[89]

In late December, Dean Angelo Sr., president of the Chicago chapter of the Fraternal Order of Police, pointed to the level of violence in some parts of the city, noting that officers seize thousands of guns a year. The department took 6,714 illegal guns off the street as of mid-December, 2015. "That is good policing," he said. "But nobody looks at it that way." Politicians are "throwing us under the bus," he added.[90]

Homicides in Chicago and Baltimore have spiked in recent years. By the end of 2015, Baltimore had suffered 344 homicides, the highest number since 1993, when the city had a population of 100,000 more people. Chicago's homicide number rose by 12.6 percent to 468.[91]

Later, at a meeting of mayors and police chiefs in Washington, Emanuel blamed the rising homicide rate on police second-guessing themselves due to fear of being accused of misconduct. Angelo denied Emanuel's accusation, saying police were "out there working their buns off." But his Baltimore counterpart had said following the Freddie Gray incident that officers were "more afraid of going to jail than getting shot and killed right now."[92]

Campus Revolts

Protests against racism are surging at public and private universities. At the University of Missouri in Columbia, the entire football team, blacks and whites, refused to play unless university President Tim Wolfe quit or was fired. The players were backing black protesters outraged at what they called Wolfe's failure to respond to their concerns over threats and insults against black students. Wolfe resigned in early November, acknowledging his "inaction" in the face of growing unrest. Chancellor R. Bowen Loftin, who supervised the Columbia campus, stepped down as well (but took another job at the university).[93]

Similar protests spread beyond "Mizzou." At Yale, more than 1,000 students marched in early November after several racially tinged incidents, including the alleged exclusion of students of color from a "White Girls Only" fraternity party — denied by Sigma Alpha Epsilon — and a controversy over a student panel's request that students not don racially or ethnically offensive Halloween costumes, such as blackface or feathered headdresses.[94]

Buildings named for former college presidents whose racism is no longer considered acceptable have become a rallying point for many students. At Georgetown, students held a sit-in over plans to rename two buildings after former Georgetown presidents who had organized slave sales in the 19th century. The university canceled the renamings.[95]

At the University of Maryland in College Park, the state Board of Regents acceded to student demands to remove from the football stadium the name of a former university president, Harry C. Byrd, who had opposed admitting black students.[96]

At Princeton, black students objected to the use of U.S. President Woodrow Wilson's name on several university facilities. Wilson, a former Princeton president, purged many African-Americans from the federal civil service during his years in the White House. In November Princeton President Christopher Eisgruber agreed to consider renaming the facilities, among them the Woodrow Wilson School of International Affairs.[97]

Some see name removal as retroactive judgment. "I don't like Woodrow Wilson any more than they do, but we can't impose modern values on historical figures,"

Is Black Lives Matter a valid slogan?

YES
Jack Hunter
Editor, Rare Politics

Written for *CQ Researcher*, January 2016

If I told my fellow allies in the fight against abortion that "unborn lives matter," few would think I was saying that other lives didn't matter. It's hard to imagine abortion opponents even being offended at such an assertion.

They would implicitly understand that I was saying certain lives seem to matter less under our legal system and in our society. If some anti-abortion activists showed poor judgment or even committed violent acts in the name of their cause, few of the like-minded would suggest that this kind of behavior discredited the cause itself.

"Black Lives Matter" makes the same important point.

Overall, it doesn't matter if Black Lives Matter leaders sometimes do questionable things. It doesn't matter if some who champion this slogan sometimes take things to unnecessary and even deplorable extremes.

Those exceptions do not discount certain realities.

Black Lives Matter is an answer to a long-standing societal question: Why are African-Americans targeted and incarcerated at disproportionate rates compared with any other racial group? Why are they more often the victims of police brutality?

And why do more Americans not realize this is happening?

From Ferguson, Mo., and the killing of Michael Brown, to Baltimore, Md., and the death of Freddie Gray, to Charleston, S.C., and the deadly police shooting of Walter Scott, to a Staten Island, N.Y., sidewalk where Eric Garner was choked to death by the police for selling "loose" cigarettes, Americans continue to see incidents, time and again, where black lives do seem to be valued less than others.

Not all of these high-profile incidents are the same. Some are murkier than others, such as in Ferguson. Some are quite clear, such as in Charleston, where a police officer now sits in jail, charged with murder.

But there is a pattern, one that is repeated too often. Many of these incidents that have captured the national imagination and begun important conversations about race have been caught on smartphone cameras.

Smartphone cameras are relatively new, but black Americans are trying to tell us that this type of brutality is not new. These problems did not begin with the advent of smartphones.

What critics like to portray as a movement needlessly stoking racial division is really just an abused minority finally giving voice to the violence they have long faced.

Black Lives Matter is an integral part of the ongoing fight to right unpardonable wrongs.

NO
Derryck Green
Member of Project 21, The National Leadership Network of Black Conservatives

Written for *CQ Researcher*, January 2016

Black Lives Matter is neither a valid slogan nor a legitimate protest movement. The slogan's implication and the movement's emphasis are incongruent; it's an intentional mischaracterization. When one hears the slogan Black Lives Matter, one is led to think of an all-inclusive phrase and social movement that's focused on several pressing issues that have a direct and immediate impact on improving the quality of black lives.

But that's not the intention of the motto. Black Lives Matter isn't all-inclusive. It's very selective, because the only black lives that matter to this protest movement are blacks who were shot and killed by white police officers. Members and supporters continue to propagate the belief, with little evidence, that cops are systematically targeting and unjustly killing black people.

This perspective is thoroughly problematic. First, police shoot more white suspects than black suspects. Second, most of the black suspects who were shot and killed by police in the past year — many of whom were defended by Black Lives Matter — were criminals resisting arrest. Defending black criminals legitimizes and glorifies black criminality. Sanctifying black criminals killed by cops largely comes at the expense of black victims — and the movement's credibility — especially when more serious issues desperately need addressing.

Furthermore, the desire to be singularly identified as people who are targeted only because they're black is to embrace victimization. Black Lives Matter doesn't want any other group intruding on or minimizing its claims of victimhood, which explains the petulant indignation to the phrase "all lives matter." If "all lives matter," blacks' special status as victims is negated and the transparent and dishonest rationale for the existence of this movement is destroyed. The movement uses victimization as leverage for its dishonesty.

The disproportionate focus on the rare, alleged cases of police brutality and shootings intentionally diverts attention from the significant difficulties blacks face. Black women accounted for 37 percent of all abortions in 2012. Black illegitimacy is at 72 percent. Black children are disproportionately trapped in substandard and underperforming schools, preserving the educational gap between black and white students. Black unemployment is twice the national rate. Blacks kill 90 percent of black homicide victims. Don't black lives suffering from these problems matter?

The selective moral outrage that favors black criminals over black lives in general invalidates the social and moral credibility of Black Lives Matter.

said Josh Zuckerman, a Princeton senior and the editor-in-chief of the conservative college magazine, the *Princeton Tory.*[98]

But lawyer Gordon J. Davis of the Venable law firm in New York argued in a *New York Times* op-ed that Wilson's race policies had real and lasting consequences, including for his grandfather, who lost his civil service job. Wilson "ruined the lives of countless talented African-Americans and their families," Davis wrote.[99]

OUTLOOK
Hope and Fear

Those who study race view the near-term future with a mix of hope and fear. For many, the country's demographic shift — already underway — is the key change on the horizon.

By 2060 non-Hispanic whites are expected to decrease from 62 percent of the population to less than 44 percent, as Hispanics come to represent more than one-quarter of the country. African-Americans are expected to be only slightly above their current 13 percent level.[100]

For Texas A&M's Feagin, the demographic transformation and what he sees as stepped-up white hostility toward African-Americans and other nonwhites are "like two trains on the same track headed toward each other," illustrated by what he calls "this dramatic increase in white protectionism to protect our privileges that you see so dramatically in Republican candidates."

Trump's incendiary language about Mexican immigrants is a danger sign for all people of color, Feagin says. "We've had coded language, but to call Mexican immigrants rapists — ordinary working people accused of being rapists — forget all the subtle stuff," he says. "This reflects the levels of white fear of losing privilege and income and wealth."

Yet one view from abroad is that Americans are facing up to their racial issues, in sharp contrast to Western Europe, which has failed to integrate Arab and African immigrants, many of them Muslims who have lived in Europe for three generations. Continuing tensions in Parisian suburbs with big immigrant populations since riots in 2005, and recent anti-immigrant violence in Germany, are only the most obvious signs of the strained relations, aggravated by recent terrorist attacks in France and Belgium.[101]

Damaso Reyes, a black Dominican-American photojournalist from New York now based in Barcelona, says the United States is far more willing than Europe to confront race in its social, political and cultural dimensions. "Black people, white people, brown people are all having conversations about race all the time, in social media, schools and history books," he says. "When a Texas history book says that 'workers' were brought to America from Africa, there is a huge outcry: 'Call slavery, slavery.' To me, that is a positive thing."[102]

For Rockeymoore of Global Policy Solutions, solving institutional racism is the most urgent task facing today's activists. "If we don't address structural racism in this country, within 40 to 50 years we'll look like apartheid South Africa or pre-1950 America in terms of opportunity or lack thereof," she says.

Georgetown's Hinkson doesn't think much is going to change in the next 20 years with regard to deep-seated patterns of racial separation. "The very fact that we haven't been able to say that integrating schools by race and class is the best way to eliminate gaps" in academic performance "tells you that as far as our schools being less segregated 20 years from now, that is not going to happen."

Fortner, of City University of New York, is somewhat more hopeful. "I'm a perpetual optimist when it comes to the American project," he says. However, he adds, he doesn't think improvement will come rapidly, given the polarization and gridlock in the political system.

"Washington is broken. If we find a way out of the current political morass, we could race to a much better future," Fortner says. "But if the system remains so gridlocked, it's going to be a slow walk to progress."

NOTES

1. Quoted in Monica Davey and Mitch Smith, "Anger Over Killing by Police Halts Shopping in Chicago," *The New York Times,* Nov. 27, 2015, http://tinyurl.com/pppahla.

2. "Chicago Mayor Cutting Short Cuba Vacation After Police Shooting," Reuters, *The New York Times,* Dec. 28, 2015, http://tinyurl.com/nhdf5cg; "Prosecutors Defend Urging No Charges in Tamir Rice Shooting," The Associated Press, *The New York Times,* Dec. 30, 2015, http://tinyurl.com/ns9eghq.

3. Maya Rhodan, "Congress Now Has More Black Lawmakers Than Ever Before," *Time,* Jan. 6, 2015, http://tinyurl.com/jqawbw3.

4. Nate Silver, "Black Americans Are Killed at 12 Times the Rate of People in Other Developed Countries," *FiveThirtyEight: Politics,* June 18, 2015, http://tinyurl.com/q6o4n38; Justin Wolfers, David Leonhardt, Kevin Quealy, "1.5 Million Missing Black Men," *The Upshot* blog, *The New York Times,* April 20, 2015, http://tinyurl.com/z7f954b; "Digest of Education Statistics," National Center for Education Statistics, 2014, http://tinyurl.com/qerhs5c; Kenneth D. Kochanek, Elizabeth Arias and Robert N. Anderson, "Leading Causes of Death Contributing to Decrease in Life Expectancy Gap Between Black and White Populations: United States, 1999–2013," U.S. Centers for Disease Control and Prevention, "NCHS Data Brief No 218," November 2015, http://tinyurl.com/jcntjbk; and Rakesh Kochhar and Richard Fry, "Wealth Inequality Has Widened Along Racial, Ethnic Lines Since End of Great Recession," Pew Research Center, Dec. 12, 2014, http://tinyurl.com/kww2vpo.

5. Kimberly Kindy *et al.,* "A Year of Reckoning: Police fatally Shoot Nearly 1,000," *The Washington Post,* Dec. 26, 2015, http://tinyurl.com/zx95ptf; (with updated statistics) http://tinyurl.com/nrsl3xr; Jon Swaine *et al.,* "Young Black Men Killed by US Police at Highest Rate in Year of 1,134 Deaths," *The Guardian,* Dec. 31, 2015, http://tinyurl.com/zc39qv2.

6. Kochhar and Fry, *ibid.*

7. "The War on Marijuana in Black and White," American Civil Liberties Union, June, 2013, p. 49, http://tinyurl.com/jycxybp; David Weigel, "The Avenger Without a Mask," *Slate,* Aug. 5, 2014, http://tinyurl.com/jvc9jkn.

8. Ta-Nehisi Coates, "The Case for Reparations," *The Atlantic,* June 2014, http://tinyurl.com/nopprgt.

9. Sandra L. Colby and Jennifer M. Ortman, "Projections of the Size and Composition of the U.S. Population: 2014 to 2060," U.S. Census Bureau, March 2015, p. 9, http://tinyurl.com/zvobj4q.

10. "National American Indian Holocaust Museum," National Congress of American Indians, Resolution #TUL-13-005, 2013, http://tinyurl.com/j2g4hay; Guenter Lewy, "Were American Indians the Victims of Genocide?" History News Network, September 2004, http://tinyurl.com/nhuz248. William D. Carrigan and Clive Webb, "When Americans Lynched Mexicans," *The New York Times,* Feb. 20, 2015, http://tinyurl.com,/n2yruap.

11. "National Museum of African American History and Culture," *Smithsonian,* updated Oct. 2, 2015, http://tinyurl.com/mrxe8b.

12. "Report of the National Advisory Commission on Civil Disorders, Summary, Chapter 2," Homeland Security Digital Library, 1968, http://tinyurl.com/jzsccqz.

13. Eliott C. McLaughlin, John Murgatroyd and Kevin Conlon, "Charlotte Jury Hears Vastly Different Accounts of Jonathan Ferrell's Death," CNN, Aug. 6, 2015, http://tinyurl.com/gv54r2g; Peter Holley, "New Video Shows Texas Police Officer Pulling Gun on Teenagers at Pool Party," *The Washington Post,* June 8, 2015, http://tinyurl.com/okvksap; Emma Brown, T. Rees Shapiro and Elahe Izadi, "S.C. Sheriff Fires Officer Who Threw Student Across a Classroom," *The Washington Post,* Oct. 28, 2015, http://tinyurl.com/hch2ajo.

14. Quoted in Richard Pérez-Peña and Timothy Williams, "Glare of Video is Shifting Public's View of Police," *The New York Times,* July 30, 2015, http://tinyurl.com/nf57czh.

15. Quoted in Alan Blinder and Marc Santora, "Officer Who Killed Walter Scott Is Fired, and Police Chief Denounces Shooting," *The New York Times,* April 8, 2015, http://tinyurl.com/pow99ay.

16. Quoted in Melanie Eversley and Jessica Estepa, "Across the USA, Videos of Police Killings Spark Protests, Drive Conversation," *USA Today,* Dec. 8, 2015, http://tinyurl.com/grt92oq.

17. James B. Comey, Georgetown University, Washington, D.C., Feb. 12, 2015, http://tinyurl.com/mckgtf4.

18. For background, see Peter Katel, "Race Relations," *CQ Researcher,* "Hot Topic" report, May 20, 2015.

19. "We The Protesters, Campaign Zero," Campaign Zero, http://tinyurl.com/p6vknog.

20. According to the most recent statistics, 51 percent of 12,253 homicide victims in 2013 were African-American: "Crime in the United States, 2013," FBI, undated, http://tinyurl.com/oxo5mhu.

21. "FBI Releases 2013 Crime Statistics From the National Incident-Based Reporting System," FBI press release, Dec. 22, 2014, http://tinyurl.com/optoe5d; Amy Sherman, "An Updated Look at Statistics on Black-on-Black murders," *Politifact Florida,* May 21, 2015, http://tinyurl.com/nmvpj4l.

22. Sharon LaFraniere and Andrew W. Lehren, "The Disproportionate Risks of Driving While Black," *The New York Times,* Oct. 24, 2015, http://tinyurl.com/pj9ukke.

23. "Full Video: Hillary Clinton Meets Black Lives Matter," "The Rachel Maddow Show," Aug. 20, 2015, http://tinyurl.com/pn9s2ex.

24. David McCabe, "Clinton Focuses on Race, Inequality," *The Hill,* April 29, 2015, http://tinyurl.com/pfkw3rb.

25. For background, see Kenneth Jost, "Housing Discrimination," *CQ Researcher,* Nov. 6, 2015, pp. 937-960.

26. Coates, *op. cit.;* Joe R. Feagin, *Racist America: Roots, Current Realities, and Future Reparations* (2014 3rd. ed.), pp. 306-308.

27. "A Policy Agenda for Closing the Racial Wealth Gap," Center for Global Policy Solutions, 2015, http://tinyurl.com/ov256s5.

28. *Board of Education of Oklahoma City Public Schools v. Dowell,* 498 U.S. 239 (1991), http://tinyurl.com/qc73rxq; Linda Greenhouse, "Justices Rule Mandatory Busing May Go, Even If Races Stay Apart," *The New York Times,* Jan. 16, 1991, http://tinyurl.com/nbrlw6d.

29. Peter Applebome, "Schools See Re-emergence Of 'Separate but Equal,'" *The New York Times,* April 8, 1997, http://tinyurl.com/om4gtqc.

30. Gary Orfield *et al.,* "Brown at 60: Great Progress, a Long Retreat and an Uncertain Future," The Civil Rights Project, UCLA, May 15, 2014, p. 12, http://tinyurl.com/n9cok4e; for background, see Reed Karaim, "Race and Education," *CQ Researcher,* Sept. 5, 2014, pp. 721-744.

31. *Ibid.,* p. 2.

32. "The Nation's Report Card: 2013 Mathematics and Reading: Grade 12 Assessment," Nation's Assessment of Educational Progress, undated, http://tinyurl.com/mn6snpf.

33. "Why Charter Schools Work," Center for Education Reform, undated, http://tinyurl.com/qdmokdf.

34. Leslie Hinkson, "Racial Issues in Urban Schools," TEDx Talks, Nov. 24, 2015, http://tinyurl.com/oxjklhx.

35. Hugh Thomas, *The Slave Trade: The Story of the Atlantic Slave Trade: 1440-1870* (1997), pp. 804-805; "The Abolition of the Slave Trade," undated, The Schomburg Center for Research in Black Culture, http://tinyurl.com/osj9pn9.

36. *Ibid.,* Thomas, pp. 501-502.

37. Sean Wilentz, "Constitutionally, Slavery Is No National Institution," *The New York Times*, Sept. 16, 2015, http://tinyurl.com/nb99yrp.

38. Patrick Rael, "Sean Wilentz Is Wrong About the Founders, Slavery, and the Constitution," African American Intellectual History Society, Sept. 29, 2015, http://tinyurl.com/q4oe3jb.

39. James McPherson, *Battle Cry of Freedom: The Civil War Era* (1988), p. 73.

40. *Ibid.,* pp. 78-79.

41. Elizabeth R. Varon, *Disunion! The Coming of the American Civil War, 1789-1859* (2008), pp. 298-304.

42. F. Michael Higginbotham, *Ghosts of Jim Crow: Ending Racism in Post-Racial America* (2013), pp. 64-66.

43. *Ibid.,* p. 64.

44. *Ibid.,* pp. 68-69.

45. Charles Lane, *The Day Freedom Died: The Colfax Massacre, the Supreme Court, and the Betrayal of Reconstruction* (2008), Kindle edition, no page numbers.

46. *Ibid.*

47. *Ibid.*

48. "Lynching in America: Confronting the Legacy of Racial Terror, Report Summary," Equal Justice Initiative, 2015, http://tinyurl.com/pu8gqwd.

49. Douglas Blackmon, *Slavery by Another Name: The Re-Enslavement of Black Americans from the Civil War to World War II* (2008), pp. 395-396.

50. Ira Katznelson, *When Affirmative Action Was White* (2005), pp. 24-52.

51. *Ibid.*, pp. 24-25.

52. *Ibid.*, p. 26.

53. *Ibid.*, p. 29.

54. "History and Timeline," U.S. Department of Veterans Affairs, undated, http://tinyurl.com/mgx7vzu.

55. Katznelson, *op. cit.*, pp. 126, 129. Also see J. Todd Moye, *Freedom Flyers: The Tuskegee Airmen of World War II* (2012).

56. *Ibid.*, Katznelson, p. 115.

57. Isabel Wilkerson, *The Warmth of Other Suns: The Epic Story of America's Great Migration* (2010), pp. 8-11.

58. Coates, *op. cit.*

59. *Brown v. Board of Education of Topeka,* 237 US 483 (1954), http://tinyurl.com/o2cl9o9.

60. Taylor Branch, *Parting the Waters: America in the King Years, 1954-1963* (1988).

61. For background, see Kenneth Jost, "Voting Controversies," *CQ Researcher*, Feb. 21, 2014, pp. 169-192.

62. Bridget Murphy, "Effects of Desegregation Busing Battles Linger in Boston," The Associated Press, in *The Huffington Post*, April 7, 2013, http://tinyurl.com/p6pwxqj.

63. For background, see Kenneth Jost, "Supreme Court Controversies," *CQ Researcher*, Sept. 28, 2012, pp. 813-840.

64. Reed Jordan, "America's Public Schools Remain Highly Segregated," Urban Institute, Aug. 27, 2014, http://tinyurl.com/pp79kye.

65. "President Johnson's Special Message to Congress: The American Promise," LBJ Presidential Library, March 15, 1965, http://tinyurl.com/qaq4l6p.

66. Quoted in James Boyd, "Nixon's Southern Strategy: 'It's All in the Charts,' " *The New York Times Magazine,* May 17, 1970, http://tinyurl.com/nuusnn8.

67. Earl Black and Merle Black, *The Rise of Southern Republicans* (2003), p. 220.

68. "Report of the National Advisory Commission on Civil Disorders," *op. cit.,* "Summary, Introduction."

69. See Nikole Hannah-Jones, "Living Apart: How the Government Betrayed a Landmark Civil Rights Law," *ProPublica*, June 25, 2015, http://tinyurl.com/8jzwt3w.

70. *Ibid.*

71. *Ibid.*

72. Orlando Patterson, with Ethan Fosse, eds., *The Cultural Matrix: Understanding Black Youth* (2015), p. 127.

73. Michael Javen Fortner, *Black Silent Majority: The Rockefeller Drug Laws and the Politics of Punishment* (2015), Kindle edition, no page numbers.

74. For background, see Peter Katel, "Fighting Crime," *CQ Researcher,* Feb. 8, 2008, pp. 121-144.

75. JoAnne O'Bryant, "Crime Control: The Federal Response," Congressional Research Service, updated March 5, 2003, pp. 3-4, http://tinyurl.com/7x9hhdr.

76. "The Punishing Decade: Prison and Jail Estimates at the Millennium," Justice Policy Institute, May 2000, http://tinyurl.com/cp2xa84; Allen J. Beck and Paige M. Harrison, "Prisoners in 2000," *Bureau of Justice Statistics Bulletin,* August 2001, p. 11, http://tinyurl.com/hpucn5l; Allen J. Beck and Darrell K. Gilliard, "Prisoners in 1994," Bureau of Justice Statistics, August 1995, p. 1, http://tinyurl.com/z9s6a4q.

77. Michelle Alexander, *The New Jim Crow: Mass Incarceration in the Age of Colorblindness* (2010).

78. *Ibid.*, pp. 58-88.

79. Lou Cannon, "National Guard Called to Stem Violence After L.A. Officers' Acquittal in Beating," *The Washington Post,* April 30, 1992, http://tinyurl.com/zocva6x; "A Timeline of Events in Rodney King's Life," CNN, June 17, 2012, http://tinyurl.com/zle595t.

80. Ben Smith and Byron Tau, "Birtherism: Where It All Began," *Politico,* April 24, 2011, http://tinyurl.com/qcm7uuq; Ari Melber, "The Nation: Confronting Trump's Coded Racism," *The Nation* (NPR), April 27, 2011, http://tinyurl.com/3qfp93p.

81. "The Latest: Medical Examiner: Gray's Spine was 'Kinked,'" The Associated Press, Dec. 4, 2015, tinyurl.com/1o428x7o; Justin Jouvenal, Lynh Bui and DeNeen L. Brown, "First Trial in Death of Freddie Gray Begins in a City Still on Edge," *The Washington Post,* Nov. 30, 2015, http://tinyurl.com/j38wwhm.

82. Sheryl Gay Stolberg, "Police Officers Charged in Freddie Gray's Death to Be Tried in Baltimore," *The New York Times,* Sept. 10, 2015, http://tinyurl.com/nanbfwv; Justin Jouvenal and Lynh Bui, "New Trial Date Isn't Set for Baltimore Officer Accused in Freddie Gray's Death," *The Washington Post,* Dec. 17, 2015, http://tinyurl.com/hyz9wss.

83. Peter Hermann, "Friends and Neighbors Remember Freddie Gray," *The Washington Post*, April 24, 2015, http://tinyurl.com/mmbvo7p.

84. "Laquan McDonald Police Reports Differ Dramatically From Video," *Chicago Tribune,* Dec. 5, 2015, http://tinyurl.com/nmo4my5; "Crime Trends in Archer Heights," *Chicago Tribune,* Nov. 19-Dec. 19, 2015, http://tinyurl.com/gwnlerx.

85. Jason Meisner, Jeremy Gorner and Steve Schmadeke, "Chicago Releases Dash-Cam Video of Fatal Shooting After Cop Charged With Murder," *Chicago Tribune,* Nov. 24, 2015, http://tinyurl.com/nfhhx98. "Changes to Be Announced in Chicago Police Training, Tasers," The Associated Press, *The New York Times,* Dec. 30, 2015, http://tinyurl.com/oqgh2d3.

86. Ashley Southall, "Reporter Who Forced Release of Laquan McDonald Video Is Barred From News Event," *The New York Times,* Nov. 25, 2015, http://tinyurl.com/q6gl2g2.

87. Rick Pearson, Bill Ruthhart and John Byrne, "Emanuel Recall Bill, Council Hearing, Show Political Flank-Covering in McDonald Case," *Chicago Tribune,* Dec. 16, 2015, http://tinyurl.com/joe2523; Amber Phillips, "Rahm Emanuel Is in Deep, Deep Trouble," *The Washington Post,* Dec. 10, 2015, http://tinyurl.com/nhg5kos.

88. Don Babwin, "1 After Another, Chicago Police Videos Made Public," The Associated Press, Dec. 10, 2015, http://tinyurl.com/nlhs8em.

89. Monica Davey and Timothy Williams, "Chicago Pays Millions but Punishes Few in Killings by Police," *The New York Times,* Dec. 17, 2015, http://tinyurl.com/ot78klo.

90. Quoted in *ibid.,* "Changes to Be Announced in Chicago Police Training, Tasers."

91. "Josh Sanburn, "Chicago Shootings and Murders Surged in 2015," *Time,* Jan. 2, 2016, http://tinyurl.com/os3q9ay; Kevin Rector, "Deadliest Year in Baltimore History Ends With 344 Homicides," *The Baltimore Sun,* Jan. 1, 2016, http://tinyurl.com/z9dxs5s.

92. Quoted in John Byrne, "Emanuel Blames Chicago Crime Uptick on Officers Second-Guessing Themselves," *Chicago Tribune,* Oct. 13, 2015, http://tinyurl.com/ofxw9wp; Josh Sanburn, "What's Behind Baltimore's Record-Setting Rise in Homicides," *Time,* June 2, 2015, http://tinyurl.com/ngdg4pw.

93. Susan Svrluga, "U. Missouri President, Chancellor Resign Over Handling of Racial Incidents," *The Washington Post,* Nov. 9, 2015, http://tinyurl.com/jv6p7kp.

94. Avianne Tan, "The Allegations of Racism at Yale That Culminated in Over 1,000 Marching for Justice on Campus," ABC News, Nov. 10, 2015, http://tinyurl.com/pkcn35y. Liam Stack, "Yale's Halloween Advice Stokes a Racially Charged Debate," *The New York Times,* Nov. 8, 2015, http://tinyurl.com/oxu7y3o.

95. Katherine Shaver, "Georgetown University to Rename Two Buildings That Reflect School's Ties to Slavery," *The Washington Post,* Nov 15, 2015, http://tinyurl.com/jsj3pdq.

96. Yvonne Wenger, "Byrd Stadium to Become Maryland Stadium After Regents Vote," *The Baltimore Sun,* Dec. 11, 2015, http://tinyurl.com/zapmvgb.

97. Mary Hui, "After Protests, Princeton Debates Woodrow Wilson's Legacy," *The Washington Post,*

Nov, 23, 2015, http://tinyurl.com/hplwgqs; William Keylor, "The Long-Forgotten Racial Attitudes and Policies of Woodrow Wilson," *Professor Voices,* Boston University, March 4, 2013, http://tinyurl.com/nas8ok9.

98. Quoted in Hui, *op. cit.*

99. Gordon J. Davis, "What Woodrow Wilson Cost My Grandfather," *The New York Times,* Nov. 24, 2015, http://tinyurl.com/p36bvol.

100. Colby and Ortman, *op. cit.*

101. Angelique Chrisafis, "'Nothing's Changed': 10 Years After French Riots, Banlieues Remain in Crisis," *The Guardian,* Oct. 22, 2015, http://tinyurl.com/ngd7rerj; Alison Smale, "Anti-Immigrant Violence in Germany Spurs New Debate on Hate Speech," *The New York Times,* Oct. 21, 2015, http://tinyurl.com/oxu7y3o.

102. Manny Fernandez and Christine Hauser, "Texas Mother Teaches Textbook Company a Lesson on Accuracy," *The New York Times,* Oct. 5, 2015, http://tinyurl.com/pwpe3oe.

BIBLIOGRAPHY

Selected Sources

Books

Alexander, Michelle, *The New Jim Crow: Mass Incarceration in the Age of Colorblindness,* **The New Press, 2010.**
An Ohio State University law professor's book helped spur efforts to change the nation's criminal justice system.

Coates, Ta-Nehisi, *Between the World and Me,* **Spiegel & Grau, 2015.**
A journalist's brief but searing memoir-essay explores life as a black man in today's America.

Feagin, Joe R., *Racist America: Roots, Current Realities, and Future Reparations,* **Routledge, 2014.**
A Texas A&M sociologist specializing in race, describes government policies that implicitly or explicitly provided preferential treatment for whites.

Fortner, Michael Javen, *Black Silent Majority: The Rockefeller Drug Laws and the Politics of Punishment,* **Harvard University Press, 2015.**
Examining the impact of the country's first drug-crack-down laws, a City University of New York professor of urban studies analyzes anti-crime sentiment in the African-American community.

Oliver, Melvin L., and Thomas M. Shapiro, *Black Wealth/White Wealth: A New Perspective on Racial Inequality,* **Routledge Taylor & Francis, 2006.**
Sociologists from the University of California, Santa Barbara, and Brandeis University, respectively, updated a 1995 book that drew attention to how profoundly discriminatory practices have affected black asset-building.

Riley, Jason L., *Please Stop Helping Us: How Liberals Make It Harder for Blacks to Succeed,* **Encounter Books, 2014.**
A senior fellow at the center-right Manhattan Institute sums up the black conservative vision: Personal choices and a culture of "victimhood" — rather than historical and economic forces — explain conditions in poor African-American neighborhoods.

Articles

Domenech, Ben, "Are Republicans for Freedom or White Identity Politics?" *The Federalist,* **Aug. 21, 2015, http://tinyurl.com/nny5h66.**
The publisher of a conservative magazine worries that Republican presidential candidate Donald Trump's focus on white grievances could push his party into European-style semi-fascist populism.

Mckesson, DeRay, "Reflections on Meeting With Senator Bernie Sanders and Secretary Hillary Clinton, and the #DemDebate," *Medium,* **Oct. 15, 2015, http://tinyurl.com/o5tumj4.**
A leading activist reports on how top Democratic candidates greeted proposals from members of the Black Lives Matter protest movement.

Rutenberg, Jim, "A Dream Undone," *The New York Times Magazine,* **July 29, 2015, http://tinyurl.com/p8hmfdt.**
A veteran correspondent chronicles a long campaign to weaken the 1965 Voting Rights Act based on the argument that discriminatory conditions have changed in the South.

Smith, Jamil, "BlackLivesMatter Protesters Are Not the Problem," *The New Republic,* **Aug. 10, 2015, http://tinyurl.com/p5b473e.**
An editor at a liberal magazine argues that activists are justified in confronting friendly presidential candidates on racial justice issues.

Walk-Morris, Tatiana, "Blacks Are Challenged to Buy From Black-Owned Businesses to Close Gap," *The New York Times,* **Nov. 15, 2015, http://tinyurl.com/ pmasdk3.**
A Chicago lawyer bought only from black-owned businesses for one year, prompting an examination of the effectiveness of grassroots efforts to close the black-white wealth gap.

Williams, Vanessa, "For Clinton, a Challenge to Keep Black Voters Energized About Her Campaign," *The Washington Post,* **Nov. 1, 2015, http://tinyurl.com/ oxaxqbu.**
A political reporter chronicles the Democratic front-runner's efforts to maintain support of a vital part of the party's constituency.

Reports and Studies

Azerrad, David, and Rea S. Hederman Jr., "Defending the Dream: Why Income Inequality Doesn't Threaten Opportunity," Heritage Foundation, Sept. 13, 2012, http://tinyurl.com/d28ppb7.
Two staff members of a conservative think tank conclude that the high rate of single-parent households among African-Americans explains the black-white wealth gap.

Orfield, Gary, *et al.,* **"Brown at 60: Great Progress, a Long Retreat and an Uncertain Future," The Civil Rights Project, University of California, Los Angeles, May 15, 2014, http://tinyurl.com/q8v3t6b.**
Four education scholars conclude that public schools increasingly are segregated by race and class, even though legally mandated segregation has disappeared.

Traub, Amy, and Catherine Ruetschlin, "The Racial Wealth Gap: Why Policy Matters," *Demos,* **March 10, 2015, http://tinyurl.com/mxltzn5.**
A liberal think tank analyzes government policies that contribute to the wealth gap and others that could narrow the divide.

For More Information

ACLU, 125 Broad St., New York, NY 10004; 212-549-2500; www.adu.org/issues/racial-justice. Litigates on a variety of race-related issues, including discrimination in school discipline and racial profiling by police.

Campaign Zero, www.joincampaignzero.org/#vision. An outgrowth of the Black Lives Matter movement; has proposed ways to help curb police use of force.

Global Policy Solutions, 1300 L St., N.W., Washington, DC 20005; 202-265-5111; http://globalpolicysolutions .com. A research and advocacy organization that focuses on equality of economic opportunity, including racial equity.

Project 21, National Leadership Network of Black Conservatives, www.national center.org/P21Index.html.
Provides an outlet for commentary by African-Americans of the political right on topics such as affirmative action and immigration.

Scholars Network on Black Masculinity, University of Michigan, Department of Sociology, 500 South State St., Ann Arbor, MI 48109; 734-647-4444; http://thescholars network.org/index.html. Studies how to improve life possibilities for black men.

The Sentencing Project, 1705 DeSales St., N.W., Washington, DC 20036; 202-628-0871; www.sentencing project.org. A criminal justice reform advocacy think tank.

12

Free Speech on Campus

Sarah Glazer

University of Oklahoma students stage a protest on March 9, 2015, the day after a video surfaced online showing members of the local Sigma Alpha Epsilon fraternity singing racist lyrics. Oklahoma President David L. Boren swiftly shut down the fraternity, expelled two students for leading the song and later disciplined 25 others. Civil libertarians and legal experts on both the right and left argue the lyrics were protected under the First Amendment. The incident helped spark a nationwide debate on how far college officials can go in regulating controversial speech.

From *CQ Researcher,*
May 8, 2015

When a racist and misogynistic email from a University of Maryland fraternity member surfaced on the College Park campus in March, university President Wallace D. Loh found himself in a bind.

The email told fellow fraternity brothers seeking sex with young women to "f— consent" and instructed them not to "invite n----- gals or curry monsters or slanted eyed chicks, unless they're hot."[1]

As the campus erupted in anger, Loh said the email expressed views "reprehensible to our campus community."[2] But he confessed to being torn between regarding the email as hate speech that should be suppressed and statements that — no matter how vile — are protected under the First Amendment to the Constitution.

"It is one of our nation's core values that the government should not be able to tell us what we can and cannot say," Loh tweeted. "Protecting speech, however, does not mean agreeing with it. And quite honestly, I am struggling with justifying this email as speech. Where do free speech and hate speech collide? What should prevail? What justification can we have that tacitly condones this kind of hate?"[3]

A university investigation decided that question for Loh on April 1 when it found that the email merited First Amendment protection.[4]

To legal experts, the implication of the university's conclusion was clear: Expelling the student who wrote the email could have been ruled a violation of the student's constitutional right to free expression if the issue came to court. Instead, Loh announced that, by mutual consent, the student would not return to campus that semester.[5]

Group: Most Colleges Suppress Speech

More than half of U.S. colleges and universities in 2014 had speech codes that "clearly and substantially" violated students' and teachers' First Amendment rights, according to the Foundation for Individual Rights in Education (FIRE), a civil liberties advocacy group.

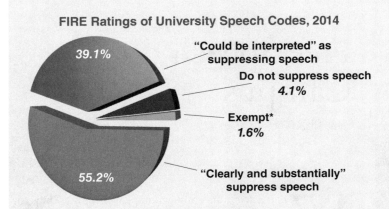

FIRE Ratings of University Speech Codes, 2014

39.1% — "Could be interpreted" as suppressing speech

Do not suppress speech 4.1%

Exempt* 1.6%

55.2% — "Clearly and substantially" suppress speech

* Private universities that say they prioritize certain values above commitment to freedom of speech

Source: "Spotlight on Speech Codes 2015," Foundation for Individual Rights in Education, Dec. 12, 2014, http://tinyurl.com/o6xlps6.

The Maryland email appeared the same week that a media storm broke over University of Oklahoma fraternity members filmed singing a racist song about refusing admission to blacks, including lyrics that seemed to condone lynching. "You can hang him from a tree, but he can never sign with me," chanted the members, whose singing on a bus taking them to a black-tie fraternity event was captured on cell-phone video and released on the Internet. Oklahoma's president, David L. Boren, swiftly expelled two students who led the singing and later disciplined 25 others. A subsequent university investigation discovered the fraternity members had learned the song four years ago on a fraternity leadership cruise, signaling a long-standing pattern of racial exclusion in the fraternity.[6]

Many educators praised Boren's action, but civil libertarians and legal experts on both the right and left criticized it on grounds that the song was protected under the First Amendment. If the expelled students were to sue the university for violating their free-speech rights, they would probably win, according to most legal experts queried by *The New York Times.*[7]

The two incidents have helped place in stark relief a much broader debate about free speech at public colleges and universities: When it comes to inappropriate speech, where does one draw the line?

In recent decades, colleges have tried to restrict racist, sexist or otherwise offensive speech by issuing written student codes of conduct, computer codes of conduct and other policies. Many of these prohibitions are required by federal law guaranteeing equal rights on the basis of gender and race. University administrators say they are simply following the law and trying to protect students from genuine harassment.

However, civil liberties groups have attacked many of these policies as unconstitutional "speech codes" that prohibit and penalize even the most minor offensive remarks or jokes, and violate students' and teachers' First Amendment rights. Speech codes at more than half of U.S. campuses violate the amendment, according to the Foundation for Individual Rights in Education (FIRE), a civil liberties advocacy group and nonprofit foundation in Philadelphia funded by private donors and organizations from "across the political spectrum," according to a FIRE spokesperson.

Complicating the discussion is the fact that while public universities and colleges comprise more than 80 percent of the nation's higher education student body, about 16 percent attend private institutions, which are not bound by the First Amendment.*[8]

---

*As tax-supported institutions, public universities are legally considered extensions of the government and therefore bound by the First Amendment's restrictions on government interference with freedom of speech. By contrast, private colleges and universities, which are not "state actors," are not strictly bound by the First Amendment. However, because most private universities also accept government funds, they must abide by federal anti-discrimination laws.

The recent incidents have escalated the controversy. Some educators and college administrators argue that it's more important to send a strong signal, through disciplinary measures, that certain kinds of speech — especially if racist or sexist — won't be tolerated on campus. And often the students themselves are pushing for even stronger measures against sexually harassing or emotionally disturbing speech.

Yet some administrators say it's unclear whether the recent incidents are constitutionally protected from university discipline. Both the Oklahoma and Maryland students' words "could be perceived as a direct threat," and threats are not protected by the First Amendment, says Kevin Kruger, president of Student Affairs Administrators in Higher Education (NASPA), an association in Washington, D.C., that represents 13,000 administrators. The Oklahoma song could be viewed as condoning lynching, and the Maryland email could be interpreted as advocating sexual assault, Kruger says.

But the legal status is "cloudy," he acknowledges. "There may not be a clear-cut case here, so it may take the courts to decide what is a direct threat and what is protected speech."

On a similar front, a small but growing movement is demanding that professors give students "trigger warnings" about curriculum material that might traumatize them and provide "safe spaces" free of trauma-inducing speech. Critics say these trends are signs that colleges are becoming overly protective of students.[9]

Freedom of expression concerns also have been raised about American universities that accept financial support from autocratic governments. Critics say such

Conflicts About Speech Are Widespread

Speech-related incidents at U.S. colleges have led to punishment ranging from student expulsions to revocation of faculty tenure.

Institution	Description
U of Maryland, 2015	University declines to suspend student after investigating racist, misogynistic email sent by student to fraternity brothers
Duke, 2015	School says student who admitted hanging a noose on a campus tree was disciplined but can return next semester
Bucknell, 2015	School expels three students who used racial slurs against African-Americans in campus radio broadcast
U of Oklahoma, 2015	University expels two students and disciplines 25 filmed singing racist chant, closes fraternity chapter
Marquette, 2015	Administrators notify professor of plans to revoke his tenure over blog post in which he claimed a student's opposition to same-sex marriage was suppressed by another teacher.
California State, Fullerton, 2014	University sanctions sorority for practicing "indecent" and "obscene" conduct after it hosts Mexican-themed recruitment event
Ohio U, 2014	Student sues after administrators ban sexually suggestive T-shirt; university agrees to revise student conduct code and pay legal fees in 2015 settlement
U of Kansas, 2013	Administrators suspend tenured journalism professor after he tweets anti-gun message
Modesto Junior College, 2013	Student sues college for preventing him from distributing copies of the Constitution outside "free speech zone;" college later agrees in settlement to pay $50,000, abolish zone

Source: Greg Lukianoff, "Free Speech on Campus: The 10 Worst Offenders of 2014," *The Huffington Post*, March 2, 2015, http://tinyurl.com/nqs7lnm; other news sources.

arrangements inevitably result in censorship of topics that offend the donor countries.

For instance, New York University's new satellite campus in Abu Dhabi, built with funding from the United Arab Emirates (UAE), came under press scrutiny in March when an NYU professor critical of UAE labor conditions was barred from entering the country.

"The lack of respect for freedom of speech permeates the whole enterprise," said Marjorie Heins, a former NYU adjunct professor who serves on the academic freedom and tenure committee of the American Association of University Professors (AAUP).[10]

At the time of the incident, NYU spokesman John Beckman said the university supported "the free movement of people and ideas" but that the UAE government "controls visa and immigration policy."[11]

Additionally, Rep. Chris Smith, R-N.J., has questioned whether academic freedom is threatened on American campuses that receive money from the Chinese government. Approximately 100 colleges in the United States house Chinese language and cultural institutes, known as Confucius Institutes, funded in part by China, which also provides teachers. In addition, some American universities are setting up satellite campuses in China as joint ventures with Chinese educational institutions.

"Is American higher education for sale?" Smith asked at a House Foreign Affairs subcommittee hearing in December. "And, if so, are U.S. colleges and universities undermining the principle of academic freedom — and, in the process, their credibility — in exchange for China's education dollars?"[12]

Confucius Institute teachers are trained in China to discourage discussion of controversial issues, such as Tibetan independence or the 1989 Tiananmen Square massacre, and to paint a rosy picture of China, charges Marshall Sahlins, a professor emeritus of anthropology at the University of Chicago who has written a book on the institutes.[13]

American universities that accept funding from Hanban, the Chinese government agency that controls the institutes, "have become dependent branches of policymaking that starts at the highest reaches of the Chinese [Communist] Party state and runs through the Confucius Institutes," says Sahlins. "It seems incredible to me that we would subcontract teaching and give research control to this operation. That's a violation of academic freedom, integrity and anything a university is based on."

Defenders of the institutes say they provide much-needed Chinese language training that American universities can't afford and that such exchanges are important for international understanding — for both Chinese and Americans. And part of that means accepting the reality that China is an authoritarian state.

Edward A. McCord, a professor in modern Chinese history at George Washington University (GWU), in Washington, D.C., says his university, which has a Confucius Institute, retains control over the political content taught at GWU but is willing to accept language teachers trained by Hanban. "We would have to cut off relations if we want no Chinese control or can't accept any Chinese scholars or students because they might be monitored" by the Chinese government, he says. "Can we live with that?"

As students, faculty and government officials debate campus free-speech policies, here are some of the questions being debated:

Should university conduct codes ban offensive speech?

In the fall of 2013, Ohio University junior Isaac Smith wore a T-shirt to a campus activities fair advertising an organization that helps students at disciplinary proceedings. The shirt bore the student group's slogan, a play on words meant to be humorous: "We get you off for free."

A dean from the Athens, Ohio, institution was not amused, however. Administration officials later told Smith the shirt "objectified women" and encouraged prostitution, and ordered him to stop wearing it, according to a legal complaint filed by Smith against the university. Smith says he obeyed for fear of punishment under the university's code of student conduct.[14]

Smith sued the publicly owned university, claiming violation of his constitutional right to free expression. In court, the university denied that its administrators had made the comments cited by Smith about the shirt's sexual innuendo or that it had forbidden the organization's members from wearing the shirt.[15] Nevertheless, in February, the university settled the suit, promising to revise its student code to conform to the First Amendment and specifying that speech or written communication must meet the legal standard of being "severe, pervasive and objectively offensive" in order to be considered punishable harassment.[16]

The settlement is the fourth resulting from nine First Amendment suits brought by FIRE, which argues that "more than half of America's top colleges maintain speech codes that blatantly violate First Amendment standards."[17]

While most universities deny having speech codes, critics like FIRE say colleges' sexual harassment policies, computer policies, codes of conduct and restrictions on where students can stage protests amount to the same thing. The AAUP shares these concerns, according to Henry Reichman, chair of the association's Committee on Academic Freedom and Tenure.

"Generally there is no right to not be offended in society as a whole or in a university," he says. "Speech codes are a bad idea. . . . It's not surprising to us that speech codes are repeatedly found in violation of the First Amendment in public universities." Reichman adds that "the answer to speech you disagree with is more speech" to express that disagreement, rather than stifling some viewpoints.

Timothy C. Shiell, author of a book on hate speech and professor of philosophy and ethics at the University of Wisconsin, Stout, says 25 years ago he agreed with universities cracking down on hate speech.[18] "But the more you look into how these things actually get implemented, the scarier it all looks," he says. "A lot of these terms are not well defined, so it becomes very subjective."

However, NASPA's Kruger contends the situation is not as dire as FIRE makes out and that "most universities have expunged their hate-speech codes over the last five to seven years," given all the court cases that have come up. He noted, "There's been a fair amount of [court] precedents that hate speech and the most repugnant speech possible has been deemed to be [constitutionally] protected."

Many observers say universities play an important role in drawing a line at the kind of inappropriate speech that violates campus community values. "If students want to learn biology and art history in an environment where they don't have to worry about being offended or raped, why shouldn't they?" University of Chicago law professor Eric Posner wrote recently.[19]

In an interview with *CQ Researcher,* Posner says he was talking mainly about private universities, which do not fall under the same First Amendment protections as public universities. Private, religiously affiliated universities, he points out, have frequently restricted students' behavior — from Catholic universities banning premarital sex to Mormon universities regulating personal grooming. The private institution, he says, "has a right to send a message to the world about what its values are, and it can therefore control students and employees if it wants to."

Ohio University student Isaac Smith displays the T-shirt that led to his free-speech lawsuit against OU in 2014. University officials had ordered Smith and other members of the Students Defending Students campus organization to stop wearing shirts bearing the organization's slogan, "We get you off for free." Administration officials said the shirt "objectified women." Free-speech advocates said the university's actions violated Smith's rights. In February, OU settled the suit, promising to revise its student speech code to conform to the First Amendment.

Some legal experts say, however, that private universities that restrict students' speech may violate their contractual obligations if they have written policies promising freedom of expression. Meanwhile, because most private universities receive federal money, they are bound by federal laws forbidding discrimination on the basis of gender under Title IX, or race under Title VI, Posner notes.[20] Under those laws, even a private university must not create a "hostile environment," which counts as discrimination, he says.

Starting in 2011 the Department of Education has issued a series of mandates that universities define sexual harassment as including verbal conduct. Since then more campuses have been adopting restrictive speech codes, FIRE contends.

The Education Department's definition of sexual harassment is "breathtakingly broad," says FIRE Vice President Will Creeley, because the department has removed the requirement that speech be "objectively offensive" from the perspective of a "reasonable person" — the widely recognized legal standard. "If all that is required is subjective offense on the part of a listener to classify speech as sexual harassment, then discourse on campus will be severely constrained," he says.

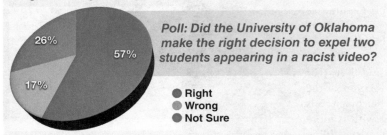

Most Support Oklahoma Expulsions

Fifty-seven percent of Americans said the University of Oklahoma was correct in expelling two fraternity members filmed singing a racist song, according to a March poll by YouGov.

Poll: Did the University of Oklahoma make the right decision to expel two students appearing in a racist video?

26%
57%
17%

● Right
● Wrong
● Not Sure

Source: Poll Results, YouGov, March 11-13, 2015, http://tinyurl.com/npbnu6o.

But Kruger calls the department's recent guidance "sound policy" because some speech "is just not tolerable." He says he agrees with the Obama administration that offensive speech among students can create an environment where "someone cannot function as a student" and that such cases "can have enormous impact on the victim."

Although many university policies forbid verbal harassment, that doesn't mean they're applying the rule so broadly that it violates the First Amendment, says W. Scott Lewis, co-founder of the Association of Title IX Administrators, a Malvern, Pa., group whose members administer the gender discrimination law on campuses. "It happens periodically, but I wouldn't characterize it as a major problem," he says.

Recent guidelines from the departments of Justice and Education encourage schools to enact policies aimed at restricting sexually themed jokes and unwelcome requests for dates, some critics charge. The guidelines could effectively "ban dating (since no one is a mind reader)," objected the free market Competitive Enterprise Institute.[21]

Lewis counters that asking someone out on a single date and being rejected "is never going to constitute sexual harassment under any policy that I've seen applied."[22] Harassment would involve persistently asking for a date or exercising a power imbalance like that between a teacher and student, Lewis added.

Shiell expresses concern that while free speech may have won the legal war in the courts, it has lost the "culture war," as universities continue to ban speech they

find objectionable, he says, pointing to FIRE's annual surveys.

As the Ohio University T-shirt incident illustrates, one person's joke can be another's intolerable insult. And FIRE's recent list of 2014's "10 worst" colleges for abusing free-speech rights shows that both liberals and conservatives can be targets. The incidents cited include a University of Kansas professor suspended for tweeting an anti–National Rifle Association message and a Marquette University professor whose tenure was revoked after he objected that a student's opposition to same-sex marriage was suppressed in another teacher's class.[23]

An important question for Shiell is, "Do you want a higher education system where people are coerced to conform to some cultural norm or where they can push back against conformity?"

Public universities can still condemn racist and sexist speech and promote politeness — within limits, Shiell says. "Courts routinely say you can have these aspirational goals of respect and civility but you can't require such things."

Should students be protected from language they find offensive?

Last April, a student approached Northwestern University film professor Laura Kipnis and told her she couldn't watch the film to be discussed in class because it "triggered" upsetting emotions for her.

Kipnis was baffled: The film had some sexual content, but it wasn't "particularly explicit," she wrote. How, she wondered, would this student survive in the film industry? "I had an image of her in a meeting with a bunch of execs, telling them that she couldn't watch one of the company's films because it was a trigger for her."[24]

Although Kipnis had never heard of "trauma trigger warnings," the incident made more sense when a news story appeared the following week reporting that similar advisories — warnings that teachers put on reading assignments or upcoming class discussions — were migrating from the Internet to colleges. Last year The

Associated Press reported that students asked six colleges — the University of Michigan, Bryn Mawr, Oberlin, Rutgers, Scripps and Wellesley — for such warnings. So far, no school has required the warnings, although some professors have provided them voluntarily, according to the AP and experts interviewed for this report.[25]

Bailey Loverin, a literature major at the University of California, Santa Barbara, first proposed that professors at her school provide a warning if they were teaching material that could cause flashbacks in students who had been sexually assaulted or suffered other trauma. Loverin, 19, acknowledged that many people had told her, "You are going to get your feelings hurt, and you should just suck it up and meet it head-on." However, she pointed out, "a girl raped just a month ago and sitting in a classroom for the first time again isn't ready to face that head-on."[26]

Like Kipnis, other faculty members have criticized such warnings, describing them as "silly" and "ridiculous."[27]

The AAUP last year condemned the idea of mandating trigger warnings on the grounds that "they interfere with academic freedom in the choice of course reading materials and teaching methods." A report issued by the association's academic freedom committee said, "The presumption that students need to be protected rather than challenged in the classroom is at once in-fantilizing and anti-intellectual. It makes comfort a higher priority than intellectual engagement."[28]

Former Barnard College President Judith Shapiro wrote of the trigger warning movement, "Aside from this being an insult to the intelligence and good sense of students and faculty members alike, it also threatens to spoil the thrill of discovery." Would a firsttime reader of *Anna Karenina* want to be told ahead of time, she asked, that Anna kills herself at the end?[29]

Apparently yes. A columnist for the Rutgers University student paper in New Jersey wrote that teachers should warn students that F. Scott Fitzgerald's 1925 novel *The Great Gatsby* "possesses a variety of scenes that reference gory, abusive and misogynistic violence."[30]

"I'm treating college students like the adults they are, and institutions increasingly treat college students like medicalized children," objected Laurie Essig, associate professor of Gender, Sexuality and Feminist Studies at Middlebury College in Vermont. She said some of her students have criticized her for showing photos of anorexic fashion models in her sociology and gender course without first warning students with eating disorders.[31]

University of Chicago law professor Posner said critics haven't considered "the justification for these policies: . . . that students are children." Perhaps, he wrote, "overprogrammed children engineered to the specifications of college admissions offices no longer experience the risks and challenges that breed maturity."[32]

In an interview, he said 18- and 19-year-olds arriving at college after a lifetime under parental control can find themselves in a "vulnerable" situation. "Universities should take these things into account," he said, whether through student codes of conduct or other means like trigger warnings.

Yet by the time teenagers get to college, they "need to confront new ideas," counters FIRE's Creeley, who supports the Supreme Court's long-held view that a university is a "marketplace of ideas." "If you haven't once been offended you should ask for your money back."

"Safe spaces" on campus — rooms where students can take refuge during debates about "triggering" issues such as sexual assault — have also come under criticism. Adam Shapiro, a Columbia University junior, protested this trend by printing a flier declaring his room a "dangerous" space. A safe-space mentality has begun infiltrating classrooms, Shapiro objected, making both professors and students reluctant to say anything that might hurt someone's feelings.[33]

While trigger warnings and safe spaces have attracted controversy, many commentators agreed a tough university response was required after the University of Oklahoma video surfaced. For many free-speech advocates, Oklahoma is turning out to be one of those "hard cases" epitomized by the phrase, "I disapprove of what you say, but I will defend to the death your right to say it."[34]

Notably, liberal outlets like *Slate* aligned with libertarian (*Reason*) and conservative (*National Review*) voices to condemn the expulsions as an inappropriate squelching of free speech.[35] In a *New York Times* roundup of opinions, most legal experts agreed that this kind of racist speech by students at a public university is protected by legal precedents, unless it can be proven to threaten actual physical harm or creates a "racially hostile environment."[36]

However, maintains Samantha Harris, director of policy research at FIRE, "the standard for what constitutes a 'hostile environment' goes well beyond one chant on a bus." For instance, she points out, "the chant was not done in front of a dorm of African-American students." While university President Boren was "absolutely right to condemn it," Harris says, without a proof of imminent physical danger to African-American students the expulsions likely violated the expelled students' free-speech and due process rights.

But both black and white students supported the expulsion. "What they said was not just offensive," said Maggie Savage, 20, a sophomore. "If you do anything to make students in a community feel unsafe, you lose the privilege of being able to attend the university."[37]

Boston College Law School professor Kent Greenfield expressed discomfort with the right-left consensus that the racist song was constitutionally protected speech. Writing in *The Atlantic,* he agreed the fraternity students "would almost certainly win" a First Amendment case but added, "If the First Amendment has become so bloated, so ham-fisted that it cannot distinguish between such filth and earnest public debate about race, then it is time we rethink what it means."

And he expressed dismay that, under the First Amendment, fear of being targeted "counts hardly at all"; what matters is a "murderous frenzy then and there."[38]

Do universities that accept money from autocratic governments compromise academic freedom?

As global demand for higher education rises, some foreign governments are offering financial incentives to attract prominent American universities to build branch campuses in their countries.[39] The practice has raised questions about how much independence such campuses have to ensure free debate — especially about subjects uncomfortable for host governments.

Abu Dhabi made an initial donation of $50 million to host a branch of New York University within the emirate, paid for a luxurious new campus and pays most students' tuition and living costs, which could total over $100 million a year.[40]

In March, the government of the UAE (which includes Abu Dhabi and six other emirates) barred NYU professor Andrew Ross from entering the country to conduct research. A professor of social and cultural analysis, Ross has published research critical of exploitative labor conditions for migrant workers in Abu Dhabi.[41]

NYU officials have said that the Abu Dhabi campus will have the same kind of academic freedom as the Manhattan campus. But "it's not at all clear if that's the case," in light of the Ross incident, says the AAUP's Reichman. "If a faculty member of NYU can't go to the campus in Abu Dhabi, that's a problem."

Universities accepting money from autocratic governments raises "a growing and complicated question," Reich-man says, both on American campuses and overseas. NYU law professor Rick Hills, who teaches at the university's Shanghai campus, has argued that while his students may not enjoy freedom of expression off campus, they can engage in free discussion inside the classroom. "If NYU were to insist that its constituents must be able to pursue in Shanghai every expressive activity that they are entitled to pursue at Washington Square [in New York], then the Chinese government would simply refuse to allow us to teach in the PRC [People's Republic of China]. Such an uncompromising posture would [deprive students] of the benefits of an education that the Chinese eagerly seek," he wrote.[42]

NYU-Shanghai Vice Chancellor Jeffrey Lehman concurs. "The written ground rules are: We have academic freedom . . . at NYU-Shanghai. We can talk about the Dalai Lama, Tiananmen Square, Taiwan and Tibet and anything we want to — and we do," he says. But, that "does not mean I somehow have a special badge that lets me walk around Shanghai exempt from Chinese law or Chinese culture or practice."

The nearly 100 Confucius Institutes established in the last decade at American campuses are equally contentious. Last year, *Foreign Policy* magazine published a forum on whether the institutes stifle academic freedom. Some experts expressed concern that their curricula amount to Chinese government propaganda and the instructors recruited in China were trained to parrot the government line — on issues such as the independence of Tibet and the outlawed spiritual sect Falun Gong.[43] However, experts vigorously disagree on whether the American universities or the Chinese government controls the curriculum and faculty.

Reichman says concern goes beyond the Chinese. "I'm in Russian history, and there's growing concern about Russian oligarchs pouring money into Russian studies" on American campuses. "Are they going to inordinately attempt to influence the research agenda?"

Other academics say such cultural exchanges are nevertheless vital to encourage freedom of thought on both sides. George Washington University's McCord, who helped negotiate GWU's Confucius Institute, says, "Even if [Chinese instructors] can't speak freely, they're here and they see our society, and I think that's good." China is "an authoritarian dictatorship, and they watch their people and punish them if they slip up," so it's understandable if Chinese instructors avoid speaking about politically controversial issues.

Kristin Stapleton, a historian specializing in China at the State University of New York, Buffalo, who served as the first director of her university's Confucius Institute from 2010-2013, said the institute "is no different from the initiatives of corporations and other private entities [that] encourage scholarship and academic programs in their areas of interest." Such arrangements should also be scrutinized, she says.

However, Bruce Lincoln, a University of Chicago history professor who organized a successful petition by 100 professors to shut down the Confucius Institute at Chicago, sees the institutes as a symptom of the "corporatization" of universities. "Money is scarce, and institutions are hungry for donors claiming ever more influence as a result of donations. We risk becoming a shopping mall where we rent out space," he says.

New York University President John Sexton shakes hands with East China Normal University President Yu Lizhong at a groundbreaking ceremony for NYU's Shanghai satellite campus on March 28, 2011. Lizhong is now chancellor of NYU Shanghai. NYU is one of several American universities setting up satellite campuses in China as joint ventures with Chinese educational institutions. But critics question whether such arrangements inevitably result in censorship of topics that offend the host countries.

BACKGROUND

Academic Freedom

Academic freedom was not a "coherent concept" in America before the late 19th century, for either teachers or students, writes Heins, a civil liberties lawyer and author of *Priests of Our Democracy*, a history of academic freedom.[44]

From the 17th to the 19th century, freedom of thought was neither valued nor practiced, and the teacher was "not to permit any novel opinions to be taught," according to educators from that period. Instead, students were drilled in Latin and Greek and were not to deviate from religious doctrine — nor were their professors. In 1654, the president of Harvard, which trained many of the era's Puritan ministers, was forced to resign because he denied baptism's scriptural validity.[45]

In the last decades of the 19th century (1870-1900), a revolution occurred in American higher education that opened the door to a freer quest for knowledge. Charles Darwin's theory of evolution challenged traditional religious thinking. In addition, German universities were becoming increasingly influential, with their belief that the independent search for truth is the main purpose of a university education and their tradition of affording professors freedom in teaching and intellectual exploration.[46]

Taking that new, enlightened view to heart, the University of Chicago's first president, William Rainey Harper, said in 1892, "When for any reason . . . the administration [of a university] attempts to dislodge a professor because of his political or religious sentiments, at that moment the institution has ceased to be a university."[47]

However, in the late 19th century, professors who expressed their political views outside the classroom came into conflict with wealthy businessmen who were donating to universities on an unprecedented scale and serving as trustees. In 1895, University of Chicago economics professor Edward Bemis was fired after supporting striking railroad workers, which Chicago businessmen saw as "treasonous."[48]

CHRONOLOGY

1915-1950s *State and federal governments suppress campus speech by targeting professors suspected of being communists.*

1915 Professors form American Association of University Professors to protect academic freedom; group investigates University of Pennsylvania's firing of radical economist Scott Nearing.

1949 New York's Feinberg law bans public schools from employing members of groups advocating overthrow of the government.

1950-1954 Sen. Joseph R. McCarthy, R-Wis., alleges that 205 State Department officials are communists; he later holds hearings accusing government employees, civilians and members of the U.S. Army of being communists. Senate censures McCarthy for his reckless tactics and unsubstantiated allegations.

1952 U.S. Supreme Court upholds New York's Feinberg law; Justice William O. Douglas' dissenting opinion marks first time a justice calls academic freedom a right protected by First Amendment.

1957 Supreme Court blocks New Hampshire legislators from investigating the political views of Paul Sweezy, a Marxist Harvard economist.

1964-1970s *Campus free-speech movement spreads nationwide, spurs protests against Vietnam War.*

1964 Students at University of California, Berkeley, protest campus limits on free speech, spawning national movement.

1966 Ronald Reagan elected governor of California promising to clean up "mess" at Berkeley.

1967 U.S. Supreme Court overturns New York's Feinberg law.

1972-1990s *Campuses adopt speech codes, which courts say violate the First Amendment.*

1972 President Richard M. Nixon signs Title IX prohibiting sex discrimination in education.

1981 University of Wisconsin, Madison, adopts the first campus anti-harassment speech code.

1989 Federal court invalidates University of Michigan's ban on racist comments. . . . University of Wisconsin institutes "hate-speech" ban.

1991 University of Wisconsin's 1989 hate-speech ban is declared unconstitutional.

1999 Supreme Court rules in *Davis v. Monroe County* that public schools are liable for student-on-student harassment if it is "severe, pervasive and objectively offensive."

2000s *Free-speech suits against colleges prompt revisions to speech codes; Chinese government funds Confucius Institutes on U.S. campuses.*

2003 California's Citrus College eliminates most speech codes after Foundation for Individual Rights in Education (FIRE) files lawsuit.

2004 Chinese government starts Confucius Institute program on overseas campuses.

2005 Palestinian groups call for boycott of Israeli academic institutions to protest occupation.

2010 Rutgers student Tyler Clementi dies by suicide after roommate posts video of sex encounter on Twitter.

2011 New Jersey enacts nation's toughest anti-bullying law.

2014 Rep. Chris Smith, R-N.J., holds congressional hearings on Chinese influence on academic freedom at American universities.

2015 University of Oklahoma expels two students for racist song; racist speech incidents follow at Duke, Bucknell, University of Maryland and University of South Carolina. . . . Sen. Patty Murray, D-Wash, introduces bill banning harassment of college students based on race, gender, religion or sexual orientation. . . . FIRE claims fifth settlement victory in free-speech suits against colleges.

In the early 1900s, socially conscious professors objected that boards of trustees dominated by business executives saw universities as for-profit businesses and felt free to fire teachers for their political views. This struggle was exemplified by the widely publicized firing in 1915 of Scott Nearing, a popular economics professor at the University of Pennsylvania and an outspoken campaigner for decent wages and an end to child labor.

The Nearing dismissal and similar incidents at the universities of Utah, Colorado and Montana spurred the newly formed AAUP to write its founding document on academic freedom in 1915.[49] The "Declaration of Principles on Academic Freedom and Academic Tenure" declared that universities are not merely businesses driven by profit or by the "resentments" of their trustees.

The declaration proposed that American universities be governed by three basic principles: freedom of inquiry and research, freedom of teaching and "freedom of extramural utterance" (speech uttered outside the classroom). Those three tenets came to define American academic freedom.[50]

McCarthyism

While universities gradually accepted the AAUP's founding principles, those values were trumped by the anticommunist fervor that gripped the country in the late 1940s and early '50s. State governments sought to keep communists or their sympathizers from teaching in tax-supported institutions. New York's 1949 so-called Feinberg law, for instance, required detailed procedures for investigating the loyalty of public school teachers and prohibited employing anyone who belonged to a group advocating the overthrow of the government.

The period between 1950 and 1954 is widely known as the McCarthy era, after Sen. Joseph R. McCarthy, R-Wis., who created a national climate of fear with sensational accusations and congressional hearings in which he denounced U.S. government officials and others as communists. In reality, anticommunist activity had started well before then. In 1947 the House Committee on Un-American Activities had begun holding its infamous hearings in which Hollywood personalities were subpoenaed to testify about known or suspected members of the Communist Party. The hearings resulted in the creation of a blacklist of suspected communists, many of whom lost their jobs and became unemployable.[51]

In this atmosphere, the U.S. Supreme Court generally upheld the ban on hiring communists. In a 1952 decision, *Adler v. Board of Education,* the court found that the Feinberg law did not violate teachers' First Amendment rights. Teachers have no right to their jobs, the court said, and because they worked "in a sensitive area" — forming young minds — their employers were entitled to investigate their political beliefs.[52] In dissent, however, Justice William O. Douglas wrote that academic freedom was a "distinct, identified subset" of the First Amendment right to free speech.[53]

The first Supreme Court case to embrace the idea of academic freedom came amid the continuing atmosphere of the Red Scare. In *Sweezy v. New Hampshire* in 1957, the court blocked New Hampshire legislators from investigating the political views of Paul Sweezy, a Marxist economist at Harvard, based on an allegedly subversive lecture he gave at the University of New Hampshire.[54] Justice Felix Frankfurter, himself a former academic, found the state's national security justification for questioning Sweezy "grossly inadequate" when "weighed against the grave harm resulting from governmental intrusion into the intellectual life of a university."

Chief Justice Earl Warren emphasized the importance of academic freedom for students as well: "Teachers and students must always remain free to inquire, to study and to evaluate, to gain new maturity and understanding; otherwise, our civilization will stagnate and die."[55]

However, the court did not declare loyalty oaths for professors unconstitutional until 1967, in *Keyishian v. Board of Regents.* Harry Keyishian, who taught English at the State University of New York, Buffalo, refused to sign a loyalty oath affirming he was not a member of the Communist Party. In a decision that finally overturned the 1949 Feinberg law, Justice William J. Brennan Jr. wrote that academic freedom is "a special concern of the First Amendment, which does not tolerate laws that cast a pall of orthodoxy over the classroom."[56]

Student Speech

In the early 1960s, students hawked political pamphlets and raised money for the civil rights movement and other causes from a lively strip of sidewalk at the Telegraph Avenue entrance to the University of California, Berkeley. Such political activity was forbidden on the campus itself,

Yik Yak Tests Campus Speech

Phone app "is being used by young people in a really destructive way."

A popular cellphone app sometimes used to spew racist rants, sexually graphic posts — and worse — has touched off a controversy over whether and how to police speech on campus.

Called Yik Yak, the app allows people to post Twitter-like messages (Yaks) anonymously to users within a 1.5-mile radius.[1] Introduced a little over a year ago, Yik Yak has been used to threaten mass violence at more than a dozen colleges. At Kenyon College in Gambier, Ohio, a "yakker" suggested a gang rape at the school's women's center.[2]

"It is being increasingly used by young people in a really intimidating and destructive way," said Danielle Keats Citron, a law professor at the University of Maryland and author of *Hate Crimes in Cyberspace*.[3]

Violent threats on Yik Yak had led to arrests on at least nine campuses as of December 2014.[4]

Some universities have blocked Yik Yak from their servers because it has been used to cyberbully students or teachers. In December Utica College, in Utica, N.Y., blocked the app in response to a growing number of sexually graphic posts aimed at the school's transgender community.[5]

Opponents of this approach say it's ineffective and may violate students' constitutional guarantee of free speech. They also note that even if a university blocks Yik Yak, students can still access it on their cell service or find other methods for making the same kinds of comments publicly through the Internet.[6]

The app's privacy policy prevents schools from identifying users without a subpoena, a court order, search warrant or emergency request from a law enforcement official.[7]

The University of Rochester, in New York state, faced that issue in March when it said it would be asking its county district attorney to issue a subpoena in response to racially offensive language. However, for the subpoena to be issued it would have to be part of an investigation of possible criminal wrongdoing "and not just hate speech that's offensive," a local newspaper pointed out.[8]

Yik Yak users defend the app, saying it represents a broad community, which, just like real life, inevitably includes some racist behavior and jeering insults.

The tech website Techdirt said universities' "shoot the messenger" efforts weren't just futile but also bad preparation for the nastiness students will face in the outside world. "By providing shelter rather than pushing students to take control of these situations, these universities are doing their students — and the future of this country — a huge disservice," Techdirt said.[9]

and most people thought the sidewalk was not university property.

However, in September 1964 a dean told students they could no longer conduct political activity there because the walkway was university property. Students protested by setting up tables for their political causes not just on the walkway but also on campus.

Eventually, the protest expanded and hundreds of students conducted a campus sit-in. Inspired by the civil disobedience tactics of the civil rights movement, the protest would become known as the Free Speech Movement and would trigger a decade of student protests. "I think about the Free Speech Movement as helping to end the McCarthy era and paving the way for the anti-war protests that came later," said New York University professor of history Robert Cohen, the author of a book about 1960s-era student activist Mario Savio.[57]

In December 1964, after the Berkeley administration failed to reach a compromise with students, a mass sit-in ensued, as more than 1,000 students stormed the administration building, led by folk singer Joan Baez singing "We Shall Overcome." Savio, a 21-year-old philosophy major who had just returned from registering black voters in Mississippi, galvanized students with his electric rhetoric. The sit-in ended with 814 arrests.

Large student protests against the Vietnam War soon erupted in San Francisco, New York and other cities, and by 1968 students worldwide were protesting the war.

A better approach, some say, is to counter hate speech by going onto Yik Yak with opposing comments, as a group of 50 professors did at Colgate University, flooding the app with positive posts after the upstate New York campus experienced a rash of racist comments.[10]

"Yik Yak allows for up-and-down voting of 'Yaks' and their related comments," a recent article in *Wired* explained. "If a Yak or a comment receives 5 down votes, it is removed permanently from Yik Yak. Yik Yak also has a robust offensive/abusive content reporting system."[11] The administrators can then take down a post if someone reports it as breaking one of Yik Yak's rules. According to cofounder Brooks Buffington, "People that are consistently posting negative material get suspended or banned."[12] In February, Yik Yak updated its system by adding options for flagging posts, including "offensive content" and "This post targets someone."[13]

The *Wired* article's author, Rey Junco, associate professor of education and human computer interaction at Iowa State University, says research has found that anonymous bystanders are actually more likely to intervene if they see bullying online than if they had to confront the bully in person.

As an active Yakker himself, he says he has seen only one case of harassment — and other Yakkers had promptly criticized it. Rather, he says, Yik Yak reflects how the community is feeling in all its diversity of opinion.

"Some of the same administrators suggesting blocking Yik Yak would do well to learn what their students are talking about — what campus culture is like," he says.

— *Sarah Glazer*

[1] Elizabeth Nolan Brown, "Schools Banning Phone App Yik Yak for Promoting Hate Speech," *Reason.com*, Feb. 6, 2015, http://tinyurl.com/k3hsntm.

[2] Jonathan Mahler, "Who Spewed That Abuse?" *The New York Times*, March 8, 2015, http://tinyurl.com/m3ln755.

[3] *Ibid.*

[4] Alexandra Svokos, "Yik Yak Threats Lead to Charges for Students," *The Huffington Post*, Nov. 25, 2014, http://tinyurl.com/lfr4rjt.

[5] Mahler, *op. cit.*

[6] See Brown, *op. cit*, and David Sessions, "Colleges Should Stop Worrying About Yik Yak and Start Respecting Their Students," *The New Republic*, March 9, 2015, http://tinyurl.com/lgtgvq3.

[7] Mahler, *op. cit.*

[8] James Goodman, "UR to Seek Subpoena of Yik Yak," *Democrat and Chronicle*, March 12, 2015, http://tinyurl.com/knr6jrk.

[9] Tim Cushing, "University Thinks Yik Yak Ban It Can't Possibly Enforce Will Fix Its 'Hate Speech' Problem," *Free Speech, Techdirt*, Feb. 10, 2015, http://tinyurl.com/kctetu8.

[10] Mahler, *op. cit.*

[11] Rey Junco, "Yik Yak and Online Anonymity Are Good for College Students," *Wired*, March 17, 2015, http://tinyurl.com/jwxek7z.

[12] Courtney Linder, "A Knack for Yik Yak," *The Pitt News*, March 19, 2015, http://tinyurl.com/lxvdvc2.

[13] Roberto Baldwin, "Yik Yak Updated With Improved Reporting System for Abusive Posts," *TNW* (*The Next Web*), Feb. 19, 2015, http://tinyurl.com/n4dmb67.

Since then, the Berkeley campus has been the site of hundreds of political demonstrations.

But the movement also created a backlash. After his election in 1966, Gov. Ronald Reagan vowed to "clean up the mess at Berkeley" and directed that university president Clark Kerr, seen as soft on students, be fired.

While the seminal Supreme Court decisions on academic freedom, such as *Keyishian* in 1967, had focused on the rights of university faculty, in 1972 the U.S. Supreme Court extended academic freedom to students. The president of a Connecticut state college had refused to recognize the radical group, Students for a Democratic Society, or to let it use campus facilities, claiming its "philosophy was antithetical to school policies." Justice Lewis Powell, writing in a unanimous decision, echoed the 1967 *Keyishian* decision in declaring the college campus a "marketplace of ideas." Powell wrote, "We break no new constitutional ground in reaffirming this Nation's dedication to safeguarding academic freedom."[58]

Speech Codes

In 1972 a landmark gender-equality clause — known as Title IX — of the Federal Education Amendments became law. It said "no person in the United States shall, on the basis of sex, be excluded from participation in, be denied benefits of, or be subjected to discrimination under any education program or activity receiving Federal financial assistance."[59]

Academic Groups Spar Over Israeli Boycott

Protest over Palestinian policy sparks debate on academic freedom.

When a professor at Tel Aviv University tried to recruit experts at American universities last year to comment on his student's Ph.D. thesis in American studies, the Americans refused.

The student was the first casualty of a boycott of Israeli academic institutions passed by the American Studies Association in December 2013 to protest Israeli occupation of Palestinian land, wrote Michael Zakim, a professor of history at Tel Aviv University. But the episode had a surprising twist: The student is Palestinian.[1]

Probably no academic-freedom issue has divided American faculty as bitterly as the boycott of Israeli academic institutions. No American college has adopted the boycott, according to David C. Lloyd, a member of the organizing committee of the U.S. Campaign for the Academic & Cultural Boycott of Israel (USACBI).[2] But several small associations of professors in academic specialties, including the Association for Asian American Studies and the Native American and Indigenous Studies Association, have adopted resolutions supporting it.

Proponents of the boycott claim it already is affecting public opinion in the United States and Israel. Critics, including the American Association of University Professors (AAUP), say such boycotts, which generally bar exchanges between American and Israeli universities, squelch academic freedom.

The American Studies Association's endorsement drew immediate condemnation from university presidents, and four institutions said they were withdrawing their membership from the association. "Academic boycotts subvert the academic freedoms and values necessary to the free flow of ideas, which is the lifeblood of the worldwide community of scholars," said Drew Gilpin Faust, president of Harvard University.[3] The Tel Aviv incident illustrates another problem with boycotts besides squelching academic freedom: It's not entirely clear how they will be carried out. For instance, most boycott supporters say it is aimed at Israeli institutions, not individuals, so it shouldn't affect a Ph.D. student looking for outside reviewers, according to Feisal G. Mohamed, a professor of English at the University of Illinois who supports the boycott.[4]

But it's difficult to separate individuals from institutions, says David M. Rosen, an anthropologist at Fairleigh Dickinson University in Teaneck, N.J., who helped organize an anti-boycott petition at the American Anthropological Association last December. "The way it really happens is, individual scholars, unless they abide by a political litmus test, will be barred" from academic exchanges, he says, including conferences in the United States and publication in journals.

Even boycott opponents expect the American Anthropological Association to pass a pro-boycott resolution at its annual meeting this November after its overwhelming rejection of an anti-boycott resolution last year. If the resolution passes, and is then approved by the entire membership, the association would be the largest to approve a boycott so far.

Under the law, all schools receiving any federal funds (which is most of them) must have policies that prohibit sexual harassment. The law laid the groundwork for lawsuits in which parents and students sued school boards for permitting sexual harassment on the grounds that such behavior constituted sex discrimination under Title IX.

In the 1980s and 1990s as more women and minorities entered college, universities began prohibiting harassing or hateful speech aimed at them. By 1995, about 350 campuses had adopted such policies.[60]

These so-called speech codes soon faced lawsuits, and courts invalidated some of them. Conservatives also claimed that such "political correctness" was a new form of censorship fostered by liberals.

In a 1989 case, *Doe v. University of Michigan,* a federal court invalidated Michigan's campus hate-speech ban on any expression that "stigmatizes or victimizes an individual" on the basis of race, ethnicity, religion, gender or sexual preference. The university had instituted the ban in response to a rash of racist incidents on campus.[61] The court said efforts to assure equal opportunity

Ilana Feldman, a pro-boycott anthropologist at George Washington University, contends that if the boycott is successful in ending the Israeli occupation, it would improve academic exchanges with Gaza, where she has conducted research.

"Many people's first question is about the consequence for Israelis, but the boycott seeks to support the academic freedom of Palestinians, which is constrained by the Israeli government at the moment," she says, through travel restrictions preventing Gazans from leaving the Gaza strip.[*5] "As a scholar, a tremendous amount is lost in our capacity to engage with Palestinian scholars and do research there," Feldman says, because the Israeli government has also barred many foreigners from access to Gaza.

An AAUP statement in 2006 declared that academic boycotts "strike directly at the free exchange of ideas even as they are aimed at university administrations."[6]

But Lloyd, a professor of English at the University of California, Riverside, counters that the boycott has actually encouraged more discussion and more press — at least about the Palestinian issue. "Until these resolutions were promoted, discussion was rare and one-sided; the Israeli view was the only view you saw," he says.

Marjorie Heins, a member of the AAUP committee on academic freedom, points out that Israeli professors and scholars who disagree with Israel's positions on Palestine also are penalized.[7]

Some academics say Israel is being singled out while China, for instance, is not boycotted for its crackdowns on civil rights in Tiananmen Square or Tibet.[8]

---

*The only legal ways in and out of Gaza are through official border crossings with Israel and Egypt, which for security reasons have severely restricted movement of people and goods across the borders.

As for the Palestinian student who couldn't find outside readers, Feldman says, "We saw very similar questions in the South Africa boycott" — an economic boycott aimed at ending apartheid that gained worldwide support starting in the 1960s. "The argument was [that] black South Africans were harmed by the boycott," she says. "I don't think there's any way around the fact that individuals can suffer negative consequences in the pursuit of much broader transformation that will be beneficial to them in the long run."

— *Sarah Glazer*

---

[1]Michael Zakim and Feisal G. Mohamed, "The Best of Intentions: Debating the ASA Boycott," *Dissent*, Nov. 5, 2014, http://tinyurl.com/pc2rv2b.

[2]The proposed boycott of Israeli academic institutions is part of a broader international campaign, the Boycott, Divestment and Sanctions movement (BDS), which began in 2005 with a call from Palestinian civil society organizations demanding, among other things, that Israel end its "occupation and colonization of Arab lands." See BDS website: http://tinyurl.com/3fnrncc.

[3]Tamar Lewin, "Prominent Scholars, Citing Importance of Academic Freedom, Denounce Israeli Boycott," *The New York Times*, Dec. 26, 2013, http://tinyurl.com/pgmujcz.

[4]Zakim and Mohamed, *op. cit.*

[5]See Eline Gordts, "Why Don't Palestinians Just Leave Gaza? They Can't," *The Huffington Post*, June 31, 2014, http://tinyurl.com/p8fkl3e.

[6]Marjorie Heins, "Rethinking Academic Boycotts," *AAUP Journal of Academic Freedom*, 2013, p. 3, http://tinyurl.com/nftld9x.

[7]*Ibid.*

[8]Ernst Benjamin, "Why I Continue to Support the AAUP Policy in Opposition to Academic Boycotts: A Response to the AAUP Journal of Academic Freedom," 2013, http://tinyurl.com/m45ys5d.

---

for all students "must not be at the expense of free speech."[62]

In 1991, a federal district court declared the University of Wisconsin's 1989 hate-speech ban unconstitutional. Wisconsin's 1981 code barring harassing speech, one of the nation's first, remained in place until 1999, when the faculty voted to end it.[63] That same year, University of Pennsylvania history professor Alan Charles Kors and Boston civil liberties attorney Harvey Silverglate founded the Foundation for Individual Rights in Education (FIRE) to litigate against attacks on academic speech. Their book,

The Shadow University: The Betrayal of Free Speech on America's Campuses, was highly critical of hate-speech bans.

"I watched with growing concern and fear and moral uneasiness as I saw the generation that had given us the free-speech movement now give us speech codes," said Kors, whose book stimulated public debate on the issue and received kudos from conservatives.[64]

FIRE scored its first victory in June 2003, when California's Citrus College agreed to eliminate most of its speech codes in response to a FIRE lawsuit.[65] In recent litigation, FIRE has succeeded in getting five colleges to modify their speech codes, with the most recent victory being a settlement announced May 4 with Western Michigan University.[66]

University of Wisconsin professor Shiell contends that hate-speech codes have "lost the legal war." Between 1989 and 2012 speech codes were struck down in at least 14 cases, including California, Michigan, New Hampshire, Pennsylvania and Texas.[67]

"Plenty of people have been arguing in the last 20 years that the First Amendment has been in error in defending offensive speech. [But] in the courtroom they have always lost," Shiell says. "Our system, as judges understand it, not only permits, but even encourages, robust and offensive actions."

Defining Punishable Speech

The U.S. Supreme Court and other courts have ruled that to be punishable, speech must constitute genuine harassment, a true threat, disorderly conduct or fit some other category of constitutionally unprotected speech. And for speech between students, the Supreme Court has ruled that to constitute harassment, speech must be "severe" and "pervasive" and "objectively offensive" — that is, judged offensive by a "reasonable person."[68]

In the recent University of Oklahoma case, for example, the university president said the students' actions had created a "hostile environment" under federal anti-discrimination law. However, the Supreme Court has set a high bar for meeting the definition of "hostile environment."

In *Davis v. Monroe* (1999), the court said harassment must be "so severe, pervasive and objectively offensive that it can be said to deprive the victims of access to the educational opportunities or benefits provided by the school." In other words, the harassment must be serious enough to have a systemic effect on equal access to education. Thus, it was unlikely that a single act of peer harassment would qualify, experts such as Shiell say.[69]

The *Davis* case centered on LaShonda Davis, a fifth-grader in Monroe County, Ga. Another student was accused of attempting to fondle her and using offensive sexual language on numerous occasions. When the school refused to take disciplinary action, LaShonda's mother sued the school board under Title IX. A lower court had ruled that the board was not liable for student-on-student sexual harassment, but the Supreme Court overturned the decision.

The court also has ruled that to constitute a true threat, a speaker must mean "to communicate a serious expression of an intent to commit an act of unlawful violence to a particular individual or group of individuals."[70]

In a 1997 case, *U.S. v. Alkhabaz,* Abraham Jacob Alkhabaz indicated an interest in violence against women through fictitious stories he posted to an Internet group. One of the stories used the name of a female classmate at the University of Michigan, although Alkhabaz did not communicate any of the stories to her. The court held there was no true threat, since there was no direct intimidation.[71]

By contrast, Richard Machado, a student at the University of California, Irvine, was convicted of a true threat when he sent and re-sent an email to 59 Asian students threatening to "hunt you down and kill your stupid asses."[72]

CURRENT SITUATION
Anti-Harassment Legislation

A bill is pending in the Senate and the House aimed at preventing harassment of lesbian, gay, bisexual and transgender (LGBT) students. It requires all colleges that receive federal money to establish policies against taunting LGBT students.

Introduced by Democratic Sens. Patty Murray, Wash., and Tammy Baldwin, Wis., and Rep. Mark Pocan, Wis., the measure also would require colleges to prevent cyberbullying and harassment based on students' race, color, national origin, gender, disability or religion. Called the Tyler Clementi Higher Education Anti-Harassment Act of 2015, the measure would amount to a federal expansion of New Jersey's anti-bullying law, considered the strongest in the nation.[73]

The bill is a response to the suicide of Clementi, a Rutgers student who jumped off a bridge in 2010 after discovering his roommate had used a webcam to spy on him having sex with another man. The roommate also encouraged others — via Twitter — to watch the sexual encounter via a video chat room.

LGBT students are more likely to be harassed in school than other students, Murray said, "yet there is no federal requirement for colleges and universities to protect their students from discrimination based on sexual orientation or gender identity."[74]

Does an academic boycott of Israel threaten academic freedom?

YES

David M. Rosen
*Professor of Anthropology, Fairleigh
Dickinson University*

Written for *CQ Researcher*, April 2015

The central objective of the Boycott, Sanction and Divestment movement and its academic allies is the suppression of dissent and free speech in America's colleges and universities. As BDS grows stronger, it becomes more strident. BDS founder Omar Bargouti's recent call for dismantling the Jewish homeland in Israel makes plain that BDS's vision for the Jews of Israel is not a two-state solution or even the one-state solution — but rather a no-state solution. BDS's radical anti-normalization campaign is designed to shut down debate and communication surrounding the Israel-Palestinian conflict and drive out the voices of dialogue and moderation.

The BDS assault on academic freedom is two-pronged: First, BSD is rebranding academic freedom not as a right but as a privilege conditioned upon accepting the BDS perspective. Second, BDS seeks to marginalize and demonize those whose views render them unprivileged to speak. The move to boycott Israeli academic institutions is part of this assault.

The leadership of my professional association, the American Anthropological Association, has embraced the boycott ethos, although a formal boycott vote won't take place until December. At last year's annual meeting of anthropologists, AAA leadership gave center stage to numerous panels of boycott advocates. This year, it refused to sponsor a panel and roundtable submitted by the only organized group of boycott opponents. An openly anti-Semitic blog post calling Israel a "criminal nation" populated by a "nation of criminals" was allowed to stand on a supposedly moderated AAA website. De facto, a boycott is in place, and its discriminatory animus is spreading across the profession.

Boycotters claim that academic boycotts target institutions, not people; but here is how it works in real life: At last year's annual meeting, an Israeli anthropologist was accosted on an elevator and denounced for wearing a nametag that identified his Israeli university affiliation. Another, long opposed to the occupation of the West Bank and Gaza, was publically mocked for suggesting at a session that there might be countries with worse human rights records than Israel's. One pro-boycott anthropologist declared scholarly objectivity to be a Zionist agenda; another celebrated the politicization of teaching, making plain the overtly prejudicial atmosphere in her classroom.

We are witnessing the emergence of the first major political blacklisting since the McCarthy era. When academic freedom is reduced from a "right" to a "privilege," it becomes meaningless. No one can speak truth to power if they need permission to speak.

NO

David Lloyd
*Distinguished Professor of English,
University of California, Riverside; Founding
Member, U.S. Campaign for The Academic and
Cultural Boycott of Israel*

Written for *CQ Researcher*, April 2015

Most discussions of the boycott of Israeli academic institutions ignore Israel's actual violations of Palestinian academic freedoms. This is not a hypothetical matter of what might happen were a boycott imposed, but an ongoing assault on Palestinian educational capacities that threatens their survival.

On the West Bank, several hundred checkpoints hamper access to schools. Campuses undergo military incursions and closures; scholars are denied the right to travel. Israeli authorities deny Gazan students the right to complete their studies on the West Bank. Worse, Israel's devastating military campaigns against Gaza have consistently targeted educational institutions, from the Islamic University to U.N.-run schools. Discrimination within Israeli educational institutions is subtle, but pervasive. Palestinian Israelis make up about 20 percent of the population but only 1 percent of university faculty.

These conditions constitute the real threat to academic freedom. Israeli universities are not bystanders, but are integrated in every aspect of Israel's regime of occupation and discrimination. Universities develop weapon systems and surveillance technology, host institutes that shape strategies like the Dahiya Doctrine, which plans the destruction of civilian infrastructure, and furnish the hydrological and topographical studies that determine the route of the illegal separation wall on Palestinian land or the sites of settlements. Israeli universities occupy land from which Palestinians were expelled or that is intended to be part of a future Palestinian state.

Nonetheless, the guidelines for the academic boycott of Israel are remarkably restrained. The Palestinian call explicitly targets institutions, not individuals. Israeli academics' right to research, teach, travel, attend conferences and express their views is fully respected. We are asked to refrain from collaborating with institutions that actively contribute to the systemic violation of international law and human rights. We are asked not to engage in joint institutional projects or host administrators acting as ambassadors for the state of Israel. Withholding consent from the violation of fundamental rights and refusing to normalize it by our collaboration is not a threat to academic freedom, but its clearest exercise.

The academic boycott will not prevent Israeli scholars from working or exchanging ideas. It will not destroy their institutions. The boycott has specific goals, consistent with human rights conventions and international law, and can be shortlived. Israel's dispossession of the Palestinians threatens to be permanent and irreversible.

Levi Pettit, right, a former University of Oklahoma fraternity member who was expelled from the university after being filmed leading a racist song, appeared at a news conference at Fairview Baptist Church in Oklahoma City on March 25, 2015. Pettit apologized for his role in the incident and said he is upset and embarrassed that he failed to stop it. Oklahoma state Sen. Anastasia Pittman, D-Oklahoma City, left, looks on.

Murray had introduced a similar version of the bill, which some education-policy experts said was too broadly worded, in 2011, but it died in Congress. Supporters believe the new bill has a better chance now that Murray is the most senior Democratic member of the Education Committee.[75]

Laura Bennett, president of the Association for Student Conduct Administration, which represents deans and other administrators, says "the bill focuses on ensuring every institution has a harassment policy, which I think is good practice." She adds, "I've seen inappropriate sexual comments depriving a student of the ability to go to class," particularly when it is "severe, persistent and pervasive," the definition used in the bill.

But FIRE's Harris said the term "bullying" is not well-defined, and the bill fails to include the standard legal requirement that the conduct be "objectively offensive" to count as harassment. Harris also questions the need for a new law.

"Tyler Clementi is the impetus for these bills, but what happened to him is already illegal," she says. "Every existing university student code of conduct and state

laws prohibit surreptitiously videoing someone engaged in sexual conduct and distributing it."

In fact, Clementi's roommate Dharun Ravi was found guilty in 2012 of all 15 counts on which he was charged, including bias intimidation — a hate crime carrying up to 10 years in prison in New Jersey — as well as invasion of privacy, witness tampering and hindering arrest. He was sentenced to 30 days in county jail, of which he served 20.[76]

However, the New Jersey Supreme Court in March found the state's "bias intimidation" law unconstitutional, portending a potential reversal in Ravi's case, which is on appeal. The law is the only one in the nation saying a defendant can be convicted if the victim "reasonably believed" the harassment or intimidation was based on race, color, ethnicity, gender or sexual orientation.

The court ruled the statute was "unconstitutionally vague" because it does not give defendants fair notice of when they are crossing a line to commit a crime. The court struck down the provision that bases a conviction on the victim's state of mind — i.e., his belief that he was targeted for a bias crime — ruling that it criminalizes "a defendant's failure to apprehend the reaction that his words would have on another."[77]

New Incidents

Since the video of Oklahoma students singing bigoted lyrics appeared online in early March, racist incidents have proliferated on campuses across the country. Most colleges have followed Oklahoma President Boren's lead in swiftly denouncing the acts and disciplining the students involved.

Bucknell University in Lewisburg, Pa., a private institution, expelled three students who made racist comments during a campus radio broadcast. Then the University of Mary Washington in Fredericksburg, Va., dissolved its men's rugby team and ordered anti-sexual assault training for the team after players were observed singing a sexist song at an off-campus party.

On April 1, Duke University announced that a student alleged to have hung a noose on the university grounds was "no longer on campus" and that "potential criminal violations" were being explored. However, after releasing a public apology from the student, the school said on May 1 that the student has been disciplined, will not face criminal charges and can return to campus next semester.[78] In April, the University of South Carolina (USC) suspended a female student and began a code of conduct investigation after she used the "N" word when writing a list of reasons "why USC WiFi Blows."[79]

The disciplinary actions have provoked almost as much controversy as the incidents themselves. "Colleges have seized on the University of Oklahoma's unconstitutional actions as a signal that they have an 'all clear' to toss free speech and basic fairness out of the window," Robert Shibley, executive director of FIRE, said in a statement April 9. By contrast, FIRE praised University of Maryland President Loh for "bucking the trend" and recognizing that the First Amendment protected the racist student email that popped up on his campus in March.[80]

But speaking from an administrator's viewpoint, NASPA's Kruger says, "Having a president make a strong statement may be worth the risk of a First Amendment suit that would follow."

China Influence

In Congress, Rep. Smith is expected to hold additional hearings on the impact on American universities of the Chinese government's involvement through Confucius Institutes on American campuses and through partnerships on satellite campuses in China. He also has asked the Government Accountability Office (GAO) to investigate whether a two-tier system exists at U.S. satellite campuses, whereby Chinese students and faculty are more restricted in their activities and research than U.S. students and faculty.

"I will also ask whether Communist Party committees operate on campus, whether fundamental freedoms are protected for both Chinese and U.S. students and faculty — religious freedom, Internet freedom, freedom of speech, freedom of association — and whether the universities are required to enforce China's draconian population control policies," Smith said at a Dec. 4 hearing.[81]

Experts at the hearing said potential solutions included more federal funding for Chinese language training so colleges won't need help from China and requiring greater openness in agreements between U.S. colleges and China.

Smith also responded favorably to a suggestion by China scholar Perry Link of University of California, Riverside: withholding visas for Confucius Institute teachers until China agrees to grant visas to American scholars, such as Link, who has been barred from China since 1995 for political reasons. During the 1989 Tiananmen Square uprising Link had smuggled a dissident astrophysicist into the U.S. Embassy in Beijing and helped to edit the "Tiananmen Papers," a 2002 collection of leaked Chinese official documents revealing how Chinese leaders responded to the protest.[82]

OUTLOOK
Open Questions

The recent student expulsions and suspensions for racist incidents on college campuses shows that both public and private university administrators are moving swiftly to punish those responsible. But whether those actions would be upheld, if challenged on First Amendment grounds, remains an open question.

Whether such casas will even come before a court is partly a practical matter: When it comes to students' free-speech rights, a student must have the will and resources to sue the university, notes FIRE's Creeley.

Some critics say college presidents are too focused on taking tough punitive actions in order to avoid suits by the victims of harassment. In the future, FIRE hopes to change that "risk-management calculation," turning the possibility of a First Amendment suit into an equal risk by continuing to file suits where it sees free speech threatened, according to Creeley.

Meanwhile, many of the recent questions raised about academic freedom will only intensify as American universities continue to expand their global reach. Referring to the recent barring of NYU professor Ross from entering the UAE, NYU-Shanghai Vice Chancellor Lehman says, "We have not had an Andrew Ross situation yet, but I expect we will at some point." If that day comes, he says, the university will do what it does when the U.S. government blocks a visa for a foreign scholar that NYU invites to New York — make a plea for the importance of bringing the scholar over.

"I happen to believe that movement [of scholars between countries] is good," Lehman says. "I hope that over time all governments will make it easier to move across borders. But that's not the world we're in right now."

America's uniquely liberal constitutional stance on free speech — unlike in France, which has outlawed antiSemitic speech or in Germany where Holocaust denial is a crime — will continue to present challenges when hard cases arise.

"Americans may laud [the French satirical magazine] *Charlie Hebdo* for being brave enough to publish cartoons ridiculing the Prophet Muhammad, but, if Ayaan Hirsi Ali is invited to campus, there are often calls to deny her a podium," observed *New York Times* columnist David Brooks, referring to Muslim students' opposition to Yale University's speaking invitation to Ali, a Somali-born political-rights activist and former Muslim who has been fiercely critical of Islam.[83]

While Americans pride themselves on their free-speech rights, it can be hard to hold to that standard when faced with speech that seems abominable. As journalist George Packer pointed out in a recent comment for *The New Yorker*, "the loathsomeness of an incident in which University of Oklahoma students were caught on video singing a racist song made it seem churlish to argue that their expulsion from a public institution might be unconstitutional."

The difficulty, he observed, is that "hate-speech regulations put actual feelings, often honorable ones, ahead of abstract rights — which seems like common sense. It takes an active effort to resist the impulse to silence the jerks who have wounded you."[84]

NOTES

1. Jake New, "Free Speech or Inciting Violence?" *Inside Higher Ed,* March 16, 2015, http://tinyurl.com/p9gut6r.

2. "An Important Statement from President Wallace Loh," University of Maryland, March 12, 2015, http://tinyurl.com/ldzv3k4.

3. Jake New, "Punishment, Post-Oklahoma," *Inside Higher Ed,* April 1, 2015, http://tinyurl.com/oh2d6uz. See also, Sonali Kohli, "Read This University President's Candid Reaction on Twitter to Frat-house Racism on his Campus," *Quartz,* March 13, 2015, http://tinyurl.com/lh37y9k.

4. "Rising Above Odious Words," statement by Wallace D. Loh, Office of the President, University of Maryland, April 1, 2015, http://tinyurl.com/lfdessv.

5. *Ibid.*

6. Jamelle Bouie, "Don't Expel Members of Sigma Alpha Epsilon for Racism," *Slate,* March 10, 2015, http://tinyurl.com/m5moa5u. Also see Allie Bidwell, "Racist Fraternity Chant Learned During Leadership Cruise," *U.S. News,* March 27, 2015, http://tinyurl.com/nksv376.

7. Manny Fernandez and Erik Eckholm, "Expulsion of Two Oklahoma Students Over Video Leads to Free Speech Debate," *The New York Times,* March 11, 2015, http://tinyurl.com/ox4ge3p.

8. Lynn O'Shaughnessy, "20 Surprising Higher Education Facts," *U.S. News & World Report,* Sept. 6, 2011, http://tinyurl.com/4y5v8o2.

9. Laura Kipnis, "Sexual Paranoia Strikes Academe," *The Chronicle of Higher Education,* Feb. 27, 2015, http://tinyurl.com/kq9aerc.

10. Stephanie Saul, "N.Y.U. Professor Is Barred by United Arab Emirates," *The New York Times,* March 16, 2015, http://tinyurl.com/kxqm4om.

11. *Ibid.*

12. "Hearing Probes China's Influence on U.S. Universities," Rep. Chris Smith, news release, U.S. House of Representatives, Dec. 4, 2014, http://tinyurl.com/ppu97a4.

13. For more detail see, Marshall Sahlins, Confucius Institutes: Academic Malware (2014).

14. *Isaac Smith v. McDavis,* Jones and Compton, Complaint for Injunctive and Declaratory Relief and Damages, U.S. District Court Southern District of Ohio Eastern Division, July 1, 2014, http://tinyurl.com/ogpevhf.

15. *Isaac Smith v. Roderick J. McDavis, et al.,* Defendants' Answer to Plaintiff's Complaint, Oct. 24, 2014, U.S. District Court for the Southern District of Ohio, Eastern Division.

16. Settlement agreement in *Smith v. McDavis,* Feb. 2, 2015, http://tinyurl.com/q4mtxuv. See also Alyssa Pasicznyk, "OU Reaches Settlement in Freedom of Speech Lawsuit," WOUB Public Media, Feb. 2, 2015, http://tinyurl.com/l29fqhk.

17. "Western Michigan U. Settles Boots Riley 'Speech Tax' Lawsuit," Foundation for Individual Rights in Education, May 4, 2015, http://tinyurl.com/m8l5h5w.

18. Timothy C. Shiell, *Campus Hate Speech on Trial* (2009).

19. Eric Posner, "Universities Are Right — and Within Their RIghts — to Crack Down on Speech and Behavior," *Slate*, Feb. 12, 2015, http://tinyurl.com/qbcr226.

20. Title IX is part of the Education Amendments of 1972. Title VI is part of the Civil Rights Act of 1964. See, "Overview of Title VI of the Civil Rights Act of 1964," http://tinyurl.com/leaxlfr.

21. Hans Bader, "Federal Title IX Enforcers Effectively Define Dating and Sex Education as 'Sexual Harassment,'" Competitive Enterprise Institute, May 10, 2013, http://tinyurl.com/qeplvpw.

22. "Dating Imperiled by Government Speech Mandate," Foundation for Individual Rights in Education, May 13, 2013, http://tinyurl.com/kaoxbuf.

23. Greg Lukianoff, "Free Speech on Campus: The Ten Worst Offenders of 2014," *The Huffington Post,* March 2, 2015, http://tinyurl.com/nqs7lnm.

24. Kipnis, *op. cit.*

25. "Trauma Warnings Move From Internet to Ivory Tower," The Associated Press, April 26, 2014, http://tinyurl.com/kwsbhzg.

26. *Ibid.*

27. *Ibid.*

28. Edward J. Graham, "Mandated Trigger Warnings Threaten Academic Freedom," American Association of University Professors, November-December 2014, http://tinyurl.com/lcurfs9.

29. Judith Shapiro, "From Strength to Strength," *Inside Higher Ed,* Dec. 15, 2014, http://tinyurl.com/kd8xgb2.

30. "Trauma Warnings Move From Internet to Ivory Tower," *op. cit.*

31. *Ibid.*

32. Posner, *op. cit.*

33. Judith Shulevitz, "In College and Hiding From Scary Ideas," *The New York Times*, March 21, 2015, http://tinyurl.com/l4ne9ye.

34. Although this phrase is often attributed to Voltaire, he apparently never said it.

35. See Bouie, *op. cit.;* Robby Soave, "To Safeguard All Students' Rights, SAE Should Sue Oklahoma U.," *Reason,* March 19, 2015, http://tinyurl.com/k73sjt4; and David French, "Congratulations, Oklahoma, in Your Outrage You Just Violated the Law," *National Review,* March 10, 2015, http://tinyurl.com/krgcnso.

36. Fernandez and Eckholm, *op. cit.*

37. *Ibid.*

38. Kent Greenfield, "The Limits of Free Speech," *The Atlantic,* March 13, 2015, http://tinyurl.com/n43twsn.

39. "Excellence v. Equity," in "Special Report: Universities," *The Economist*, March 28, 2015, p. 4, http://tinyurl.com/k863uxj. For background, see Reed Karaim, "College Rankings," *CQ Researcher,* Jan. 2, 2015, pp. 1-24; and, Robert Kiener, Future of Public Universities, *CQ Researcher,* Jan. 18, 2013, pp. 53-80.

40. "A Pearl in the Desert," in "Special Report: Universities," *The Economist*, March 28, 2015, p. 11.

41. Stephanie Saul, "N.Y.U. Professor Is Barred From United Arab Emirates," *The New York Times,* March 16, 2015, http://tinyurl.com/kxx3qaj.

42. Rick Hills, "Is It Legitimate to Compromise on Academic Freedom Abroad?" *PrawfsBlawg,* March 20, 2015, http://tinyurl.com/qd2579o.

43. Stephen I. Levine, *et al.,* "The Debate Over Confucius Institutes in the United States," *Foreign Policy,* July 11, 2014, http://tinyurl.com/le7yobw.

44. Marjorie Heins, *Priests of Our Democracy* (2013), p. 17.

45. Geoffrey R. Stone, "A Brief History of Academic Freedom," in Akeel Bilgrami and Jonathan R. Cole, eds., *Who's Afraid of Academic Freedom?* (2015).

46. *Ibid.,* pp. 3-4.

47. *Ibid.*, p. 5.

48. Heins, *op. cit.,* p. 18.

49. *Ibid.*, pp. 20-23.

50. Marjorie Heins, "An Old Story: The Corporate University," *Dissent,* Nov. 14, 2012, http://tinyurl.com/pnxfy77.

51. Heins, *Priests of Our Democracy, op. cit.,* p. 74.

52. *Ibid,* p. 3.

53. Marcia Clemmitt, "Academic Freedom," *CQ Researcher,* p. 846.

54. Heins, Priests of Our Democracy, *op. cit.,* p. 179.

55. *Ibid.,* p. 180.

56. *Ibid,* p. 4.

57. Lisa Leff, "What Was the UC Berkeley Free Speech Movement?" *The Huffington Post,* Dec. 2, 2014, http://tinyurl.com/lbj8kg7; Robert Cohen, *Freedom's Orator: Mario Savio and the Radical Legacy of the 1960s* (2009).

58. Heins, *Priests of Our Democracy, op. cit.,* p. 240.

59. "Title IX," *Encyclopaedia Britannica,* http://tinyurl.com/bhfkweu.

60. Clemmitt, *op. cit.,* p. 847.

61. "Harvard Law Review: Recent Case," Lexis Nexis, April 1990, http://tinyurl.com/qhrdetg.

62. Clemmitt, *op. cit.,* p. 847.

63. *Ibid.*

64. "Alan Charles Kors," National Endowment on Humanities, http://tinyurl.com/ntsb3c4.

65. *Ibid.*

66. "Western Michigan U. Settles Boots Riley 'Speech Tax' Lawsuit," *op. cit.*

67. Timothy C. Shiell, "The Case of the Student's Racist Facebook Message," *AAUP Journal of Academic Freedom,* 2014, http://tinyurl.com/ohy48pv.

68. *Ibid.* For "reasonable person" legal definition, see Cornell University Law School Legal Information Institute, http://tinyurl.com/nsjx6gz.

69. *Davis v. Monroe,* cited in Shiell, *op. cit.* Also see "Davis v. Monroe County Board of Education," *Encyclopaedia Britannica,* http://tinyurl.com/qdg97of.

70. Shiell, *op. cit.*

71. *Ibid.*

72. *U.S. v. Machado* (1999), cited in *ibid.*

73. "Tyler Clementi Higher Education AntiHarassment Act of 2015," govtrac.u.s., http://tinyurl.com/p5dr35x.

74. "Murray, Baldwin, Pocan Introduce Tyler Clementi Anti-Harassment Act," press release, Sen. Patty Murray, U.S. Senate, March 18, 2015, http://tinyurl.com/p236x28. Also see, Carlos P. Zalaquett, "Cyberbullying in College," SAGE Open, March 19, 2014, http://tinyurl.com/ndeehfe; the study found 19 percent of college students experienced cyberbullying.

75. Tyler Kingkade, "Democrats Renew Push for Colleges to Establish Cyberbullying Policies That Cover LGBT Students," *The Huffington Post*, March 18, 2015, http://tinyurl.com/kdmsv8.

76. Kate Zernike, "Jail Term Ends After 20 Days for Ex-Rutgers Student," *The New York Times,* June 19, 2012, http://tinyurl.com/pbewfqj.

77. Kate Zernike, "Part of New Jersey's Bias Intimidation Law Is Ruled Unconstitutional," *The New York Times,* March 18, 2015, http://tinyurl.com/qhztk5r

78. The Associated Press, "North Carolina: Investigation Into Noose at Duke Ends," *The New York Times,* May 1, 2015, www.nytimes.com/2015/05/02/us/north-carolina-investigation-into-noose-at-duke-ends.html.

79. Peter Holley, "University of South Carolina Student Suspended After Racist Photo Goes Viral," *The Washington Post,* April 5, 2015, http://tinyurl.com/kcg83ro.

80. "Colleges Rush to Violate Free Speech, Due Process in Response to Speech Controversies," Foundation for Individual Rights in Education, April 9, 2015, http://tinyurl.com/kcnyhw5.

81. Rep. Chris Smith, Opening Statement, House of Representatives, Dec. 4, 2014, http://tinyurl.com/pskomnx.

82. Daniel Golden and Oliver Staley, "China Banning U.S. Professors Elicits Silence From Colleges," *Bloomberg Business,* Aug. 10, 2011, http://tinyurl.com/orazy7n. Also see Andrew J. Nathan, "The Tiananmen Papers," *Foreign Affairs*, January/February 2001, http://tinyurl.com/oxr2r6o.

83. David Brooks, "I Am Not Charlie Hebdo," *The New York Times,* Jan. 8, 2015, http://tinyurl.com/nhpxtsc. Also see, Rich Lizardo, "We Invited Ayaan Hirsi Ali to Yale — and Outrage Ensued," *The American*

Spectator, Sept. 16, 2014, http://tinyurl.com/ nm9ttge; Richard Pérez-Pena and Tanzina Vega, "Brandeis Cancels Plan to Give Honorary Degree to Ayaan Hirsi Ali, a Critic of Islam," *The New York Times,* April 8, 2014, http://tinyurl.com/mc2w2sq.

84. George Packer, "Comment: Mute Button," *The New Yorker,* April 13, 2015, http://tinyurl.com/ nf987xg.

BIBLIOGRAPHY

Selected Sources

Books

Bilgrami, Akeel, and Jonathan R. Cole, eds., *Who's Afraid of Academic Freedom?* **Columbia University Press, 2015.**
A sociology professor (Akeel) and a philosophy professor (Cole) from Columbia University provide academic essays, some of which discuss the boycott of Israeli higher education institutions.

Fish, Stanley, *Versions of Academic Freedom: From Professionalism to Revolution,* **University of Chicago Press, 2014.**
A law professor at Florida International University asks whether academic freedom authorizes professors to question the status quo inside and outside of the university.

Heins, Marjorie, *Priests of Our Democracy: The Supreme Court, Academic Freedom and the Anti-Communist Purge,* **New York University Press, 2013.**
A civil liberties lawyer traces the history of academic freedom from the late 19th century to today.

Articles

Bouie, Jamelle, "Don't Expel Members of Sigma Alpha Epsilon for Racism," *Slate,* **March 10, 2015, http://tinyurl.com/m5moa5u.**
An African-American columnist says the University of Oklahoma should educate students about a 1921 anti-black race riot in Tulsa, Okla., so they "see what their words actually mean," instead of expelling them.

Fernandez, Manny, and Erik Eckholm, "Expulsion of Two Oklahoma Students Over Video Leads to Free Speech Debate," *The New York Times,* **March 11, 2015, http://tinyurl.com/ox4ge3p.**

Numerous legal experts say racist singing by University of Oklahoma students, two of whom were later expelled, was constitutionally protected speech.

Greenfield, Kent, "The Limits of Free Speech," *The Atlantic,* **March 13, 2015, http://tinyurl.com/ n43twsn.**
A law professor at Boston College asks whether Americans should rethink the First Amendment if it protects racist chants such as those sung by University of Oklahoma students, some of whom were later expelled.

Kipnis, Laura, "Sexual Paranoia Strikes Academe," *The Chronicle of Higher Education,* **Feb. 27, 2015, http://tinyurl.com/kq9aerc.**
A film professor at Northwestern University says university sexual-harassment codes and "trigger warnings" leave students ill-prepared for the outside world.

McCord, Edward A., "Confucius Institutes: Hardly a Threat to Academic Freedoms," *The Diplomat,* **March 27, 2014, http://tinyurl.com/q3qzeym.**
A historian of China at George Washington University finds little evidence that Confucius Institutes threaten academic freedom on American campuses.

New, Jake, "Punishment Post-Oklahoma," *Inside Higher Ed,* **April 1, 2015, http://tinyurl.com/ oh2d6uz.**
After the University of Oklahoma expelled students for a racist song caught on video, other college presidents quickly disciplined students involved in similar incidents.

Sahlins, Marshall, "China U.," *The Nation,* **Oct. 29, 2013, http://tinyurl.com/kdkmr53.**
A professor emeritus of anthropology at the University of Chicago says Confucius Institutes censor political discussion of China on American campuses.

Schiell, Timothy, "The Case of the Student's Racist Facebook Message," *Journal of Academic Freedom,* **2014, http://tinyurl.com/ohy48pv.**
A professor of philosophy at the University of Wisconsin-Stout examines a racist Facebook message through the lens of landmark court decisions to determine if it is constitutionally protected free speech.

Scott, Joan W., "Changing My Mind About the Boycott," *Journal of Academic Freedom,* **2013, http://tinyurl.com/kn5xltc.**
A professor emerita of social science at the Institute for Advanced Study, in Princeton, N.J., explains why she supports a boycott of Israeli academic institutions.

Reports and Studies

"Spotlight on Speech Codes 2015: The State of Free Speech on Our Nation's Campuses," Foundation for Individual Rights in Education, 2015, http://tinyurl.com/o6xlp56.

A report by a group advocating free speech on college campuses concludes that more than 55 percent of colleges restrict speech protected by the Constitution.

"Subcommittee Hearing: Is Academic Freedom Threatened by China's Influence on American Universities?" U.S. House of Representatives, Dec. 4, 2014, http://tinyurl.com/plp6t9j.
Foreign Affairs Subcommittee Chairman Rep. Christopher Smith, R-N.J., leads a hearing on whether Confucius Institutes on American campuses and satellite campuses in China undermine academic freedom.

For More Information

Association of American University Professors, 1133 19th St., N.W., Suite 200, Washington, DC 20036; 202-737-5526; www.aaup.org. Professional association representing faculty at American colleges and universities that promotes academic freedom and shared governance.

Association of Title IX Administrators (ATIXA), 116 E. King St., Malvern, PA 19355-2969; 610-644-7858; https://atixa.org. Professional association for school and college Title IX administrators responsible for coordinating the anti-sex discrimination law.

Foundation for Individual Rights in Education (FIRE), 170 S. Independence Mall W., Suite 510, Philadelphia, PA 19106; 215-717-3473; www.thefire.org. Educational foundation that works across the ideological spectrum on behalf of individual rights, freedom of expression, academic freedom, due process and freedom of conscience at colleges and universities.

Human Rights Watch, 350 Fifth Ave., 34th Floor, New York, NY 10118-3299; 212-290-4700; www.hrw.org. International organization that defends human rights worldwide.

International Campaign for Tibet, 1825 Jefferson Place, N.W., Washington, DC, 20036; 202-785-1515; www.savetibet.org. Advocacy group that promotes human rights and democratic freedoms for the people of Tibet.

Scholars at Risk, 194 Mercer St., Room 410, New York, NY, 10012; 212-998-2179; http://scholarsatrisk.nyu.edu. International network of education institutions and individuals hosted at New York University that promotes academic freedom and defends scholars' human rights.

Student Affairs Professionals in Higher Education (NASPA), 111 K St., N.E., 10th Floor, Washington, D.C. 20002; 202-265-7500; www.naspa.org. Association of professionals in student affairs at the college and university level.